Out of China

ROBERT BICKERS

Out of China

How the Chinese Ended the
Era of Western Domination

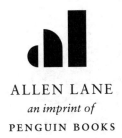

ALLEN LANE
an imprint of
PENGUIN BOOKS

ALLEN LANE

UK | USA | Canada | Ireland | Australia
India | New Zealand | South Africa

Allen Lane is part of the Penguin Random House group of companies
whose addresses can be found at global.penguinrandomhouse.com

First published 2017
001

Copyright © Robert Bickers, 2017

The moral right of the author has been asserted

Set in 10.5/14 pt Sabon LT Std
Typeset by Jouve (UK), Milton Keynes
Printed in Great Britain by Clays Ltd, St Ives plc

A CIP catalogue record for this book is available from the British Library

ISBN: 978-1-846-14618-3

For Kate, Lily and Arthur

Contents

List of Illustrations

Every effort has been made to contact all copyright holders. The publishers will be pleased to make good in future editions any errors or omissions brought to their attention.

26. 'Overtake Britain in Fifteen Years', poster, 1958. (Courtesy of the Shanghai Propaganda Poster Art Center)
27. Poster for the Joint Stock Theatre Group production of *Fanshen* by David Hare, 1975.
28. Poster for the film *The World of Suzie Wong*, 1960.
29. Poster for Jean-Luc Godard's *La Chinoise*, 1967.
30. 'Le Petit Livre Rose de Mao', *Lui* magazine, 1967, photographs by Frank Gitty. (Francis Giacobetti)
31. Womenswear feature, *China Reconstructs*, June 1956.
32. Wang Guangmei humiliated by Tsinghua University Red Guards, 10 April 1967. (Original source unknown)
33. Effigies of Lyndon Johnson, Harold Wilson and Moshe Dayan, Beijing, 1967, photographer unknown. (Courtesy of Emerita Pilgrim)
34. Glenn Cowan in China, 1971. (Frank Fischbeck/The LIFE Images Collection/Getty Images)
35. Wham! in Tiananmen Square, 1985. (Rex/Shutterstock)
36. Portrait of Queen Elizabeth II being removed from display at HMS *Tamar*, Hong Kong, 16 June 1997. (Stephen Shaver/AFP/ Getty Images)
37. Schoolchildren at the National Museum of China, 2011, photograph by the author.

Images 1, 2, 3, 4, 6, 13, 15, 18, 21 and 22 can also be viewed with similar photographs and additional information at the *Historical Photographs of China* project website: http://www.hpcbristol.net. I am grateful to the British Academy and the Swire Trust for their support for this initiative, which I direct, and to Jamie Carstairs (project manager), Alejandro Acin, Shannon Smith and Gao Yuqun for their contributions.

List of Maps

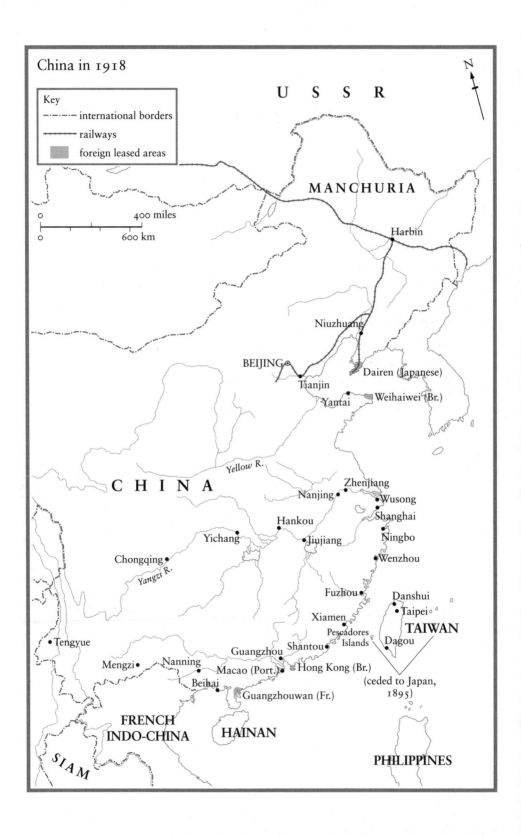

China in 1918

Key
— · — · — international borders
—+—+—+— railways
▓ foreign leased areas

U S S R

MANCHURIA

Harbin

400 miles

600 km

Niuzhuang

BEIJING ⊙

Tianjin

Dairen (Japanese)

Yantai

Weihaiwei (Br.)

C H I N A

Yellow R.

Zhenjiang

Nanjing

Wusong

Shanghai

Hankou

Ningbo

Yichang

Jiujiang

Wenzhou

Chongqing

Yangzi R.

Fuzhou

Danshui

Taipei ⊙

Xiamen

TAIWAN

Pescadores
Islands

Dagou

Tengyue

Guangzhou

Shantou

Mengzi

Nanning

Macao (Port.)

Hong Kong (Br.)

Beihai

(ceded to Japan,
1895)

Guangzhouwan (Fr.)

FRENCH
INDO-CHINA

HAINAN

SIAM

PHILIPPINES

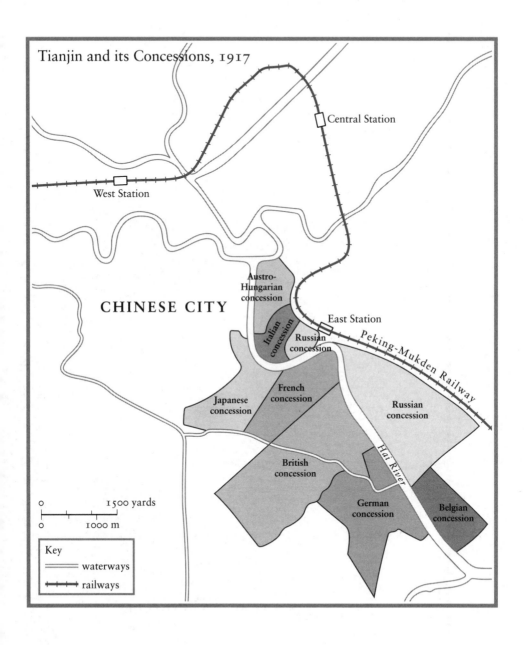

Tianjin and its Concessions, 1917

Central Station

West Station

CHINESE CITY

Austro-Hungarian concession

Italian concession

Russian concession

East Station

Peking-Mukden Railway

French concession

Japanese concession

Russian concession

Hai River

British concession

German concession

Belgian concession

0   1500 yards

0   1000 m

Key

waterways

railways

The Northern Expedition

MONGOLIA
(Independent 1924)

SINKIANG

INNER MONGOLIA

GANSU

QINGHAI

•Lanzhou

SHAANXI

Datong•

SHANXI

HENAN

Xi'an•

2

2

2

TIBET

SICHUAN

•Chengdu

HUBEI

4

INDIA

Kunming•

YUNNAN

5

GUIZHOU

•Guiyang

5

4

Changsha

HUNAN

Guilin•

GUANGXI

6

7

BURMA

Tonking
(to France
1885–1953)

7

MANCHURIA

JILIN

FENGTIAN

☐1☐

☐1☐

REHE

☐1☐

• Shenyang

• Beijing ☐1☐

ZHILI

• Jinan

☐1☐ • Qingdao

SHANDONG

• Kaifeng

JIANGSU

ANHUI

☐3☐ • Nanjing

• Shanghai

• Wuhan

• Hangzhou

• Nanchang

☐3☐

ZHEJIANG

JIANGXI

☐3☐

FUJIAN

☐3☐ • Fuzhou

GUANGDONG

Guangzhou

Joseon
(Korea,
to Japan
1910–45)

JAPAN

Formosa
(Taiwan,
to Japan
1895–1945)

SOUTH CHINA SEA

0 _____ 400 miles
0 _____ 800 km

Key

☐7☐ Guomindang home territory
☐6☐ Guangxi group of warlords
☐5☐ Faction of Tang Jiyao
☐4☐ Zhili faction of Wu Peifu
☐3☐ Zhili faction of Sun Chuanfang
☐2☐ Feng Yuxiang's Guominjun
☐1☐ Fengtian faction of Zhang Zuolin
☐ ☐ Non aligned or fragmented
→ advances of Guomindang
→ advance by Yan Xishan
→ Guominjun advance

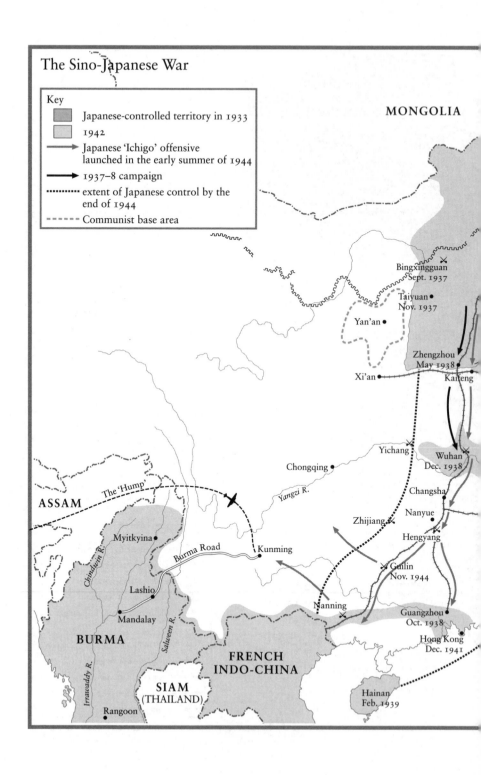

The Sino-Japanese War

Key

- Japanese-controlled territory in 1933
- 1942
- Japanese 'Ichigo' offensive launched in the early summer of 1944
- 1937–8 campaign
- extent of Japanese control by the end of 1944
- Communist base area

MONGOLIA

Bingxingguan
Sept. 1937

Taiyuan
Nov. 1937

Yan'an

Zhengzhou
May 1938

Xi'an

Kaifeng

Yichang

Chongqing

Wuhan
Dec. 1938

Yangzi R.

Changsha

ASSAM

The 'Hump'

Zhijiang

Nanyue

Hengyang

Myitkyina

Chindwin R.

Burma Road

Kunming

Guilin
Nov. 1944

Lashio

Salween R.

Nanning

Mandalay

BURMA

Irrawaddy R.

Guangzhou
Oct. 1938

Hong Kong
Dec. 1941

FRENCH
INDO-CHINA

SIAM
(THAILAND)

Hainan
Feb. 1939

Rangoon

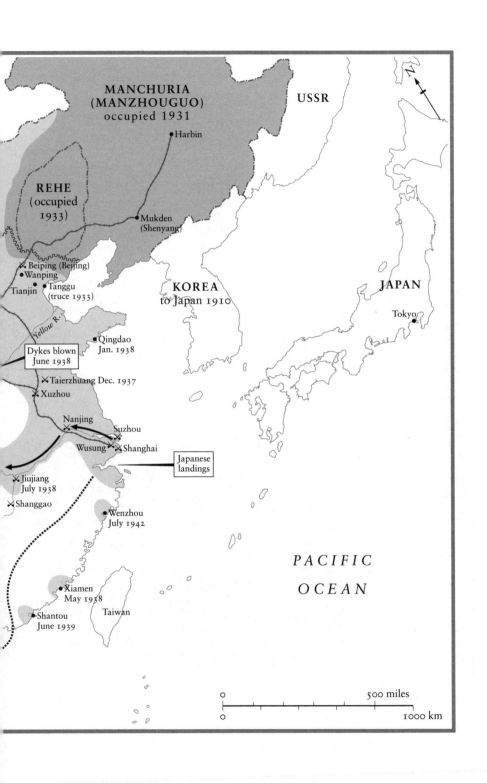

MANCHURIA
(MANZHOUGUO)
occupied 1931

USSR

●Harbin

REHE
(occupied
1933)

●Mukden
(Shenyang)

KOREA
to Japan 1910

JAPAN

✗ Beiping (Beijing)
●Wanping
Tianjin ●Tanggu
(truce 1933)

Tokyo●

Yellow R.

●Qingdao
Jan. 1938

Dykes blown
June 1938

✗Taierzhuang Dec. 1937
✗Xuzhou

Nanjing
✗   ●Suzhou
Wusung✗ ✗Shanghai

Japanese
landings

✗Jiujiang
July 1938
✗Shanggao

●Wenzhou
July 1942

PACIFIC

OCEAN

●Xiamen
May 1938
●Shantou
June 1939

Taiwan

0   500 miles

0   1000 km

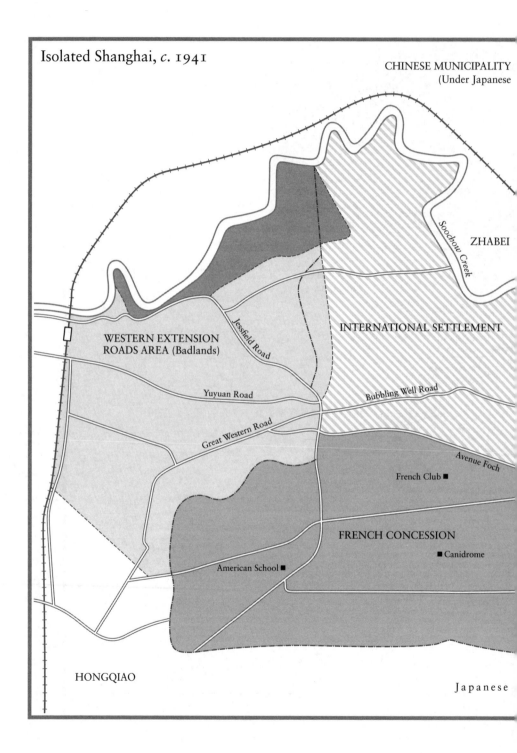

Isolated Shanghai, *c.* 1941

CHINESE MUNICIPALITY
(Under Japanese

ZHABEI

Soochow Creek

INTERNATIONAL SETTLEMENT

WESTERN EXTENSION
ROADS AREA (Badlands)

Jessfield Road

Yuyuan Road

Bubbling Well Road

Great Western Road

Avenue Foch

French Club ■

FRENCH CONCESSION

■ Canidrome

American School ■

HONGQIAO

Japanese

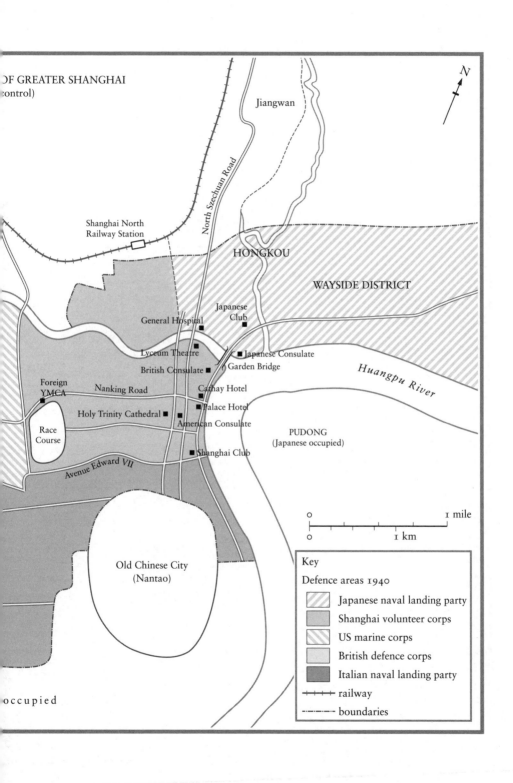

N

Jiangwan

North Szechuan Road

Shanghai North
Railway Station

HONGKOU

WAYSIDE DISTRICT

General Hospital

Japanese
Club

Lyceum Theatre

Japanese Consulate

British Consulate

Garden Bridge

Huangpu River

Foreign
YMCA

Nanking Road

Cathay Hotel

Holy Trinity Cathedral

Palace Hotel

Race
Course

American Consulate

PUDONG
(Japanese occupied)

Shanghai Club

Avenue Edward VII

1 mile

1 km

Old Chinese City
(Nantao)

Key

Defence areas 1940

Japanese naval landing party

Shanghai volunteer corps

US marine corps

British defence corps

Italian naval landing party

railway

boundaries

occupied

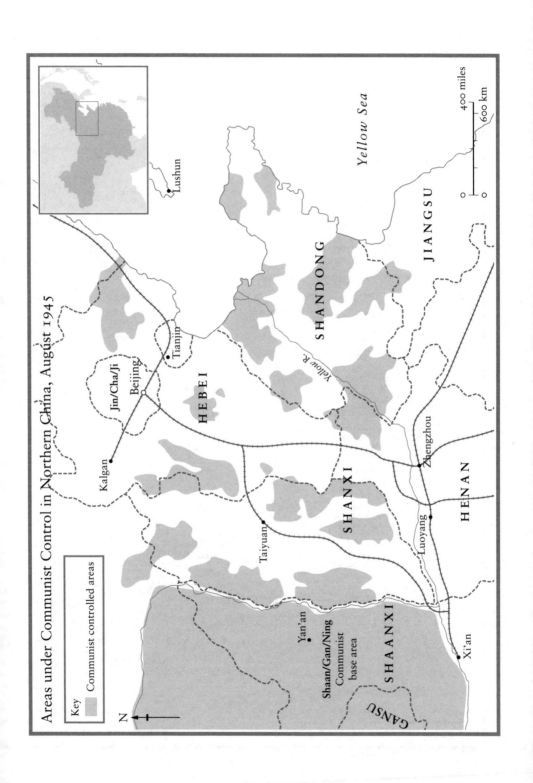

Areas under Communist Control in Northern China, August 1945

Key
Communist controlled areas

Flash Points and Conflicts on China's Periphery since 1949

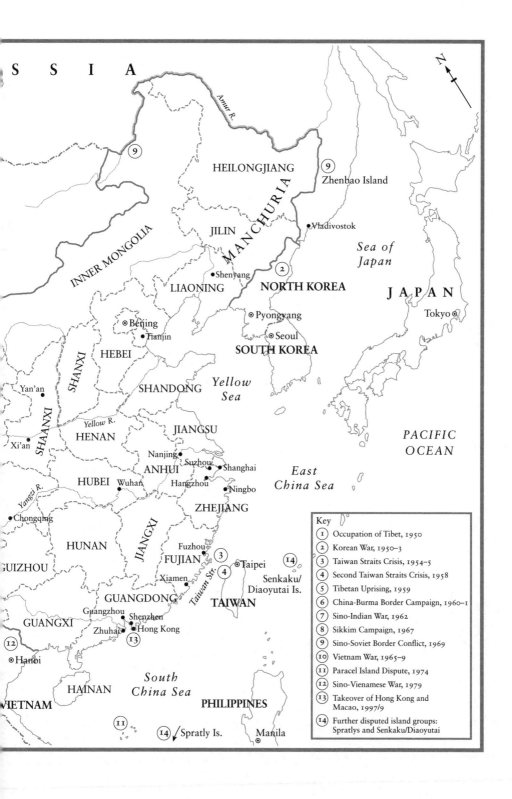

Key

1. Occupation of Tibet, 1950
2. Korean War, 1950–3
3. Taiwan Straits Crisis, 1954–5
4. Second Taiwan Straits Crisis, 1958
5. Tibetan Uprising, 1959
6. China-Burma Border Campaign, 1960–1
7. Sino-Indian War, 1962
8. Sikkim Campaign, 1967
9. Sino-Soviet Border Conflict, 1969
10. Vietnam War, 1965–9
11. Paracel Island Dispute, 1974
12. Sino-Vienamese War, 1979
13. Takeover of Hong Kong and Macao, 1997/9
14. Further disputed island groups: Spratlys and Senkaku/Diaoyutai

Acknowledgements

For the third time now, my editor at Penguin, Simon Winder, has cheerfully encouraged me as I have developed, researched and written a book. His interests and knowledge, ranging as they do far from the German heartlands of his own recent books, have also kept me very much on my toes. I am very grateful to him, as I am to all the team at Penguin and to my patient copy-editor Richard Mason. My agent Bill Hamilton has been immensely supportive in helping me steer this in, and I am also grateful to the late – unique – David Miller, for enabling it to embark and for all his support and encouragement. For assistance with research and references I am greatly indebted to Catherine Ladds, Gordon Barrett, Jamie Carstairs, Chih-yun Chang, Jon Chappell, Sabrina Fairchild, Isabella Jackson and Hirata Koji, and to Cecilia Mackay for her advice on and assiduous searching out of the illustrations. For sharing copies of their work I would like to thank Amy Jane Barnes, Chris Hess, Di Yin Lu, Cagdas Ungor and Jake Werner. For allowing me to see and to quote from the L. K. Little diaries my thanks go to Liz Boylan and family. I am extremely grateful to Bill Callahan, Andrew Hillier, Jon Howlett, Rana Mitter and Frances Wood, who each read some or all of the manuscript and provided a helpfully and unmanageably diverse and contradictory set of suggestions. Of course, the love, patience and encouragement of Kate, Lily and Arthur, Bob and Joan, and my friends and wider family, has as usual helped as much as it has hindered the completion of the book. I would not have it any other way.

This book has drawn on research undertaken over a number of years in a number of archives and libraries. It has been supported by a variety of research projects including an ESRC Research Grant (RES-062-23-1057), and a sequence of awards to the British

Inter-university China Centre through the Language-Based Area Studies scheme (RES-580-28-0008, AH/K000055/1 and AH/L006731/1). Investment in arts and humanities research does not always provide swift returns, and this book draws also on research finds from Arts and Humanities Research Council awards made in 2003 and 2008. Mike Basker and Kate Robson-Brown, neither of them hugely endowed with spare time, allowed me to step back from administrative duties to complete the manuscript, and I could not be more grateful to them for agreeing to this. More widely, my colleagues at the University of Bristol have helped me bring this to completion, especially Tim Cole, Josie McLellan and Simon Potter. As before, and as with all works of scholarship, this one is indebted to the work of a large number of my fellow historians, not least those now pioneering new research into the difficult terrain of 1950s and 1960s China. It is difficult work in more ways than one, for as this book progressed, securing access to already-opened records in many archives in China became more and more challenging. Many files that I have seen in the past and have used here are no longer accessible. Some archives have shut down completely. Of course, China is not alone in finding that the difficult legacies of the past also include the unpredictable and unpalatable contents of the records of those histories. But this is now combined in China with a systematic drive to shut down access to records and to proclaim afresh – at the highest levels of the state – the unquestionable supremacy of a single interpretation of history. I must conclude with a note of bemusement, then, that still, and in fact increasingly, despite such trends, those working in the humanities across the world are routinely asked to demonstrate the value or utility of their disciplines.

Robert Bickers
Bristol, 1 October 2016

Pronunciation Guide

Most Chinese words in this book have been transliterated using the internationally recognized pinyin system of romanization. An exception has been made for some names rather more widely known in former usage, such as Chiang Kai-shek or T. V. Soong, and for words within contemporary quotations or institutional names (for example Peking University, Shameen Municipal Council). I have in the first instance given the former standard usage as well. While my practice will serve to make place names, in particular, more obvious to the great majority of readers not familiar with the older terms, it does have one drawback that needs highlighting: the language of the world of the foreign communities in China is thereby partially obscured, when it was integral to the way in which they saw themselves – and where in fact they thought they were. As readers will see, they did not live in Xiamen or Jiujiang, or Shantou or Chongqing, but in Amoy, Kiukiang, Swatow and Chungking. Up to a point, in their minds, they did not actually live in 'China'. That was how they wrote and talked. In fact it was even more complex than this, for the French occupied the Kouang-Tchéou-Wan Leased Territory, for example, which was known to English speakers as Kwangchowan (and in pinyin Guangzhouwan). Germans visited Tsingtau, Britons and Americans Tsingtao, and it was always known in standard putong-hua as Qingdao. To appreciate this most fully you actually need to hear former foreign residents speak, but I hope nonetheless that this book captures some of that language and through it the assumptions and self-assurance of this other time and place.

List of Abbreviations

BAAG   British Army Aid Group
CCP   Chinese Communist Party
CER   Chinese Eastern Railway
CNRRA China National Relief and Rehabilitation Administration
IPR   Institute of Pacific Relations
NRA   National Revolutionary Army
PLA   People's Liberation Army
PRC   People's Republic of China
PUMC   Peking Union Medical College
RIIA   Royal Institute of International Affairs
ROC   Republic of China
SMC   Shanghai Municipal Council
SMP   Shanghai Municipal Police
UNRRA United Nations Relief and Rehabilitation Administration

Introduction

Nationalism matters in China, and what matters in China matters to us all. Over the last three decades there has been a series of angry demonstrations and protests, fierce denunciations and confrontations that have seemed to herald a new and assertive phase in China's relations with the rest of the world. These episodes have been sparked by territorial disputes, the accidental bombing in 1999 of China's Serbian Embassy by NATO warplanes, protests over the 2008 Olympic torch relay, encounters between US and Chinese military aircraft, and by many other controversies.[1] They have involved sharply worded statements from leaders and diplomats, as well as carefully planned and contained actions by the Chinese government. There have been peaceful demonstrations as well as violent attacks on foreign properties in Chinese cities. We have also seen a vogue for crude nationalistic polemics urging China to 'say no' (or worse) to foreign governments. But in large part such outbreaks are the spontaneous responses of ordinary people to events. This is not just the state talking.

The depth of feeling and the strength of the language used have continually taken foreign observers aback, but what has also puzzled many is the fact that in every round of protests there has been the significant presence of references to the past: anger is one thing, but this historical consciousness is surely another. Some of these episodes have also been sparked by disputes over the past itself and representations of it, over the content of Japanese textbooks, for example, or items of Chinese provenance that have come up for sale at international auction houses. Disputes, accidents and other events are the ordinary stuff of relations between states, but why are the responses to these in China often so violently expressed, and why are they routinely framed the way they are? Why does the past matter? The era when China was subject to foreign invasion, when parts of the country fell under Japanese or British control as colonies, when British, American or French gunboats patrolled the Yangzi River, and Japanese, Britons, Russians and Germans governed parts of a dozen major cities, has been over for seventy years. Is it not simply history, done and dusted with now?

China's new nationalism needs to be understood. It has unfolded in tandem with the country's epoch-shaking economic development, and it is in large part a logical consequence of that new and hard-won strength. We can reasonably expect an economically strong China to assert itself in the world, and while this might take a little getting used to, it will happen. But we cannot make proper sense of this phenomenon, or learn how to engage with it, unless we understand how deeply it is rooted not in China's present power, but in its past weakness. These disputes have been couched in the context of the country's modern history, and its experience at the hands of foreign powers since the 1840s. China looks out at the twenty-first century through the lens of history; it judges the events of the present and the challenges it faces by those of the nineteenth and twentieth centuries. If we too look through that lens we can see how far and in what ways the roots of China's new nationalism lie in the capital cities of foreign empires, and in their colonies and other offshoots in China itself. But rather than simply acknowledging this, the contention of this book is that we can only make sense of the present if we actually understand this past and if we know more about it. This is not simply a discourse, it is a history and it lives on.

Take the simple matter of a signboard that once stood at the entrance to a public park on Shanghai's riverside embankment, the Bund.[2] This was placed on display in a Shanghai history museum from the 1950s until 1989. That year the museum began to prepare to move into a new building, and not realizing that the signboard was actually a fabrication, one of the staff later described how he had expressed his confusion to older colleagues at finding it amongst scrap material waiting to be thrown out. Museums all over the world use reproductions in their displays, mocking up copies of the material stuff of the past to better give visitors in the present a feel for it. There would be little interest in this tale, which was narrated in a short magazine article some years after the event, were it not for the fact that what was thrown away was not simply a careful copy of an original – but a fake. There had been a signboard, but it did not present the words that were written on the museum's version, which in starkly simple Chinese and English announced 'Huaren yu gou bude runei': 'Chinese and Dogs Not Admitted'.

There is no evidence that such a sign ever existed. For some decades prior to 1928, Chinese residents of Shanghai were certainly forbidden by racist admissions policies from entering this park, as well as others in the parts of the city that were controlled by its foreign-run municipalities. The history of the regulations is well known, and there are photographs of signboards. But it was very widely and genuinely believed that these specific insulting words had once been used (and 'dog' is a particularly incendiary term of abuse in Chinese). The history of that belief can partly be traced through newspapers and reports. However, the story of the sign was an urban myth conveying a simplified version of a complex story that had gained significant political traction. It once mattered, internationally in fact, that the signboard should be known to have been phrased this way; it mattered in slightly different ways over the decades starting from the 1920s, into the 1990s and beyond. It matters today.

This wryly written yet serious anecdote appeared in April 1994 in a new popular history magazine published in Shanghai, *Shiji* (*Century*), and the article was quickly picked up by newspapers overseas. Its author, Xue Liyong, had prefaced his piece with a short account of the actual history of racist exclusion, and of the reaction to previous assertions that the signboard story was a myth. Many people claimed to have seen the signboard with their own eyes, he noted, but it was probable that they had in fact seen and remembered the museum's fake. This was a reasonable and carefully composed argument, but the piece provoked a storm. By acknowledging that the museum's signboard was a fabrication, and by rejecting the myth, Xue Liyong was deemed to have asserted that the story of discrimination itself was untrue. Xue and those who came to his defence with additional essays and at a quickly organized seminar on the issue were stamped on. On 7 June 1994 at least four newspapers in Shanghai published the same lengthy essay that had originally appeared in a Communist Party newsletter and which rebutted Xue's sceptical account. It marshalled evidence from contemporary reports and from memoirs apparently proving that the obnoxious wording of the notice was a verifiable historical fact. *Shiji* was forced to republish this essay as well, and to issue a recantation and an unambiguous apology. *Guangming ribao*, a national newspaper of intellectual debate, ran a pungent comment piece: 'Western colonialists in China committed monstrous crimes,' it read, 'too many to mention in fact; the sign placed at the entrance to the parks reading "Chinese and Dogs Not Admitted" is prime evidence of their guilt.'[3] The author directly addressed those concerned: 'Some people do not understand the humiliations of old China's history, or else they harbour sceptical attitudes and even go so far as to write off a serious historical humiliation lightly; this is very dangerous.'

I had already blundered into this issue myself, not in Shanghai, at least not at first, but in the grand meeting room of the Royal Society of Antiquaries at Burlington House, on London's Piccadilly, in March 1991. I had been asked to give a lunchtime talk about my research on the history of relations between Britons and Chinese in Shanghai to a group that met there once or twice a month called the China Society. This had been formed in 1907 for the 'encouragement of the study of China's language, literature, history and folklore, and of all scientific, artistic, commercial, and social Chinese matters'.[4] The then Chinese envoy to Britain was its first speaker. Over the years it had hosted some very eminent speakers and had members from across the diverse worlds of people working with China: British businessmen, diplomats and politicians, missionaries and academics, and many Chinese visitors as well. As the audience assembled on that mild, wet spring morning, I began to realize, however, that by 1991 this society had largely become a gathering place for elderly Britons who had formerly lived in China, if not been born there. I was about to address the subjects of my research, and I had chosen to begin with reference to the story of the controversy about the Shanghai park, its regulations and the alleged wording of the sign.

My text shows my last-minute attempts to better frame the talk to fit the audience, but to little avail. They made it quite clear afterwards what they thought of me: I was accused at best of harbouring unnecessarily sceptical attitudes about the British record in China – about their record, their families, their life and their worlds – and at worst of lying, and of fabricating the evidence I offered to support my argument. They were tired of hearing about it, and of being told they had presented a problem, and they were tired of the blasted sign. They had all had Chinese friends, they said, and later some gave me examples, showed me photographs, and provided introductions to old friends in China. They were still in touch, they would say, with the old family servants. How could anyone think that they would inflict such a grotesque insult on the Chinese? Who did I think they were?

Well, hard truths need discussing, although this was not quite the right audience for them. But I had chosen to talk about the sign because it had become such a potent emblem of the enduring and problematic legacies of China's experience of foreign power: that is, the legacy of the actual record, the uses to which that record has been put, and in what ways, and the problems of forgetting and of denial. You cannot avoid encountering the issue in historic archives and newspapers. The wording of the sign had been a subject of claim and rebuttal since at least the year the China Society was established, when a note about the allegation was published in a British newspaper in Shanghai. The story had been fought over in Shanghai itself, of course, and in the pages of the press internationally. In 1907 the story was circulating in pamphlets in China's southwestern Sichuan province. Press packs containing photographs of the signboards then actually in place were issued to journalists by the International Settlement's secretariat in the 1920s and 1930s. Foreign nationals who had formerly lived in China argued over it in the pages of Hong Kong's *South China Morning Post* at regular intervals from the 1950s into the 1980s.[5] At the same time, tour guides and a noticeboard in Shanghai retold the story to visitors to the People's Republic. In an iconic scene from a 1972 Hong Kong film that was a tremendous international success, *Fist of Fury* (*Jingwumen*, also known as *The Chinese Connection*), the actor Bruce Lee destroys the sign with a powerful karate kick. Chinese audiences reacted with unabashed glee.

Despite that kick the sign lived on. It is one of the symbols of China's degraded status in the past that is still regularly rehearsed in its present. But because the sign is a myth, it is also vulnerable to those who would seek to belittle the importance of that past, writing it all off as a fabrication. And because it has become an iconic symbol of a history that 'cannot be forgotten', and about which ideologically driven directives are given, it is also tempting to ignore it. Why should we take propaganda seriously? And the reality, too, behind it can easily be forgotten because it has been left behind in the great historical withdrawal from empire. The International Settlement was surrendered in 1943. The wider world of the foreign-dominated treaty ports is long, long gone, reconvening only in such gatherings as those of the China Society, and not even there any more. Time has taken its toll; the society is defunct. We live in the twenty-first century; China is not what it was. So hasn't the slate been wiped clean?

Far from it, and this is not the only part of the wider story of the nature, impact and legacy of the exercise of foreign power in China that is still alive today, and which has become more and more important within the new Chinese nationalism that has been developing since the early 1990s. We might note that Bruce Lee's character in *Fist of Fury* spends much of the film fighting Japanese, including three who had insulted him at the park gate, one of whom had suggested Lee pretend to be his dog in order to gain entry. It is hard in the Chinese context to think of a more combustible combination. The intermixing of issues of personal and national dignity, colonialist practice in a Chinese city, and hostility towards Japan and the Japanese, remained potent. And we should note that *Fist of Fury* was itself made in a British colony on Chinese soil.

We need to remember and understand the world that gave rise to this myth. I do not mean simply that we need to know what happened so that the sins of the past can be atoned for properly in the present. Instead, I mean that it is vital we all understand the internationalized landscapes of twentieth-century China with all their contradictions, their violence, their cosmopolitanism and their ambition. This book provides the story of that foreign establishment and its aftermath down to these history battles of the 1990s, and to the very end of that presence with the return to Chinese sovereignty of the colonies at Hong Kong and Macao. The more we understand that story, the better we can understand China's present – and future – use of the past. In my previous book, *The Scramble for China: Foreign Devils in the Qing Empire, 1832–1914*, I set out the history of the growth of the foreign presence in China, from its origins amongst angry British traders in a tiny area to which they were confined by law in Guang-zhou, to the vast establishment that had secured almost a commanding hold over the country by the onset of the First World War. That book looked at these traders' arguments, and at the world they built within the borders of the Qing. It looked too at how their ambitions and initiatives were resisted by the officials of the dynasty, as well as by its subjects – but also at how people collaborated with foreign inter-ests and used them for their own purposes. It was generally always a collaborative enterprise, if only sometimes a genuine partnership of equals. There were limits to what force could achieve. I also explored how this period has been presented subsequently in histories. In this book I trace these stories onwards from the end of the First World War, through the rise of a powerful Chinese nationalism, the inva-sion by Japan, and the rise of the Chinese Communist Party to power in 1949. I will show how these elements fared in the 'New China' of the Communists and how the legacies of the past were dealt with, and represented; and how foreign powers with a strong legacy in China before 1949 engaged with it afterwards during the Cold War, and the years after the death of Mao Zedong in 1976. At the time of writing we are still less than twenty years on from a time when China still hosted two foreign-controlled colonies on its soil. This is still today's story.

In the case of the Shanghai signboard we have a myth, certainly, but we have, too, a wider story of how an international consortium of foreign nationals, supported by an array of treaties and agree-ments, enforced by a military presence, established a municipal administration that controlled the heart of what would be China's most important city in the early twentieth century. That administra-tion built the famous riverfront, the Bund, established a public garden on its northern tip, and enacted a set of regulations that prohibited dogs and bicycles, the picking of flowers, and the entrance of Chinese (except servants accompanying foreigners). It recruited Britons, Sikhs, Russians, Japanese and Chinese into a police force that enforced these rules, amongst others. The society and culture of the foreigners who lived in the International Settlement were infused with racist and chauvinist attitudes, practices and policies, both conscious and unconscious. It was also of course necessary there to find compromises, and collaborations, to negotiate and accommodate Chinese residents and partners in business and in other enterprises. Residents' associations, social and political organizations, and individuals, engaged with this world of foreign power, or ignored it, as they saw fit. Those park regulations had a history themselves, and they were contested. They were fought over in the vibrant multi-language press in the settlement, at public meetings and through social and political organizations, and in June 1928 they were changed to allow entrance to all on payment of a small charge. This issue captures many of the elements in China's modern experience with which this book is concerned: the story of protest and resistance, of representation and incomprehension, and of the tangible presence in China of this complex foreign-administered world, and its long and contentious legacy.

My core subject here is this foreign presence and how it fared throughout these periods, but that also requires a discussion of the growing importance of issues of national and individual dignity, and of the discourse of what is routinely called China's 'National Humiliation', and of the persistent ambiguities in China's relations with the West (which I here use to embrace Japan as well). So this is the story of who controlled Shanghai, for example, and when and how, and who set out to build a new China that could contest that foreign power, and where, and when and how. There is a tale that needs remembering about foreign China helpers, and China critics, about humanitarians, political activists and mercenaries, as well as banking experts and technicians. It is also the story of who controlled how China was represented, and how, who by, and where. Hollywood and Piccadilly were important sites of that story as much as Shanghai, Guangzhou, or the 90 per cent of China's counties that had some form of foreign missionary presence. It is the story of China's foreign relations as they were made manifest in its cities and in its countryside; the story about who spoke for the country, how and where, and about how the 'problem' of China was articulated, and what solutions were proposed for its resolution. It is also about the lure of the West, of the eager embrace of foreign things, ideas and practices – of how China started to dance, for example – and also of their rejection: who bombed the dance halls, and why, who burned the books, or suppressed the music. It is also a story of the routine ways in which the foreign was incorporated into the life of twentieth-century China.

This world did not cease to exist on 1 October 1949 with the establishment of the People's Republic of China, as I found out on my first visit to Shanghai in 1991. 'Call me T. T.,' said Mr Chen, the seventy-seven-year-old retired deputy director of a once British-owned utility company, to whom I had been given an introduction by one member of my audience at the China Society back in London. T. T. Chen had been the first Chinese graduate engineer employed by the company, and his flawless pre-war English diction was itself part evidence of his background in Shanghai's anglophone community in the old city. Such families patronized English-language schools and colleges (T. T. had attended St John's University, an American missionary institution), and they found employment within the world of foreign-owned firms and institutions, but they were no less Chinese, and no less ambitious for their country. When I first encountered Chen, he lived in the same home the British company had provided for him, although over the decades he had steadily lost more and more of it as other residents were moved in, and he was reduced to the use of one room when we met. For three years after 1966, Chen had been jailed in the house, his personal history and foreign connections having served to damn him by the standards of the tumultuous Cultural Revolution. T. T. was accused of being a foreign spy. An important part of modern China's history can be seen in the story of the reputation of such families and communities and in how individuals like Chen suffered as a result of the twists and turns of state policy after 1949, and in the face of China's attitude towards the past.

China is more than Shanghai, and the world of its T. T. Chens. How 'New China' after 1949 aimed to redress the imbalance between rural and Westernized urban worlds, between indigenous and foreign influences, and between self-reliance and external aid, is a core theme in the book. Moreover, before the 1940s few but cranks and aesthetes would think of looking to China as a model for anything, but after 1949 it suddenly became a revolutionary beacon. New China seemed to offer a new world that could teach the old one, and it caught the imagination across the globe. And at the same time as this new vision of China bewitched and inspired observers from Paris to Peru, it became practically isolated as almost never before in its history. As the country started to reopen in the 1970s, it became clear that the business of the past was still unfinished and formed a prominent and explosive issue in the diplomacy of the present, and in the fashioning of a Chinese identity for the twenty-first century.

This book brings together the various perspectives that in effect came to claim ownership of the story of the Shanghai park sign: the careful scholars who sought to present a robust and true account of their country's history in the pages of *Shiji* magazine; the ideologues who emphasized the primary importance of a political understanding – for we need to get to grips with that too; the residents of the foreign communities – for we need to know what they were doing, and why – as well as their successors in the story of China's foreign relations after 1949. This is not a comprehensive history of modern China as such, but it is a vital part of modern China's history, and the themes are of paramount importance in understanding that wider story: they shape it, and in turn of course are also shaped by it.

The book draws on research in archives across China, Britain and the United States. Access to some of the Chinese records used here has been restricted since I first looked at them, primarily because the evidence from the past that was uncovered proved to be too much at variance with the official version of history that is promoted today. It undoes or contradicts, we might say, the official version of the story of the sign. However, a significant amount remains accessible there, and the records overseas attest in their sheer profusion alone to the scale of the foreign enterprise in China.

In June 1994, just three days after the affair of the park sign was decisively concluded by the textual barrage delivered through Shanghai's mass-circulation press, I was actually sent an invitation to speak about the subject at the city's Institute of Modern History. Historians are persistent people. At that point I was unaware of the storm over the *Shiji* article, and did not realize until after I had given my talk that autumn that I had been invited to speak in order to contribute to the argument that had been proposed by the Shanghai sceptics. Like them, I believe that we need to accept the story of the sign as a myth.[6] Like them, I also believe that we need to have a firm understanding of the history of this period that goes further than the rosy memories of former expatriate residents, and of the ideologically rigid hostility of post-revolution interpretations – and indeed of many pre-revolutionary ones. The story of China's interaction with the West needs discussing, properly, and it needs remembering outside China. It is too readily lost to sight overseas: forgetting is an essential attribute for societies in the former heartlands of empires. It has been far too easy to forget or ignore as a simple detail of history the nature and impact of the foreign presence in China. It has been easy, too, in the United States, to believe that this was a European and Japanese phenomenon, and that America was not complicit in this world, or was involved in a different enterprise, helping, not oppressing China. As we shall see, the story is also much more complex, and it remains vibrant and relevant today.

What follows in this book is not a history of nationalism in twentieth-century China, but a history of the role of imperialism and anti-imperialism within that wider story. Although, as we will see, their impact and legacy have been and still are profound, for political reasons they have again and again been made to bear a far greater weight in understandings of modern China's history than is objectively justified. They do so still; and this is a potentially dangerous thing.

After publishing *The Scramble for China*, I asked a former British diplomat how far his Chinese peers had made use of the sort of events and themes narrated in that book when interacting with him and his colleagues. Did they talk much about them? He looked at me, smiled, and replied: 'For years they talked about little else.' Other topics are certainly now discussed, but this one is still there, still alive, and it is still kicking.

I

Armistice

All of China seemed to have come to the party, city sophisticates had bagged good spots on restaurant balconies, country people walked hand in hand below, staring open-mouthed at the sights. Gawpers struggled to keep their balance in the trees. It was Saturday, 23 November 1918. Shanghai looked set on fire. Across the turbid Huangpu River, bright red lights proclaimed Allied triumph in English and Chinese: 'Shengli', 'Victory'. A quarter of a million red flyers had been papered across the city from way south in Longhua, east into the industrial Yangpu suburbs and north into Zhabei. A drawing of the German Kaiser, battered by his enemies, took up most of the page. All were welcome to celebrate, announced the Chinese caption. The President of the Republic of China had announced three days of public holiday to celebrate the Armistice, and so hundreds of thousands gathered in Shanghai to watch the parades. 'Big Willie' and 'Little Willie' – Kaiser Wilhelm II and his son – Admiral Tirpitz and Field Marshal von Hindenburg were each carried in effigy through the streets and made to kowtow to various buildings on the riverside Bund as they went – the Shanghai Club, the Chinese Maritime Customs, the Hongkong and Shanghai Bank, the *North China Daily News* building.

There were scores of floats.[1] The world joined in arms paraded along the streets of the French concession and the foreign-run International Settlement: there were Canadians and New Zealanders, the French and Belgians, Brazil, Serbia, the Indian community of Shanghai – their float a 'wonder of gold and embroidery, a robed prince seated on a throne beneath a splendid domed canopy' – then Italy, and seven American floats – led by Liberty – including one each representing the Philippines and Hawai'i. A string band led the Portuguese. Torch-bearing Indochinese policemen escorted the French. Men from Shandong province who had just returned from service under the British in the Chinese Labour Corps in Mesopotamia processed along. Chinese Boy Scouts marched behind their own brass band. It is unlikely that anyone could hear any tunes that were played that day, but that was beside the point – it was a day for joy, and of relief. And there was plenty of simple entertainment in amongst the symbolic tableaux of smashed mailed fists, and crippled Prussian eagles. Chinese clowns bobbed along on donkeys; stilt-walkers strode about behind them. Hundreds of schoolchildren followed, and behind them under symbolic police guard came the effigies.

The Teutons were manhandled west along Nanjing Road, the city's premier commercial street, forced to stop again and again to bow for the crowd's delight. Then they were frog-marched onto the Shanghai racecourse and hanged from the four corners of a wooden tower on which 'House of Hohenzollern' had been painted in big 'Germanic' letters. The Belgian Consul General Daniel Siffert, who had escaped from occupied Brussels early in the war, stepped forward to do the honours, setting light to the waiting bonfire. And so up, up in flames went Hohenzollern. And down, down went the edifice of 'Prussian Militarism', and the philosophy of 'Might is Right'. Cleansed by fire, a new world of respect, justice and negotiation would emerge. For good measure they also hanged an effigy of a Dachshund, as a symbol of 'Teutonic' conceit about the primacy of German 'Kultur'. Dachshunds had had a very bad war; peace as yet was proving no better.

Victory parades were held across China. Hapless Wilhelm and his son were taken on Skimmington rides and set alight in Xiamen – Amoy – on the south coast, and in Jiujiang deep inland along the Yangzi River. Some 20,000 people paraded in Changsha; 10,000 in Anqing; 5,000 in Guangzhou (Canton). Where there were no bands to hand, people made their own rough music with bells, horns, tins and drums, composing a cacophony of delight. Such was the joy that, having marched once, people set about marching again that same night, and the next. In Beijing on 28 November thousands of Allied soldiers assembled in the Forbidden City in the great courtyard in front of the Taihemen – the Gate of Supreme Harmony. Indian, British and Chinese troops and the US Marine Corps filled the cavernous square, which was sharply lit by the brilliant winter sunshine. Walking through them at 11 o'clock and up on to the Sumeru terrace at the top of the central marble steps to the main entrance to the Great Hall, on the north side of the courtyard, came the silk top-hatted and smartly tailed figure of Xu Shichang, President of the Republic. Barely a month into his third such stint, Xu was a scholarly man who had held a high position under the former monarchy, but who was now a rare civilian holding an office that was to be dominated by soldiers. As Xu processed, China's then current national anthem was played, and he was followed by his cabinet and by the capital's diplomatic corps, all cock-hatted and braided. The gold threads and 6,000 bayonets all glinted in the light, and the standards of the victorious Allies were carried forward to be arrayed along the balustrade of the terrace. Taking off his white gloves Xu read a statement extolling the great principles on which the Allied victory had been based. In both Chinese and European culture, he announced, you could find similar maxims highlighting the principle that 'might can not conquer right'.

In the shuffling of the watching crowd, and as an aeroplane flew nearby, his words could hardly be heard, but in the reports on the speech the message is very clear. China had chosen in 1917 to join the Allied cause, President Xu claimed, because of the commitment of the powers to the principle that justice and respect should shape relations between the nations. 'Hereafter,' he said, 'right will shine with the brilliance of celestial bodies and the merit of the Allies shall be everlasting.' Then the circling aircraft flew directly overhead, dropping celebratory messages on red paper, volleys were fired and the troops marched out through the city. Many in the crowd then took advantage of a day's free entry into the former palace of China's emperors, where the last of them, Aisin-Gioro Puyi, still lived. The abdication in February 1912 of the 268-year-old Qing Dynasty was still so fresh in people's minds that some must have sensed a delicious chill in trespassing on an emperor's private realm. For some days there had been parades and celebrations in Beijing: Allied troops had marched backwards and forwards; two weeks earlier students had paraded through the city carrying banners proclaiming in English and Chinese the victory of justice, and demanding that 'Destruction is Over. Reconstruct', that 'Militarism Must Go!!!', and 'Long Live Freedom'.[2] Peace offered relief, but opportunity too, to confront the greater problems facing the world in 1918, and facing China in particular.

On display in Beijing and in Shanghai, at Changsha and Guangzhou, amongst officials and the populace, Chinese and foreigners, there was an apparent historic unanimity of purpose and of language. Their words matched and – more tellingly – if you looked from European diplomats to President Xu, or from the Chinese Boy Scouts to their British peers, then there seemed also to be a single shared culture. Certainly in amongst the photographs of the 28 November events you can see Manchu women in their distinctive costume, their hair worn the traditional way, but they stand out as different to the norm on the streets. The exotic, alien China of Western caricature that had such a grip on the foreign imagination seems a world away from the city *en fête* celebrating the Armistice. And this new, modern China seems to be on a level par with the victorious Allies.

How things had changed: barely eighteen years earlier, troops from most of those same powers, as well as defeated Germany and Austria-Hungary, had marched in triumph through the same court-yard in the Forbidden City. The soldiers of the expeditionary force had celebrated, with hard boots and martial tunes, their defeat of the forces that had been unleashed upon them in north China by the Qing court, as well as the great peasant Boxer uprising against foreign power that had thrown China into turmoil.

All that was now gone with the winds that blow down from Mongolia across the capital: it seemed that by November 1918 China had earned a rightful place amongst the community of nations. But in fact the seeds of China's twentieth-century tragedies, and the scale of the task that faced those who wished to shape the country, lay also in those same words and in the slogans shouted out by marching students. The route back from the devastation and abject humiliation of 1900 was still unclear. Chinese and the foreigners marched together but mentally lived far, far apart. The clothes, the tunes and their words were deceptive. 'We Celebrate' headlined the advertisements in Shanghai's British-owned *North China Daily News* in mid-November, ahead of the parade. But for all that it looked like a cosmopolitan and inclusive festival, that 'We' was fatally compromised and insular: residents in China of the Allied powers living in the treaty ports – those cities opened to foreign trade and residence under various Sino-foreign treaties – had no true conception of any new equality with their host. This view was widely shared outside the country, amongst politicians and diplomats, analysts and journalists. They all went through the motions in speech, but not in actions, and their hearts were set against it. Within six months this would all become starkly clear.

In fact the Allies would soon start to forget that China had been on their side in the Great War. They did not even fly China's flag during their celebrations in Tianjin's British concession.[3] The great War Memorial that would be unveiled on the Bund at Shanghai in 1924 failed to recognize China's dead. The thousands of Chinese Labour Corps workers who had died in France and in the Middle East, and at sea, would have no such monument, saving gravestones in Belgian and French cemeteries. Or if they did remember, the Allies did so with bitterness at China's seeming utilitarianism, opportunism and greed: those Shandong labourers had come at great cost to the Allies. There had been no real sacrifice on China's part, as the self-styled Allied defenders of freedom had sacrificed their millions of young, including over two hundred foreign residents who had sailed to their deaths in action just from the treaty ports. The Chinese, in the view of some, deserved no thanks for their part in the war.

China still hoped, and dreamed, nonetheless. The republic had joined the conflict on the Allied side in the expectation of plenty – or at least justice – at the conference table, hoping to recover the former German territories in Shandong province seized in November 1914 by the Japanese, who had held fast to them thereafter. It also anticipated that the solidarity of victory would enable the Chinese to roll back a wider Japanese move on China, which had traumatized the country in 1915. For, while Britain, France and Russia struggled to gain their military balance as the year began, Japanese diplomats had pressed on the then president, Yuan Shikai, a list of what became known as the 'Twenty-One Demands', which aimed to force the republic to accept Japanese rights to significant commercial and political privileges, and effective control of Manchuria in the northeast as well as the provinces of Shandong and Fujian. Some of those parading in November 1918 had been marching three years earlier as a great anti-Japanese boycott took hold, to protest against Japan's lunge for primacy amongst the foreign powers feasting on China. Although some of the most egregious demands had been evaded, Yuan had acquiesced to others. And the British and French had also secretly agreed in 1917 to support the Japanese cause for the formal transfer to them of German possessions after the war, not just in China, but also the former German-owned islands scattered across the western Pacific. But President Woodrow Wilson had seemed to have made it clear in his 8 January 1918 address to the US Congress that colonial as well as European questions needed resolving at the war's end. The principles underlying Wilson's 'Fourteen Points' offered a path forward for China, so it was widely believed, in China. Wilson had telegraphed his congratulations to Xu Shichang on his installation as President on China's national day on 10 October 1918, and had expressed strong hopes that the country would pull back from its incipient civil war, unite, and 'assume its rightful place in the councils of nations'.[4]

Wilson's hint to Xu was reinforced by further diplomatic notes, and made a great impression in Beijing. It was also followed up by his personal emissary, Charles Richard Crane, a Chicago businessman involved in Russian affairs, and a former nominee as American Minister to China. Crane was on a fact-finding mission to China and Japan, and arrived in Shanghai just after the victory celebrations there. He delivered precisely the message his Chinese audiences expected to hear in his public speeches: 'I think it is important for China at this time not to scatter too much the opportunity which lies immediately before her, the opportunity which I am sure she is going to have at the Peace Conference.'[5] China's diplomats and current-affairs commentators were already planning for that conference, with very high hopes for it. Now they heard almost directly from Wilson himself, it seemed, promises of change to come: 'You know what the principles of the President are. You may be sure he is going to continue to observe those same principles at the Peace Conference that he has applied to the other problems in the world. I will tell Wilson,'

Crane promised, how 'loyal you are to his ideals'. He lectured them, as he had in private and in public throughout his trip, on the need to end civil strife. Just a month earlier Xu Shichang had issued a mandate recommending unity and peace, and on 17 November had ordered forces answering to his government to cease military action ahead of a peace conference that aimed to repair the political fissures arising from the republic's difficult history. So Chinese crowds celebrated two armistices in their November days and nights of carnival and light: Europe's, and their own.

These hopes seemed well founded, and many Chinese felt more anchored now than ever before in the global community. This went far beyond the promises held out by Wilsonian rhetoric. Almost 200,000 men had gone overseas to serve in the Labour Corps. With them went many young intellectuals, as translators, or as educators or social workers. Over the previous seventy years hundreds of thousands of Chinese had moved overseas, to settle or work, following gold rushes into Australia or California, indentured to work in plantations in Cuba or Hawai'i, on railway construction in North America, or mining guano in Chile and Peru. Merchants formed large communities across Southeast Asia. China's foreign trade had always partly been based on its traders sojourning abroad. The scale of the new migration, happening as the Europeans were themselves colonizing and settling their new territories, posed problems for those who looked for them. Racists sought those territories, and so too did those seeking to define and shape the new societies in the great zones of European settlement. They wanted 'White' states, 'stocked' from Europe. So immigration politics in Australia, Canada and the United States had led to laws and regulations that inhibited a free flow of Chinese migrants, and in some instances attempted to repatriate them.[6] The Great War's Chinese Labour Corps drew on those seven decades of foreign-organized shipment overseas of labourers, but at the same time marked a radical new departure. The Chinese went in common purpose with the Europeans – as equals of a kind – and Chinese intellectuals and labourers worked together. China did not send troops to Europe, but its contribution did release tens of thousands of Allied troops for the front lines.

Education programmes also sent increasing numbers of Chinese students overseas to schools and colleges. Many began to find their own way to Japan, Europe or North America to study. Students undertook advanced degrees in engineering, medicine and the sciences, went to military colleges in Japan, or to business schools and commercial colleges. A project would soon start to send some 1,600 students to France, many of them earning money to pay for their studies by working in factories. China's future leader Deng Xiaoping was one of them, spending a year making rubber overshoes in a factory near Paris. Political science, law and history students investigated the puzzles in international relations and in the history of recent Sino-foreign interaction that bedevilled their country. More than any generation before them, Chinese intellectuals in 1918 had an acute grasp of the technical details underpinning the issues they faced. Many in the republic's Ministry of Foreign Affairs were now getting ready to deploy this at the Paris Peace Conference. Qing officials had never been supine in the face of foreign pressure, and had in many ways, and at many times, handled their foreign problems adroitly. They knew what they were dealing with. But the military power and technological edge of the foreigners, and the great internal crises facing the dynasty, had compromised their ability to act. Now, however, China's aspirations seemed to match the world's; the leader of the now-supreme Allied power was personally offering a better future for China; and its talented young diplomats were ready to claim what was theirs.

So were the generals in Beijing. Well, wrote one caustic observer in the first week of December 1918, now we are smashing windows and our generals puff themselves up in all their plumed martial finery and claim a share of the Allied victory. But what did they do; what did any of the Allied generals achieve? Whose victory was this? The writer was twenty-nine-year-old Li Dazhao, chief librarian at Peking University, who had studied political economy in Japan for three years, and who was heavily engaged in the city's febrile intellectual debates about constitutionalism and reform. Allied nationals in the city had reacted to the news of victory by first setting out to wreck the premises of the Deutsche-Asiatische Bank and German-owned businesses in the Legation Quarter, where foreign embassies had been concentrated since the Boxer uprising. They had also attempted to demolish the Ketteler Arch, a huge monument demonstrating China's regret at the murder in 1900 by Qing soldiers of the German Minister to China. Li Dazhao saved his fire for his compatriots, for those who joined in the smashing of German shops, shouting 'Hurrah' in the streets, and for politicians like Xu Shichang and the generals who backed him, who strove to bask in the reflected glory of Allied might. Like an increasing number of others, Li Dazhao was appalled at the sabotage of constitutionalism by Yuan Shikai, who had become China's President in 1912, had overseen the country's first ever democratic national election, and then nullified the result by arranging for the assassination of the incoming Prime Minister-elect, Song Jiaoren, in March 1913. Song's National People's Party, the Guomindang, was then driven out of the new assembly, which was drenched with bribes, and sometimes surrounded with thugs, until it had made the 'right' decision, as Yuan established a military dictatorship. Yuan Shikai died in 1916, but his legacy was a broken republic and civil war, and a growing disenchantment with the promises of Western liberalism.

If China's place in the world seemed to have changed, its confidence was shaken by its internal chaos. By 1918 the seven years of the Republic of China had also seen two attempted monarchical restorations, a revolt by the Guomindang that had been crushed – British financial assistance to Yuan playing a key role – and the party's subsequent banning and regrouping around an alternative but often precarious government based in the southern port city of Guangzhou. Yuan's former military subordinates had assumed power, but were hardly united. The consistent factors in a byzantine story were, first, that all the functions and offices of a central government continued to operate in Beijing, and were recognized internationally, although this administration was wholly subordinate to the military, operating in alliances that were far from stable. The state was bankrolled by foreign loans, and by the revenues of the foreign-staffed Maritime Customs Service, whose chief, the Englishman Sir Francis Aglen, would sometimes be referred to as 'China's Supreme Minister of Finance' as a result. But there were other foreign loans too, secret ones to politicians and generals, and these loans often came with conditions. Opposition to Yuan's own attempt to become emperor had provoked regional declarations of independence that had persisted, as the opportunities provided to provincial militarists by a weak centre, or strong local cultures of independence and new thinking about federalism, saw such provinces increasingly assert their autonomy. There was also a widespread fear of foreign intervention. All the warring parties, in whatever constellation of alliance they had moved into, pledged themselves to the same task of maintaining or restoring national unity. They feared that a divided or chaotic China would invite foreign intervention, and the loss of territory to control by the Western powers.

For their part, foreign observers viewed all this as farce. They made jokes about the 'warlords', and about how they evaded fighting – for how can a 'warlord' be a warlord without an army, which might be lost through battle? One satirical *Child's Primer of Things Chinese*, published in Tianjin in 1923, and penned by an American doctor working in north China, began its Lesson III, 'Civil War', with the lines:

> Now here, my Child's a how-de-do!
> Watch Wang-lo-tsin and Hu-Ar-Yu,
> Ac-comp-anied by ten thous-and men,
> March up the hill and down a-gain!

But this was no 'pic-nic in a dell', as the stanzas concluded, for the financial and human costs of military rule were immense, and steadily increasing.[7] The militarists at the centre pledged themselves to defend the nation, and took both the Customs revenue and cash from Japan; in the localities soldiers defended themselves, and took all that they could lay their hands on. The price was paid by a traumatized populace, and generated a widespread feeling of powerlessness and humiliation. The generals and the politicians did not look as if they would or could save China.

Whose 'victory' was this? Well, Li Dazhao provided a simple answer to his query, in a text sprinkled with new foreign words as yet untransliterated or untranslated, reporting developments and thought so new that the Chinese language had not yet caught up: the victory was that of Bolshevism. The German people had overthrown the militarists, as the Russian people had overthrown the Tsar. This was a world-historical movement; the Russian revolution was the first falling leaf presaging autumn. The journal in which this essay appeared, *Xin Qingnian – La Jeunesse* (*New Youth*) – was rapidly becoming the great agenda-setter for radical thought. Li was the first of China's thinkers to express support for the October Revolution in Russia, and to espouse Bolshevism for China.[8] The red flag would fly elsewhere too. Li Dazhao did not look to the Paris Peace Conference for China's future, nor the world's.

The same issue of *Xin Qingnian* contained the latest essay in a series of 'random thoughts' penned by a former medical student, Zhou Shuren, a product of the new Western-style educational institutions that had emerged in the late Qing, and of study overseas. Now working in a government office in Beijing, he had refocused his energies on politics, on a literature for politics in fact, publishing earlier in 1918 under the pen name 'Lu Xun' the first of the stories and essays that would help revolutionize China's culture. His comment now, in 'Random Thought No. 35', was an oblique response to the opportunities presented by the peace. Since the republic began, he wrote, 'we have been hearing people declare that we should "preserve our national characteristics"'.[9] But what does this mean, he pondered, and why are we in such a mess? 'Some say this is because we failed to preserve our national characteristics and opened ourselves up' – that is, allowed the opening of the treaty ports. But was all well before then, he mused? 'A friend of mine has said most aptly, "If we want to preserve our national characteristics, we must first make sure that they can preserve us."' As 'Lu Xun', Zhou Shuren raised no Bolshevik red flag, but he was quietly setting out an agenda for revolution nonetheless. And he did not look to Woodrow Wilson for self-preservation, but to a process of rigorous self-examination, a root-and-branch analysis of Chinese culture. 'All we ask is whether a thing has the power to preserve us, not whether it is characteristic or not.'

Preserve us from these dreary intellectuals, many other people thought. For every revolutionary who later rehearsed in memoir a story of radical awakening and enlightenment, inspired by *New Youth* and its champions, there were other students immersed in the sybaritic pleasures and excitements of youth. We should acknowledge the sense of crisis, but not assume that it in any way dominated everyday life. The war had unleashed an economic boom for China, especially in the cities, and that brought with it social and cultural change. Expressing this most dramatically were the two great department stores that opened their doors during the conflict within ten months – and 50 yards – of each other on Shanghai's Nanjing Road. The Sincere Company's five-storey, Beaux Arts-style building, equipped with lifts, clock tower and roof gardens, housed retail space and a hotel, and 10,000 people visited it on the day it opened in October 1917.[10] Its owner, Ma Yingbiao, was born near Guangzhou, but had emigrated to Australia, where he had been impressed by the department stores he saw in Sydney, establishing his own in Hong Kong in 1900. The Wing On (Yong'an) store opened by fellow Australian returnees, the Guo brothers, on 6 September 1918 was just as sumptuously built and stocked – and just as crowded. Its customers emptied the store of half its stock in its first three weeks, their demand far outstripping the predictions of its owners. Both stores saturated Shanghai's press with advertisements: they were presented in these as modern – often a synonym for Western, but not always, and the meanings would be changing; they were sites of entertainment and display; they sold lifestyles, new ways of living and consuming for a new youth.

Nanjing Road's new stores helped shape a market, but that market was already emerging. President Xu wore his top hat and tails. Chinese men and women changed their clothes, shoes and headwear; they changed the ways they exercised their bodies, and tended to them; they changed how they lit and lived in their homes, what goods they used and how they were displayed.[11] They rode bicycles, listened to gramophones, learned to play foreign musical instruments, and they sang and danced together to different tunes. All this changed their patterns of consumption and interests. Focused on the cities of China, this changing culture percolated along the shipping lines, railways and postal routes into the hinterland. Advertising reflected and helped shape this. A foreign company, British American Tobacco (BAT), was the largest player in this field, but others – Chinese and foreign-owned – followed its lead. Like BAT they employed Chinese artists who evolved a new, consciously modern visual style – 'modern' women, with unbound feet, fashionable clothes, a cigarette to hand – and a nationwide marketing system that took the women portrayed in its popular New Year posters in particular into households far from the Nanjing Road.[12] This new world of consumption would become a major political arena in the two decades after the end of the war, but as the wartime economy boomed it was dominated by the bright shining lights of Shanghai's stores, and the hotels and the new forms of urban pleasure they represented and sold. Lu Xun worried about Chinese culture and China's 'national characteristics', and argued that they should be re-examined root and branch. Urbanites in Shanghai and other cities took a different route, fashioning through consumption a 'modeng' – modern – Chinese culture: even the word was foreign.

Many remained outside Wing On looking in, of course, poverty – genteel or absolute – holding them back. But rather than a stark divide between a 'Westernizing' urban elite, for example, and a 'traditional' majority culture, the evidence shows a steady diffusion of the new across the country. The shacks of even the very poor hosted BAT's visions of a glamorous new life, as often as did the wealthier homes; both were lit with lamps developed by the American-owned Standard Oil Company, or British-owned Asiatic Petroleum, to burn kerosene they imported from abroad.[13] China, however, had its share of natural disaster, at times more than its share, and man-made disaster too, and life in the Chinese countryside, or on the margins of city life, could be hard. But those who wished to change China – missionaries and radicals alike – had a vested interest in exaggerating its problems. 'Wherever one goes, it is the same weary tale with interminable reiteration,' wrote one influential missionary writer in 1899. 'Poverty, poverty, poverty, always and evermore poverty.'[14] Such views of Chinese rural life and culture as unchanging, and 'medieval', have remained influential, and obscured the dynamism of the urban world, as well as the realities of life in the countryside.

So the Chinese and their country were changing. They did so in ways that provided sharp contrasts to the patterns of living, consuming, and social and personal relations that had characterized their world as the twentieth century dawned. Of course, we can find 'change' wherever we look for it, in any country at any time, and much of what was changing China was also having an impact in the

Americas or Europe. What gave change in China its particular character was that it was bound up with understandings of stark differences between Chinese and 'foreign'. It felt and looked markedly different to the world of twenty or thirty years before, and it would take much, much longer for habits of distinction to relax. Moreover, this passage to a new Chinese world seemed compromised or distorted by the political impasse in which China found itself. The Qing had retreated to the private quarters of the Forbidden City, but the country seemed to have had only half a revolution. Student banners in 1918 opposed China's own militarism through attacking Prussia's; they urged reconstruction not destruction for China, they demanded China's freedom from imperialist domination, its other great problem. Those foreign soldiers in Beijing, the foreigners in Shanghai who had organized the great victory celebration, these had been China's allies in war, but they remained its problem, both in war, and now, more clearly again, in peace.

If we look across the country at reports of the peace celebrations more widely, we can see evidence of the hopes vested in victory by the Chinese, and of the implicit impediments to their realization, not least of all in the shape of the foreign presence now embedded across China.[15] Since the 1840s, a coven of European powers led by the British had secured from China through treaties either resting on force of arms, or on the threat of it, a wide range of privileges and possessions. China's sovereignty had been deeply impaired. In the 1890s these powers had been joined by Japan, and throughout most of the decades before 1918 the United States had willingly shared in the spoils of the great 'Scramble for China'. Extensive tracts of territory had been carved off and incorporated into the Russian Far East; realms that had once pledged allegiance to the Great Qing Dynasty had fallen under foreign colonial rule, such as Indochina. Britain and Germany had seized colonies at Hong Kong and at Qingdao; Japan had taken the island of Taiwan. The Japanese, British and French had secured 'Leased Territories' at Guangzhouwan and Kowloon in Guangdong province, and at Dalian ('Dairen' in Japanese, formerly Russian Dalny) in Manchuria. That latter northeastern territory had been the subject of a struggle for domination between Russia and Japan, which was resolved through Japan's shattering victory over the mighty power of its adversary in the war of 1904–5. Where they did not have territorial control, foreign powers claimed 'spheres of influence' in which their commercial and strategic interests should be paramount. In brief, they demanded first share of any potential gains: mines, railway concessions, the right to issue loans, establish steamship lines, found hospitals or colleges – anything and everything.

The colonial expansion of Europe and its partners in the nineteenth century was a global phenomenon, and China was one of but a handful of existing polities that escaped wholesale incorporation into one empire or another. Like other survivors its territorial integrity and sovereignty were degraded nonetheless. Some felt that this 'semi-' or 'hypo-' colonization was the worst of possible outcomes. For Sun Yat-sen, a veteran anti-Qing revolutionary, and leader of the alternative government based in Guangzhou, such a geographically partial and plural subjection to foreign control was actually worse than total loss of independence, for all took and none gave. No single power felt to any extent the degree of responsibility for China and its people that a colonial sovereign might be expected to have. It was not a colony, but a 'sub' colony: a lower-order category of analysis.[16] Analysts and historians might well query Sun's assumption that colonial powers routinely exercised any such duties of colonial care; but the rhetoric of all of the late nineteenth-century empires certainly placed the 'White Man's Burden' at its heart – if it could be said to have any heart. The able statesmen of the Qing and their successors had to juggle the competing and often contradictory demands of at least a dozen active foreign powers.

What this meant in practice was that China played host to a cosmopolitan foreign establishment lodged in towns and cities and along railway and steamship lines from the borders with Burma and French Indochina in the southwest to the fast-developing Manchurian provinces in the northeast. So as a Chinese man or woman, you could take a walk in Tianjin as recently as 16 March 1917 from the northeast gate of the port city, and traverse a Japanese, a French, a British and then a German concession. You could cross over to the north bank of the Hai River into the Belgian concession, then saunter along through the Russian, then Italian, and then lastly the Austro-Hungarian-controlled district. You would come across street signs in at least eight languages, and policemen from all those states and some of their colonies (Sikhs from British India, Annamites from French Indochina). There were different by-laws and regulations to observe as you went, and different cultures of interaction with 'natives' like yourself, some more dully, routinely, violent than others, but all capable of it. So you had to keep your wits about you. If you took a break and sat down in the parks or squares that could be found in each concession – that is, if the regulations did not prevent your entrance (because you were a 'native') – you would also find in most of them a monument in national style, commemorating their civil and military dead during the 1900 siege of the concessions by Qing forces and Boxers. These were memorials to victory – but also to your defeat at their hands.

There were other deliberate architectural statements in the various concessions, highlighting the culture of this power or that one in the shape of consulates, municipal buildings, churches and barracks. Not all of these areas were fully developed by any means, for colonialism's grubby reach often exceeded its grasp – and its available resources – but several powers were still hungry to expand. Even China's jurisdiction over the difficult, winding river at Tianjin was impaired, for an international 'Conservancy Board' took decisions concerning its management and improvement. These foreign concessions had been established at different times, and the pattern of foreign residence and business hardly matched evolving political realities, but here was a slice of Consul Siffert's Belgium in a north Chinese city, and there was a bit of Britain, and a morsel of France. The world had come to squat on the banks of the Hai River. There was certainly a long precedent in historic state practice in China for corralling foreign visitors and sojourners into clearly delineated areas, and making them responsible for their own behaviour. So to an extent this pattern of concessions was not unfamiliar: but most of the new ones had been granted under various forms of duress, and while the Chinese state ultimately retained nominal ownership of the land – in Chinese the concessions were 'zujie', meaning leased areas – this freehold sovereignty was a fiction. Foreign powers and foreign residents were apt to treat them as permanently alienated colonies, whatever the letter or even the spirit of the treaties intended.

The roster of concessions at Hankou, 600 miles along the Yangzi from the sea, was smaller, but the effect along the riverside bund there was the same. Some cities had but one concession – Zhenjiang or Jiujiang, for example. Some hosted a couple. Guangzhou had a British and a French concession abutting each other on Shamian Island (Shameen), which had been deliberately reclaimed from the river and built for the purpose. At Xiamen – Amoy – in southern Fujian province, a tiny British concession faced a much larger International Settlement on beautiful Gulangyu Island in the harbour. Some cities opened to foreign residence and trade, such as Ningbo or Fuzhou, had no concession area, though there was often an informal foreign settlement area. These mostly port cities – the great exception was Russian-dominated Harbin, which had grown out of a railway junction – formed a network of foreign enclaves, linked together by coastal and riverine shipping lines, and by some of China's new railways. They were protected by garrisons of foreign troops, and naval patrols on the great rivers. Subjects and citizens of a number of foreign powers also enjoyed extraterritorial rights in China. They were not subject to Chinese law, but to the jurisdiction of their consular services: foreign courts sat in China, foreign jails were built there, foreigners were occasionally hanged there by their consular police. Extraterritoriality also delivered two things yet more intangible, for an aura of untouchability surrounded most Europeans and Americans, regardless of their actual status, in many Chinese eyes, and many foreign residents and visitors adopted in their interactions with Chinese an assumption of a vulgar extraterritoriality: they could get away with murder. Sometimes they did.[17]

The infrastructure of this world is written all over its daily press, in English – American- or British-owned – French, German, Russian and Japanese, which is full of advertisements and news of banks, shipping and railways; telegraphs, posts and insurance; consulates and courts, councils and chambers of commerce. Its own urban consumer culture is all to the fore as well in the department store notices, car agency ads, and listings of the showings at the cinemas, and of sweet deals from restaurants and hotels. There are, too, the offerings from the specialist shops: S. Moultrie or Robinson's selling sheet music, pianos and gramophone records; Kelly & Walsh or Edward

Evans publishing or importing books; F. Venturi shipping in fine wines and brandies. A browse through the *North China Daily News* of the victory week offers more evidence of its thicker texture: the pastry cooks and bakeries, the 'Sweetmeat Castle' on the Nanjing Road, travel agencies offering trips to 'luxurious hotels' in Japanese-controlled Dairen, and small ads seeking a specialist gardener, a position for a 'Lady Stenographer', rooms for bachelors, cars for sale, as well as shotguns and stamp collections. The recently established American Club holds social events and hosts Chamber of Commerce meetings in its Nanjing Road home; establishment of a Rotary Club is under discussion; the Shanghai Volunteer Corps' American Company holds its annual summer camp and rifle meeting. An undertaker has Italian marble and Scotch granite 'always on hand'. The cemeteries, churches and hospitals were always busy.

Some 27,000 foreign nationals lived in Shanghai at the war's end; a third of that number were Japanese, just under a quarter were British, and there were some 3,000 Americans. These formed the three largest foreign communities. Across China some 40,000 foreigners lived in the forty-eight 'treaty ports', and another 180,000 Russians and Japanese lived in Manchuria or Dairen.[18] The International Settlement Council at Shanghai, itself a large employer, recorded foreign occupations across eighty categories in its regular census: actuaries, architects and auctioneers; dentists, divers and drapers; photographers, plumbers and police were all listed. The Protestant cathedral had its Cambridge University-educated dean; the power station and waterworks needed qualified engineers; hospitals needed trained nurses and doctors; the orchestra needed an experienced conductor. They lived, worked and played in and amongst, and in various forms of collaboration with, some two million Chinese residents living in Shanghai across its foreign-controlled zones and in the districts outside them.

Overlapping with this world within China's own borders were the colonies that had been ceded from it, and that sat formally within foreign empires. The oldest and oddest of these was tiny Macao, held by Portugal, which dated its origins to 1557 (although the Chinese had consistently refused to acknowledge its legality). Administered by a governor appointed from Portugal, it sat on a peninsula and two nearby islands. The parliament in Lisbon – to which it elected a deputy – fixed Macao's budget; its highest law court sat in Goa in Portuguese India; and it was garrisoned with Portuguese colonial troops from India or Africa. Its church was subordinate to the Archdiocese of Goa. Macao was a sleepy free port, home in 1920 to about 85,000 people, nine-tenths of them Chinese. But the Portuguese of Macao – the Macanese – actually worked across the treaty ports in China and dominated some sectors: they were its printers and its clerks, notably its bank clerks. These were Macao's mestizo settlers, of mixed Chinese and Portuguese heritage, who had developed their own distinctive patois and culture. They were fiercely proud of being Portuguese, the more so because they had little direct connection to Portugal. The town's heart lay in its waterfront, a mile and a half long, the Praia Grande, its skyline dominated by the ruined facade of an early seventeenth-century church that nurtured the rich air of decay and of history with which the colony was smothered. The 'pleasure resort for South China', as one 1920 guidebook described it, was a three-hour ferry ride from Hong Kong.[19] So it was for many residents of the latter indelibly associated with adultery, and with its licensed gambling and brothels.

The Boys' Association of Macao trampled on Germany's flag and then burned it as part of the colony's three days of victory festivities in its streets, churches, clubs and its mosque in 1918. The Portuguese of Macao descent had also packed out Hong Kong's Catholic cathedral three days earlier, as the British colony had marked victory with a day of meetings, services and dinner dances. At least seventy-five British Hong Kong residents were by then known to have died on active service in the war; six hundred or more had gone to fight.[20] They came from its businesses, its administrative services, and from the recently established University of Hong Kong. The colony had been taken by the British in 1841, and its territory had been greatly expanded in 1898 with the addition of the Leased Territory to the north (which had taken a short but vicious little war to enforce). By 1920 Hong Kong's population of nearly two-thirds of a million lived mostly in Victoria, the city on the island's northern shore, and in the Kowloon suburbs across the harbour. There were barely four and a half thousand Britons of all ages. Punjabi Sikhs worked in the police force and as watchmen. Parsees, who had once been prominent in business and in society, were dwindling in number. The Germans, who had had their own large club, and who had, like the Parsees, hosted one of the celebratory events that marked the colony's golden jubilee in 1891, had been interned or deported after October 1914. Some 1,500 Japanese and 500 Americans were counted in 1920. There were just over 2,500 Portuguese, mostly then living in the new garden city-style suburb in Yau Ma Tei. Hong Kong had long lost to Shanghai the paramountcy in China's foreign trade that it had itself seized from Macao in the 1840s, but it remained an important entrepôt, had a slowly developing industrial sector, and was an offshore base for many British interests in China itself.

The Crown Colony was marked by its snobbery, the elite British clinging to fine-grained social distinctions as their houses clung to the higher slopes of the island, and by the fast turnover in its British population, which was almost entirely refreshed every five years. As a result it was thought by the chief census officer John Lloyd, who was a member of the small cadre of officials – the Hong Kong Cadets – recruited specifically for the colony's administration, entirely to lack any 'public spirit'.[21] When governors arrived and departed they did so ritually at Queen's Pier, landing close by a statue of Queen Victoria that itself demonstrated the way in which Hong Kong was tied to the British Empire, for copies of the same monument graced the cities of Kimberley and Toronto. Close by was the Hong Kong Club, the headquarters of the Hongkong and Shanghai Bank, the languid sprawl of a cricket ground, and the Royal Naval Dockyard. The administrators of the colony so lacked a sense of humour as to have erected a statue to Sir Thomas Jackson, its most prominent late nineteenth-century banker, but this also reflected the growing power of the Hongkong and Shanghai Bank in China's finances. The flags of the bank and the colony flew side by side when the statue was unveiled. Queen Victoria and Sir Thomas were well lit by strings of lanterns as Hong Kong celebrated on 13 November 1918, when its Europeans promenaded, some in fancy dress, with 'the most complete, albeit decorous, abandon', watched, one report noticed, in a reversal of roles, by crowds of Chinese who 'marvelled at the spectacle'.[22]

Victory jamborees and processions of flag-waving schoolchildren took place much further afield in November 1918, in cities and towns without concessions or any large foreign communities. At Anqing the crowd crammed itself into the compound of the provincial military command to hear speeches from Anhui province's leading officials, but four foreigners also took a turn, representing their countries, and highlighting how much further into China than the port city enclaves the foreign presence reached. Kado Sotomatsu, the Japanese consul, led off. But the man speaking for France was a Jesuit missionary, Father Jean Noury; and for Britain, Robert Young, who worked for the China Inland Mission at Shucheng, seventy miles north of Anqing; and for the United States, John Knight Shryock, who had arrived in the city to work for the Protestant Episcopal Church of America just two years earlier. In many parts of China, missionary voices, not diplomatic ones, spoke for the world beyond the republic's borders. This was a mixed blessing overall.

There were missionaries or a mission presence of some sort in nearly every one of China's 1,704 counties.[23] They represented every possible denomination, and they came from all over Europe and North America. Established state Churches had their offshoots, such as the Church of England's Church Missionary Society, but there were specialist organizations, such as the China Inland Mission. Through contacts with individual evangelists and outposts, communities overseas often became deeply intertwined with China. Mission work in China became an embedded feature of Norwegian rural life, for example, and news from China missions a steady strand in the activities of towns in the American Midwest and English provincial cities.[24] The Catholic Church had a long-established infrastructure across China, and large communities of adherents in Shaanxi province, Shanghai and elsewhere. Chinese orphans were ever in the minds of French congregations.[25] Societies sometimes competed for converts, but by 1918 had mostly settled down and demarcated areas of activity amongst themselves. In Anhui province there were nine Protestant societies at work, with about 150 foreign staff. Only the China Inland Mission and the Protestant Episcopal Church of America had stations in Anqing itself: the former established in 1869, which included a men's Chinese-language training school for new arrivals, and the latter in 1894. By 1918 the city had a cathedral, a church, two schools and a hospital, and half a dozen rural 'out-stations'. Members of the two societies did not, in general, interact much with each other, nor with the Catholics.[26] Only three Protestant societies had more than a thousand converts, and those three had a total of 6,000 believers by 1917; there were about ten times as many Catholics. The population of the province stood at seventeen million in 1910.[27] By any rational measure the results were unimpressive; it looked like failure.

The cultural and intellectual impact of the mission enterprise far exceeded its actual gains, however, at least as they were tallied up in mission yearbooks and in a triumphalist, thoughtlessly and tellingly titled 1922 report, *The Christian Occupation of China*. This was prepared for the decennial China Missionary Conference held at Shanghai that year. The missionary enterprise had three substantial fields of impact beyond simple conversion. Firstly, it had served as an influential vector for the transmission of foreign cultural, scientific and philosophical knowledge to China. Secondly, converts had formed communities that had in some places become highly influential, displacing or living in parallel with existing rural or urban elites, in cities like Fuzhou, for example.[28] Thirdly, missionary educational, medical and, increasingly, social initiatives had their own dynamic. Mission education was often sought after because it provided tuition in English and foreign-style mathematics, which were increasingly desirable skills for those wishing to work within the urban port cities. The religious content or framework of missionary education would start to create tensions between students motivated by secular ambition, and those staffing the institutions, who saw them as serving an evangelical purpose. At the same time, the growth in social gospel thinking, and the professionalization of education, meant that increasing numbers of foreign missionary staff were more secular-minded than otherwise. Organizations such as the Young Men's Christian Association became important sites of social welfare and, implicitly, political discussion and action. The unintended consequences of the missionary enterprise were to prove influential as the years unfolded.

So, to a new arrival, stepping off the launches that brought passengers from the mail steamers, this looked like empire. If that person had traversed the railway lines eastwards from Europe, or sailed across the Pacific from San Francisco or north from Australia, Shanghai would have appeared to be simply one more colony amongst others, and a gateway to a wider structure of colonial power in China. That it was not was a problem for China, in Sun Yat-sen's analysis, also because nationalists had to engage with – or confront, oppose and potentially fight – more than one single colonial ruler. Yet it was also China's opportunity: for a united front of the foreign powers was never easy to maintain, and they could be played off against each other. However, thinking of the foreign establishment in China as a colonial society also presents other problems. It presupposes that the thousands of foreign residents were colonialists, in mind and function, when most were not, at least not as we instinctively think of them. They did not seek to serve their states, nor aim to advance imperialism. Rhetorically they might often profess to both, but they were in fact mostly migrants and sojourners, traversing the oceanic and transcontinental transportation highways in the search for jobs or opportunities. A man does not leave Canada to work for an insurance combine in China in a conscious bid to advance empire; an Englishwoman does not find a place in a Shanghai hospital to help colonize the city, nor does a Japanese trader who sets up a small store in Shantou. Rhode Island native Lester Knox Little did not join the Customs, nor Thomas Millard found Shanghai's *China Press* newspaper, to help subordinate the Chinese state to American interests. Instead, the main factor would have been personal advancement against the backdrop of a world of opportunity that was certainly (and violently) shaped by colonial power – that much always needs remembering.[29] Each made their choice alone.

This is not to say that amongst these were not many – a majority – whose world view was shaped by empire and imperialist instincts, and by the rising tide of 'scientific' theories of, and justifications for, racism, and their popularizations, in the later nineteenth century. The ways in which foreign residents in China thought about, and acted on, their views on race and relations between 'races', was routine for its time. They were ordinary men and women, so they were in the main ordinary racists. There was little that was distinctive about the easily aired, fluently obnoxious views held by the foreign residents, nor about the ways they dealt with the Chinese people they lived amongst and worked with. And, given some hold on power locally – as was secured at Shanghai, in Tianjin, Hankou and other cities, backed up with treaties and agreements and by simple brute foreign military force – they sought to preserve it. Amongst those who paraded in 1918 were people fresh to Asia, as well as third-generation families in China. For all of these, a world shorn of empire's protective armour was unimaginable: think of a tortoise without its shell. In China foreign residents believed they knew what would happen if they let down their guard: they called it 'Boxerism'. The events of that 1900 Boxer uprising – hundreds of foreign men, women and children killed, thousands of Chinese Christians slain – had left a permanent fear of Chinese popular nationalism, which could only ever be, in the eyes of foreign residents, murderously xenophobic. They saw all foreign 'weakness' – which they were quick to spot, and guard against – as encouraging, directly or indirectly, the 'fanatical' Boxer who lurked in the Chinese shadows.

While the Qing state had mostly failed when it fought, its opening to foreign power had been less dramatic and sustained than later political analysis would usually claim. Opponents and critics of the Manchus would routinely state that Qing weakness and incompetence had recklessly imperilled China; while nationalistic agitation would lack bite if its cry had been tempered to fit the objective facts of the limits to foreign power. The Qing had more or less effectively managed their unwelcome guests, and Chinese society – and the Chinese economy – had proved resilient and adaptable. China had not been extinguished. It had survived. The greatest problem for the Manchus in the nineteenth century had been the Taiping Rebellion (1850–64), which, although shaped and arguably sparked by the disruptions caused by the assertion of foreign power after 1839, had been a domestic crisis.[30] The peoples of the Qing Empire and of the republic that had then taken over most of the land within its borders, had mostly – if often warily – come to terms with the steady enforced integration of their realm into a world dominated by empires. On an individual level this found expression in their ready adoption and adaptation of foreign goods. The Boxer uprising was the great exception, not the rule. Measured assessment carries little weight, however, if it is not believed, and if it is politically inconvenient and out of sync with its time. For all that it was hemmed in and contained, foreign power still seemed to many to lie at the heart of China's problems – and of its unfinished revolution of the body politic, and of the mind.

This paradox had already found bloody expression in Shanghai earlier in 1918. On the night of 19 July, Chinese and Japanese had fought in the streets of the Shanghai International Settlement's northern district of Hongkou, not far north by rickshaw from the site, but four months later, of the carnival of peace. A dispute three days earlier between Japanese sailors and a Chinese shopkeeper had spiralled into a lethal ethnic clash: organized groups of Japanese residents had attacked Chinese policemen and civilians; police based in the local station feared further attacks, and on the sultry Friday evening of 19 July groups of Japanese men attacked them in the streets nearby. Several people were injured, and two Japanese bystanders, a draper and an off-duty policeman, were shot dead. An investigation blamed a virulent culture of antipathy between Chinese and Japanese for fuelling the events.[31] Japan's 'Twenty-One Demands' in 1915 had aimed to re-orientate the republic towards its eastern neighbour, and diplomatic demands had their counterpart and prompt in a fast-changing reality on the ground. The size of the Japanese population in Shanghai had been rising steadily, doubling between 1910 and 1915. Wartime volunteering by Europeans from the concessions and settlements had left gaps in the ranks of the police, for example, that Japanese diplomats were happy to help fill. The Japanese share of foreign trade in Shanghai also doubled between 1914 and 1918. The general picture from Customs Service statistics was of a similar increase in the scale of the Japanese presence across China since the start of the war, but the broader context was of a twenty-fold increase in Japanese residents and firms since 1903.[32]

The canker in the sweet rose of victory in November 1918 did not stem simply from the underlying intransigence and resentment of the Europeans, but from the fact that they were also increasingly being challenged by Japan, this imperialist interloper, which had defeated the Russian Empire in the war of 1904–5 for predominance in China's northeastern Manchurian provinces, and attacked Germany's Shandong possessions in 1914. British reports indicated that the Chinese police concerned in the 1918 Shanghai affray had been recruited from Shandong province, and were acutely sensitive to Japanese aggression there, declining to bow to it on the streets of the settlement. But this was no longer a Shandong problem. Most worryingly for many observers was that the Japanese diplomats seemed to have no control over their countrymen, and that they responded in the aftermath of the riot with aggressively partisan demands. They wanted more Japanese in the settlement police, and a greater formal say in the running of the settlement. They wanted, it seemed, their own colony in Shanghai. The 'Hongkew disturbances' were hardly Shanghai's first riots. But they were the first arising from the deliberate actions of a part of the foreign community – 'Never mind the reason; go for the Chinese' one of the groups was heard being told on the night of 19 July – and they involved an assault on the colonial status quo.[33] The constables were attacked because they were Chinese, but they were also employees of the British-dominated International Settlement. The assertion of Japanese power in China, by its diplomats and by ordinary Japanese residents, was already targeted at the republican state, but now also, and thereafter increasingly, at the other foreign powers in China.

Legal disputes over the July riots were still in train when a new round of conflict with the Japanese swept Shanghai, as it had swept across China. This had its origins in Paris, not in China, although the great optimism displayed on city streets across the country in November 1918 was also a critical factor. Woodrow Wilson went in person to Paris to the conference that would shape a peace treaty and that new world order called for on China's streets and from the podiums. China sent a large delegation too. It brought with it a wide range of issues for discussion: proposed 'questions for readjustment' covered the renunciation of spheres of influence, withdrawal of foreign garrisons, abolition of extraterritoriality and return of foreign concessions. All of this was extraneous to the main order of business at Versailles. But the Chinese in Paris, at home and observing from across the world, took confidence from Wilson's Fourteen Points. From the sympathetic reception given them by American officials and diplomats, they also believed that their specific case for the return of German possessions in China would meet with success – and this did fall squarely within the remit of the Paris Peace Conference.[34]

The delegates brought together in the Chinese delegation were talented and articulate advocates for their country, representing different generations of China's response to its challenges. Shanghai-born Lu Zhengxian (Lou Tseng-Tsiang) was Minister for Foreign Affairs, and had graduated from the old 'Interpreters' College', the Tongwenguan, established in 1862 to create a cadre of new officials versed in foreign languages and knowledge. Joining the nascent diplomatic service in 1892, he had served in Russia and at negotiations in The Hague and elsewhere, had married a Belgian general's daughter, and served as the Minister to the Netherlands. Wang Zhengting (C. T. Wang), the Guomindang's representative in the delegation, had been born, like Lu, into a Protestant family. He had studied in Japan, and at Michigan and Yale Universities in the United States. Heavily involved in national politics since the outbreak of the revolution in 1911, he was also a leading light in, and in 1919 national chairman of, the YMCA in China. The star of the team, however, was the youngest, Columbia University-trained Dr Gu Weijun – better known as V. K. Wellington Koo (and named after the Duke of Wellington). Koo's doctoral thesis concerned 'The Status of Aliens in China', and his clear ambition was to change it. Joining the Ministry of Foreign Affairs, he had swiftly risen to become an ambassador, first to Mexico, and then to the United States in 1915. He was a charming and persuasive speaker. China was not wholly new to participation in international conferences – Lu had represented Chinese interests at The Hague peace conference in 1907 – but this was a gathering of a different order. The delegates were clearly up to the task, but it is not entirely clear that they were intending to participate in the same meeting as the British, the French, the Americans, and certainly not the Japanese.

Although the Chinese delegates supported Japan's proposal for a racial equality amendment to be added to the proposed League of Nations Covenant – a bid that was thwarted by the British and the United States – the two sets of representatives clashed over Germany's former interests in Shandong. The Chinese wanted them transferred back from what they assumed was temporary Japanese occupation; the Japanese demanded them as spoils of war. It did not help that the Chinese representatives – even Foreign Minister Lu – were unaware of the fact that on 28 September 1918 the militarists controlling Xu Shichang's government in Beijing had secretly recognized a Japanese military presence in Shandong in exchange for Japanese loans. Koo's well-articulated claims for restitution, grounded in diplomatic precedent and garnished with claims that Shandong was the 'cradle of civilization . . . a Holy Land for the Chinese', fell by the wayside. China had little standing at the conference, its assumption of the shared mantle of Allied victory proving even less persuasive when articulated just thirty miles from the furthest reach of the German advance in 1914 than it did back in the foreign concessions.

In late April 1919, as the Shandong question was being discussed in detail by the leading Allied powers, the 'Council of Four' was temporarily three in number, for Italy had withdrawn and the conference seemed to be in crisis. Wilson, not in the best of health at this point, feared that everything was falling apart, that his plans for the League of Nations would be thwarted and that war would restart. The Japanese, angry at the rejection of the racial equality proposal, were intransigent over Shandong, and the British and French were compromised by commitments they had made in 1917 to support such a claim in return for Japanese naval assistance in the Mediterranean: 'Japanese help was urgently required,' noted British Prime Minister David Lloyd George in justification, for at that point in the war Britain 'had been very hard pressed'. Wilson was eventually persuaded to accept the Japanese claim, not without some anguish on his part, but having secured from them what he confidently felt was a very clear commitment to restore eventually to China the core rights transferred from Germany. This was not embedded in the treaty, but was given in a form that the Japanese delegates argued was all that their own public opinion would accept: after all, they had fought Germany from the start of the war, and needed to show some fruit for their sacrifice. The compromise secured what Wilson is recorded as describing as an 'even break', 'the best that could be gotten out of a dirty past'. Most of the American delegation was appalled, but his chief advisor Edward House assured Wilson that 'it is no worse than the things we are doing in many of the settlements in which the Western Powers are interested.' Get the League of Nations established, ran one consistent thread of argument in support of accommodating the Japanese, then let it sort out these and other colonial issues. Even so, Wilson did not sleep that night, 'my mind was so full of the Japanese-Chinese controversy'.[35]

During the discussions, Lloyd George – 'slippery as an eel' in the view of Wilson's press secretary Ray Stannard Baker – also advanced a position that would be more familiar to his compatriots in China. He had every sympathy for China, stating just a week earlier that 'the way in which [the Japanese] have terrorized the Chinese to force them to' agree to the Twenty-One Demands 'is one of the most unscrupulous proceedings in all history'. But 'China's stagnation', he argued on 29 April in a meeting with Wilson, French President Georges Clemenceau and the Japanese delegation:

> justifies a great part of what foreigners have done there. The Chinese are like the Arabs, a very talented race, but at a stage that doesn't allow them to progress further. China would have been destroyed by the Taiping Rebellion if Gordon hadn't been there to organize her army. It must be acknowledged that China isn't in the same situation as the great powers represented in this conference.[36]

This state only exists, Lloyd George was saying, because we propped it up in the middle of the nineteenth century – he was referring to the involvement of Charles George Gordon in a small force of foreign-officered troops who had supported Qing operations against the rebels. This was poor history on all possible counts, but much of what passes for a historical justification of any status quo tends to be equally inaccurate. The myth is the point, not the facts. And China's claims could barely be heard amongst the clamour, as the French sought revenge against Germany, the Italians sought territory from the former Austro-Hungarian Empire, Germany was in danger of starvation and revolution, and Bolshevism menaced Europe.

This was no betrayal: it was a routine episode in practical politics. Objectively, the specific losses in Shandong were hardly going to prove disastrous. The Qing and now the republic had learned to live with and make use of the foreign concessions. New treaty ports had been opened within the previous decade. A new settlement at Qingdao 'under the usual conditions' was what the Japanese technically secured at Versailles, as well as Germany's economic privileges.[37] In fact, within three years the Japanese did transfer the territory back to

China, and no new settlement was ever developed.[38] Moreover, former German and Austro-Hungarian assets elsewhere in China were unaffected. These had been confiscated in 1917 by the republic and this offered precedents for future restitutions – while the collapse of the Russian Empire left a further range of possessions in China vulnerable.

China had come to a different conference, however, one it believed would entirely reshape existing international relations. The preamble to one draft of China's formal claim for restitution, to be lodged with the conference in March 1919, had stated that 'the repudiation of Imperialism as a rule of action in the transactions of nations' lay at the heart of the objectives at Versailles.[39] But it did not. This was a powerful statement from one of the handful of states outside Europe or the Americas that remained independent. But almost nobody at the conference believed this statement to be true. The conference seemed instead to endorse the practices of empire, tarnishing in the process the very practice of diplomacy as a vehicle for effecting change. The Chinese expected the Paris Peace Conference to change the world; Wilson expected the League of Nations to do that. This confusion underpinned the crisis. The apparent corruption of the principles that all had assumed underpinned the Peace Conference proved catastrophic in China, that, and the fact that the negotiations had exposed the secret, self-serving machinations of the militarists who had taken over the republic.

When news reached China on 2 May 1919 of the acceptance of the Japanese claims, it shocked the nation. The hopes of those who had marched to welcome victory in November were dashed. Such was the uproar that the Versailles Treaty was not signed by the Chinese delegation on 28 June. They had received instructions only to sign with a caveat, which had been rejected, for it been agreed that no nation could be allowed to sign the treaty in this way. The delegates – happily for them – were also penned into their hotel in Paris by angry Chinese students.[40] That demonstration in Paris was of a piece with developments in Chinese communities across the world, but nowhere were they as significant as they proved to be in China. The news of the demonstration arrived in China on 3 May, and students in Beijing gathered in protest on 4 May in front of the Tiananmen – the Tianan gate – south of the Forbidden City, only a few hundred yards from the site of November's dazzling victory ceremony, and at the heart of the republic's capital. Whatever you do, the capital's garrison commander told the students as they readied themselves to march, do not provoke 'foreign intervention'.[41] Their anger that day was not directed at the foreign powers, however, but at those ruling China, who they felt had betrayed her. Whatever their thoughts on Lu Xun's question about whether China's culture could preserve the country, until 2 May they still had cause to assume that China's government and its representatives ought to be attempting to do so. Instead it seemed to have betrayed them, and to have sold Shandong for Japanese Yen to fund the civil war.

The 3,000-strong demonstration involved students from a dozen institutions in the capital, and ended with a small riot. They marched to the Legation Quarter intending to present letters of protest to the Allied ministers, but it was a Sunday – and a beautiful spring one, so the diplomats were largely out of town in the Western Hills. After some hours of confrontation with police, the students marched to the home of Cao Rulin, then Minister of Communications, but formerly Vice Minister for Foreign Affairs, and deeply involved in the 1915 negotiations with Japan and the secret loans of 1918. Some of the marchers broke into the compound and set part of the house alight. Cao himself fled to the safety of a hotel in the foreign-controlled Legation Quarter. He would not be the last to do so: imperialism's friends and foes alike found it convenient to have such safe havens just a short hop away. The Chinese Minister to Japan, who was also in the house, was less lucky, and was badly beaten.[42] Three dozen of the students were arrested, and as their peers organized themselves to try to secure their release, a national student movement was born. The marchers did not set out on the afternoon of 4 May to change the nation. But their able diplomats at Versailles had failed to, and they perceived the government in Beijing as unwilling to confront Japan, and China's wider difficulties.

This became a nationwide assault on imperialism, and on China's prevailing culture. Demonstrations began to be held across China, and across Chinese communities overseas. The most potent weapon available was the boycotting of Japanese goods or the services of

Japanese firms. This was a tactic first developed in response to American anti-Chinese immigration legislation, and had already been used twice against the Japanese – in 1909 over disputes about Manchuria, and in March–April 1915 over the Twenty-One Demands. 'Why did Korea perish?' asked one Shanghai placard. 'Because her people lacked the sense of unity and heroism and patriotic shame.'[43] A patriot would not buy a Japanese product. Between May and June 1919 in cities across China radically new coalitions of interest groups came together in protest. The student movements led the way, but to achieve any success they had to join with and encourage others: merchants who traded Japanese products, shippers who moved them, dockworkers who unloaded them. After all, 3,000 students had assembled at Tiananmen, but 10,000 people poured into the Sincere Department store on its opening day, and thousands more every day thereafter. If the potential political power of those consumers could be harnessed, then perhaps it could be a more potent force than the disgraced armies of the new republic. Where sympathies were not already found, and persuasion failed, boycott committees used blockades or intimidation. They marched, leafleted and plastered public walls with posters. In Shanghai, when news arrived of the arrest of hundreds of students in Beijing, their peers launched a concerted week-long city-wide strike on 5 June that involved merchants and shopkeepers as well as industrial labourers. Local authorities, Chinese and foreign alike, responded with new press regulations, bans on demonstrations and the display of boycott movement badges, and sometimes with violence.[44] Such responses encouraged old demands to resurface, and triggered new ones, while the very forms of organization that had sprung into being became the vehicles for challenging the status quo, and foreign and Chinese authorities alike, across China.

As they articulated their grounds for a boycott, the students and their supporters more and more started to follow Lu Xun's advice, and the explanation for China's political, if not moral, impasse was more and more conceived of as being cultural. What sort of a culture encourages its leaders to so lack self-respect and a sense of national honour as to sell their country in order to pursue their own selfish, short-term objectives? If China's culture could not save it, then it needed renewing. The May Fourth Movement, as it became known, embraced an already developing current of intellectual change, the 'New Culture Movement', which advocated a reassessment and renewal of the Chinese language and literature, social and gender relations. New men and new women, with new ideas and new talents, were needed to save the nation. Everything was 'New' or 'Young'. Scores of magazines and journals were established – by one calculation just over 600 new titles appeared in a very short period of time. All seemed to have the word 'New' in their title. Imports of paper for printing soared. The often rapidly repositioned existing press filled its pages with translation, as much as with new articles and essays on the need for reform.[45] Simple mimicry at Versailles, to put it crudely, had failed. Wellington Koo had performed in an outstanding fashion as a modern cosmopolitan diplomat, better educated than most of those present. It got China nowhere. More was needed. This new movement was broad, vibrant, chaotic and eclectic. Often contradictory, it embraced the new, wherever it found it, for the old had failed.

That other peace conference, China's own, which Xu Shichang had set in motion when he had called a halt to military operations in November 1918, equally bore little fruit. Delegates from the Beijing government and from the Guomindang-led south met intermittently in Shanghai between February and May 1919. Their failure was directly intertwined with the failure at Versailles, for the Shandong question, and the issues of the acceptance and use of Japanese loans by the northern military, were placed high on the agenda by the Guomindang delegates. Barely two weeks after the May Fourth incident, and as students demonstrated in the streets of Shanghai, the negotiators chose to resign their commissions and the Peace Conference collapsed.[46] The great problems besetting the still young republic, and those engaged with it, had been starkly highlighted in the victory celebrations and the attitudes of those participating in them. The country's degraded and impaired sovereignty, the arrogance and condescension of many foreign observers and residents, its unresolved political revolution, and the power of its militarists all came into sharp relief. But there was also the idealism of its young, the commercial savvy of its energized merchants, and the often brilliant talents of its professional classes. There was, too, the sympathy and commitment of some of China's foreign allies, in and amongst the missionary communities, amongst professional advisors working at the heart of its government, visitors like Wilson's personal emissary Charles Crane, and the many foreign servants of some of the agencies of its state.

But they all faced a challenging task. For others, the situation in China seemed to have got simpler. With the departure of the SS *Antilochus* from Shanghai on 3 April 1919, the last of almost 2,200 German residents in the country had been forcibly expelled. The process was chaotic, and the atmosphere vindictive.[47] Japan was not alone in seeing new opportunities in China. Many on the Allied side now felt that they had freedom from German competition, and that the Great Game of jockeying for concessions could begin afresh. At Shanghai, the International Settlement authorities even lobbied for an extension to the territory they administered. But in November 1918, on the streets of Beijing, Shanghai, Anqing and many other cities, people had expressed their desire for a new order in relations between nations that would salvage Chinese honour, and the hopes of the new republic. The revolution that had created the new state in 1911–12 had been bloody, but far less destructive than might have been the case if both the revolutionaries and their enemies had not feared foreign intervention. Born in compromise, its infancy was marred by the counter-revolution of Yuan Shikai against the Guomindang, and the corruption of the new state. The experience of the first six months of the new post-war world had wrecked many of the hopes for the republic, or at least degraded any confidence in Wilsonian methods to achieve change. Might seemed to have conquered right after all. So, some started to think, if we are to restore to China its dignity, independence and power, then we will need to do so by force.

2

Making Revolution

The world seems simpler when looked at along the barrel of a gun. You certainly know that you have the ability to change something, the course of a life not least, your own, somebody else's. At the very least you can defend yourself, and when negotiation and compromise fail, then there are moments when recourse to violence seems the inevitable and only path to a different future. China needed change, and after the disappointment of the Versailles Treaty many believed it needed a new revolution. All that urbane talk, all those marches and boycotts, the excited chatter in all the new magazines and in lecture halls had left the country exactly where it was in November 1918: under the heel of the generals, disunited, vulnerable. China was steadily fragmenting into a set of unstable and shifting fiefdoms where power lay in the hands of militarists – the warlords – who fought each other for supremacy, sucking their territories dry with their demands for revenue. Reformers despaired. These militarists would need to be fought if China was to be saved. And those diagnosing the country's ills would increasingly see another set of interests lurking behind and propping up the soldiers: the 'powers', or the 'imperialists' – as they were increasingly being routinely described.

To use a weapon effectively you need to be trained, and to deploy violence to maximum effect you need to be organized and disciplined; you need money, numbers, a secure base. The Guomindang leader, Sun Yat-sen, had never been a man of peace. In the years before the accidental and unplanned uprising against the Qing in 1911 – launched after a careless revolutionary blew up an underground bomb factory with a discarded cigarette – he had organized and launched a series of violent revolutionary actions against the

Manchus. Instead of provoking the hoped-for wider rebellion against the dynasty, these had usually just added new names to the roster of revolutionary martyrs. Sun had also never been shy of seeking foreign assistance, or permission to base his organization overseas, or requesting supplies of munitions – often seemingly unperturbed by the onerous conditions that might accompany financial support.[1] By the summer of 1926, Sun's party was ready again to fight its way to power, and it was in a new set of alliances that would eventually change global politics, let alone China.

The Chinese did not lack for foreign friends, even if most foreign governments had turned their backs on Sun Yat-sen. And a whole class of advisors had emerged, sometimes well intentioned, sometimes serving two masters – one Chinese, the other their own nation – and sometimes simply parasitic. There were good salaries to be earned (or backhanders to be found) as a political or military advisor, or in helping draw up new codes of law, planning administrative reforms, or running publicity campaigns. Since the appointment of Horatio Nelson Lay as Inspector General of the Imperial Maritime Customs Service in 1859, foreigners had been employed at the heart of the modern central state, as well as by leading provincial figures.[2] There were earlier precedents for this, most recently in the form of the Roman Catholic scientists, cartographers and musicians employed at the Qing court, but now the numbers and roles multiplied.[3] Lay's successor, Ulsterman Robert Hart, had become the most well known of these, overseeing during the six decades in which he held the post the development of a complex institution that eventually employed some 11,000 foreign nationals between 1854 and 1950. Others who served ranged from men with guns or expertise for hire working as mercenaries for local figures during the great Taiping Rebellion of 1850–64 that convulsed China (or for the rebels – artillerymen were much in demand), to powerful figures like Gustav Detring, an anglophile Prussian who served for decades in Tianjin as an advisor and fixer for the senior Qing official Li Hongzhang.[4] Admirals and midshipmen worked for China; freelancers and hoodlums banded together with Chinese pirates or robbers in times of chaos.[5] In the nineteenth century, Frenchman Prosper Giquel directed the Fuzhou naval yard; Sir Halliday Macartney and American Anson Burlingame served as official envoys for China overseas; Baptist missionary Timothy Richard, working with the provincial governor Cen Chunxian, helped establish Shanxi University in 1902. Some found great satisfaction in assisting in the rejuvenation of China; some found more pleasure in the liberal salaries they could earn. For others yet, serving China was a way to serve humanity (or else their god), or the aims and objectives of their own governments, in China, or back home.

Modern China's history is not a history made by foreigners; but its domestic history was an internationalized one, at times very heavily spiced with them. At particular points they made decisive interventions: Guangzhou was the site of some of these. In the early 1920s the city hosted some odd encounters. An undated photograph taken by a rising and well-connected young figure in the Guomindang, Fu Bingchang, who was Commissioner for Foreign Affairs in the city, shows one such (Fig. 4).[6] In the foreground, clutching a cigarette and a briefcase, is the pith-helmeted figure of Mikhail Gruzenberg, better known by his cover name Mikhail Markovich Borodin. The charismatic forty-year-old Russian was the leading agent in China of the Comintern: the Communist Third International, an organization created to foment and support communist insurrection across the globe, but which also in practice furthered the foreign-policy aims of the new Soviet Union. He had already served in the United States, Mexico and Britain (and spent time in a Scottish jail). Standing watching, leaning on a stick with a straw boater raked at an angle across his head, is Morris Cohen, another former jailbird, born near Warsaw to parents who then emigrated to England. A slightly younger man and a veteran of the Canadian Army in the First World War, Cohen had also been, in his life to date, a boxer, thief, confidence trickster, gangster and real-estate dealer. Presently, likely as not (for no one was really quite sure), he would work as a gun-runner, fixer and bodyguard. Both men worked with and for the Guomindang, at the heart of the new capital of the Chinese revolution. Now entering a dramatic new phase, the business of solving China's problem had brought to the country the high- and the low-minded who found a place – for the moment – within the emerging dispensation.

Sun Yat-sen's own crew of foreign advisors was an eclectic and internationalized one. Partly it was used to mediate between the

revolutionary and foreign officials, although the men concerned –
Morris Cohen least of all – did not always impress the diplomats.
Emerging from his associations with Chinatown circles in Edmonton, Canada, Cohen had arrived in Shanghai in December 1922 as an
agent for a railway contract, but was soon acting as Sun's bodyguard
and describing himself as his 'Aide-de-Camp'. Such foreign brawn
was augmented with brain, or at least expertise, in the shape of Robert Stanley Norman, an attorney from Oakland, California, who had
long acted for Sun there. Norman had arrived in Guangzhou with
his family in May 1922 to act as his legal advisor, and intermediary
with foreign officials. Pilots and aircraft manufacturers were also recruited. Foreign journalists routinely found roles advising Chinese
figures. G. E. Morrison, former *Times* correspondent, had worked
for Yuan Shikai; Thomas Millard, founding editor in Shanghai of
The China Press and what would become the *China Weekly Review*,
advised the three-time Chinese President Li Yuanhong. Sun's enemies
had their foreign advisors too. Frank Sutton, a decorated British war
veteran, ran the Shenyang arsenal for Manchurian power-holder
Zhang Zuolin; refugee Russian imperial troops held important posts
in his army. Zhang's subordinate Zhang Zongchang took on three
Russian armoured trains, and Russian engineers built more for him.
Increasingly, as well, overseas born or overseas-educated Chinese
came to the fore. Eugene Ch'en (Chen Youren), a Trinidadian barrister and British colonial subject, whose impeccable English – he spoke
no Chinese – routinely confounded his interlocutors, came in though
this route to take a leading role in the Guomindang. More so even
than the likes of shady Morris Cohen, Ch'en would discomfort and
puzzle British officials especially, arousing in many of them visceral
disdain at a Chinese, black anglophone, whom they saw as a renegade
colonial subject.[7]

The collapse of the Shanghai peace talks in 1919 had left the southern coalition, in which the Guomindang played a key role, even
further isolated from the formal institutions of the republic; although
in a bizarre twist, from July 1919 until March 1920 the coalition
received, with the agreement of the central government, a share of the
Customs revenue surplus.[8] Establishing an alternative – in their eyes
legitimate – national government in Guangzhou had failed. The

wheel of fortune turned: Guangdong province was dominated after October 1920 by a veteran revolutionary, General Chen Jiongming, who nominally served as governor. A progressive, if idiosyncratic, reformer, much taken with anarchist philosophy, Chen's slogan 'Canton for the Cantonese' reflected the hostility of local interests to the depredations of extra-provincial troops, as well as his own federalist leanings. Whereas Sun Yat-sen aimed to reunite the nation, Chen, and an increasing number of others, wished to explore a federal solution to China's problems.[9] From his base in the east of the province, Chen had moved to expel the forces from neighbouring Guangxi province who had occupied Guangzhou and expelled Sun's regime. Chen allowed Sun to return to Guangzhou in November 1920, and to re-establish what the Guomindang presented as the legitimate national government of the republic, wheeling out a few hundred members of the old parliament elected back in December 1912 who voted to make Sun president in May 1921.

An estimated 120,000 people processed through the city on the day of Sun's inauguration.[10] Chen's troops, schoolchildren, even martial-arts practitioners and actresses had their place in the great demonstration. Naval gunboats fired salutes from the river, and great triumphal arches had been erected, decorated with electric lights. But after such a heady Guangzhou spring, tensions between Chen Jiongming's provincial ambitions and Sun's aim to use the province as his base from which to launch a war of national reunification mounted. The end came in June 1922 when Sun and his government were expelled after he had stripped his host and protector of his offices. Outgunned and outnumbered, Sun fled, and not for the first time with foreign assistance, shipping out of Guangzhou on a British gunboat, but not before his own gunboats had bombarded Chen's troops, killing civilians as they did so. Sun returned – yet again – in February 1923, having bought the services of mercenary units from Yunnan province, who drove Chen out.[11] So it seemed to go and so it threatened to go on and on, revolution as French farce with rapid exits and plot changes. But it was a dark and sanguine comedy, for lives were lost in each act, and rarely were they those of the principals.

During his 1922–3 exile in his house in Shanghai, safely located in the French concession, Sun was visited by Soviet emissaries, including

Adolf Joffe, the USSR's ambassador to Beijing, building on earlier contacts. The framework for a collaboration had started to emerge. There was nothing covert about this, although the International Settlement police had diligently kept watch and recorded all that they could. There was also nothing new about foreigners with schemes to propose pitching them to Sun, who was well known for his keen interest in grand infrastructure projects for national reconstruction. He planned 100,000 miles of new railway lines, a million miles of new roads, three mega-harbours, new canals, new telegraph lines, massive new heavy industrial plants, reforestation, irrigation of the dry northwest.[12] In some ways, as a programme for national development this was far ahead of its time, but it suggested to most contemporary observers that Sun was simply a fantasist. Still, there might be money in it. And Sun stated that foreign expertise would be needed for every initiative. So one man would outline a scheme to him to raise funds for industrial development projects by selling bonds on the American market; another one would propose a scheme to do so to finance harbour construction. Would Mr Henry Ford, Sun wrote in a June 1924 letter to the industrialist, like to consider visiting China, where there was 'an opportunity to express and embody your mind and ideals in the enduring form of a new industrial system'?[13] Thank you for the invitation, his office responded, but Mr Ford had no plans to visit China.

Shanghai's local press documented the meetings with Joffe, and the policy agreement the two men signed on 26 January, just as the ground was being laid for Sun's return to Guangzhou. What made this encounter distinctive was that it was a record of an understanding between a foreign ambassador to a sovereign state and one of that state's rebel opponents.[14] It affirmed the Soviet Union's readiness to disengage from its remaining possessions in China, disavowed any intentions to detach Mongolia from Chinese control, and accorded with Sun's view that national reunification was the political priority for China, not the introduction of communism. This last clause precisely fitted Soviet analysis of China's current situation and its strategy in China, which was to work within a national revolutionary movement, in this case to establish a 'United Front' with the Guomindang. Nonetheless, Comintern representatives had already worked to fashion politically sympathetic Chinese such as Chen Duxiu, editor of *New Youth* magazine, and the study and labour groups that were intensely active, into a new, formally established Chinese Communist Party in 1921. This twin-pronged China policy was in turn developed in tandem with the Comintern's wider international political strategy.[15] China was not yet ready for social revolution, it was believed: that would come in time, but first the ground must be prepared. Sun Yat-sen was the most likely ally for the Comintern's China venture.

The Guomindang's turn to the Soviet Union was not preordained. Sun had appealed for support to the Americans and to the British in his bid to have his southern government recognized. Neither was prepared to give much credence to his claims to legitimacy. But this promiscuous revolutionary would continue to explore any and every option. Sun had even made a triumphant visit to Hong Kong on the way back to Guangzhou in 1923, lunching at the Governor's, and taking tea at the Hongkong and Shanghai Bank, before speaking at Hong Kong University. 'We must carry this English example of good government to every part of China,' he told the students, to loud applause. But if British colonial administration was a rhetorical exemplar – and modern scholars have questioned quite how effective it actually was in practice – and if his hosts found themselves flattered by his comments and confirmed in their own perceptions of their achievements, it was of no practical help to him. No loans were forthcoming, and no recognition was accorded his regime. The British, like other foreign powers, also remained largely confirmed in their own assessment of Sun as yesterday's man, and a verbose troublemaker. He talked peace and reconstruction, but then his gunboats machine-gunned and shelled Guangzhou. So they debated the virtues of other figures on the national scene, mostly the militarists: Feng Yuxiang, the 'Christian General' who caught the attention of the Japanese; Zhang Zuolin in Manchuria, an old-style strongman who the British rather liked; and Wu Peifu, who was increasingly the real power in the Beijing government.[16] Joffe's agreement, however, led to the despatch of Soviet advisors, munitions and money to Guangzhou. And so on 6 October 1923, fresh from prison in Glasgow, Mikhail Borodin arrived in Guangzhou, having hitched a ride from Shanghai on a vessel carrying 200 sheep so as to avoid trans-shipping at Hong

Kong, where the British might arrest him. Borodin was happy to tell reporters that he was leading a trade mission, but he did not then let on that he carried instructions to help Sun Yat-sen launch a national revolution.[17]

The international situation had developed promisingly in China's favour. Although in great part by 1926 it remained in practical terms in stasis, the underlying rules of the game that had ensnared the Qing and their successor regime appeared to be changing. The young Bolshevik regime in Russia had made its dramatic pronouncements – the so-called 'Karakhan Declaration' – repudiating Tsarist privileges and concessions in China, and while these had in reality not all been implemented – for as it consolidated its rule the Soviet Union did not, for example, surrender its railway holdings in Manchuria – the impact on Chinese public and political opinion had been significant. Secondly, the 1921–2 Washington Naval Conference, designed to prevent a Pacific arms race, also involved the signing of a 'Nine Power Treaty', which affirmed the American government's 'Open Door' policy for China. This doctrine had been given its most famous articulation in an August 1899 note originally drafted by an English senior member of the Chinese Customs, Alfred Hippisley. It sought assurances from the powers involved in the aggressive late 1890s 'scramble for concessions' in China that they would not exclude other foreign powers from new spheres of influence, and asserted the continued primacy of the institutions of the Chinese state. All would still be free to share the spoils of the new phase of plunder. Reaffirmed in 1922 in order to restrain Japan, these somewhat vague principles prompted the signatories to the Nine Power Treaty to agree to 'respect the sovereignty, the independence, and the territorial and administrative integrity of China', and to 'refrain from taking advantage of conditions in China in order to seek special rights or privileges'. At the same time, Japan agreed to relinquish the gains it had been so uncompromising about in Paris: German rights in China then transferred to it were to be surrendered in full within six months.[18]

Those negotiating in Washington had not gone there to abolish what were now routinely being described in China as the 'unequal treaties' – not least by Wellington Koo, who had led yet another large and optimistic Chinese delegation to the conference.[19] Once more, high hopes had been raised, and Koo and his colleagues lobbied for the negotiators to revise wholesale China's position. But the agreement of the powers in principle to call a halt to further foreign incursions was important, for the inescapable logic of agreeing to respect China's 'sovereignty . . . independence, and . . . territorial and administrative integrity' was that where these had already been compromised, such infringements would need to be re-examined, and corrected, when conditions were right. Expressions of pious intent predicated on the restoration of suitable conditions in China were made, and noted. These generally included internal peace, stable central government, and rule of law. In this way, Japan's actions in Shandong, like the Soviet declaration, quietly called time on the other treaty ports and concessions. The British even committed themselves to returning the leased territory of Weihaiwei, ostensibly to encourage the Japanese to do likewise, although this Shandong base had long been surplus to their strategic requirements in East Asia.[20] But as the unsettled conditions at Guangzhou showed, the realization of these preconditions for revision of the current agreements seemed so remote a possibility that it was easy enough for foreign diplomats to make such statements. This was such a republic of dreams that even foreign diplomats could safely relax and enjoy the reverie.

So talking, yet again, had not got China anywhere, at least not immediately. And whereas in 1919 Wellington Koo and his colleagues had charmed their interlocutors and public opinion, and won at least the moral argument, in Washington in 1922 Chinese demands were thought to be tiresome, and their ambitions for the conference were entirely oblique to the matter at hand. Nevertheless, detailed precedents were set during the negotiations to which Chinese diplomats would return, notably commitments from the treaty powers to allow China's Customs' tariffs to be raised, if only temporarily, for these were not under its control. This would be discussed in three months' time, it was agreed, by a further conference, which did not in fact meet until October 1925, and on the understanding that China would abolish taxes on goods in transit within the country. This served for many to indicate that China in fact had a right to see the restoration of sovereignty over the setting of its tariffs. This was hardly what was intended by the powers, but by acceding to a process through which negotiation in one area might commence, foreign diplomats created a space towards which nationalist demands and aspirations might increasingly be channelled.

That space, the powers trusted, was capacious enough to satisfy Chinese honour, but bounded enough to perpetuate foreign privilege. For example, the establishment of an international commission of judicial experts agreed at Washington was also delayed until 1926. It was charged with investigating the possibility of the foreign powers relinquishing extraterritoriality, and after nine months, much talk, and more paper, as well as tours of inspection of prisons and courts across the land – an awkward process given the continuing violence and political instability – it reported, to no one's great surprise, that until China's legal system was truly independent the end of extraterritoriality could not be countenanced.[21] Thus, again, the status quo was reaffirmed, but with piles of neatly assembled and nicely printed evidence and reasonable argument to back it up. Where once the powers had routinely resorted to gunboats, now they resorted to commissions. The results looked very much the same, but at least nobody was killed.

The southern leaders had been represented in Paris in 1919, but Sun Yat-sen was excluded from sending representatives to the Washington Conference, at which only the internationally recognized republican government in Beijing was present. The foreign powers did not wish to seem to recognize the legitimacy of the rival regime in Guangzhou, and its fluctuating fortunes hardly impressed them. In the developing and confusing maelstrom that was the China of the 'warlord' era, in which militarists fought or feinted at national, provincial and local levels, Sun's government looked like just another of the warring factions, flimsily dressed up in the clothes of a legitimate regime. Denied recognition, Sun would denounce the Washington agreements, and concentrate instead on building up a secure revolutionary base at Guangzhou. To prepare that, the Guomindang oversaw and encouraged the growth of China's model modern municipality, staffed by energetic young men mostly educated abroad who were committed to scientifically and rationally developing the great southern metropolis.[22]

The city of Guangzhou had formerly symbolized all that foreign opinion saw as dark, decayed and decrepit about China. It was in this view an obdurate city, administered by reactionary officials in league with a xenophobic population. It had certainly been the site of some of the bloodiest and most sustained campaigns of the mid-nineteenth-century 'Opium' wars, and it had held out against foreign access even when this was required by treaty. This had caused British officials on occasion to resort to force in order to make their feelings clear. This was the only language it seemed that the British actually understood. This approach had not endeared them to the recalcitrant city and its suffering populace. Representations of Guangzhou in word or image were also hostile. Foreign photographers captured its narrow, gloomy, winding streets, and these became emblematic of its perceived tradition-bound, pre-modern stasis. While a darkened street was a sensible way of dealing with the city's hot and humid climate, for foreigners it came to symbolize backwardness and decay. Many such criticisms were also later taken up by Chinese reformers.[23] Guangzhou's floating brothels and large population of Tanka boat dwellers added to the mix. The city was for most the antithesis of cosmopolitan, internationalized Shanghai.

But any objective visitor to Guangzhou in the 1920s would find a city that defied such archaic caricature. It was a confident, self-consciously modern metropolis with an estimated population of 1.3 million that was undergoing a process of rapid urban renewal.[24] Chen Jiongming, who more often than not before 1923 ran the city, was a reformer, and in 1921 a pioneering municipal government was established at his initiative, with Sun Yat-sen's son, Sun Fo, as mayor. Already, between 1918 and 1922 the city walls had been pulled down, and a new road system built in their stead. Stone blocks reclaimed from the walls were used to pave and line an extended and increasingly vibrant bund. The city of benighted alleys was now a city of parks, wide new roads, tall government buildings and high-rise department stores. Such contrasts were highlighted in detail in new guidebooks.[25] These developments would continue apace despite the twists and turns of politics locally. Entrepreneurs, many of them émigrés, were also reshaping Guangzhou. Its own Sincere Company store pre-dated Shanghai's by five years; its Sun Company building was a twelve-storey palace to consumption on the now high-rise-fronted bund. New districts were being laid out; old ones were being renovated. Guangzhou's urbanites wore fashionable Western-style clothes, played foreign sports, went to their cinemas to watch foreign films, danced cheek to cheek – or at least arm in arm – to Western tunes played on up-to-date Victrola gramophones, and considered themselves no less patriotic for their personal embrace of each other and of China's internationalized modern culture. There was a lively local press, and Hong Kong newspapers were sold as well. Still, some worried about decadence, and others saw the city as a trap that ensnared and depraved the young and innocent. For others, however, it was a paradigm of Chinese modernity, not a city misshaped and thwarted – as Shanghai seemed to be – by overwhelming Western power.

Guangzhou was a city partly shaped by imperialist power, nonetheless, for it hosted two foreign-controlled concessions on the small 50-acre island of Shamian – Shameen the foreigners called it – that had been reclaimed from riverside sandbanks after the 1857– 60 'Arrow War'. Pennsylvanian Quaker Nora Waln moved to a house on Shamian in 1924 when her British husband, George Osland-Hill, was appointed Postal Commissioner in Guangzhou. (Over a hundred foreign nationals held senior positions in the Post Office, and it was co-directed by a Frenchman, on the basis of Qing-era agreements.) Waln, who had come to China in 1921 to work for the YWCA, would later pen a well-received book, *The House of Exile*, which purported to chart her deep immersion in the life of a Chinese family, but she was mostly embedded in the life of the foreign establishment and the degraded Chinese state. In Guangzhou, Waln lived in the British concession, complete with its 'Shameen Municipal Council', and smaller French neighbour.[26] It was a pretty site, and a leisurely circumnavigation of it would last her barely twenty minutes, taking in a public garden with its neat lawns, tennis courts that were 'the envy of south China', and a playground, a Church, consulates and banks, trading houses and shipping offices, all shaded by scores of banyan trees to which pigeons flocked. Shamian was connected to the mainland by two bridges, but this was also designed as a way to control access. Waln noted, as others did too, that even though it was a site that attracted tourists and sightseers, Shamian remained a place of exclusion and restriction: Chinese could not even use its benches, excepting servants supervising foreign children, and then only until the late afternoon.[27]

Like most such foreign-controlled enclaves, large or small, Shamian housed offices of the usual China coast firms – Butterfield & Swire, the Hongkong and Shanghai Bank, Jardine Matheson and Co., Standard Oil, the Japanese OSK and NYK shipping lines, as well as the Canton Club, a Masonic Hall and the Victoria Hotel ('one of the two worst . . . in Asia', a journalist recalled). The Customs and Post Office headquarters were on the Guangzhou Bund, but their Commissioners lived on the island, along with about 350 other foreign nationals and just over a thousand Chinese. The view from Shamian could be archaic. Victor Purcell, a young language student in the British Colonial Office, lived there in 1922, finding it idyllic, and out of sync with the times. 'I can hear the continuous coo of the pigeons in the dense foliage of the trees as I write,' he recalled, wistfully, forty years on. No cars traversed the island. The British Consul General was carried around it in a sedan chair with eight bearers – as certainly befitted, in an earlier age, his status. But Chinese officials in Guangzhou no longer used sedan chairs; they were driven in smart new imported cars along the wide boulevards, armed bodyguards on the running boards. The Consul General's display of prestige was stuck in a pomp-and-glory long ago past; so too, at times, was British thinking. It hardly helped that some of those Purcell met had family connections stretching back to the old pre-'Opium' war Guangzhou, nor that the church and churchyard were providing new homes to gravestones and memorials now being cleared away from the old foreign cemetery that lay in the path of new road development. History hung heavily over Shamian, and there seemed world enough and time for boorish japes with no serious consequences for Purcell and his peers. 'Zest rather than danger', a guidebook noted laconically, 'is added to residence there by reason of the occasional disturbances in Canton, and the presence of pirates in the canals of the delta.'[28]

Guangzhou hosted a foreign presence in other important sites. Each of these seemed very different, but each shared an underlying ambition to help change China: the Canton Christian College, and the headquarters of Mikhail Borodin's growing Comintern advisory team. While the American Presbyterian and Baptist missions had various centres in the city, and on Shamian, the college, known in Chinese as Lingnan University, was the most significant missionary enterprise based in Guangzhou. Established in 1888, it occupied a large and prominent campus on Honam (Henan) Island on the opposite bank of the Pearl River to the city. An inter-denominational enterprise, Lingnan's funding was originally supplied mainly by American donors, but by the 1920s – unusually for a missionary institution – it mostly came from Chinese sources, not least overseas ones. Its faculty were in large part American, who outnumbered Chinese staff by two to one. Lingnan was emblematic of great changes underway in the missionary world internationally, and also in China, though there things always seemed to lag a decade behind. The college represented both the new and the more traditional faces of missionary life. While religious worship on Sunday remained compulsory, many in its student body were active participants in the nationwide anti-Christian movement that had swept across campuses and schools in China since 1922 and forced many college administrations onto the back foot. This was leading to significant changes in curriculums, daily routines, personnel, names and even ownership of institutions. But even at progressive Lingnan some old ways still stuck. 'We had to listen to the idiotic preaching of the missionaries for two hours every day and during the whole of Sunday morning,' remembered one student, and most of them 'hated this compulsory religionizing'.[29] Some of the college's senior staff considered themselves missionaries first and foremost. However, other, younger men were barely observant Christians: they were there as educators. One young American lecturer, Earl Swisher, contrasted the Western comforts of academic life at Lingnan with the hard conditions endured by a Canadian woman missionary, living alone on a 'Gospel Boat' moored upstream along the Pearl River in amongst Tanka boat people. That was real mission work, he thought, out of another age, like the Consul General's sedan chair. The college did not take advantage of its American status to secure extraterritorial protection for its properties (unlike, for example, the British Sun Company store, which ran up the Union Jack when Sun Yat-sen's gunboats fired on the city in 1922), but it was still nonetheless an organized target of anti-imperialist political boycotts and strikes.[30]

At their headquarters the Russians were hardly roughing it, although the first of the military advisors accidentally drowned on a visit to the front line. They were mostly based in houses at Tongshan, a suburb in the east of the city, and although they kept themselves apart from other foreign communities in Guangzhou they were hardly alone in this. Missionaries and businessmen did not mix, and the social niceties of home were always exaggerated abroad. But Victor Purcell, who lived in the same apartment block with some of the group for a while, only met them when a fire threatened the building, and they probably did not, as he did, dip into a bar-cum-brothel-cum-casino run by Petroff, a White Russian refugee of a different political stripe, where narcotics were easy to secure. There were other advisory teams in north China, and almost 270 different men and women worked in these groups between 1923 and 1927. The political agents were also joined by film teams, and later on, in a surreal moment in revolutionary Wuhan, by a troupe of dancers led by Irma Duncan, the activist daughter of the dancer Isadora Duncan. The Soviet advisors at Guangzhou lived very much as other foreigners did in China, although their sexual mores were the stuff of public gossip. They took rickshaws and toured the city, shopped and went to the movies. They patronized the tailors, and like all expatriates in China located a reliable seamstress, in their case a francophone African woman married to a Cantonese man. And they sampled the local food. Children were born within the community, and when trouble flared, families were despatched to the safety of Hong Kong. Borodin later sent his children to the American school in Shanghai.

Tensions developed in the group between newer arrivals from Russia, who thought their longer-established colleagues had succumbed to these minor pleasures of colonial-style life, and between the military and civilian officials. In their memoirs the advisors would romanticize their relations with the Chinese: 'unlike the advisor condottieres from the capitalist countries,' wrote Alexander Cherepanov, 'we made friends in China easily.'[31] But there was plenty of scope for a profound mismatch of cultures: their music is awful; the food smells; they cannot run meetings, complained another of the Russian advisors of his Chinese colleagues, nor could they hold their drink.[32] With the exception of the last, these were standard foreign moans.

Asked by Lingnan University's president in December 1925, in a private meeting, whether he actually liked the Chinese, Borodin 'seemed surprised' by the question, and 'after some thought [he] said that he had not given the matter any consideration'.[33] It was ideologically an irrelevant question. Like the missionary educators at Lingnan, the Soviet advisors were technical experts, although like most of those they held a wider brief as well. They too were missionaries for a revolution, albeit a political one, not the spiritual or ethical revolution of the religious evangelists.[34]

Shamian, however, not Tongshan or Lingnan, remained the most prominent site of foreign power in Guangzhou, and though it seemed innocuous and quaint, it proved to be a site of vivid controversy. The crises that it engendered exemplified how, more widely, small sites of foreign control could have an impact on their host cities – and on Sino-foreign relations – out of all proportion to their size and identifiable utility. In times of disorder, if they could not get out to Portuguese Macao or British Hong Kong, Guangzhou's people sought refuge for themselves or their possessions in the concessions, as they did elsewhere in China, and as Cao Rulin, the Minister of Communications, had done in Beijing on 4 May 1919. Shamian's council would lock the gates it had erected on the bridges, and its police force would guard them, while marines would be landed if necessary, and a gunboat or two would moor in the Pearl River nearby. Boats full of Cantonese would crowd the island's waterfront, nonetheless, seeking what safety even that slender shadow of extraterritoriality might provide. Since 1920 the foreign authorities had been tightening up the rules. The 'Land Regulations and Bye-Laws', which governed the British concession, did not proscribe Chinese residence, but they had always regulated it. All Chinese residents, who were assumed to be either servants or employees of foreign households and businesses, were required to register with the police. A more archaic rule, still on the books in 1924, insisted that Chinese visiting the concession after sunset had to carry a lantern.

Neither of these regulations prevented a Vietnamese nationalist from attempting to assassinate the Governor of French Indochina at the Victoria Hotel in June 1924. He missed, but killed five other French citizens with a grenade. Further restrictions were rushed in requiring all those wishing to cross the bridges to Shamian to have a pass. While the bombing prompted the new rules, it was also argued that if the concessions were known as a site of the storage of goods then they would attract looters in a crisis – and the ebb and flow of Sun Yat-sen's government certainly generated enough of those. But the regulations were also designed to keep Chinese sightseers and 'undesirables' out of Shamian, and to stop people using the concessions as a short cut to and from the fast-developing Bund.[35] This sparked a furious reaction locally. A month-long protest strike by Shamian's Chinese employees and a boycott saw the desertion of the small police force, and forced the authorities to revise the rules. You did not have to be a Bolshevik to be outraged by the quotidian petty affronts of imperialism, and the assumptions that underpinned them. Indignation knew no political boundaries, and the indignant formed a broad church of protest.

Disputes over access to the concessions and restrictions on Chinese within them had long been a source of minor and generally localized disturbances in Sino-foreign relations in China. But the new politics of the post-'May Fourth' world saw such incidents through new lenses, and forms of social and political mobilization that had evolved and been tested during the 'May Fourth Movement' were now deployed against the foreign authorities. There were labour unions and boycott committees to deal with, strike pickets and propaganda teams, and these were disciplined and effective. A whole new repertoire of protest was now in play, as the latest protesters learned from the last movement, and as channels were opened to link previously disconnected social groups, channels that were reactivated with each fresh controversy and getting stronger each time. The great turning point was the Hong Kong seamen's strike between January and March 1922. Undertaken by the newly established Seamen's Union to press shipping companies to raise wages in the light of post-war commodity price inflation, the stoppage developed stark political dimensions and forms when the Hong Kong colonial government responded by trying to break it. It outlawed the union and then police shot dead a number of seamen. A general strike was called, and amongst the 100,000 who stopped work in the colony were the staff at Government House: this could not get any closer to the heart of

British power. The Governor backed down, and the strikers won. Not for the first time, nor for the last, the actions of those opposing what they saw as organized political radicalism actually inflamed it.[36]

Sun's government at Guangzhou had supported the strikers, thousands of whom relocated upriver to the port from the colony, and in assessments afterwards British observers articulated new concerns about the increasingly proficient organizational ability of the labour movement in China more widely. They believed that Sun was now deliberately aiming to harness labour unrest in his support, and that the new political climate meant that workers and others were much readier to act in their own interests, and even out of sympathy with other protesters, than had been the case previously.

New strategies were needed to head off unrest, and this included encouraging new attitudes amongst employers. Legitimate labour demands should always be seen to be sympathetically considered by firms, recommended the Shanghai International Settlement's acting Commissioner of Police in a secret report in the immediate aftermath of the Hong Kong strike, however unreasonable they seemed. But he also believed that smarter intelligence was needed about what might be developing. We can no longer issue bombastic proclamations or expect a show of force to solve things, he wrote.[37] This was a prescient report, and as a result intelligence-gathering activities in Shanghai were stepped up and state of emergency plans refreshed. Generally, of course, such institutions and organizations are always better prepared to handle the last crisis than the next one. But this was a sensible and unusually forward-looking analysis and set of recommendations. The report's prescience was rendered superfluous, however, on 30 May 1925, when a British Inspector in the International Settlement police, Edward Everson, panicked in the face of a large and boisterous demonstration, and ordered his Sikh and Chinese subordinates to open fire on the crowd at point-blank range. Twelve died; students and labourers lay in pools of blood on the Nanjing Road close by the department stores, those sparkling twin beacons of Chinese modernity. What had originated in a protest against conditions in a Japanese-owned mill exploded instead into a sustained and nationwide anti-British movement.[38] Inspector Everson thought that the crowd was on the verge of taking the police station he commanded, and in his eyes he saved the station that day – but the British lost the conflict that ensued. The echoes of this cruel day in May were heard across China, and across the globe. They were certainly heard in Guangzhou – and the city was ready.

Since 1923, Borodin and his growing team of Russian military and political advisors had been helping Sun Yat-sen build up the capacity of the Guomindang. Soviet funds and munitions had poured in, and potential local opposition was quashed. At a January 1924 party conference Borodin had secured support from Sun for a restructuring of the Guomindang's organization along Leninist party lines, as well as for allowing individual members of the fledgling Chinese Communist Party to join the Guomindang, and the appointment to important positions of several of these active and energetic young men, each of whom, one advisor thought, did the work of ten others.[39] These cosmopolitan adventurers conversed in the lingua franca of the Chinese revolution, which was also the language of its prime enemy: English. Sun had lived abroad or in Hong Kong for most of his early life, and Borodin had spent most of his adult years working outside Russia. Photographs show Borodin standing next to Sun at the official inauguration of the Guomindang's new military academy at Huangpu (Whampoa), south of the city. The 'trade commissioner' had swiftly moved into a strong and influential advisory role in the party. In October 1924, Borodin had co-ordinated the Guomindang's devastating strike against local forces challenging Sun's exactions on the city, a coup that left parts of it in ruins. A Russian warship had just arrived with a cargo of weapons and ammunition, and over the next two years 80,000 rifles, 24 aircraft, 200 artillery pieces and 300 machine guns would arrive from the USSR.[40] Arms were important; the advisors and pilots who came with them were important too; but the new party structure, and its work through new mass organizations, was the key to the growing power of the Guomindang. As one early commentator noted, the Russians had found the Guomindang to be a 'community of belief rather than a party'.[41] But it was now transformed into a self-consciously vanguard party working through a hierarchical and centralized organization, derived in essence from military command structures. While faction and clique could certainly overlay and distort this, at its strongest moments the new party structure was able to mobilize and target mass support to its political aims like no other party in China's political experience.

That structure certainly weathered on 12 March 1925 the early death from cancer of Sun Yat-sen at the age of fifty-eight. He passed away in Wellington Koo's house in Beijing, to which city – in a characteristically sharp change of course – he had gone for talks with the new central government. Borodin amongst others was at Sun's side at his death, and immediately the sometime President's legacy was contested.[42] The Soviet ambassador Lev Karakhan was chief mourner at one memorial service; a second, Christian, ceremony was held by the family at the same time. In fact memorial gatherings were held across China, as Sun's life instantly came to symbolize and galvanize yet further the country's struggle against its shackled place in the world. Sun Yat-sen's career had been one of frantic failure, but he had talked, lobbied and publicized himself into a unique position as a talismanic political leader. He seemed to stand above – if not actually apart from – the Guomindang, the most recent of the vehicles he had attempted to use to achieve his aims, and secured approbation from many who otherwise disdained the busy revolutionary regime at Guangzhou. Sun, the professional revolutionary, had almost despite himself become a figure who actually transcended politics. His death, coming so soon after his journey north, which had seen a number of bitter public exchanges between him and foreign diplomats and observers, generated a politically charged atmosphere across China into which were fired the shots at Shanghai.[43] Wang Jingwei, one of Sun's closest political associates, had drafted his leader's brief and pointed political testament, which was to become a canonical text in the developing revolutionary struggle. Its overriding focus was on the struggle for liberty and for equality with other nations. 'Above all,' it concluded, the abrogation of what were described as the 'unequal treaties' was a critical task. Power in the Guomindang now fell to a political triumvirate of three Japanese-educated veteran revolutionaries: Wang Jingwei, who led the more leftist elements within the party; Hu Hanmin, around whom more conservative groups came to coalesce; and San Francisco-born Liao Zhongkai, a continuing strong advocate of the relationship with the Russians, who had been responsible for working out the details of the alliance with the Communists.

Sun's final documents included a letter of farewell to the Central Committee of the Soviet Union, enjoining the Guomindang to continue to work with the one foreign state that treated China as an equal. This supported the position of Liao Zhongkai and the left, who had drafted it, but it was not signed by Sun and was little respected by their opponents.

In June 1925 massive protests spread across China against the shootings in Shanghai. In Guangzhou the Guomindang were dealing with yet another militarist incursion allied to Chen Jiongming, and their efficient – Russian-led – triumph in the field allowed them to then turn their focus on attempting to harness the outpouring of popular rage that the Shanghai massacre had unleashed. After communist activists persuaded labour unions in Hong Kong to go on strike in protest, a rally was held in Guangzhou on 23 June, which was followed by a large parade, including amongst many other contingents a Boy Scout band, a hundred-strong contingent from Lingnan University and armed cadets from the Huangpu Military Academy. The day was windy, and the atmosphere festive. It had always been exciting, this revolution. Guangzhou, its 'Mecca', attracted the ardent young from across China. They could live, work and read Chinese futures there. Nowhere else were communist books and magazines on open sale; and there were posts for new arrivals in the organizations being set up. Days and nights of hectic politics were intertwined with an equally hectic living out of social and cultural revolt in the new recruits' personal lives. 'Love has not yet been achieved, comrades must still bend every effort,' the young radicals joked, spoofing Sun Yat-sen's widely known statement about the tasks of the Chinese revolution not yet having been accomplished. Rallies and demonstrations punctuated the calendar and were all part of the busyness of revolution. Three months earlier, on 8 March, 10,000 had marched through the city to mark International Women's Day.[44] So 23 June, although a day of rage, was yet another day of normal politics, yet another act in the steaming grand theatre of Guangzhou revolution.

After the speeches, the demonstrators snaked their way along the new Bund and what was known as the Shaji (Shakee) Bund, which bordered the canal separating the city from Shamian. The concessions, from which Chinese workers had already – yet again – withdrawn in a protest strike and boycott, and from which many foreign residents had been evacuated, were guarded by British and French marines and armed civilian volunteers, who were stationed in trenches and behind sandbag emplacements protected by barbed wire. They more than half expected the island to be attacked, and had designated the Asiatic Petroleum Company buildings as a last-ditch redoubt. The Commissioner of Customs, a Briton, Arthur Edwards, had shut down the office, despite instructions not to from the Guomindang authorities, a move that would later come back to haunt him. A larger than usual foreign naval presence waited nearby: two British and two French ships, one American and one Japanese. The British Consul General was co-ordinating the defence. He had written to the municipality's Foreign Affairs Commissioner the previous day to ask him to guard against any attempt by agitators or student would-be martyrs to assault the settlements, 'so that it may not be said hereafter that British Imperialist rifles wantonly massacred inoffensive Chinese youth'. Unusually for him – and his habits were public knowledge at the time – he was probably sober that afternoon, but all were tense, the day was hot, and tempers hotter.[45]

We do not know who opened fire, whether it was the cadets, buoyed up by the army's victory over Chen Jiongming, or the foreign soldiers and volunteers, but we do know that in the ensuing twenty-minute slaughter, as French and British machine guns raked the column at 30 yards range across the canal, at least fifty-two Chinese and one Frenchman lost their lives. It was an hour before the fighting stopped, as surviving cadets responded as best they could. Postal Commissioner George Osland-Hill, revolver in one hand, tiller in the other, evacuated some of the remaining foreign women and children onto a motor boat as bullets flew overhead. Scores of people were wounded. Red Cross workers appeared, and observers on Shamian could later see photographers capturing grim memento mori, individual portraits of each of the dead as they lay in the doorways or by the heaps of rubble where they had tried to seek shelter from the storm of bullets. A 'Shaji Incident Investigation Committee' made up of individuals from across Guangzhou society and politics provided details of the victims. Half of them were cadets, but others were university students, shop assistants, labourers and schoolchildren: they ranged in age from fifteen to seventy.[46] Another photograph captures the grim, yet clearly satisfied faces of European men in the porch of the Victoria Hotel after the shooting. American journalist Hallett Abend would note that the hotel still bore evidence of the previous year's bombing, and that dried blood still caked the walls in its restaurant. Now fresh blood congealed on the street opposite the pretty, bougainvillea-dotted island.

The acts of violence at Guangzhou, and of the Hong Kong and the Shanghai International Settlement police, were contingent events. Tempers were inflamed; the situation was brittle; things happened. People lacked patience, restraint, or common sense. The absence of these qualities also stemmed from an embedded culture amongst many foreign officials and residents in China that still expected a show of force to solve problems, and which patently seemed to belittle the value of Chinese lives. Machine-gunning at a range of 30 yards hardly displayed civilized restraint. In most foreign eyes, every gathering was a potential mob. Each demonstration, however well marshalled and organized, equipped with banners and slogans agreed in advance, was for many foreign residents a potential xenophobic riot. What was a wholly contemporary political movement was viewed as an archaic one. The British and others often did not see party cadres, military cadets and unions. They only saw the same rioters whose attacks were the stuff of treaty port history: the Yangzi riots of 1891, riots in Shanghai in 1905, and so on. Most of all they saw 'Boxers'. They did not see nationalist, mobilized, political anti-imperialism, they saw 'Boxerism': by which they meant xenophobic, murderous violence. This was strongly rooted in foreign cultural understandings of China, from sociological treatises to pulp fiction. Victor Purcell, in most other respects a perceptive observer, did not see Guangzhou as a modernizing city, but as a pre-modern one. This is not to say that British officials and others did not perceive the role that Soviet political friends of China were playing, nor did they fail to note the rapid spread of the new organizations of the Chinese Communist Party (CCP) or the reorganized Guomindang, but they saw these as flimsy, superficial shells housing a deeply rooted, backward-looking anti-foreign reflex. Borodin was less a Comintern agent than a familiar bogeyman straight out of popular fictions – and in fact he was quickly a figure thrown straight back into a new wave of such fictions.[47] He was a messianic leader, a puppet master manipulating his toys to attack the British. But viewing the bodies of those slaughtered in Shanghai and Guangzhou (and also at Hankou on the Yangzi in an incident on 11 June), Chinese protesters in Beijing posted placards turning the caricature back on the British: 'Who are the Boxers?' they asked.

Hate is a strong word, but it is the apposite one to describe the emotions engendered in many Chinese by the Shaji Massacre. It is, however, a barren emotion unless channelled. Moving slowly centre stage in the Guomindang was Chiang Kai-shek, the Commander of the Huangpu Military Academy, a Japanese-trained thirty-eight-year-old from China's eastern Zhejiang province who had become politically close to Sun Yat-sen. One scholar has found 100 statements and draft slogans in Chiang's papers aimed at focusing popular anger at the British in the immediate aftermath of the killings. The French role at Shamian, as with the Japanese role in Shanghai, was carefully set aside in what became an effective targeted mass political campaign against the British. 'All the British "enemies" should be killed', ran one of those draft slogans; the British were 'barbarians'; they must be 'annihilated', 'destroyed'. They were the principal obstruction to the Chinese and to the world revolution against imperialism. 'They slaughter Chinese like pigs or dogs,' Chiang wrote on 23 June, 'not regarding them as human.' 'I was born to deal with this national humiliation.'[48] The Guomindang prepared for immediate war against the principal foe, the British, but the Soviet advisors counselled against an offensive, arguing that Guangzhou was too isolated, and that the British would eventually defeat them. This was probably over-cautious, for the evolving mass politics of nationalistic opposition to imperialism might well have brought a victory, but it would none the less have been pyrrhic. The new army of the Guomindang would not have survived intact; the goal of national reunification would have moved far out of reach. Instead, although it took sixteen months, and caused great hardship in Guangzhou, a boycott and a general strike crippled British trade locally and at Hong Kong. There had been 'nothing like it since the Opium War' claimed a rising star in the CCP, Zhou Enlai.[49] Restraint proved the wiser course. The

'May Thirtieth' incident and its associated calamities was the single greatest wound suffered by the British in China before 1941 and dramatically undermined their position – and it was entirely self-inflicted.

Chiang Kai-shek did not get his war with the British; but the CCP increased its membership tenfold in a year. Tensions that had been evident from the start of this alliance of convenience steadily developed, between a more cautious grouping that was worried about the role of the Soviet advisors – for Borodin now moved to the fore as the most influential figure in the revolutionary party – and those who believed that a social revolution was necessary for both strategic and political reasons.[50] Some veteran Guomindang figures outside Guangzhou viewed developments there with alarm. And in August 1925 the leading pro-communist, Liao Zhongkai, was assassinated, a move that symbolized the nature of the potential rift between left and right. A commission of inquiry would assert that it had ultimately traced the trail of guilt back to the British, but scores of those associated with more conservative politics were arrested, others fled and the right-wing leader Hu Hanmin was forced to absent himself for a while.[51] But although the development of the Guomindang's capacity, and especially its armed force, continued apace, and despite the affair bringing Chiang Kai-shek further to the fore, the strengthening hold of Soviet advisors and the energetic and able young communists was exacerbating unresolved problems about the leadership of the party after Sun. Its work, though, continued apace, and the party now acted to reorganize its administration into what it grandly and ambitiously termed the National Government of the Republic of China on 1 July.

Chiang Kai-shek was to prove capable both of giving speeches at the Huangpu Military Academy outlining the necessity of anti-imperialism and radical mass politics, and of striking back against the left. In March 1926, fearing an attack from his opponents in the Guomindang, Chiang launched a coup against the Russians. Troops loyal to him arrested Communists, and surrounded the advisors' headquarters. This was smoothed over, but Chiang had made his point. In the aftermath, General V. A. Stepanov, newly installed as chief of the military mission, outlined some self-criticisms: the advisors had been too pushy, taking a lead instead of guiding Chinese colleagues; propaganda work in the army had followed too radical a programme, focusing on communism, land issues and anti-imperialism; and power had been too quickly centralized. The young communist activists were too eager and quick to try to control the Guomindang, rather than work within it to transform it. 'We normally pay no attention to Chinese habits, customs, and etiquette,' Stepanov continued. 'This may be a minor blunder but it is sufficient to cause unpleasant feelings against the Russian advisors among the Chinese.' Chiang might be reading about Napoleon and have a 'lust for glory and power and craving to be a hero of China', the Soviets stated, but the Huangpu cadets were intensely loyal to their commander, and they mostly came from reasonably well-off backgrounds. Most had a stake in a socially conservative politics, however much they were national revolutionaries.[52]

If different terms are substituted, Stepanov's self-criticism could easily pass for one of the even more agonized self-criticisms that were also being made within the mission community, initially as a result of the anti-Christian movement, but also because of the ambiguous position of missionaries more widely in China; they mostly sheltered under the flags of extraterritorial convenience, and so found themselves complicit in the wider foreign establishment in China. They too were part of the world of Shamian, however much they felt distant from it. The actual, or perceived, overbearing attitude of foreign personnel in their relations with Chinese co-workers helped inflame the anti-Christian movement. The shootings at Shanghai and Guangzhou forced foreign staff to take a public stand and identify themselves, and in many cases in doing so they failed to please either the Chinese or the wider foreign community. At Lingnan in the immediate aftermath of the Shaji Massacre, the one Briton on the staff, an old-school Congregationalist evangelist, was spirited off campus and out of Guangzhou via Shamian. Earl Swisher was one of a number of American faculty members who signed a statement condemning the killings, but their text accepted the Chinese claim that the first shots came from Shamian, and stated that the marchers were all unarmed. Swisher and his colleagues were drummed out of Hong Kong by the British when they tried to take refuge there from the rapidly spreading general strike that shut down the college.[53]

Chiang Kai-shek's assertion of his leading role in the Guomindang was demonstrated as he pushed forward plans for a 'Northern Expedition'. The tensions between Sun Yat-sen and Chen Jiongming had partly arisen from the fact that for Sun, Guangzhou was a provincial means to a national end, a base from which his military force would achieve the reunification of China, whereas for Chen and many other interests locally, such ideas distorted or even impaired the city's and the region's development and prosperity. The Guomindang's National Revolutionary Army (NRA), as it was officially constituted and named in 1925, was 150,000 strong by August 1926. It was a well-trained and well-organized force, a Party army loyal to the Guomindang, in which political work – directed by communists mostly – was vitally important. But the officer corps was heavily shaped also by strong ties of personal loyalty to Chiang. These overlapping cultures would prove important, but not before the NRA had marched out to set China ablaze and to bring about a national reunification under the rule of the Guomindang's new National Government.

There is a bitterness that chokes the romance of the Northern Expedition, but it was nonetheless by any standards a magnificent and daring enterprise.[54] Put briefly, from their base in the south the soldiers of the NRA struck north on 9 July, carrying all before them. They took Changsha in Hunan province on 11 August 1926, then dashed further north to the great Yangzi cities, besieging Wuchang for forty days until it fell on 10 October. Jiujiang fell on 5 November, and Nanchang, capital of Jiangxi province, three days later. A second force launched itself east from Guangzhou and into Fujian province, then pushed northeast from there. The NRA eventually enveloped Shanghai; and the Guomindang made Nanjing the seat of their new capital, opening a fresh chapter in Chinese history. For a country that had endured large-scale destructive internecine warfare between militarist factions in 1924–5 involving upwards of half a million soldiers – a set of conflicts led by men who paraded in public their credentials and ambitions for patriotic national reconstruction, but who were in practice prolonging the country's fragmentation – here was the real thing.[55] The following year the NRA mopped up the north, moving into Shandong province, and sending troops on to Beijing. The opposing forces of the militarists crumbled, were defeated in the field, manoeuvred themselves out of the way, or switched sides. Feng Yuxiang had thrown in his lot with the Guomindang a year earlier, and a Soviet mission had also been active at his headquarters in Kalgan (Zhangjiakou). Their foreign mercenaries fled if they could; expert advisors like Zhang Zuolin's arsenal director Frank Sutton sashayed overseas as fast as passages could be purchased. For two further summers the new Nanjing-based regime would have to fight the forces of rebellion or reaction, but it grew stronger as each year passed thereafter. The Russians remained vitally important into early 1927: they advised on strategy, and some led units in the field. They flew reconnaissance missions and strafed enemy positions and transport. Several died in action. But it was the politically committed and courageous performance of the NRA in battle, and the practical popular support it was given, that won it victories. Crucial too was the hectic parlaying that went on between Guomindang agents and their enemies. The troops of the NRA fought hard, and many opponents, sensing the changing wind, fell into step with it rather than suffer annihilation. This was to dilute and weaken the political coherence of the army, but the flag of the Guomindang's state, of the National Government of the Republic of China, flew now instead of the five-barred flag of the discredited Beijing government.

This was the cue for panic in the foreign concessions in China, in legations and consulates, amongst China trade lobby groups, in the press and within clubs and business offices, and in foreign ministries across much of the world. Those long-incubating political tensions between the left and the right, between the Communists and more conservative factions, between civil and military leaders, between Chiang and the Comintern advisors, were to pull the coalition apart at its moment of victory, but not before it had delivered a revolution that utterly unnerved the foreign powers. Hysterical tomes tumbled into bookshops, their titles matching the panic of the foreign-language press: *A Bolshevised China: The World's Greatest Peril?*; *What's Wrong with China*; *Is China Mad?* However, the fact was that it also utterly unnerved more conservative factions within the Guomindang. The mobilization of anti-imperialist sentiment, and the harnessing of all that bitterness and anger over the Twenty-One Demands,

Versailles and the Shandong Question, the Nanjing Road and Shaji shootings, had in large measure delivered a mass base for the Nationalist revolution. The astute linking of militarism and imperialism, as mutually reinforcing threats in analyses of China's predicament, proved potent. They made for powerful pairs of slogans that were painted on walls across China, printed on posters and handbills and chanted at rallies. But this drive also proved potentially uncontrollable. And while many Guomindang leaders, and those now quickly becoming sympathetic to them, supported the cause of the national revolution, they had little stomach for a social revolution, and even less for their allies on the left, and for Russia. The National Government at Guangzhou moved to Wuhan in December 1926, Borodin and his team with them, but power in the movement was moving towards the army, and towards Chiang Kai-shek. Whilst political activism more radical than any seen in Guangzhou now inflamed Wuhan and its province, Chiang Kai-shek and others established a rival – they claimed legitimate – government in Nanjing.

The Northern Expedition brought the Guomindang into skirmishes with the foreign powers, and almost into full-scale armed conflict with them. Sensing a head-on conflict, Eugene Ch'en negotiated to bring an end to the Hong Kong strike-boycott in October 1926, but relations did not improve. British and American warships would lay down a barrage on NRA troops who had attacked foreign-owned property and killed foreign civilians at Nanjing. Tens of thousands of foreign troops were dispatched to defend Shanghai, Hong Kong and Tianjin. A large British Royal Navy flotilla was assembled and patrolled the Yangzi. A state of war seemed to be developing, but war between whom? For some observers – including many Britons – the confrontation between the Guomindang and the British, who were sullen and bitter after two years of conflict with the Chinese nationalist movement, was in fact a proxy war with the USSR. China was but one more front on which this conflict was being fought. The 1926 General Strike in Britain seemed to have opened another front, and in May 1927 British police raided the Soviet trade commission – ARCOS – in London, seizing documents, and shutting down an organ that was clearly engaged in subversive political work. Diplomatic relations with the Soviet Union were broken off. There was a great deal of belligerent talk. But the changing reality on the ground led the British to evolve and broadcast in December 1926 a new China policy, reinforced in January 1927 with a further set of substantive and unilateral proposals for reform.[56] This was too late.

Most dramatic of all the evolving events, however, was the stand-off on the banks of the Yangzi River at Hankou on 3–4 January 1927. The small, 75-acre British concession there had been a source of tension and dispute for some years, most notably over such familiar issues as Chinese access and residence, and the erection of gates and walls in 1911 that enabled its British Municipal Council to guard access during times of strife. Disagreements with the city administration and the chamber of commerce over this were exacerbated by other routine controversies about the treatment of Chinese, and were then inflamed by the killing of eight people in Hankou by British civilian volunteers during the May Thirtieth protests. Anti-imperialist slogans helped fire and channel the mass movements that took the NRA to victory. Its political cadres moved in with the army, and the concession areas became the target of sustained political attack in late 1926. Anti-Guomindang action on the part of British concession authorities at Tianjin, which led to the arrest and handing over of party agents for execution by their enemies, inflamed the situation. So, over two long days in January 1927, a small unit of British marines held back a politically charged crowd. To avoid a catastrophe unfolding they were then withdrawn and NRA forces moved in to guard the concession. Two days later the council formally handed over administration to a newly established Guomindang municipality. The same day, the even-smaller British concession at Jiujiang was seized by demonstrators, and much of it was looted. The withdrawal of the marines from the Hankou Bund on 4 January was, in its understated way, a moment of great symbolic importance in the wider and steadily unfolding history of Asian nationalism's contest with foreign empires. For the first time in history, an outpost of European empire had fallen to its nationalist opponents; and it would never be retaken.

What next, where next? This was all the stuff of nightmares. They had feared a rush at Shamian in 1925, and they had long indulged in fantasies of Chinese attacks on their settlements, finding in the Boxer uprising only a generation earlier the fulfilment of all those dark dreams. Now, as the NRA moved north, and with the atmosphere still rank from the May Thirtieth Movement and Shaji Massacre, every one of the hundreds of sites of the foreign presence in China, every concession, settlement and mission station, every foreign-run school or hospital, every foreign-owned steamer even, became a site or potential site of the nationalist upsurge against imperialism. Every relationship with Chinese co-workers, or servants, employees or communities, was put to the test. Students and servants went on strike; congregations demanded autonomy from mission societies; consumer boycotts hit British trade badly. An accident on the street could quickly turn into a political incident. And war of course brought disorder with it. Defeated or deserting soldiers turned bandits – weapons flowed out of military formations into criminal hands – robbers took advantage of collapses in order; victorious units put into practice the anti-imperialist slogans they had imbibed. A bigger flight to the coast than had ever been seen ensued. Starting in late 1926, thousands of foreigners made their way to Shanghai, Guangzhou and Tianjin, and many sailed out of China, with significant numbers of them, especially missionaries, not returning. Barely 500 out of 8,000 Protestant missionaries remained at their posts during the evacuation.[57]

This felt like a global crisis. The potential for a domino effect was widely assumed. After China, Vietnam? Or Korea, perhaps India, as the key prize? The man who would become better known as Ho Chi Minh, Nguyễn Ái Quốc, worked as a translator for Borodin at Guangzhou, and established the forerunner of the Communist Party of Vietnam there in the spring of 1925. The Indonesian revolutionary, later communist leader, Tan Malaka, also spent time in the revolutionary city. South Asian nationalists were active at Wuhan, printing literature that circulated across China. The British government of India despatched an intelligence agent to Shanghai to co-ordinate surveillance of activists. It felt like a world war against communism. American, French and Japanese forces were strengthened. Italian, Spanish, Portuguese and Dutch marines and ships were available. The British sent a 20,000-strong 'Shanghai Defence Force' to protect the International Settlement, their largest deployment of forces between 1918 and 1939; Royal Navy reinforcements arrived, many spoiling for a chance to bloody the noses of the 'reds'. 'I trust,' wrote

Winston Churchill, to British Prime Minister Stanley Baldwin, 'that there will be no false logic and false sentiment and false humanity against using gas?'[58]

At Shanghai the International Settlement authorities waited. Defence plans were put into action, and barbed-wire barriers erected; foreign military reinforcements were housed in readiness. The news from Hankou was worrying. The foreign police in Shanghai continued to work closely with the military authorities allied to the enemies of the Guomindang, to identify and arrest the party's agents in the settlement and the French concession, and hand them over. Most were promptly executed. In late January 1927 the police force's political unit, the Intelligence Office, discussed commissioning cartoons for propaganda handbills and posters to bring home 'the wickedness of Chiang Kia Shek [sic]', 'representing him as an unscrupulous, avaricious and blood thirsty traitor'. It would be best to portray him as a 'tortoise, a leech, a cobra, a wolf and a "running dog"', they concluded.[59] Ten weeks later, on the night of 11–12 April, the police closed the protective barriers and gates, allowing through only a convoy of trucks that headed north into the district of Zhabei, carrying hundreds of armed men loyal to a powerful local underworld figure, Du Yuesheng. As dawn broke next morning these gangsters attacked labour headquarters and other sites housing the organs of a Guomindang-allied, communist-led uprising, which had seized Shanghai just ahead of the arrival of Chiang's forces. NRA units came forward to support the attacks: a counter-revolution had begun. This was all planned. Chiang Kai-shek had arrived at Shanghai on 26 March, and Du Yuesheng and his associates were some of the first people he had met. The revolution splintered, the once competing, now fighting, factions coalescing around rival centres of power and self-proclaimed National Governments at Wuhan and Nanjing. On 13 April, on Shanghai's northern Baoshan Road, a peaceful march protesting against the crackdown was machine-gunned by NRA troops. Almost ten times as many died at the hands of the Guomindang as had been killed two years earlier on the Nanjing Road by the International Settlement police.

The Soviet intervention in Guangzhou had been crucial to the revived fortunes of the Guomindang. It led to the reorganization of the party and the creation of its army. Soviet arms, cash and advice were vital to its reformation and the revolution that had secured for it the control of central China and the at least nominal allegiance of much of the rest. For the first time a foreign power had intervened directly and overtly in China's civil conflicts. Its aims were greatly compromised. The Russians mixed ideological communist internationalism and a strategy to outflank the young Soviet Union's European enemies by striking a blow at their colonial possessions and setting China on fire. The 'missionaries of revolution' generated a moment of intense, internationalized political conflict centred first at Guangzhou, which became a headquarters for a wider revolutionary initiative, and then across southern, eastern and central China. The impact on foreign governments (and their security agencies) and on public opinion was immense. While this proved transitory in some ways – for the global economic crisis, Sino-Japanese tensions and the rise of European fascism would obscure memories of what has been articulated as 'the tragedy of the Chinese revolution' – a strong legacy would remain. Crucial to this were the anti-Stalinist history of that name by Harold Isaacs and André Malraux's novels *Les Conquérants (The Conquerors)* (1928), set in Guangzhou, and *La Condition humaine (The Human Condition/Man's Fate)* (1933), set during the Shanghai rising and coup. The novelist's books would imprint one version of the events of 1926–7 on European culture, reconfiguring them as sites of individual, existential crises. Malraux had never visited China when he wrote these novels, instead turning, from a safe distance, the agonies of a political catastrophe into art.

Mikhail Borodin too was an artist of sorts, but he had been supremely pragmatic as he pursued the Comintern's policies. This – as much as the guns and the cash – contributed in no small measure to his success, and to what remained strong bonds amongst the core leadership of the Guomindang, even though this was now splintered across different armed camps. Borodin's approach was sharply criticized and challenged by some of his colleagues, not least in the crucial period after Chiang's purge at Shanghai. Leading the charge was a newly arrived Comintern representative, Manabendra Nath Roy, a veteran anti-British Indian revolutionary, 'a star of Asia', in the words of Chinese Communist Party leader Zhang Guotao, but also a 'scholar' and ideologue, full of 'empty talk'. By contrast, Zhang thought that Borodin 'attached the utmost importance to reality'.[60]

Reality closed in, and gave little quarter. The Soviet establishment in China had been assailed in the north, east and south. On 6 April 1927 the leading foreign diplomats at Beijing, still controlled then by the Manchurian militarist Zhang Zuolin, gave permission to the city police to raid the Soviet Embassy. British troops manned the wall of their neighbouring legation to ensure that no one sought refuge there. An enormous cache of documents was seized – which is the reason now that so much is known about the inner workings of the Soviet teams in China – and twenty-two Russians and thirty-six Chinese were arrested, including senior Communist Party leaders and members of the Guomindang. The Russians would eventually be freed. At least twenty of the Chinese were swiftly executed, including one of the founders of the Communist Party, Li Dazhao. At Tianjin and Shanghai, Soviet consulates were raided or blockaded. Diplomatic couriers were detained, and correspondence was seized. Borodin's wife, Fanny, was arrested, and only later sprung from jail by a well-bribed judge. Between 9 and 15 April forces allied to Chiang Kai-shek and the conservative Guomindang factions attacked leftists and communists in Xiamen, Ningbo, Nanjing, Shanghai and even back in Guangzhou, home of the revolution. Not even the headquarters of the Hong Kong Strike Committee survived. Hundreds of people were killed in this wave of repression. Terror begot terror: leftists struck back in Wuhan and Changsha, arresting and killing political and alleged 'class' enemies. But when the leftist Guomindang leaders in Wuhan, their military strength ebbing, were shown by Manabendra Nath Roy – still failing to grasp reality – a telegram sent by Joseph Stalin to the CCP, ordering their own removal from office and the acceleration of a rural revolution across the areas under their control, they too decided that they had had enough, turned on their allies, and made moves to reconcile themselves with Chiang Kai-shek.[61]

One of the last photographs of Borodin taken in China shows him hunting grouse from a makeshift camp in the Gobi desert in September 1927. Earlier that month a convoy of five cars and five trucks had set out from Yinchuan in Ningxia province, carrying a motley complement: Soviet advisors who had left Hankou with Borodin in late July, his bodyguard, his cook, two of Eugene Ch'en's sons, and an American communist journalist, Anna Louise Strong.[62] They had been seen off with due courtesies from the Guomindang leaders in Wuhan. Sun Fo, Wang Jingwei and others had come to the railway station, notwithstanding the fallout from the Stalin telegram. Given a safe passage through territory controlled by Feng Yuxiang, they were heading north to Russian-controlled Mongolia. The game was up. Although it looked like any one of a number of foreign expeditions that tramped around the sparsely populated northwest in the 1920s and 1930s, few of the others will have travelled with a radio operator. This was a party in flight, not exploring. The Russian venture in China had collapsed, and those who could got out of the country. Comradeship and the shared experiences of four hard years counted for something, and Borodin was steered safely to a route that avoided those who now placarded Guomindang-held cities with posters offering rewards for his capture. Many of those who did escape would, in time, perhaps regret their successful flight north to Ulan Bator, which they reached in late September. Very few of them would survive Stalin's purges, the dapper Mikhail Borodin not excepted.[63]

As the move against the left intensified across China in the spring and summer of 1927, the Communists themselves – on the orders of the Comintern – staged a series of open revolts, throwing off any pretence of working with or through the Guomindang, seizing and losing Nanchang, Shantou and other cities and towns. If these futile gestures were not so bloody we might think of them as farce. On 11 December a mixed force of armed workers, rural dwellers and military cadets seized control of most of central Guangzhou and proclaimed the establishment of a Guangzhou Soviet. A grand programme of social and economic reform was announced. Red flags flew. But popular support for the revolt was not forthcoming from the exhausted city. Shops stayed shut. The workers of Guangzhou kept their own counsel. The city bore two days of communist control, and then on 13 December army units loyal to the Guomindang landed on the Bund from Henan Island and assaulted the under-armed communist forces. Days and nights of slaughter followed. The Russians who survived the attack, including the vice consul, were marched through the streets and then executed. Thousands of people were seized and shot. Some were captured rebels, but mostly they were suspected sympathizers or hapless bystanders. Many were bound, shoved on to boats and drowned in the Pearl River. Photographs of carts loaded with bodies circulated across the globe. Lingnan University's Earl Swisher saw the revolution and the revenge up close. The streets, he reported, were 'piled with dead', women's bodies lay stripped after slaughter and mutilated.[64] One symbol of Guangzhou's smooth modern cosmopolitanism had been the chic Western clothes and hairstyles of its emancipated young women. But now this was seen as an obvious sign of communist affiliation, and the Chinese revolution that had secured its great, stirring triumph in 1927 concluded the year by executing scores and scores of its bobbed-haired youth in the streets of one of its greatest metropolises.

3

Good Earth

The revolution had been checked in the cities. The foreign advisors who had come to help, and had assisted in giving it form, organization, resources and even a language of revolution, had fled, or lay dead in Guangzhou's streets, languished in jail, or had, in what would become a recurrent political irony, sought what they hoped would be the security of the foreign concessions. The foreign interests in Shanghai, and their diplomatic backers, had now formed a rough alliance of purpose with the Guomindang, first sealed in blood during Shanghai's sanguine April coup. In this Cold War of the 1920s they had joined together to fight the USSR, the Comintern and its agents in China. It would not be an easy relationship, and would remain brittle, not least because Chiang Kai-shek and his allies remained no less committed to rolling back foreign power than their former comrades in arms from the Communist Party. For now, the new regime worked to consolidate its power, authority and finances, dunning the wealthy of Shanghai for loans and contributions through a mixture of extortion, exhortation and persuasion. A little bit of kidnapping helped, but expunging the taint of communism helped too. It looked and felt like a counter-revolution, especially as the foreign diplomats and concession and settlement authorities started to work with the Guomindang. So, if the new world of the cities had failed the revolution, might not the old world of the countryside redress the balance?

Peng Pai set out to find out. 'One day in May I started the peasant movement,' begins the engaging account of a one-man campaign of rural reform published in 1926 by Peng, the twenty-nine-year-old son of a prominent family of landholders in eastern Guangdong province's Haifeng county. Peng's family were relatively comfortable and well connected, their fortunes established by his grandfather who had profitable timber, nut-oil and real-estate interests, which he parlayed into land ownership and all the affectations and ambitions of rural gentry status. Fifteen hundred people lived on the land the Peng family owned in Haifeng. The revolutionary militarist Chen Jiongming – Sun Yat-sen's sometime ally – was also a native of the county, and in 1918 after a largely old-style classical schooling Peng was one of a number of local students selected to go and study in Japan at Chen's initiative. At Waseda University in Tokyo, Peng encountered the internationalized modern, studying political science and subjects a world away from the Confucian education of his early years back home. Like many students who went overseas during these heady years, Peng also threw himself into political activity: Waseda was a hotbed of socialist activism and those Chinese studying in Japan were also electrified by the Shandong controversy and the fiasco at Versailles.

Peng returned to China in 1921, and Chen, by then provincial governor, appointed him as the educational commissioner in their home county, Haifeng. Chen's aim was for young men like Peng to feed back their new learning and to lead a wholesale reform of schools in Guangdong province. New schools with an overtly 'modern', scientific curriculum would underpin the revitalization of China. Chen's modernizing zeal encompassed pulling down the walls of Haifeng town and laying out a new highway to link it directly to Guangzhou in the west and Shantou in the northeast.[1] But instead, Peng, who seems to have joined the communist Socialist Youth League in Guangzhou shortly after returning home, instigated a series of radical initiatives in Haifeng county and its neighbours that would capture the horrified attention of observers the world over.[2] For the movement whose roots seem so innocuous grew into a bloody rural revolution, its name a byword for savage butchery.

It is easy to be seduced by the bright, shining modernity of China's great cities, but in the 1920s this was still an overwhelmingly rural society, with the vast majority of its people living on the land as farmers. Patterns of land ownership varied greatly, as did the nature of local rural society across the country's vast landmass, which encompassed a sub-tropical climate in the south in which two rice crops a year could be grown, together with the harsh, dry landscape of the northwest, where barely a single grain harvest could be managed. Subsistence farming coexisted with pockets of highly commercialized agriculture. In some areas people seemed tied to the land, but in others there were rich traditions of seasonal migration to seek other work. Differences such as those between the great north China plain, which stretched south from the capital, and the mountainous lands of the southern and southeastern provinces, for example, also meant that rural China encompassed a very wide range of different social structures. In eastern Guangdong province and Fujian, its neighbour to the north, clans such as the Pengs dominated the land, and sometimes fought to defend it from competitors. China's population is estimated in 1920 to have already reached at least 450 million, roughly a quarter of the world's total, and larger than Europe's, and over eight out of ten Chinese lived on and tilled what was in places a very densely populated land.[3]

There was some movement from the land into the cities – Shanghai annually sucked in new recruits to its underclass of rural immigrants from the north of Jiangsu province. There was also a sustained pattern of migration into such regions as Manchuria from Shandong province, into the provinces devastated by the Taiping Rebellion in the nineteenth century, into highland areas as pressures on the plains grew more intense, and of course overseas. Peng Pai himself provided some probably quite impressionistic figures for the impact of emigration on Haifeng. He estimated that five-sixths of its emigrants went abroad, mainly to colonial Southeast Asia, travelling along the foreign-owned shipping lines that formed the sinews of empire. Three-quarters of the remainder worked in Hong Kong in construction, as small-time traders, or pulling rickshaws. Most of the rest did similar jobs in Guangzhou, and some had headed north to Shantou for similar work. Their labour was their commodity, that and their ready pluck to leave the lands to which they remained tightly bound by kinship ties, and by duties to their ancestors. They maintained their affinity overseas through their distinctive dialect – Cantonese was not spoken in the east of the province – and remitting funds back home, and they returned to the county when they could. Haifeng is situated on the coast east of Hong Kong, cut off physically from the rest of

Guangdong province by the Nanling mountains. Seven-tenths of its territory is mountainous, and this effective isolation had an important role in shaping local society and identity. Moreover, most of the population were 'Hoklo', descendants of migrants from Fujian province to the north, while around 30 per cent were Hakka – 'guest people' – like the Hoklo also ethnically Han, but with a distinct language and customs and also descended from migrants. Peng himself was a Hakka, though his family was so assimilated that he did not speak the language.

The language Peng learned at Waseda, however, was a new one concerned with reform and with revolution within a socialist framework. There had been great interest there in particular in questions of rural education and agrarian reform, and it is this strand of socialist debate and thinking to which Peng, like others, was drawn. An idealistic 'New Village Movement', inspired more by Tolstoy than Marx, was the most striking initiative that attracted an eclectic range of Chinese observers such as Peng, Li Dazhao, one of the Communist Party's founders who had also studied at Waseda, and most prominently in this period the writer Zhou Zuoren – Lu Xun's brother – its most articulate and enthusiastic advocate.[4] While motives varied, and even understandings of what a 'new village' might mean in practice differed, there was common ground when it came to articulating a problem. For many of them the defining challenge of China's twentieth century was not its cities, which could surely look after themselves, for they were, each in their own way and to different extents, connected into the world economy. Industrialization was slowly gathering pace, boosted by both the world war and then the demands of peace. Nor was it China's political predicament, for that would surely evolve as the republic's political structures matured, and as education rejuvenated the nation. Rather, it was the great rural heartland of the country and the world of these hundreds of millions of farmers that seemed to present the greatest challenges to any rebuilding of China. They were too many, too under-educated and too poor. They seemed trapped in cycles of poverty, and if they were trapped, then China too was surely trapped with them.

In Peng Pai's analysis a relatively stable rural economy had been undermined since the 1911 revolution, with a steady impoverishment of more established farmers and concentration of land ownership into a smaller elite of landlords. This new elite was often intertwined with a new and rapaciously kleptocratic republican political establishment, which did not hesitate to use violence to enforce debt collection and the extraction of a bewildering array of new taxes and impositions. The new schools, for example, were an expensive addition to the rural tax bill, wherever they were established. Peng also identified what was a standard element in Leninist analysis: imperialism had destroyed the local handicraft industry, 'imperialist' control over the customs tariff kept prices high and 'imperialists' allied to militarists fought out their battles on Chinese soil, paid for by various forms of extortion from the rural poor. Peng's picture of the change in relationships between landowners and farmers served his political analysis, but other accounts do at least support the wider view of a rural society undergoing bewildering and rapid change, and in which various forms of violence had become embedded.[5]

The Shanghai Taipan strolling along the Bund to lunch at his club would have been bewildered at the charge that his presence had such a deep impact far away (in his mind) in China's countryside. That was a world he would generally never see, except for the relatively prosperous counties neighbouring the city where he might holiday on a houseboat, or ride or hunt. He might accept that his presence was helping to foster the 'modernizing' of China, through some sort of trickle-down effect. But really, in general he did not concern himself with thinking about China beyond the Bund. The opponents of imperialism viewed China whole, however, and through this theoretical lens.

The idea has taken hold that China's rural economy and rural society were 'backward', and 'traditional', and that China was a 'land of famine' in which rural people lived always on the verge of disaster, and had always done so. In the oft-repeated words of British socialist R. H. Tawney's classic social survey published in 1932, 'there are districts in which the position of the rural population is that of a man standing permanently up to the neck in water, so that even a ripple is sufficient to drown him'.[6] This dramatic image has been extrapolated out to encompass the entire world of the rural Chinese, their plight significantly exacerbated by the actions of a greedy and violently oppressive landlord class, and by the depredations of petty or major militarists. Certainly, life could be as hard in China's countryside as in any other. Many rural households did live within an economy of intense routine scarcity. Moreover, climate deviations from general norms, such as the El Niño effect, could have a devastating effect. This was the cause of the 1876–9 north China famine that led to at least ten million deaths, and in 1920–21 at least half a million people died in the same area as a result of drought. Flooding left an equally savage mark, the waters killing large numbers, and many more dying in the aftermath as a result of food shortages and crop destruction. The capacity of the Chinese state to provide emergency relief had been greatly eroded in the last stages of Qing rule because of internal rebellion and external threats. Nonetheless, in general, food production had increased as the population grew: new types of crops and the breaking of virgin soil had been key factors: there was no 'land of famine'. But even so, many came to believe that there was a systemic problem that needed redressing if China was to progress.

Foreign analysts such as Tawney reinforced this view. Missionary involvement in famine relief in the 1870s, and in later episodes, was accompanied by globally circulated publicity efforts, aimed at raising awareness and funds to help famine-struck districts. This proved to be a key way in which the idea of China as a uniquely famine-hit land started to take hold.[7] It was exacerbated by the routine language and devices of missionary reports, which contrasted what they portrayed as the hidebound, traditional, oppressive worlds of those they sought to convert and save, with the modern spiritual uplands to which missionaries wished to help lead the rural Chinese. Identifying a China that was 'unchanging' was simply an unreflective and often unconscious cliché in the missionary repertoire. Not only in theirs: even a social scientist like Tawney felt able to state – at a conference in Shanghai in the first instance – that 'what elsewhere is a memory is in China a fact'. Eileen Power, an influential British historian of medieval Europe, felt she had encountered that past made present when she visited China in 1921.[8] To any visitor fresh off a smart steamer from overseas, to a missionary or a traveller like Power, or even in fact like Peng Pai himself the same year, the Chinese countryside resembled the European past: unmechanized, 'feudal' in its social and family relations, trapped in superstitious rituals and beliefs and fearful of change. It looked that way to many young urban Chinese as well who had never been abroad, who looked out from the cities and saw a world from which they were increasingly disconnected.

But whereas the consumers of revolutionary chic in Guangzhou, all dolled up in their swanky department-store finest, had played politics and pursued romance, Peng Pai had put his money where his mouth was and set to work to make change happen, almost literally, for he reformed even his own family lands. While research now suggests that we must temper any idea that there was a systemic crisis in the Chinese countryside, any analysis would have to accept that there were many problems, different in scale and complexity in different places, and that these, as much as imperialism and 'warlordism', deserved the attention of reformers and revolutionaries.[9] Indeed, the disputes that characterized the last stages of the Comintern-Guomindang alliance in Wuhan in 1927 revolved around the question of rural revolution. This was Manabendra Nath Roy's particular field of expertise, and reports such as Peng Pai's offered much food for thought about the capacity of China's countryside and its populations to undergird the struggle. This was not simply a question of urgency or priorities, but one of tactics: might not the rural masses provide an unstoppable force for revolution?[10] Could China be regenerated from the countryside rather than the town? Back in 1900, as large numbers of men in rural north China combined in armed bands aiming to extirpate foreign influences during the Boxer uprising, observers such as Robert Hart pondered what such energy and power might do if properly organized and led. Imagine, he wrote, 'Twenty millions or more of Boxers armed, drilled, disciplined, and animated by patriotic – if mistaken – motives.' They could 'take back from foreigners everything foreigners have taken from China, will pay off old grudges with interest, and will carry the Chinese flag and Chinese arms into many a place that even fancy will not suggest to-day, thus preparing for the future upheavals and disasters never even dreamt of'.[11]

For the Chinese Communists this vision remained mostly couched in orthodox Marxist-Leninist terms, and it was to serve the revolution: it would be a rural force led by urban proletarians, and intellectuals like themselves. But here was power, untapped, latent.

Peng Pai had quickly alienated Chen Jiongming and the local Hai-feng elites by his actions as educational commissioner, losing his job in the summer of 1922 after organizing a May Day demonstration amongst school students. As he tells it, he then decided, against the advice of his friends, who thought it a complete waste of his time, talents and education, to go to work amongst rural people in Hai-feng. 'I went to a village,' Peng wrote:

> wearing a student-style Western white suit and solid cap. A village peas-
> ant in his thirties saw me coming. As he was working with manure, he
> said to me, 'Sit down, sir, have a smoke. You came to collect tax, right?
> People around here haven't put on any opera.' I replied, 'I'm not here
> for theatre tax, I'm here to make friends with you. Because your life is
> hard I came to have a talk.' 'Ah,' replied the man. 'It's fate that our life
> is hard. Sometime I'll invite you to tea, sir. We don't have enough time
> to talk to you, forgive us.'

'With that,' Peng continued, 'he took off.' Who can blame him? The incongruous image of this encounter between a white-suited, earnest young student, and a farmer hard at work turning manure, leaps off the page. The gulf between their worlds seems unbridgeable. Others whom the neophyte revolutionary encountered similarly assumed he was a rent or tax collector, or another type of emissary with an impo-sition in mind. Dogs barked at him. Doors were locked. At home that night Peng's family, angry at his venture, refused to speak to him.

The landlord's son had found that he spoke a different language to his tenant neighbours, it was too elegant and rhetorical, so much so that his words failed to make any sense to them. His clothes further marked him out. Reflecting on this, Peng reworked his tone and delivery, and reconsidered his choice of clothing. Then, having suit-ably dressed down – or so he thought – he positioned himself at a local crossroads by a temple, which many farmers passed and rested at as they moved to market and back. For two weeks he took up posi-tion there daily and spoke out, arguing that landlords lived unfairly off their hard-working tenants, giving 'proof of landlord oppression of peasants', arguing that it 'was necessary for peasants to unite' to fight this. Peng gradually attracted a regular crowd, but largely, it transpired, because people were bemused at the sight of the landlord family's seemingly insane son embarrassing himself in public – for this was the tale that was being put about, and which his extended family did not contradict. He also found himself on the receiving end of sharp comments about the rent-collecting practices of the Peng family, some thirty individuals in total. But eventually one or two of his audience agreed to talk with him in private. They gathered by lamplight one night in Peng's home on the outskirts of Haifeng town. 'Why,' he asked them, 'is it so difficult for me to get a hearing for my ideas?' 'Change your clothes and change your language,' they said. 'Moreover,' they reminded him, 'people do not have time to spare, and they do not know you.' Peng needed to be introduced, they said, by someone farmers trusted. 'Some of us often discuss your comments after we have finished work,' they continued, 'and we are interested in what you have to say. But you are doing it all wrong.'

China's rural inhabitants were of course quite capable of articulately defending their own interests. The long history of tax revolts, or other forms of collective resistance, points to this. Country people did not need citified radicals like Peng Pai in order to understand their own situation or find ways to defend it. In Haifeng itself there was a robust tradition of collective self-defence through 'Red Flag' and 'Black Flag' organizations, which defended their members' interests, and fought for resources or to redress wrongs; and triad organizations had also been active. Peng also claimed that in 1895 there had been a revolt in the county, which although suppressed, was widely remembered. An older farmer, Yang Qishan, celebrated locally for his martial-arts prowess, was already recognized by local people as a natural leader, and he sought out Peng to explore what the landlord's son was up to. Without such allies within local society, Peng was unlikely to have made any headway. Moreover, aside from the seeming hypocrisy of calls for action against landlords coming from this scion of one of the more notorious local families, people voiced a pragmatic caution: Peng Pai, well educated and well connected, could get away with saying such things. The social elite would ultimately protect its own, and the long-established tradition of tolerating the protests of the educated young, grounded in the profound respect accorded education, would also buffer him. Indeed, Peng was always treated with elaborate politeness, tea being offered, cigarettes too, when he met even those opposing the Peasant Union, at least in its early phase, and he still found it easy to secure audiences with Chen Jiongming. But ordinary rural folk could pay a much higher price for protest.

Despite this inauspicious start, there was enough interest in what Peng had to say for the small group that met in his home to establish what they called a 'Peasant Union', and to agree to accompany Peng on his trips into the villages. 'Success is on its way,' he gleefully wrote in his diary that evening. They went to villages at night, after the day's work was over, for in the rural economy people really had no time to spare during the day. Peng's new associates would introduce him, and instead of lecturing his audiences as before, he would engage in question-and-answer sessions with them, gaining more attention and bigger audiences with magic tricks and a gramophone. Christian missionaries and British American Tobacco's cigarette salesmen used the same devices as they sold their respective wares in the country-side. There was precious little to do in the rural evenings, despite such recent innovations as lamps fuelled with imported kerosene oil, which brought some light to the dark, so Peng now had no difficulty in securing audiences. But they would not join the Peasant Union. Peng built rhetorically on their own cautious responses: 'Joining the Peas-ant Union was like crossing a river; on this bank, misery; on that bank, happiness; but who wants to drown in the water?' he said. 'If all join the union together,' he reasoned, 'then each would be able to help each as they forded their way to a different future.' The nascent organization started to intervene directly in small disputes to success-fully secure redress for its members. Actions spoke loudly to the power of combination.

Out of Peng Pai's naive and initially maladroit venture into the villages near his family home emerged an organization that gained traction rapidly with local farming communities, to the consterna-tion and eventually the violent opposition of local power-holders. By the autumn of 1922 a reported twenty new members a day were join-ing, and the union and its district branches set up welfare departments including a clinic. On 1 January 1923 a Haifeng General Peasant Union was established that claimed to represent some 20,000 house-holds, and therefore an estimated 100,000 people, about a quarter of the population of the county. On 3 March the union organized a 'Peasants' New Year Celebration'. Some 9,000 people, two-thirds of them already members, enjoyed a rally that included lion dances and fireworks, the usual fare of a New Year festival, but also political speeches and a decidedly radical play about rent disputes that further reinforced an overtly revolutionary message.[12] Peng assumed the chairmanship of the union, and Yang Qishan was vice chairman. Ostensibly, and to outside eyes, this was a mutual aid and self-defence organization. The union had a department that arbitrated disputes between members, between members and non-members, and undertook educational initiatives. But an agenda for radical social change was also discussed within the union leadership. As news of the venture spread, other young, educated people came to support it. In a rent dispute that year Peng mobilized 6,000 people to march on a magistrate's office to protest the illegal jailing of union members, who were subsequently set free. Unions began to be formed in the neighbouring counties, notably in Lufeng, and fierce debates started to be held within the union about strategy. Now that it had reached such a size, and secured such loyal support, what should it do with its power?

Despite Chen Jiongming's support for the association – which waxed and waned in inverse proportion to his military fortunes and his need for a secure base in Haifeng – the local elites rallied, cracked down on it in July 1923, and jailed many of its leaders, including Yang, who was also badly beaten. The cause was an escalating dispute arising out of a series of natural disasters, several typhoons that one after the other ravaged the coast, destroying crops and causing damaging floods. Customarily, landlords would lower rents to allow tenants to recover, but in an atmosphere made fractious by the success of the union, leading landlords now refused to do so. In protest, the union campaigned for a rent strike, the first in a series of events that led to the crackdown and the dissolution of the union that July. Its headquarters was attacked by armed men and police, its archives destroyed amid charges that it was fomenting rebellion as well as the communalization of wives (a recurrent and culturally controversial charge in a conservative society). Peng fled to Guangzhou to seek support from Chen Jiongming, but nothing tangible was forthcoming.

However, loyalty to the organization remained embedded within the rural society of Haifeng and Lufeng. Although the activists attempted to revive the union, its opponents persuaded Chen to finally and definitively order the closure of all such associations in March 1924. Peng Pai took a post in Guangzhou within the reorganized Guomindang's new revolutionary apparatus, as secretary of a new 'Peasant Department'. Peng had discovered what other rural activists would also discover, that rural activism was a slow business that required great patience, and sympathetic allies from within. His was not the first of these ventures, nor the only one in the province. Others too were inspired by debates about socialist agrarian reform.[13] They found, like Peng, that rural communities were slow to start to mobilize. They had too much to lose, and were too conscious of the ways in which power could be deployed against them, legally or illegally. The jailing and treatment of Yang seemed to show this afresh. But these rural activists nearly always had some form of existing organization that might come into play. When pushed *in extremis* they could certainly act to defend themselves, but the type of organization that Peng and his associates wished to set up proved harder to realize, for they appeared to be challenging 'fate', as Peng's first interviewee had put it, not some clearly identifiable wrong.

Here we need to think about terminology. For the Communists, but for some others too, the country people of China, its farmers, were 'peasants'. But 'nongmin', the term Peng and the Communists used, was a new word, imported like very many others from Japanese. It was created there as a translation term for the new concept of 'peasant' that was encountered in foreign works. A very large number of foreign books published in Chinese were in fact translated indirectly, from versions translated into Japanese, and terms such as 'peasant', as well as 'communist' and 'socialist', for example, all entered the Chinese language this way. Accompanying the term 'nongmin' was an integrated system of analysis of 'feudalism' and 'feudal society', their characteristics and historical trajectory. Before the 1920s most foreign observers would use the term 'farmers', and the most common Chinese term in use was the direct equivalent of this: 'nongfu'. Turning farmers into peasants this way served a specific vision of society and, implicitly, laid out an agenda for change. It turned what was historically honoured (at least rhetorically) as the bedrock of Chinese society, and much of what was traditionally regarded as good, into a benighted, backward 'class' (another new concept) that needed salvation. Likewise anything 'feudal' was old and bad and oppressive, and in Marxist analysis was bound to fall to a rising bourgeoisie, while 'feudalism' alongside 'warlordism' and 'imperialism' was identified as a target of the revolutionary assault.

At Guangzhou, Peng became the first director of a new 'Peasant Movement Training Institute', and the sole teacher of its first cohort of mostly young, male urbanites.[14] Over the next two years the institute trained some 770 activists, who would then go on to undertake organizational work in a countryside that was largely and incomprehensibly alien to most of them. In Peng's class there was a strong emphasis on practical training and experience. He led the students into the countryside around the city, and took them through all the discoveries he had made in Haifeng: about dress, about speech, and how to build trust and find local interlocutors. Members of the last cohort, the largest, trained under the directorship of a young Hunanese farmer's son, Mao Zedong, would even make a trip to Haifeng itself in 1926. Peng had lectured them in Guangzhou on conditions in the county and the wider East River area, but now they got to see things for themselves. This class was also able to learn from his report on the movement in Haifeng down to 1924, which he started to publish in January in 1926, in a new journal edited by Mao, *Zhongguo Nongmin* (*The Chinese Peasant*).

The network in Haifeng had proved resilient. On both occasions in 1925 when the Guomindang's new army struck east to fight Chen Jiongming and his allies, the organization that seemed broken in 1923 was revived. Peng led graduates from the institute into the field. As the army moved in, he and his team came quickly behind, holding meetings to which large numbers of country people came. Amongst others, Yang Qishan, now released from jail, led bands of farmers who attacked Chen's troops and made their retreat difficult.[15] Over 30,000 people were reported to have attended a victory rally at the headquarters of the reconstituted union, which now became the real power in the land. And blood started to flow. Many of its opponents who had not fled were put on trial, and killed. The land of some of them was confiscated to support the activities of the organization. A general rent reduction of 25 per cent was ordered, and an armed force of local people established. Religious institutions of all kinds were attacked. Clan loyalties brought in en masse yet more supporters – and by now most of the Peng clan had joined their miscreant in his venture – but these also worked to add to the enemies of the new dispensation. Unsettled conditions caused by the fighting brought more violence and provided opportunities for smuggling and banditry – often the recourse of the defeated soldier who put his weapons to freelance use. Instability at Guangzhou led to the recall of Peng and the forces he had to hand, and as the armed power of the revolutionaries was withdrawn, Chen Jiongming and his supporters returned, extracting bloody penance from those they caught.

Haifeng was now entering a cycle of violent revolution and counter-revolution. The Guomindang forces returned in October 1925, but the damage had been done. Many union activists had been killed, and many simply suspected of being implicated in the movement, or related to those who were, were targeted as local elites marshalled armed bands or directed Chen's troops to suppress the opposition. Before the decade was out the pendulum would swing, swing and swing again, as Haifeng and its neighbours were fought over, and as local society was turned inside out. With each swing more violence would ensue, as revenge was taken by first one side, and then the other, and as the social order was completely broken. Chiang Kai-shek's move against the Communists in Guangzhou in March 1926 significantly changed the atmosphere, and emboldened the local enemies of what was widely viewed as a 'bolshevik' regime. But as the Northern Expedition moved north to the Yangzi, and as Chiang's anti-communist stance became clearer and clearer, those centres of Red power that did exist galvanized themselves to continue and to intensify the struggle. The Chinese Communist Party followed the instructions it received from the Comintern, and launched its series of darkly farcical urban insurrections, during each of which much blood was spilt, and from each of which its forces had to make their undignified escape. But in Haifeng and surrounding districts in October 1927, Peng and his associates seized power from the Guomindang's administration, and on 21 November they triumphantly proclaimed the establishment of a Hai-Lu-Feng Worker Peasant Soldier Soviet Government. Then they embarked on a systematic programme of land confiscation, burning of title deeds, and killing of landlords and other 'counter-revolutionaries'. By all accounts, the affable narrator of the 1926 report took a hand in this himself. At the culmination of the three days of celebration that marked the establishment of the soviet, the landlord's son who had stood by the side of the road back in 1922, pestering passers-by to listen to him talk about bettering their lot, took a long knife to the neck of one of the captured enemies of the new government. Peng then cut off the man's head, and immediately afterwards, together with other leaders of the regime, sat down to enjoy a feast.[16]

'On returning home,' Peng told his audience at the closing event of the festivities:

> each representative must kill at least 10 counter-revolutionaries and he must also lead peasants and workers to kill 10 more to a total of 20 per representative: with 300 representatives, the final count will be 6,000. But that is not enough since more will still be left behind . . . We must kill! kill! kill! until the water in the harbour of Shanwei and in the bay of Magong turns red, and all the clothes of each brother are tainted red with the blood of the counter-revolutionaries![17]

So they killed, killed, killed their enemies – priests, Christians, spies, landlords, soldiers, clan leaders; they killed to settle scores and pay back the perpetrators of earlier killings; they killed to demonstrate their commitment to the cause; they killed out of fear of not proving their commitment to it; they killed to ensure that none would survive to exact a later revenge; they killed to show the hesitant that the victims no longer had any power over them; they killed because the sanguine public theatre of the embattled revolution demanded it; and they killed simply because they could. Refugees came away with tales of children instructed to kill their elders, allegations of a policy of killing the old, of episodes of cannibalism: the triumphant feast of victory. Magnified and sensationalized in the telling and retelling, exaggerated for propaganda purposes by their enemies, and turned into horrifying copy for news agencies, tales of the extreme violence in the soviet made headlines around the world. Some 5,000 people are estimated to have been killed, not too far short of Peng Pai's target. But, after all, this was a revolution – and its opponents at Guangzhou in December 1927 had themselves shown little mercy to those they defeated, who included militiamen sent from Hai-Lu-Feng to join the uprising – and the swings of the pendulum had already shown the supporters of the soviet what mercy they might expect locally if overthrown.

Revolutionary terror was hardly invented in Hai-Lu-Feng. The word 'terror' of course is most familiar to us as describing the most violent phase of the French Revolution, umbilically connected to its defining tool – the guillotine. But the consolidation and defence of Bolshevik power in Russia was a key example in the normalization of terror in Communist Party thinking, language and practice in China.[18] Local cultures of violence were also a factor, such as the flag tradition in Haifeng. But all this killing did not save the Hai-Lu-Feng Soviet Government. To secure itself, Peng led a policy of aggressive and initially successful territorial expansion, driving eastwards, but this further solidified a new coalition that coalesced to suppress it. So its enemies returned in February 1928 and after ten days of fierce fighting Guomindang forces captured Haifeng town, and destroyed the structures of the soviet regime. The peasant army stood and fought, but this militia was no match for its professionally trained opponents. In the aftermath yet another wave of reprisals was carried out, but Peng and a core of supporters regrouped in the mountains further to the northwest and established a new soviet there at Da'nanshan. This survived for four more years, preying on the surrounding lowlands, raiding local villages, towns and police, and army posts. It attracted a range of supporters: activists beaten out of the cities, local Hakka who opposed provincial anti-opium campaigns that threatened their livelihoods, opportunists and bandits.[19] Kidnapping and extortion provided one key source of funds. Peng Pai left for Shanghai in late 1928 to take a senior role in the Communist Party apparatus, but was betrayed, arrested and executed in 1929. Many of those of his family who had worked with him were also captured and killed over the next few years.

The ultraviolence of the Hai-Lu-Feng soviet was to become a characteristic feature of the embattled and paranoid bastions of rural communist power. In the mountain fastnesses to which defeated communist insurrectionaries retreated after 1927, especially in those highlands in eastern Guangdong, and in Fujian and Jiangxi provinces, there would also be regular episodes of savage internecine strife, as well as a programme for popular mobilization that had at its heart a murderous settling of accounts with an overthrown class of landowners, 'petty tyrants' and 'local bullies'.[20] Rural mobilization had been a core part of the strategy of the National Revolutionary Army's Northern Expedition. Graduates of the Peasant Movement Training Institute had gone into the field to help prepare the way for the armies, and rural activists had in places materially assisted the army's advance. In its wake, most notably in Hunan province, they set the countryside further aflame, helping to establish 'peasant unions' and agitate for rent reductions and land redistribution. For the Guomindang, however, it had been a military tactic, not a social or revolutionary policy in and of itself. It was aimed at undermining their enemies and their enemies' supporters.[21] The Whampoa Military Academy cadets who formed the nucleus of the officer corps of the NRA were drawn from the sons of the rural elite: they sought military victory, not social revolution. For a small and growing number of communist activists, however, the experience offered a vision of a different route to the future.

Mao Zedong proved the most articulate and visionary advocate of this new path. Characteristically, activists found, as Peng Pai had discovered, that farmers were slow to start to act, but also that when they did start they moved very quickly, as if dam gates had broken. 'The present upsurge of the peasant movement is a colossal event,' proclaimed Mao, like a 'fierce wind, or Tempest, a force so swift and violent that no power, however great, will be able to suppress it. They will break through the trammels that bind them and rush forward along the road to liberation.'[22] 'Choose quickly,' he urged his comrades, and urged 'every Chinese': where will you stand as they do so? And these peasants, once moved, had gone quickly to commit acts of greater and greater violence. 'And what of that,' he wrote, for after all:

A revolution is not a dinner party, or writing an essay, or painting a picture, or doing embroidery; it cannot be so refined, so leisurely and gentle, so temperate, kind, courteous, restrained and magnanimous. A revolution is an uprising, an act of violence by which one class over-throws the power of another.

The passage comes from Mao's own report on the peasant movement in Hunan, published in March 1927. If Peng's often affable account captures the imagination for the way in which it charts the path to enlightenment of its well-meaning narrator, Mao's does so because of its sense of an almost uncontainable excitement, and its joy at the topsey-turning carnival of revolutionary action. The peasants paraded their enemies in dunce hats through the streets, they 'lolled on the beds' of the daughters of the landlords, they knew no fear and no lingering deference. Mao discovered in Hunan a powerful force that had accomplished in months, he claimed, what Sun Yat-sen had failed to achieve in forty years of activity. 'Go look at the villages,' he urged his comrades, you will 'feel thrilled as never before'. If unleashed, the power of the rural poor could sweep all before it, and when unleashed, it would also be immensely violent. The practice of terror, tempered and directed by party activists, was to form a key part of the rural revolution of the Communist Party. It was 'necessary to create terror for a while', argued Mao, to destroy the enemies of the revolution, but this thinking would also soon become a defining characteristic of the party's own internal practices.

Mao's report needed some careful editing in later years. It was revised in subsequent official editions to ensure that it had outlined adequately the key role in the Hunan movement of proletarian leader-ship, for otherwise it was a clearly unorthodox document in Marxist terms. Mao's grasp of Marxism in general at this point was not assured. Like most in the Communist Party and its allied movement, he was attracted to action and revolution first, and ideological preci-sion would follow. The son of a man he identified as a 'poor peasant', Mao had been born in Shaoshan, Hunan province, in 1893. By dint of intellectual capacity and curiosity, and inspired by Robin Hood-type heroes of popular culture, and some encounters with rad-ical teachers, he negotiated a series of schools and arrived in Changsha, the provincial capital. There he formed a study group, then found his way to Beijing in 1918, where he worked in the library at Peking

University. From the anonymous vantage point of overseeing the reader-registration desk, he encountered many of the prominent intellectuals of the time. He had been introduced to the university librarian, Li Dazhao, and through this connection entered a broader network of radical discussion groups and activists attracted by Marxism and the unfolding Russian revolution. He would always be attracted to anarchistic violence, but Mao would be one of those corralled by Comintern representatives into formally establishing a Chinese Communist Party in 1921. Aside from an unexceptional flirtation with the modish 'New Village Movement' discussions in 1919, Mao had not, until 1926, shown much interest in the rural question, and the world of his own rural upbringing. His experience in Hunan changed that, but his conclusions were rejected by the Communist Party's leadership in 1927, and his clarion call for an intensified rural struggle was overshadowed instead by its choice of a policy of urban insurrection. Moreover, in late April 1927, as the Communists reeled from Chiang Kai-shek's deadly and ever-widening purge, it was deemed necessary to control and rein in the extemporary violent revolution in Hunan.[23]

As Mao published his triumphant manifesto on Hunan, another telling contribution to the discussion about the problem of China's rural economy was being prepared for publication. Its author, an American agronomist, John Lossing Buck, had snatched up his draft manuscript from his house on the campus of Nanjing University on 24 March 1927, as ill-disciplined National Revolutionary Army soldiers, who had that day seized the city, moved through the campus attacking and killing foreign nationals. Fired up with anti-imperialist zeal, they took direct action against the enemies of the revolution. Buck and his family hid from the attackers in the house of a family servant, while other foreign nationals were evacuated as American and British warships laid down a covering barrage. As order was restored, they were taken on board a US destroyer and transported to Shanghai.[24] Buck's book was published in 1930 as *Chinese Farm Economy*, and was the first fruit of a long-term research endeavour that would continue to generate a great deal of data about the predicament of Chinese rural society. With Buck's work two strong strands came together, the new republic's zeal for investigation and

the generation of statistics, and a developing concern within missionary and Chinese Christian work for rural problems. The survival of
the Buck family in March 1927 also meant that a third strand would
soon blossom: Buck's wife, Pearl Sydenstricker Buck, was already
mulling over the characters and incidents that would find expression
in her Pulitzer prize-winning 1931 novel about Chinese rural life, *The
Good Earth*.

Pearl Buck attempted to communicate the textures and mentalities
of Chinese rural life. Lossing Buck (as he was always known) wanted
facts. To solve a problem, in most instances, you first need to be sure
that there is one; and to know its precise contours, and to enact legislation or support policy, you need data. To build a state you need to
know what it is that the state represents, controls and marshals. The
new Republic of China established in 1912 had been most attentive
both to the forms of what it felt a state should have – an anthem,
flag, honours and decorations, ceremonial uniforms – and to data,
voluminous amounts of data.[25] The Guomindang's Nationalist Government seemed even more fond of surveys and investigations than
the regime it overthrew, certainly to foreign diplomats, who wearied
of complaints from foreign firms and other interests about the endless
barrage of statistical queries. This was not simply a Chinese phenomenon, but the frequent foreign charge that China lacked data was one
that stung – 'Chinese like other Orientals care absolutely nothing for
statistics' was a not uncommon aside – and the new government's
departments, Chinese universities and other research institutions
embarked on all sorts of survey and data-generation initiatives.[26]
Even Peng Pai's 1926 report provides one glimpse into the statistical
mentality of the moment, for he was careful to provide in his text
what purported to be survey data about land ownership and forms of
tenancy, education, emigration and so on. Surveying was much easier
than doing, of course, but data was nonetheless felt to be needed,
about the rural world of China not least of all.

Lossing Buck had arrived in China in 1915 to work as an agricultural missionary for the American Presbyterian Mission (North) at
Nansuzhou, in Anhui province. A farmer's son – almost a requirement for the US missionary enterprise – Buck was a Cornell University
graduate, and the Nansuzhou initiative seemed a good fit with his

private interest in agricultural work. Such initiatives might help develop the Church, even help fund it, but Buck was steadily moved to focus on his development work as an end in itself, rather than as a means to evangelization. In 1920, when funding for his model farm and local agricultural education programmes at Nansuzhou was discontinued, Buck took up a post in the College of Agriculture and Forestry at Nanjing University. There he steadily developed a statistical initiative that attempted to provide hard data with which to understand the problems, some of which he had encountered in Anhui.[27] China needed 'reliable statistics', he asserted, if it was to take its 'place in world statistics', but also because there needed to be 'self-knowledge before there can be self-improvement'. Reflecting on his findings, Buck concluded that China's farmers needed most of all to gain access to credit. In his eyes they also needed education, but in general, as long as there were no meteorological or other emergencies, they seemed to get by reasonably well, at least as far as his survey subjects were concerned. In practice, as we have seen, this was based on the idea of there being a peaceful and stable status quo that was absent in much of rural China in the 1920s. Buck was selective in the information he sought, and seems to have ignored evidence presented to him about the fracturing of social relations in the countryside. Even being shot at by bandits did not much turn his head from his carefully assembled statistics.[28]

The data does not reveal the harshness of the experience of living in Nansuzhou, which lay not far from the Nanjing to Tianjin railway line, some 300 miles northwest of Shanghai. Pearl Buck's private letters, and *The Good Earth* itself, do however communicate much of the draining, alien texture of the rural world the Bucks encountered.[29] Marjorie Clements, a young English Congregationalist, arrived a decade later at Cangzhou, 375 miles further north, and in her own letters displayed this all too common despair at 'dirt, noise and confusion', disease, thoughtlessness and 'immorality' (as it appeared to her).[30] Too much can be made of this, however, and like most missionaries she saw only what she wanted to see, including what she did not want to see (or smell, or hear) but could not but avoid: instances of violence, poverty, and a lack of understanding of standard hygienic or other practices. Although missionaries like the Bucks or Clements lived in the 'interior', amongst rural communities, they remained as culturally bound to their home societies as did the foreign communities on the coast, in Shanghai for example, or in Zhenjiang on the Yangzi where Pearl Buck had spent much of her childhood.[31]

The plight of the farmers, their 'ignorance', and the incipient violence and 'filth' of Chinese rural life exercised the epistolary and literary talents of many foreign observers. They are common themes, common enough to suggest veracity in reporting, but then you can find similar strands in most writing about country life in most places, whether it was J. W. Robertson Scott's angry essays on English rural poverty in the journal The Countryman in the 1930s, or even Pearl Buck's comments about Lossing Buck's own family farm in New York State.[32] The shock facing urbanites on encountering rural society anywhere was profound, but even the shock of encountering the life and raw world of the urban poor could be shattering. Henry Mayhew's sketches of city lives in London Labour and the London Poor seemed like despatches from another planet to the Victorian Londoners who read them, as did In Darkest England, William Booth's accounts of the life of his country's 'submerged tenth'. Exposés of life on the breadline were as much a feature of Edwardian and post-world war British life as they were of reports on China. Even such key themes as dirt, ignorance and the noxious smells pervading the life and world of the poor can be found in reportage from European cities. George Orwell put it bluntly in The Road to Wigan Pier: 'The lower classes smell.' This was the belief of those who believed that they were not working class, he wrote, and with good reason: cleanliness costs, retorted Orwell, so of course they smell. Orwell's comment was illustrated with a Chinese example, from W. Somerset Maugham's On a Chinese Screen, which set out the same argument for the English poor. The Chinese do not notice, Maugham claimed, whatever their station in life, for they 'live all their lives in the proximity of very nasty smells'.[33]

The question of how this rural China was to be understood and on what terms was not a new one. The Connecticut-born Congregationalist missionary Arthur H. Smith, who was based in north China for almost fifty years after 1872, had published a pioneering account of Village Life in China: A Study in Sociology in 1899. The village was 'the empire in small', he claimed, 'and when that has been surveyed, we shall be in a better position to suggest a remedy for whatever needs amendment'. His was, we might think, a predictable answer: there were many problems, and Christianity 'alone in time can and will solve them all'.[34] By August 1927, Lossing Buck had moved definitively away from the view. He was arguing that 'conducting rural community surveys' ought to be undertaken to find out 'what problems the church should attack'. He also advocated undertaking the promotion of 'better agriculture and rural community improvement' as a 'definite Christian act in itself'.[35] The missionary enterprise more broadly was evolving, and the rise of 'social gospel' thinking and organizations played a role. Many missions had always undertaken medical and educational work, mostly as part of a strategy to engage with potential converts, but also and increasingly in many cases on the basis that these were – as Buck argued rural work should be – a Christian good. But this type of activity began to become more prominent in China, as in other mission fields as the twentieth century progressed. A wider range of social welfare initiatives, not least those associated with the YMCA movement, also developed. The student-led anti-Christian movement of the early 1920s, and the association of missions with the wider foreign presence and imperialism, also accelerated this change. Crisis in the missionary establishment, precipitated by the Nationalist revolution of 1926–7, led to a strategic reorientation in many quarters towards engagement with social reform and social welfare activities led by the Chinese National Christian Council. If missions were to survive, such thinking went, and to have any chance of proselytizing, they would have to be seen to be genuinely aiding China in practical terms.[36]

Lossing Buck's career developed dramatically as he scooped up large grants from the US Social Science Research Council, and from the Rockefeller Foundation through its funding of the Institute of Pacific Relations (IPR). This non-partisan research organization was established in Honolulu in 1925 in the spirit of Wilsonian internationalism, to better understand the problems of Pacific rim countries, to build coalitions among the like-minded, and dialogues between its various antagonists.[37] *Chinese Farm Economy* was published under its auspices, and Buck then led a much larger team that worked on collating and assessing data from almost 17,000 farms across China. This was published in a three-volume survey of *Land Utilization in China* in 1937. His work also attracted the attention of the National Government, and some funding from it as well. A large cohort of Chinese students was trained by Buck and his growing number of Chinese and overseas colleagues at Nanjing. Their publications were widely distributed and findings disseminated through forums such as those held annually by the IPR. The world of statistics now knew a great deal about, for example, the economy of that sample of 17,000 farms, the size and types of landholdings, types of crops grown, as well as the minutiae of household economies, and even inventories of furniture they owned (and whether made from planed or unplaned wood, painted or varnished). It was avowedly descriptive, and offered no recommendations for policies, nor even beyond five lines of text any assessment of where problems might lie.[38] And as the book was being prepared for the press, a devastating new war with Japan was erupting. At the same time that it was being researched and written up, the Communists were engaged in what they later termed a 'Land war', the conflict in places like Da'nanshan, and most dramatically in what became the Jiangxi Soviet Republic, where they instituted revolutionary land policies. Lossing Buck described the Chinese rural world; the Communists were aiming to change it.

But they were not the only people trying to change that world. Lossing Buck himself, when he did point to solutions in his early work, highlighted another important approach to the predicament of rural China: education. Debates about the role of rural education had inspired Peng Pai, and the Peasant Union in Haifeng had embarked on a number of educational initiatives that are easy to overlook, for they lack the drama of rent strikes and land confiscation, the raising of militia, and the violent excesses of soviet power. But Lossing and Pearl Buck both returned again and again to issues of education, and in north China, Yan Yangchu – better known as James Yen – was building an important movement for rural reconstruction. Yen was born in Sichuan, educated in missionary schools, and in 1916 went to Yale University. A Christian, he became involved in YMCA activities, and was one of many young Christian intellectuals who went to work with the Chinese Labour Corps on the Western Front in and just after the First World War. There he quickly moved from running literacy classes for the labourers to founding a vernacular newspaper for them. As it did for many of his peers, the experience suggested to Yen the supreme importance of a new mass-education movement in the rebuilding of Chinese society.[39] Democratizing and expanding education lay at the heart of the New Culture Movement, and May Fourth thinking: even the very written language, it was argued, needed reform. Classical or literary Chinese was largely and quite rapidly abandoned as a result, as a movement to write in and teach using the colloquial language gathered pace. Yen learned of two kinds of ignorance on the Western Front: first, he found it in the behaviour of the Chinese workers, whose personal deportment – spitting not least of all – 'shamed' China in the eyes of foreigners. But much more importantly, he learned about his own ignorance of the great mass of his compatriots, who were hard-working, able and eager to learn when given the opportunity.

The shock of the encounter with rural China that we find expressed by Pearl Buck or Marjorie Clements was equally strong for men like James Yen. What the foreigners found uncomfortable and alienating was difficult too for the hundreds, if not thousands, of young men and women who were inspired by the movement Yen led. The Yale graduate, like Peng Pai, looked overseas for inspiration – and like Peng's comrades in Guangzhou, for funding too – but whereas Peng was inspired by an increasingly radicalized socialist agenda, Yen grew steadily more and more involved in a cross-Pacific network of connections, which would eventually reach into the White House. But he began in the countryside, 120 miles southwest of Beijing, in Ding Xian – Ding county – then commonly transliterated as Ting Hsien. Returning to China in July 1920, Yen had first been involved in masterminding a Chinese YMCA-inaugurated 'Mass Education Movement', which used a wide range of mass-mobilization strategies in order to attempt to embed a new and sustainable infrastructure to raise levels of literacy. This initiative used inspirational rallies and exhibitions, and created new 'thousand character' primers for its volunteer teachers to use in classes to which people flocked in large numbers. The story of the movement is impressive, and it used imaginative marketing and publicity initiatives in order to garner support and funds. Yen, with his American connections, was one of its greatest assets, and he was able to secure substantial funding from supporters in the United States. Literacy was the key to reforming the citizen, and the nation, enabling men and women to better their personal lot, as well as China's cultural and political standing. And imagine, Yen told audiences in America in 1928: literacy helps people raise their income, and even if that rise is small, 'they will be able to buy all your expensive farm machinery', and if all 400 million Chinese could each put a little more cash towards buying 'only two copies of the *Saturday Evening Post* in a year, can you imagine the additional income of the *Saturday Evening Post* people?'[40] The far-fetched, yet cannily homely reference, played on a long-standing vision of the massive potential of the China market in foreign eyes. Dollars rolled in. But Yen and others found that the focus on the education campaign alone had its limitations, and that there was a compelling logic towards a deeper and more wide-ranging approach to the problem.

Yen started to think about identifying a 'model' district, which would serve to incubate through example a nationwide programme of what he came to describe as 'rural reconstruction'. Serendipity led to the choice of Ding Xian, which had a recent record of educational initiatives, largely through the efforts of a powerful local elite family. Its population of some 400,000 was similar in size to Haifeng's, but they lived in a very different landscape: the flat, dry north China plain. The farmers grew millet, mostly, wheat and cotton, and themselves consumed three-quarters of what they grew.[41] The county became a focus first for a concerted Mass Education Movement programme, and then for a wider programme of public health, infrastructure and appropriate technology initiatives, amongst others. Rather than spreading its energies too thinly, relying on inspiring examples and exhortation, Yen aimed to demonstrate in this model district what might be done if political will and resources allowed. Ding Xian was also minutely surveyed and analysed, even its folk sayings and popular plays were recorded. It was reasonably close enough to Beijing to attract visitors, and developed an instructive itinerary to show off its achievements. In the aftermath of the Nationalist revolution and into the early 1930s the 'rural problem' became a mainstay of intellectual and public discussion. The fractures exposed by Haifeng and in Hunan were important counter-examples, Ding Xians gone wrong. Unconsciously echoing Robert Hart's comments, Yen would identify the circles from which he aimed to recruit as those which had provided the Boxers. The difference was that these young people would not fight with weapons, but with words.[42]

James Yen's work was part of a network of cross-Pacific connections and transnational initiatives. His confrères in the movement were often, like him, US-trained, and strongly embedded in an intertwined network of philanthropic, educational and development activities and interests: Rockefeller, the publishing magnate Henry Luce, who would become a prominent supporter of Chiang Kai-shek, and the YMCA. While Yen always remained a Christian, and his initiative worked with missionary networks, it was more closely identified with the social gospel movement, and with what was, after the anti-Christian movement of the early 1920s and the anti-missionary episodes of 1926–7, an organized Chinese Christianity that worked autonomously. It was also staffed by many, like him, who accepted Christianity, but rejected any notion that foreign Christian or mission institutions had a leading role to play. The 'Christian Occupation of China', as the title of a mammoth 1922 missionary survey had it, was being dismantled.[43] But another important rural experiment was entirely independent of any Christian or mission roots, or socialist ones, although it was equally inspired by the education movement. In fact, it was also significantly shaped by Peng Pai's activities in Haifeng, but in opposition to them.

Liang Shuming was the son of a sometime minor Qing official, Liang Ji. The father was famous for committing suicide in November 1918, just as the war in Europe ended, in a somewhat amorphous protest about the corruption of the times in which he found himself.[44] The son also found himself out of sympathy with the times, in which Marxism or a heavily Americanized liberalism seemed to have captured the imagination of so many of those who wished to bring to fruition the project to rejuvenate China. Liang Shuming had been involved in the republican revolution in the Beijing area in late 1911 and then as a journalist on a newspaper supporting the new dispensation, but had then become disenchanted. His thinking gradually shifted towards Buddhism and towards outlining an agenda for

Chinese reform that was grounded in Confucian education and cultural practices. This, he would later argue, was not simply necessary for China, but had a relevance far beyond its borders. Like Peng Pai, and like James Yen, Liang went to the countryside to try to put some of his thinking into practice. In Zouping County, Shandong province, eschewing funds from the types of transnational sources favoured by Yen, Liang embarked upon an otherwise similar rural reconstruction initiative. On a visit to Guangdong in the summer of 1927 he had witnessed at first hand the ways in which communist activists managed to galvanize rural communities. Whoever won the farmers, he concluded, would win China: so rural mobilization was vital for the country's salvation, not least for its salvation from those same Communists.[45]

By the early 1930s the Chinese countryside might seem to be bursting with different species of experimental initiatives and model districts, schools and agricultural stations. The rural or agrarian question seemed never to have been so prominent, nor to have exercised so many different strands of thought.[46] There were hundreds of initiatives, great and small. Rural issues, themes and locales formed an important strand in the work of an influential set of modern writers, such as Shen Congwen, and in journals and magazines in which articles about agrarian questions sat alongside pieces about Shanghai film stars and society events. The various initiatives attracted energy, funds and political support, though the latter were not always connected. Both Liang Shuming and James Yen would be co-opted into the new establishment of the Guomindang republic. So too would be the National Christian Council's rural movement. Through Chiang Kai-shek's Wesleyan College-educated wife, Song Meiling, sister-in-law of Sun Yat-sen, whom Chiang married in Shanghai in 1927 after publicly proclaiming his conversion to Methodism, the former 'Red General' would often call on the good will, funds and connections of the missionary movement. As the menace from the Communist Party's rural revolution began to grow, 'rural reconstruction' also came to be associated with finding ways to rehabilitate territories captured back from communist control, or to bring about reforms that would make it much more difficult for communist mobilization. But there was to prove to be no political will within the Guomindang for any

substantive land-reform programme, even after it actually promulgated a new Land Rent Law in 1930. It was precisely fearful of what
Mao Zedong celebrated in his 1927 Hunan peasant-movement report,
but it also had no taste for alienating its supporters. Moreover, the
party's aim to control and shape political activity in the new state
meant that it grew intolerant of any autonomous initiatives.[47] Continuing political instability would eventually also see the curtailing of
the Ding Xian and Zouping model experiments as the threat from
Japanese aggression grew in the 1930s. For all this frenetic activity,
the plight of the farmer in the decade of the global economic depression and Japanese invasion only grew worse.

Instinctively, most of us would find that the vision of the Chinese
rural world conjured up in the decades before the communist revolution is a dark one. The picture is assembled through an eclectic
mixing of the portrayals to be found in Pearl Buck's writings, in missionary accounts, Chinese Communist Party reports, as well as those
of its foreign supporters, most influentially William Hinton in his
book *Fanshen* (1966), an account of land reform in Shanxi province
in 1948. We see a society caught in an acute crisis; economic circumstances are dire, and steadily getting worse; the position of women is
ghastly – treated as chattel, feet bound, uneducated – bandits and
soldiers scour the land. Drought and famine are ever close at hand;
landlords feed off the labour of their tenants; taxes multiply like bac-
teria. It is a harsh world. Buck in fact was pilloried for decades in the
People's Republic of China for her portrayals of the life and world of
Wang Lung, the protagonist of *The Good Earth*. For its critics the
book offered no hope that the peasantry – the farmers – could save
themselves, and accorded them no dignity or political consciousness.[48] Mao Zedong's epiphany in Hunan, that vision of peasants
making not only their own history, but China's, and remaking the
world afresh, also reinforced this growing orthodoxy, the picture
of a world of suffering and hate, relieved only through liberating
violence.

But it is also worth shutting out all these hectoring voices, and look-
ing at other reports from the countryside. Yang Maochun – or Martin
Yang as he was better known – was an academic sociologist, born in
Shandong province in 1904. His birthplace, the village of Taitou, was

close to the city of Qingdao, then still a German colony. After a mission education, Yang studied at Yenching University in Beijing, before working as a schoolteacher and then at Cheeloo University (formerly the inter-denominational Shantung Christian University) in Jinan, Shandong's capital. Yang had been inspired by Liang Shuming in the 1920s, and had participated in the rural reconstruction effort he led at Zouping. In 1945, while working in the United States, he published a path-breaking ethnographic account of his home village, which included an elegy for a country childhood in the shape of an autobiographical chapter 'The Story of Tien-sze'.[49] Yang's world was certainly a fragile one: it was upset by poor harvests, fatal family sicknesses, and by foreign violence – rumours of German depredations, and by Japanese forces who occupied the area in 1914 when they attacked the colony. The family economy was based on 'working hard and living frugally'. But the memoir is also an account of a young life lived close to nature, and of advancement through education, inspired too by an eclectic range of influences, including biblical ones and stories from the classics of Chinese popular fiction, but also moral tales derived from the life of the British admiral Horatio Nelson. When he wrote, Yang was cut off from his home, which had been occupied again by the Japanese, and his work is certainly coloured by that fact, but in its vision of the rural world, and in the recommendations he made about how the 'village of tomorrow', as he put it, might look, Yang articulated a different path to that future.

The trouble is that all of these visions were in their own ways true, but the most powerful of them became in time the one provided by Mao Zedong. As the rural revolution designed by the Comintern failed and failed again, and as Mao rose to take a dominant position within the battered but tenacious Communist Party organization, the road to violent political and social change offered through the power of the rural masses was chosen. The general turning of attention to rural China was less a response to any existential crisis that impressionistic evidence or modern statistical data might reveal there, than a set of strategic decisions mostly concerned with China's national political fate. It was China's crisis, not that of the farmers, which galvanized its would-be saviours.

4

Talking it Over

Now it was time to talk. Violence had done its job; Guangzhou had won the country. The Guomindang had established a National Government that was quickly recognized as the de facto, and steadily more widely as the de jure, government of China, although quite how far its remit reached in practice was repeatedly challenged internally and overseas. But even if much of the country remained only nominally under the authority of the new government, the same had been true of its internationally recognized predecessor in Beijing. And moreover, this new regime was an active and energetic state-builder, where Beijing had not been, and even this partial control had a profound impact on people's understandings at home and abroad of China's predicament. After 1927 the Guomindang acted like the government of China, and enacted a drive to restore the country's sovereignty, and its pride. As a result it was taken seriously by commentators, by analysts and diplomats, by the press, and by many of the people it ruled.

There was a job to be done. Despite the mass anti-imperialist activism of the Northern Expedition, nearly all of the legal and physical apparatus of foreign power remained intact, even if the British and others felt that their prestige – no less a part of their armour of self-defence than military force – had been besmirched by the loss of their concessions at Hankou and Jiujiang. British settlers in China felt that their diplomats had abandoned them, cutting and running, tails between their legs, but they were generally no worse off than before; and the remaining islands of foreign power bristled with troops and warships. Foreign flags flew high and proud. Treaties were still in place, and negotiations to revise them or implement the changes recommended in the Washington talks were in abeyance. Festering resentment aside, and there was much of that, most foreign residents went about their daily round much as before, their privileges and prerogatives intact. Only in the educational sphere had there been substantive changes, with a switch to Chinese management required of foreign-run schools and colleges under a new registration regime introduced in 1928 by the Ministry of Education.[1] But as foreign power was not rooted in missionary education this did not much concern most foreigners. As a result, any one of China's vast number of people enthused and inspired by the nationalistic upsurge from 1919 to 1927 might have stood on the Bund at Shanghai, watching the foreign Taipans, Missees and Griffins go about their daily business, and wondered whether those heady years had been but a dream. Nothing seemed to have changed.

The warlords still seemed to be in place too. The National Government began its rule with a set of back-room compromises with powerful provincial militarists who, as a result, retained their satrapies and, it was noted, their armies, despite flying the flag of the new republic, and accepting positions in the structure of the new Party State. Chief amongst these were Zhang Xueliang in Manchuria, Yan Xishan in Shanxi province and Feng Yuxiang, who retained control of Henan, Shaanxi and Gansu. The new regime shared out the spoils of office – Feng became Minister of War, Yan became Interior Minister – but even Sun Yat-sen had always been a pragmatist, ever eager to talk, compromise, sup and work with the imperialist and any other devil if it meant some possible step forward on the path to China's renewal. Sun had also always talked promiscuously to all who might provide resources: be they weapons, experts, or money. Once the ends had been secured, he aimed to review and refresh the means.

The Guomindang's Nationalist revolution was no less a revolution for being unfinished. Most revolutions, after all, remain unfinished, quickly finding their ideals needing to be compromised in the face of deep-rooted power. This is an old story: the hard-core Jacobins dominate for a while, but the pragmatists eventually gain the upper hand, while Robespierre and other revolutionary purists get the chop. It is also easier to topple a ruler than a ruling class, and so the short sharp shock of the seizure of power is often followed by the much slower work and more difficult business of remoulding state and society – and that work often starts to falter. The Guomindang remained a revolutionary party, dedicated to rolling back foreign encroachments and refashioning China and the Chinese – their minds, bodies, clothes, customs, even their calendar – despite the fact that its rhetoric and ambitions were compromised by the purges it implemented in consolidating its hold. The rooting out of the Communists continued apace, and Chiang's party also moved against the more activist elements within its own ranks, closing down particularly vigorous party branches. It also gutted the movement of many of those young cadres who had been fired up by the events of 1919 and the succeeding decade, and inspired by the possibilities for national and personal renewal offered by Guangzhou in its revolutionary prime.

Some have argued that the origins of the Guomindang's eventual failure to hold on to power in the late 1940s lay in its early purging of the party of all that was most vital and alive at the moment of its triumph. The regime was thereby doomed to failure, it is asserted, and so historians for a long time simply viewed it as an interregnum, if not one of history's bad jokes. The Nationalist 'regime' (often labelled as such, with obvious derisive intent) was rarely studied, routinely condemned, and as a result little known.[2] As far as scholars were concerned, the real story was the slow revitalization and coming to power in 1949 of the Chinese Communist Party. The course of China's history between the Communist Party's darkest hour in 1927 and its victory two decades later seemed bereft of any interest other than identifying the source of communist power, and the mechanisms through which it mobilized the support that eventually brought it to victory.[3] That is a vital story, but the Guomindang's twenty-two years of rule on the Chinese mainland were in fact vibrant, full of promise and busy with strong currents of change. The state was challenged from within and from without; it faced uprisings, civil war and foreign invasions; and it made catastrophic errors. The Nationalists evaded some key problems that they might have done better to grapple with – land ownership, for example – but in other areas they were bold and persistent. The National Government helped rebuild and reshape the Chinese state, and shared much more with its Chinese Communist Party successor than with its early republican predecessors. Its leaders were never wholly and definitively united: they slip out of office, and then back in, with bewildering rapidity, but all at least aimed to awaken, and to save, China and strengthen and extend the reach of the state. And the longer the government lasted, despite the twists and turns it took, the more its vision of China persisted and shaped that of Chinese people at home and abroad in the diaspora.

The Guomindang did not entirely change when it came to power, but it did change its friends, especially its foreign friends. And it began to talk to them, and talk, and talk, and talk: if revolutionary power would not move them, the thinking went, then perhaps negotiation would undo the position of the foreign powers. Revolutionary power had proved too volatile and unpredictable; mass activism had proved too capable of running loose from those directing it. For all that it continued its rhetoric and pronouncements about regaining sovereign rights, steeped in the era's dominant May Fourth Movement thinking, and the political mobilization of the Guangzhou years, the new regime wanted a managed process that would be negotiated, signed and sealed, and then smoothly implemented. Talking had been tried before, and had failed, at Versailles and in Washington, but there was now diplomacy in a new vein, for the Guomindang could talk from a position of comparative strength. So it played the diplomatic game of nations, and its foreign ministers at Nanjing – first the Japanese-educated Huang Fu, then Wang Zhengting (C. T. Wang, as the foreigners knew him) – parlayed formally with foreign diplomats and envoys, with some success until late 1931. These were talented, cosmopolitan men, and they were well supported by their diplomatic staff.

First they talked about Hankou, Jiujiang and Nanjing, and other unfinished business of the revolutionary upsurge of 1926–7. True to type, and to established diplomatic practice in China, foreign interests affected by disorder or depredation totted up their losses and filed their itemized and often generously calibrated claims for compensation with their consuls and diplomats. The latter then worked to secure financial redress from whichever authority looked most likely to deliver it. With the consolidation of Guomindang rule, these claims now made their way to Nanjing, and diplomatic files are rich with detail of losses of stock, damage to property and looting of personal items. If you want to know details about the way a missionary lived, or what could be found in a China trader's up-country office, then you can find this information in such records, carefully costed to the last penny. Those filing such claims would eventually include the staff of the former British concessions at Hankou and Jiujiang, for these had been surrendered for good. Activist press commentators would lambast the diplomats for the apparent neglect into which these former British outposts fell, but even the most belligerent of them knew that the deed could not be undone.

The British and the Guomindang first properly met and talked together over the question of what to do about the seizure of these middle Yangzi concessions in January 1927, and a modus vivendi was negotiated by Owen O'Malley, Counsellor at the British Legation, and Caribbean-born Eugene Ch'en, a leading left-wing Guomindang figure, who continued to confound his interlocutors. O'Malley was a diplomatic high-flyer who had no prior Chinese experience before his appointment in 1925. He later remembered Ch'en simply and obnoxiously as 'a nigger from Trinidad'.[4] Despite these gulfs in their background and political stance, and despite this fundamental contempt on the British side (primed further by briefings from the colonial authorities in Trinidad alleging that Ch'en had been responsible for various financial frauds before he left), the two men contrived a deal allowing for joint Sino-British administration of the British concessions. Ch'en made it clear that this set no precedent for any future discussions about other concessions, and the British vouchsafed that they had no intention of reoccupying Hankou and Jiujiang by force, and that the Shanghai Defence Force sent to the city in 1928 would only be used for self-defence. Hankou, in this way, became the first of Britain's imperial possessions in the twentieth century to be cast adrift in the face of Asian or African revolt. This role in the great unfolding of Britain's empire has largely been forgotten, but the 'surrender' embittered the China coast British at the time, and worried British officials more widely about its impact on nationalist thought elsewhere – especially in India and Afghanistan.[5]

There was considerable disagreement amongst British diplomats, as well as within the already splintering revolutionary leadership, about the wisdom of making any deal, let alone the content of this one, but the agreement held. Neither man lingered long enough in post to have to review it: Ch'en fled the anti-leftist purge; O'Malley was 'permitted to resign' after being implicated in a currency-speculation scandal. British concession employees filed those claims for lost pension rights, and debenture holders for compensation, but mostly to little avail. Others accommodated themselves to what effectively proved to be a solely Chinese administration of Hankou, under the same terms as those allotted to residents in the former German concession there, and they found that the sky did not in fact fall on their heads. They joked that their lives were now 'SAD', for their little bit of Britain on the Yangzi became a Special Administrative District of the Guomindang's city government. The pun was of course invisible in Chinese, and in many other ways the conversations about China held by its foreign interlocutors, however powerful, often remained invisible and irrelevant to those reshaping the country from within.

Once their position was secured, the Guomindang turned to look at the other settlements and concessions, at extraterritoriality and all the apparatus of foreign power. In putting out feelers to the Nationalists during the revolution, the British and others had reiterated their willingness to discuss treaty revision once stability was assured. This standard formula and catch-all caveat seemed to offer a sop without being in any sense a commitment, for surely the circumstances would never prove right. This was 'China' after all, land of pious platitudes and no action. A favourite Chinese aphorism deployed by British officials in their internal minutes on documents was 'You ming wu shi': meaning something merely nominal, which has a form, or literally a name (*you ming*), but no substance (*wu shi*). They scribbled it everywhere, often not even bothering to complete the phrase. 'Yu Ming ... !' they would smugly scribble in the margins of reports and despatches, using the contemporary transliteration.[6] There could never, surely, be 'stability' as the foreign diplomats and lobby groups defined it.

But as the regime settled in through 1927 and into 1928, and as it survived large-scale onslaughts from its opponents in 1929 and 1930, it became clear to foreign diplomats that the serious talking had to start. The Guomindang were here to stay. It certainly also helped that

Chiang's anti-communist credentials had been demonstrated on the bloody streets of Shanghai, Guangzhou and other cities in 1927–8. But before they would formally recognize the National Government, the British, along with the Americans and the Japanese, demanded a formal settlement of the 24 March 1927 Nanjing Incident, when NRA troops had attacked foreign nationals, killing several, as they captured the city. Foreign consulates had been ransacked, and a widely believed rumour that European women had been raped inflamed foreign opinion. A stumbling block proved to be the fact that the Guomindang required an apology for the naval barrage laid down by an American warship, under cover of which an evacuation had been organized, but which left a score of Chinese dead. A British vessel had also opened fire. Intransigence all round meant at first that the talking got nowhere.[7]

Despite the impasse over Nanjing, the entrenched stances adopted by the Americans, the British and the Guomindang in public and in their diplomatic exchanges were undermined, and steadily reshaped, by the increasingly friendly interaction between officials in private. The more they encountered each other, the more they found at least superficially that they liked each other, or at least the more they found that they could generally get on, relax together and do business. The Chinese Foreign Ministry officials, mostly educated overseas, certainly proved to be men they could talk with. C. T. Wang, for example, was a Yale University graduate, fluent in English, and fond of good clothes, fine cigars and fine wines. Hard talk done for the day, these cosmopolitans can be noticed in less formal diplomatic reports playing drinking games together off duty, or simply drinking.[8] The ever-awkward exception to this rule was Chiang Kai-shek himself, whose stiffly reticent personality never made for easy interaction. But in December 1927 in Shanghai, in a lavish Protestant ceremony, Chiang had married Wesleyan College-educated Song Meiling, whose confident charm – and intellect – more than compensated for his own deficiencies, and who was in time to become an important foreign-relations asset in her own right.[9] With a Methodist, anti-communist President, and an Ivy League-trained elite, it would surely be possible to find a lasting solution to the perplexing problems of China. Over the Nanjing Incident the diplomats eventually found formulas that satisfied the honour of all sides. Neither the British nor the Americans apologized for the actions of their naval personnel, but they did regret that circumstances had necessitated the use of force to protect their nationals. This was meaningless – *you ming wu shi* – but it sufficed. Notes were signed and exchanged; reparations were paid. If remembered at all today, the incident survives only in Alice Tisdale Hobart's account, *Within the Walls of Nanking* (1929), and the city is instead associated with another horror yet to come, the catastrophe that engulfed its residents in December 1937 when Japanese troops captured the city.

One thing to note also was that the foreign diplomats failed to act in concert, despite attempts to get agreement in principle to do this, although they did liaise and exchange ideas, alert to what they felt might be divide-and-rule tactics on the part of the Chinese. On the other hand, each of the foreign diplomats felt they had a particular special relationship with China that they did not wish to see compromised by too much association with their 'dear colleagues', as the British Minister, Sir Miles Lampson, a man formidable in height, girth, personality – and condescension – would usually refer to them. American diplomats felt that they had pioneered the 'Open Door' policy, and had worked to support China against bumptious British imperialism and its more freshly rapacious Japanese counterpart. For their part the British felt that 'Chinese' appreciated what they felt to be their bluff plain-speaking, which Britons contrasted with what they saw as the high-minded vacuities of US policy and the idealism of the 'American character'. This was most clearly expressed, the British felt, by the American missionary establishment, which was universally loathed by British observers, who generally felt that Christian missions were a source of problems that they could well do without. The Japanese believed that they had a unique cultural edge on the Europeans and Americans, and therefore a necessarily closer and more intimate relationship, and many saw the Chinese as natural allies in an Asian anti-imperialist struggle. The Japanese also had a different balance of interests in China, especially in the northeast, and many had very different ambitions as well. Everybody felt, then, that they had a unique special relationship, which they did not wish to have tarnished through unduly close association with their colleagues, however dear.

On the morning of 20 December 1928, Lampson formally presented his diplomatic credentials to President Chiang Kai-shek, and so the British became the first to formally recognize the National Government with accepted ceremonial. Sir Miles was driven through three miles of Nanjing's streets from the British Consulate, which only relatively recently had still had large anti-imperialist slogans gracing its walls, his route lined by NRA soldiers and police, and he was met at the seat of government by a Chinese band playing 'God Save the King'. Cock-hatted and plumed in his formal best, the British Minister was greeted by Chiang, and the two traded pleasantries through interpreters, as a British cruiser, HMS *Suffolk*, fired a twenty-one-gun salute from the Yangzi. The two men then exchanged small talk on the state of King George V's health, before Chiang withdrew. Sir Miles then sat down to lunch with senior Guomindang ministers, and the currently tamed regional militarists Feng Yuxiang and Yan Xishan. Barely two and half years had passed since the Shaji Massacre, and Chiang's outraged demands for war against the British 'barbarians'. Yet now all was sweetness and light in Nanjing, and the British, first among the foreign powers, had formally recognized the Guomindang's National Government with all the theatre of diplomacy.[10]

The ceremony followed the signing at 1.30 early that same morning, after two weeks of negotiation, of an agreement for the restoration of a key facet of China's sovereignty: its ability to set the level of its own import tariffs. The 1842 Sino-British Treaty of Nanjing, signed aboard a vessel close by where the *Suffolk* fired its salute, had brought the first 'Opium War' to its formal conclusion, and among its terms was the imposition of a single 5 per cent ad valorem tariff limit. 'Most favoured nation' clauses in other treaties had entrenched this, but on 25 July 1928 the American Minister, John V. A. MacMurray, had relinquished the concession, following up commitments that all the powers had made at the Washington Conference and subsequent meetings. For the foreign powers this was a heavily symbolic issue. It had long been seen as a foundation of the treaty system, preventing discrimination against foreign goods, but to unpick any single part of the web of treaties that bound China was also to risk the whole. For the Nationalists it was a simple question of Chinese sovereignty, but it was also a pragmatic one: customs revenues were to remain the single biggest source of China's state finances until 1941. The restoration of tariff autonomy allowed them an enhanced ability to shape the development of the Chinese economy, and to raise much-needed funds, and tariffs could also be a potent political tool as well. They could be used to protect nascent Chinese industries while they grew. Crucially, the new agreements were reciprocal ones. Even though British diplomats joked in private about how very unlikely it was that Chinese manufactured goods would ever be pouring into the British Isles, China was accorded the right to reciprocal treatment.[11]

The British had really had no choice but to acquiesce, given earlier commitments, but here was the pre-eminent foreign power in China, not only in their own eyes, but by any objective assessment, permitting the unpicking of its foundational treaties. It was also significant that their treaty followed five months on from the break-through signing of the US-Chinese agreement, which was to come into effect on 1 January 1929. The British were not setting the agenda, although Lampson offered a rearguard argument that initial British intransigence had actually paved the way for his American colleague. But it became steadily obvious that the Nationalists looked to America, first and foremost, when they looked to a decisive and amenable international partner. There did not seem to be room for a partnership with British power. The 'spirit' of American policy at Versailles and in Washington was appealed to by Chinese negotiators, however much the substance of it might need to be conveniently forgotten.

Despite this, however, even MacMurray could not persuade the Guomindang to allow the reopening of the American Consulate in Nanjing, closed since the incident in March 1927, to be accompanied by 'ceremonies calculated to lend dignity and mutual cordiality to the occasion'. The Americans outlined a plan for the occasion that centred around the flagship of the US China Station, accompanied by five or six destroyers, making its way to Nanjing with the incoming consul and the Commander of the US Navy's Yangtze Patrol, Rear-Admiral Yates Stirling Jr. There would be salutes, and the landing of military personnel for honour guards and parades. This proved too much for influential interests within the Nationalist elite, who rejected the proposal as too redolent of the infrastructure of imperialism that they were pledged to remove, and instead the consulate reopened on 15 December 1928 without any fanfare.[12] The fact that Nanjing was now definitively the capital of the republic heightened anxieties around this issue, for Beijing was downgraded, and even formally renamed (it became 'Beiping', meaning 'Northern Peace', losing the word 'capital' – *jing* – from its name).

MacMurray had argued that it would demean the United States in Chinese eyes not to insist on such formality, and that it would 'imperil' American consular officers, who would not be seen to have formal recognition by the Guomindang.[13] Symbols remained obsessively important for all concerned, even for America, a power that conspicuously disowned the trappings and pretentions of imperialism. The resulting minutely detailed choreography of visits, negotiations and exchanges of notes was complex; the public performance of diplomacy could look awkward, if not tortuous. Since their arrival in China in the 1830s, foreign envoys and diplomats had campaigned to secure courtesies, treatment and recognition from the Chinese appropriate to their status, as they saw it, and tried to force the Qing to adopt new procedures and language in its interaction with them, but with mixed success. The whole issue was entangled with ideas about national pride, culture and increasingly 'race', as much as it was ostensibly about the operation in Sino-foreign relations of agreed international diplomatic norms and practices. MacMurray, who had deeply imbibed the settled customs and attitudes of the diplomatic establishment in China, now asked his superiors in the State Department how he should in future acknowledge the officers of the Guomindang authorities if they were to be prevented from such dignified and important ceremonial? Accord to them 'the courtesies of a fully recognised foreign state' came the curt reply.[14]

The old diplomacy lingered, not least in the foreign imagination, but also because the legations remained in Beijing. So did the diplomats in fact: they were comfortable there; their establishments were grand and in keeping with their pretentions. Prestige mattered: the British occupied an old *fu*, a gorgeous, princely palace; by contrast the American Legation, opened in 1906, was designed by a US Treasury architect, and would not have looked out of place in Washington, except that the compound was a defensible fortress. The missions were situated in the 'Legation Quarter', an extraterritorial enclave administered by the foreign envoys sitting in committee. The early 1920s had really been a rather pleasant time to practise diplomacy in Beijing, despite the turmoil enveloping China beyond the city's walls. Owen O'Malley's wife, writing as Ann Bridge, caught their insular world nicely in *Peking Picnic*, her best-selling roman à clef of 1932. There was time for curio hunting, flirting, and unhurried excursions out to temples and springs with picnics carried by a column of servants, and a bandit or two could not very much threaten such lotus-eating. China was noise elsewhere. This was a world in which Sir Francis Aglen still held the purse strings of the Beijing government, and the British and their peers patronized this warlord or that one, but in which nothing serious ever really seemed to happen – and John MacMurray had enough leisure time in which to perfect his skills with the brand-new Cine-Kodak camera he had brought with him out to China.[15]

Then, as the Nationalists neared Beijing in June 1928, Japanese officers of the Kwantung Army blew to smithereens the train carrying the retreating warlord Zhang Zuolin, the 'Old Marshal', who was withdrawing to his Manchurian powerbase. Zhang died in the explosion. He had been seen off from Beijing by Lampson and MacMurray, who had both lamented the departure from the scene of such a reliable old-stager. 'He looked you straight in the eye,' remembered the British Minister, 'and made no bones about the point he was after.' This was usually money, or weapons.[16] The Japanese knew this full well, as Zhang had until recently been a long-term and ultimately pliable client of theirs, whose power buttressed their own position in Manchuria – as theirs in turn buttressed his (as did their financing). The triumph of the Nationalists, and a sense that Zhang had served his purpose, spurred the conspirators who killed him, and who hoped that a wider crisis might ensue that they could take advantage of. This time it did not.[17] Lampson and many others refused to believe that Japanese agents had committed the attack, but all would come in time to regret rather more deeply the Japanese intervention into Beijing's picnicking, and China's problems.

The 'sufficiency of leisure' enjoyed by Ann Bridge's senior British diplomat in the opening pages of her novel was but a fiction by

1932 and the book's publication. A torrent of paper now poured into the legations, and the mail steamers and ocean liners seemed daily to disgorge fact-finders, commissions and emissaries who called on the diplomats, querying and lobbying. A great age of investigation, conferences and reporting had commenced in China. The Nationalists certainly set the pace, for well trained as many of them were in social science and law, the state they envisioned building was to be founded on accurate knowledge, garnered through the surveys and statistics that they now adored.[18] They bombarded businesses and legations alike with questionnaires and requests for data. And they knew the importance of being better briefed than their opponents. A cynic will always point out that it is easier to survey and analyse than to act, and that the former are often deliberate substitutes for the latter. There were many foreign cynics in early Nationalist China, and there were many useless reports. *You ming wu shi*, the diplomats would lament. But the modern state needed knowledge, as those same diplomats knew, who memorized Chinese faces from the photographs on their office walls before sallying forth to greet their visitors. Their junior staff churned out translations of Guomindang documents and conference and newspaper reports, and the consular networks formed the core of an extensive intelligence-gathering system whose fruits were deployed as and when needed in discussion with the Chinese.

In the palavers about reform in the years after the Nationalist revolution four distinct strands can be identified: changes in the administration of the treaty ports themselves; a private sphere of largely foreign-inspired personal initiatives; bilateral negotiations amongst the diplomats; and the activities of the League of Nations. At the heart of many of these discussions was the 'problem' of Shanghai. It was not the only issue, but it seemed the thorniest, and loomed largest internationally. The trouble was that as an international settlement it was nobody's problem, and yet it was everyone's: it was under no single foreign state's control, and over a dozen nations were recognized as treaty powers with an interest in its status. But even in conclave they had no political control over it, due to its ambiguous constitutional position. This had most chillingly become obvious in the aftermath of the May Thirtieth incident in 1925, when the British, American and Japanese nationals who formed the Shanghai

Municipal Council showed little inclination to work with the diplomats to try to ameliorate the crisis that their police force and its
sanguine incompetence had caused. Diplomats, do-gooders and the
League of Nations would all try to solve this problem. Effecting transition without violence was the ambition, but the option of solving
the problem of China by force was never too long absent from the
political scene.

Even the most conservative foreign interests in Shanghai eventually
realized that they needed to do something. They also found them-
selves shown up by reforms instituted by their peers in Tianjin's
British concession, or their neighbours in Shanghai's French one. A
Chinese representative joined the Tientsin British Municipal Council
in 1919; its parks were opened to all residents in 1926; and the Land
Regulations were revised in 1928 to allow the appointment of five
Chinese councillors. Symbolic but significant Chinese appointments
were made to its administration. If this was not example enough,
Shanghai diehards also consistently found themselves out of step
even with formal British colonies at Hong Kong or Singapore in the
way they treated the majority population. Proper colonialism, as Sun
Yat-sen had also argued, did at least bring with it responsibilities. Many foreign Shanghai residents believed they owed none to the
Chinese population of the International Settlement, because they
considered that ultimately Chinese had no right to reside there.
'Shanghai' – as the foreign diplomats termed its foreign residents,
neatly obscuring the city's majority Chinese population – proved sullen as a result. Foreign ratepayers rejected a proposal to end the racist
restrictions on access to settlement parks in 1927, although it was
passed the following year. And, having agreed to create two positions
for Chinese representatives in 1928, those ratepayers initially rejected
a further increase to a total of five in 1930 in a heated and ill-tempered
meeting.[19]

British diplomats had not generally much intervened in the ordinary running of the International Settlement, nor did they have any
formal mechanism through which they could do so. In the British
concessions they had authority, but they had none in Shanghai.
Moreover, unlike their Japanese counterparts they had no authority
over their nationals in any corporate sense. Japanese residents, who

comprised half of the 36,000 foreign nationals living in the International Settlement in 1930, were required to join their local Japanese Residents' Association, and this together with the Japanese consular police network had significant authority over them.[20] But the British and the Americans only had jurisdiction over individuals, and only over their individual behaviour. With the Shanghai Municipal Council they could and did engage with significant political issues, liaising with their compatriots who ran the settlement, mostly to some effect.[21] From 1927 onwards the British and Americans began to intervene more regularly, and to seek to manage the process of reform and even the composition of the council. This was not easy, for the company managers, property developers and professionals who dominated municipal affairs guarded their autonomy jealously. But pressure was now steadily applied to the council to introduce reforms. When in 1930 the ratepayers rejected the proposed increase in Chinese councillors, the Consul General immediately went into action to secure a rerun of the vote and a hastily convened 'Emergency General Meeting', lobbying hard to ensure a better result. The English-language press was also a worry, so editors were encouraged to be less inflammatory, proprietors urged to reconsider editorial appointments (with one notable scalp, the removal of the editor of the *North China Daily News*), and in at least one case an egregiously racist small-time newspaper editor was hauled into court and the newspaper suppressed.[22] Steadily, also, the diplomats built up a coalition of what they felt to be right-minded individuals, representing firms who could see beyond narrow Shanghai concerns to the bigger picture of British interests in China. These men would come to dominate the Shanghai Municipal Council by the later 1930s.

Such moves aimed at improving the situation in Shanghai were important: the British presence there, not least, but not only, its press, was widely perceived as representing British thinking about China more widely, and of being under the control of its diplomats. This was not true, but the presence of a bellicose and autonomous community of Britons in the heart of China's most important modern city was a conspicuous problem. Diplomatic encouragement of reform did remove or temper some sources of tension, but the changes in Shanghai were nonetheless insular. Clearly there was a need to encourage change more widely, and others took on this task as well. In May 1928, for example, when the SS *Empress of Asia* docked at Shanghai from Vancouver, two Britons disembarked who came from very different spheres: W. J. 'Tony' Keswick, scion of the great Shanghai agency house Jardine Matheson and Co., the most historically promi- nent of British firms, and Sir Frederick Whyte, a former Liberal Party Member of Parliament, and more recently President of the Legislative Assembly in India. The two had evidently talked on board, and Whyte had presented Keswick with a copy of his just reprinted book- let *China and Foreign Powers*, which had appeared in 1927 under the auspices of the Royal Institute of International Affairs (known as Chatham House) and was being widely discussed.[23] Both men repre- sented different facets of a drive to try to secure a new balance in Sino-British relations, through improving interpersonal relations, communication and understanding among the elites on both sides. Keswick, then just twenty-two, had come out to work in China three years earlier, and with his younger brother John was seen as repre- senting a new generation of British business leaders in the making, who would be free of the taint of the fractious 1920s. In their case they were entertaining high hopes, for the Keswicks led a firm tainted like no other with the opium trade and the mid-nineteenth-century British assault on China, but they were indeed to prove more affable and flexible than their predecessors. A wider easing of relations began between many of the foreign elites and their Chinese peers, smoothed in this sphere as in others by the common culture and in many cases experience (of university overseas, for example) that they shared.[24]

Keswick may or may not have read Whyte's booklet, but his firm was one of ten that were contributing to the costs of Whyte's mission to China, for Sir Frederick had a roving brief to try to build elite connections and understanding. Republican China did not lack for such visitors, some self-appointed, some invited by Chinese organiza- tions or by the government, and others, like Whyte, tasked by foreign interests to attempt to resolve the difficulties facing China in the international sphere. Whyte was no China expert, but he had been asked to provide a disinterested survey of Britain's relations with China at the second conference of the Institute of Pacific Relations in Hono- lulu in 1927. In China, Whyte networked and talked, building up contacts deliberately, rather than allowing accident to bring people together – for such was the social and political gulf between elite Chinese and foreigners resident in China that they had almost no opportunities simply to interact. As an outsider to the scene Whyte was also not tainted, in Chinese eyes, by involvement in the local infrastructure of foreign control.[25] In the crisis years of 1925 to 1927 in Shanghai, for example, the local heads of such firms as Jardine Matheson, the Hongkong and Shanghai Bank, Asiatic Petroleum and Standard Chartered had all served on the International Settlement Municipal Council when it was at its most hostile to both the Guomindang and to Nationalism in general. Police under their command had raided Nationalist agencies in the settlement and arrested party activists, handing them over to their political enemies, in whose hands they did not fare well. Shanghai foreign businessmen had overseen the May Thirtieth disaster, and had barely co-operated with the ensuing inquiry. For some years they had fought against the activities of the local Chinese Ratepayers' Association, which had lobbied for fairer representation and taxation policies. The Shanghailanders' reputation stank, and tainted thereby were the foreign firms that now wished to build bridges. So, the businessmen congratulated themselves when Whyte was invited to become an official Advisor to the National Government in 1929, although this apparent advantage was then comprehensively undermined in 1930 when he bolted for Japan with the wife of a Belgian steel magnate, and when she committed suicide shortly thereafter.[26] Without a culture and an infrastructure for communication and collaboration Sino-foreign relations remained at the mercy of such random and unfortunate events as this one, or the suicide in 1929 of the Japanese China expert Saburi Sadao, who had established early ties with the Nationalists. Saburi had just been nominated as Japanese Minister to China; his successor was rejected by the National Government for his association with the 1915 'Twenty-One Demands', Japan's wartime attempt to secure a commanding position over the Beijing government. The impasse that followed Saburi's death was not helpful.[27]

Whyte's diversion to Chinese matters came through the interweaving of two initiatives by non-governmental organizations fresh on the international relations scene, the Royal Institute of International

Affairs (RIIA), established in 1920, and the Institute of Pacific Relations (IPR), founded in 1925. Both were influenced by the Wilsonian moment in Paris, and by a strong and novel sense that problems could be solved only if they were in the first instance properly researched and understood, and if they were then discussed as widely as possible by expert stakeholders, not least those well outside the foreign-affairs establishments. The founding of the RIIA was driven by the crusading zeal of Lionel Curtis, a British imperial idealist and talented organizer, who drew inspiration from the months in Paris during the Peace Conference when experts from across the world had debated the issues, formally and informally. He and others were also struck by the difficulties they encountered in securing accurate documentation about the problems under discussion. Out of this grew both the RIIA in London and the Council on Foreign Relations in New York. Curtis brought together diplomats and politicians, academics, journalists and figures from the business world, arguing that the real world problems faced by commercial interests needed understanding and discussing as much as did broader issues of global strategy.[28]

From 1926 onwards Curtis had started to focus on China. His vehicle for this initially was the IPR, which had its genesis originally in a plan for a regional YMCA conference that evolved into a plan for a conference on 'problems of the Pacific peoples' in Honolulu, which then grew into the initiative to launch a research institute there. Like the RIIA this was fairly elitist, and the IPR's biennial conferences were closed talking shops, but the bringing together of elites from across the 'racial divide' – which was very much an IPR theme – was itself a significant step forward. While the IPR was significantly shaped by evolving American strategic concerns about the Pacific, it became an institution through which Chinese and Japanese voices were heard on a footing equal to those of the colonial powers. The fact that the first article in the first issue of the IPR's journal *Pacific Affairs* was by the Chinese intellectual and educational reformer Hu Shi was symbolic but no less important for that. And through its focus on a region, the Pacific, and one newly defined as such, the IPR was also a radical departure from the norm. While Curtis personally viewed the IPR as a vehicle for British imperial interests – his abiding vision was of a Commonwealth, rooted in a federal British Empire – it became the foremost non-governmental vehicle for research and discussion about the 'Problems of the Pacific', as the reports on its conferences were titled. This was a very substantial change. The region was not the 'Far East', a Europe-centric description that had Asia on the periphery of international concerns; it was now a region with its own centre of gravity and its own concerns. Curtis had a significant impact on the activities of the IPR, and the RIIA was its British agency, but at its conferences in Kyoto, Honolulu and China, British as well as American observers were confronted with stark statements from Asians about the issues facing the nations that formed this new Pacific community.[29]

From the IPR's 1929 conference in Kyoto, Curtis hopped over to Shanghai, which was, he announced at a public dinner, 'the hard knot at the centre of the problem', that is, the problem of 'the belated contact of an ancient and brilliant civilization with the other three-quarters of the human race'.[30] Untangling that knot was to be the task of a South African judge, Richard Feetham, invited by the Shanghai Municipal Council, at Curtis's suggestion, to investigate and report on a solution to the issues facing the International Settlement. If the facts could be properly elucidated, ran the argument, then a logical and incontestable plan could be proposed. The thread from the RIIA through the IPR in this is clear. The Shanghai worthies who gathered at the banquet in the city's newly completed Cathay Hotel were conscious that they were being outflanked politically by the talented Chinese jurists, foreign-affairs researchers and historians, who were compiling the surveys and monographs that undermined many of the claims to legitimacy on which such bodies as the SMC rested. Moreover, as the council's chairman, Harry Arnhold, remarked in introducing Curtis, they had failed in their efforts to influence world opinion, being 'frequently treated as naughty boys, with a naughty boy's mentality, which in our case is called the "Shanghai mind"'. This was a flippant take on the devastating incidents and exclusionist policies that had so tarnished the SMC's reputation internationally. The 'Shanghai Mind' label had come from the *Manchester Guardian* journalist Arthur Ransome, who visited China between January and August 1927. Ransome is better known for his later, hugely successful children's books, but amongst the

China hands he was remembered as the coiner of a catchy phrase that stuck. Shanghai, he had announced in a May 1927 article, was the 'Ulster of the East'; the British there did not want 'adjustment' to the post-war world, they wanted war, and they viewed all Nationalists as Boxers. There was enough truth in his strictures to continue to sting men like Harry Arnhold for years afterwards.[31] Their fight back against all these challenges involved initiatives like the Feetham investigation, as well as their grudgingly instituted municipal reforms.

It was all perfectly rational, but was in fact little different to an unworldly plan – seriously communicated less than a year earlier by a representative of various SMC councillors to the Foreign Office in London – for establishing Shanghai as a free port along the lines of Danzig, administered by the League of Nations. Variations on this theme had been suggested by foreign interests in Shanghai since the 1860s; they were even less likely to be successful in 1929 than they had been then.[32] Feetham spent an expensive year and a half – he was very well paid, at SMC expense – nosing around the council archives, and soliciting what data he could, but was hamstrung from the outset by the fact that most Chinese interests simply refused to have anything to do with the initiative, and if they did respond to his consultation process they simply and definitively demanded the rapid retrocession of the entire settlement. Their involvement would hardly have mattered, for Feetham had already made it clear to British diplomats a year in advance what his conclusions would be, and that he would propose a 'self-governing Sino-foreign municipality'.[33] The SMC, British diplomats concluded on reading the report, got what it had paid for, and there was little need to take the report seriously. Chinese opinion was of course similar. It was of 'no value whatsoever' remarked one senior Foreign Ministry official; it was simply 'idyllic' said the Minister of Finance.[34]

The Feetham report was premised on the belief of men like Harry Arnhold and the foreign interests controlling the International Settlement that they could shape their own destiny. This was a Shanghai fantasy. Diplomacy was in command, at least where the British and the Americans were concerned. Elsewhere in China, as we shall see, views similar to Harry Arnhold's were held by men who actually had the means, and the intent, to put them into operation.

What most interested the Chinese, however, was not the IPR or the RIIA, but the League of Nations. Their diplomats had helped draft its covenant and were enthusiastic and attentive participants in its annual assemblies in the 1920s. While it would continue to disappoint them on one score – China was never given a permanent seat on the council that set League policy – it remained vitally important to the way in which China's diplomats viewed international affairs. Firstly, they aimed to use it, mostly indirectly, as part of their strategy to secure treaty revision. Secondly, it was a venue through which the claim for recognition of China's status as a great civilization could be demonstrated. The National Government's predecessors, including Qing diplomats in the last decade or so of the dynasty's rule – and there was significant continuity of foreign-affairs personnel across these administrations – had begun routinely to interpolate China into the circuit of international convention-making and organizations. Over such issues as international maritime safety standards, the 1899 and 1904 Hague conventions on warfare, and on opium, Chinese representatives came to the conference table arguing by their very presence that China was a state that needed respecting as such, and not simply the bad joke, the 'dying' civilization or 'sick man of the East' of its critics. The League of Nations offered a far better forum: a means to codify international law and practice that would demonstrate the profound inequities of those agreements the Qing had signed in the nineteenth century, and which were still in place. These 'unequal' treaties would be discredited, and would simply come to be seen as archaic and redundant in the light of such new international norms. The League was routinely reminded of China's predicament and its aspirations for treaty revision, but the moral argument was accompanied elsewhere by the parallel and practical business of bilateral negotiation.[35] For their part, however, it is very hard to find references to the League in British deliberations about China before 1931. Foreign and Chinese diplomats drank and chatted together easily, and made real progress in meetings, but it should not surprise us that they were still not operating with the same frames of reference.

In the 1930s there were development initiatives, focused around the work of League-appointed agricultural and other advisors, but the most significant achievement was one in which China's rights-recovery aspirations perfectly met the technical work of the League, and wider discourses about modernity and the functions of a state. This was in the arena of public health, and specifically quarantine. As far as they had been developed at all, Chinese quarantine functions had been handled by the foreign-led Chinese Maritime Customs Service. The establishment of a National Quarantine Service, headed by the widely respected plague prevention expert Wu Liande in 1930, saw the transfer of those functions from the Customs. These were 'by their very nature matters that properly attain to the sovereign rights of a state', noted the British Inspector General of Customs, Sir Frederick Maze, a man clearly incapable of irony, in a note to his staff outlining the transition of responsibilities and the history of Customs Service quarantine work.[36] Moreover, extraterritoriality had actually impeded the inauguration in the past of quarantine procedures, for it was deemed to be a hindrance to trade that was forbidden by the treaties. Establishing the new service was functionally important as a global health measure – pneumonic plague had hit Manchuria within the past decade, for example, and cholera outbreaks were recurring – but it was also part of the performance by China of its fitness to be considered a modern state, one that undertook all the activities deemed appropriate and proper, and as a result one that should be treated with the respect due to an equal. For similar reasons Penang-born, Cambridge-educated Wu Liande pointed out to foreign shipping managers in Shanghai that his staff were well trained and experienced. They had the necessary 'knowledge, manners and deportment', and were trained in Europe, America, China and Japan. They were equal to the world's best, and like China, he might have added, should be respected as such.[37]

At the League, Chinese diplomats tried to reshape international understandings and practices that would highlight the injustice of China's legacy of nineteenth-century treaties. In Nanjing they set in motion a mix of bilateral initiatives and grand strategic announcements. The National Government tried to set the pace too for discussions about revision of the treaties. In April 1929 it issued a mandate stating that extraterritoriality would cease on 1 January 1930. This certainly prompted the major powers – Britain, America and France – to respond, but January came and went, and 1930 came and went, all without substantive change.[38] Certainly there was reform. By the time Sir Miles Lampson and C. T. Wang came to be cruising along a tributary of the Yangzi River in May 1931, hammering out a draft treaty under which the British would surrender extraterritoriality, the British world in China had shrunk. The tiny and long-redundant concession at Zhenjiang (Chinkiang), which was not far distant from where they sailed, had been surrendered on 15 November 1929; the yet tinier British concession at Xiamen (Amoy) had been quietly given up in September 1930 (having really rather ceased to exist five years earlier when its last employee had been dismissed); and on 1 October 1930, while Lampson lay in a hospital bed there enduring a bout of malaria, the British Leased Territory of Weihaiwei was finally handed over to Nationalist control by its administrator, Sir Reginald Fleming Johnston.[39] Other, yet more minor accretions to the British estate in China had been pared away, including the Ningbo Sino-foreign committee and the 'International Committee' at Chefoo (Yantai).[40] A nominal concession area at Yingkou (Newchwang) had long ago mostly collapsed into the Liao River and was discreetly retired by British diplomats as a concept in the 1920s. Many of these territories – if the eleven lots and four acres of British Xiamen deserve such an appellation – had long been more trouble than they were worth. They were sites of boycotts and disputes over the behaviour of their municipal personnel – they did not attract talented high-flyers – and over the positioning of every wall, gate, jetty and flagpole.[41] Their surrender simplified things in one way, but British subjects resident in each place still enjoyed extraterritoriality, and now Lampson and his team could focus on that, and on the significant holdings that remained: the International Settlement at Shanghai (and its tiny cousin on Gulangyu Island at Xiamen), and concessions at Tianjin (large) and Guangzhou (modest). They itched to regain some sort of guarantee, a 'reserved status', for Hankou, but this was not to be had.

Houseboat diplomacy was something new. Wang Zhengting and Lampson aimed to talk away from the prying eyes of the press, for it was no secret that Lampson had come south to Nanjing to reopen discussions on treaty revision. They took several long day trips out on his senior consular colleague's boat *Wanderer*. They had oddly chosen as the discreet floating site for their talks something that was as quintessentially a symbol of the routine perquisites of foreign life at Shanghai as the rickshaw on the city's streets. The houseboat holiday from the city was a fixture in the annual round of the foreign community; even working-class foreigners in the police force clubbed together and hired the council's boats. Small convoys of them would sometimes be towed up the Wusong River, passing the British Consulate, to head out west into the maze of waterways that cut through the alluvial plain between Shanghai and Lake Tai, sixty miles away. A small literature had developed celebrating the idyll of the experience, and the perceived idiosyncrasies of the houseboat 'lowdahs' who captained the vessels and their crews. Generally the vacationers were looking to shoot, hunting wild fowl mostly, on whose populations their cumulative impact was substantial. They treated the land as theirs to tramp over, though a code of practice evolved that included a 'closed' season.[42] In their stalking across the land of local farmers, the houseboating hunters exemplified the problem of extraterritoriality, for as they walked their British status, invested in their person, walked with them (and they were advised always to carry their passports as well).[43] Moreover, extraterritoriality, or at least a relative immunity, had a way of enveloping any who travelled with those who possessed it, and of being attached in cautious Chinese minds with any who looked as if they might possess it, that is, those who looked 'white'. Hunting analogies had also surfaced at an IPR meeting at the RIIA in London in July 1929: 'Supposing you bought a shooting estate,' argued one speaker, '[the Chinese] cannot give you the same protection that we in this country could give to some Chinese gentleman who bought a moor in Scotland.'[44]

Wang Zhengting was hunting bigger game than grouse on the *Wanderer*, though he himself was often at this time a hunted man, harried by more impatient nationalists in and outside the National Government, hence the discretion. It all seemed to pay off. On 6 June 1931, Lampson and Wang exchanged the texts of a draft treaty, and in July an American draft treaty was also exchanged. Shanghai was to retain a 'reserved' status for ten years, and Tianjin for five, but that was to be all: the new treaties would remove the poisonous legacies of their predecessors. Other powers were more cautious. The French thought the British quite foolish to act, and told them so. The Japanese had initially stood outside this process, but were forced to engage as well, though their focus for a 'reserved' area was to be Manchuria.[45] The Dutch had simply surrendered their position in late April, bowing to strength. Lampson expected the treaty to be signed in time to come into effect before the 1 January 1932 unilateral abrogation announced by the National Government on 4 May. But less than a week before the exchange of drafts, a young Briton had been seized and later killed 150 miles to the east, and as events unfolded in the aftermath of this incident the process was stalled. John Thorburn was making his way alongside the main railway line between Nanjing and Shanghai in the dead of night, and was assumed to be a spy, a conclusion not helped by the fact that he was wearing what seemed to be military uniform, was armed, and had shot at and wounded two gendarmes when approached. The nineteen-year-old seems to have been setting off on a naive quest for adventure, but was caught and then killed by the military police, who then disposed of his body and covered up the incident. His disappearance soon became a cause celèbre around which Britons in China mobilized to try to thwart treaty revision. They turned out in numbers never before seen at protest meetings in clubs and at race courses (when clubs proved too small to hold them). A high-profile press campaign was launched, arguing that the incident proved that Britons and other foreigners were not safe without extraterritoriality. The fact that hapless John Thorburn had of course possessed this status when he was nonetheless seized and killed could not shake this belief.[46]

Even as the foreign-controlled world in China had shrunk with the surrender of the outlying concessions and other gobbets of Chinese territory, the population had steadily grown, and it was also evolving. The days of masculine pioneering were long past. As the International Settlement at Shanghai grew to fit the 'outside roads' territory it laid claim to west of the city, and as land values rose and older estates were carved up into plots for smaller homes, the new houses built were filled with families. They had their servants, and generally rather more of those than their peers back home. Their memoirs are populated with their Amahs, Boys, Cooks and Garden Coolies; and they lived what was recognizably a British or American suburban life imported from home (and it was always 'home'). There were tennis, lawn bowls and amateur dramatics, flower shows, dog shows and charity work. The police court dealt with parking offences and faulty brake lights. This was certainly flavoured with things Chinese of course, as was their local argot with its mix of pidgin English and Anglo-Indian: tiffin (lunch), chit (a bill, or note), maskee (never mind), 'Missy have got?' (Is Madam at home?). A little book of verse for children written by the daughter of a local broker offers a glimpse of the world from the British Shanghailander house: 'Amah's very useful (and doesn't scold a bit)/I *never* have to dress myself and Mother needn't knit'; 'I carry small-piece master/To school near Bubbling Well' runs the poem 'Rickshaw Coolie'. The little master wears a pith helmet. And there was of course the garden, the subject of handbooks and newspaper advice columns, with its 'weedy-women': 'They'll sit on the lawn/In a long blue row,/And chatter like monkeys/As hard as they go.'[47]

John Thorburn had joined this world at the age of sixteen, seeking to 'make good', and holding (and losing) a series of menial sales jobs in foreign-owned showrooms. This was a colonialism of refrigerator salesmen. For all that Shanghailander activists would talk about their rootedness, a substantial majority of residents were migrants like Thorburn, and like his father, who had arrived in 1917, seeking one of any number of privileged and reserved openings for foreign nationals. The young man got to whet an appetite for soldiering with service in the Shanghai Volunteer Corps, and he and his young Shanghailander friends were found to have been plotting various 'wildcat' schemes of adventure. They were not alone. The week Thorburn disappeared two yachts crewed by young Shanghai foreigners had sailed to Yokohama, and two young Russians had set off to push a wheelbarrow around the world.[48] The mythic Shanghai of the salacious exposés that were starting to become popular focused mostly on prostitution (preferably 'white'), narcotics and espionage. Well they might, for the trade in all three was brisk and blatant. Residents joked self-deprecatingly about the more mundane reality of their daily lives – arguing with cook over the bills (for the servants would 'squeeze' so) – but they also liked to have the exotic edge their

Shanghai status gave them. And visiting tourists bullied rickshaw pullers, haggling over fares, and demanding someone find them an 'opium den' (fatally, on at least one occasion), although they usually settled for the circuit of cabarets and being fleeced by the Russian hostesses for expensive bottles of fake champagne.[49] Thorburn's attempted foray into a *Boy's Own* adventure story of his own devising was the cause of his downfall, but the greater underlying problem for the diplomats was the stubborn, settled domesticity of the rooted world he had left behind, the fondness for the comforts of Amah and Rickshaw Coolie – and the substantial investments in property, utilities and trade, together with the service industries that supported them. Those defending that establishment leapt on the opportunity his disappearance provided to defend their rights (as they saw them) and privileges (as the treaties set them out).

The Thorburn case proved a tricky one, and helped stall the treaty process, but other factors also came into play, not least the formation of the coalition National Government in Britain in 1931 and the political instability that ensued, but then new developments in China completely altered the situation. The British had been fixated on their Shanghai problem. But Shanghai was not China, and the major catastrophe that faced the Nationalist state came elsewhere, in Manchuria, although its precursor took place further south. Harry Arnhold and his peers in Shanghai had long believed that they could shape their own future, and had a right to, if not, in some articulations, a 'birthright' to protect in the city. British and American diplomats were by 1931 entirely unsympathetic with such views, and worked to disabuse their nationals of such notions. In Manchuria, Japanese Kwantung Army activists also believed that they had a right to shape their future, and with that, Japan's. Japanese diplomats attempted to correct this notion, and were threatened, sidelined and ignored.

We need to backtrack a little in time to understand the root of the new crisis. The Japanese had already proved brittle in their reaction to China's new scene, and the triumph of the Guomindang. Their military had shown itself pugnacious, and, as with Zhang Zuolin's assassination in 1928, not securely under any political control. As NRA troops had approached Jinan, capital of Shandong province, on their way north in the spring of 1928, the Japanese government sent a defence force to protect their 2,000 nationals in the city. This was a routine manoeuvre in the world of foreign power in China. British troops reinforced Tianjin, and the Tangshan coal mines further north, so all were anxious about the arrival of the nationalistic NRA. Despite initially reaching an agreement with the Chinese units that entered the city in late April, whereby the Japanese force stood down their barricades and defences, fighting broke out. Before a truce was arranged and the NRA withdrew most of its force, both sides had committed foul atrocities. The Guomindang's newly installed Commissioner for Foreign Affairs was seized, his eyes gouged out and ears cut off, and he was then machine-gunned alongside most of his staff. Japanese troops in turn found the hastily buried bodies of fellow citizens, some of whom had been castrated. A week later, his force greatly augmented, the Japanese commander on the spot issued an ultimatum entirely on his own initiative aiming to clear the locality of remaining Chinese units. Before any compromise could be reached his troops pounced on the Chinese. Estimates of Chinese civilian and military casualties range as high as 11,000: only thirty-eight Japanese troops were killed.[50] Many foreign commentators were quite indifferent, if they did not actively side with the Japanese. The 'conduct of the Japanese soldiers has been admirable', reported a British military observer from Jinan. Yes, their behaviour was 'distinctly harsh', but, he continued, 'the Chinese have at last obtained what they have been asking for'. And in return they have received 'the most salutary lesson since the Boxer rebellion'.[51]

Public opinion across China was outraged, but the National Government was too weak to take on even the heavily outnumbered Japanese forces in Shandong. In his diary, sometime repository of his diatribes against the British, Chiang Kai-shek now pledged to outline every day a 'way to kill the Japanese'.[52] In public, the Chinese bent over backwards to placate their attackers, whose own version of events was widely accepted internationally. Locally, many treaty-port foreigners were dismissive of Chinese claims about Japanese responsibility for the outbreak, or even of the veracity of reports about atrocities. The savagery of the fighting, even when the odds were so stacked in favour of the better-equipped Japanese, and the fact that the local commander had acted independently, without any direction from Tokyo, were both worrying signals of just how unstable and unpredictable the Sino-Japanese relationship could become, and how problematic the Japanese presence in China, and Japanese ambitions, remained. While the Jinan Incident was settled by an agreement reached a year later, in which both sides acknowledged their responsibility, and the Japanese agreed to remove all forces from Shandong, the assassination of Zhang Zuolin demonstrated that autonomous Japanese interests on the ground in China aimed to shape the course of events themselves. Japan's diplomats and politicians would struggle to keep up.

Much more was at stake. Japanese interests in China by 1931 were extensive and growing rapidly. While China was never a significant element in British overseas trade, Japan sourced a fifth of its cereals imports there in that year, and a quarter of China's import and export trade was in Japanese hands. There was a Japanese infrastructure and a presence in China south of the Great Wall that seemed to mirror and match those of the British and French, and to a lesser extent the Americans: almost 20,000 Japanese residents in Shanghai's International Settlement, the largest community of foreign nationals (and a third of the total Japanese population in China outside Manchuria), two Japanese members on the Municipal Council, Japanese concessions at Tianjin and Hankou, Japanese shipping lines operating on the Yangzi and along the coast. The Japanese presence was, however, markedly different in terms of occupation and social composition, with a strong presence of small shopkeepers and petty traders. In Shanghai there were bathhouse keepers, 1,000 clerks, 1,600 factory employees (mainly foremen), 13 watchmakers and 350 domestic servants.[53] Their mentality was akin to that of the settler-minded Britons who called themselves Shanghailanders, but their numbers were proportionately much larger. They were much more tightly supervised and organized by the organs of the Japanese state in China, but they were also much more activist, and through such organizations as the local branches of the ultra-nationalistic Seinendan (Youth Corps), more violent. This was more than a settlement of shopkeepers.

Like Britain and France, Japan also had leased territory – though seized from Russia (which had taken it from China) after the war of

1904–5 – at Dairen (Dalian). But this was not sleepy Weihaiwei or inconspicuous Guangzhouwan. It was being systematically developed as a major port city, 'a sort of Japanese Hong Kong', as one British journalist described it, with a population of 400,000 by 1930, one-quarter of them Japanese. 'You might fancy yourself on the outskirts of a large English or German town,' mused another British visitor, the historian Arnold Toynbee. The houses of its clerks reminded him of south London, but its grand public buildings 'would not be scorned by American railway kings'.[54] Dairen was China's second-busiest port, and two-thirds of the world's soybean production transited its harbour, rolling into the port on the South Manchurian Railway (SMR). The railway extended the Japanese reach deep into the north-east, and over one hundred towns and cities came under its jurisdiction due to their proximity to its 700 miles of track, and in each of these was a Japanese quarter. There was in addition a growing agrarian community, mostly migrants from Japanese-ruled Korea, Japanese imperial subjects whose presence was encouraged and facilitated by the agents of the imperial state. For Japanese residents and visitors, Manchuria felt comfortably familiar.

These shoemakers, traders and bathhouse operators meant that Japanese residents could live in much more of a familiar Japanese world in China than other foreigners. The greater intimacy of the relationship between the Japanese in China and those in their home-land was also helped by swifter transport links that not only meant quicker and cheaper means of travel for individuals, but also of moving goods. Fish from Japanese markets could be rapidly conveyed to shops in the Japanese-dominated Hongkou neighbourhood in Shanghai.[55] This made Japanese China contiguous with the home islands in practical and emotional ways that were vastly different to those experienced by Europeans or North Americans, who were separated by weeks of travelling from their home countries. This proximity was dangerously seductive. And Japan had already fought one major war over – and largely in – Manchuria, when it defeated Russia in 1904–5. Arnold Toynbee was disturbed by the museum commemorating the war that he visited in the Leased Territory at formerly Russian-held Port Arthur, and the town itself: 'this landscape,' he mused pre-sciently, 'electrically charged with the sentiment of a whole nation, may prove the most dangerous obstacle of all' to any settlement of the Manchurian question.[56] To the seductions of contiguity were added for some the emotional duty to those who fell in that war, and the temptations of greater gains yet to come fuelled by beliefs that Manchuria was under-populated, under-developed, and historically stood outside China 'properly' conceived. And unlike other foreign institutions in China, the South Manchurian Railway also had an army.[57]

Manchuria was not yet a Japanese issue alone. Distant Belgium, for example, could be bullied out of its concession at Tianjin (which became a Special Administrative District in 1931) and its 1865 'unequal' treaty when that came up for renewal, but the neighbouring Russians were not to be shifted from their own prize asset in the northeast: the Chinese Eastern Railway (CER). Opened on 1 July 1903, and shaving some 600 miles off the journey to Vladivostok by taking a southeasterly route through Manchuria, the railway was a small state within a state, and had occasioned the creation of the city of Harbin out of its key junction with its southern branch to Shenyang. The CER had its own flag, education system and armed force. It had a small river fleet, and over 16,000 employees. It dominated northern Manchuria, and this had always been the point. Tsarist administrators continued to run the CER until 1924, when it was formally taken over by a Sino-Soviet administration. But in practice it remained a Russian-controlled institution. Zhang Xueliang, the 'Young Marshal', who had succeeded his father as the dominant Chinese militarist in the three provinces that formed Manchuria, was determined to assert Chinese control over the CER system, and more precisely his own. In December 1928 he began what became a series of challenges that over the following months included the arrest and detention of Soviet diplomatic officials.

Three years earlier, Soviet advisors working through the Comintern had helped fashion in Guangzhou the force that united China. But as much as it had been a vehicle for revolutionary internationalism, the Comintern always remained part of the foreign-policy armoury of the USSR. In 1929 foreign-policy considerations triumphed, and it was policy of a kind that would also appeal to a diehard Shanghailander in his club on the Bund; former Guangzhou advisor General Vasily Blyukher led a Soviet invasion of Manchuria in November. Zhang Xueliang's troops were noted to have fought quite well, though they looted rather better, but they had no stomach for standing their ground against Soviet aircraft, which flew unopposed to bomb and strafe them. Cossack cavalry proved highly effective too. The incursion was swift, well executed, and utterly successful. Over the course of the year the diplomatic war of words had drawn in the central government in Nanjing, which had been emboldened by Zhang's initiative and had assured him of military support, but now the Guomindang folded. The Soviet position in the CER was restored. Yet again, as over Jinan, the Nationalists secured no international sympathy when their country was attacked and invaded by a foreign power.[58]

There were two further forces present in the Manchurian provinces, quite different, but each inextricably linked to other powers outside: Chinese popular nationalism and the Japanese Kwantung Army. Nationalism took two forms. There was the impact of formal policies, such as the economic challenge being posed, now possible because of the recovery of tariff autonomy, which began to drive Chinese shippers away from the SMR and shipment of goods through the Kwantung Leased Territory. And there was the continuing populist nationalist wave that the Guomindang attempted to ride securely in their public mandates and diplomatic démarches in the period 1929–31, which had its consequences on China's streets, in its newspapers, chambers of commerce, and schools and universities. The calendar was peppered with official 'humiliation days', marking this event or that one, and these created a nationalistic rhythm for the year. Nationalism had its own life as well outside official events. With each such day came articles, public meetings, heartfelt speeches, songs, slogans and posters. These raised expectations that were hardly met with the recapture of Weihaiwei or redundant Zhenjiang. They also reinforced, in a circular process, the predisposition of national and regional leaders, such as Zhang Xueliang, to act to restore China's sovereignty, as he had tried to in 1928–9 over the CER. No one in public life could afford not to align themselves with the nationalistic consensus. But more important than any of these was the simple development and consolidation of an everyday sense of national identity, an imagined national community shaped by these processes, by schooling, through the maps and geography textbooks published by the great Commercial Press in Shanghai, by transport networks that moved more people more easily around, by newspapers, advertising and 'National' consumer products, and through popular culture.[59] This growing sense of there being a single China, shared in common with other Chinese, across the scores of languages and regional cultures within the borders of the republic, from Manchuria to Yunnan, in its turn highlighted its antithesis, a heightening awareness of how this China was degraded by foreign power: what damaged Yunnan, damaged Manchuria, because it degraded both. This was by no means an even or a matured process, and it was fractured in myriad ways, but it was unstoppably in motion.

Conversely, this mood steadily embittered the proponents of a different future for Japan's presence in China: relatively junior Japanese officers already at odds in their minds and attitudes with what they saw as their effete government and corrupt democratic society, and not infrequently with their military superiors. Two such men set in motion a conspiracy for catastrophe in 1931: Kwantung Army officers Kanji Ishiwara and Seishiro Itagaki. Events this year moved them to strike. On 4 May – a day of humiliation, naturally, as the anniversary of the Versailles Treaty betrayal – the National Government promulgated the set of regulations extending from 1 January 1932 Chinese jurisdiction over all foreign nationals who had previously enjoyed extraterritorial privileges. The announcement came a day before the opening of a National People's Convention, part of Sun Yat-sen's planned process of constitutional development. The announcement did little to help the various sets of negotiations over treaty revision then actively in train, although it did reinforce the pressure on the diplomats. But so did events on the ground, which, as far as Britons or the Japanese were concerned, demonstrated that conditions in China did not augur well for foreign lives under Chinese rule. And while Britons mobilized that summer over the disappearance and death of John Thorburn, Japanese officials totted up over 500 incidents of Chinese 'failure' to protect their nationals. But the two most damaging occurrences were the murder of a

Japanese intelligence office, Nakamura Shintarō, in Inner Mongolia in July, and a near-contemporaneous series of clashes at Wanbaoshan near Changchun between immigrant Korean and Chinese farmers. This sparked an organized anti-Chinese pogrom in Korea, and resulting outrage in China that found expression in a sustained and effective anti-Japanese boycott, the biggest such movement since the May Thirtieth campaigns that had struck British trade.[60]

No friction could develop, no stand-off or incident, no controversy over a canal (as at Wanbaoshan) could take place between Chinese and foreign nationals that was not viewed through a nationalistic lens. For Kanji Ishiwara, Seishirō and their co-conspirators each contingent event was part of an unfolding project that would degrade and destroy the Japanese enterprise in China. And that enterprise was absolutely vital to the future of Japan: little mattered more, as they saw it, and their concerns were magnified by the damage the Japanese economy was already suffering from the onset of the global economic depression after 1929.[61] Moreover, Zhang Xueliang was clearly not turning out to be the effective collaborator with Japanese interests that his father had been. Zhang's entrenching of control over Manchuria also alienated many in the coalition of semi-secessionist Chinese military and civil interests that had supported his father. His nominal allegiance to Nanjing dismayed such interests as much as the Japanese. To their further alarm in October 1930 his Nationalist loyalty was shown to be even more substantive when he turned his troops on Yan Xishan, who was in rebellion against the National Government, in a decisive intervention that sealed Yan's defeat.[62] The small group of officers around Kanji and Seishirō began plotting a violent provocation that would precipitate action by the wider Kwantung Army, and drag in the Imperial Japanese Army and government into a decisive struggle to secure Manchuria's present and future for Japan.

This was a classic operation on a colonial frontier by men 'on the spot' to further the interests of the imperial state – as they saw them. Sometimes these operations fail: Jameson's 'raid' on the Transvaal Republic in 1895 was one notorious example, an unofficial attempt to bring the republic under British colonial control on the pretext of a 'restoration of order', after that order was in the first place unsettled through a contrived uprising. But more often than not such actions succeeded because those acting knew that they had wider support, and that there was a taste for some decisive action to resolve the frustrations of an impasse. And anyway, Paris, or London – or Tokyo – were distant and powerless to act before reality had been reshaped on the frontier.

All that well-intentioned talk, talk, talk about China melted into the warm air of 18 September 1931. We have records in abundance of the IPR conferences and independent commissions, position papers and meetings; academics and businessmen met and exchanged views in a leisurely fashion, and toasted each other at their pleasant dinners, assuring themselves of their own reasonableness and openness, but none of that helped save China from Ishiwara Kanji's plot, and the violence it set rolling. Reality was remade on the South Manchurian Railway line just outside Shenyang (Mukden) as a small bomb was exploded and then, responding to this notionally shocking act of sabotage, units of Kwantung Army troops fired on and routed Zhang Xueliang's garrison force. This series of actions was not enthusiastically supported by either the Imperial Japanese Army or the government in Tokyo. So great was their antipathy towards Japan's diplomats that the plotters kept the Japanese consul at Shenyang under armed guard during the operations, not for his own safety, but to keep him out of the way.[63] The Kwantung Army forces thereafter kept pushing, putting into action contingency plans for reacting to Chinese attacks, and securing through a series of lightning strikes – and the treachery of forces hostile to Zhang Xueliang – victories that placed much of southern Manchuria in their hands with dizzying speed. Civilians and soldiers in Tokyo kept trying to rein the adventure back in, but to little avail. They were ignored or evaded, or presented with too tempting faits accomplis. The sweet taste of success brought others on board, and then in early December the government in Tokyo fell, and more hawkish figures assumed command. These decided to seize the opportunity engineered for them by Kanji Ishiwara and the men on the spot.

By August 1932 most of Manchuria, aside from the CER zone, was secured. Zhang Xueliang had withdrawn his forces from the province, pursuing, alongside the National Government, a policy of non-resistance that aimed to allow other pressures to come to bear on the aggressors. Now indeed was the moment for the League of Nations to play a decisive role, and now indeed they talked at Geneva, and talked, and formulated resolutions, and attempted in the spirit of the new order of international arbitration mapped out by Woodrow Wilson to negotiate a fair and lasting resolution. On 10 December a Commission of Inquiry was appointed, led by the British peer Victor Bulwer-Lytton, Second Earl of Lytton. Its members traversed the troubled provinces and visited Tokyo and Nanjing. By the time they had arrived, Manchuria had been proclaimed the independent Republic of Manzhouguo (*Manshūkoku* in Japanese). The last Qing emperor, Puyi, was installed as head of state, having been spirited out of a playboy exile in Tianjin by Japanese agents. Nobody believed that any of this was real: it was a puppet state, a 'wei' regime in Chinese, a term of decisive negation.[64] And in Shanghai, where Lytton and his colleagues arrived on 15 March 1932, they were greeted by the ruins of the suburb of Zhabei. The spiral of nationalistic outrage and provocative and often pre-emptive responses from Japanese units based in the city had precipitated its own vicious five-week war across the north of the city.[65] The air reeked of the stench of the unburied dead, but the clubs of Shanghai also stank, the bars and smoking rooms rancid with foreigners gloating at the bloody good hiding that somebody had at last had the guts to give the Chinese. Zhabei was payback in too many foreign minds for Hankou, Jiujiang and Nanjing. The foreigners climbed to the tops of Shanghai buildings to watch the Japanese fighter-bombers.

We might assume that a report drafted by, amongst others, a former Governor of British Bengal, who was himself son of a former Viceroy (Lytton), a one-time Governor of German East Africa, the French Inspector General of Colonial Troops, and a career US soldier who had participated in the conquest of the Philippines, would simply accept and reinforce the colonial perspective offered by the Japanese.[66] The arguments presented by the conquerors were familiar ones from the repertoire deployed by those – not least the British, Germans, French and Americans – seizing new colonies: pacifying turbulent frontiers, restoring order, bringing prosperity, development and 'civilization'. But while Lytton and his colleagues softened some of their language, the conclusion of the report delivered in October 1932 was blunt and to the point. They did not believe in Manzhouguo's independence, and they had not enjoyed the oppressive atmosphere that enveloped them there. They castigated the Kwantung Army's assault on the provinces, and while they carefully argued that Japanese interests should be recognized and respected, for they were based on internationally recognized treaties, they demanded that Manchuria be returned to China, albeit in a form that acknowledged an autonomous status. But it must be a state genuinely controlled by China. Japanese representatives in Geneva asked for time to consider the report and its recommendations in full, and then walked out of the League's Council Chamber and out of the League altogether in March 1933. Lytton's report signified nothing except the failure of the League of Nations. Manzhouguo proceeded on its path as a model Japanese colony in all but name. Hundreds of thousands more Japanese settlers were soon encouraged to move there, and its cities were refreshed as a quintessentially modern public architecture was encouraged.[67] Puyi was installed as Emperor of Manzhouguo, or Kangde Emperor, on 1 March 1934 (but not, he lamented, as Emperor of the Qing). The ceremony was somewhat less than modern, although in keeping with changed times he wore military uniform as Manzhouguo's senior officials kowtowed to him in formal recognition of his new status. Far south in Guangzhou a 'monster parade' was held in protest, and another boycott was launched. The enthronement was both a 'farcical comedy', and an 'act of high treason', declared Wang Jingwei, President of the Executive Yuan in Nanjing.[68] The 'Far Eastern Crisis' certainly had many such multifaceted moments as the accession to the throne of Puyi, the Kangde Emperor, but there was nothing funny about its impact on the credibility and authority of the League of Nations, and the post-war international order: it was crippling.

Until March 1933 many felt that the problem of China could be resolved through discussion and negotiation, through research, reports and considered recommendations backed up with persuasive evidence. It was always an international problem, and not simply a Chinese, let alone a Manchurian problem. A new breed of internationalist global trouble-shooters was emerging, and into China they popped (more than adequately recompensed for their pains), and they talked with the other types like them they found there, or encountered at IPR or other conferences, or in Geneva or at Chatham House. This illusion would persist, but men like Ishiwara Kanji would actually effect change, and events not discussions were their method. For its part the National Government secured tangible gains from its assertive drive to restore China's sovereign rights, even if these were overshadowed by the disaster in Manchuria. Despite its internal difficulties – a major rebellion almost annually, a developing communist insurgency in south central China – the National Government succeeded in dismantling key planks in the infrastructure of foreign power in China. The roster of foreign-controlled concessions was whittled down. The government also increasingly acted as if it had secured the restoration of rights, even where it had not, helped by the ambiguities in many instances of the minor privileges secured by foreign interests. The Guomindang continued to act as if it ran the country, enacting and enforcing new laws that did not exempt foreign firms and individuals, in education and public health, for example, and over trademarks or cinema censorship. The foreign game in China had been always to maximize the reach of extraterritoriality, and to deploy it as supporting the exemption of foreign interests from almost any sphere of Chinese control or responsibility. The Qing and early republican officials had always pushed back against this, but over the decades an accretion of precedents had developed, and their very existence seemed to provide them with an authority to persist. Now they were successively scrubbed away. But the formal process of treaty revision was suspended after the seizure of Manchuria. Realpolitik suggested it be set aside while the National Government attempted to marshal a coalition of support for its resistance to Japan as it faced the greatest single threat any Chinese government had had to face from foreign imperialism.

Tangible foreign interests underpinned resistance to reform or aggressive expansion in China: bricks and mortar spoke. The foreign-owned infrastructure had been built up over many decades, and new investment was still being attracted to China. The most symbolic expression of this was the Cathay Hotel itself, opened in 1929 at a prime spot at the intersection of Shanghai's Nanjing Road and the Bund and marking the arrival on the Shanghai scene of Indian tycoon Sir Victor Sassoon, who was relocating his investments from India to real estate in China. There was an almost ninety-year history of such development, and a strong settler element within the foreign communities, some of whose families had been in China for three generations already, with a few closing on four: branches of the Sassoon family had been involved in the China trade since the 1840s. Beyond the ultimately narrow, if often deeply felt, concerns of such settler interests, there were calculations based on national interests, and in some cases on perceptions of national survival. Opposing any 'surrender' to Chinese nationalism was entirely rational, even if it was short-sighted. But a wider problem underlying the question of responding to China was the more intangible one that coloured and poisoned attitudes towards it: the widespread contempt with which China and Chinese culture was held by the 1930s, a contempt once memorably described as 'the barbed wire thread which wove together the whole fabric of foreign imperialism in China'.[69] This could not be revised or reformed by treaty, but it also needed to be confronted.

5

China in the Mind

It was a declaration of war, in its way. On 28 November 1935 the 'International Exhibition of Chinese Art' opened at Burlington House in London, home of the Royal Academy of Arts. Never before had such an extensive and comprehensive collection of Chinese exhibits been brought together, including 780 items loaned by the National Palace Museum, housed in Beijing's Forbidden City, the former palace complex of the Qing emperors. The 3,080 exhibits came from over 280 different donors, and attracted 410,768 visitors in four months. The catalogue sold more than 100,000 copies; bookshops were soon full of other volumes on Chinese art; there were public lectures and radio talks, and the press was full of these unknown glories of China. There had never been anything like it before, and it transformed understandings of the country, and of Chinese civilization and culture.

The first sight that greeted a visitor was a nearly 19-foot-high, 1,300-year-old statue of a Maitreya Buddha, carved from a single slab of marble. Then, arranged across fourteen rooms, packed with objects, visitors moved through over 3,000 years of Chinese history from the Shang Dynasty to the end of the eighteenth century. It was a riot of unfamiliar form, and new colour. Most striking of all were the paintings on display, for this field of art was largely unknown outside China and little understood by foreign audiences. Beyond a small circle of collectors Chinese art was simply porcelain, and a narrow range of China's historic ceramic culture at that, or the scattering of small objects lumped together in foreign minds as 'curios'. The British, for example, were fond of collecting snuffboxes. This narrow understanding of the arts of China was challenged by the breadth of material on show: screens, calligraphy, statues, reliefs, bronzes, jades and paintings.

Canvas covered the 'dowdy' walls of the galleries, to better foreground the objects on display, but there was still a sharp contrast between the exhibits and the 'machine made', vulgar Renaissance foliage of the cornice. To some Chinese eyes too much was crammed together, and the crowds made it difficult to view and savour individual pieces, but this was a problem of success and plenty, and of the historic embarrassment of Chinese riches on display. The organizers and reviewers recommended thinking of this material not as Chinese, but as art. 'If you approach these pots with the receptiveness you would give a Greek lyric,' recommended one, 'I think you will find them equally delicate and rewarding.' Not everybody was convinced. 'Where,' asked art critic Clive Bell, 'is the Chinese Rembrandt?' It all goes downhill after 1500. But did we really once approach such statues using terms like 'ugly idol', asked another writer. And the displays summoned 'shocked amazement that Western soldiers, merchants and missionaries should have thought to bring civilisation to a people with such a tradition as was here set forth'. The political implications of the Burlington House show spilled out into nearly every report about it.[1]

The exhibition proved a revelation. Quite dramatically, Chinese culture was presented to the popular imagination as something of great value, with its own integrity, making its own contributions to culture universally. It thereby demanded preservation. 'No wonder,' mused F. T. Cheng (Zheng Tianxi), the official representative accompanying the loans from Beijing, 'some people have observed that it had the effect of hastening the war that Japan afterwards launched on China.' Why? Because 'the former feared that the Exhibition had evoked too much sympathy for the latter'.[2] A London-trained barrister who would later serve as ambassador to Britain, Cheng joked with serious intent. For the National Government, its involvement in the exhibition was a crucial move in the struggle for national survival in the face of Japanese aggression, and the seeming indifference of foreign opinion to its plight and to its worth as a civilization.

The threat of 'national extinction' (*wangguo*, literally 'loss of country') had worried Chinese intellectuals for decades. The term first became current in the 1890s, in the bewildering days of the 'Scramble for Concessions' after defeat at the hands of Japan in the war of 1894–5 led to the loss of Taiwan, and then the seizure of Jiaozhou Bay by Germany in 1897. In a paroxysm of greed Russia, France and Britain had staked out their 'spheres of influence' and rapidly secured new concessions of their own, small but symbolic territories alienated, it seemed, for ever from Chinese control. There was a geo-strategic logic to many of these moves, if looked at solely from the viewpoint of the small groups of European politicians, diplomats and military officers who formed the policy-making establishments across the major powers. For Chinese observers it looked like the end of the world, and it caused a catastrophic collapse in faith in the competence of the Qing. The 1900 Boxer uprising and resulting war saw further European and Japanese gains secured: the British seemed to be detaching Tibet from Qing control; in 1904–5 the Japanese and Russians fought their war in, and for, Chinese Manchuria; while after 1908, Korea had been fully detached by Japan from Chinese suzerainty.[3]

The Qing had survived in their partially dismembered state until 1911, the great bulk of their territory intact, even though the dynasty's sense of itself had been shredded. The new republic's singular achievement was to find itself established with most of the multi-national empire of the Manchus still in one piece, and now incorporated into the historic core, China. Outer Mongolia was lost, as an independent republic was established, but the Republic of China now acquired the boundaries of the former realm of the Qing at least nominally. Supreme amongst the considerations of revolutionaries and defenders of the throne alike in 1911–12 had been fear of providing an opportunity for a definitive foreign carve-up should some resolution of the crisis not be found quickly. Through the two decades of turmoil and lack of effective control that ensued, as militarist satrapies were established, and as autonomous regimes flourished in Xinjiang and Tibet, the sovereignty of the republic remained nominally intact: its borders held.[4]

The establishment of Manchuko changed everything. This seemed to be a permanent alienation, backed up by a rapid and extensive programme of settlement. It was also reinforced by science, by archaeological and historical research by Japanese scholars who demonstrated, helpfully, serendipitously, disinterestedly – of course – that

Manchuria had never been Chinese. It was historically part of an ethnically Korean empire, and Korea too was now incorporated into Japan's empire. But even though Han Chinese mass settlement in the northeast was of comparatively recent vintage – the historic ban on immigration was only lifted in 1878 – it was nonetheless a fact. Manchurians were as Chinese as their peers across the nation. Lord Lytton's report was blunt: Manchuria was 'an integral part of China'. And it said this more than once.[5]

Accompanying these developments always was a noisy chatter abroad about 'dying nations' and the rights of succession to them – and to their empires; there was also a wider cultural discourse in which it had become the norm to assume that China's civilization and its culture were degraded, or degenerate. At the end of the nineteenth century this had become entangled with a developing 'scientific' discourse about race, and Social Darwinist thinking. The extinction of China seemed perfectly to fit these models. Ever since the first British envoy to reach China, Lord George Macartney, had concluded in January 1794 that the Qing Empire was 'an old, crazy, first-rate Man of War', which might 'drift some time as a wreck', but eventually be 'dashed to pieces on the shore', the dominating voices had been negative.[6] China would inevitably fall.

The reality of dismemberment on the ground had been reinforced by a sustained assault on the very notion of China as a civilization. The books and essays published by members of Macartney's mission had helped bring about a definitive and fairly swift shift in attitudes towards China and its culture, driving them away from what had been a mostly uncritically positive attitude in the eighteenth century. That had been the heyday of chinoiserie styles, the Pagoda in London's Kew Gardens, and a belief that China's government took the form of a rational, enlightened despotism.[7] Instead, increasing foreign familiarity bred heightened disdain as more and more first-hand accounts of China were published, as foreign intercourse through the China trade grew, and then foreign residence developed after the Opium Wars. Sinophilia was dislodged by Sino-scepticism, and then replaced with simple contempt. China was decrepit. The defining visual account of China, John Thomson's landmark photographs, first published in 1873–4, surveyed its capital, the treaty ports and different 'types' across society, yet the presentation of exquisite but crumbling ruins, and fading grandeur, was striking. An English aesthetic privileging antiquarian and historic topographic subjects coincided with a colonial reflex. Degradation was a justification for mastery.

Triumphant foreign power had much to gain from belittling its victim, but the problem for China was deeper than any simple model of foreign cultural superiority would suggest. When Macartney delivered his verdict about the Qing state, he did so with a confidence that in 1794 would probably not in fact have been realized on the battlefield. The dynasty was itself strong and confident when it met the envoy and his entourage. But in 1839–42 the industrializing British, with their steam-driven warships and more advanced weaponry and state organization, indeed trounced Qing troops, however well and hard those fought. The modern world, as contemporaries saw it, had triumphed over an archaic one; and this was only natural.

This presentation of China as archaic, and at best static, at worst actually retreating from what were seen to be global norms of progress and modernity, became pervasive. China was 'the European Middle Ages made visible', announced the President of the American Sociological Association in 1911.[8] In fact, China's peoples and its rulers readily embraced much of what they found useful from abroad; they were quite 'modern', on their terms. Foreign things and ideas found ready audiences. John Thomson's photographs captured a culture and society in transition, even though it was the ruins that spoke. But the desire to effect change on China's own terms and at its own pace was viewed by foreign observers and interlocutors as simply a smokescreen for conservative reaction, if not xenophobia. Because Qing officials cautioned foreign diplomats and advisors not to rush them, they were viewed as hostile to the modern world that was now camped on their doorsteps in the concessions and settlements in the great coastal cities. Pragmatic statecraft was interpreted as stubborn ignorance.

After 1900, the Qing in its 'New Policies' had set in motion a process of rapid change, issuing new decrees and reforms that transformed the shape of China's government and its education system, abolishing the civil service examination system that had been based on mastery of the Chinese classics, and mandating the study of 'Western learning'. But this late flowering of reform generated popular expectations about further changes that it declined to meet. This, combined with vivid memories of its failures in the era of the 'Scramble for Concessions', had helped seal the dynasty's fate after the October 1911 military uprising that led to its overthrow. Even though its successor, the new Republic of China, had embraced all the forms of a 'modern' state, down to those top hats and tails mandated as ceremonial wear, and on display at the victory celebrations in 1918, nobody abroad really took it seriously for a moment. The belief that China's was a degraded culture and civilization was only heightened by its ready adoption of the foreign during the republic. Instead of being received as modern, Chinese culture was widely viewed as mongrel, and lacking roots in either world. There was effectively no form that the Chinese could adopt which would not be transformed by hostile Western observers into yet another sign of failure.

There was little challenge to such views from scholars overseas. China had little presence in universities as a subject in any field of learning, although as a country with a civilization and history outside Western Europe and its worlds of overseas settlement it was hardly alone in this. The few individuals holding academic posts relating to China in European or North American universities were usually retired missionaries, diplomatic officers, or former employees of the Chinese Maritime Customs. The quality of their scholarship was in some few instances quite formidable, but the work of most was always unlikely to pass the test of time, and has not. Moreover, it was also usually conducted in a separate 'Oriental' faculty or department, and China had no presence in the mainstream academic disciplines, in history or political science for example.[9] In the early twentieth century the professionalization of universities and academic research was still an evolving process, but the absence of China as a subject was even then notable, and noted. Such China scholars as did hold posts rarely had much to say about contemporary affairs, and were mostly engaged in teaching the language, but rarely other than to those preparing to work in the mission field, business or diplomacy. The study of China was a practical matter, not an intellectual exercise. It could offer nothing meaningful to knowledge.

It was left to the press and to self-appointed experts to instruct audiences overseas about China. The Nationalist revolution of the 1920s had led to a great outpouring of journalism and reportage from foreign writers. While some of this was excited and positive there was, for every balanced account of the events of 1925–7, or Arthur Ransome's castigation of the reactionary foreign settlers in Shanghai, a score of critics who rushed to press. These were men like 'old China-hand' J. O. P. Bland, whose strictures about the deficiencies of the 'structural character' of the Chinese people shaped his 1932 book *China: The Pity of It*,[10] or the American Shanghai journalist Rodney Gilbert with his contribution *What's Wrong with China* in 1926. There was, it might be pointed out, no question mark in his title, and his answer was fairly comprehensive, for example that:

> Chinese poetry is sentimental moonshine ... Chinese canonical philosophy is stuffy and ponderous, revealing at every turn a childish ignorance of first principles ... Chinese history is rambling, ill assembled, ill presented and often prejudiced, while Confucian ethics as expressed in the classics are either childish platitudes or arbitrary rules based upon traditional prejudices.

Gilbert, it need hardly be added, was incapable of reading the literature he so comprehensively dismissed, but, he added, with a logic characteristic of this genre, this made him all the more objective.[11] These examples are low-hanging fruit from an orchard ripe with prejudice and nonsense. However, such views and such commentators were taken perfectly seriously.

It was certainly also true that China – and its poetry, philosophy, ethics and history – had its defenders, interpreters and advocates. But Sinophiles were an eccentric minority. The translations of Chinese and Japanese poetry published from 1917 onwards by Arthur Waley were widely read, and the former British Museum assistant was a figure at the heart of modernist London and its culture. But Gilbert and Bland were read where it seemed to matter most: by those who interacted with China, and by businessmen and military men setting out to take up positions there. They were read, too, by Chinese readers, aghast at the travesties of their culture and society they found being peddled by mainstream foreign publishers and such widely respected experts. For the moment, Gilbert and Bland mattered much more than Arthur Waley.

It might also be noted that Waley himself never once visited China. But Bland, for example, wrote with an authority based on almost thirty years of working there, including a decade as the Shanghai correspondent for *The Times*; Gilbert spent seventeen years in the country, mostly working as a journalist. Any visitor to China could write a book about it (and many, many did so).[12] But China coast journalists like these dominated public discussion about the country and its travails, and until the 1930s virtually held a monopoly on news reporting from China.[13] Waley's was a China of the mind, but treaty port editors such as H. G. W. Woodhead, 'Putnam Weale' (Bertram Lenox-Simpson), or O. M. Green, like Bland and Gilbert, were the experts on China that publishers and magazine editors turned to for timely volumes or essays on Chinese upheavals. These writers were happy to provide material, not simply because this was their livelihood, but as activists and lobbyists. These pungent advocates catalogued China's ills and alleged deficiencies as a robust defence of the privileges of the foreign communities in China. Weale worked for the Shanghai Municipal Council as a publicist in 1927. O. M. Green, having been engineered out of his role as editor of the *North China Daily News* by British diplomats in 1930, worked on a retainer in London as a lobbyist for the Shanghai diehards. Woodhead was a prime mover in the agitation within the British China coast communities against treaty revision in 1931 and over the Thorburn case. Gilbert's earlier career as a quack medicine salesman in China perhaps came in useful. It was but a short step from selling 'Dr Williams' Pink Pills for Pale People' to touting his fake wares as an authority on China.

Even when China was viewed positively from a distance, it could disappoint or baffle when encountered in the flesh. The British potter Bernard Leach's experience in Beijing in 1914–16 is suggestive of the problems facing any sustained and informed engagement with China. Leach, who would become one of the most important British ceramic artists of the twentieth century, moved to the Chinese capital from Japan, in part making a pilgrimage to the heart of the culture from which came the pots he revered. Leach was entangled with a Prussian musicologist and pedagogue, Alfred Westharp, who, amongst other concerns, aimed to bring together the 'Occident' and 'Orient' (an ambition to fuse 'East' and 'West' was a recurrent fad). This difficult personal relationship would come to define Leach's months in the country, and would in the main drive him away from it, but there were other difficulties. It was impossible to avoid visiting China at any point after 1911 when the country seemed not to be in some sort of turmoil. Leach's arrival coincided with the crisis of the Japanese 'Twenty-One Demands' and Yuan Shikai's dictatorship. It was also, in the main, difficult to escape from the quasi-colonial world of foreign power and society that enveloped foreign nationals even in Beijing. And while Leach thought China 'deep', and Japan 'shallow', the life of its people 'hard', but 'natural' and 'not evil in the way our great mechanical cities are evil', China failed Bernard Leach artistically. He would soon return to Japan to work and study, and his oeuvre owes much more to Japan, and to Japanese techniques and styles, and to the networks of potters there with whom he worked, than to China and its longer heritage. He found no like-minded potters in China. Japan proved alive to Leach artistically when China did not.[14] In the *fin de siècle* and after, *Japonisme* had an impact on artists overseas and modern currents in art that was far greater than any Chinese influence. Leach was not blind to China's artistic triumphs, and remained keenly interested in Chinese philosophy, but it was Japan that shaped him.

Others adopted a response to the problems of China that was far less tortured than Leach's. In short they felt that modern China could not be entrusted with its own past, and so they parcelled it up and took it overseas. Archaeological expeditions such as those led by the Hungarian-British Aurel Stein in 1907 and the Frenchman Paul Pelliot in 1908 led to huge volumes of material newly discovered at the Dunhuang cave complexes in Gansu province being taken abroad. Nobody much seemed to mind at the time.[15] It was really quite simple, the Swedish art historian Osvald Sirén was told as late as 1921, just search

for likely looking spots. When you have found what you think will suit you, your interpreter buys the land. It is then yours to do whatever you like, and I do not see how any power can prevent you from digging there if you so desire.

If the authorities carp, the advice continued, offer them half the finds.[16] Sirén never found that likely spot, and was content to purchase from dealers and through intermediaries, but thereby acquired a great number of significant items that went overseas. By the mid-1920s attitudes in China began to change, and such expeditions were robustly and effectively challenged and thwarted. But by this point a great deal of material that had by then started to be conceived of in terms such as 'national treasure' had already vanished. Amongst the many perverse and contradictory defences of this was that such cultural patrimony was better appreciated and safer overseas, and that foreign scholars were in fact best equipped and trained to interpret and conserve it. Modern China had failed its own past; Aurel Stein or Paul Pelliot could help save it for the future.

The problem was deeper yet. It would not have surprised foreign readers to find that Chinese culture was decrepit: for its people were deficient too. There was no shortage of material available telling them so. Those overseas who wished to learn more about China, or who were preparing to go there, could turn to various texts written by the authorities who dominated discussions. Amongst other widely recommended experts on China was Arthur Henderson Smith, whose essays on *Chinese Characteristics* were first published in the late 1880s and included 'The Disregard of Time', 'The Disregard of Accuracy', 'Intellectual Turbidity' and 'Indifference to Comfort and Convenience'. The frustrations of missionary living amongst farming communities in the north China countryside clearly shaped this popular pseudo-sociological account of 'the Chinese' that nonetheless still had a place on reading lists in the 1920s.[17] But even by the time those interested had sought out such guides, the damage had been done.

English-speaking readers, and not those alone, would also have already encountered an almost uniformly negative vision of the country and its people from the 'Chinese' themes and racist caricatures that were firmly embedded in popular culture. Anxieties about immigration, fuelled by racist labour agitation and exclusion laws in North America and Australia, certainly helped shape this vision of Chinese abroad. The 'Heathen Chinee is peculiar', as Bret Harte's verse had it.[18] In this world, Chinese villains stalked London nights, 'tongs' (gangs) fought violent battles in American Chinatowns, and opium- and later cocaine-dealing criminals seduced and defiled young white women. Chinese men, even if poets, were a threat to any 'alabaster cockney child' such as Lucia in Thomas Burke's story 'The Chink and the Child', centrepiece of his 1916 collection *Limehouse Nights*. Adapted as the hit D. W. Griffith film *Broken Blossoms* (1919), the story was very widely known, playing on – and reinforcing – notions of racial threat that were common currency. Such notionally Chinese figures litter the archives as much as they litter fiction, film and the press.[19] And the British author Arthur Sarsfield Ward, writing as 'Sax Rohmer', had earlier launched the first of his many stories about the 'devil Doctor', Fu Manchu – the 'yellow peril incarnate in one man' – on what proved to be an immensely receptive global reading public in 1912. The tales of this xenophobic Chinese master criminal, driven by his desire to revenge the death of his parents at foreign hands dur- ing the Boxer war, were relayed across all forms of popular media, including cinema, the stage and then radio; they had many imitators and the books were widely translated. Fu Manchu strode out on a life of his own in Western culture.

This was not simply the stuff of juvenile fiction. Similar portraits, using similar key words and tropes, would also surface in regular media storms about drug-trafficking or people-smuggling.[20] It became almost impossible to view Chinese except through the lens of Sax Rohmer, a south Londoner who, naturally, had no experience of them at all. European and anglophone popular cultures had become satur- ated with racist portrayals of Chinese villains. While there were other richly mined genres of popular fiction about China, some whimsically harmless – such as Ernest Bramah's silly but popular Kai Lung stories with their willow-pattern aphorisms – most were ultimately negative, and could usually be placed somewhere on a continuum with the excesses of Sax Rohmer and his acolytes. Other genres included the presentation of China as spectacle in which purported authenticity was at a premium – W. Somerset Maugham's 1922 hit play *East of Suez* falls into this category, with an opening wordless scene set on a crowded Beijing street including sixty Chinese extras.[21] Or it was a

1. Ready for burning: victory celebrations at Shanghai Race Course, 1 December 1918.

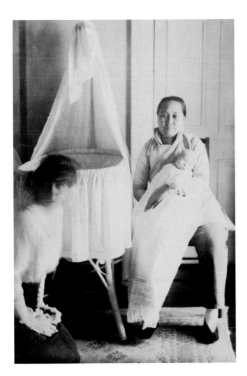

2. Foreign mother's helper: the Chinese Amah.

3. Young Tientsin: Margot Fonteyn, 1928.

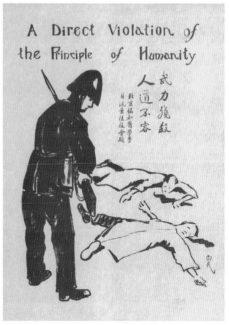

4. China helpers: Mikhail Borodin (*right*), and Morris 'Two-gun' Cohen, Guangzhou, *c.* 1926.

5. Massacre on the Nanjing Road: 30 May 1925.

6. Traders in training: Shanghai Volunteer Corps, *c.* 1924.

7. Weedy-women and a Shanghai lawn, *c.* 1930.

8. An American Shanghailander: Chuck Culbertson (*right*), on the polo field, 1940.

9. Jazz-band leader Buck Clayton (in white suit) and friend in Shanghai, *c.* 1934.

10. Buddha in Piccadilly: setting up the Chinese Exhibition, 1935.

11. Hollywood's China, with Nanjing's assistance: Paul Muni and Luise Rainier in *The Good Earth* (1937).

12. 'Western Civilization' in the eyes of Wang Dunqing, *Modern Sketch* (March 1935).

13. Shanghai besieged: refugees trying to enter the International Settlement, August 1937.

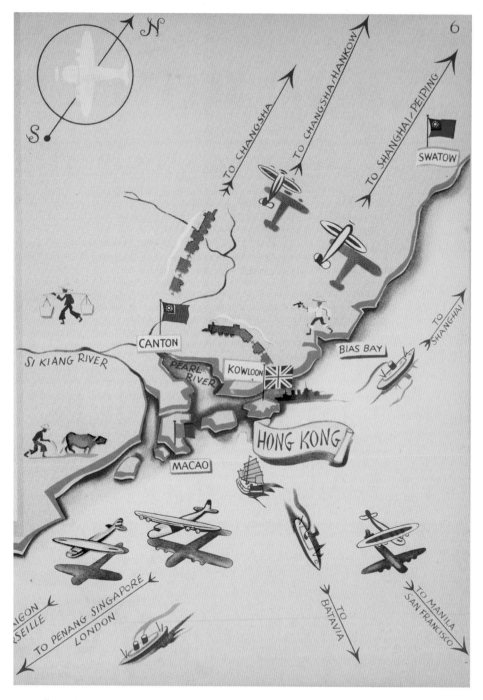

14. 'All roads lead to Hong Kong': illustration by Friedrich Schiff from Ellen Thorbecke, *Hong Kong*, 1938.

15. In the midst of battle, British hostage Mavis Lee, and her dogs Mitzi and Otto, accompany Japanese envoys to beleaguered Hong Kong island, 13 December 1941.

16. Hong Kong's war: British Army Aid Group Officers' Mess, Guilin, 1944

17. The sweet taste of Sino-American friendship, 1943

18. Watching Chongqing burn from the British Embassy garden, 1940.

source of topsy-turvy comic relief, as in such stage shows as Oscar Asche's 1916 hit *Chu Chin Chow* ('of China, of Shanghai, China', as the title refrain went), and other variations of the Aladdin story. And after all, 'Topsyturvydom', another China expert told his readers, was another one of those Chinese 'characteristics'.[22] 'Chinese' conjurors performed in vaudeville – some genuinely so, others as Caucasians in 'yellowface'. Chinese acrobats, dwarfs, giants, impersonators, and women with bound feet all held the stage.[23] Hindsight might prompt derision at all this, as it certainly did for some higher-brow contemporaries, but Chinese readers and audiences who encountered such caricatures did not laugh, and those encounters were difficult to avoid given the grip of the genre on the anglophone imagination.

What was to be done? Of course, Chinese culture and society, and even the Chinese 'character', had their own critics; this was, after all, a key motivation for the New Culture Movement that began to unfold after 1915, and then exploded spectacularly in the May Fourth Movement of 1919 and thereafter. But that was China's business. Lu Xun or Li Dazhao could take their fellow countrymen to task; what right had Arthur Smith to, or Rodney Gilbert? So Chinese intellectuals and Nationalist leaders took the struggle for rights recovery and national salvation into the cultural sphere, and fought there as hard as they fought for the abolition of extraterritoriality, for tariff autonomy and treaty revision. They had markedly better and swifter success.

Their cultural initiative was of its moment. The interwar period saw a great flowering of international organizations and cultural diplomacy.[24] Chinese representatives at the League of Nations had been enthusiastic supporters of the establishment of the League's International Committee on Intellectual Co-operation in 1922. After all, they argued, 'China was an intellectual country at a time when Europe was in a rudimentary state of civilization'.[25] This could hardly be doubted, although ancient history set no precedents and even on this committee – the forerunner of UNESCO – the Chinese were denied a seat. Within the League, China remained focused on securing what its officials considered appropriate recognition of its proper political status within the global order, and the country's different civilization was presented as one imperative factor in that recognition. It did not establish its own Chinese National Committee on

Intellectual Co-operation until 1933, in the aftermath of the seizure of Manchuria and the Shanghai war, and this would mainly work with the League on more technical issues; but at the Institute of Pacific Relations the Chinese had adopted an earlier and more comprehensive strategy to project culture.

The fourth general meeting of the IPR was to have convened at Hangzhou in September 1931. At the Kyoto meeting, two years earlier, there had been an extensive discussion under the heading 'The Machine Age and Traditional Culture', but the conference's main focus had been on political questions, notably extraterritoriality and concessions – and Manchuria. The Chinese delegation had submitted no papers on cultural matters, unlike their Japanese counterparts, who also expected the historic city, Japan's former capital, to speak for itself in that regard. Perhaps feeling outmanoeuvred, the Chinese IPR secretariat launched a determined effort to present a detailed account of Chinese culture at Hangzhou, a city that might also be expected to speak for China's cultural heritage. This took the form of a set of papers, first published – in English – ahead of the meeting and 'presenting China at her best', as the preface put it, 'by acquainting . . . readers with facts and actual achievements which defy refutation'.[26] Hu Shi, Cai Yuanpei – head of China's recently established state-level academic research institute, Academia Sinica – and the scientist V. K. Ting (Ding Wenjiang) were amongst the prominent set of contributors.

Ting's essay exemplifies the concerns of this influential group of intellectuals. He argued that an 'unscientific' version of Chinese history rooted in myth, generated and perpetuated by older generations of Chinese scholars, had been accepted with alacrity by European diplomats and missionaries who used it to justify their own activities and assumptions of cultural superiority. 'No doubt,' he added dryly, 'modern Sinologists are more sophisticated', but 'the old tradition dies hard'. And, 'as a matter of fact, nothing is further from historical truth'. Scientific research showed otherwise. China, he argued, had consistently been agile and adaptable, quick to learn from foreign influences, and 'the charge of unreasonable conservatism or degeneration . . . is utterly unfounded'. His targets were 'ignorant missionaries and traders', but also included Chinese who were 'despondent' and despairing of their own culture as a result of the country's political crisis. Fellow contributors reinforced his picture of Chinese civilization, and added furthermore that it remained a culture in transition. The 1931 IPR meeting itself proved to be a conference in motion. The rapidly unfolding events in Manchuria that autumn forced the organizers to move the event into the International Settlement at Shanghai, where the discussions were held instead in the awkwardly symbolic confines of the International Recreation Club on the Bubbling Well Road.[27] It was to be a continuing irony in the 1930s that colonial power provided such safe havens for China's efforts to combat imperialism.

The IPR volume was concerned to place scientific achievement – and infrastructure – in the vision of Chinese culture it presented to the world as 'irrefutable' fact. This was an argument about the authenticity and value of a uniquely Chinese civilization, but also about what that actively contributed to universal notions of culture and the human tapestry. China was of the world, and an attack on China – such as, implicitly, Japan's – was therefore an attack on the world. That assault continued. During the Shanghai war the great Oriental Library of the Commercial Press at Shanghai was utterly destroyed. The wrecked press itself had supplied the great majority of textbooks for schools across China. In letters sent to Albert Einstein and other intellectuals overseas, Cai Yuanpei pleaded for international condemnation of such 'wholesale destruction of China's educational and cultural establishments'. Chinese librarians petitioned Lytton on his arrival in the city, for 'it is a loss ... to our country, [and] to the whole world as well'.[28] The Lytton report summarized the continuing conflict in the autumn of 1932 as 'a war in disguise'.[29] Culture was in the front line.

London seems an unlikely battlefield in China's war against Japan, and its struggle for sovereignty and for respect. But it was important to take the argument overseas into the heart of one of the powers that had shaped the global order that the Nationalists were fighting to change. They had some unlikely, awkward, but genuine allies, for the original impetus for what became the 'International Exhibition of Chinese Art' in November 1935 came from a small group of prominent British collectors of ceramics, and in the main reflected significant shifts in collecting over the previous two decades. The leading figures included Sir Percival David, whose family business concerns had included the India–China opium trade until its final suppression in 1917; George Eumorfopoulos, a wealthy trader; the poet Laurence Binyon, who had recently retired from the post of Keeper of Prints and Drawings at the British Museum and was a scholar of Chinese art; and Robert Lockhart Hobson, the museum's Keeper of Oriental Antiquities.[30]

Why was art important? One answer was that it was intimately intertwined with the history of foreign violence in China. The collapse of the Qing state and the turmoil of the republic had created perfect conditions for a rapid expansion of the market overseas for Chinese *objets d'art*. The original field of collecting had largely grown out of the export trade that greatly expanded in the eighteenth century, and had created a strong market for Chinese objects, notably porcelain. This was in the main restricted to materials made specifically by the Chinese for export, and targeting European tastes. War changed all that. The nineteenth-century conflicts had seen extensive and systematic looting by the armies of the victors and their camp followers. The sacking in 1860 of the Yuanming Yuan – the Qing Summer Palace northwest of the capital – and systematic looting more widely across the city in 1900 during the Boxer war had swamped museums, auction houses and collections abroad with very different types of material, and greatly whetted the appetite for more. The fall of the Manchus led to much more material finding its way from private collections of officials of the old regime, or even from the imperial palace. Puyi, the last Qing emperor, and his brother took or sold a significant amount. The absence of any effective export controls or antiquities laws until 1935 also meant that material was taken from known historic sites, or from newly discovered ones. The looting never really stopped. Through agents in China such as the Briton Stephen Bushell or the American John C. Ferguson, or through networks of dealers overseas, such as C. T. Loo (Lu Qinzhai), and Yamanaka and Co., a steady stream of material found its way overseas to collectors and museums.[31] David and Eumorfopoulos were significant beneficiaries of this changing market, and in turn also significant advocates for its worth as an object of study and appreciation. The new materials radically altered the way Chinese art could be understood overseas. David funded university positions in Chinese art (and would later donate his entire collection to the University of London); and in 1934, Eumorfopoulos sold a large part of his collection, at well below the market price, to the British Museum and the Victoria and Albert Museum.

So the time seemed right. And moreover the 1935 exhibition also fitted into a sequence of nationally themed Royal Academy shows, the most successful being the 'Italian Art' exhibition held in 1930 and attended by almost 600,000 visitors. In this way too, China could secure its place amongst the ranks of nations. If Persia had been on show, as it had been in 1931, then China should also be displayed. In February 1934 the idea was first formally put to the Chinese Minister in London, Guo Taiqi, with the argument that 'the Chinese spirit . . . has proved a stimulating challenge to the Western mind', and was 'in an increasing measure a ponderable factor in the relations of China with the West'.[32] This was perfectly phrased. In October the project secured the formal approval of the National Government and its agreement to collaborate with their plans, and to co-sponsor the initiative. But it would do so on its terms, and those terms were set by the wider cultural diplomacy that was unfolding.

The exhibition proved a triumph, receiving adulatory press coverage and setting the British and others achatter about the 'treasures' of China temporarily in their midst. Thousands of people came from overseas – 500 students in one group alone from Germany. It was 'worth crossing the Atlantic to see', advised *The New Yorker*.[33] Chinese themes saturated the media. Excitement had been heightened by the unorthodox shipping arrangements decided on for the National Palace Museum collection, which was transported to Britain on a Royal Navy China Station cruiser, HMS *Suffolk*. The crates were unloaded at Portsmouth by being carried across the decks and under the guns of the giant battlecruiser HMS *Hood*. The symbolism could hardly be more apt: this was an intensely political venture, entangled awkwardly with the physical infrastructure of imperialism, and not only in Chinese minds.

The National Palace Museum collection had already been treated as an object of political importance. In 1933, amidst anxieties about possible Japanese expansion out of Manchuria into north China, over 21,000 items were moved from Beijing and stored in a warehouse in the French concession at Shanghai.[34] Chiang Kai-shek gave the London exhibition a strong endorsement, and the Premier, Wang Jingwei, presided over the formal opening of the preliminary exhibition organized in Shanghai before the material sailed on HMS *Suffolk*. T. V. Soong (Song Ziwen), H. H. Kung (Kong Xiangxi) and other senior leaders attended, as did all the foreign ambassadors accredited to China, including Japan's. A portrait of Sun Yat-sen hung over the gala dinner. This was all but a state banquet, with the Guomindang's underworld allies in attendance for good measure.[35] And, just to rub it in, Lord Lytton, public face of the international condemnation of the seizure of Manchuria, had been appointed chairman of the formal organizing committee of the Royal Academy show.

Despite this formal government support, Beijing-based intellectuals launched a public campaign to try to prevent the loan to London, further arguing that if it did go ahead only Chinese scholars should make any decisions about what was to be selected, and criticizing any involvement of Paul Pelliot in the organizing committee. The Dunhuang expeditions were by now viewed as theft of 'national treasures'. Rumours would also circulate that the Palace collection would be sold or left in Britain as collateral for a new loan.[36] How China was represented, and who by, and on what terms, became an even more controversial point. It could certainly not be left to those 'ignorant missionaries and traders', nor in many cases to the Sinologists, however 'modern'. It should not be left to those who had robbed China of its cultural patrimony. It should not even be in the hands of those friends of Chinese culture who had set the exhibition in motion, the protesters argued. David and Eumorfopoulos sparked a storm in China largely unnoticed back in London, by altering a number of the attributions provided to them by the Chinese organizing committee, implicitly asserting that they, and not China's experts, knew China's culture best.

Meanwhile, the Japanese government took umbrage at Lord Lytton's involvement and initially refused to co-operate. Surely, Robert Clive, the British ambassador to Japan, quietly suggested to the Vice Minister for Foreign Affairs Shigemitsu Mamoru, the decision cannot be based on the appointment of Lord Lytton, 'that seemed to me altogether too petty'.[37] But this stance was also reinforced by lobbying from the influential Japanese art historian Taki Seiichi, 'who appears to be extending the spirit of nationalism to the domain of art', as Clive put it. In the end, and after more informal lobbying by British diplomats, the Japanese imperial household led the way in providing significant contributions from Japanese collections. But the Japanese would counter with their own blockbuster show – tellingly entitled 'Art Treasures from Japan' – and held in Boston in 1936, a year after the Chinese exhibition. While the Japanese show was successful, it failed to achieve the impact of its Chinese counterpart.[38]

'All London is China mad,' wrote Nora Heysen, then an Australian art student, to her parents in 1935:

> People wear Chinese gowns, the shops are filled with Chinese materials and the antique dealers are filling their shops with Chinese articles of every description and the bookshops with books on Chinese art.

Heysen pronounced herself 'stupefied with such beauty' after visiting.[39] Reviewers generally reported themselves 'humbled'. 'One cannot but hang one's head in shame,' announced one reviewer. There was a lot of talk about China's 'spiritual' civilization and the West's 'materialistic' culture. Others had more functional responses, as Heysen had noted. The Chinese exhibition was the talk of the town, claimed the American magazine *Vogue*, 'every one laying odds that it will influence fashion as much as the Italian exhibition in Paris did'.[40] 'Queen orders Jewel Blue dress' ran one report, 'Fashion World Rhapsodizes' read another. A trade body, the British Colour Council, recommended that textile manufacturers prepare relevant colours (available, for example, at Barker's department store in South Kensington) for the 1936 season fashions: 'Mandarin Blue', 'Chinese Green' and 'Manchu Brown'. 'Chou Green, adapted from the colours of a 1,000-year-old vase' was tipped for autumn the following year, along with 'Canton', 'another green', a 'pale milky jade'. The impact was felt widely in the interior design world, as Chinese wallpapers and wall hangings leapt into fashion. Storekeepers made sure that the housewife could find those 'Eastern touches' in the shops.[41]

Britain had a long history of assimilating Chinese products, tea not least of all. Robert Hobson argued that while you could already find

Chinese objects in every house in the land, they were 'grotesque'; '"bazaar" goods made to tickle the fancy of the foreigner'. At the Royal Academy visitors were confronted with 'real Chinese art'. Nonetheless, the Academy restaurant's Chinese cocktail (a mix between a Bronx and a White Lady), and the young Chinese women in red cheongsams who manned the postcard stall, might not quite have fitted with the 'authentic' Chinese culture – as he understood it at least – that Hobson was aiming to share with the Western public.[42] We can link this discovery of Chinese culture, too, with the cultural pilgrims who started to sojourn in the country in the 1930s, seeking to taste it 'before it should perish', as one of them, Osbert Sitwell, put it. They hastened through Shanghai because it was 'not China' (when, of course, it was), rented courtyard houses in Beijing hutongs (alleys), observed the changing of the seasons in their neighbourhoods, tasted theatres and brothels, and later sniped in their memoirs about the foreign residents who had not, like them, 'gone native'. As well as the sex tourists and snobs were some, like historian John Fairbank, whose studies bore fruit in work that came to be central to the shaping of understandings of China after the war. The Bernard Leach impasse seemed now to have been overcome.[43] But much of the impact of the Burlington House exhibition took place in realms far removed from the aesthetic sphere in which it was conceived.

F. T. Cheng's speech at a press lunch ahead of the exhibition opening had deftly weaved the political implications of the show into what became fairly routine descriptions of the importance of the material. 'You will see,' he told the journalists:

> not mere objects of art of China but, with your mind's eye, will see the culture and civilization of China as well; for these things were not created by the bayonet but were produced by the love of beauty, and nothing is, of course, more beautiful than peace, virtue, righteousness and affection.[44]

There were attempts to arrange for the exhibition to move on to the United States as well, politics and culture again intersecting in the moves that were made by the Metropolitan Museum of Art, the State Department and Chinese diplomats, but which had borne no fruit before the scheduled return journey of the collection to China.[45]

'Our sole aim is to make the West appreciate the beauty of Chinese Art', ran the disingenuously phrased preface to the preliminary exhibition of the Chinese government loan, held in Shanghai in April 1935. But the political message was reinforced at each and every iteration of the show: at a related exhibition in Manchester that began in early April 1936, opened by Ambassador Guo, who thanked the locally based liberal newspaper the *Manchester Guardian* – renamed the *Manchurian Guardian* by critics of its support for China, he noted – and with Cheng in attendance rehearsing his bayonet/peace/ righteousness formulation; and at the unveiling of the Victoria and Albert Museum's permanent display of the Eumorfopoulos collection a fortnight later.[46] This was not simply a metropolitan or intellectual episode. Associated lectures and talks were held across the country. Slide shows and magazine reproductions took the exhibition into the provinces, and it was covered by the press nationally. The 'Chinese exhibition' was a cultural and intellectual landmark in the development of a balanced, sympathetic, even 'scientific' understanding of Chinese culture. It was certainly the indispensable social highlight of the season: 'the Mayfair darlings, poor things, have just got to go and struggle with it', joshed *The New Yorker*. But it was also a popular hit, made a success by the hundreds of thousands of ordinary Britons who threaded their way along the queues into Burlington House.

While the doors of Burlington House were still open, Lin Yutang's landmark book *My Country and My People* was published in Britain. This was to become a best-selling, hugely influential and witty salvo in the third front of the culture war. China wrote back against the China hands, and Chinese writers began to move centre stage in the presentation of the country and its predicament to the world. Lin would become the most famous of these, but others, including playwright Shih-I Hsiung (Xiong Shiyi), artist Chiang Yee (Jiang Yi), and journalist and novelist Hs'iao Ch'ien (Xiao Qian), would become powerful advocates for understanding China as the Chinese understood it – or at least as this eclectic and diverse group of self-appointed cultural brokers wanted people to. Explaining China in English had long been a project of China's revolutionaries and radicals. Sun Yat-sen and Wang Jingwei alike published books in English outside China. The aim was to communicate Chinese perspectives to anglophone audiences in China and abroad and to secure support, and this included an increasingly important group: overseas Chinese who could not read, and often who could not speak, the language. The most overtly political of these periodicals was *The People's Tribune*, but more effective was *The China Critic*, established by a group of overseas-educated writers in 1928 in Shanghai, and aiming to provide a 'fair presentation of all issues arising between China and the world'.[47] It was probably funded, at least initially, from Guomindang sources, but it took on a life of its own as the first Chinese-edited English-language periodical published in Shanghai, and secured a high circulation. This initiative was augmented in 1935 by *T'ien Hsia*, a monthly cultural journal.[48] 'There is one activity of the League of Nations which has not been given the prominence it deserves,' wrote the then Premier Sun Fo in his introductory essay in its first issue, 'the work of the International Institute of Intellectual Co-operation.' To advance such work in China, Sun announced the establishment of 'the Sun Yat-sen Institute for the Advancement of Culture and Education', which published the new journal, aiming 'to bring about international cultural understanding'. The journal lacked the spark of its earlier companion; not least, it lacked humour.

Lin Yutang was from 1930 onwards one of *The China Critic*'s star writers. Born into a third-generation Christian family in Fujian in 1895, he was initially, like his father, directed towards the priesthood. Lin studied at St John's University in Shanghai, taught English literature at Tsinghua University in Beijing, and then in the four years starting in 1919 studied for an MA at Harvard, worked for the YMCA in France with the Chinese Labour Corps, and secured a PhD in classical Chinese phonetics at Leipzig. This career was more mobile than most amongst the 145 students who sailed with him for the United States on 16 August 1919, although in outline it was of a pattern with the rapidly growing outpouring of young men and women who went to study overseas. They were reminded of their status in US immigration law even before they disembarked: they were 'herded to an isolated spot on deck and lined up for a physical examination' by officials, like cattle.[49] Lin returned to a post at Peking University and then Xiamen, worked for the Left-Guomindang's Wuhan government, and later Academia Sinica, all the time engaging in a spirited literary and journalistic career that brought him great acclaim in China, where he established and ran several journals, and that with the publication of *My Country and My People* would make Lin one of the most prominent of China's interpreters overseas.

Whoever spoke for China needed to speak English, if an audience was to be found abroad. But Lin's genius was to deploy humour as his tool. He was never less than deadly serious, but his fluent English prose was playful, ironic and witty, and projected a persona like none other that anglophone audiences had encountered as 'Chinese'. The book was midwifed by Pearl Buck, whose *The Good Earth* had had a powerful impact on readers internationally after its publication in 1932, eventually selling over two million copies. Buck provided a preface heralding 'the most important book yet written about China. And, best of all, it is written by a Chinese.'[50] The material was partly drawn from Lin's essays in Chinese in the journals he edited, and was a taste thereby of a wider debate in Chinese letters about the importance of humour.[51] Lin set out his wider political project at the onset, and skewered the 'Old China Hands'. 'It is,' he ventured, tongue in cheek from the start, 'the lot of the great to be misunderstood, and so that is China's lot.' His country was 'greatly, magnificently misunderstood'. Still, would it not be better to be understood than to be recognized as great? Of course, so 'who', he asked, 'will be the interpreters?' The 'Old China Hand', 'very well informed within his limits', but 'the limits of a man who cannot talk three syllables of Chinese' had become the default authority. For each exception to this rule there were 'ten thousand Rodney Gilberts, and . . . ten thousand H. G. W. Woodheads'. And so 'the result is the constant unintelligent elaboration of the Chinaman as a stage fiction, which is as childish as it is untrue'.[52]

Lin proposed to show the 'common human values' that underlay the experience of being Chinese. 'This is,' he argued, 'the basis of all sound international criticism.' He was quite happy, then, to discourse on the 'Chinese character', the joy of taking afternoon naps, reading novels slowly, the importance of theatre, the literary revolution in China, and the need for 'moments of blissful madness'. Lin would spend the three decades from 1936 living in the United States, building on his success – he topped *The New York Times* best-seller list, the first Chinese author ever to do so – especially through another book, *The Importance of Living*. This was an eclectic romp through China's philosophers and literature (as well as Walt Whitman, amongst others) and Chinese life 'at first hand'. Lin's China was accessible, fresh, attractive, and at once familiar, yet unfamiliar. His method seemed whimsical but his aims were never less than serious.

The Chinese vogue overseas in the mid-1930s was also in evidence on theatre stages, on radio and in schools. Shih-I Hsiung's *Lady Precious Stream*, a free adaption of a Beijing opera story for the Western stage, had a three-year run after its first night in London in November 1934. It was showcased in New York, adapted for radio, and into versions that could be performed in schools, and it was translated into several other European languages. The play was seen in London by several men who had been or would serve as British Prime Minister, by members of the royal family, and by such cultural lions as J. B. Priestley and George Bernard Shaw. The Chinese Embassy adopted it early on: guests at a December 1934 private performance there included the British Foreign Secretary, the Chancellor of the Exchequer, three other cabinet ministers, Lord Lytton, H. G. Wells and other prominent figures. Bernard Shaw had apparently prompted Hsiung's enterprise in the first place: 'Try something different. Try something really Chinese and traditional,' Shaw had reportedly advised him after reading a conventional modern drama that Hsiung had sent him.[53] There was little 'traditional' about the play, which was calibrated for foreign tastes and expectations, and Hsiung would later disown it. It was also entirely modern in that, however commercial a venture it was, *Lady Precious Stream* became part of a sustained exercise in cultural politics.

As Burlington House opened its doors, the painter Chiang Yee's book, *The Chinese Eye: An Interpretation of Chinese Painting*, was published in London. Endorsed by Hsiung, this was a popular survey aiming to provide 'some data for understanding and appreciating Chinese painting'.[54] Chiang had arrived in Britain in 1933 with very little English and a very just regard for his former position as magistrate in the city of Jiujiang. He was therefore shocked at the casual racism he encountered from French soldiers on his voyage to Europe or from children on London's streets. Chiang quickly became a prominent figure in London's small circle of Chinese expatriates and foreign Sinophiles. He taught Chinese at the School of Oriental Studies and stumbled by accident into prominence as a Chinese artist by virtue of being virtually the only one living in London. But it was as a cultural intermediary that he began to thrive. A number of popular travel books followed, the 'Silent Traveller' series, commencing with an account of the Lake District seen and described, and painted, by a Chinese visitor. Chiang's oeuvre would serve in turn both to provide accessible accounts of Chinese painting and calligraphy from a Chinese artist – not a foreign critic, collector or art historian – and a series of oblique representations of landscapes and cities closer to home in the Western imagination, Oxford, London, New York and Paris amongst them. An old conceit in English literature had been the portrayal of mores and customs by a visitor from China. Oliver Goldsmith's *The Citizen of the World, or, Letters from a Chinese Philosopher, residing in London* (1760–61) was the most famous of these. Now, topsy-turvily, came the real thing. Chiang was also to respond to a growing demand for books for children about China, a market previously dominated by earnest missionary texts, or adventure tales in which pirates featured prominently.[55]

Lin Yutang, Shih-I Hsiung and Chiang Yee were pragmatic entrepreneurs, who made the most of a favourable moment, and they also in each case benefited from the advice or assistance of foreign interlocutors. They were lucky beneficiaries of a turn in cultural relations. Their individual trajectories intersected with the proactive cultural diplomacy of the Nationalist state, and they found ready audiences, sympathies already prepared for them as a result of the Manchurian crisis, and the runaway global success of Pearl Buck's *The Good Earth*.

The China represented was entirely complicit in, and incorporated into, the Nationalist state, however independent and critical it claimed to be. From the left came other viewpoints, sometimes critical of this group. Where was today's China? Chinese culture as shown at the Royal Academy had had a cut-off date of 1800. *Lady Precious Stream* was a refashioned Beijing Opera tale. Although Chiang Yee had helped organize and was exhibited in a well-publicized exhibition of 'Modern Chinese Painting' in 1935 in London, he too was not seemingly presenting modern China, or *Living China*, as the title of one collection of translations of leftist stories had it. This 1936 volume, edited by Kansas-born journalist Edgar Snow, who had worked in Shanghai since 1928, was one of a number that presented other voices – such as Lu Xun – and pointed out, too, the repressive side of the Nationalist government. One of the authors translated was Rou Shi, one of five members of the communist League of Left-Wing Writers executed in Shanghai in February 1931. This was a state that showcased and protected China's culture abroad, and one that did not hesitate to shoot writers at home.[56]

Snow's volume did not make much of an impact. Lin Yutang sold some 55,000 copies of *My Country and My People* in the United States, running through seven editions in the first four months alone. Even Chiang Yee's handbook leapt off the shelves, needing five reprintings by the end of the year. *Lady Precious Stream*'s three-year run meant that it secured a substantial audience. But this was still quite modest. Just over 400,000 visits were made to the Burlington House exhibition, thousands more will have read about it in the press. But in the 1930s almost a billion visits a year were made to the cinema in Britain, and the number of admissions to movie theatres in the United States in 1935, the year the 'International Exhibition of Chinese Art' opened, was 2.33 billion. The reach of any single film could vastly outstrip even the largest exhibition of Chinese art ever assembled. And China was increasingly on display on screen in the 1920s and 1930s.[57] As far as the numbers went, cinema mattered more. The National Government knew this, and worked in that field also to reshape foreign representations of China on screen.

Cinema was big business in republican China, and growing all the time. By 1927, Shanghai had twenty-six cinemas. All the major American firms had opened offices in the city, and Hollywood's exports had grown in value seventeen-fold between 1913 and 1925. Most of its movies had a Chinese showing.[58] Film was also politically brittle. Cinemas themselves had become sites of protest in the city's French concession and International Settlement in the 1920s as pugnacious foreign nationalists contested the representation of what were deemed to be 'offensive' stereotypes, and political conservatives attacked radical portrayals of their countries. Internationalized Shanghai had grown accustomed to the movie-theatre fracas: to Italian marines cutting up rough over this film or that one, or the French over *All Quiet on the Western Front* (and its scenes of fraternization). But the fury in Shanghai that greeted Harold Lloyd's 1929 comedy *Welcome Danger!*, a routine portrayal (by then) of Chinatown threats, plots and ritual murder, took everybody by surprise, not least its star. It 'was not intended as a reflection against Chinese dignity, but was simply made in the spirit of fun,' Lloyd told the American Consulate.[59] Thereafter the Shanghai branch of the Guomindang instituted a censorship policy that aimed to resist such examples of good clean racist 'fun'.

Chinese students studying overseas had for a while been the first to report on and protest about problematic stage shows or films. In 1928 they prompted their diplomats in London to protest formally about a raft of Chinese-themed plays and shows on the London stage, to the bemusement of the Foreign Office and of the Lord Chamberlain's department, the agency that censored British theatre. Officials gave the complaint short shrift. It was quite unavoidable, as China was so 'picturesque', but such shows were 'too obviously staged in the realms of fantasy' to be taken seriously by any 'discerning' theatregoer. The Chinese, the Lord Chamberlain felt, should get a sense of humour. There was no other redress possible, other than satirizing such caricatures, as Shu Qingchun, who wrote under the pen name Lao She, did in his novel *Er Ma* (translated into English as *Mr Ma and Son*), which was set in London and partly revolved around just such a controversy about the making of a Chinatown film.[60] Shu was teaching in London at the time of the controversy. *Er Ma* is a caustic account of the casual and 'yellow peril'-inspired racism encountered by Chinese studying in London, and it identifies the film both as symptomatic of the problem and exacerbating it.

In 1920, Chinese students in New York complained to the consulate about two films they took objection to, to little effect. But when Chinese students in Germany reported in 1933 that a new movie, *Tod über Shanghai*, 'ridiculed China and the Chinese people', action was possible in China. The Foreign Ministry formally protested, and the Guomindang's National Film Censorship Committee, which had been established in 1931, suspended vetting all German films.[61] Appeals to the need for good cultural relations free of 'misconceptions' fell on deaf ears: hitting the industry's bottom line would prove much more effective.

Foreign films were banned in China if they portrayed Chinese with opium, or gambling, Chinese people as vicious, violent, comic or backward, in subservient or menial roles – no laundrymen or servants allowed – or if films otherwise denigrated them or China. This left little out, for it was a fairly comprehensive summary of the variety of ways in which the Chinese and China were represented on screen. It left no margin either for satire of such themes: censorship does not recognize irony. The censors moved from requiring passages deemed offensive to be cut out, to simply banning offending films in their entirety. This regime also encompassed the French concession and International Settlement, despite the Guomindang having no authority there: cinemas and distributors voluntarily opted in on economic grounds. Censorship also encompassed other subjects: radical politics, sex, 'superstition' (which did for *Ben Hur*) and 'strange' (or grotesque) topics. The foreign administrations themselves, as was the practice across the colonial world, policed the representation of foreign women in film. In 1936 and 1937 some thirty Hollywood films were banned, roughly one in ten of those likely to be shown. The industry's own codes made some of these problematic anyway: nobody was happy – audiences and studio aside – when Mae West announced that she was an 'Occidental woman with an Oriental taste for love' in *Klondike Annie* (1936) where her character had a Chinese boyfriend. In 1933, Chinese diplomats campaigned against Frank Capra's *The Bitter Tea of General Yen* through the State Department, and through its consulates in colonial Southeast Asia, leading the film's studio, Columbia, to issue an apology and securing the addition of a prologue. This described the film as a 'literary fancy' depicting the 'sentimental conflicts of two civilizations': it was not pretending to 'depict actual conditions in China'.[62] As Hollywood was doing increasingly well out of its steadily growing Chinese market, it had to respond. China disciplined Paramount Films in 1936 over *Klondike Annie* and *The General Died at Dawn*. Facing a total ban on the import of its movies – thirty-five of which had been shown in China in 1935 – the studio's head undertook that 'nothing will be incorporated in any picture which we may produce in future which will in any way affect adversely the sensibilities of the people of your country and of its government'.[63]

Economic and political pressure was the first strand in this pugnacious new strategy. The second was headquartered from Suite 551, 1151 South Broadway in Los Angeles. This was the local office of the Consulate of China established in late 1932, with Hollywood in mind. Individual films could be cut, or banned; the products of entire studios could be threatened. But there was also a concerted effort to deal with the problem at its root. If studios wanted a smooth passage through the censorship process, or if they wanted to shoot in China, they found themselves required to engage with it. Film-makers, like theatrical producers, had long striven for Chinese authenticity – at least outside the Fu Manchu genre. Even D. W. Griffith had hired a Chinese technical advisor to help with costumes and settings on *Broken Blossoms*. Now it was made clear to the studios that if film-makers wished to shoot in China, they would need official assistance, and that would not be forthcoming if scripts gave offence. So a twenty-three-year-old Chinese diplomat who had never been to America before, Yi Seng Kiang (Jiang Yisheng), was appointed Vice Consul with a motion-picture remit. Film-industry trade papers of the 1930s provide glimpses of his work. They note Kiang dropping by the studios to advertise his presence and to advise Harold Lloyd, for example – who clearly had not learned his lesson – that Cantonese was not spoken in Sichuan, the setting for a new film – *Cat's Paw* – with a Chinese theme; and giving interviews about the problem of film representations about China. (*Cat's Paw* was banned anyway.) The script of 'China Roars' had been 'approved' by Kiang, the trade press reported. Kiang 'okays Chinatown script for *Shadow of Chinatown*' (a Bela Lugosi vehicle); he filed legal complaints through an attorney about the use of the epithet 'chink'; and he took on radio stations for playing 'Minnie the Moocher' and 'Lime House Blues' ('In Limehouse/Where yellow chinkies love to play').[64] This was like building a dam, mid-torrent, but Kiang's remit was widely known, and the studios clearly engaged with him.

The National Government next turned Hollywood film-maker. MGM, aware of intellectual and popular criticisms of Pearl Buck's novel, proactively sought discussions with Kiang, and through him the Foreign Ministry, to try to secure support and co-operation in the making of a film of *The Good Earth*. Buck's genius – which won her one of the more controversial Nobel prizes for literature – was to have convinced its readers that the book was utterly authentic. Its treatment of sex was too gritty to be filmed unrevised under Hollywood's Hays Code, but the producer Irving Thalberg aimed to make the film as realistic as possible. After extensive diplomatic negotiations, the National Government set out its stance:

1. The film should present a truthful and pleasant picture of China and her people.
2. The Chinese government can appoint its representative to supervise the picture in its making.
3. MGM should accept as much as possible of the Chinese supervisor's suggestions.
4. If the Chinese government decides to add a preface to the picture, MGM undertakes to do accordingly.
5. All shots taken by MGM staff in China must be passed by the Chinese censor for their export.
6. The Chinese government hopes that the cast in the picture will all be Chinese.

With caveats, MGM formally signed an agreement to accede to these demands in March 1934. The negotiations were conducted through American diplomats in China, and on the Chinese side ultimately with Chen Lifu, a senior and powerful figure in the Guomindang, and a leading supporter of Chiang Kai-shek. Never before had a Hollywood studio formally made such a commitment with a foreign government.[65]

Few films of the time were more keenly watched in their making because of the political sensitivities involved. Two envoys were sent from China – at MGM's expense – to supervise the film's development. Kiang had already had a role in vetting the script even before the concordat. A former member of the National Film Censorship Council, Major General Ting-hsiu Tu (Du Tingxiu), arrived in California in 1934 to keep a closer eye on things, and on the way, in an echo of Lao She's *Er Ma*, he and Kiang took control of the business of supplying extras from the Chinese communities in California. Theodore (or 'Teddy') Tu, as he was known, was a jovial character who had spent five years studying in the United States, arriving in

1920 with a large cohort of students on the same scheme that had despatched Lin Yutang a year earlier. Tu was a baritone, and he studied music and education at Lawrence, Northwestern and finally Columbia universities, along the way performing at the American Academy of Music in Philadelphia and Boston Symphony Hall. Returning to China in 1925, he taught 'Christian General' Feng Yuxiang's troops to sing, and then played a leading role in the new National Conservatory of Music established at Shanghai in 1928, and very much a project of Cai Yuanpei's. Tu went on to compose the tune of the official anthem of China's Boy Scouts, help organize the landmark 1931 National Games at Nanjing, provide the official English translation of the National Government's National Anthem, serve as YMCA Secretary in Nanjing, and issue a string of recordings of hymns and Chinese folk songs.[66] None of this prepared the 'Caruso of the East' – as he was often named – for Hollywood, but it indicates the extent to which the project to police China's image overseas was also intertwined with the National Government's drive to remould its citizenry through music and physical education, youth organizations and education. These had come together in the militaristic 1934 'New Life Movement', which had a hybrid character, recasting selected elements of Protestant Christian practice and combining them with 'traditional' Chinese culture. Tu's army rank was a courtesy one, but strong currents in Guomindang thought were aimed at militarizing society entirely.

Tu did not prove a reliable technical advisor, as Paramount found out: he advised on the making of *The General Died at Dawn*. Others dropped by the making of *The Good Earth*, including Hu Shi – who was in California for the IPR's biennial meeting – and Lin Yutang.[67] MGM provided preview screenings for Kiang, and the Chinese Embassy in Washington, and for Lin, who cabled his approval to the Chinese authorities.[68] Hu Shi thought the film banal and melodramatic, but overall the response, if not gushing, was resignedly positive. It could have been worse, and would have been, without the intervention. Quite whether foreign audiences noticed any change was a moot point, although P. G. Wodehouse, whose father had been a senior colonial official in Hong Kong, and who was one of a team of reviewers hired by MGM to comment on the first night, was positive – as befitted his salary – even though, he announced, he had 'never been a pushover for Chinamen'.[69]

In the end the leads were all played by Caucasian actors, but otherwise the 1934 agreement held. No preface was demanded, but diplomacy being the better part of valour, MGM provided one anyway:

> The soul of a great nation is expressed in the life of its humblest people. In this simple story of a Chinese farmer may be found something of the soul of China – its humility, its courage, its deep heritage from the past and its vast promise for the future.

After only minor cuts the film passed smoothly through the censors. MGM got its film shown, and crucially, the rest of its productions were safe in the China market – where its business was as extensive as Paramount's. Vice Consul Kiang planted a Chinese beech tree outside the cinema where the movie had premiered, with a plaque commemorating the event. But the greater legacy was the intervention by the National Government, which had managed significantly to shape a film that had been seen by an estimated 23 million Americans by 1955, and by another 20 million viewers across a further 183 territories. Government officers were embedded in the creation of a movie that was estimated by researchers in 1958 to have more significantly shaped American attitudes towards China and the Chinese than any other single work of art had ever done.[70]

The culture war mattered. The denigration of China and of Chinese culture, and the denial of that culture's worth, was pervasive in the 1920s. It was deeply rooted in European and American culture, and increasingly so in Japan as well, even though there it was connected through thick webs of historical and cultural affinities.[71] China provided antithesis: archaic versus modern; banal versus sublime; inferior versus superior. Politically reactionary China experts 'ten thousand' at a time – in Lin's words – lambasted the country in the press internationally, and on the airwaves.[72] The sustained effort by the Nationalist state and by individual cultural entrepreneurs to present different visions of China overseas was part of the wider cultural reformation of the country that also took place at home. Hu Shi and Lin Yutang were no less critical of their own country and people, but they were theirs to critique. The place of China in foreign minds was absolutely intertwined with the colonial power in China that persisted into the 1930s, and was now advancing from Manchuko in the north as Japanese penetration intensified. Rooting out colonialism involved challenging its cultural and intellectual foundations. Burlington House and Main Street movie theatres alike were front lines in that contest.

Fu Manchu never stopped stalking the screen; racist portrayals in film of Chinese, or others, would persist for decades to come; the 'picturesqueness' of China retained its hold on European and American imaginations. But it would turn out to matter enormously nonetheless that between 1919 and 1937 foreign attitudes towards China and Chinese culture underwent what became a dramatic shift away from the negative and instinctively hostile towards a more sympathetic consensus. When the full-scale Japanese invasion unfolded after July 1937, public opinion globally was mostly sympathetic to China. The Japanese played catch up, with increasing difficulty. The new image of Chinese and China that evolved certainly had its own problems. The impact of MGM's *The Good Earth* was to construct a new image of hard-working, noble Chinese farmers, aspirant Americans in many ways, and people who could be helped. There was nothing in the movie to suggest that the hero, Wang Lung, had problems that had any significant political context, or real-world solution. The Chinese writers translated in *Living China* had different ideas, and as filming wrapped up in Los Angeles the book's editor, Edgar Snow, arrived in Yan'an, the headquarters of the resurgent Chinese Communist Party, to conduct the interviews published the following year in *Red Star over China*, a book that would broadcast an alternative China to the world.

The National Government's diplomatic offensive was important in setting this process of change in motion, as China's struggle to be recognized as having a status that needed respecting moved from its bilateral negotiations with individual treaty powers, and then into the League and other international organizations. But the Japanese assault in 1931-2 also brought to China a new cohort of journalists. The 'war in disguise' that followed and the rural insurgency of the Communists, who were driven out of the cities by 1932, meant that there was always news from China that needed reporting.[73] The cultural about-turn was crucial also, and the sustained and unprecedented programme of cultural diplomacy undertaken by the Nationalists was key to this change. The National Government formally negotiated with MGM, and with the Royal Academy of Arts; it funded Lin Yutang's sallies in *The China Critic*, and indirectly midwifed his career as the English-speaking world's favourite Chinese writer. It despatched a cultural apparatchik to Hollywood; and policed foreign film imports.

Of course, this new image of China, of noble peasants, of a people who were 'wise', 'spiritual', deeply cultured and artistic, adept with brush and ink, and infused with a love of connoisseurship, was as much a caricature in its way and as unrepresentative as any other. It was clearly of immense political help, as truce after truce with the Japanese in north China broke down, and as the Japanese Army spread its zone of influence and concern. But it was politically conservative, if not reactionary, and it was also hardly chic, jazzy or modern, or *modeng* as they had it in Shanghai. At the Burlington House exhibition, Chinese culture stopped at 1800, but in the studios, ateliers, coffee shops and nightclubs of China's roaring cities, culture was being remade faster than ever before in the country's history, with never a Ming vase or a painting to be seen.

It was against a background of these positive modern developments that a disaster unfolded in the north and then around and across the city of Shanghai.[74] On the evening of 7 July 1937, Chinese and Japanese troops based around the small village of Wanping, southwest of Beijing, exchanged shots. Otherwise obscure, the village neighboured an internationally famous twelfth-century architectural gem, the 900-foot-long Lugou Bridge, garlanded with 500 stone lions, and known in English, because it was the one thought to have been mentioned in Marco Polo's book – as the Marco Polo Bridge. The encounter was unplanned and accidental, and the local commanders moved after four days of escalating action to secure a ceasefire. This sort of misunderstanding had happened before. It was a continuing danger in a front-line region now thickly pocketed with troops under different commands, and owing different allegiances. But both Chiang Kai-shek and the government of the new Japanese Prime

Minister, Prince Konoye Fumimaro, decided that the time had come to seize control of events. Each side feared the intentions of the other; each feared that the other would in the future, soon, be aiming to confront them anyway. Discussions in each camp took place in a febrile atmosphere of public hunger for a once-and-for-all resolution of the issue: the 'China problem', the Japanese problem. Within two weeks China and Japan were at war. One cruel but helpful conse-quence of China's drive to assert its integrity, identity and value as a culture and a civilization recognized and accepted internationally, was that the harrowing eight-year conflict that now unfolded was indelibly linked to the name of Wanping's bridge, site of the Marco Polo Bridge Incident.

6

Monkeys Riding Greyhounds

The writer got to the point swiftly:

> Dancing friends: some of you can dance the foxtrot, others the waltz. Why don't you go up to the front to kill? Some of you spend lavishly on brandy and whiskey. Why don't you give the money to our troops so that they can buy more munitions to kill the enemy?
>
> Dancing friends: why spend your money for cosmetics when your bodies smell the odour of a conquered people? The only way to remove that smell is to give our warm blood to the nation. You have been amusing yourselves over the Lunar New Year. Our meagre gift tonight – bombs – will help to give you added pleasure.
>
> Dancing friends: if you like them, we shall meet each other in the ballroom.[1]

It was the evening of 1 March 1939. The first bomb exploded against a window of the Oriental Hotel on Shanghai's Nanjing Road at 9.25. A little over an hour later a second was thrown into the forecourt of Ciro's palatial nightclub on Bubbling Well Road, and two more exploded outside the Cathay and Paradise clubs, and in front of the entrance to the Great Eastern Ball Room on Nanjing Road. It was an act of theatre – the devices loud rather than lethal, for they consisted of firecrackers packed into cigarette tins – and it came with this sweet commentary to Shanghai's 'dancing friends' on mimeographed leaflets that were thrown into the streets of the International Settlement.

The performers were a self-styled 'Blood and Soul Traitors Extermination Corps', a moniker that had been used at various times in the decade by anti-Japanese hit squads. A vicious, fascist-inspired network of Chiang Kai-shek loyalists now operated within the Guomindang state, and in the summer of 1938 it had sent armed units into embattled Shanghai, which the Japanese invasion had otherwise now left isolated, to remind people where their loyalties ought to lie. The leaflet elaborated on this:

> The country is on the verge of being eliminated; you are now but slaves living in this 'isolated island'. Are you dreaming, do you believe that the country can be saved by dancing or do you imagine that you have won the final victory and are celebrating the same by dancing?[2]

The treason these units policed was threefold. There was actual collaboration with the Japanese; there was a more widespread apparent passivity in the face of conquest and lack of commitment to the armed resistance to the invasion; and then there was a subtle treason of the soul, that 'odour' of Westernized modernity. The foxtrot and the waltz had once been acts of social and cultural revolution for educated urbanites, the types who flocked to Guangzhou in the mid-1920s and played at revolution: the country might indeed be 'saved by dancing', and by being in all ways modern and Western. That was part of their thinking back then. Now these steps were seen by some as acts of treachery.

The Japanese invasion was in its twentieth month.[3] The reach of the attackers stretched over six hundred miles inland along the Yangzi River. Chiang Kai-shek's gamble on war had gone hideously awry. He had chosen to confront the Japanese at Shanghai in August 1937, but the three-month battle that ensued saw his forces lose nearly 200,000 men, including 30,000 officers. Facing strong resistance in the city, the Japanese had simply landed large new forces north and south of Shanghai, and forced the battered Chinese to retreat. They left a city whose northern suburbs lay in ruins. The capital, Nanjing, had fallen in December 1937, and a temporary capital at Wuhan was seized in October 1938. The National Government was now based at Chongqing in Sichuan province. Japanese forces controlled Hebei, Shanxi and Shandong provinces, as well as Jiangsu and Anhui in central China. By March 1939 the front line was deep in Henan and Hubei. In the south the enemy had just taken the city of Guangzhou. Despite some victories, the defenders had been rolled back away from the coast and any easy communication with the sea. The conflict had already cost hundreds of thousands of casualties, caused extensive destruction of cities and towns, and across the scarred countryside. At least half a million country people had died when the Nationalist forces attempted to stem the Japanese advance by breaching the Yellow River dykes. They had been given no warning. At Nanjing in December 1937 tens of thousands of Chinese soldiers and civilians were murdered as Japanese troops were allowed by their commanders to despoil the captured Nationalist capital, which had been abandoned by its defenders.[4]

How, then, could the dancers dance, and how could the bombers bomb? Answering this question highlights the peculiarities of China's bitter war. Whilst it faced its gravest existential crisis ever, and just as Wang Jingwei, one of its great political leaders, defected to the enemy and started to form a Japanese-sponsored government – China still harboured within it the fruit of its historically multiply fractured sovereignty, ten foreign-controlled settlements, concessions and leased territories. These were symbols of its degraded sovereignty, but they also now became hugely valuable wartime assets, gaping holes in Japan's zone of control from which war could still be waged – both the war of words for international public and political support, and a war of assassination and bombing against collaborators. And the issue of the status of Shanghai dragged British and American diplomats back to the China problem again and again, as the Japanese also contested their own control of the International Settlement there. But it kept China visible, too, in ways that the struggle inland failed to do, even though the Nationalists initially exercised very little censorship on the foreign press, aiming that way to get their story told sympathetically. The destruction around Shanghai and then the events at Nanjing had shocked the world – W. H. Auden slipped the traumatized Chinese capital into a list of places whose names had suddenly become redolent of evil – but shocks like these passed and were soon forgotten.[5] Surmounting such indifference was vital for the Guomindang: the National Government needed to be clearly of the world of the West if it wanted to survive, and wanted to be so, but its ambivalence about that Westernization and its manifestations – the music, those dancers, their clothes, their odour – was so great as to be almost unresolvable. It fought for the West's attention, and fought against the West at the same time as it fought the Japanese.

The intertwined problems of the war and of the West that beset China in the 1930s and 1940s were most clearly seen on the streets and in the darkened dance halls of Shanghai. The city became a front line in multiple conflicts – over different forms of modernity, between competing and warring political regimes, and between imperialism and its opponents. Shanghai seemed to stand outside the Sino-Japanese War, because of its internationalized status, but also because of its raucous urban culture. 'Blood and Soul' or 'Blood and Iron' zealots hated Shanghai (but lived it to the full, off duty), and the Chinese Communists, driven out of it by 1933, deeply distrusted it, thinking it a collaborator city.[6] Its fragmented administration, and the British, American, French and Italian troops quartered there, provided havens from conflict. But as in-between zones, where no single sovereignty was effectively exercised, and there was no single set of laws, the French concession and International Settlement were sites of opportunity, where authority was always playing catch-up, if it was not itself complicit in whatever was the profitable speculation of the moment. Shanghai had never been more globally prominent than it was in these decades in the period before the Japanese invasion, as China had never been so globally prominent either. Globe-trotting tourists dropped in – liners on world cruises had started calling at Shanghai from the mid-1920s – roving reporters and special correspondents, itinerant entertainers, playwrights, novelists and poets swung by. There were around 60,000 foreign residents by 1935. It was more American than it had ever been, more Japanese, and more European. It remained still utterly Chinese, and in that it was eclectic, polyglot and utterly problematic.

The anomalous position of Shanghai after the onset of the Japanese invasion in July 1937 prompted a new wave of studious analyses of the 'Shanghai problem'. Chiang Kai-shek deliberately took on Japanese forces locally in a bid to fight in open sight of the Western powers there, and not hidden away in the north, where the fighting had erupted. Residents in the foreign areas had climbed to their roofs once again to watch the battles. The war could get no closer than it did, devastating the northern suburbs, and bringing death and destruction into the heart of the International Settlement: one Chinese bomb fell into Nanjing Road on 14 August 1937. The street was packed with refugees and hundreds were killed on the doorsteps of Sir Victor Sassoon's Cathay Hotel. Even though parts of the city resembled one of Bruegel the Elder's grimmest scenes of butchery and death, the war left it behind after three months. Chiang's forces – his best, German-trained – were crushed in the battle around Shanghai, and driven inexorably westwards.

Left behind, housing hundreds of thousands of refugees, were the French concession and the International Settlement, as well as other settlements and concessions in Tianjin, Xiamen and later Wuhan, all similarly isolated. The war years actually brought an economic boom to the city, and a population increase of almost a million. The Shanghai anomaly meant that Chinese government organs remained in operation in the settlement; Chinese and Japanese still sat on the Shanghai Municipal Council (SMC), and worked side by side in the Municipal Police Force and the Chinese Maritime Customs. Pro-Nanjing newspapers and magazines rolled off the presses. Although the Japanese military detached the northern part of the settlement from SMC control, they avoided a head-on confrontation with the Americans and the British, and did not seize the settlement. The multi-national condominium of foreign interests persisted for another six years after 1937. The boundaries, institutions and rhetoric of the International Settlement were, at least nominally, preserved and perpetuated, even as the Japanese and their collaborators violently contested control over areas outside the formal boundaries of the settlement where the SMC had long exercised authority.[7]

Researchers at the Institute of Pacific Relations and the Royal Institute of International Affairs got to work, believing, as ever, that objective analysis could help provide a template for a solution.[8] Hope sprang ever eternal in the academic heart: their reports were extensively documented, rigorously argued, and delivered compelling conclusions. But they were wholly redundant. Soldiers did not stop to read them; those aiming to revise definitively the imperial status quo in China were not going to linger long to look over the arguments of foreign think tanks and professors. The League of Nations was, of course, now entirely irrelevant. Meanwhile, Shanghai's leading foreign interests blithely assumed, as they had so many times before – because war was part of the routine in Shanghai – that they could secure agreement for recognition of the city as a neutral zone, somehow situated outside the unfolding conflict.

Unreal as such analyses were, it is important to understand two deeply embedded ideas that partly informed their work: the didactic example provided by Western-style governance in Shanghai, and its internationalized, 'cosmopolitan' character. Both linger still in memoir and myth about the history of the International Settlement. At the heart of the rhetorical defence of the status quo at Shanghai had been the idea of its being a 'model settlement': the SMC was in this view a model of administrative modernity and municipal efficiency, guided by the disinterested public service of its leading public figures who sat on the council and its committees, and underpinned by the rule of law. It was a beacon for China. It would teach the Chinese how a 'modern' city should be run. This conceit set a standard to which the opponents of imperialism actually worked as they fashioned new administrative structures in the city. Whilst Nationalist diplomats assailed their counterparts over the 'unequal treaties', and sought the surrender of extraterritoriality and other foreign privileges, a Special Municipality of Greater Shanghai and a modern police force had been established in 1927 to both administer the parts of the city in Chinese hands and to prepare for retrocession. The municipality was to do this by directly contesting foreign power, but also by exemplifying model administrative practice themselves.[9] The most important physical manifestation of this drive was the construction of a new civic centre at Jiangwan, northwest of the city's core, set out on an American-style grid of roads surrounding a cruciform-shaped centre, with a substantial municipal headquarters overlooking the public square at its heart in which was to be built a tall pagoda. Around it were arrayed a museum, stadium and hospital, and an auditorium. This was functional – a new centre for a city full to bursting – and heavily symbolic of the aspirations of the Guomindang's republic.[10] It all looked so grand and impressive on paper, but it was to be another of history's lost city futures. The municipal building was one of the few that had been finished by 1937: so the Japanese took to staging victory parades past its wrecked facade, demonstrating what they thought of those dreams of Chinese nationhood.

The lack of Chinese sovereignty under the treaties made Shanghai, in particular, a regional and then a global hub for refugees. It had always been a refugee city: flight from civil war had been crucial to its real-estate development since the 1850s. During the First World War, Germans and Austrians from hostile states and cities across Asia had made it their home; after the war, Korean and Indian nationalists had holed up there. Russians came in great numbers, some directly from the collapse of the anti-Bolshevik regime in Siberia, others from the Chinese Eastern Railway zone, and from Harbin. A new wave of German and Austrian Jewish refugees started arriving after *Kristallnacht* in November 1938 and the intensification of anti-Semitic policies and laws in Nazi Germany: over 15,000 of these new refugees eventually made it to Shanghai, further straining resources in a city struggling to manage an influx of almost a million Chinese residents after mid-1937, as well as Japanese civilians moving from the war zones.[11] In August 1939 the International Settlement and French concession introduced the first-ever restrictions on landing at Shanghai: up to this point it had remained an open city. The Great Depression had pushed many Americans to seek work there; increasing political repression in Japan saw large numbers of leftists and liberals seek out the greater freedoms that could be found in Shanghai, even after the onset of the Pacific War.

This mix of peoples was such that by the 1930s an extraordinarily diverse culture had developed. Viennese bakeries operated side by side with Japanese restaurants, Italian and American cafés. There were newspapers in French, Japanese, Russian, German and English – the last aimed at general or specific British, American, Chinese or Anglo-Jewish readerships. There were eight 'national' companies in the Shanghai Volunteer Corps (nine, if the Shanghai Scottish are counted). The Municipal Council funded an orchestra with an Italian conductor, and Russian, German, Hungarian, Filipino, Portuguese, Chinese and Italian musicians. Couture à la mode, fresh from France, was to be found on Avenue Joffre; there was a British publishing house, and a Russian opera company and choir. And as one flippant handbook reminded its readers, 'There are also some Chinese in Shanghai.'[12] There were twenty-one foreign consulates in 1935, eleven national chambers of commerce, and one government in exile (and there were activists for others hiding out there). This multi-national mix had its echoes in other Asian port cities, but never on the scale attained in Shanghai. The guidebooks were smug about it, and many histories have been mesmerized by it.

An authentically cosmopolitan culture was certainly created by those who came off the ships and trains at Shanghai. It was also proclaimed by fiat. The International Settlement's administration was bumptious enough to have its own flag, which at one period flew tall from a flagstaff on the Bund, proclaiming ownership. At its centre was the municipal seal, created in 1868, which incorporated the flags of a dozen nations and the Latin motto 'Omnia Juncta in Uno' ('all together in one'). Nothing better illustrated the power of the cosmo-politan ideal that was rehearsed in the press, in descriptions of the settlement in guidebook and memoir. But in addition, nothing better symbolized its political contingency either: the German and Habs-burg Empire flags had been replaced after 1917 by blank spaces, and there was never a trace on it of China, excepting the council's Chinese name. And Latin did not mean much on the banks of the Huangpu.

These two ideas were intertwined. Here in Shanghai was a model united nations showcasing exemplary, cosmopolitan co-operation. Similar rhetoric was used about the internationally staffed Chinese Maritime Customs Service. The cosmopolitan ideal was appealing to new arrivals, not least the Russians and those fleeing anti-Semitic violence in Europe. While the idea was also drawn on by the Chinese who overwhelmingly populated the International Settlement, this cos-mopolitan ideal was in practice a politically exclusive one. At its heart was an idea that might best be described as Anglo-cosmopolitanism: a tolerance of multi-national collaboration in an enterprise as long as it was shaped by British power. The SMC's official language was Eng-lish; its senior staff were British; British councillors held sway; British social and cultural mores largely dominated the life of the settlement. The multi-national Shanghai Volunteer Corps was led by an officer seconded from the British Army, and it was supplied with arms and ammunition from British Hong Kong. It was, Edgar Snow cynically remarked in 1930, a 'poorly disguised British colony'.[13]

The 'model settlement' idea was also powerful, and reinforced by every example of Chinese maladministration that the defenders of foreign power could find – and they kept themselves always busy finding more. But like the cosmopolitan idea it was also little more than empty rhetoric – *you ming wu shi* – as the British diplomats still liked to joke: all name, no substance. The Shanghai 'problem' so beloved of scholars and analysis was simply that it was systemically corrupt. Whilst trading remained the fundamental function of the city, opium and land had been the prime generators of much of its wealth and their symbiotic relationship was captured in the Chinese slang term for the drug: *tu*, meaning 'mud'. Opium was recycled into land and property investments: 'mud' turned mud, both were hugely profitable. But the settlement had also been a vehicle through which different forms of financial speculation could be undertaken with little effective legal oversight. Fraudulent practices associated with the 1909–10 boom in rubber stocks involved, amongst others, the council's British chairman. He could not be prosecuted, for there was no chance, British diplomats admitted, of finding enough men who had no connection to the business to form a jury. And the British Supreme Court in Shanghai only required a jury of five.[14] The termination of the legal opium trade from India galvanized one long-serving municipal councillor – Edward Isaac Ezra – to continue the traffic in 'Indian imports' (as his obituary euphemistically put them) by illegal means instead.[15]

A fairly tightly interconnected cabal of landed interests held extensive influence within the International Settlement. New wheezes caught on fast. In 1927 a number of city residents, including two municipal councillors and one of the most senior members of the Municipal Police, had formed a company to introduce mechanized greyhound racing into the International Settlement, quickly followed by two more companies, one of them in the French concession. Dressed up as a sport, this was simply a gambling vehicle – an 'animated roulette board' in Winston Churchill's pithy phrase (which might really apply to the city at large) – and a hugely profitable one at that.[16] Council members fought a three-year campaign to protect the stadiums when the Chinese authorities, and then British diplomats, moved against them, citing all those high moral principles about defending extraterritoriality, whilst Chinese customers handed over their dollars and the companies took a 20 per cent cut. Tens of thousands of tickets were bought every racing night. Eventually, the settlement's American chief administrator fought back against this powerful clique using similar rhetoric. 'The Chinese are sparing no pains or effort,' he had told councillors in October 1930:

> to make a case against the Council the object of which is to show in general that instead of administering a 'Model Settlement' as it was once called, all sorts of abuses take place under the privileges of extra-territoriality which would not take place under a purely Chinese administration.[17]

This hit where it hurt, and was backed up with impressive detail: for there was nothing exemplary about the crime rate in the International Settlement, which was greater than in the surrounding territories. This was, if a model of anything, a model of structurally flawed governance.

There was a deeper problem yet. Into every Shanghai Municipal Police station flowed monthly payoffs from 'local businesses' – gangsters – allotted by rank from station head down to the lowliest Chinese constable.[18] But this was insignificant compared to the structural corruption of the French concession. From 1918 to 1925 the head of the Chinese detective branch in the French concession police had been a leading local mobster, Huang Jinrong, and between 1925 and 1932 the authorities secretly permitted the Shanghai Green Gang to operate an opium monopoly and develop extensive gambling interests. In fact they subcontracted policing to the gangsters. Police Chief Étienne Fiori told his counterparts in the International Settlement in 1931 that they were 'fools not to do the same' and reach an arrangement with the gangsters whereby 'whilst tolerating their opium and gambling activities – at a price – the French authorities used them for maintaining order in the French area'.[19] The combine had offered the same deal to the International Settlement, which many found tempting in practical terms, and financial ones, but it was politically impossible, even though government opium monopolies operated in formally held British, Dutch and French colonies. (One-fifth of government revenue in British Hong Kong came from taxes on opium sales in the 1920s.)[20] This 'pact with the devil', as the French themselves described it, became so open a scandal that the French Foreign

Ministry finally took action in 1932. An agreement was reached whereby the Green Gang was permitted to continue its monopoly, but from outside the concession, and the French authorities helped transport the combine's opium stocks there.[21] For the leading French officials involved, the price for failing to provide effective protection was fatal: three died mysteriously within a week of each other in March 1932.

Americans were for sale as well. Lawyer Norwood Allman, a former US consular officer, and from 1925 to 1933 Honorary Consul for Mexico, held out against an SMC crackdown on gambling in 1928–9 for as long as he could: for one of the few Mexicans in Shanghai was a leading operator in the roulette business.[22] This did not harm Allman's later career as a respectable and respected municipal councillor. In a different sphere, powerful local American interests had secured the effective connivance of the US legal apparatus in Shanghai for over two decades with what proved to be an extensive but fraudulent financial operation. Frank Jay Raven, a municipal councillor from 1931 to 1934, a model of personal propriety and a pillar of the American community, had created a network of property and finance companies centred around the 'American Oriental Bank' that had been insolvent for three years before its collapse in 1935. It brought down with it three Chinese banks, and severely undermined the financial standing of many US missionary organizations in China, which had lodged funds with Raven's company. 'Shanghai is not alone in producing this kind of criminal adventure', the leading local British newspaper pointed out in the aftermath of the trial. But the 'peculiar conditions prevailing here' should have warranted greater caution. It was 'often referred to as an American Bank', admitted the liquidator, but was in fact just 'a bank established in Shanghai by an American' and not subject to any US banking laws.[23] So there was a loophole large enough to allow Raven to establish a bank protected by extraterritoriality, but outside any US legislation. And to reinforce this Raven and his legal team had effectively silenced or suborned the American legal establishment in China. That was hardly difficult when the court attracted staff like Samuel Titlebaum as US Deputy Marshal, a man who after being found guilty of embezzlement in 1941 was then discovered to have assumed a false identity to secure his job (not least, so as to obscure a prior conviction). Although Title-baum was jailed, his real name remains unknown.[24]

It comes as no surprise to find Shanghai deemed a 'city for sale' by one reporter, in a popular 1940 exposé that was simultaneously published in New York and Shanghai, such was the market locally for works like these (and so swiftly did pirated editions appear there). But the city itself was innocent: colonialism's key weapon in its armoury in China had been extraterritoriality, and it was this that facilitated each one of these scandals. Shanghai's International Settlement and French concession held no monopoly on crime. Morally or criminally corrupt legislators or officials could certainly be found elsewhere. But there was no denying that extraterritoriality and the fragmented administration of the city at once facilitated routine crime, and also provided a vast opportunity for such frauds as those perpetrated by Frank Raven, and the grey areas of sovereignty and authority in which the greyhound racing combine acted. To shut the latter down, finally, the International Settlement authorities had to take the step of barricading the stadium with the police riot squad to prevent anyone entering. This was sheer farce: one part of the foreign administrative machine taking action to suppress the activities of another, but it was embedded at the heart of the political culture of the International Settlement. The net result, of course, was a boom for the *Canidrome*, the greyhound stadium over in the French concession.

But if extraterritoriality made governing China effectively more difficult – for these problems were played out across the country in one form or another where extraterritoriality reached – it also made resisting Japan easier. The same processes that allowed any citizen of a treaty power to rent out their nationality to Chinese interests made it easy for pro-Nationalist newspapers to place themselves nominally under American or British ownership after 1937 (ten of them by 1940). This in turn enabled National Government agencies to continue to operate in the settlement, and anti-Japanese agents to travel on foreign-owned shipping lines among the treaty ports. Unoccupied Shanghai became for a while a major source of manufactured goods for Chiang Kai-shek's embattled China, an intelligence hub and a finance centre. For all its stark polarities, the Sino-Japanese War was in many ways an odd one. The front lines were often porous – goods and people easily crossed them – and there was a continuum of loyalties along which were placed the non-Guomindang allies of Chiang Kai-shek, and collaborators with the Japanese such as Wang Jingwei. Wang had split from Chiang, convinced that only a negotiated peace could save China, and in 1940 established a rival 'Reformed National Government' in Nanjing. It was not a black-and-white war.[25] And in the heart of occupied east China, foreign journalists were able to counter the propaganda efforts of the Japanese simply by reporting the facts as they found them, or in some cases actively waging a spirited campaign against the Japanese.[26] For the Nationalists, embattled in heavily bombed Chongqing a thousand miles west along the Yangzi, Shanghai was a vital gateway onto the world outside the war.

The Guomindang's campaign to abolish extraterritoriality and secure the return of the concessions had been on hold since the Japanese invasion of Manchuria. There was no apparent end in sight to foreign control in Shanghai, and the other islands of ruptured sovereignty in Tianjin, Hankou and Xiamen, let alone colonial Hong Kong and Taiwan. So, alongside the extraordinary pressures of coping with the war on its doorstep, the Municipal Council and French administration got on with the business of administering their territories. In 1938 its annual report shows that the SMC burnished its social and industrial welfare credentials by engaging with the International Labour Organization in Geneva, opened new premises for its public library, relocated old cemeteries, launched traffic-safety campaigns in its schools, and experimented with Shanghai's first roundabout. Its annual ratepayers' meeting devoted most of its time to discussing the future of its municipal orchestra, a motion to abolish it being overwhelmingly defeated.[27] So this was Shanghai business as usual. And so it went without saying that as the city continued to manufacture and to trade, to play its roles in the resistance against Japan, or in the simple business of keeping the Chinese economy alive, it continued to play as hard as it worked.

The targets of the terrorists in March 1939 were dance halls and nightclubs, for China's war years were also China's dancing years. Shanghai danced as the bombs fell, and danced even as grenades were thrown into the dance halls, restaurants and hotels. Shanghai's people danced as the core of the city became a 'lone island' (*gudao*) after 1937, surrounded by Japanese forces, but still, precariously, neutral territory under foreign control. They danced after the bombing of Pearl Harbor on 7 December 1941, when the Japanese finally marched in and raised the Rising Sun flag from the high-rise buildings that Shanghai movies used to symbolize the city's modernity. From that day in December they danced – many with different partners now – until August 1945 when the city reverted to National Government control. These were years of cocktails, modern music, modern style and modern bodies. China was never more cosmopolitan, more hectic, or more violated and damaged.

The Chinese dance craze had begun as the Nationalists assumed power in 1927–8.[28] Establishments aimed solely at Europeans long pre-dated this, but from this point on new clubs and halls started to be opened by Chinese owners, aimed at a rapidly growing Chinese dancing market. When Swedish-American bandleader 'Whitey' Smith arrived in the city in 1922, he claimed that the 'Chinese hadn't learned to dance western style yet'.[29] By the time he left in 1937 they could not be stopped. Faster and cheaper cross-Pacific shipping connections brought goods, ideas and people more swiftly from the United States (and more swiftly from there than from Europe). Dance halls had mushroomed in American cities during and after the war, and the impact overseas was swift. 'Cargoes of Jazz are laden on all vessels passing through the Golden Gate,' announced a young American journalist, Burnett Hershey, in 1922, and 'Shanghai without jazz,' he ventured, 'would not be Shanghai.'[30] Music travelled on song sheets, on gramophone recordings, with musicians and in the tastes of a dancing public. New dance steps travelled with them too, and with stage dancers who showcased new styles. Back to China too had come the cohorts of students who had sailed overseas to study. They returned with their degree certificates, and their lessons from the school of life lived abroad: changed outlooks, clothes, hairstyles and habits, and a taste for jazz and dancing.

Nothing undermined British cultural dominance more comprehensively and swiftly than Shanghai's jazz world. Treaty-port foreigners had formerly danced in hotel ballrooms, but in the 1920s and 1930s dedicated dance halls and clubs were added to a fast-evolving nightlife scene. Those that attracted the attention of the vigilantes in

March 1939 included the Great Eastern Ball Room, located in the Wing On Department Store, which had been built at the height of the Chinese dance-hall boom in 1928. This was a populist venture, aimed at students and urbanites, and the Great Eastern became famous for the star dance hostesses it retained. Its neon sign, topped with an image of a ball-gowned woman and her tuxedo-wearing dancing partner, hung over the Nanjing Road. Taking up the fifth floor of the Sun Company Department Store, the Paradise Ball Room, another target, was an elaborately and elegantly laid-out taxi dance hall, which provided sixty dance hostesses whom patrons bought turns with by ticket. By contrast, Ciro's was a lavishly designed dedicated nightclub, which had opened in 1936 and was aimed at the Chinese and foreign elites. The art deco building with its neon-lit tower was part of Sir Victor Sassoon's portfolio of Shanghai property investments, and a counterpart to his Bund-side Cathay Hotel.

These were sites in which the sexes mixed in public, which was still daring in Chinese society, and they were representative of the complexity of the multi-national environment of the city. The Great Eastern was popular with Japanese customers as much as Chinese ones; its owners were Chinese-Australians. African-American, Filipino, Russian and Japanese musicians could be found playing in the clubs, and were later joined by refugee Jewish Germans. In 1934 the first all-Chinese band started performing at a ballroom opened under gangster patronage in a newly built Chinese-owned hotel.[31] Cabarets and taxi dance halls employed Russian hostesses, who became the subject of a hugely popular vein of salacious foreign reportage. 'Half-naked, poured into their evening frocks,' wrote the journalist Henry Champly: 'To the strains of the universal jazz they revolved in the arms of Yellows in long robes or in national uniform.'[32] Chinese commentators paid equal attention to the subject. Exposed in print, this world was hardly hidden physically: the clubs were all of them lit – the Paradise employed its own neon light designer – and were in this and many other ways bright shining beacons of hedonistic modernity. So they were also sources of acute anxiety, to European racists like Champly, and to Chinese social commentators and educationalists, as much as to the patriots who threatened them.

The Canidrome Ballroom exemplifies the complex interplay of

politics and culture, technology, modernity and crime that marked Shanghai's 1930s. The Champ de Courses Français, as it was formally known, was the chief beneficiary of the crackdown on greyhound racing in the International Settlement. Elaborately constructed on a large site in the French concession, on a former property of the owners of the *North China Daily News*, it opened in late 1928. It consisted of a stadium that could hold 20,000 spectators, the racetrack, sports fields, and an art deco hotel with a ballroom overlooking the blindingly lit course. Races were dizzyingly short, but deliriously popular, and the company's returns from the bets placed on them were huge. The French concession authorities took a cut of the revenue, but through an arm's-length party, for it was against French law for government agencies to benefit directly from gambling.[33] Shanghai Green Gang interests were known to be involved in the business, working through French proxies on the board of directors. Each and every Chinese spectator was breaking the law, under which it was an offence even to be present when gambling was taking place – but still the dogs ran. Entrance to the stadium cost half a dollar, not an impossible figure for even many of the urban labour force, but upstairs the ballroom was a more exclusive site.

When African-American Buck Clayton gave his first performance on 13 April 1934 with his 'Harlem Gentlemen', Madame Chiang Kai-shek and her sister Soong Ailing – whose husband was Finance Minister H. H. Kung (Kong Xiangxi) – were in the audience. The dance floor alone was bigger than any American club he had ever played in: it was like being 'in a different world', Clayton recalled. As part of its bid to get the crowds back in after the battle for Shanghai, the management introduced a grill room with a 'teletrack' display – 'a step towards television', it boasted – that allowed diners to keep up with the progress of the races without leaving their tables.[34] A different novelty tactic involved hiring an animal trainer and his troupe of monkeys. The monkeys were tied to the dogs and rode them as jockeys, complete with blouse, jodhpurs and cap. 'The whole show was a riot,' boasted the race manager.[35] This was a perfect mix: jazz and art deco, gangsters and the political elite, technologically up-to-the-minute mechanized gambling and uncouth stunts, all under the umbrella of French colonial power. Small wonder that Shanghai attracted sensationalist reportage, novelists and film-makers looking for inspiration. They got it. There was no need to make anything up: Shanghai itself always outdid any imaginary counterpart.

The Good Earth's hearty chaperone, Theodore Tu, and his earnest official brand of physical and spiritual national renewal – the YMCA, the Scout movement, his Victor Company recordings of 'What a Friend We Have in Jesus' – were outflanked. 'Go to bed early,' urged the New Life Movement's comprehensive instructions for its new model citizens: be punctual, queue properly, do not gamble or visit prostitutes, salute your elders, be polite, wear your hats straight and shoes properly, breathe fresh air, do not get drunk, do not litter or smoke, do not call out loudly in teahouses or theatres, on boats or in buses, be frugal. But such injunctions were mocked by the urban crowd, and Tu's patriotic songs, belted out by youth choirs in the besieged west, could not be heard in Shanghai, which buzzed instead to any number of American jazz recordings, or the increasingly popular 'Yellow music' – Shanghai pop songs – pressed onto disk at EMI's local plant, broadcast on the new radio stations that mushroomed in the 1930s, and that accompanied Shanghai's prodigious movie output. Militarizing a society that dances was tricky. Until the bombs flew, politics struggled to be heard, and when the bombs stopped, the music began again.[36]

There had been continuing attempts to rein this urban culture back in before the war. Films were censored, radio and print were policed, and the patriotic and moral guardians of the nation shouted themselves hoarse. In late 1934, as part of the wider New Life Movement, students at some of Shanghai's universities formed teams to track down their classmates and teachers who were patronizing the city's dance halls.[37] But tinkering with a movie or banning a song made little difference. Shanghai was already too confident in its worldliness and lackadaisical about its failings. Social satire of the time joked knowingly about the dilemmas faced by men about town in Shanghai who were faced with so much choice. Cartoonist Xiao Jianqing's 1936 volume *Manhua Shanghai* (*Shanghai in Cartoons*) takes the reader through the city of plenty: flesh for purchase in the dance halls, cabarets, or bathhouses, or through guide agencies or on the streets, or simply on view in stage shows, or in the *modeng* outfits of the female university students.[38] Launched in 1934, and heralding a wave of imitators, a deliriously colourful new graphic magazine, *Modern Sketch* (*Shidai manhua*), gave the New Life Movement cadres and Blood and Soul corps much to fulminate about.[39] Over its three years of publication the monthly tossed together sex and politics, social satire and hard-edged criticism, silliness and eroticism. Its artists were inspired by the work of George Grosz, John Heartfield and James Thurber, amongst many others, including Mexican and Japanese cartoonists. The magazine was as utterly eclectic as the city, and utterly modern. One article introduced and explained 'modern speech', including the words 'Tango', 'Jazz', 'Waltz', 'Charleston' and 'Foxtrot', as well as 'coffee', 'curry', 'toast', 'Agfa', 'Kodak' and – never forgetting – 'imperialism'.[40]

It is impossible to tease apart sex and politics in *Modern Sketch*. Both stand out dramatically. Although there were some women artists, the female body as imagined by men was relentlessly on show, as it was – eroticized to greater or lesser extent – across the visual culture of China's 1930s.[41] The women on display were naked, transparently or barely dressed, showed off modern swimwear, pleasured themselves for the reader, or were simply reduced to their breasts alone. The 'woman question' had been placed at the heart of Nationalist discourse by influential writers like Lu Xun, but this public spectacle, masquerading as modern liberation, could hardly have been foreseen. Across China's visual culture more widely, beer, cigarettes and whiskey, Coca-Cola and kerosene were advertised through images of women in swimsuits and in *qipao* (cheongsams), all smiles, allure, short sleeves, short hair and visible legs. *Modern Sketch* intersected with China's booming film industry, and the world of its stars – Ruan Lingyu, 'Butterfly Wu' (Hu Die) – and movie magazines. Cabarets, nightclubs and dancing were splashed across its pages.

The politics of *Modern Sketch* were sometimes safely generic – pillorying archetypes such as the complacent bourgeois, the corrupt bureaucrat. These were targets nobody could object to; but the magazine could also hit more dangerous ones. In 1936 it was banned for six months for attacking China's ambassador to Japan, and the Japanese were increasingly an object of attention. Their country could not be named – it was always 'XX Country' – for the National Government had played a holding game through the mid-1930s, endeavouring not to provoke its enemy until it was strong enough to. Meanwhile Chiang Kai-shek's forces had launched a series of campaigns aimed at destroying the communist insurgency in central China, excising what he termed in 1933 the 'disease of the heart', before he turned to the 'disease of the skin' that was Japan.[42] Dropped in among the social and cultural skits in the final issue of *Modern Sketch* in June 1937 was a cartoon of an 'XX Country' battleship, bristling with guns, dragging the angel of peace across the lawless Pacific.

There was a third element to Chiang Kai-shek's equation, a disease of the soul we might name it: the Westernized culture on display in the rambunctious pages of *Modern Sketch* or on the dance floors of Shanghai, a culture protected by the armed power of the treaty nations, and the fine detail of those treaties. Most people never danced, of course, or read *Modern Sketch*, or could even read – though they could listen to the radios that could be found in four out of ten households in the city. Many had cash to spare to get into the Canidrome to watch the dogs, but vast numbers did not. Theirs was the Shanghai story as well: urban destitution, squatter villages on the settlement edges and refugee camps. A mass influx of a million people into the International Settlement and French concession took place swiftly after July 1937, and they did not leave. They needed feeding and they needed work. Their bodies needed collecting from the streets. The politics of managing this crisis consumed the energies of the foreign authorities in the city.[43] They were at least in this sphere allowed to get on with the job.

Although National Government 'special service' units disciplined their citizens with bomb, gun and knife, they did not attack the authorities in the International Settlement. The Guomindang's rhetorical opposition to imperialism and the 'unequal treaties' remained, but active contestation of foreign privilege remained on hold. That nationalistic language was instead stolen by the Japanese, and especially by their collaborators and proxies, who attacked 'Anglo-American hegemony'. It was the Japanese who directly confronted and challenged the status quo in the International Settlement. Between 1937 and December 1941 an unequal struggle played itself out in the foreign-administered heart of the city. This had three facets. First, the Japanese military worked to force the SMC and French concession authorities to suppress Chinese nationalist and patriotic activity: they aimed to gag radio, cinema and the press, and clamp down on any manifestation of support for the National Government. National day, and the roster of public 'memorial days' commemorating such 'national humiliations' as the Twenty-One Demands, or the start of the Manchurian Crisis, were obvious targets. As the rearguard insurgency unfolded, the Japanese succeeded in suborning the foreign security apparatus to their own ends. Secondly, as Japan remained a treaty power – for war against China was never declared – with representation on the SMC and personnel in all its branches, Japanese diplomats lobbied for greater and proportionate representation of their interests within the International Settlement. Thirdly, with much less effort, they allowed the British, French and Americans to shoulder the burden of running China's most populous city, bloated further with refugees, at this time of acute crisis. They secured all the benefits of conquest, with far less of the cost. It was occupation on the cheap, the British and Americans serving as their proxies in the business of governing the conquered. On the whole, the sympathies of most foreign non-belligerents came swiftly to lie wholly with the Chinese, but expediency and *force majeure* created unhappy de facto collaborations.

The projection of Japanese military power into the International Settlement began almost straight away. On 3 December 1937, General Iwane Matsui, who had led the Japanese forces during the battle for Shanghai, oversaw a 6,000-strong victory parade along the Nanjing Road to the Bund through the heart of the settlement. The route had long been the site of such military theatre: the British and Americans, and the Shanghai Volunteer Corps, regularly paraded along it – the 'Kaiser' had done so in 1918, so the Japanese intention was doubly symbolic. Despite precautions, a small stay-behind unit of Chinese fighters managed to bomb the parade.[44] Three days later, in just one of many such incidents, Japanese forces openly operating within the settlement – in contravention of long-standing agreements – seized four Chinese suspects from a hotel and took them into their zone of control. As the Chinese insurgency started to grow, Japanese pressure on the International Settlement to co-operate in security matters grew accordingly. The SMC issued regulations prohibiting the broadcast or publishing of anti-Japanese propaganda, and restricting the raising of the Chinese national flag to only a few days a year. However, despite such actions and extensive surveillance it could not prevent attacks that increased in tempo and ferocity to astonishing levels as undercover units bombed and shot the enemy and their associates. In response to Japanese demands the council finally agreed in February 1939 that the Municipal Police would actively collaborate with Japanese police organs. They conducted joint raids, and the settlement authorities handed over arrested suspects to the Japanese. The council pleaded with Chongqing through British diplomats, asking Chiang Kai-shek directly to order his men to assassinate collaborators outside and not inside the settlement, so as not to destabilize it terminally and provoke a Japanese takeover.[45] There was no let-up. In February 1941 the SMC established a Western Shanghai Area Special Police to be run jointly with the puppet Special Municipality of Greater Shanghai. Britons and other staff from the Municipal Police found themselves working for the collaborators and their Japanese puppet masters.

At the same time, the SMC found the gentlemanly agreement that had for decades underpinned the sharing of control over the council itself under stress. The British had always held the largest number of seats on the council, although no longer an absolute majority, but the apparent cosmopolitanism of council membership – five Chinese, two Japanese, two American and five British members – obscured the fact that Britons still held the majority of jobs in the council administration, and within the police force. Now there were sustained pressures to open up senior positions to Japanese, to which the SMC was forced to accede. Moreover, the property-based electoral franchise was structured in favour of the British, whose voting numbers were enhanced by the larger landholdings of British firms in the settlement. Sheer weight of numbers alone of nationals resident in the settlement would favour the Japanese in elections. But an established tradition required electors to cast votes to ensure the accepted balance of nationalities on the council. The Japanese put forward two candidates only, and British voters headed their lists with these so that they would be returned. In 1939 this started to unravel, as the

Japanese Residents' Association (JRA) – which organized Japanese votes – began a campaign for a more representative council.

Few things appear in the historical record of foreign power in Shanghai that are more absurd than the battle of the ballots that followed. Ahead of the 1940 council election, Japanese firms nominally parcelled up their larger properties into smaller units that would each have a vote once they were formally registered at the consulate. The Japanese electorate doubled in size as a result. As war broke out in Europe, British diplomats in China responded in kind to the Japanese challenge at Shanghai, and worked to facilitate a proportionate British response. As a result the 1940 election results did not change the balance of control, but in the aftermath this vote-splitting accelerated wildly. By February 1941 there were ten times as many British votes as there had been in 1939 – and there were fewer Britons actually living in Shanghai. To give them credit, British diplomats and their allies knew how to rig an election.[46] Such was the bitterness engendered that Hayashi Yukichi, seventy-year-old chairman of the JRA, shot the council's chairman, the Briton W. J. Keswick, at the annual ratepayers' meeting in January 1941. Keswick survived, but the council did not. To avoid an explosion of fury, the American and British consuls hastily reached an agreement with Japanese diplomats, suspended the electoral process, and appointed a new provisional council to run the settlement.

At the same time as its authority was challenged and its administration was under pressure, the SMC found itself hoist by the petard of its own right to govern. As well as policing for the Japanese, it still found itself bearing the brunt of the continuing costs of the aftermath of their war locally. The one million refugees had to be helped. While many lodged with friends and family, another 140,000 were in scores of refugee camps, a quarter of a million sheltered precariously in a 'safety zone' organized by a French Jesuit priest that abutted the concession, and some 75,000 lived on the streets.[47] As the city's economy started to right itself, and as hundreds of new small workshops were started up, most refugees no longer remained a direct charge on charities or the authorities, but indirectly their well-being became the responsibility of the foreign administrations. The city needed feeding, homes needed fuel, and public health needed protecting. Rents spiralled. The SMC became actively involved in procuring food supplies, and attempting to regulate prices, and its resources were stretched to the limit. Economic fragility manifested itself in labour relations, prompting strikes, and the Japanese and their proxies worked behind the scenes to exert additional pressure on the British and Americans from this direction as well, by fomenting labour unrest in foreign-owned factories. This effort and long-term financial ineptitude meant that the SMC was effectively bankrupt by 1939, and was forced to go cap in hand to the British government to try to secure a loan.

Money was tight all round. The exchange rate depreciated, cut into foreign earnings and raised prices. The Institute of Pacific Relations reported that speculators threw 'vast sums' in and out of commodities, the stock exchange, gold and property. 'Millions of dollars nightly' crossed gambling tables.[48] These were casino years. The French concession funded much of its social-welfare activity through the Canidrome revenues. The International Settlement had always raised a good proportion of its revenues from licences and now instituted a temporary voluntary entertainment tax. The Shanghai Race Club regularly contributed a share of its earnings from betting to the council directly or to good charitable causes. The puppet administration and various intelligence and policing agencies established after 1937 took this to the limit. Like the gangsters that many of them were, or became, they funded themselves from casinos. The western districts of the city, outside the settlement and concession, had long been within their orbit as zones that the foreign administrations had earmarked for expansion. They had built roads and other infrastructure, collected taxes from houses built along the lanes and streets that became popular residential areas, and policed them as well, laying down their markers. Now the western districts were re-landscaped as a wild new garden suburb of violent crime, Shanghai's 'badlands'.

The badlands have attracted no end of myth-making, and with good cause: this was Al Capone's Chicago, but without the restraint. Casinos and nightclubs flourished, catering for the dancing, chancing city, brothels sprang up, and Japanese-sponsored narcotics gangs found safe havens. Disputes were settled with extreme violence. To an extent, of course, this was simply Shanghai's business as usual. In a zone in which no single authority was ever able to monopolize power, the vacuum was filled by speculators, opportunists and criminals. Shanghai's badlands were simply the product of the routine mechanisms of China's degraded sovereignty stripped to their bare and violent pure essentials. For all its land regulations and fine and fancy rhetoric, model settlement platitudes, and for all the undoubted disinterested effort and dedication of many of its staff, the International Settlement had always been a badland.

But still the appearance of normality was maintained, though it was relentlessly challenged, and there was little that could not be fraught with danger. The collaborationist regime launched a campaign of 'rights recovery', and anti-imperialist propaganda, that was entirely in the rhetorical mainstream of Chinese nationalist politics – which is where Wang Jingwei positioned himself and his collaborationist 'Reformed National Government'. But now anti-imperialism served Japanese interests, and was targeted solely at the British and Americans. Interactions between foreign soldiers and civilians with the Japanese military could often be tense, and there were numerous incidents of violence and disagreement. Soccer was not exempt. On 15 March 1941 the Canidrome stadium hosted the championship final of the local soccer league. The leading Chinese team, Tung Hwa, was playing the SMP's foreign staff eleven. The French referee had cause to send off a Chinese player, and the whole Tung Hwa team walked off in protest. Then the 20,000-strong crowd rioted, invaded the pitch, throwing sticks, stones and bricks, and set light to the stands. The police suspected 'professional agitators', but economic and political tensions would also have fuelled the outburst: 'Swine', 'Dogs', 'Foreign gangsters' yelled the crowd.[49]

From the start of the conflict, Kenneth Bonner, a Canadian colleague of the police soccer team, recorded the savage pace of violence in scrapbooks of news cuttings. The battle for Shanghai seamlessly moves across the pages from the clash of armies to the tit-for-tat terror war, indistinguishable even in its casual violence from the wave of armed crime that unfolded alongside it and often fuelled it. 'Bombs Explode, Bullets Fly as Shanghai Marks First War Anniversary' screams one headline: 'Six Bombs Hurled . . . Three Dead when Police and Gangsters Wage War through Louza District . . . Another Ta Tao Official Slain . . . Salt Tax Chief Riddled . . . Gunmen Shoot Pro-Japanese Chief . . . Bomb Breaks up Wedding Party . . . Bomb

Thrown in Gambling Den . . . Chinese Die after Ballroom Shooting . . . Nanking Foreign Minister Shot'. A year's end round-up was headed 'Unmuzzled Terror Era'.

Unmuzzled: they killed or kidnapped each other's bankers; they killed each other's journalists. They bombed courts, banks and newspaper offices. They shot puppet officials and suspected loyalists; they shot court officers and cabaret stars. The SMP's most senior Japanese and Chinese officers were assassinated, as were lowly constables ('you people work for foreigners as slaves . . . we are heroes to serve the country, to work for heaven and to exterminate you', read a leaflet left at the scene of one murder).[50] Most murders simply spoke for themselves. They killed the head of the Russian Emigrants' Association, and his successor; they killed the chief of the French police's Chinese detective branch, and his successor; as well as the interim director of the French concession, and a leading French lawyer. They attempted to shoot the British chief administrator of the International Settlement, who thereafter rode around Shanghai in the British ambassador's bullet-proof car. Kenneth Bonner snipped out the stories and pasted them in, but nothing could contain the violence. Like the monkeys on the Canidrome greyhounds, the settlement authorities all properly costumed were yoked to dogs of war and terror. The whole show was a riot.

The Japanese seizure of the International Settlement on the morning of 8 December 1941 in some ways came as a blessed relief.[51] The extraordinary thing about the almost two years that then followed was that the International Settlement, its council and its agencies, remained in place, and most of the existing staff as well. Local Japanese interests had no stomach for handing the settlement over to their notional collaborationist allies. In the early hours of 8 December the Japanese announced that they would be coming in, readying the settlement administration and police to receive them. The British and American councillors resigned in January 1942, and were replaced with neutral or Axis nationals. Some British heads of section resigned as well, and senior police officers were 'retired'. It was all perfectly proper and formal. But most stayed on in post, for they had nowhere else to go, and nothing else they could do to earn a living. This suited the Japanese, who had no desire to pay for the subsistence of their enemies. Other

Britons still served on the council's various committees, and the chief administrator, Godfrey Phillips, stayed on in post for three months.[52] Shanghai was no longer a 'lone island' in a sea of Japanese-occupied territory, but Allied nationals were now marooned. The new German and Swiss councillors acted much like their Anglo-American predecessors. They were jealous of municipal sovereignty, and cautious about the budget. They were mindful of symbolism. Departing enemy staff were given fulsome praise and appropriate pensions. The Shanghai Volunteer Corps was disbanded, but with appropriate sensitivity, and its standard was retired with all due ceremonial. English remained the council's official language. Even Japanese staff used it in internal documents, such was the power of culture even in defeat.

Relief proved in much shorter supply in Hong Kong. Since 1937 the city had been changed by the unfolding war as well. Its first taste of the disruption in the north came when 3,500 British women and children began to be evacuated from Shanghai on 16 August 1937, and were shipped down to Hong Kong. Several hundred Americans sailed to the colony as well, or to Manila, and 900 Indians sailed direct to Calcutta on a vessel chartered by the government of India. At Hong Kong those without friends in the colony were billeted in the Happy Valley racecourse stands, where the 'absence of Amahs' was described as having greatly added to the problems facing the refugee Shanghailanders.[53] Their arrival briefly woke up a sleepy backwater. British Hong Kong had long been eclipsed by the galloping growth of Shanghai, and had settled for a quieter life. It remained an important entrepôt, through which 40 million tons of cargo on 20,000 ocean-going ships had flowed in 1936, the last year of peace. But its one million residents – all but some 22,000 of them Chinese – lived in a city that lacked the ragged edge of Shanghai, and which except for those heady years of Sun Yat-sen's government in Guangzhou, and the unsettling 1925–6 strike and boycott, seemed far removed from the turmoil in China. 'It's just the natives fighting,' Vandeleur Grayburn, the Chief Manager of the Hongkong and Shanghai Bank, told Christopher Isherwood and W. H. Auden when they called on him in 1938. While he was probably playing up to the role he knew his Marxisant visitors had already allocated him, Grayburn wrote privately that 'it is ridiculous to call it a war, it is simply a gangster's game'.[54]

As the Japanese advanced into central China, Hong Kong became an important adjunct to the refugee central government that moved first to Wuhan and then to Chongqing. Until the Japanese attacked and occupied Guangzhou and its surrounding regions in October 1938, it remained an important supply route, but even thereafter it was a vital point of contact as China's airlines flew the dangerous route out of the colony over Japanese-occupied territory. Somewhat against its wishes, the British territory soon found itself hosting important official Chinese agencies – thirty-two of them by one count – and these sought to supply and succour the embattled Nationalist Government.[55] Until Japanese pressure forced the British to ban direct shipments, two-thirds of China's munitions supplies were channelled in from the colony. Some of Shanghai's businessmen moved down south as well, and relocated their factories to the security of the British possession. Hong Kong became a centre for film production as Chinese studios relocated their activities to the security of the colony, and it also became the focal point for the Chinese government's propaganda campaign to rally the support from the Chinese diaspora and sympathetic foreign publics. Increasing Japanese pressure and official British conservatism meant that the colonial administration imposed a more stringent censorship that aimed to fend off any Anglo-Japanese confrontation such as had occurred in Tianjin or in Shanghai. As tensions with Japan rose in June 1940, however, the British government had ordered the evacuation of all British women and children, but although 3,500 did leave, many returned, or pulled strings to be able to stay, training as nurses or taking up other occupations deemed to be essential. The evacuation also exposed tensions. By law anybody born in the colony was a British subject, but the order was applied only to those of 'European race'. A number of Eurasians of Anglo-Chinese descent found themselves stranded en route to Australia and recalled to Hong Kong in the belief that its racist immigration rules would prevent their landing.[56] Most refugee traffic came towards Hong Kong, however. Some half a million Chinese had made their way across its loosely watched border by December 1941.

Across that same frontier early on the morning of 8 December 1941 came some 50,000 Japanese troops. The British had very brief notice of the attack and put into action a contingency plan, demolishing bridges and withdrawing to hold what was possibly the worst-named defensive position in military history: the Gin Drinkers' Line. Hong Kong's defenders fought hard, and they fought for longer than the Japanese expected. But they had been cast outside the sphere of British imperial interests that would have been protected years earlier, for after the fall of Guangzhou the colony was effectively surrounded by Japanese possessions. It was also entirely at the mercy of Japanese aircraft, as was demonstrated later on the first day of the fighting, when bombing commenced. The struggle by Hong Kong's defenders was designated a holding action, its defence a matter of honour – and a signal to the Nationalists in Chongqing that the British meant business. Prime Minister Winston Churchill ordered a fight to the last, and the Commander in Chief and his forces held on until Christmas day 1941, but it was a hopeless struggle. A very few managed to break out and escape, most famously a team led by a one-legged Chinese admiral.[57]

The defenders' cruellest critics tarred them all as blimps and Gin Drinkers (even though the defensive line of blockhouses and entrenchments was named for a bay at one end). 'What was the use of calling Hong Kong a fortress,' declaimed one local critic, Leslie Ride, in the heated aftermath of the defeat, 'when many families were still there, when the Club was still open, and when you could ring up your wife just as you could from the office (but with a better excuse for not coming home to dinner).' Ride asserted that 'The Hong Kong Government was rotten to the core. No one would believe that Japan would attack this island of beauty, this Pearl of the Orient, this sanctum of the taipans.'[58] It fell the moment it was attacked, he claimed, not when the British abandoned their defensive line, not when gangsters and collaborators rose up and attacked them in Kowloon, and not when the Japanese landed on the island. Ride was hardly exaggerating. When the Japanese sent three officers over from Kowloon on 13 December to parlay for a surrender, they came with two British women as hostages. One of these was Mavis Lee, the wife of the Governor's private secretary, who had brought along her two dachshunds, Otto and Mitzi. 'I couldn't bear to leave them behind,' she told a reporter as she was served sandwiches brought from the Hong Kong Club.[59]

Vicious recriminations immediately followed the British catastrophe in Asia, with metropolitan critics and reporters alike raging about 'Maginot Mentalities', and Singapore as 'Blimpapore' – a bastion of reaction and incompetence fuelled by whisky soda, pink gin and racism.[60] The battle for Hong Kong exposed the colony's institutionalized bigotry, and the limits of its inclusion within the polity of its British Chinese subjects, or those from other communities – the Portuguese (as they were known, or Macanese), Anglo-Chinese Eurasians, Indians and others. Until Madame Chiang rented a house on the Peak, the only non-European who lived there – servants excepted – was the wealthy Eurasian businessman Robert Hotung, for it was reserved by a 1904 ordinance for 'non-Chinese'. Half of the small island of Cheung Chau was similarly reserved in 1919. It was not a 'racial' issue at all, stated one of the supporters of the decision in the colony's Legislative Council, before he proceeded to justify the move on the grounds of the needs of a particular 'race'. To make matters even worse, the initiative had come at the request of British and American missionaries. No Chinese were admitted to the Hong Kong Race Club, nor were they recruited to the ranks of the Hong Kong administrative service – the elite cadre amongst local officials. And in the year or so prior to the Japanese attack, two scandals had unfolded exposing corruption amongst British officials in the immigration and air-raid precaution departments, and possibly hinting at a wider problem. As people tried to survive the defeat and its aftermath, many of these fissures between the British and their subjects in Hong Kong, and within their communities, came to the fore.

The Japanese attack, and its aftermath, was accompanied by several bloody incidents in which captive defenders, wounded men, nurses and doctors were butchered. Thousands of Chinese civilians died, and thousands of women were raped. Japanese forces systematically looted the colony and struggled amongst themselves for the spoils. Ritual humiliation of the captured British was enacted. Accounts tell of men forced to pull Chinese and Indians in rickshaws, and Britons being paraded around the streets. On 5 January 1942, British subjects were ordered to assemble, and then after first being lodged in some 'filthy little brothels', were moved into a hastily organized internment camp next to the colony's prison at Stanley. Perhaps we might be interned on the Peak, pleaded some. 'Think of it,' wrote one observer, the American journalist Emily Hahn. 'Hong Kong was full of government servants who behaved like kings, sitting as they did on that heap of coolie labour. Remember this. And then, all of a sudden, this!' To help the business of remembering 'this!', the Japanese sponsored the making of a film, variously known in English as 'The Battle of Hong Kong', or 'The Day England Fell'. British prisoners were taken from camp and made to parade around Hong Kong's Statue Square and to re-enact surrendering from positions on the Peak. The camera lingered on their dejected faces, and the caricatured paraphernalia of British imperialism: one man was forced to dress up in riding breeches.[61] The film was screened in Tokyo, and in Shanghai, and in Hong Kong on the first anniversary of the Japanese attack. Mavis Lee and her dogs featured in a postcard circulated by the military press agency.

Aside from the battle at Hong Kong, which cost the lives of 1,700 of its defenders, the Japanese lunge for the remaining British concessions and settlements in China was mostly orderly and peaceful. The only other active Allied resistance occurred briefly at Shanghai, when the commander of the British gunboat HMS *Peterel* was ordered to surrender by a Japanese landing party: 'Get off my bloody ship,' he replied. *Peterel* went down in minutes, honour intact, but seven men at least dead. Ninety miles northwest of Hong Kong, at Guangzhou, the war began for the Customs Commissioner, the American Lester Knox Little, when a refugee German Jewish doctor brought him news of the outbreak of the conflict early on the morning of 8 December. The previous night Little had walked back from a social visit to his home in the British Shamian concession 'through blacked-out streets, a city of the dead'. He was given notice of his dismissal from the now-collaborationist Customs, and along with the rest of the small community of Allied nationals – mostly missionaries or staff from Lingnan College – was then placed under house arrest. It was a pleasantly warm winter. He gardened, practised his piano playing, sunbathed and read. As Little sat 'quietly smoking a pipe on the verandah after lunch,' he noted on the seventeenth, 'it seemed utterly inconceivable that a great battle is going on at Hong Kong'.[62] On New Year's Day 1942 he watched Japanese officials in morning coats and their wives and children in kimonos walking through the streets paying calls. After four months he and other civilians were moved into Shamian's Victoria Hotel and then on to Shanghai, picking up further groups of Allied civilians from Shantou and Xiamen on the way north.

The foreign presence in China underwent a regrouping, and a series of involuntary relocations. The war itself had long driven many foreign nationals into the comparative safety of the concessions. Many missionaries had stayed on in the stations, but some had been forced to leave. Japanese residents had fled from their concession in Wuhan after the onset of the conflict and from other Nationalist-held cities in which they lived. Now Allied nationals were interned or imprisoned, but at a pace that differed across the captured cities. The process of house arrest like Little's, or concentration in a hotel or school, was the pattern across most of the smaller treaty ports, and cities in Manchuria. The defining characteristics of the experience for these groups were discomfort, uncertainty and tedium. Some were able to enact quiet acts of defiance. To mark St George's Day and Shakespeare's birthday in 1942, the cloistered British staff at Yenching University in Beijing invited their American colleagues to join them for one of the oddest of picnics at the home of a sometime Chinese Prime Minister in a disused Buddhist temple. After lunching on sausages – 'a delicacy in these hard times' – they were addressed by the former Beijing newspaper editor William Sheldon Ridge. 'Now all the youth of England are on fire,' Ridge assured them, his *Henry V* to hand, and St George – England – would get his dragon. They sang 'God Save the King' and 'The Star-Spangled Banner', and danced to folk songs.[63] It was all they could do, that and wait.

The rump British community in Beijing would eventually be concentrated in the otherwise underused British Legation compound in the foreign-controlled Legation Quarter. British diplomats had remained attached to the comfort and dignity of their former princely palace in the one-time capital, but in late 1936 they had formally transferred the embassy to Nanjing. Pride and prudence led them to keep the former legation, for where else might they store decades' worth of archives, and perhaps the pendulum might swing again north, and the location of the capital with it. The complex served as a temporary refuge for British residents as the Marco Polo Bridge Incident unfolded in 1937, but the small Legation Guard allowed under the 1901 Boxer Protocol that had established international control of the quarter was withdrawn in August 1940. By December 1941 the legation housed only a small consular staff, but also rented out rooms to some of the Britons remaining in the city. In one of these in the winter of 1942–3 one of the odder literary compositions of the Pacific War was written. *Décadence Mandchoue* was a richly detailed erotic fantasy masquerading as a memoir and was written by Sir Edmund Trelawny Backhouse, long banished from Britain by his respectable Quaker family. It seems a fitting end to the fantastical story of the pro-consular pretensions of the British diplomats who had inhabited the legation and had in their time bullied warlords and hectored Chinese politicians. Sir Edmund was a forger and fraud who nonetheless had established a reputation as a Sinologist, and who now sat in the legation compound and recounted in precise detail his sexual encounters with, amongst many others, Aubrey Beardsley, Lord Rosebury, Paul Verlaine, Oscar Wilde and the Empress Dowager, Cixi. It clearly helped him pass the time, as much as dancing to 'Down among the Dead Men' helped the Yenching staff pass theirs.[64]

As Allied nationals elsewhere across Southeast Asia experienced the full vicious force of Japanese conquest in the aftermath of Pearl Harbor, their peers in Shanghai went to the horse races and off to the dogs, hosted their parties, and shopped for bargains that might be had from the antique dealers of the city as people tried to raise funds. Japanese occupation officials and arriviste puppet administrators went scouring the markets to secure these trappings of status. The collector of Chinese porcelain Sir Percival David, who had been instrumental in organizing the 1935 Burlington House exhibition, had arrived in the city just in time for Pearl Harbor and joined the hunt for bargains.[65] The cinemas stayed open, and the cabarets too, and the bombs continued to fly: the Grantown ballroom was attacked on 7 March 1942. These were days of 'hectic violence', it was later recalled, but the Japanese grip tightened, and was now unrestrained by foreign press coverage or any legal niceties. Some individuals – pro-Nationalist journalists, suspected intelligence operatives – were quickly hauled into Japanese military police custody and were brutally treated, but they were a minority overall. Reports and photographs of the 1942 spring meeting of the Shanghai Race Club would poison the reputation of the Shanghai British on the other side of Asia's battle lines. But, they later said, the Japanese forced us to hold the meet, organized a massive parade to celebrate the fall of Singapore, and interrupted proceedings by marching onto the race-course with a military band and around the tracks. It was 'Allied Annihilation Week', in aid of which 70 per cent of the profits were to go to the Japanese Army, the remainder to be retained by the Race Club. The march done with, the racing and the betting resumed.[66]

For most Allied nationals in Shanghai this anomalous situation lasted for the best part of the next fourteen months. Their memoirs and papers show them living a straitened and insecure but essentially famil-iar life, although successive Japanese regulations limited their access to money, saw many of them turfed out of their jobs, and some their homes, and prohibited their use of private cars: bus and tram travel ('in closer proximity than would normally be the case') was an unfamiliar and humiliating novelty for many. So was housework, shopping for food and cooking. With Red Cross assistance roughly 2,500 people sailed to Portuguese East Africa or India in 1942 and 1943 as part of an exchange of civilians with the Japanese. Many would never return. In October 1942 the 8,000 remaining in Shanghai were ordered to wear armbands denoting their nationality in public, were banned from cinemas, theatres and restaurants, and were subjected to a curfew. Some three hundred men deemed by the Japanese to represent a secur-ity threat were arrested in November 1942 and interned. In February and March 1943 a dozen 'Civilian Assembly Camps' were established in Shanghai, Yangzhou, and in Weixian in Shandong (for north China internees), and all but the very elderly or sick were ordered to move into them, including most of the Yenching University picnickers. The loca-tions chosen were ill-prepared and poorly equipped, but in the main the experience of most internees over the following two and a half years was mostly simply uncomfortable, and tedious, rather than harrowing or dangerous. It also involved a quite surreal re-creation of their life outside in the huts, warehouses and school buildings into which they were moved. And all without a 'very useful' Amah or No. 1 Boy: 'What a business, unroping, unpacking and carrying all our FOUR Beds OURSELVES,' wrote one young British woman in her diary as her family arrived at camp in Yangzhou. But at least she had been able to prepare for camp life with a fresh perm.[67] Allied civilians in China were generally spared the ritual humiliations visited on colonial officials in Hong Kong or in Southeast Asia, where conditions were generally much harsher. And overall the death rate by 1945 was actually reckoned to have been 'below normal for the European population of Shanghai'. The longer-term impact on health is another matter, and another year of war would have seen death scythe through the camps. But when they were first inspected the health of the internees was seen to be 'surprisingly good'.[68] They had also been spared the violence of invasion and trauma of defeat.

Escape was entirely feasible, for anti-Japanese guerrilla units were operating not very far away and could easily be reached, but only a few made their way out. These were generally single men, and they were bored, so off they yomped, making their way to the west. (One of those who did so had been a friend of John Thorburn's, and so he finally got his taste of adventure.)[69] The most vulnerable foreign communities were those that were not interned, either because they had to fend for themselves in an increasingly difficult wartime economic environment, or in the case of Indians because they were additionally the target of specific drives by the Japanese to harness them into the wider war effort. Agents of Subhas Chandra Bose's Indian Independence League and Indian National Army were active amongst the 3,000-strong community in China.[70] In a half-hearted sop to pressure from Nazi agencies in the city, the Japanese authorities in Shanghai also demarcated a 'special area' within the city's Hongqiao district, and on 18 March 1943 ordered Jewish refugees who had arrived since 1937 to relocate into it. Life grew tougher. Many Indians were destitute by the war's end. Most of those in the police were dismissed in 1944–5. Malnutrition and – later in the war – American air raids took Jewish lives in the Ghetto, as it was known. But a diverse range of educational, cultural and religious activities flourished in the adverse conditions of the tiny half-mile-long, three-quarter-mile-wide 'designated area'.

The years of the Pacific War saw the retrocession of nearly all the remaining concessions and settlements, sometimes twice over, for good measure: for the formal treaties abolishing extraterritoriality and these islets of foreign power, signed by the British and Americans in Chongqing on 11 January 1943, had their doubles in Nanjing and in the performance of anti-imperialist nationalism by the stooge administrations that took over the International Settlement and the French concession that summer.[71] Like the British and American diplomats in Chongqing, those administering the International Settlement in Shanghai had no choice in the matter. But the language of cosmopolitanism and of a 'model' of governance was still rehearsed. The council even organized a competition to design a new municipal seal, as the existing one still had no Japanese flag on it.[72]

Cosmopolitan rhetoric was no less vital. Japanese military and intelligence agencies jockeyed to enrich themselves from confiscated enemy assets, as did the puppets. So Japanese commercial interests and diplomats tried to counter this by using the same old language of their former partners in empire even as the old municipal flag was symbolically lowered. In a talk broadcast on radio just after the retrocession, the departing council chairman, Okazaki Katsuo – a career diplomat and former Olympic athlete (and future Japanese Foreign Minister) – pleaded with his Chinese successors to work in consultation with civic and commercial interests of all nationalities. 'It is my firm conviction,' he added, 'that there exists a close and inseparable link between the prosperity of this great city and sound methods of revenue-raising, budget-making, borrowing and public accounting.'[73] Japanese businessmen and diplomats were as loath as any of their British predecessors had been to hand over their apparatus of sound Shanghai governance to the Chinese.

But this was a time for nationalist acts, and speeches – and music too. To mark the retrocession to Chinese control, a 'Greater Shanghai March Song', nominally penned by the collaborationist mayor Chen Gongbo, was performed for the first time at a 'special patriotic concert' by the former municipal orchestra:

> Greater Shanghai! Greater Shanghai!
> Our wealth is ever growing;
> Our civilization is ever progressing.
> Let us rejuvenate China,
> Safeguard East Asia
> And perfect our freedom and independence.

A newspaper article on 1 August 1943 – retrocession day – urged its readers to 'make Shanghai a model municipality', so that 'we may not disappoint our Japanese friends' (whose presence somewhat qualified that 'freedom and independence'). Neither these nor Chen Gongbo's exhortations were much heard. Even under occupation the city's hectic culture vaulted on. From 5 o'clock that same afternoon the Canidrome was to run the first of the day's twelve races. The Weida nightclub was opening, promising a six-piece Hawaiian band and 'Hawaiian atmosphere', 'genuine drinks' and 'charming hostesses'. At Waldemar's Dancing Academy on Avenue Joffre those few yet to dance could rehearse their steps before trying them out on the Weida's taxi dancers. The 1937 French gangster movie *Pépé le Moko* was showing at the Doumer Cinema – for those not weary of vice – and *Opium War* (better known as *Eternity*, or *Wanshou liufang*) was about to open at the Nanking and Majestic, for those not weary of propaganda accounts of Britain's pioneering role in the perfidious trade. Puppet President Wang Jingwei had been given a preview of this Japanese-Chinese production in May. The summer's hit tunes, heard and played even in Chongqing, came from this film, and from its star, the Manchurian-born Japanese singer, known by her Chinese name, Li Xianglan. The vapid nationalism of Chen Gongbo was smothered by the catchy, American-infused jazz-pop of Li's 'Maitang ge' – the 'candy-selling song' – as was the song's own anti-opium message.[74]

The complexities of Shanghai's wartime 'liberation' from 'Anglo-American Shackles', and the triumphant anti-imperialist propaganda that accompanied it, are highlighted by this comprehensive assimilation of Western forms into the theatre of retrocession. *Shenbao*, the leading Shanghai daily, issued an expanded commemorative edition bursting with congratulatory notices from retailers of Western-style clothes (including 'Smart' brand shirts), and pipe tobacco, amongst others. Hollywood gossip was retailed in the *Shanghai Times* (Jackie Coogan was getting divorced, again), even though American films were no longer on the screens. The SMC's informal farewell took the shape of a cocktail reception in the Tower nightclub at Sir Victor Sassoon's – confiscated – Cathay Hotel. Both the 'Greater Shanghai March Song' and the Hawaiian music in the nightclubs were facets of the powerful cultural turn to the West, and principally to America, that urban China had experienced in the 1930s, but which seeped across China through the movement of goods and people along the railways and shipping lines, and through the postal networks and radio waves. So this was a peculiar kind of victory over Anglo-Americanism.

Victory it was, though, and for the National Government too, as its own new treaties terminated the privileges of the British and the Americans. But in Chongqing there was less ceremony and more humiliation. The British military collapse in the face of the Japanese onslaught enraged Chiang Kai-shek and the Nationalist leadership, and comprehensively undermined the British position in their eyes. With the fall of Hong Kong and then of Singapore, the British position in China, which had been functioning on borrowed time since September 1931, fell to pieces.

7

Allies of a Kind

How can you fight a war without typewriters, or paper to type on, or tables on which to put the machines, or chairs to sit at, or even buildings in which to work? How can you fight a war without typists, or the money to pay them even if you had them, or when they would not be able to find housing, or easily find food, or cooking oil, or clothes, or even a toothbrush? This was the conundrum that faced Cecil Henry Bencraft Joly, appointed Officiating Inspector General of the Chinese Maritime Customs in December 1941. It was compounded by the fact that the Customs Service had lost all of its archives, the greater part of its staff and most of its stations. There was little trade to assess, and almost no revenue to collect. It had thereby lost anything remotely resembling a rationale for continuing to function, let alone function under the leadership of a foreign Inspector General. In 1937 the Customs Service had still delivered almost 45 per cent of the revenue of the National Government, and its continued staffing by foreign nationals could be tolerated as a result. By 1941 this had shrunk to a little over 1 per cent.[1] As Joly viewed the situation in late December from chilly, overcast Chongqing, a city still reeling from the shattering effect of over 200 Japanese bombing raids, the prospects for the once high-riding service did not look good.

The seemingly bleak future for the Customs heralded an end to the world of the treaty ports more widely and those who benefited from them. Joly was one of those. His family was embedded in the British China establishment. He had been born in Macao in 1892, when his father had been consul there. Joly's brother and brother-in-law both served in the Customs. His wife had been born in Tianjin, where her father had been a Chinese railways accountant. Joly's sister was married to an American employed by Standard Oil, and his widowed mother had once kept the family afloat by teaching English to the Crown Prince of Korea.[2] This family's interests had for decades depended on the opportunities provided by the treaties. It now fell to Cecil to defend those, and not just for himself, but for over 950 foreign nationals in the Customs, some 12 per cent of its staff.[3]

The post to which Joly had been appointed had been fraught with political symbolism long before an 1898 exchange of notes between the Qing and the British asserted a formal British claim that the Customs Inspector Generalship should be held by one of their nationals. This had been based on the fact that the British held the greater share of China's foreign trade, and expected to do so for decades to come, such was the complacent confidence of what would prove to be their fleeting paramountcy. But since the Japanese seizure of Manchuria in 1931, the more important factor in perpetuating British dominance of Chinese foreign trade had been the pressing need of the Nationalists to protect the republic's international creditworthiness. Continuing foreign leadership of the service was seen as vital to China's ability to raise the loans that were secured on its revenues. Moreover, any opening of the question of the replacement of the British would leave the service vulnerable to an assertion of Japanese claims – for Japan's trade with China had challenged that of Britain's by 1931 – and as more and more ports fell to the invaders, the personal neutrality of the foreign staff, even though they remained Chinese government employees, proved useful in protecting China's interests. At the start of December 1941, Joly had been Commissioner of Customs at Tengyue, in happier times a backwater post close to the Burmese border in Yunnan province. Now he had been summoned to Chongqing, the temporary capital of the republic, to deal with a political disaster.

When the Japanese took over Shanghai's International Settlement they secured complete control of the Inspectorate General of Customs, its staff, archives and equipment. Despite orders to the contrary, this had not been relocated to Chongqing by Sir Frederick Maze, the Inspector General, who had argued that he could do more good for his masters by staying on in Shanghai. More cynical colleagues put his decision down to the city's relative security – nearly 12,000 people had died in the bombing of Chongqing – and his fondness for its comforts ('fleshpots' was the term one of them used). So Maze and the Customs were an easy catch. All Allied nationals in the service were dismissed on 13 December 1941 by order of Wang Jingwei's collaborationist government, which now formally operated from shattered Nanjing.[4] Some Britons were perplexed by this course of events. Owen Gander, for example, a Marine Assistant in Shanghai with twenty-seven years' service, could not understand why 'the position of foreigners in the service should have been affected by the political situation'.[5] This divorce from the reality of the position of the treaty ports was quite a common one in the early weeks of the Pacific War. Decades of sitting out revolutions and petty warlord conflicts had bred an assumption that the Customs was an entirely disinterested bureaucratic agency, which would be allowed to continue to function whatever the nature and outcome of any conflict. Maze himself advised the Chinese and neutral staff that staying on in post – which over one hundred of the latter did throughout the war – was likely to be in the Chongqing government's long-term best interests, and assured them that his replacement, Kishimoto Hirokichi, was 'eminently fitted for the difficult task for which he has been selected'.[6] Kishimoto, who as Chief Secretary was the highest-ranking Japanese in the Customs Service, was actually quite popular with Chinese employees, as he had long stood up for their interests. The options for those serving in the occupied areas were circumscribed anyway. While escape to free China was relatively straightforward, men could hardly trek west through a war zone with their families in tow. Recognizing this, the National Government ordered only senior staff to leave their posts and report for duty in Chongqing by the end of 1943. In this war a certain degree of accommodation with the enemy was frequently thought the most rational course.

There began what became a peculiar bifurcation of the history of the Customs Service, which continued under Kishimoto to exhibit all the characteristics of its historic self. It retained most of the staff, nearly all the stations, and all the records of the service. Kishimoto's organization also had the typewriters. Moreover, Sir Robert Hart – who was Maze's uncle, the Customs being rich in such family ties – remained a focal point for service legitimacy and his 1860s directives continued to shape its ethos. But increasingly, like Joly's makeshift legitimate Inspectorate in Chongqing, Kishimoto's service had no foreign trade to assess, and so also lacked an underlying rationale for its continuing existence. The Japanese triumph in the Customs, so long lobbied for, proved a hollow one.

Cecil Joly was overwhelmed by the task he faced on his arrival in Chongqing, and found himself outmanoeuvred by National Government interests that had long set their sights on undermining foreign domination of the Customs Service, and which were energized by outrage at the collapse of the British in the face of Japanese attacks after Pearl Harbor. As Hong Kong and Singapore fell in late 1941 and early 1942 respectively, so did any residual prestige that their colonizers retained. As his diplomats barely had credibility to spare with which to aid him and thought that it 'would do more harm than good' to do so, Joly's main ally in his negotiations for resources came to be Arthur Young, a Californian who had been financial advisor to the Bank of China since 1929.[7] The British ambassador in Chongqing, Sir Horace Seymour, was sanguine about the prospect of treaty revision as momentum grew for its renunciation in 1942. It would be 'of little practical importance to British trade with China at the present time', he noted wryly.[8] There were only eleven different companies still extant in Chongqing and Kunming. Half of them had no business, and stocks held by the remainder were fast running down. One firm was run by a Cypriot. Swires had only a single steamer, Jardines had a silk buyer working for the Ministry of Supply, and the Hongkong and Shanghai Bank office was somewhere in transit from Fuzhou. The Chinese courts had started to act as if there was no extraterritoriality anyway. The centenary in August 1942 of the signing of the Treaty of Nanjing was marked in Chongqing with editorials demanding its abrogation. And the Guomindang and nationalists in China generally remained resolutely anti-imperialist. There were certainly posters to be found depicting Chiang Kai-shek and Winston Churchill side by side as allies in the struggle against fascism, but one diplomat's visit to Lanzhou was marred when he came across large propaganda murals depicting the Opium War, the May Thirtieth Massacre in Shanghai, and foreign troops entering Beijing after the Boxer uprising in 1900, the British and Japanese flags flying together.[9] This shift in power from the beleaguered British to the Americans presaged a more general passing of the imperial baton. The fall of the

Philippines did not dent American prestige in China to the same extent: but the United States had long evaded, where the British had long trumpeted, the label of empire.

Sir Frederick Maze managed to scrape his way out of Shanghai on one of the repatriation vessels, and travelled as quickly as he could from Portuguese East Africa to report back for duty. But he was given a chilly reception in Chongqing, and was quickly paid off. Maze came to 'rob the till and run away', muttered his colleagues.[10] In March 1943 the Dartmouth College graduate Lester Knox Little was offered the post in his stead. Cecil Joly had by then 'fled aghast'.[11] The formal British claim on the Inspector General appointment was one of many items abandoned, almost incidentally, in an exchange of notes added to the landmark treaty signed at Chongqing on 11 January that year, abolishing extraterritoriality and all the remaining settlements and concessions. The United States signed a similar agreement on the same day, but its economic and military power meant that those Nationalist interests which oversaw the Customs Service saw virtue in prolonging its foreign-led character for a while yet. Little, who had been repatriated from China on one of the exchange ships, arrived in Chongqing in August. 'War news good,' he noted on arrival. 'Outlook for Customs very dark.' His first task was 'provision of living wages for staff'. 'All is lost,' his colleagues told him, 'even honor.'[12]

Chongqing was a steeply mountainous city of 'crowded, narrow, dirty, stinking streets'.[13] It perched high above and astride steep sandstone slopes overlooking the confluence of the Jialing River to its north, with the Yangzi on its southern boundary. The city had barely registered as a treaty port for decades after it was formally opened in 1891, except as the objective of the pioneering efforts over ten years of British trader Archibald Little to effect the first steamship voyage to the city through the Yangzi Gorges and rapids.[14] Aside from that saga, which had been entered in the little pantheon of British achievements in China by its publicists, Chongqing was famous mostly for its foul weather and worse streets. Its thickly crowded lanes, 'thousand noises' and stench quite 'baffled' Somerset Maugham, who visited it in 1921.[15] In 1931 there were twenty-four foreign firms in the city, and a survey in 1936 found 138 foreign nationals, mostly missionaries and the largest portion of them Americans. The Japanese had established a concession, but like many such it had never been developed. This was one of the remoter outposts of the treaty system: living there required 'strong nerve, and self-control', thought one Briton visiting from comfortable Shanghai in 1931. It was a place where the arrival of 'a new brand of whisky is an event that will be talked about for days'. But the isolation of life in China even for those living on the Upper Yangzi was being eroded by technology: in May 1937, Chongqing's British residents were able to listen live through shortwave radio broadcasts to the coronation of King George VI.[16]

Longings for communion with the wider world of British patriotism grew easier to assuage, and that early physical isolation began rapidly to be eroded too. Cargo junks were entirely superseded by steamships after 1924, a year after the first year-round steamer service commenced between Chongqing and Yichang downriver. From October 1931 there were scheduled flights to Shanghai via Wuhan, cutting the journey time from two weeks to two days. Reports from Chongqing in the mid-1930s convey a sense of its belated embrace of the municipal progress that had been a feature of city life across China in the 1920s, as it shut down opium dens, built roads (and controlled their traffic), constructed a water plant, and imported street lamps from Britain in an ambitious bid to 'rival Shanghai's brilliance'. But while the foreign shipping companies started to run Yangzi River cruises, it still took three months in 1936 to ship the equipment for a second power plant from Shanghai. And pockets of darkness certainly remained despite the new lights, not least an easy popular belief in rumours that rapidly spread in the spring of 1937 that foreigners were killing foundlings and eating them.[17]

As Chiang Kai-shek's forces chased the retreating Red Army into Sichuan when it beat its retreat from the Jiangxi Soviet after October 1934, the province's local power-holders found themselves subject to the attentions and pressure of the Nanjing authorities for the first time. This was unwelcome, for Sichuan's militarists preferred a long-distance patriotism. They had largely enjoyed a profitable autonomy since the 1911 revolution, although it cannot be said that Sichuan's people shared its benefits. The militarists had also successfully challenged foreign interests, gaining a major share of the shipping business on the Upper Yangzi from foreign companies. Part of Cecil Joly's challenge in 1941 had been that the Chongqing office had itself long been suborned by the city's power-holder, General Liu Xiang, whose own shipping line had grown used to ignoring the Customs Service.[18] Foreign staff had not been stationed there since 1926. Establishing the authority of the service proved an uphill struggle even after the government focused attention on Chongqing.

This murky, muddy city was an unlikely site for a capital, but its physical isolation had determined this choice. So first the nation and then the world came to Chongqing. On 20 November 1937 the National Government announced that the city would become its headquarters, and government officials and their families headed upriver on heavily overcrowded steamers, followed by foreign diplomats on their gunboats. An orderly withdrawal in the face of the Japanese advance turned into a flood, especially when Wuhan was captured in October 1938, and Chongqing's peacetime population of half a million grew rapidly and in time at least doubled in size. But because of the great rivers the city was already the most densely populated urban environment in China, bloated in recent years with refugees from Sichuan's politically unstable countryside and a terrible famine in early 1937. So many steamers initially came up the river that there was no chance of finding a mooring, and once ashore there was little accommodation or food to be had.

The government had moved its ministries and military command, and then the rest of the country had followed it, and not just its people alone. It relocated its arsenals, and many other factories came too. Nearly 200,000 tons of arsenal equipment alone was shipped west between 1937 and 1940. In 1939, the American journalist Randall Gould found that Shanghai's Mei Ya silk-weaving factory had shipped equipment upriver and started production again; so, too, had a Henan cotton mill (complete with its relocated power plant). Barefoot workers were installing in crude, makeshift buildings electric furnaces and steel foundries transported from downriver – for there were no construction materials to be had. The newly assembled Hua Lien Iron and Steel works was already producing machine guns. National Central University had been reconstructed in just six weeks after its staff had evacuated Nanjing. They had even shipped upriver its experimental livestock herds, bringing their cows to Chongqing. The city's buses had been driven from Nanjing. Twelve thousand crates of the National Palace Museum's collection were moved by ship and a forty-nine-day drive by a convoy of trucks.[19] The Chinese-owned English-language newspaper the *Hankow Herald* somehow got its equipment west and published a 'Chungking Edition'.

The war came too, of course, and it came by air. At noon on a clear May day in 1939, Japanese bombers dropped their loads into Chongqing's crowded streets, and next day nearly forty more flying leisurely in formation made a second raid on the still-burning city. There had been almost no preparation despite earlier attacks on the airfield, and some 5,000 people died in the inferno that gutted a long, wide swathe of the old city. In the aftermath, dazed and now homeless survivors camped out on Chongqing's streets, while 200,000 others fled the burning city. Four-fifths of its core was destroyed; bodies of Sichuanese and outsiders alike floated downriver. Despite being identified by large painted flags, foreign diplomatic buildings were also hit by Japanese bombs, and the victims included Chinese who had broken in and sought the shelter they thought the neutrality of the compounds offered. The destruction of newspaper offices and the radio station in the government's Central News Agency offices seemed to threaten to smother news of the atrocity, but the city was now crowded with foreign journalists and photographers, and their story electrified world opinion. 'The most frightful example of bombing of a big city in the history of modern war,' remarked *Life*, and it was a city 'far older than Rome' and an outpost of a civilization under siege.[20] Images of piles of charred corpses, and of whole blocks of the city laid waste – 'a monstrous twisted dump' – appalled even readers starting to grow inured to reports of aerial bombardment from the Spanish Civil War.[21]

Chongqing dispersed, dug deep and rebuilt. The city spread out further west and across the river as residents, businesses and government offices moved out of the battered core. Air-raid shelters were excavated from the rock on which the battered city tenaciously sat, but the pulverized centre also offered an opportunity for reconstruction. Buildings soon sprang up that were 'larger and fancier' than any before, and were designed in a 'modern international style'. Mostly these were lath-and-plaster constructions, for the shortage of building material continued, although others were built with recycled bricks from the ruins. As a result Chongqing looked like a huge theatre set, one observer thought. The city once routinely dismissed as 'medieval' in its layout now reflected the cosmopolitan population it housed. Cinemas, cabarets, ice-cream parlours and even a roller-skating rink opened up. Three orchestras were established and before his death in 1939, Theodore Tu organized mass patriotic-song concerts. Some of the National Palace Museum treasures were put on temporary exhibition, and displays of Chinese art and photography were held. Two cinema studios managed to produce films. The refugee rich from Burma came with their cars, and in one case, an American observer reported, evening clothes and a pet leopard. For most refugees, however, the consumer delights offered by the advertisements that plastered the walls were impossibly out of reach.[22]

When the writer Lin Yutang later visited Chongqing, he found silver and silk shops from Shanghai, medicine shops from Beijing, makeshift offices of the great newspapers of Shanghai and Hong Kong, Beijing's famous Dasanyuan Cantonese restaurant, and the Guanshengyuan eatery from Shanghai's Nanjing Road. For those with money there were Shanghainese pastry shops, Fuzhou shredded meat and Yunnan ham on offer. The Commercial Press, and Chung Hwa, Kaiming and World Book publishers had all set up shop. 'In a word,' he concluded, 'you find all the different cities telescoped into Chungking.'[23] In these crowded streets the new world of the Nationalists, their coastal, cosmopolitan China, met a Chinese heartland, the 'Da houfang': the Great Interior. 'Down-river people' – the incomers – encountered the wary Sichuanese. The challenges presented by the babble of dialects and languages that ensued were solved as people whose tongues were mutually unintelligible communicated in writing, or even in English.

Chongqing became China's major window on the wider world for the rump republic of the National Government as the war developed. Lin Yutang found that its scores of bookshops were jammed with readers too poor to buy, who stood and read all day.[24] Pirated translations of Ernest Hemingway or John Steinbeck were nonetheless printed to feed a hunger for foreign literature from an audience now cut off from its former libraries and bookstores. But supplies were limited and the selections quite random. To his chagrin, Lin noted that one of his own recent books was wholly unknown in the city. After the fall of Hong Kong in late 1941 and Burma in May 1942, Chongqing's sole supply lifeline was American air transport over the Himalayas, a landmark logistics operation that delivered hundreds of thousands of tons of supplies, and moved thousands of people, at a cost of 600 planes and 2,000 lives. In such circumstances there could be no prioritizing of books.[25] One American cultural programme nonetheless designed new lightweight microfilm readers, and then sent them to China along with sets of specifically filmed collections of scientific works, as well as important Chinese classics held in safe-keeping at the Library of Congress.[26] Chongqing's contrasts and absurdities also needed the caustic attention of a monthly like Shang-hai's *Modern Sketch*, but supply shortages meant that there were no illustrated magazines at all, barring one published by the US Office of War Information. Copies of *Life* magazine were 'regarded as a treasure'. Instead, Chongqing's people lived out a hothouse simulacrum of modern China's urban life against the backdrop of its lath-and-plaster buildings.

But even if it did not bring books, Chongqing's air corridor brought witnesses and reporters first from Hong Kong, and then, after Pearl Harbor, from over the 'Hump'. 'Almost everyone who writes an article' gets sent there, remarked Emily Hahn. Martha Gellhorn arrived in April 1941 to report for *Collier's*, her new husband, Ernest Hemingway, tagging grumpily along. ('China,' he announced privately, was a 'shit filled country'.) The photographer Margaret Bourke-White came with her husband, playwright Erskine Caldwell. Many such brief visitors got a 'quick airport-warphanage-dugout-hospital-Madame-airport' tour, as Graham Peck put it (Madame Chiang frequently associated herself with aid for war orphans – 'warphans'). But others stayed more or less for the duration.[27] Gellhorn's reports and those filed by Theodore White for *Time*, Harrison Forman for the *New York Herald Tribune*, Günther Stein and others kept Chongqing's story alive as the war spread globally and helped 'keep the city on the map day in day out'. Most of the reporters were 'loyalists', as Emily Hahn put it. They wrote for victory, and not for defeat, wove together a story of defiance from the rock of Chongqing, and at the start they probed little into the problems of their ally, at least at first, and at least in print.

Gellhorn found the city inspiring, despite its privations and weather – but 'I never want to travel again,' she announced. Hahn thought the depressing impact of its climate – a 'viscous fog', as another described it – was quite bearable for anyone who, like her, had ever lived in London. For his part, Chongqing's privations rather reminded Indian journalist D. F. Karaka of his undergraduate life in Oxford.[28]

So sprang into makeshift existence one of a number of new foreign communities in China. Reporters and diplomats were joined by men and women on missions. They came to reassure, fact-find, advise, lecture and listen. As their armed might had failed them in 1941–2, and as they failed to satisfy the National Government's exorbitant demand for a £100 million loan (they got £50 million), the British called on culture to rescue their position, appointing for the first time a cultural attaché to co-ordinate activities including exchanges, scholarships, gifts of books and equipment. A Sino-British Science Co-operation Office was established, with scientist Joseph Needham as its head, but literature was called into service as well. Robert Payne taught English poetry at Fudan University's refugee campus north of the city, hampered by the absence of books. (The poet and critic William Empson had managed for two years at the Kunming campus of the exiled Beijing universities through a prodigious recall of the texts he taught.) For its part the US Office of War Information saturated wartime China with material that in significant part projected Western cultural values using magazines, film shows, exhibitions, leaflets and radio broadcasts. Refugees and escapees also dribbled in from the occupied treaty ports and Hong Kong. Most were shipped on to India by their diplomats, but others made themselves useful locally. Some White Russians set up restaurants. A tap-dance teacher advertised in the *Hankow Herald*. An English Sinophile, John McCausland, worked for Chungking Radio, broadcasting with 'the cultured, well-modulated voice of the perfect English gentleman', but otherwise refusing to speak the language. He and a Dutch colleague had both taken Chinese citizenship. The tenuous nature of Chongqing's links outside China was exemplified by the fact that the station's broadcasts were transcribed and recorded for relay by American networks by a dentist and his wife in Ventura, California.[29]

The flights over the Himalayas also brought men and women who would shape the way free China (as it came quickly to be termed) was visually perceived. The British fashion photographer Cecil Beaton was sent by the Ministry of Information in the spring of 1944. It was all a long way from *Vogue* magazine, for which he had worked through the 1930s. In this China he found 'no Pekin picnics, no ponies for polo, no wealth of peonies from which to choose the one perfect specimen'. This was not Anne Bridge's China, nor that of the Beijing aesthetes like Harold Acton. Instead Beaton was kept hard at work photographing munitions factories and parades, but he brought some of his distinctive *Vogue* aesthetic into his portraits of politicians and their wives, Chengdu policemen, street peddlers, commandos, firemen and nurses. These were widely circulated in the glut of books explaining China that now poured off wartime presses in Britain and America, and which aimed to continue the shift in public perceptions of China. Look at the photographs first, one author directed his readers, for they showed the common humanity of 'East and West', and that 'Chinese and British . . . were meant to be friends'. Wartime censorship and politesse kept Beaton's more caustic comments out of his own published accounts of the visit, but these were still strident, undercutting his powerful images of a poor but confident society mobilized for war. But 'I felt I had come out of jail or was freed from the Gestapo,' he wrote in his diary when he reached India.[30]

Saul Steinberg of *The New Yorker* arrived in July 1943 to join a US Navy Psychological Warfare team, sending back to the magazine drawings of the China Theatre life of the US Fourteenth Air Force, drawing demolition guides for Chinese partisans and illustrating an official handbook distributed to servicemen about living in China. American Air Force bombers were by now flying from large airfields in the southwest that had been constructed in a crash building programme. Some 60,000 Americans would be based in China as part of this effort by the end of the war. Their meat-heavy diet, and their demand for as many of the comforts of home as could be shipped in, placed great strains on the Chinese – there simply were not enough 'cows, pigs and chickens' for them, argued Madame Chiang in 1943. It was the single largest, most rapid and dynamic irruption of foreign nationals ever into provincial China. *The New Yorker* published Steinberg's sketches of this meeting of cultures – and economic power – in which the considerable tensions it increasingly generated are subsumed in affable mutual incomprehension. 'Don't try and buy out every store', ran one of the handbook's instructions: Chinatowns at home have better curios; and be careful where you eat.[31] Advice and information for servicemen was also delivered in Frank Capra's powerful film *The Battle for China* (1944), the sixth of his 'Why We Fight' series commissioned by the US Army. 'China is history, China is land, China is people,' the narration asserted. Japanese footage of the bombing of Shanghai, Wuhan and Chongqing was intercut with a powerful narrative about the march of 'thirty million people' westwards to Chongqing, and of ships heading upstream 'weighted down to the water's edge with the precious tools for new China'. 'Flaming Chungking became the symbol of their indestructible spirit.' Like all the films in the series, *The Battle for China* mixed enemy newsreel with material culled from feature films.[32] As a result some of the unused footage from *The Good Earth* had an airing in Capra's film, showing the great march to the west in the face of the Japanese advance. It was, up to a point, an improvement on his 1933 film *The Bitter Tea of General Yen*.

It would be unfair to conclude that the wider narrative of China's resistance that came out of the press corps at Chongqing, and the visitors on their rapid tours, was a similar mix of fact and fiction, but there was certainly wishful thinking in the reporting that emerged. The press also worked with a steadily tightening censorship, and with a realization that there were increasingly serious criticisms to make, and concerns to communicate to China's supporters overseas. When critiques were published, National Government agents hit back with charges that the foreign reporters were 'whoring, drunken ignorant men', filed complaints to the diplomats and simply tightened the censorship.[33] More proactively they used a much sweeter pill, accentuating the cultural campaign inaugurated at Burlington House as far as wartime conditions allowed, and harking back to older forms of diplomacy by sending pandas to foreign zoos. This sparked what would become in time an important identification of China with these most charismatic of animals. Two baby pandas arrived at the Bronx Zoo just after the Pacific War commenced, heralded as 'furry emblems of China's gratitude' for the work of United China Relief. In

Britain, Chiang Yee set about illustrating an account of London Zoo's panda, Ming, whose arrival in 1938 had sparked hysterical public excitement.[34] But then the Nationalists also sent overseas their single best publicity asset, Song Meiling: Madame Chiang Kai-shek. She had been told she was 'worth 10 divisions to China', Meiling told Martha Gellhorn in 1941, but a barnstorming tour of the United States in 1943, which took in rallies at the Hollywood Bowl and Madison Square Gardens, and included an address to a joint session of Congress, was worth many more divisions than that. 'I speak your language,' she told her audience there, 'not only the language of your hearts, but also your tongue . . . basically and fundamentally we are fighting for the same cause.'[35]

The travails of Chongqing were already being rehearsed at meetings overseas by Chinese activists like Yao Nianyuan, who helped rally foreign public opinion to China's cause and raised funds for relief initiatives. At events across Britain and later in the United States and Australia, Yao, who decades later would become well known under her pen name Nien Cheng, talked of the horrors of a war conducted not between soldiers, but in large part 'by Japanese aeroplanes on Chinese civilians'. At 'Stricken China', an exhibition in the south-coast town of Hastings in September 1938, a miniature idealized Chinese garden was constructed, with little shops stocked with Chinese handicrafts, the whole contrasted with films and photographs of 'the death, destruction, grief and pain' brought by Japanese bombers. Communists, missionaries and internationalists joined together with the Chinese students, diplomats and others sojourning overseas as the war unfolded, who had unexpectedly found themselves advocates for the country's cause. 'The people of Chungking have learned to face death every day,' Yao later argued at a widely reported Rotary Club talk in Canberra, so they 'are tough and China can take it'.[36] By then she spoke from experience: Yao's own home in Chongqing had been destroyed just before her departure for Australia with her diplomat husband. Still, it was easier said at a distance, out of reach of the bombers, but for what it was worth Chongqing gained a horrified hold on the foreign imagination that was only loosened as the war in Europe exploded. The name of a city barely heard of before 1937, one 'marked on no man's map', became a byword for terror.[37] Writers like

Xiao Qian also reinforced a message that this was, as the title of one of his books put it, *China but not Cathay*. A civilization and a culture were under attack, but not a distant one, neither exotic nor 'picturesque'.[38]

For their part, British diplomats and exiled defenders of the treaty ports also liked this message of shared humanity and solidarity – but in their case because it rather allowed them to assert that it had really always been thus. Now Britain and China were allies, however, they argued, they have always been friends. Books about China rushed into print included some old familiar names. Since his removal from editing the *North China Daily News* in 1930, O. M. Green had been a persistent defender of the treaty port communities. His *The Foreigner in China* (1942) paid homage to the men who had built prosperity on the mudflats of Shanghai. While extraterritoriality and the concessions had not, strictly, been defensible in the long term, they had, Green argued, once been vital. And had they not been run fairly and helped to midwife a modern China? They had 'forged an "invisible link" between China and the West', one British diplomat claimed in a speech in October 1943 in Chongqing. This was part of a wider emphasis on a new narrative of friendship, co-operation and assistance, of how a 'handful of British (and Americans) in China – missionaries, officials, merchants' – had built this partnership.[39]

By contrast, in Lanzhou, Nationalist propaganda teams painted the May Thirtieth Massacre on city walls showing British police gunning down Chinese students on Shanghai's streets. Some of the cultural and scientific support offered by the British was funded by the Boxer Indemnity, so this was British charity using Chinese money, rooted in the humiliation of 1900. In England, Xiao Qian found himself staying with descendants of 'Chinese' Gordon, and discovered that one Aid China exhibition of Chinese antiquities was assembled from Boxer war loot. The past was not so easily to be forgotten, rewritten, or avoided.

Yet China was not alone in that struggle against empire, and during its war against Japan it grew more and more conscious of a wider role in global affairs that might now finally be within its grasp. For the future Indian Prime Minister Jawaharlal Nehru, Chongqing in 1939 was 'the symbol today of magnificent courage in the struggle for freedom'. Ill-equipped with name cards, and daunted by the prospect of a succession of Chinese feasts, the Indian National Congress leader visited the city in August 1939. Nehru sat in shelters through five air raids – on one occasion with Chiang Kai-shek himself – and concluded that the Chinese were a 'significantly grown up people'. Indian nationalists could 'learn a lot from them'. Such interaction offered the nightmare scenario for the British of a pan-nationalist alliance that could in time challenge them. They had for years thwarted as far as they could exchanges between Indian nationalists of any stripe and the Guomindang, but now from China's capital Nehru declared in a radio broadcast that 'The days of imperialism and aggression are numbered, in a world that is sick of both.' There was little the British could do except what they did quite well: set up a sophisticated intelligence operation in India to keep such ties under close surveillance. The former Shanghai Municipal Police chief Kenneth Bourne was one of its commanders, his team monitoring the activities of Chinese diplomats and residents. At his own initiative Chiang Kai-shek would reciprocate Nehru's visit in February 1942, although by then the situation had so dramatically changed for the worse that his objective was to try to persuade Mahatma Ghandi not to obstruct the war effort against Japan. Chiang offered full support to India's struggle for self-determination. He thought that he had to, he told Franklin D. Roosevelt, for he professed himself 'shocked' at the political situation he found there, and at the political intransigence of the British.[40]

However, the British would remind anybody who now listened, and many who did not wish to, that India was their business, and that they had no imperial possessions in China. Well, there was certainly Hong Kong, but that was entirely another matter, and part of a different world of colonies and empire. It was not, they said firmly, China. British war aims did not include parting with it, and the Japanese-occupied colony would be an abiding concern throughout the war. Part of the new exodus to Chongqing that began almost immediately after Pearl Harbor came from Hong Kong. One of the first to arrive in the capital was one of the unlikeliest. Phyllis Harrop was Lady Assistant in the colony's Secretariat for Chinese Affairs, a role that involved working with the police to investigate sex trafficking. A brief marriage to a German enabled her to secure German papers and escape the captured colony for Portuguese Macao in late January 1942, and then ship on from there to Fort Bayard in the French-leased territory at Guangzhouwan. From that surreal spot – rather like a 'Parisian suburb', she thought – Harrop and a small group made their way into Nationalist-held China in sedan chairs, on bicycles, and then in trucks and by train and air to Chongqing. On the way Harrop had already sent ahead the first eyewitness account of Japanese atrocities in their assault on Hong Kong and ill-treatment of prisoners afterwards. Her status as a government official gave these some weight, and together with reports from another escapee, the Professor of Physiology at the University of Hong Kong, Leslie Ride, formed the basis for a 10 March 1942 British government statement that shocked British opinion. Harrop became the public face of the vicious violence unleashed in Hong Kong: 'My Chinese houseboy was bayoneted,' she told journalists. 'My amah was raped.'[41] Britons and Chinese had suffered equally at the hands of the enemy. 'Remember Hongkong' demanded one newspaper strapline. The humorous weekly *Punch* published a grim cartoon of a sword of vengeance being sharpened.[42]

We need to understand the political geography of Harrop's story if we are to understand the strangeness of the south China front around Hong Kong. While the Japanese held the island and the urban districts on the Kowloon peninsula, they did not venture much into the countryside. Communist guerrilla units were able to operate there as a result. While Macao came under a great deal of Japanese pressure, it remained neutral, as did Portugal, but very isolated, and the British consul, John Reeves, newly arrived in June 1941, managed to keep active and cheerful throughout the conflict. Guangzhouwan's French administration was Vichy in its affiliation, but also mindful of incurring the wrath of the Japanese. Nonetheless, with some bribery, and with false papers, and because some neutral coastal shipping remained active, Harrop was able to make her way out of Hong Kong. Guangzhouwan would be taken over by the Japanese in February 1943, but Macao remained intact, though compromised. Reeves operated from the consulate, which was separated from Japan's by only a low wall, and his major responsibility came to be co-ordinating the provision of aid for many of the 10,000 people who fled from Hong Kong to the colony or who were shipped out by the Japanese and were housed in makeshift refugee camps; they were mainly Hong Kong residents of Macanese descent, but there were also Indians, Malays and other Allied subjects, including Filipinos. It was a huge and difficult task, but Reeves had the time of his life. He kept his consulate flag flying (and a new one was smuggled in to be ready for the day of victory), ran a newspaper (writing the editorials and limericks), and even chaired a Rehabilitation Committee to plan for a post-war Hong Kong. 'I loved it,' he wrote later of his experiences. Undercover Nationalist bodyguards watched his back, but he generally kept his revolver to hand (even when playing hockey). Macao's war was a bitterly harsh one nonetheless. Its population of about 150,000 had already been swollen by 100,000 Chinese who had fled the Japanese occupation of Guangzhou in 1938, and during the Pacific War it rose to almost half a million. Over 27,000 people died of starvation in the hapless colony in 1942 alone. The Japanese largely got what they wanted from it, and so did the colony's gangsters.[43]

Although Reeves's communication with the world of the Allies was mainly through radio, he was in touch with the other significant British presence in south China, the British Army Aid Group (BAAG), established by Leslie Ride after his escape from Hong Kong.[44] BAAG's objective was to facilitate escape from Hong Kong, open communication routes into the camps where Allied civilians and servicemen were held, and secure intelligence about Japanese activities. It also aimed – rather more discreetly, for it was forbidden from undertaking any political work – to provide a forward base that maintained a British presence as close to the occupied colony as possible. From improvised beginnings in 1942, when it was headquartered on two former brothel boats in Shaoguan, 200 miles north of the colony, BAAG grew and developed an extensive network. This helped British, Indian and Hong Kong Chinese servicemen, civil servants and civilians escape from the territory, and assisted American aircrew who had been shot down during Fourteenth Air Force raids on the colony's infrastructure and its shipping that began in 1942. BAAG was a uniquely home-grown organization, staffed in large part by Hong Kong people from across its diverse communities, who were even clothed in uniforms made in – and smuggled out of – occupied Kowloon. It flew no flag for the 'Taipan mentality', as Ride had put it, but it aimed to raise the Union Jack nonetheless. Although BAAG co-operated with communist units operating in the New Territories and with the Nationalists, Ride hoped to be able to make a dash into Hong Kong when the Japanese capitulated. It was important to try to make sure that a British unit – not the Nationalists, and certainly not the Americans – liberate the Crown Colony.

Life in the camps in Hong Kong for Allied nationals was harsher than it was in Shanghai, and it began almost from the start of the Japanese occupation. It was morally far less hazardous and politically less difficult than life outside, however. Hong Kong was 'not part of China', announced its Japanese Governor, General Rensuke Isogai, on arrival in the colony.[45] Japanese Pan-Asian ideology and liberationist rhetoric might had led Wang Jingwei's collaborationist government to assume that the British possession would be returned to China, but instead – in an echo of the story of Qingdao during the First World War – Hong Kong was annexed by Japan, and was promptly recast as a Japanese possession. The bronze statue of Queen Victoria installed to mark her jubilee in 1897 was removed and shipped off to Japan, and an imperial proclamation was put in its place.[46] Japanese firms and settlers would shortly start to arrive in a city cleansed of more than its British monuments: streets and districts were given new Japanese names, language schools were instituted to teach the colony's new official language, public ceremonial lauded Japanese military victories and their anniversaries, and the rituals and festivals of the Japanese year. As in every city that fell to the invader, a few local figures in Hong Kong aligned themselves with the new power, but others came forward as well, prompted to do so by British officials and motivated by the desire to see order restored and residents buffered as far as possible from the privations of the war. Most had little choice. The Japanese regime was at once bureaucratic, capricious and brutal. As in other occupied cities, different branches of the military and other agencies competed for authority and for spoil. Hong Kong's population, bloated with Chinese refugees after the fall of Guangzhou in 1938, was steadily reduced through repatriation schemes that first encouraged, and then forced, people to leave. As residents were moved on, they added to strains on food supplies elsewhere, not least during the widespread famine in Guangdong province in 1943–4 that took a million lives.

In Hong Kong's Stanley internment camp, and despite the odds, the British in particular began to re-establish what became a hothouse parody of their interrupted society and government outside the wire.[47] The usual tensions between officials and the business community were intensified in an initial atmosphere of vicious recrimination, but the Colonial Secretary Franklin Gimson – the senior government official in the camp – established his authority in the name of the King (the Governor had been packed off to Taiwan, where he spent his time tending goats with his captured peers from colonial Southeast Asia). Gimson's charges formed committees and set about reconstructing a sort of life, but with novel touches for the former colonial elite, not least as women and men alike learned to cook, and make, mend and wash clothes. Teachers taught and children studied; exams were set and marked and would in time be recognized with formal qualifications. The twin pillars of colonial life – alcohol and servants – were missing. The internees gardened, put on plays and concerts, held religious services, gossiped, played cards, and grew very, very bored. At least forty babies were conceived and born in the camp, twenty marriages contracted, and a few broken. The internees were ill-clothed and ill-fed, and there were few medical supplies. Fewer died than might be expected.

Like Reeves in Macao, they also got to work thinking about the future. In fact, there were no fewer than three rehabilitation and post-war planning initiatives. Reeves's group had probably the most representative membership, for it included Indians, Chinese, Portuguese and Eurasians as well. Franklin Gimson had probably the best-informed group, as it included many of the officials who had been administering the colony, but in London the Colonial Office's Planning Unit was the only one with any formal standing.[48] All conducted post-mortems, and argued that the shock of defeat and the hiatus in British rule offered an opportunity to bring about profound reform. Whilst the Japanese did raise the prospect of handing Hong Kong back to China in 1944 (in a set of peace concessions offered secretly to Chongqing), the British had no intention of doing so. Hong Kong was now certainly a matter of honour for them, but it was also viewed as a significant economic and strategic asset, and it would be likely to be even more important in a post-war China in which the British operated without extraterritoriality. Already, throughout the 1930s, more and more British companies in China had relocated their legal domicile to Hong Kong in the face of Nationalist policies. A British Hong Kong was going to be more important after the war, not less. Still, there was a widespread consensus that there ought to be a more democratic or representative system established in future, with greater Hong Kong Chinese participation in the running of the colony. This, the planners in Stanley felt, could only entrench more deeply the type of loyalty and commitment shown by the Chinese in the colony who had fought, and died, in the ranks of Hong Kong's Volunteer Reserve regiment.

There was of course a fourth planning group that discussed the issue of Hong Kong. This one met in Chongqing in the Europe department of the National Government's Foreign Ministry.[49] It does not seem to have achieved very much, but the intransigence of the British, who steadfastly refused to discuss Hong Kong either during the 1942 treaty negotiations or notably at the Cairo Conference of Allied leaders in November 1943, did suggest that there was little point. 'We mean to hold our own,' Winston Churchill had famously announced in November 1942, and he had not become Prime Minister in order 'to preside over the liquidation of the British Empire'.[50] The plain fact remained that, even in the face of a redoubtable push from President Roosevelt himself, Hong Kong was kept off the agenda. In other areas, the Cairo Conference delivered for the Chinese some firm commitments about the return from Japanese control of Taiwan and Manchuria, and the transfer of Japanese property in China as reparations. Except for the 425 square miles of Hong Kong and Macao's eleven, the prospects for a historic reunification of China had never looked better.

The Cairo Conference was a singular achievement and at the same time a profound disappointment for the Chinese. It brought international prominence for China as one of the 'Big Four' Allied powers (although the discussions had to be staged in two sessions across Cairo and Tehran, as the USSR was still a neutral in the Pacific Theatre and Stalin only went to the latter session). But in operational terms the Chinese did not secure the focus on the Allied 'China The-atre' of operations that they had hoped for and which might ease the blockade through the reconquest of Burma. Nonetheless, Chiang Kai-shek wrote in his diary afterwards that the conference and the 1 December 'Cairo Declaration' formed 'the greatest triumph in the history of China's foreign affairs'. Not only China, but 'the whole world' treated it as such, he claimed. It was by any standards a remarkable moment in global politics when China's leader partici-pated in the discussions as one of the great Allied powers. Photographs of Chiang, Roosevelt and Churchill provided a startling glimpse of a differently ordered world. (It was not clear who invited Song Meiling, however, or what status she had, or why she too posed with the Allied leaders.) Roosevelt put a great deal of personal effort into making sure that Chiang felt the conference was a success, while Winston Churchill and the British were perplexed and irritated that so much time was taken up with China. The actual military discussions with the Chinese delegation were a 'ghastly waste of time', thought British commander General Alan Brooke.[51] But the fact was that an impov-erished Asian nation had been included because China was needed at the Cairo Conference if the grand alliance was to hold. Churchill still thought it an 'affectation' to pretend that China was a 'great power'. He had no option, however, but to listen to Roosevelt's rhetoric about China's post-war role, and accept Chiang's participation. But when the American President apparently suggested over a private lunch with the British Prime Minister that he might return Hong Kong as a ges-ture and lease it back, the idea was rebuffed. And an uncomfortable reminder of an earlier era for Chiang would have come when the British ambassador to Egypt, Lord Killearn, paid a courtesy call. This was the former Sir Miles Lampson, British Minister to China through-out the Nationalist revolution. Eighteen months earlier Killearn had surrounded the Egyptian royal palace with British tanks and forced the King to dismiss the government. British policies in China had always been on a continuum with such other naked displays of colo-nial brute force elsewhere, as Chiang well knew, having encountered them in Guangzhou in the 1920s. It was a symbolically mute meeting, in addition, for neither man spoke the other's language.

The Cairo Conference proved to be the high point in Sino-American relations during the war. Almost immediately afterwards US diplomats began to act to head off grandiose projects from the Nationalists to request a massive new loan from Washington.[52] There was simply no reason why any more American cash was needed, and while Chongqing's resistance meant that substantial Japanese forces were held down in China, there was something profoundly disquieting about Chinese attitudes, expectations and action.

Money was the issue all over. For his part, all Cecil Joly had really wanted by 1943 was his pension. The number of foreign employees on the Customs Service books had been drastically reduced after Pearl Harbor. Not only did Lester Little pay off all the outdoor staff in unoccupied China – the mariners, tidewaiters and surveyors – but on 31 July 1943 most of its British and American employees in Japanese-held China were compulsorily retired (again, for Chongqing did not recognize the legitimacy of any of the actions of the Kishimoto inspectorate, including its dismissal of the same men in December 1941). They were by then mostly in Shanghai's internment camps or had been repatriated. The threat of war after 1931 had prolonged their role in the Customs; the onset of the Pacific War terminated it for most men. Little and the dozen foreign senior staff in Nationalist China still found themselves serving a useful function for the government. But the rules of the game had changed. The service marked its ninetieth anniversary in 1944 and Little would read out loud at meetings from Hart's 1864 instructions on the spirit of the service, but this history and that spirit were becoming an irrelevance. The Customs was no longer the semi-autonomous, foreign-led fiefdom that it had been even in Sir Frederick Maze's day, and men like Little found themselves having to brush up their Chinese skills, for the language of the service shifted abruptly to Chinese. This left most foreign officers utterly tongue-tied.

Little's abiding objective was to secure a fair outcome from the chaos for all of his employees, but particularly for his foreign staff, whose days were quite clearly numbered. For all the high-mindedness of Churchillian imperialism, and the internationalism that others talked (the Customs was a little 'League of Nations' some said), the private details of pensions and pay-offs were the reality for those entangled in the last days of institutions like the Customs. They wanted what was owed them, and they wanted it in hard currency so that they would not be vulnerable to the artificially low official exchange rate. They would point to their contracts and terms of service. Solipsistic to the last, they failed to notice that there was a revolution under way in China's relations with the West, and that changes in the Customs were part of this. Those expectations for proper recompense were to carry little weight in a China free of the treaties, one which no longer needed Cecil Joly and his colleagues. Most people would be disappointed. Employees of the now-abolished treaty port administrations would secure no redress until the British government made *ex gratia* payments to them in the 1950s. The Customs fared a little better in time, for Lester Little had some access to hard cash.

When Little arrived in Chongqing in 1943, air raids had been growing less frequent. There was less terror, but it was for him still a city of 'filth and stench and latrines and pigs and sewers', through which he made his way by sedan chair to the office every day. There the Inspector General battled to find funds to feed his staff and their families – 'thirty thousand mouths', as he put it – and cushion them against the continued assault from nationalists in the government. One minister announced in November 1944 that the Chinese staff were 'all slaves of the foreigner'. Little oversaw what revenue was collected – a third of which in 1943 came from legitimate trade with Japanese-occupied territory, as he told the American Vice President Henry Wallace when he visited Chongqing in June 1944 and planned for post-war reconstruction. Most of Chongqing was kept busy, it seemed, either playing the black market – where a $50 piano could fetch $3,000 – or preparing for the post-war rehabilitation of China after the defeat of Japan.[53] There was much talk of battle, but little evidence of it. Instead, the discussion was of aid and loans. Would America restock China's fleets with war-surplus vessels? Would it provide funds to rebuild harbours, lighthouses or railways? China was ready to take. It had fought the war alone for four years. It was morally owed the assistance, or at least this was how its critics characterized the position of its leadership.

The war itself seemed incidental, until in May 1944 the Japanese Army's Ichi-go offensive began to split China in half. In the face of the biggest offensive the enemy had yet launched, the Nationalist armies, ill-trained, ill-equipped, ill-prepared and ill-led, collapsed. The chaos, misery and destruction that ensued, as hundreds of thousands of people fled the advance, shocked Chiang's allies to the core. Soldiers abandoned their arms and ran (some generals ran faster); bandits preyed on the refugees; Henan's country people, sick of impositions, rose and attacked Nationalist soldiers.[54] Lester Little filed away in his private archive a copy of one harrowing report, sent by Luoyang Commissioner Li Donghua, who had led the evacuation of a party of 100 staff and their families by mule cart and then on foot. They were robbed by villagers and bandits, by their cart drivers, retreating soldiers, and even by their own guards. Roads had been washed away. Li briefly fell into enemy hands, saw two other captives butchered, and escaped. Of a party of 120 bank officials who set off with his group only six could be accounted for. The Japanese machine-gunned those they caught up with, or killed them with grenades. One night the sky was lit by fires from burning buildings and trucks. 'The scene reminded me of a war picture in the cinema,' Li commented.[55]

In despair, the Americans pushed for Chiang to effect a reconciliation with the Communists, whose growing strength was headquartered from Yan'an, 500 miles to the north of the capital. This small market town in the hilly northwest was the capital of what had been designated as the ShaanGanNing Border Region under the terms of the 'United Front' agreement between the Communists and the National Government in 1937. After a battering by Japanese bombers in 1939, Yan'an had largely been left untouched. Communist forces that had survived what they would celebrate as the 'Long March' – their year-long, arduous retreat from Jiangxi province – had arrived in October 1935. Like Chongqing, the town was relatively inaccessible. In Yan'an they had created a model new society and a showcase for their wider vision for China. Their story had first been dramatically told in news articles and a widely circulated book, *Red Star over China* (1937), by the American reporter Edgar Snow, who had made his way to the communist base in 1936 from Shanghai. Other accounts quickly followed as journalists and leftist activists travelled to Shaan-GanNing. Foreign access to Yan'an in wartime was officially blocked by the Nationalists, however, but those who had been there had published largely uncritical accounts of what seemed to be another China, and another future. In Yan'an there was no corruption. Instead, although poor in resources, there was a highly motivated and tightly organized organization, embedded in local society. Yan'an drew to itself an estimated 100,000 refugees, many of them well-educated and highly skilled men and women who chose to join the Communists, not, in most cases, because they were ideologically committed, but because they thought that here was the heart of a real resistance. Many of them were inspired by Snow's book.

During his visit to Chongqing, Henry Wallace had persuaded the Nationalists to allow official American access to the blockaded region, and journalists also made it. A US military observer group, known jokingly as the 'Dixie Mission' – as it was in 'rebel' territory – arrived in Yan'an in July 1944, ostensibly to use communist networks to extract pilots shot down over occupied China and to provide intelligence. Yan'an's climate was clear, but much more than the fog of Chongqing appeared to lift. It was a 'different country' with 'different people'. There were no police, no beggars, 'no signs of desperate poverty'. There was a 'sense of mission', an easy intermingling of leaders and led, of men and women. The Communists danced in the evenings and the gramophone, remarked one foreign resident, would likely be a lasting symbol for him of life there. There was 'none of the claptrap of Chongqing officialdom'. So reported John Stewart Service, Second Secretary to the American Embassy, who accompanied the Dixie Mission when it arrived. Born in China in 1909 to missionary parents then working for the YMCA in Chengdu (who would lose their life savings in the Raven Group scandal), Service began working as a clerk in the Foreign Service in China in 1933. He and his family had lived through warlord turmoil in Sichuan, which provided a further sharp contrast with Yan'an under the Communists. 'We have come to the mountainous north,' he reported a foreign journalist saying, 'to find the most modern place in China.'[56]

'This is the kind of China which I have always hoped to see,' reported one former missionary after visiting Yan'an.[57] A *New York Times* correspondent who visited the city in 1944 reported meeting a man who had fought on the republican side in the Spanish Civil War;

a pastor and former YMCA worker who had graduated from the American-run St John's College in Shanghai; a missionary-trained doctor from Fuzhou, and many other medical staff who had studied abroad; other Chinese from overseas; and a former seaman who had 'sailed all the world's oceans'.[58] This was the cosmopolitan China that was already familiar. Yan'an offered many such surprises, but these seemed to be people with whom business could possibly be done. The revelations at Yan'an strengthened the impression that many had already gained from the suave diplomacy of Zhou Enlai, who had led the communist mission at Chongqing earlier in the days of the United Front. These were pragmatic people, not doctrinaires. 'The Chinese Communists are not Communists,' concluded one of the visiting pressmen, Harrison Forman. It was a refrain that was taken up by more and more observers.[59]

The Communists were in fact so pragmatic in Yan'an that they had prepared for the arrival of their Western visitors by embarking on a rapid programme of improvements, ordering the replacement of anti-Guomindang posters and slogans with pro-Allied ones, and setting out very carefully to present a moderate face to the world. It worked. It was a 'Chinese wonderland city', joked another journalist in a facetious report about what seemed to be, after Chongqing, a topsy-turvy land. Service and others were not just dazzled by their own first impressions, for they had also sought out informants from amongst the small coterie of foreigners working in Yan'an. One important source was the Briton Michael Lindsay, who was working for the Communists teaching radio engineering and advising on radio communications. Lindsay was well connected – his father was A. D. Lindsay, Master of Balliol College at Oxford University, and a notable establishment figure – and he had come to China in late 1937 as an education advisor at Beijing's Yenching University. He and his wife, Li Xiaoli, had begun to work with the communist underground in the former capital, and then fled Beijing for guerrilla-held territory at the onset of the Pacific War. The couple's trek across Japanese lines to the communist bases was one being made by thousands of students and teachers from Beijing. Unlike other foreigners in Yan'an, and like many of those who made their way there, Lindsay was no communist. He simply believed that 'any thinking person had a duty to oppose the Japanese army'. Lindsay assisted the Communists deliver news reports directly to the United States by helping them design a radio transmitter and starting transmissions on what would in time become Radio Peking.[60]

The despatches of 'Jack' Service broadcast a positive story to the American State Department, one that reinforced the steadily growing disquiet about the Nationalists, and in many cases distrust and even disdain. By 1944 few foreign observers believed that the Nationalists had any stomach for a real fight. Instead, the government feigned resistance and husbanded its slowly increasing military strength for an expected post-war struggle with the Communists. In fact, Chinese troops fought well in Burma and in the spring of 1945 they had defeated a new Japanese offensive in western Hunan and recovered significant territory lost during the Ichi-go campaign in Guangxi province. But the widely discussed corruption of the Nationalist leadership inflicted grave wounds on its reputation amongst the Allies. Madame Chiang took a floor of the Waldorf Astoria in New York on her visit in 1943 (and an entire floor of a Manhattan hospital). While she was photographed in her furs at the Waldorf, the Communist Eighth Route Army seemed to be taking the fight to the enemy. Well, hardly, noted Peter Vladimirov, Comintern representative to Yan'an, in his diary. In fact, their strategy was to avoid large-scale combat with the Japanese and focus instead on denying the Nationalists access to recovered territory.[61] Some of the reporters urged caution, but it was Jack Service's view of communist capacities that held, and a wider distaste for Madame Chiang and the corruption that she seemed to represent.

The war's China Theatre came under American command, and there was little for the British to do. So they focused instead almost exclusively on positioning themselves for peace, and in this were in synch with the Guomindang and the Communists (and many of the puppets). For the British the key aim was to rebuild their empire in East and Southeast Asia, including the reoccupation of Hong Kong, and assume as much of their position in China itself as possible, given that the privileges provided by the nineteenth-century treaties had been lost. The Japanese takeover of Shanghai, and then the internment of Allied civilians there from February 1943 onwards, was a gift to the diplomats and other leading elements that had long been weary of the burdensome distractions of the pretend-Raj that China had provided. There was now no opposition to the return of the concessions to China and the abrogation of extraterritoriality, not that the National Government was in a mood to brook any, but the eventual implementation of change could take place without local hiccups. So Jardine Matheson, ICI and BAT could focus on getting ready to resume their place after the war and secure their Chinese markets, preventing as far as possible those becoming too used to competing products.

The most spectacularly successful British operation in China during the Pacific War was the most cynical and revealing of them all. Operation 'Remorse', run by bankers and traders in uniform for the duration of the conflict, was established by the covert warfare Special Operations Executive in 1943. 'Remorse' established a huge black-market organization that generated £77.7 million worth of additional resource for British activity in China: a profit, in short, of £2.7 billion at 2015 prices.[62] At issue was the National Government's requirement that its allies purchase its *fabi* currency at official exchange rates that bore little relation to reality. This meant that when Allied agencies purchased goods in *fabi* they cost much more than they would have done in the United States or in Britain: a $5 shovel used in airfield construction cost the Americans $25 in China. They felt they were being bilked, and they were right, but diplomatic representations failed to effect a change in Chinese policy: any such change would fuel inflation, they were told.[63] So the British for their part decided to bypass the process – which they and others thought simply profited corrupt officials – and to play the black market instead. First they sold rupees and sterling, bank drafts and all sorts of currency instruments, but then started to deal in precious stones, watches, pens and other high-value/low-bulk items, and at one point some particularly fine motorbikes. These goods were flown into unoccupied China from India and then distributed through an extensive and efficient network of agents and offices masquerading as outposts of the British Ministry of Production. It fulfilled orders placed as far into enemy-held territory as Shanghai, with goods sourced from as far away as Switzerland and South Africa. The *fabi* generated by 'Remorse' was

distributed to British and other Allied organizations for their operational use – which was how officials squared it with, if not their
consciences, then at least the rules of engagement. It was used to help
ensure secrecy by bribing anyone in sight who might be of some use
to the British effort in China, and who might be tempted. 'Softening'
people was the term used, but 'smothering' might be more apt: it was
later estimated that at any one time six tons of *fabi* notes were in
transit in 'Remorse' vehicles.

The objective, ostensibly, was also to fund the extraction of intelligence, and to fund what operations the British could manage to
undertake. At the end of the conflict 'Remorse' funds were airlifted
to internment camp inmates, and into Hong Kong to help rebuild the
colony's currency, but running through the internal records of this
vast enterprise was also the clear objective of keeping the British
flag flying in the war-torn China market. Diamonds were the British
businessman's best friend in China, and this staggeringly successful
venture – capitalism in the raw – helped these khaki-clad merchants
of war to ready themselves for the end of hostilities and the new
scramble for China that would ensue.

It is hardly surprising, then, that it was during the later stages of
the war that Lin Yutang lost his sense of humour. As Chiang Kai-shek
had never had one, his own attacks on his erstwhile allies were more
predictable. The responses of both exemplify the deep frustration of a
wide spectrum of Chinese nationalist thought over the country's apparent position in Western eyes. For their part, in their now increasingly
internationally known headquarters in Yan'an, the Chinese Communist Party had never held any such illusions. Most existing accounts
of wartime relations between China, America and Great Britain
chart the steadily developing disenchantment of the Westerners with
their difficult ally. But this was a process that had its own dynamic
on the Guomindang's side as well. The Americans and the British
rather hoped that they had wiped the slate clean by signing the new
friendship treaties in February 1943, but this was an illusion.

Lin Yutang's book *Between Tears and Laughter* was published in
the summer of 1943. It began angry, and stayed that way for 243 bitter pages; there were no jokes. Five million Chinese soldiers have not
died, he wrote, 'to keep the British in Hong Kong', the 'booty of the

Opium War'. The British had deliberately starved China of resources by acceding to Japanese demands in 1939 to close the Burma Road – its sole logistical lifeline once it had lost the coasts – and by now focusing on regaining their own Southeast Asian colonies first, before supporting the China front. The British, he charged, even refused to allow the National Government to develop its own air force. America was little better in Lin's eyes, as in the earlier days of the conflict it had allowed shipments of 'oil and scrap iron to Tokyo to bomb Chinese women and children'.[64] His cynicism about British war aims was hardly unusual, and widely shared within the US government in fact. It was also a perfectly sound understanding of British aims.

Lin was also bitter about the hypocrisies of the Atlantic Charter's elision of colonialism: Roosevelt and Churchill committed the Allies to respect the right of 'all people' to self-determination: but this was not intended, certainly by the British, to apply to the European empires. Lin also took his argument further, developing a rejection of the West itself, aside from its science, and its 'materialistic civilization'. Still, Lin allowed that 'all you need to do to make an Englishman a gentleman again is to ship him back west of the Suez Canal'. So there was hope for England. Meanwhile, China should see its allies for what they were, arm and strengthen itself, and then 'nothing the Western nations can do can stop her or keep her down'. Pearl Buck and Richard Welsh, her husband and their joint publisher, had urged Lin to maintain his earlier, funnier, persona, in communicating Chinese perspectives, as a Chinese, to a Western readership. But Lin had tired of performing as the wise and witty sage, and like many in China, had tired too of the Allies. 'Shrill, abusive and intemperate', ran *The New York Times* review of his book; Lin was 'smug, condescending and self-righteously superior'. It was, however, in many of its observations about British war aims and the pre-Pearl Harbor appeasement policies of the Allies, entirely spot on.[65]

Lin could be dismissed as a lightweight, and as a cultural but not a political critic, and more space was given to reports and commentary on the corruption and authoritarianism of the Guomindang. Concerns about this were not assuaged by reports on the tone and content of Chiang Kai-shek's political credo, delivered in a book published in March 1943 and designed for reading by party and government officials, and students and schoolchildren. *China's Destiny* (*Zhong-guo zhi mingyun*) outraged the diplomats in Chongqing. The British produced translations and synopses that they shared with the Americans, and reports flew to London and Washington, and out to the press, about what was characterized by some as a manifesto that could have been produced in any of the dictatorships (perhaps not by Hitler, one diplomat mused, but certainly by Franco).[66] Its anti-democratic tone was less problematic for the British than its sustained critique of the record of foreign and particularly British imperialism in modern China. More than half the text was a lesson in retelling that history. Chiang's book began with an account of the Manchus and their weakness in the face of the foreign onslaught. The succession of unfair treaties, and the depredations of the cosmopolitan collection of powers that sought advantage in China, were rehearsed in detail, while the injustices of the concessions and the International Settlement in Shanghai were all itemized. These were places, he argued, in which gambling, prostitution, narcotics and gangsterism flourished – which could hardly be denied – in which speculation was king, and which had destroyed any respect for law on the part of the Chinese people.

China's Destiny was a signal that the surrender by the British and Americans of their privileges was not going to be the end of that story: imperialism's impact on China served too important a function for Chinese nationalists. And this was not enough, as the book also seemed to lay claim to a greater China than was currently controlled by the republic, including Tibet and Mongolia, and it seemed to suggest continental Southeast Asia too, and all areas shaped culturally by Chinese civilization. Plans to print an English edition by the British Ministry of Information were quickly shelved. 'I never saw a more pernicious use of history for political reasons,' wrote the historian John Fairbank in his diary, 'a tract unworthy of a statesman'. Another reader, Robert Payne, judged it 'disturbing' and 'intolerant'.[67] The book outraged liberal intellectuals and leftists in China as well, who distanced themselves from it as far as they safely could. Yet the episode provided further fuel for those of China's allies who were beginning to question whether a country led by the Guomindang was worth saving, or could in fact be worked with in the post-war world.

More shocking were reports of widespread corruption throughout the Guomindang state, and amongst some of those close to the Generalissimo, as well as of murderous repression by its secret-service units, which was hardly restricted to the streets of isolated Shanghai. If Franco provided the text, Himmler seemed to be running the intelligence services. Such reports were presented as warnings by diplomats on the spot and by such high-profile China commentators as Pearl Buck, most pointedly in a May 1943 article in *Life* magazine, which up till then had been vociferous like all the Luce press in its support for Chiang's China.[68] The point that took everyone by surprise, however, was that the Guomindang remained committed to an anti-imperialist agenda, and at the same time aspired to regional predominance. If anyone had been actually listening to China's diplomats in the 1930s, this would hardly have been so unexpected: it had been rehearsed at the League of Nations and repeatedly during and since the party's rise to power. The impact of this ideology, deployed through Chiang's book, but more widely in the educational and other vehicles used to mobilize the Chinese in the war against the invader, was also magnified by the more cynically deployed anti-imperialist rhetoric of the Japanese and their collaborator regimes.

Anti-imperialist nationalism might well succeed in shipping 'Englishmen' back west of Suez, but the Westerners would leave their culture and values behind, as occupied Shanghai had seen. The city's particular forms of social and cultural modernity would remain embedded: the cocktail, the ballroom, gossip about Jackie Coogan, the Canidrome (still holding races as the war ended) and jazz. In June 1945, with the end of the Pacific War just a few weeks away, a perfectly Shanghai modern event took place in the Grand Theatre. Li Xianglan had the lead part in a jazz symphony, inspired by George Gershwin, and composed by a conscripted Japanese musician, Hattori Ryoichi. The musicians came from the former SMC orchestra, and were in the main Russians and Western European Jewish refugees. The symphony finished with a section that provided China's first taste of a boogie-woogie beat, heard in a modernist hall designed by a Hungarian architect, and sung by a Japanese woman born in Manchuria.[69] Such a quintessential melange of influences, cultures and people would outlast the war, but there was growing opposition to hybridity. A body of thought was developing, and finding expression in Lin Yutang's book and *China's Destiny*, that identified the problem of China as being not imperialism but the West itself, that disease not of the skin nor the heart but of the soul. It was not Western power but Western culture that had despoiled the essence of 5,000 years of Han Chinese history, and humiliated, degraded and enslaved the Chinese. As Lin Yutang put it, in his own introduction to the official English translation of *China's Destiny*, published in January 1947, there was a need for 'cultural and moral reconstruction' to accompany 'political revolution'. From such seeming platitudes, great horrors would yet evolve.

8

Foreign Experts

The former concession areas in Guangzhou on Shamian Island had been restored to their pre-war calm and beauty by the end of 1947. Some tensions existed where foreign property owners had been unable to remove politically well-connected Chinese tenants who had moved in when the Japanese had surrendered, but most had regained possession. Inflation and import restrictions notwithstanding, the outlook looked positive enough for National City Bank of New York to reopen its Guangzhou branch on the island to join some eighty foreign firms operating in the city. There was talk of turning the area into a cultural centre, as the infrastructure developed under the former 'Shameen Municipal Council' was so robust. Less prosaically, its magnificent camphor trees inspired one of the staff at the British Consulate to poetry that found an outlet in the pages of the *South China Morning Post.*[1] It was, one visitor remarked, 'a quiet place, where it is always Sunday morning'. So it was a shock, then, when on Friday, 16 January 1948 a large crowd surged across the bridges to the island, pushed aside police barricades and surrounded the British Consulate. An attempt was made to pull down the Union Jack that flew in its grounds, and then bricks and garden ornaments were thrown at the windows. Before troops restored order two hours later, the consulate had been invaded and set alight, the consul and vice consul hiding from the violent mob under their cook's bed before escaping. The offices of Chartered Bank and Butterfield Swire were also set on fire, and the flames could clearly be seen three hours later as reporters rushed in on flights from Hong Kong. The consulate flag had been pulled down on Shamian, but the marchers were actually demanding that it be pulled down in Hong Kong:

'Down with British imperialism,' they shouted. 'Return Kowloon and Hong Kong.'

A wave of student-led protest had erupted nationally after the colonial authorities in the British colony had started evicting some of the 2,000 people who had set up shacks on the site of the former walled city in Kowloon. For months there had been controversy about these squatters, as the British saw them, but more importantly there had been dispute for decades about who exercised sovereignty over the six-and-a-half-acre district, which before the extension of the Leased Territories in 1898 had contained the local Chinese government offices.[2] The Chinese authorities had always maintained that their jurisdiction had been retained within it; the British rejected this claim, and had fitfully asserted their own over the years, but had been careful as they did so. Rather than turn the land over to urban development, as Kowloon grew rapidly during the interwar period, they had aimed at using the site to create a park, and in the 1930s had evicted the several hundred people who had made homes there. After the war, as refugees again moved back across the border, the Walled City – shorn of its walls, the stones from which were used to build the airport runway – attracted new residents. Despite protests from the Guangdong authorities, the colonial government, still set on its park, and intent on asserting its authority, sent in bailiffs protected by armed police holding placards reading 'Disperse or we fire' to evict the residents from their 'jerry built city' and destroy their 'matchwood cabins'. English-language newspapers joked that the 'invasion' used one gate as a 'point of attack' and was so well choreographed that it looked like an assault by a 'Roman Legion'. The police faced token protests, but found slogans pasted on the walls: 'Respect our sovereign rights: protect our property', 'Let us unite together to protect our sovereign rights', 'Let us unite as one to face the outsider', 'Recognize who is our enemy'. 'Where is this tearful little Miss to go?' asked one local Chinese paper over a photograph of a child with the remains of her house.

The squatters moved straight back in, and they raised China's flag. The police had bungled the whole thing, claimed the colony's governor, and as a sometimes violent stand-off developed in Kowloon, outraged students across China – in Guangzhou, Shanghai, Tianjin, Nanjing and Beijing – answered the call for help. At Tianjin activists demanded that all students in north China protest against this 'British atrocity'. At Shanghai, Jiaotong and Tongji universities went on strike. In Nanjing protesters assembled outside the British Embassy, the Chinese Foreign Ministry and other government buildings, calling for the return of Hong Kong to Chinese sovereignty.[3] Posters reading 'Resist Imperialism', 'Remove Imperialists', 'Down with Imperialism' were pasted up on foreign-owned business buildings and hotels by some of the 10,000-strong crowd that demonstrated along Shanghai's Bund. They carried China's flag and also chanted anti-American slogans, chalking slogans on US military vehicles and only dispersing when representatives were allowed into the British Consulate grounds to present a petition to staff. 'Get out, you dirty British' and 'Get out you dirty American beasts' were painted with pitch on the walls. So the slogans defied easy removal by labourers sent to scrub them away, but the sentiments were now indelibly written all over China's political scene. 'We never expected the burning of the Consulate,' said the perplexed British consul later, 'the world is at peace and we are situated in a friendly country.' 'The War of Resistance is over,' one Guangzhou group announced, 'the unequal treaties have been abolished, but British imperialists invade our territory again and wound our compatriots, and the Shaji Massacre is not yet avenged.'[4] The British abandoned the initiative in Kowloon. Gangsters moved into the political vacuum before a fire in 1950 destroyed the rebuilt shanty town.

The authorities in Guangzhou and in Nanjing blamed communist agitators for the Shamian riot. In fact, events had been organized by a nationalistic faction within the Guomindang that aimed to harness anti-imperialism as a diversion from China's domestic turmoil, and embarrass T. V. Soong, the provincial governor. It had all got out of hand, for the country was awash with protest and discontent of which the brief outburst in January was a potent manifestation. The events were certainly fomented, concluded American officials, but the 'sincerity' of the demonstrators 'could scarcely be doubted'.[5] The civil war with the increasingly strong and very confident Communists was not going well, and the day before the events on Shamian communist forces in the northeast had launched what became a decisive offensive in their struggle to consolidate a hold on Manchuria. But perhaps it was made most definitively clear that the Guomindang's party was truly over when even the taxi dancers of Shanghai rose up in protest later the same month.

Shanghai cabaret interests had been resisting by whatever means they could a nationwide ban on dance halls that should have come into effect in September 1947. This ban was partly fuelled by continuing moral disdain for the modern commercial leisure world in general, and partly by a drive to impose austerity on an economy spiralling out of control. Dancing was deemed an extravagant luxury in the midst of a civil war and galloping inflation: prices in Shanghai in January 1948 were almost twenty times what they had been a year earlier, and they were just getting into their stride.[6] But the ballrooms were employing about 200,000 women and men by late 1947, and had barely paused even when bombs and bullets flew. And what else could a dancer do? 'I have eight mouths to feed,' one protester explained; 'This is a death sentence for us,' cried another; 'We don't want to become prostitutes,' they shouted. By the end of the day a mob from around an estimated 5,000 protesters had stormed the municipal government office that was tasked with enforcing the decision, and comprehensively wrecked it. Riot police had to quell the disturbances, and a few of those involved were put on trial and jailed, but from 1 April the order was repealed and the ballrooms opened again.[7] The government would have to tolerate a city that danced as China burned.

The reports with their photographs of rioting dancers provide one of the more arresting vignettes of civil war China, and a telling one, demonstrating how this still relatively new culture was embedded into the urban leisure world, how much a feature of the economy it was, and also how it still had many opponents who abhorred it. This violent carnival of the dancers in Shanghai on 31 January was also symptomatic of the by now fragile hold on power of the Guomindang, and the exasperation with the times even of those within a world that hardly had a political culture. Yet even though all China was in this state of febrile uncertainty, the country's future had once seemed better than ever back in August 1945. Chiang Kai-shek had finished the war as leader of one of the 'Big Four' powers, allied in victory and shaping and commanding the new world order of the United Nations. His prestige was never higher, despite the intensification of criticism from his partners overseas, not all of which had been *sotto voce*, and a general unravelling of foreign confidence in the regime in the latter part of the conflict.[8] The National Government had never been militarily stronger, and it had regained Chinese sovereignty over Manchuria and colonial Taiwan, and over the Japanese concession districts. It brushed aside all remaining foreign territorial claims except British Hong Kong and Portuguese Macao, and reinforced the abolition of the 'unequal treaties' when it came back into possession. At a local level it had blithely failed to honour its handover commitments, and the wartime Japanese-organized fait accomplis stood, with no compensation for employees or creditors of the former foreign concessions and settlements. Even private foreign firms found it very difficult, as they had feared, to get their plants and businesses back. The costs for China of resisting the invader, and of pinning down a million Japanese soldiers and a sizeable part of the enemy's war machine throughout the Pacific War, had been horrendous, but the gains in August 1945 looked to have been immense. China stood proud and tall: a genuinely independent state with few equals, its humiliations, dismemberment and junior status removed.

In barely four years of civil war all of this was lost. The National Government fled to Taiwan, established a Provisional Capital of the Republic of China in Taipei, and prepared, fruitlessly, to 'recover the mainland'. As the Chinese Communist Party proclaimed a Central People's Government of a 'People's Republic of China' in October 1949, the Guomindang began intensifying what became a violent purge within its ranks of those suspected of having helped it 'lose China'.[9] In the United States and Europe a different shakeout took place, personified in Senator Joseph McCarthy's witch-hunt for those alleged to be communist agents or sympathizers who had facilitated this shattering world-historical event. Amongst the targets of what became a widespread crackdown on the American left were the Institute of Pacific Relations and critics of the Guomindang government within the State Department. John Service, who had uncritically championed a US engagement with Yan'an, was hounded for years. Liberals and leftists were swept up in a profoundly anti-democratic clampdown, even as genuine Soviet spies were also uncovered.[10] The Cold War chilled the democracies, but in Asia there was more than frost: it was an active and dangerous armed conflict, pitching forces from America, Britain and fourteen other member states of the United Nations against Chinese troops and Soviet pilots in Korea from 1950 to 1953. At one point in 1951 American planes inadvertently bombed a Russian airfield near Vladivostok. And Chinese supplies, training and advisors were deployed in support of the Viet Minh in the independence war against the French, who were in turn aided by the United States.

Helped by the Soviet Union, which declared war on Japan on 8 August 1945 and invaded Manchuria, the Chinese Communist Party had grown as rapidly in confidence, strength and support as the Nationalists equally steadily and swiftly shrunk into themselves. No amount of mediation or US military or financial aid could save the Nationalists from their own disunity, timidity and incompetence, and from their spirited, determined and fiercely well-organized, well-disciplined and increasingly well-armed opponents. The Guomindang's terror apparatus, assisted and equipped by America, continued as violently and seemingly arbitrarily as ever, but for all its murderous vigilance it wreaked its greatest harm on the National Government's cause. Its extra-legal killings, such as that of the poet and scholar Wen Yiduo in July 1946 – 'with American silent revolvers', one of his friends noted – shortly after he had delivered an impassioned, angry elegy at the funeral of another victim, were symptomatic of its viciousness, and its looming failure. 'How many days are left for you,' Wen had declaimed. 'You're finished! It is over for you!'[11]

With the Japanese surrender had come the long-prepared-for scramble to secure an advantageous position in China. Communist forces, now calling themselves the People's Liberation Army (PLA), immediately moved out of their bases and rapidly doubled the territory the party held. But American troops landed in Tianjin to take over from Japanese forces in the north, and then 110,000 Guomindang soldiers were airlifted to Nanjing and Beijing in US aircraft to secure them. From north China the Nationalists advanced along the railways into Manchuria, taking over the cities as the Russians pulled out – cities shorn of all industrial plant except breweries, distilleries and cigarette enterprises, reported one American observer, for their occupation troops had needed supplies of those. But the Communists had ferried tens of thousands of troops across the Bohai Gulf from Shandong, and while US mediation efforts brought the two sides to the negotiating table, the Manchurian countryside largely fell under communist control. Chiang Kai-shek committed his forces to a strategy to hold the cities, but the Communists, who steadily increased their forces, besieged these. The civil war waxed and waned, and was interrupted by US-brokered ceasefires. The Communists lost Yan'an, but then largely gained Shandong. In the winter of 1947 they launched an offensive that firmly consolidated their hold on Manchuria, cutting off the cities by destroying the railway lines along which they could be resupplied. Perhaps 200,000 civilians starved to death in the besieged 'living tomb' of Changchun before it fell to the PLA in September 1948. With it fell any hope of retaining Manchuria. Quickly following their advantage, the Communists thrust southwards. No longer a guerrilla force, this was now a battle-hardened, well-trained and well-equipped army, and it routed – or suborned – the demoralized Guomindang forces. In January 1949 the PLA seized Beijing, Tianjin and most of eastern China north of the Yangzi River. In May it crossed the Yangzi.[12]

Crushed on the battlefield, an army of half a million men destroyed, the Nationalists went into retreat. A population weary after nearly two decades of unremitting conflict turned towards the prospect of a peace under the Communists, most giving the party at least the benefit of the doubt. 'The Chinese people have stood up!' Mao Zedong stated at a meeting three weeks before the proclamation of the new state in 1949, but this claim – of self-reliance, self-determination and self-liberation – was rhetorical, not analytical, and what the Chinese Communist Party's victory ushered in was not an era of total self-reliance, but initially just a change of partners, and a new phase in the attempted development of China in collaboration with foreign allies and foreign experts. It was out with the old and in with the new, and at the same time China went to war against the West, delivering a series of stunning victories over the US-led United Nations forces in Korea.

Against the backdrop of the end of the war, and the triumph of the

Chinese Communist Party, we can examine the history across the middle of the twentieth century of initiatives to aid China. Never had a country been on the receiving end of such a diverse range of official and private ventures that aimed to help it develop, or reconstruct itself after decades of civil war and foreign invasion.[13] The costs of these good intentions were high. They were at the same time welcomed, although guardedly, by the Chinese state, and resented and then repelled for reasons of realpolitik and national pride. In this sphere, as in many others, there were more continuities across the change of regime in 1949 than there was rupture. Philanthropic and humanitarian initiatives first developed that were embedded in the missionary world. These were then augmented by political, educational, military and scientific missions, by private relief initiatives organized by charitable foundations, and then by the activities after the Second World War of the United Nations Relief and Rehabilitation Administration (UNRRA). The seizure of power by the Chinese Communist Party ushered in a new era of sustained co-operation with the USSR and the Communist Eastern bloc states. Foreign experts flooded in who spoke new languages, or spoke in old tongues but with the new jargon of socialist internationalism and fraternity. In many ways, however, they were as paternalistic, condescending and self-serving as any of those they replaced. In July 1960, as relations between China and the USSR cracked apart, this fresh set of foreign experts was abruptly withdrawn. Scores of projects were left unfinished, and with the exception of only a few allies, China was only then genuinely alone for the first time in a century to determine its own path.

From the outset of the establishment of the Western presence in China in the 1840s, the notion that an enhanced foreign presence would somehow aid the country had been present. Diplomats and merchants talked glibly about how commerce would inexorably enrich the country, if not raise its level of 'civilization' – as Europeans and Americans conceived and took it upon themselves to judge that standard. More trade would make the state strong and prosperous, and the people too, while 'ignorance', 'superstition' and 'cruel' social practices would decline. Protestant missionaries, who had embarked for China on the earliest ships, aimed to aid the Chinese to salvation, and to recast Chinese society itself through Christian precepts and values. Most of those traders would talk whatever highfalutin tosh would further their interests, and many missionaries were focused on a rapid salvation of the souls of individuals alone. But the notion of them all bringing a wider benefit became a rhetorical necessity for those defending the foreign enterprise in China, or lobbying for its expansion beyond the first five treaty ports, and then the greater though still restricted number opened after 1860. It was in many places a sincerely held belief nonetheless. Sir Robert Hart, who had assumed effective control of the Imperial Maritime Customs Service in 1863, placed the uplift of China at the heart of his mission for that service, which as a result came to oversee a wide range of projects. Although he directed a secular agency Hart was a profoundly religious man, and this also shaped his view of what he ought to try to achieve for China. The Customs Service delivered its core functions: it assessed duties and managed the process by which goods arrived and left China. But it developed as a cabinet of experts for the Qing, and a recruiting board for expertise that the state lacked. In the 1860s this mainly focused on activities that would strengthen the military capacity of the state, but its reach grew far broader. It supported translation projects, an interpreters' school, and public-health, medical and scientific initiatives. It built lighthouses, charted rivers and harbours, and established a Western-style Post Office.[14] Customs commissioners busied themselves out of hours with development or educational projects, with campaigns against foot binding, or projects to counter female infanticide – the latter two being issues that loomed large in the foreign imagination. Only good, surely, could come from this, for all concerned.

For pragmatic reasons, parts of the mission enterprise developed medical and educational initiatives from quite early on. At first, this was simply a way of securing audiences. Pity the hospital patient with a headache: waiting rooms at missionary clinics were never quiet, for they were sites that held moderately captive audiences, who then became targets for evangelical exhortation. Children at mission schools learned their lessons, but also their hymns and prayers, and Christian codes of conduct and modes of deportment. The development of social gospel thinking in the later nineteenth and early twentieth centuries led to an intensification of such activity as an end in itself and its expansion into other spheres. Hospitals, schools and colleges themselves started to become important sites of missionary endeavour, not as adjuncts to mission, but as the prime vehicles for Christian activity. The YMCA was the major force in a steadily widening portfolio of educational, social and industrial initiatives.[15] As the most widely dispersed facet of the foreign presence – with a Protestant presence in over 95 per cent of China's counties, for example – missionaries had also been ideally placed to respond to crisis, and to lobby through their international support networks for aid during episodes of famine or flooding.[16] Their high-profile involvement in the Shandong Famine Relief Committee during the 1876–9 north China famine, or the International Famine Relief Commission in 1921–2, amongst others, helped embed missions further into the public life of Qing and then republican China, and also reinforced the place of secular activity within the world of mission work.[17]

The late Qing reforms and those of the early republic had also seen the efflorescence of foreign advisors and experts.[18] Robert Hart had formerly been unique – not being a diplomat – in having the ear of senior officials. But by the 1920s every government office seemed to have its advisors, and the game of empires in China also became the game of planting such experts in this office or that one. It became a fixture of loan negotiations, and lay at the heart of the colonization of the central state apparatus that was explicit in Japan's May 1915 Twenty-One Demands. In 1914 there were Dutch, German, Italian and Japanese finance advisors to the Chinese government, and American and Japanese constitutional experts. The Ministry of War had a German, Japanese and French expert, and the Ministry of Communications was advised by the Germans, French and Danes. The former *Times* correspondent, Australian George Ernest Morrison, had the ear of President Yuan Shikai, and another Briton, former Shanghai International Settlement police chief C. D. Bruce, provided advice on police matters. The government's legal advisor was Belgian.[19] There were other advisors at provincial levels and in lower offices of state. They all watched each other's advisors like hawks, noting the possible advantage that might accrue to this state or that one. Some of these men were genuinely committed to their role; some did their jobs professionally enough; others bided their time and accrued their often generous salaries.

The 1920s and 1930s were the golden age of opportunity for advisors and experts, which saw high-level placements organized by governments, and freelance operatives touting their expertise to any two-bit general who would pay them. Foreign experts secured well-paid sinecures in the central state, appeasing their diplomats, and a range of overseas military and other experts accounted for their own share of the resources of the competing militarists, including the Guomindang itself. At one extreme, Sir Francis Aglen, Hart's successor, effectively held the purse strings of the republic, and he was therefore, inescapably, a man whom presidents listened to. At the other end of the spectrum men like Frank 'One Arm' Sutton (the other was left at Gallipoli) brought cynical greed and much experience to bear on military tactics, and in his case, a devastating refinement of the trench mortar for Zhang Zuolin's armies.[20] This melange of refined and vulgar expertise continued into the era of the National Government after 1927. German military advisors were vital to the training of the National Government's army after 1933. Soviet Russian and then volunteer American pilots – the Flying Tigers – flew against the Japanese invaders. The British collared the navy. American Arthur Young served as a senior government economic advisor from 1929 onwards, but a Bank of England mission, nonetheless, helped reform the national currency in 1935–6.[21] Like his predecessors, Chiang Kai-shek would make purely symbolic appointments for political reasons, but also maintain a diplomatic balance of power. In 1936 the British still held the Customs Service, and foreign advisors from the United States, France, Germany, Austria and Yugoslavia held important posts in five of the ministries, the Americans holding by far the majority of the jobs.[22]

Advisors came, could be the subject of rancour and dispute, and they could also be withdrawn. The German military mission was terminated at Japanese insistence in May 1938.[23] The sour wartime saga of US General 'Vinegar Joe' Stilwell's relationship with Chiang Kai-shek – the 'peanut' as the American too publicly nicknamed his superior – has had many retellings. Appointed Chiang Kai-shek's chief of staff in January 1942, Stilwell lacked the patience needed to make the relationship a success, let alone real experience of leading in the field. Strategic differences and operational disputes, set against a wider context of intra-Allied political fractiousness, were compounded by personal animosity. In Stilwell's case this was generously apportioned: the British and their commanders, notably Louis Mountbatten, were as much a target as Chiang – but Stilwell did not instruct his deputy to make contingency plans to assassinate Mountbatten, which he did in Chiang's case. In September 1944, President Roosevelt demanded that Stilwell be appointed Commander in Chief of the Chinese armed forces, an impossibly humiliating and unrealistic idea. Stilwell was then abruptly withdrawn.[24] Expediency could make for stranger partnerships. The Japanese China Expeditionary Force commander General Okamura Yasuji seems to have started advising the Nationalist defence ministry on anti-communist strategy almost immediately after surrendering his forces in 1945, a role that was formalized in Taiwan in 1950.[25]

Many of these men – without exception men – were influential in their spheres.[26] Outside the immediate orbit of the Chinese state, meanwhile, grew another large sector in which foreign philanthropists and humanitarians helped shape republican China, building on the pioneering social gospel, educational and medical initiatives of the missionaries. One facet of this was shaped by policies dealing with the legacy of the punitive indemnity imposed on the Qing as part of the 1901 Boxer Protocol. This was designed to compensate the foreign powers for the costs of the military operations and the occupation of north China, and to compensate for losses of property and in lives. Customs revenues were to pay for the loan taken out to make the indemnity payments. But the indemnity was based on luxuriously generous estimates – twice as much as could possibly be reasonable in the American case – and was almost immediately regretted by some of the diplomats. In 1908 the US government approved a reduction of the sum demanded by almost half, and, as a great deal of it had already been paid, the redirection of the remainder to educational initiatives.[27]

At first these focused on the programme to educate Chinese students in the United States, and to establish a college, which later became Tsinghua University, to prepare them for their studies. This scheme would take Hu Shi, for example, Lin Yutang and Theodore Tu across the Pacific, among a final total of some 22,000 students who were scattered across the continent.[28] In 1925 these arrangements were revised to create a China Foundation for the Promotion of Education and Culture. Among the initiatives it funded were the establishment of the National Library of China (1929), a doubling of the resources available to the National Geological Survey (which almost uniquely amongst Chinese scientific institutions at this time was internationally recognized for the quality of its work), and wider capacity-building in scientific research and teaching across a range of universities, as well as fellowships for academic visits overseas. Unusually for a foreign-funded body this was wholly in the hands of its distinguished board of Chinese trustees.[29]

At the same time the British were moving to remit their own portion of the indemnity, diverting the greater part into a new Chinese Government Purchasing Commission to procure infrastructural equipment from the United Kingdom (mainly for railway construction), to fund scholarships at the University of Hong Kong, and establish a Universities China Committee in London to support academic exchanges.[30] Other contracting powers similarly established educational, scientific or cultural programmes, or developmental schemes that directed the spending to their own industries. The National Palace Museum, the newly established central government research institution known in English as Academia Sinica (*Zhongyang yanjiu yuan*), and a score of universities and other educational institutions in China, received support.[31]

None of this was in the slightest bit disinterested. Remission aimed to take the sting out of nationalistic objections to the continued servicing of the underlying debt (which was scheduled over four decades), and prevent unilateral renunciation of the commitments, and the impact which that could have on markets. But in each case the projects were designed to further cultural diplomacy objectives, or to lock China into purchasing relationships that benefited the home markets of the countries concerned. And these foreign soft-power programmes had the perfect virtue of being paid for by China itself. The ability of the Qing and its successors to make their own spending decisions was sharply constrained. Initially, the repayment commitments reduced the available revenue left to the state by just under one-half, but even as that proportion declined the hypothecation of customs revenues to debt servicing severely hampered the state. It was later argued, facetiously, that this was all for China's longer-term good, given the propensity of the militarist-controlled Beijing government for unproductive military expenditure that simply fuelled further civil conflict. But the Boxer Indemnity degraded the sovereign autonomy of the Chinese government and was a source of rumbling discontent.

The cumulative effect of this significant investment into the cultural, scientific and educational sphere was huge, nonetheless, even if this was in many ways simply a continuation of the great game of appointing advisors by other means, and on a different scale. Such programmes created, it was hoped, ties of affinity, and language, and an American- or a Japanese- or a British-facing elite, with whom business could be done and understandings reached. The experience of study overseas certainly did not always endear students to their hosts, not least as racist US Chinese exclusion laws – the only immigration legislation in US history that discriminated on the basis of perceived 'race' – were not repealed until 1943.[32] But in general, connections were certainly made that persisted, and institutions were created or supported that had a profound impact in China.

This state-driven initiative dovetailed with private-sector investment. By 1921, Protestant mission societies had founded over 250 hospitals, nine medical colleges and fourteen universities in China.[33] But missionary work was never well funded; and 'hospital' was in many ways an aspirational description for many of the institutions concerned. In contrast, by the time the United States ordered a trade embargo with the People's Republic in December 1950, the private Rockefeller Foundation had spent US$55 million on Chinese projects over the previous four decades (equivalent in 2014 prices to $400 million).[34] The objective was 'the gradual development of a system of scientific medicine in China'.[35] It had supported some seventy-five Chinese institutions: hospitals, universities and colleges, providing foundational support for departments in the natural sciences, sociology, economics, agricultural and soil science, public health and rural reconstruction. Initiatives such as those led by the social reformer James Yen at Ding Xian, or agronomist John Lossing Buck at Nanjing University, received important investment. Beijing's Yenching University secured about a quarter of its budget from the foundation in 1927–37, and Tianjin's Nankai University was another important legatee. The foundation's own funds were a legacy of the Rockefeller family's controlling interest in the Standard Oil Company, which until 1909 had a near monopoly on the market in the United States, and which had made for John D. Rockefeller a private fortune greater than the entire US federal budget for 1913. The Standard Oil Company of New York (SOCONY) was the largest American company operating in China. It had also secured possibly the strongest secular role in domestic understandings of the US presence in China through Alice Tisdale Hobart's best-selling 1933 novel *Oil for the Lamps of China*, and its 1935 film adaptation. SOCONY's success was derived from its innovative marketing practices in China, but it was also, of course, a beneficiary of its extraterritorial status, and from the low tariff that was embedded in the mid-nineteenth-century treaties. Rockefeller gave, but like the Boxer Indemnity programmes, though less directly, Rockefeller took.

Forty per cent alone of the foundation's China expenditure had gone on an endowment for its flagship Peking Union Medical College (PUMC), opened in 1921 on a large site half a mile from the Forbidden City. More funding had gone to the college for its annual operating costs. PUMC was another foreign 'model' institution, a lavishly funded medical training and research hospital, embedded within a state-of-the-art hospital. Its patients were ordinary urban residents of Beijing, but Sun Yat-sen's terminal cancer was diagnosed there, and it was the site of the autopsy performed on his body, his first funeral service, and of the embalming of his body in 1925. Chiang Kai-shek and Song Meiling had been patients. The college was established on a grand scale in a former imperial palace complex, with new buildings in an 'adaptive' style that was becoming predominant in missionary architecture, melding some facets of Chinese architectural design (roofs, mainly) with the European/American norm. The architect Harry Hussey had been particularly inspired, he said, by the British Legation complex.[36] The college had initially been established in 1906 by a consortium led by the London Missionary Society, American Board of Commissioners for Foreign Missions and American Presbyterian Mission. Yet Rockefeller funding transformed this from the workable but mediocre standard that was generally the norm in underfunded missionary institutions into something quite out of the ordinary, even by international standards: a Johns Hopkins for China, an elite institution.

There was nothing adaptive about PUMC's mission, which was to serve as an exemplar of scientific medicine for China. It established 'a standard of work to which all other schools in China must reach', it was declared, not least if they wished their graduates to join it. PUMC conducted some world-leading research, and trained an elite cadre of doctors – 313 of them by 1943 – and it refreshed and updated the skills of a greater number of mid-career missionary and other doctors from across China.[37] It was viewed by one Chinese observer, even at its dedication ceremony, as privileging 'quality, and not quantity', and 'if it had only one student, that student was to be a sound one'.[38] This elitism was both a virtue and a problem. How appropriate PUMC's mission was, given that it soaked up a tremendous proportion of Rockefeller Foundation support, remained a controversial point over the course of its history of working in China. Its graduates moved into influential and leading positions in China's health sector, but their uphill task there was not aided by the foundation: barely 3.6 per cent of Rockefeller funds went to Chinese institutions. And PUMC's expatriate staff, in particular, were well paid and well housed, living lives in their palatial 'self-contained island' – with its own power, gas and water supply – not too dissimilar to those that could be enjoined by comfortably well-off merchants in the model settlement at Shanghai. The director lived in the sole remaining building of the original Manchu palace complex, but with all modern conveniences.[39] Despite explicitly being cast as a model institution, PUMC also evaded National Government medical and educational regulations that required Chinese nationals to be the directors of all such institutions: PUMC's were merely nominal. The board of trustees did not have substantive independence until the later 1940s. It was an American institution, run from the United States, and its endowment was invested there.

All had been in agreement at PUMC's formal opening and

dedication in September 1921 about the virtues of scientific medicine.[40] But why, others argued, should that science be directed by foreigners, and was it appropriately directed to serve China's needs? One of those asking this question was the physicist Zhu Kezhen (Coching Chu), one of the second batch of American Boxer Indemnity students, who had arrived in the US in October 1910, his queue newly shorn off by a Japanese barber in Shanghai. Zhu eventually graduated with a PhD in meteorology from Harvard University in 1918, and by then was already a leading figure in a group of young nationalist students who had established the Science Society of China, a body that aimed to save the nation through science. He would return home to direct a new Institute of Meteorology at Academia Sinica (1928–36), become the President of Zhejiang University in 1936, and after 1949 would serve for over two decades as one of the leading science administrators in the People's Republic.[41] Zhu pioneered the use of Chinese historical texts to reconstruct the country's climate history, but he would find it quite impossible to secure copies of the much more recent data generated by an agency of the Chinese state: the foreign-led Maritime Customs Service. A 1931 account of his institute and its work had argued that unless it could 'freely draw its observation material from a weather-reporting organization under its own control', it 'eventually will be forced to play a very subordinate role in the development of synoptic meteorology'.[42] The quandaries of nationalism included this struggle over science.

Robert Hart had offered the resources of the Customs Service to 'science' – as defined and represented by the British Royal Society – in 1873, and the prime outcome had been the development of China's first meteorological network, based at the stations and lighthouses of the Customs.[43] This systematically harvested data for research, and grew to be incorporated into an East Asian storm-warning system. The institution with which the Customs collaborated closely for over sixty years was the observatory at the Jesuit Zikawei (Xujiahui) College in Shanghai, which was at once part of a global network of research institutes run by the society, and part of an overlapping system of scientific bodies working for the French colonial empire.[44] This was an effective arrangement, for its time, but, as Zhu would later point out, its research and its forecasting served only China's maritime economy, and thereby and overwhelmingly the interests of foreign coastal shipping and ocean-going trade. There are strong parallels with PUMC, which also seemed focused on Western scientific priorities, and not on China's developmental needs, as identified by the Chinese. China, it could be argued, needed public-health campaigns, or midwives, not a cadre of specialist physicians.

From their inception the meteorological work of both the Customs and Zikawei Observatory had been clearly bound up with the foreign presence in China, and remained so into the 1930s. The observatory conducted pioneering research into typhoon systems that primarily affected maritime communications. But China's wider problem of the recurring vulnerability to extreme weather phenomena, which caused drought or flooding, was not addressed by the Jesuit scientists. How might China be better prepared to cope? Meanwhile, Zikawei broadcast daily weather forecasts in Russian, English and French, but, extraordinarily, not Chinese, and its institutional patrons were entirely foreign, comprising the French Navy, the Shanghai French concession authorities, the government of French Indochina, the French Ministry of Foreign Affairs and various foreign shipping companies. And of course these organizations and authorities expected some return for their patronage. The French Navy received twice-daily weather forecasts and contracted the Jesuits to carry out geophysical surveys on its behalf. In the 1930s data were still routinely sent to the central observatory in Tokyo, and even after the outbreak of war in 1937, to the Japanese naval authorities in Shanghai.[45] In a sphere that was increasingly seen as vital to national defence, the privileged access of foreign military organizations to potentially sensitive data generated by a Chinese government agency was a contradiction that was no longer tenable. No state could tolerate this, but China had had to.

On coming to power the Nationalists were committed to imposing their authority over meteorological work and to channelling the data collected into the service of China's needs. This was part of a wider programme of the marshalling of natural resources, development of strategic productive capacity and scientific research, all aimed at building up the military capacity of the new state.[46] Cutting-edge meteorological research and weather forecasting were to be taken out of the hands of foreign-run observatories and placed under the control of local and central government. But China's patchy sovereignty obstructed its developmental ambition here as elsewhere. While they continued to apply pressure, the meteorologists worked around their difficulties – as Nationalist agencies had in other areas – in this case establishing meteorological stations independently of the Customs, which were also much better equipped.[47] Zikawei Observatory, rather than being heartened by this progress, was clearly alarmed by the government's plans. It had in the late nineteenth and early twentieth centuries been at the forefront of meteorological research in China, had managed to gain privileged access to raw meteorological data, and the Jesuits had even represented 'China' at congresses of the International Meteorological Organization. Unwilling to see its standing eroded, Zikawei's director even proposed in May 1937 that the League of Nations finance the establishment of a nationwide meteorological service in China under Jesuit control. The proposal came to nothing, but it is indicative of the otherworldliness of such foreign institutions, shared with those who dreamed of a Shanghai Free City, or who argued in all seriousness that the British concession at Tianjin was a 'neutral country' during the Pacific War.[48]

The war brought all these problems to the surface. In the face of the Japanese occupation of Beijing, some PUMC students and staff made the trek to the southwest and to what became the Southwest Union University (*Lianda*). Most famously, the entire nursing-school team walked out of the city and a thousand miles south to Chongqing in 1942. But most faculty stayed put: as an American-owned institution, the college remained untouched by the Japanese until Pearl Harbor, when teaching ceased, only resuming six years later in 1947. Many of those who relocated kept themselves aloof from developments. PUMC students mostly came from wealthy families, and had been educated in missionary colleges; they could afford the fees, which were five times those of study at government or other schools. More than half of the graduates studied abroad for a while after graduation, and in total about half of them went into medical teaching. PUMC's comfortable confines encouraged the 'monastic isolation' of this elite cadre from the world outside, and the emerging wider infrastructure of health in China. And while the ratios of foreign and Chinese staff changed from a rough equality in numbers in

1925–6 to one in ten by 1940–41, foreign nationals still dominated half of all senior positions and only in 1947 was a Chinese appointed director. PUMC was hardly rooted in its Chinese soil, and it lacked legitimacy as a result.[49]

Zikawei faced escalating political problems in the aftermath of the war. The politicization and militarization of meteorological work, which was a global phenomenon, and the heightened nationalistic tone of wartime and post-war life, meant that Chinese government agencies were keen to protect their own spheres and reclaim sovereign rights where these were seen to be imperilled. The foreign presence in the Customs Service was an obvious target after 1941 and only the need to sweeten potential foreign aid donors, and thereby secure resources for the reconstruction of China's shattered maritime infrastructure, kept any foreign nationals in the service at all. Senior appointments of foreign staff were still being made after Lester Little took over, such as the Briton E. A. Pritchard to the post of Shanghai Commissioner in June 1946 for just such expedient reasons, despite a chorus of public criticism. The Finance Minister T. V. Soong was critical of what he reportedly termed such 'narrow chauvinistic nationalism', but the regime could certainly deploy just that weapon when it wanted to, and it remained wholly committed to its nationalist principles.[50] Zikawei also provided an obvious target, and was the subject of conflict in 1947 with the Nationalist Government's Central Meteorological Bureau. In February 1947 the observatory was ordered to close 'to maintain [Chinese] national rights', but although it had to bow to the national administration and was placed under the orders of the Shanghai Meteorological Bureau, Chinese control remained incomplete.[51]

As they streamed back into the liberated cities in the late summer of 1945 after the Japanese surrender, the Nationalists had scrambled to help themselves to what they found there, devastating fragile economies in a wave of confiscations and extortions. Foreign businesses had had to fight to get their properties back: these had been seized by the Japanese in 1942, and so in 1945 passed into the hands of Nationalist 'Enemy Property Administrations'. In the immediate aftermath of the surrender the Japanese military as well as criminals – the distinctions collapsing rapidly – systematically looted what they could find.[52]

Formally, or informally, Nationalist officials made hay from their positions of power, a favourite quip being that they quickly set about securing for themselves a round quintet of confiscated 'possessions': house, car, gold, cash and women. This was just the start. Once the essential comforts of an official's life and marks of his status were secured, they also took mill, shop, dockyard and factory, and caches of any goods that they could get their hands on, and of the hundreds of thousands of tons that now started to arrive. The post-war international relief effort in China became a byword for graft and corruption on a previously unheard-of scale – even for China.[53] Politics also intervened. Why, the Chinese asked, should horse racing resume in the heart of the city? It was an activity intimately bound up with the old order of concessions and extraterritoriality. It cannot have helped that the Chairman of the Race Club was Cornell Franklin, an American lawyer and sometime chairman of the Shanghai Municipal Council. Racing never resumed.[54] Most firms eventually succeeded in reacquiring their assets; however, the civil war years and the hyperinflation brought great strains to labour relations, and to the business of operating in a battered and divided country.

While Nationalist officials arrived from western China to help themselves, some 2,200 foreign nationals from thirty-eight different countries also started arriving to work for the largest single aid initiative that China had ever seen. The United Nations Relief and Rehabilitation Administration (UNRRA), working through its Chinese partner, the China National Relief and Rehabilitation Administration (CNRRA), provided roughly $520 million worth of supplies and services to China from January 1945 until the end of the programme in December 1947, the greater part of it provided by the United States. Four hundred Chinese would travel overseas for study and training. Hundreds of foreign staff were seconded to Chinese state and CNRRA positions by UNRRA (an activity that was firmly placed by the organization itself in the context of the history of foreign advisors and employees in the Customs Service and Post Office, for example).[55] Over 2.4 million tons of material was shipped in, three-quarters of it through Shanghai. Jealous to preserve its newly acknowledged sovereignty, the National Government demanded that the work be done under Chinese administration through CNRRA and not by UNRRA directly, and political tensions persisted in this vein throughout its lifetime. This figured even in its name in Chinese, *Xingzheng yuan shanhou jiuji shu*: the Relief and Rehabilitation Administration of the National Government Executive Yuan (its presidential cabinet). The biggest source of controversy, however, was around corruption, and alleged incompetence. Aid rotted in Shanghai warehouses, or was taken out and sold on the market in Shanghai to feed the city, while Hunan province starved and *Life Magazine* published photographs of an unfolding catastrophe that affected 33 million people. Officials sold CNRRA flour to restaurants, and soldiers seized what they wanted. A rice-shop owner smiled for *Life*'s photographer, as a starving child begged in front of her.[56] 'The whole of Shanghai is living on UNRRA supplies,' claimed the British writer and lecturer Robert Payne in 1947, and the 'smell of corruption' pervaded the local CNRRA office.[57]

'We used to say,' quipped one Chinese academic later, that CNRRA stood for 'China Never Really Received Anything'.[58] This was unfair. CNRRA, for example, had a significant impact on the rehabilitation of the area that had been devastated by the 1938 breaching – on Chiang Kai-shek's orders – of the Yellow River dykes. It prepared the way for the redirection of the river back onto its former course, and re-establishment of farming in areas also harried by the 1942–3 Henan famine that claimed an estimated four million lives.[59] UNRRA certainly delivered in China, but it was also beset with profound logistical problems, exacerbated by the fact that China's transport infrastructure had been all but destroyed during the war. However, it did not always even attempt to deliver beyond the ports. The Shanghai businessman Liu Hongsheng and his Cambridge-educated son Liu Nianyi, for example, secured influential positions within CNRRA through cultivating US intelligence connections with a view to the advantages that would accrue. They were skilful and adept administrators, and worked voluntarily, but at the same time UNRRA ships were directed by Liu Nianyi to wharves controlled by his family's enterprises, which also gained preferential access to equipment and materials that helped the Lius rehabilitate their own business.[60] It was hardly surprising that CNRRA secured a poor reputation. In the course of its history it would see the arraignment of its chief cashier, deputy director and chief secretary, who all faced criminal prosecution over their handling of supplies or finances.[61] UNRRA itself admitted to having to conduct a 'very large' number of investigations into alleged abuses, but the number of prosecutions was ultimately small. Most abuse went unchecked.[62]

Foreign staff were not exempt from such charges either, but the problem was greater than this. While reserving his sharpest thrusts for Guomindang officials, one bitter, American-educated CNRRA provincial director nevertheless had this view of its foreign staff in late 1946:

> A few are good men, but most of them are 'tourists', who want to 'see China'. They do precious little work, but enjoy the drinking and dancing of Shameen. Some are crack-pot idealists, e.g., a 'welfare worker' who proposes to 'weigh every baby' and 'examine its food under a microscope'.

They are attempting to deploy 'Park Avenue ideas in a Chinese country village,' he claimed.[63] Those who were not humanitarian tourists included former staff of the foreign concession administrations, and American and British ex-employees of the Chinese Maritime Customs (a quarter of UNRRA's 400 British staff had been recruited in China). Arguably they had good local experience and connections, and perhaps – although this should never assumed – some knowledge of its languages. But the shuffling of former servants of the dismantled infrastructure of foreign power into the aid sector hardly sent out the right message, and it was a source of controversy with the National Government. 'Superior attitudes' amongst staff seconded to Chinese agencies were criticized in UNRRA's own wrap-up report.[64] The dissident former US foreign-service officer George W. Kerr summed it up as simply 'the latest but not the last of a century-long series of American philanthropic attempts to improve the conditions of the Chinese people'.[65] It was the secular culmination of the social and philanthropic work of the missionary enterprise, and of the Rockefeller initiative.

Part of UNRRA's remit was to work to repatriate foreign refugees in China, including Europeans and overseas Chinese from Southeast Asia, and it worked alongside the US military's massive 'Operation

Beleaguer', the programme to transport Japanese military and civilians back to Japan. There was a great movement of people generally after the Japanese surrender, and the size of the foreign presence was steadily whittled down. The staff of the foreign concessions and settlements generally had to leave, as very few found alternative employment; the foreign contingent in the Customs Service further declined rapidly in numbers. Some of the foreign communities were shipped out en masse. Shanghai's December 1945 population of 72,500 Japanese were expelled in the course of the following year. This was a less bloody and bitter experience than that of the Manchurian Japanese: 179,000 died there in the year following the defeat from starvation, disease and brutality: almost one in five of its civilian Japanese residents. Almost 70,000 Japanese servicemen also died.[66] A thousand British Indians from the disbanded foreign-run police forces were repatriated swiftly. Up to 4,000 Russians took up Soviet citizenship and sailed to the USSR. A good number were then shipped straight on to the Gulag. Over 5,000 German Jewish refugees secured US entry visas in 1946, and almost 3,000 gained access to Israel in 1948–9. The most bizarre episode involved the transport in early 1949 of almost 5,000 stateless – but clearly more cautious – Russians to the Philippines, where they remained encamped in US-issued tents on Tubabao Island, some for up to two years before gaining clearance to move to Australia or the United States.[67] Urban China's polyphonic chorus started its diminuendo.

Those who remained had to get used to living without privilege, specifically without extraterritoriality. Britons and Americans now found themselves on a legal par with other foreign nationals resident in China. They were at least subjects of the victorious Allied powers, but all were now equal in the eyes of Chinese law. One explosive difficulty, however, was the fact that the large official American presence was not: diplomatic and military personnel (some 10,000 troops still in late 1946) were excluded. A significant test for the new order was the trial of a Hong Kong-born British Eurasian, Charles Archer, for the murder in August 1947 of a Chinese blackmarketeer, Yu Shengxiao. Archer and an accomplice, a US marine, Thomas Malloy, had been involved in bullion deals with Yu, and he had been shot dead. Each blamed the other. Malloy was court-martialled, and jailed for life, a sentence that was to be served in the United States. Archer, who had coincidentally been on an earlier occasion the last Briton jailed under the old extraterritorial system on 2 December 1941, was tried and convicted by a Chinese court. 'First Briton on Murder Charge for 173 Years' ran one headline. Archer was also sentenced to life imprisonment. A British official (a former Shanghai police officer, Harold Gill) pronounced the proceedings 'extremely fair'. But Archer received a harsher sentence than Malloy, a British commentator later claimed, for it was to be spent in a Chinese jail. It was, in fact, to be spent in a Chinese jail built by the British-dominated Shanghai Municipal Council.[68] Manslaughter and murder cases had long been incendiary points of conflict over the decades before extraterritoriality had been imposed. Perceived injustices from the 1820s and earlier were regularly called in as evidence by the defenders of extraterritoriality. But there was little that could be complained of in the Archer verdict – unless it was the fact that in Britain, in all likelihood, he would have been hanged.

A greater problem proved to be the continued immunity of American military personnel. Few cared about a criminal like Yu Shengxiao, but when a Peking University student from an elite family background, Shen Chong, was raped by a US marine corporal, William Pierson, on Christmas Eve in 1946, it sparked a massive nationwide protest.[69] The American military presence was already under fire for the ill-discipline and poor behaviour of its troops in China. They were associated with black-market dealing, like Malloy, drunkenness and street violence, and prostitution. The stock image of the 'jeep girl' filled newspaper caricatures: young Chinese women who consorted with these relatively rich and uncouth foreign soldiers. Comparison was even made with the behaviour of Japanese troops, and officially inspired campaigns against 'jeep girls' had already been launched during the war, with the women serving, for many, as a proxy for an attack on their American companions. Although Pierson was court-martialled and given a fifteen-year sentence, this was nullified on appeal in the United States. The fact that he was not tried by even a joint Sino-American commission, that he eventually went free, and that the defence argument had painted Shen as a willing partner, deeply angered nationalists. The then Peking University

President, Hu Shi, begged the students not to confuse the legal problem of jurisdiction with the political problem of the presence of American troops. But they did. The Communist Party was also shrewd in its political use of the case, as it was over the killing of a rickshaw-puller in Shanghai a month after Yu Shengxiao's death. The crime in Beijing and its handling were of immense and long-lasting importance in the fashioning of a new image of the United States in China. Not only did America support Chiang Kai-shek's government, but its soldiers were drunks, brutes, rapists and murderers. The Guomindang had failed to protect China's sovereignty, and it had failed to protect Shen Chong.

The arrival of communist forces in Shanghai on 25 May 1949 prompted the immediate flight of some foreign nationals, but others left in a more orderly fashion when the blockade of the Yangzi River imposed by the Guomindang allowed, providing material for iconic photographs by Henri Cartier-Bresson, who left with them. Catholic priests, bearded, long-gowned and solar-topeed, made their way to the USS *General W. H. Gordon* in September 1949 in Shanghai; others took their final rickshaw trip to the docks.[70] But many thought this would be business as usual, and just another change of government. Foreign businesses and most of the private sector had seen several such changeovers, and had always adapted. The largest foreign firms, sometimes initially quite gracelessly, had generally managed to establish workable if not amicable relationships with the Guomindang. Standard Oil and British American Tobacco, for example, had agreed voluntary tax payment arrangements that they had no obligation to do under the treaties. BAT was China's single largest taxpayer in the 1930s.[71] There seemed to be no reason why the transfer of power in 1949 should be any different. Moreover, an influential vein of analysis presented the Chinese Communist Party as 'agrarian socialists', not doctrinaire Marxists. The Americans were officially more wary, and to avoid imperilling staff, and so as not to 'court insult', the State Department ordered the closure of all but their Shanghai and Tianjin consulates in the summer of 1949.[72] The troops that padded into Shanghai in their soft-soled shoes on 25 May 1949 looked harmless enough. Cartier-Bresson caught telling moments with his Leica camera as country boys and urban sophisticates looked at each other, and as soldiers of the People's Liberation Army stared bemused at shop windows filled with American-made refrigerators.

With almost indecent haste the British government formally recognized the new regime on 6 January 1950. 'They have trade to offer', reasoned the Foreign Office in marshalling its case in October 1949 for the British cabinet in favour of the decision, and 'we have an immoveable stake in their territory which can only be maintained by trade'.[73] The Guomindang had now no capacity to recapture the mainland, from which it had been all but driven out. The British had never really liked Chiang anyway, as he, of course, had certainly never liked them. With measured calm the Central People's Government noted the announcement, pledged itself to establish diplomatic relations with all friendly powers, and then went profoundly silent. The character of the odd dialogue that did eventually ensue was that the British assumed their relations with China could be viewed and developed as a bilateral state-to-state arrangement in the usual manner of diplomacy. The British had recognized the Central People's Government; and really, they argued, what more could it want? It was impossible, however, for the Chinese Communist Party not to view the British presence as imperialist, and as the residuum of the century of the exercise of foreign power in China. The entire relationship with the Western powers was viewed through this prism, at once intensely ideological and at the same time deeply nationalistic. They might or they might not develop a working state-to-state relationship. But first the new government had to dismantle the remaining infrastructure of imperialism, expunge as far as possible its influence and, as Mao Zedong put it to Stalin in June 1949, its 'lackeys', and prevent any possible re-establishment of an imperialist presence.[74] That had its tangible side – the Shanghai Club, the Cathedral School, ICI's headquarters and factories, the *North China Daily News* – but it had its life in the Chinese mind and Chinese society as well.

The United States was less than happy about the British recognition. It held to its mission to support the Guomindang, to which it had committed vast amounts of aid, credit and material assistance, and a great deal of goodwill. UNRRA had been followed by the 1948 China Aid Bill, which was to be a continuation of that effort, and an attempt to help resolve the political crisis by providing a 'respite', as President Truman called it in February 1948, from China's immediate economic crisis. In total, America calculated that it had provided $1.6 billion in grants to China between 1945 and March 1949 in military and economic support, and a further $400 million in credits. United States policy was aimed at materially assisting the National Government, whilst it tried brokering a compromise between it and the Communists. Successive missions had been undertaken in this vein, most notably by General George Marshall in 1945–7, but no progress was made. The United States had no stomach for active military intervention, and did not think its strategic or even its economic interests required it. But it also did not wish to withdraw entirely from supporting a partner of such long standing, despite the 'painful contrast' with Nationalist officers provided by the communist cadres and soldiers that American foreign-service officers in China itself started to encounter in the 'liberated' areas. Nor did the United States want to disengage from supporting the significant elements in the Guomindang and liberal establishment in whom it placed greater faith than in Chiang Kai-shek and his security state. But its vision was clouded by an idealistic paternalism that owed little to any understanding of its own complicity in the history of the foreign degradation of China after 1842.

American policy initially owed much instead to the power of the Luce press, and the cultural hold of the vision of China and the Chinese as presented there and by the missionary lobby, and encouraged by China's wartime publicity machine in the United States. The power of the influence of 1,000 missionaries home on leave every year, talking, lecturing and writing about China; the impact of years of publicity by China United Relief, the major umbrella wartime aid organization in America; and the influence of Pearl Buck's work, and of MGM's *The Good Earth* – all had secured a place for China in the American imagination that could not easily be reconciled with abandoning its people and their fine and ancient culture to a new tyranny.

The Chinese Communist Party's explicit alignment with the USSR simply added to the difficulties of finding a pragmatic policy, but in August 1949 the State Department released its 'China White Paper', a massive survey of its relations with China that was designed, in the words of one of its authors, to 'call the dogs off from the China

Lobby', and – in its eyes – exonerate it from responsibility for the 'loss of China'. The blame for that lay instead with the National Government. The United States could have done no more. And in January 1950, Secretary of State Dean Acheson announced that America would not even intervene to defend Taiwan from attack.[75] The Nationalists had lost the mainland, and they would not be helped to retain Taiwan.

The Communists feared a foreign counter-attack nonetheless. They would probably seize major coastal ports, Mao thought, and garrison them with large forces. In May 1949, Mao had claimed that British navy vessels were operating with the Guomindang and had inflicted 'great losses' on the PLA.[76] This was almost certainly a reference to the 'Amethyst Incident', the last overt Western military action in Chinese territory. The frigate HMS Amethyst was shelled and disabled by PLA troops near Zhenjiang on the Yangzi in April. Three other ships attempting to reach it had been beaten off by artillery, with the loss of some thirty men. HMS Amethyst spent 100 days pinned down before making a successful dash for the sea that became a legend of British late imperial daring. Meanwhile, Shanghai's Hongqiao cemetery had seen 2,000 foreign residents assemble on 23 April for the burial with full military honours of some of the dead. A Royal Air Force flying boat flew past in salute. This was the last time British rifles were fired in Shanghai, and that British Empire servicemen paraded there. All the rituals of a century of treaty port life were consciously performed for the final time at Holy Trinity Cathedral, on Shanghai's streets and in the cemetery.[77] But trenches and ditches were also being dug, and barricades erected nearby for an armed defence of the city by the Nationalists. The last train out of Nanjing arrived that same morning, and reports quickly followed that communist troops had entered the capital. The Royal Navy pulled out of Shanghai the following day; the last American military personnel left two days later.

It was time to be gone in more ways than one. Foreign reporters found that popular opinion in the city largely applauded the PLA attack on the British ships, for 'the foreigners who had kicked the Chinese around for 100 years had finally got what they deserved'. The American ambassador John Leighton Stuart also noted the 'undertone of national pride' amongst Chinese over the incident.[78] Even in the midst of civil war there was time for satisfaction in Nationalist circles at the defeat that their enemy had inflicted on the once high-riding Royal Navy. Characteristically, the British would themselves deftly extract a victory from this defeat for naval pluck and valour, and the *Amethyst*'s crew would parade through London to the sound of cheering crowds in November that year, but it was a ragged and unsettling end to almost 110 years of military supremacy and confidence in China.

Counter-intuitively the new regime achieved the withdrawal of the rest of the foreign presence – that 'immoveable stake' – largely by not allowing it to happen. This process has been described as 'hostage capitalism': foreign enterprises were ordered to continue working, forbidden from laying off staff, instructed to raise wages and benefits, and prevented from closing down.[79] At first the new regime simply lacked any capacity to run the territory it had occupied with any attention to detail other than that which was vital for consolidating its power. It needed to prevent an economic collapse, and prioritized the resumption of production and the building of the ties needed to stimulate this with China's business circles, whatever their nationality. Gradually, as conditions and its personnel allowed, it took a more active stance. The onset of the Korean War and the imposition of an American trade embargo on 2 December 1950, and a freeze of all Chinese assets in the US two weeks later, changed the game. In retaliation thereafter, American-owned institutions were steadily expropriated, and foreign enterprises generally found conditions hardening against them.

Zikawei's troubles, for example, had multiplied when the Communists took over the city in May 1949. On 12 December 1950 it was formally taken over by the communist authorities, and fully incorporated into the Shanghai Meteorological Observatory. 'Is there a meteorological service in China?' Stalin asked Mao in December 1949. 'It should be established,' he continued, on receiving a negative answer. Well, Zhu Kezhen would claim in 1951, there had been one, but the entire system had only ever served Zikawei, and that served only Anglo-American shipping interests. All of this foreign activity, Zhu later wrote, served only the economic interests of the foreign imperialist powers and their assault on China. It was not until 1949, he continued, and significantly not until the takeover of the Zikawei Observatory in 1950, that the 'cultural aggression' of the imperialist powers on the meteorological front was terminated.[80] PUMC operated as normal, initially, but the remaining overseas staff found, as others did in foreign-financed institutions, that their colleagues and students were the focus of political mobilization efforts that began to target the position and actions of foreign nationals, as well as their history. With the onset of the war in Korea and the development of a 'Resist America Aid Korea' campaign in July 1950, foreign colleagues became the targets of denunciation meetings, and on 16 January 1951 PUMC was nationalized. An American researcher there, Malcolm Berhson, was arrested in July on trumped-up charges of being a spy. He would not be released for four years. As the anti-American campaign grew more intense, the criticism grew wilder. PUMC had been a 'centre for espionage', an exhibition claimed the following year, and the foreign staff had used Chinese patients as guinea pigs in medical experiments: 'it is still an open question how many Chinese were murdered'.[81]

PUMC and Zikawei were high-profile seizures of autonomous foreign institutions that had secured influential or commanding positions within their spheres in China. The moment of their enforced takeover was contingent on the rapidly evolving Korean conflict, but was also the logical culmination of a decades-long process of rights recovery, and the expansion of the concerns and reach of the central Chinese state. Even the best-intentioned foreign experts and helpers still operated within a paternalistic framework of relations with China. Humanitarian endeavour there was hardly alone in this, but the pre-eminence of nationalistic politics made it acutely vulnerable. Pragmatism kept useful foreign institutions in operation, however, until national defence or other considerations became paramount. After all, as the Japanese had found during Shanghai's 'isolated island' period, it was far better to have the costs involved met by others, if they remained willing to shoulder them, and better to retain the capacity provided, than to close it for purely political reasons. Nationalism had its pragmatic side.

Actual confiscation or nationalization of foreign institutions had not in fact ever been the norm. Rarely did the state, Nationalist or Communist, seize foreign assets. The major exceptions had been war-related: the post-1917 and post-1945 seizures of enemy property after the declaration of war on Germany and Austria-Hungary, and the Japanese surrender. But it was also true nonetheless that the wider context for the takeovers of PUMC and Zikawei was the steady thinning out of the foreign presence in China nationally after the establishment of the Central People's Government. By late 1951 the great majority of Western nationals had left China; after this only one British company, Shell, and two banks, remained operating in the country. Everyone else had gone. This was a complex process that was shaped by the economic priorities of the communist regime, and by the Korean War. There was no immediate rupture, and the expectation of all sides was that connections would persist, although some British, French and United States officials were deported and their consulates forcibly closed. A course had now been set that led to China being isolated and self-reliant as almost never before in its history.

Foreign consulates closed as a result but also because of hostile pressure from the new government. In turn these closures reinforced the drift away of their former charges. Having rebuilt their torched building in Guangzhou (at their own expense, the era of reparations long past), the British closed it down in early 1953 (there were only twelve Britons in the city), and it joined the consulates at Chonqging, Xiamen, Kunming, Qingdao, Nanjing and Wuhan that had been sold off a year earlier.[82] The official foreign presence in China was sharply whittled away. But there were two singular exceptions to this pattern: Hong Kong and Macao remained under colonial rule. 'I am not interested in Hong Kong,' Mao had told foreign reporters in 1946. There would be enough to do in China. Later messages stressed that as long as the Chinese in Hong Kong and Macao were not ill-treated, then the new regime would be, for the present, content to allow the status quo to persist. Both colonies would have vital economic and diplomatic roles to play for China, and they would be bases through which it could also extract intelligence. As the PLA occupied Guangdong province, its commanders were careful to avoid any confrontations. The takeover of the border posts on Hong Kong's northern boundary on 17 October 1949 was a 'tranquil' affair, although there was more tension in Macao as refugees and fleeing Guomindang soldiers poured into the tiny colony.[83] The economic roles envisaged for both cities became even more important with the onset of the Korean War trade embargo, but this tolerance had its limits. In 1952, when the Portuguese government bowed to American pressure and toughened border controls to comply with the embargo, the Chinese responded with a series of violent military actions on the border and a blockade that led Lisbon to back down and argue for Macao to be exempt. In 1955 the colony's preparations to mark its 400th anniversary were abandoned in the face of Chinese pressure: postage stamps were pulped, and construction of a monument to Sino-Portuguese friendship was stopped. Chinese displeasure in this instance was communicated informally but tersely through Hong Kong's governor, who assumed that it was also meant for him to note, and through powerful local intermediaries who largely ran Macao behind the scenes. Both colonies were far too useful to China for it to allow their foreign rulers to endanger the status quo through maladministration or through too ostentatiously performing any pageant of colonial triumph.

One sector of the foreign establishment in China had always of course been centrally committed to its own eventual redundancy and withdrawal. Protestant mission societies aimed in theory to establish self-supporting and self-governing churches, after which they would have no major role to play. In practice missionary culture had often become bound into the wider world of colonialism internationally, and in China had relied on extraterritorial privilege and the infrastructure of foreign power. Elements within this diverse world – one estimate counted 109 different societies active in 1949 – displayed all the assumptions associated with the life and culture of the secular foreign establishment. Missionaries lived European- or American-style lives in foreign-style houses in gated compounds.[84] Those working in the more secularized sphere of mission activity in medical, social or educational work might be difficult to distinguish from the foreign personnel of treaty-port institutions. 'Do missionaries ever get lice?' one communist cadre was reported asking.[85] Did they really sacrifice themselves for their beliefs? Undoubtedly, missionaries would reply, who had their martyrologies to hand listing their dead at the hands of Boxers, bandits and Communists, but they were on far shakier ground when it came to charges of complicity in empire, and of cultural imperialism. Their own language hardly helped. Calling their 1922 survey of the missionary presence *The Christian Occupation of China* had been problematic even then, but the language of the Church militant was taken literally by its new enemies. An oft-repeated description of the pioneering American medical missionary Peter Parker, that he had opened the gates of 'China to the gospel at the point of a lancet when Western cannon could not heave a single bar', was the first item raised in the vitriolic public indictment of foreign staff at Lingnan University in Guangzhou at a denunciation rally in December 1950.[86]

There had never been any shortage of self-criticism. Pearl Buck was the most prominent critic from within the mission world. 'Is there a Case for Foreign Mission?' she asked in a controversial 1933 pamphlet. Her conclusion: only if the talking and the preaching stopped and there is Christian – social – action instead. The student Anti-Christian Movement of the 1920s, the upheavals of the Nationalist revolution, and the assertion of Guomindang state power in education and healthcare shook this branch of the foreign establishment like no other. As a result, a steady process of reform within churches and religious institutions had been taking place since the early 1920s, with Chinese Christians moving to take leading roles, but by 1949 the foreign mission communities were still large. Most societies and most individual missions believed that they could ride out what they thought to be just one more in the sequence of China's changes.

In most instances the initial transition to communist rule across the country went smoothly as far as Protestant missionaries were concerned, but this was not to last. In seeking clarification of their status within the new dispensation, Christian organizations came to understand that they needed to distance themselves quite definitively from foreign missions and in fact from any foreign connections. Meetings with Zhou Enlai in May 1950 set out the broad parameters. They must dispense with any financial support from overseas, and any subordination to foreign nationals. This was articulated in what became known as the 'Christian Manifesto', published in July 1950 and drafted by leading figures in the Protestant Churches, which placed Christianity firmly within the history and potential future of imperialist aggression against China. Christianity had been 'related' to imperialism, and so Chinese Christians needed to disassociate themselves from foreign connections. The vehicle that emerged from these self-criticisms and that aimed to divest Chinese Christianity of the imperialist stain was the 'Three Self Patriotic Movement' (*Sanzi aiguo yundong*), established in 1951, which required churches to be self-financing, self-governing and self-propagating.[87] In the churches, schools and colleges where foreign missionaries worked, the situation was already more brittle and turning difficult, and for their Chinese colleagues, it was increasingly dangerous to continue the association. In an atmosphere of denunciations and paralysing suspicion the London Missionary Society decided in September 1950 to withdraw completely by the end of the following year. In December the China Inland Mission announced that it would evacuate all staff, almost a thousand workers and their families. On 18 January 1951 twenty, mostly missionary, colleges funded from overseas were appropriated by the government. The missionary withdrawal rapidly became an undignified rout.

There was a singular exception. The Catholic Church had no intention of pulling out foreign nationals. Its adherents in China were far greater in number than those of the Protestant Churches, and it had a far longer history there. Its response was militant and confrontational, and it was savaged as a result. Scores of foreign priests were arrested. In echoes of nineteenth-century tumults, Irish, Canadian and French nuns who ran orphanages in Nanjing and Guangzhou were pilloried, tried and jailed for neglect of their charges, and then deported. Two thousand babies had died at Guangzhou in two years, it was alleged. Are we back in the bad old nineteenth-century days of rumours of infanticide and of pogroms, perplexed diplomats asked, and are we reliving the 1870 Tianjin massacre of foreign nuns and other outbursts?[88] The Papal Nuncio, Antonio Riberi, was expelled from China in September 1952, the only foreign diplomat who was forced out of the country. He left a Church that was split, and hit by wave after wave of repression.

Other sectors of the foreign presence had a better time of it, though experiences could still be rocky. Government regulations controlled the withdrawal of foreign nationals whatever their role in China had been. For businesses, however, exit-visa controls were used to keep foreign staff in place. Overseas head offices had to start remitting funds to China to cover operating costs, and their branches or subsidiaries were even forbidden from taking on loans locally. In factories and offices new labour union activity, and a potential politicization of every action, every foreign fault or perceived slight, led to confrontations.

Chinese enterprises had similar experiences, except that Chinese nationals also faced the murderous dangers in 1950–52 of a series of campaigns against 'counter-revolutionaries' and others (known as the *zhenfan* campaign). This drive began in March 1950, targeting in particular former Guomindang members, although the category was quite vaguely defined. A wave of terror engulfed 'historical' counter-revolutionaries, rumour-mongers and 'collaborators with imperialism', and many other categories. It could encompass any member of the Guomindang, or Nationalist state functionary, any associate or employee of a foreign firm or other institution, including religious ones. The state provided quotas for executions, Mao Zedong arguing that the new regime would need to execute no more than about 0.1 per cent of the population, although in many localities this target was significantly exceeded. The figure of the Nationalist 'special agent' (*tewu*) – nearly always wearing a fedora hat and looking like a Chicago gangster – was dominant in the language and poster campaigns. Spy fever gripped the country. Nationalist guerrilla forces were certainly still fighting on within the country, and raiding the coast with active American covert support.[89] But most of those consumed by the *zhenfan* campaign were not guerrillas, nor were they *tewu*. The most chilling episode for foreign diplomats was the trial and public execution in Beijing of two alleged foreign spies, one Japanese and one Italian, for leading a supposed American plot to try to assassinate Mao Zedong. The message was clear: no one was safe.[90]

Shanghai's Canidrome became notorious as a site of the most spectacular phase of the crackdown after the Japanese surrender. The greyhound racing continued throughout most of the occupation, but ended with the return of the Nationalists. The ballroom stayed open; the stadium hosted sports events: the American army and navy teams had kicked life back into the pitch in a December 1945 derby.

In October 1950 patrons could still dance away in the ballroom to the boogie-woogie sounds of a nine-piece jazz band led by 'Tayong', the 'Trumpet King'.[91] But on 21 February 1951 new 'Regulations of the People's Republic of China on Punishment of Counter-Revolutionaries' were issued. Large-scale initiatives were launched nationally involving mass arrests, mass trials and mass executions. On the night of 27 April, Shanghai police pounced, arresting 8,000 people. The following afternoon, in front of a crowd of 10,000, nine 'big' counter-revolutionaries were arraigned one by one in a pen on the sports field where Shanghai's foreign communities had played soccer, and around which the dogs had run. Now, instead, 'running dogs' – of imperialism – were vilified and the crowd demanded the death sentence. The men were shot the next day. An estimated 2.8 million people listened to the proceedings on 28 April as they were relayed by radio into workplaces, schools and homes. Another 285 people were tried at the Canidrome on 30 April, and then immediately taken away and killed in front of large crowds. News reports abroad lit on the sanguine use of what had been a leisure venue. It also housed a 'Three Self' rally on 10 June at which leading Christians aggressively denounced their former foreign missionary co-workers (and the Chinese Methodist Church announced the expulsion of Chiang Kai-shek and Song Meiling). Three weeks later the same venue hosted a mass rally to celebrate the thirtieth anniversary of the founding of the Chinese Communist Party.[92]

A campaign against the triple evils of corruption, waste and bureaucracy in late 1951 was then joined in February 1952 by a quintet of evils: bribery, theft of state papers, tax evasion, cheating on government contracts and stealing economic information. There was little these campaigns could not be thought to cover, and in the context of the Korean War these were also considered to be counter-revolutionary crimes, and treated as such.[93] Three thousand people were executed in 1951 alone in Shanghai; the government itself announced in 1956 that 800,000 people had been killed nationally. 'If they had not been killed,' Mao Zedong later told an audience, 'the people would not have been able to raise their heads.'[94]

On the surface, though, the foreign landscape looked much the same. Expatriates still played golf at the Hungjao links (but accidentally hitting a forecaddie with the ball could prompt a major incident, as one wild-swinging foreign golfer found).[95] The *North China Daily News* published its centenary number in August 1950. Felicitations came from the Hongkong and Shanghai Bank, Jardines, Chartered Bank, Lever Brothers and ICI, as well as more locally rooted firms: Arnholds, the Shanghai Land Investment Company, Kelly & Walsh. Capstan Navy Cut cigarettes were advertised, Pan American still publicized its Stratosphere Clipper flights. A later issue of the *North China Daily News* printed advertisements for the Cathay Fur Store, Christmas gifts from Hall & Holtz and White-away's, caviar from 'Gastronome', Christmas cakes from Bianchi's, pianos at San Lazaro's. Church services continued, and the Royal Asiatic Society still organized public talks. Clark Gable, Myrna Loy and William Powell were starring in *Manhattan Melodrama* at the Roxy. The cabarets were mostly still open, and the taxi dancers still worked. But only tea and coffee were served there, *Manhattan Melodrama* was sixteen years old, and another column of advertisements listed exit visas that had been granted, while a news item reported the farewell given by the Filipino community to departing friends. The Ewo Brewery, owned by Jardines, was still brewing beer, but in the atmosphere of terror and repression no one dared drink it.[96] On 31 March 1951 the newspaper appeared for the final time, thanking its 'glorious international brotherhood' of readers as it said farewell. In other columns, the auctioneers L. Moore & Co. advertised the disposal of a property and all its furnishings belonging to Sir Robert Calder Marshall, sometime chairman of the British Chamber of Commerce.

Who bought those furs? The residents of the 'Little Kremlin' or 'Forbidden City', it was said, the guarded and gated compound in Shanghai's Hongqiao district where a large, new and growing community of Russian advisors was quartered, partly in the former residence of the Shanghai manager of Jardine Matheson.[97] Somebody might have smiled as the billeting decisions were made. The Taipan was supplanted by the scientists and technicians on what was called *komandirovka* ('work assignment'). Into Avenue Joffre the Russians poured, first buying suitcases, and then filling them up, steadily clearing out the stocks that remained of imported luxury goods. Canadian

Silver Fox furs were particularly popular. These avid shoppers were the advance guard of what has been estimated to have finally totalled about 20,000 Russian and East European advisors who came to China between 1949 and 1960. This was the single largest cohort of 'China helpers' ever dispatched. They worked at the highest levels of the new Chinese state, in factories and on large-scale infrastructure projects. They worked in China's universities, trained the PLA's new air force and its navy, and reorganized its healthcare system. Some 38,000 Chinese headed in the other direction on study tours and placements in the USSR and Eastern bloc countries. New students and established intellectual figures flocked to Russian language classes. For those challenged by this, large numbers of Russian language books were translated; these new textbooks, manuals and literary and artistic works made up over 40 per cent of books published in China between 1954 and 1957.[98] 'Sino-Soviet Friendship' had its own association, exhibitions and journal, and a massive exhibition centre opened in Shanghai in 1956 on the site of the former residence of opium and property tycoon Silas Aaron Hardoon.[99]

Over the course of its history it has been estimated that the Soviet programme in China amounted to US$25 billion (at 2012 prices), equivalent to about 1 per cent a year on average of the USSR's GDP.[100] These numbers alone cannot convey the breadth and reach of the work undertaken. In 1953–7, during the period of the First Five Year Plan for economic development, the contribution of Soviet bloc aid included the construction of 108 industrial plants, and supply of equipment for another 88 that the Chinese would build from their own resources, and the delivery of some 4,000 major pieces of technology.[101] This material did not end up in the hands of the canny Liu family; Hunan shop owners did not grow fat as a result. It all made an 'enormously astonishing impression' on one Soviet visitor, the scientist Aleksei Vasil'evich Stozhenko, as he reported in a letter in 1956:

They have placed before themselves the task of catching up to global science (including our own) in 12 years. But everything suggests that they will accomplish this even sooner ... In 4 years they have constructed several times more than [we have] done in 20 ... they have the most contemporary equipment, about which our institutes can only dream, including even those in Moscow . . . under the leadership of our advisers. Our scientists have realized their dreams on foreign soil.[102]

Stozhenko was tremendously impressed too by the Chinese: 'They are hard-working and disciplined . . . highly talented in all the sciences, decisive and active, with initiative, polite and courteous not only to us Russians but to each other.' And they were honest, he announced, every last one of them.

But all the characteristics of the historic foreign presence in 'Old China' – as it was increasingly and officially described, contrasting with 'New China' – could be found in this new establishment. Advisors lived in segregated compounds, including around the Victoria Hotel on Shamian Island in Guangzhou, which was reserved as a government area, and proved no more open to city residents after its retrocession than it had ever been. A massive 'Friendship Hotel' in Beijing that was opened in 1954 and that had 1,500 rooms, a Russian school, an estimated 750 cars and drivers, held weekly dances and film shows and served as a Russian island in northwest Beijing's university district.[103] Russian advisors enjoyed privileged access to goods through a system whereby 'Friendship Stores', inaccessible to Chinese, were set up in each city. Supplies for bachelors at times seem also to have included young Chinese women, at dancing parties at least. Advisors who came with families worried about the moral health of their children, just as in their own time treaty-port families had, anxious about the 'spoiling' effect of a privileged life on children. The standard of living available to the advisors was far greater than their local colleagues: they lived off their expenses, and saved their salaries back home, leapfrogging queues in Russia to buy cars or consumer goods. They did not learn Chinese, and it was not easy to find out much about China: the chemist Mikhail Klochko recorded that there were no books about the country in the Friendship Hotel's library.

Advisors seem to have been under the surveillance of Russian security operatives, and were also spied on by the Chinese. Some certainly needed watching. Reports of individuals displaying boorish behaviour encompass the USSR's ambassador himself, as well as many lower-level advisors. There were reports of more serious incidents, including rape. In a twist that shows how unequal the relationship actually was, following a familiar pattern, advisors were not subject to Chinese law. They were under Soviet jurisdiction. This was an early demand from the Russian side during the negotiations about the programme. These new friends of China held extraterritorial status through secret protocols to a treaty contracted, as its text ran, 'in the spirit of friendship and cooperation, and in conformity with the principles of equality, mutual benefit and mutual respect for national sovereignty and territorial integrity'.[104]

UNRRA's importing of 'Park Avenue methods' had its critics in 1946–7; now Russian practices were imported wholesale into a Chinese environment. In universities, doctoral examinations were held in ways that minutely replicated Soviet practice: a covered table, a vase of flowers in place.[105] Precise imitation was also problematic, because in most sectors of Chinese society, but especially in higher education, the prevailing model was American or Western European and it was deeply entrenched. Contradictions and problems also arose from the differing industrial environments from which the advisors came. Russians found in many instances that Chinese factories were equipped with imported American or European equipment that was much more advanced than their own. UNRRA and private Western enterprise between them had left this legacy for the new regime. The Chinese in turn started to find that some of the industries of the Eastern bloc had more modern and sophisticated equipment than the Russians did. But the biggest problems that started to emerge with the entire programme were political, as the Chinese and the Russians began to vie for leadership of the Communist bloc in the years after Stalin's death, and as the economic and political programmes initiated in China after 1956 started to diverge wildly from the Soviet economic model.

The relationship with the USSR had never been an easy one. In its negotiations with the Chinese Communist Party in early 1950 over what would become the Sino-Soviet Friendship Treaty, Stalin was concerned to make sure that the USSR would lose none of the advantages it had secured through its August 1945 treaty with the Nationalists, and in this he was largely successful. The USSR had acquired a treaty port in 1945 when the Nationalists allowed it use of the Lüshun naval base – better known overseas as Port Arthur, first acquired by imperial Russia in 1897 – as well as the former Japanese Darien leased territory (Dalian). These were not finally relinquished until May 1955, and no charge levelled at the former treaty powers about their occupation of bases in China was absent from the record of the Soviet presence in Dalian.[106] The USSR retained control of the Chinese Eastern Railway (now known as the Chinese Changchun Railway) until 1952. China's claim for the restoration of its Qing-era sovereignty over 'Outer Mongolia' was rejected. Sino-Soviet 'joint stock companies' were established at China's prompting to exploit Xinjiang's natural resources, but became the cause of angry frustration over Russian aims and ambitions. The power of popular nationalism was such that university students demonstrated in opposition to the Xinjiang agreements, quite taking the new government aback and forcing it to launch a campaign to justify its actions.[107]

There was little national dignity to be had in any of this, despite the elaborate performance of solidarity and fraternity. And even though the Soviet aid programme was significant, the sums involved were loans, not grants, and were repayable with interest. Against them could be set China's losses through the systematic looting of Manchurian industry that took place in 1945 and after under the Russian occupation when an estimated 50 per cent of industrial plant was removed to the USSR.[108] China's soldiers died in the tens of thousands in Korea – Mao's eldest son amongst them. They had little by way of timely and effective support from the USSR, which also scuppered any plans to invade Taiwan.

But despite these losses, the fact that the country's army had taken on and had fought the Americans to a standstill in Korea greatly enhanced the prestige of the new government at home, and most clearly burnished the reputation of Mao Zedong himself. The mass campaigns that accompanied the conflict had ridden a nationalist upsurge that had its roots both in the struggle against Japan and in the assertion of a new place in the world for China. But that place remained an awkward one. New China's position within the socialist bloc was uncomfortable. Internationally its status was hardly what had been envisaged. States that in 1949 were likely to have worked towards a compromise with the new regime were now resolutely hostile. The Chiang Kai-shek government retained China's seat on the United Nations Security Council, and would do so for two decades yet.

The greatest problems came with the death of Stalin in 1953, and Nikita Khrushchev's attack on his predecessor in the secret speech of 25 February 1956. The Chinese had no inkling that this was coming and were profoundly dismayed. After 1956, Mao steered the state and party away from the Soviet command-economy model towards mass mobilization programmes such as the 'Great Leap Forward', through which the Chinese economy was meant to overtake Britain's within fifteen years. In foreign relations, PLA forces became embroiled in the crises over the continued Nationalist hold over the offshore islands of Jinmen (Quemoy) and Mazu (Matsu). Mao alarmed Khrushchev with his increasingly bellicose language and a posture that seemed to relish the possibility of war with the United States. Ideological and strategic differences exacerbated the workaday tensions in the alliance, and set the People's Republic and the USSR, with nearly all the rest of the Communist bloc in tow, on course for rupture. For Mao the USSR's leadership was 'revisionist', weakly steering the Communist bloc away from the necessary climactic confrontation with capitalism and imperialism. Abuse and invective poured out of the state news agency and thickened the air at rallies, congresses and summits. By August 1960 the Russians had had enough. They abruptly withdrew all their personnel and shut down their aid and assistance programmes.

One state alone, however, would remain true as the Central People's Government built New China in and amongst the remnants of the old. One state alone had refused to join the USSR's condemnation of the Chinese at what became a landmark 1960 conference of the socialist bloc parties. From that point onwards the two new partners exchanged high-level leadership visits, and China itself provided technical assistance. In 1964 the two nations signed a formal treaty of alliance. When the Premier of this new ally visited Beijing in 1966, the Chinese mobilized a million people to greet him. The road from the airport to the city was lined in its entirety with 'cheerful crowds in holiday dress'. 'Firmly oppose US imperialism,' they chanted, and 'Firmly and thoroughly oppose modern revision-ism'. Six thousand performers danced for the delegates in Tiananmen Square, and a 1,600-strong choir sang 'Workers of all countries unite'. Children released balloons that crowded the sky.[109] This, after all, was the proper way to treat the Premier of a state that accorded China in full the dignity and respect it deserved and had fought so long and hard to secure. Stalin had not even bothered to meet Mao off the train in December 1949. Roosevelt had made Chiang Kai-shek weep with rage. The nationalist and ideological course that Mao had worked his way towards resulted in the most eccentric of history's grand alliances. China's decades-long struggle for recognition and respect culminated in a bizarre episode during which a crowd equal in number to more than half the population of their visitor's country was organized to meet these favoured foreign friends from Albania.

9

Light of Asia

Mao Zedong was certainly born a countryman, but he performed the peasant increasingly as he grew more powerful, dispensing with his years of urban schooling and life in Changsha and Beijing. There was no better way to unsettle an audience than through his staged uncouthness, earthy language and deportment. Mao's father was a poor man who by dint of canny hard work became relatively well off for a farmer in Shaoshan, a region of Hunan province. In Mao's own analysis his father became a 'rich peasant'. This was a technical term in his eyes, not a mere description. It was one of a restricted number of categories that after 1949 were soon attached to every one of the inhabitants of the People's Republic.

Mao's struggle against the tyranny of his bullying father's behaviour was a central theme of his life that he had delivered to American journalist Edgar Snow across several nights of discussion in July 1936. The Shanghai-based reporter had taken advantage of a temporary truce between forces encircling the Communists to seek his scoop. They had established a new base then centring on Bao'an, in a mountainous district of Shanxi province. Mao's audience included other party leaders and his wife, who were also learning more about the origins of their leader and the sources of his deeply rooted belief in the need for constant struggle. Through defying his father, Mao said, he understood for the first time what might be gained from defending rights 'by open rebellion'. Snow's notes were checked by his subject before being allowed to stand (and were revised further before publication at Mao's request), for the world was to learn about Mao Zedong from these discussions, and so in fact was China, through articles published in the *China Weekly Review* in November

1936, and *Life Magazine*, and in Chinese translations that quickly started to appear that year.[1] Snow's book *Red Star over China* sold 125,000 copies in Britain, and over 65,000 in the United States, and was the subject of wide coverage internationally.[2] It was, and remains, an engaging book: it was a romance of a whispered-about revolution that was ever after able to shout. But this was a carefully managed exercise, and set the pattern for decades of controlled presentation of the Chinese Communist Party, its leadership, its ambitions and their implementation. Nothing was left to chance.

Red Star over China also provided a foundation myth for the party. Here was a man from the rural world in which 90 per cent of Chinese lived, and he was leading them to revolution. His family had lived frugally, Mao said, but had never wanted. Although when young he worked on the family plot himself, his father could also afford to hire labour, and this enabled Mao to have the common schooling in the classics that was almost the only form of education in such rural areas. His father needed a bookkeeper and some educated help for his increasingly complex business, so Mao read and learned his classics; but he also retreated into the 'romances of old China, and especially stories of rebellions'. All his classmates read these books, but few of them learned from them as Mao did. Sitting in Bao'an in 1936, he claimed that he started to notice something 'peculiar' about these tales: 'All the characters were warriors, officials, or scholars; there was never a peasant hero.' He came to the conclusion that because peasants had no power, the stories 'all glorified men of arms, rulers of the people, who did not have to work the land, because they owned and controlled it and evidently made the peasants work it for them'.[3]

Mao Zedong's political consciousness was slowly stimulated, he said, by elements of the new thought that had penetrated even into Shaoshan, of the need for self-strengthening with Western technology, of the threat of national extinction, and of the inspiring victory of Japan over Russia. But in July 1936 he also placed his emerging thinking in this stark contrast between his own rural world and that of Chinese literature and culture, even in racier, populist genres, and between the countryside and political power. Mao was fashioning a narrative on those summer nights in Bao'an, but he was also shaping a revolution. After the Chinese Communist Party assumed power, it reshaped Chinese society, its economy and culture to place the rural world, and the life and values of the peasantry, at the beating heart of the nation's existence, its image in the world and its history.

This new position of the peasant was one of the sharp distinctions that were drawn between 'Old China' and 'New China', and between the 'Old Society' and the 'New'. In a culture of thought that was historically structured around dichotomies, this pairing of 'old' and 'new' became the template into which was stamped every sphere of life, and every individual's understanding of themselves, their own histories, and that of their country. The past was certainly not forgotten. It was inescapable, but it was to be remembered only so far as it was to be used. Individuals were to find themselves unable to escape it, but they were also to be transformed and made afresh – if their histories allowed. Communist China's rearticulation of itself and ambition to remould individuals was not unusual or novel: it had also driven the Nationalists (at its most obvious in the New Life Movement). But the re-presentation of China after 1949 was much more totalistic and far-reaching than anything that the Guomindang had ever attempted or even imagined possible. In New China the rural, the urban and the country's place internationally were made afresh. 'New China' was a powerful idea that was communicated in a massive range of propaganda across media, but it was also a set of processes that turned lives upside down and inside out, reshaped cities and landscapes, and offered a powerful challenge to the international system.

When it came to telling the New China story it certainly helped that nobody loved the Nationalists. Their own limitations and failures had guaranteed that, but it was also the fruit of their own success. They had been successful at cultivating a better image of China overseas, and this had undergirded the pro-China publicity campaigns of wartime agencies like United China Relief in America, and British United Aid for China. Chinese scholars, writers and artists overseas had helped inculcate in Western minds and opinion new understandings of China's historic and contemporary culture, and of the Chinese. But the Nationalists had then betrayed all this – or at least so went what became the dominant narrative. They had betrayed their country by ill-prosecuting its defence against the Japanese, and instead feathered their nests, created a Gestapo state, and prosecuted a murderous war against liberals and against the party of peace: the Communists.

One misfortune was that the Nationalists' critics had all the best writers. Anger improved their style. New Zealander James Bertram's *Unconquered* (1939) and American Jack Belden's *China Shakes the World* (1949) were inspiring accounts of what they found in the communist areas. They added new layers to the story presented in *Red Star over* China, and *The Tragedy of the Chinese Revolution* (1938) by Harold Isaacs, which laid bare the bloody origins of Guomindang rule. *Thunder out of China*, the pungently written 1946 account of the wartime China Theatre by *Time* magazine correspondents Theodore White and Annalee Jacoby, was the most lacerating indictment. White was one of the scores of foreigners who made their way to the communist areas after Snow, but he was hardly one of the starry-eyed ones. In this Book-of-the-Month Club hit – it sold 450,000 copies – White and Jacoby gathered all the charges together: corruption, incompetence, and the cruelty that had led to starving peasants turning on Nationalist troops during the Ichi-go offensive.[4] And, widely circulated through the British Left Book Club, and reinforced by reports from a host of other pilgrims to the communist headquarters, there was *Red Star over China*'s portrait of this new man, Mao, and his new hope for China.

As a result, many overseas were prepared to give the Chinese Communist Party the benefit of the doubt. Their victory would at least bring peace. This was in line with much opinion within the country itself, and amongst Chinese abroad. The fact that the CCP's victory was swiftly followed by involvement in the Korean War did not dismay the hopeful. Instead, circles that opposed what they saw as the remilitarization of the West, the rearming of Japan and the unfolding Cold War were even more determined to give the Communists that benefit. In this view, the political and social revolution inside China was the necessary precursor to a new era of peace and development, and was needed for its self-defence. Because it was not really clear what was happening, reports about the violence involved were not believed, or not registered, or accepted as the necessary price to be paid by the enemies of justice in the good cause of establishing a better China. Many foreign observers were prepared to believe just about anything, it turned out, including the false allegation that American forces had used biological weapons in China and North Korea in 1952.[5]

What was most striking about the new state was its rural foundations: a peasant revolution, led by a peasant who had complete control of the world's most populous country. No other such state existed, or had ever existed in world history. This process involved some profound inversions. The farming people of China had been routinely patronized; they had been present in every account of China, but, as Mao had found out as a child, they were never of account. They were deeply respected in theory and in China's dominant cultural values, but they were ignored in the practice of political power. The state did not connect to them, except through tax collection, and even that it farmed out, so that the rural world was administered largely at several removes from the state itself. Rural people had never been passive in the face of injustice, and the history of uprisings and resistance was a rich one. At one end of the scale peasant rebellions had toppled dynasties, and at the other there was a crowded record of violent anti-tax outbreaks. The greatest challenge against the Qing had not come from foreign aggression, but from the Taiping rebels in 1850–64, who had come out of the mountainous countryside in southwest China's Guangxi province. The biggest assault on the foreign presence in China came in the shape of young rural men from the northwest who formed the backbone of the 1899–1900 Boxer uprising.[6] Peasants had power. Peng Pai had grasped this in Haifeng, and unleashed it during the Nationalist revolution. Mao had seen it in Hunan.

They also had culture. One of the distinctive features of the republican era had been the discovery of China's popular cultures by the country's intellectuals.[7] This was overwhelmingly rural in its focus. Folk songs and legends, proverbs and children's rhymes and tales, were all collected and explored by some of the most prominent scholars, men like Gu Jiegang and Lu Xun's brother, Zhou Zuoren. Peking University President Cai Yuanpei had supported the establishment of a Folk Song Collecting Bureau there in 1918. Lu Xun himself was a leading advocate of using popular forms in the visual arts, notably woodcuts, picture books and block-printed *nianhua* ('New Year pictures'). The wider context was partly the Tolstoyan-inspired belief in the value of rural culture and life as an authentic source of China's identity, and a salve for its ills. Romanticism, nationalism and the urgent task of cultural renewal were all part of the mix. For these thinkers the 'Shanghai-ization' of China – the spread of hybrid urban culture from the coastal cities – should be countered, for it was complicit in China's fall, and it was demeaning. The 'humiliation' visited on China by imperialism could be cleansed by the authentic, wholesome culture of rural China. And this was also a political project: art forms drawn from the people, and familiar to them, could also help mobilize them. There was no room here for *Modern Sketch*.

The novel Chinese story that emerged first in Edgar Snow's books, and then in the reports from the 'New' China published by other reporters and political pilgrims who made their way there, intrigued and inspired audiences overseas. China's own problems were being solved, but there seemed to be much for the rest of the world to learn as well. Here it seemed was evidence of the proving of an alternative model of economic development that might help solve problems of poverty internationally. And China's was a path of growth that eventually diverged from that of the USSR and from the Western model. Nor was it geared to wasteful over-consumption, it seemed. The new state was self-sufficient, and there was contentment with sufficiency. This Chinese model accorded dignity to farming people, pioneered new forms of gender relations, and new models of practical democracy. So New China was in some eyes a beacon for the world. If we are to understand how this happened, and how China's peasants excited radicals across the world, and even in time shaped the practices of, for example, the Women's Liberation Movement in the United States and Europe in the 1970s, then we need to understand what happened in China's countryside after 1949, how it was reported and who by, and how those reports were shaped.

Quite how to husband and nurture peasant power and culture to best effect had been a pressing issue for revolutionaries since the 1920s. Peng Pai's Soviet had turned unsustainably sanguine. Disagreement over the handling of the agrarian question had been crucial to the collapse of the Guomindang-communist alliance. The CCP itself was still focused thereafter on a policy of fomenting urban revolution. It would cling on to this through defeat after bloody defeat until it formulated a new rural revolutionary strategy between 1930 and 1935 in what it styled its Jiangxi Soviet Republic, and then in the ShaanGanNing Border Region headquartered at Yan'an. Tensions over land policy split the left. But the experiences of Peng, Mao and others were vital to the reformulation of party strategy after it was driven out of the cities. Practices and processes were tried and tested in the bases of Communist Party power in north China in the 1930s and 1940s, and were then deployed rapidly across the nation in the 1950s as land ownership was reformed, and the existing political structure in every village and hamlet was pulverized.

Mao's steadily more unorthodox thinking – in Marxist terms – started to place rural China at the heart of the development of the new state in the middle of the 1950s. The nationalist political project, in and outside the Guomindang, had been aimed at rebuilding China as a strong power through scientific and technological development, and through building up its industrial capacity.[8] This project engaged with the countryside only in order to try to control it in the fight against what it routinely termed 'communist banditry', or to extract conscripts from it. Sun Yat-sen had advocated giving 'land to the tiller', and the National Government even passed an agrarian reform law in 1930 that restricted rent levels, but this was never implemented – except by the Communists themselves in their wartime 'liberated areas'. In retrospect the Nationalists would blame the Japanese invasion for their failure, or the disruption caused by the communist insurgency: it seemed that the time was never right, and that their hands were always tied. But the fundamental issue was that the Nationalists were driven by a vision of modernity that was almost entirely urban. The Communist state certainly shared this vision in its early years, and it lay at the heart of its First Five Year Plan in 1953–7 and in its USSR-derived model of state-directed growth. But alongside this it also kept a focus on the land, and increasingly a wholly different idea of modernity came to the fore. Peasant China, not its urban counterpart, was modern China. Mao Zedong, unlike many in the party's leadership, not least those who were prominent in the planning in the early years of the People's Republic, had never been abroad before 1949, and had up to then seen little of China's cities.

While the Guomindang's vision had been projected overseas with increasing success – at Burlington House, through its news management and through its sympathetic supporters and their publicity campaigns – the discovery of rural China had certainly been crucial to the changing image of the country overseas. The key text had been Pearl Buck's novel *The Good Earth*. Her characters Wang Lung and O-Lan, his wife, and their struggles had had a tremendous impact on the American public. Buck wrote about them, she said in 1949, because they were 'the voiceless ones', the 'solid body of the Chinese people'; they were its 'foundation'. They would persist through hideous adversity and 'remain what they were yesterday, as they are today, and will be forever'.[9] The essential characteristic of her view of China's rural people was their passivity. Wang Lung had no mastery over his own fate: he was at the mercy of the weather, of locusts, of soldiers and of other human 'parasites'. He only recovers from adversity because he was one of a mob that looted a rich man's home. Wang was given no conception of politics, asking a street-side revolutionary orator who was decrying the power of the rich how – as they were so powerful – they could be persuaded to make it rain, so that he could farm. There is no suggestion of society, or of community, or much by way of solidarity in the book. There is only family; and the word 'peasant' does not even appear in *The Good Earth*. Neither Buck's book nor her image of China were welcome in the country after 1949, and she had long been the subject of leftist and communist criticism for what was presented as her 'reactionary' picture of China's rural people. The Wang Lungs of New China, far from being passive, confronted their problems and made their own history. They were, in fact, the only possible drivers of historical change.

Theodore White and Annalee Jacoby took this further in *Thunder out of China*, placing the plight of the peasant up front in their book, arguing that an urgent solution was needed before 'the peasant takes the law into his own hands and sets the countryside aflame'. They also threw light on how the Chinese Communist Party was working to engage the peasantry in the districts it controlled.[10] Other dramatic reports alerted overseas opinion to the fact that something powerfully different and inspiring was underway in China, and that peasants could certainly become political. Industrial co-operatives and agrarian reforms were recurrent topics of books that offered a counterpoint to the despair about the Nationalists which characterized most work.[11] This was unprecedented, 'un-Chinese' even, if your vision of China had been shaped, as most were, by the unremittingly hostile portraits of the old China coast experts.

Some influential foreign observers had optimistically characterized the Chinese Communist Party as an agrarian reform movement, believing it in essence not truly a communist party at all.[12] The Soviet leadership in Russia was also initially suspicious. In his first meeting with Stalin, in Moscow in December 1949, Mao focused on the outlines of a state-strengthening programme that would have been familiar to any American-trained Guomindang technocrat. It placed military modernization and industrial development at its core, while the countryside and China's rural people were not mentioned.[13] Mao's requests for assistance were the prototype of the Soviet-style development model. But that required reconstruction of the economy, which in turn relied on agricultural growth to feed the countryside and the cities, supply light industry with raw materials (such as cotton), and fund imports of machinery and technology through the exports of agricultural products that formed three-quarters of its foreign trade.[14] The countryside was vital to this plan in ways that had never been considered by the Nationalists, but first it had to be secured.

The initial task of the new authorities was to disarm the countryside and to suppress any active local resistance, continuing banditry or egregious local 'despotism' or 'bullying'. Existing social, political and economic relations were then hacked apart by a combination of the redistribution of land and productive property, sustained public humiliation of those designated 'landlords' or other categories of 'bad element', and mass killing. 'Landlords' were identified where very few, or none at all, actually existed: it was necessary to invent them, so they were conjured up out of unpopular local personalities against whom people had scores to settle or those who had no connections or allies.[15] Work teams coaxed and coached villagers to make sure that they understood their past situation. At 'speak bitterness' (*suku*) meetings, men and women stood up and told their communities of their sorrows and sufferings at the hands of landowners and 'bullies', who were then dispossessed of all but a fraction of their land and possessions. Many were then killed. Perhaps two million people died at the hands of their accusers, and great numbers committed suicide. In his account of the Hunan peasant movement in 1926, Mao had pointed to the extremes of violence that could be let loose unless the process was properly guided. But he would also frequently dismiss such results as the understandable consequences of historic injustice, as would influential foreign observers.[16] Those killed were in effect blamed for having thus brutalized their killers. Land reform mobilized the nation, instilling a new consciousness of being a 'peasant', of shared class identity and of a shared experience of oppression. This was also a matter of pride. New leaders emerged from amongst the poor and marginalized, and began to enter the Communist Party. And land reform left the population in every village in every one of China's counties complicit in the murderous overthrow of the old dispensation.[17]

In the sanitized version of this tale in which the peasant threw off the 'feudal' yoke of history and stood tall, resistance to reform mainly came from the hesitation with which cautious individuals and communities approached the tasks required of them. But in many parts of the country they initially had reason to fear that this new regime would be as short-lasting as those that had successively swept through their land in recent decades. In much of south China in particular, there was no process of liberation anyway, just military conquest by the PLA. Resistance in the southwest, especially, continued well into the early 1950s. There were uprisings against the Communists, while large guerrilla forces, gangs of displaced soldiery and bandits remained active. Even with power secured, this process was not without its twists, turns and defeats. At least 3,000 cadres were killed in 1949–50, as communities resisted tax collection. Work teams were small, vulnerable, and also often very young and inexperienced. Relationships between tenants and landowners were so intertwined and complex that changes made by daylight were undone covertly at night. But steady pressure, and two million killings, had a strong cumulative impact. 'Rich peasants' were initially left in possession of their property, but were consistently made targets for further mobilization activity. The fraught tensions that this brought into everyday life were immense.

Land reform brought into the spotlight new heroes from amongst the farmers of China. One of these was Li Shunda, son of a Henan province carpenter, who settled in Shanxi province's Pingshun county in 1930.[18] Li Shunda's story was one of a number that became central to the projection of a new peasant China at home and overseas. Xikou village, his home, was set in the dry and stony Taihang mountains, and was such hard land to farm that the villagers had more than once considered abandoning it altogether. Only refugees from extreme poverty elsewhere – like Li's family – would think of settling there. In the story that was developed, a party work team came to the village when it was first occupied by the Communists in 1938, and assembled a Peasants' Union which Li Shunda joined. All the elements of the narrative of historic injustice and of liberation were present: landlords were lazy, sadistic, and cheated their tenants. 'We suffered hunger and cold,' ran the story. 'Our usual food was corn husks and wild herbs.' Tenants were cautious but slowly persuaded to act. Li, as a poor peasant, was a persuader who also worked by example. He was recognized as a 'labour hero', formed a Mutual Aid Team, pioneered new work methods, and organized the team to reclaim unused land to boost production.

Xikou's peasants held their absentee landlords to account, spoke about their bitterness, itemizing extortion and violence inflicted upon them: their words being their truth. They set ambitious targets for themselves that were publicized nationally in 1951, and garnered the status of most successful Mutual Aid Team across the country in 1952. Li travelled to the USSR in 1952 as one of a delegation of seventy model peasants led by the Vice Minister of Agriculture. Kitted out in their first Western-style suits in Beijing – which will have made for uncomfortable wearing for a Shanxi farmer – they travelled by train, stayed in a Moscow hotel taller than any building in Shanxi province, attended the May Day parade and caught a glimpse of Stalin. On his return Li toured China speaking about his experiences at Xikou, and the vision of the technological farming future he had seen in the USSR at model collective farms in the Ukraine, and in Siberia. The future was tractor-shaped, but only a truly collective enterprise could afford to deploy machinery. 'Now I completely understand what socialism is,' Li reportedly said on his return.[19] He also brought back home what was quite likely to have been Xikou's first gramophone player, and reported that all the Russian women had looked like actresses, even when working in the fields.

This was New China's new peasant fairy tale, relayed internationally through its publicity machine, presented to visitors at model collective farms and communes, and discussed in the journals and newsletters and at the meetings of overseas groups with an interest in China and in its politics. But this particular story, and the wider one, was mired in problems behind the scenes: misreporting of production levels, poor management, inadequate preparation for too rapid an expansion, and the simple frailties and minor failures of any human enterprise. In 1952 the Xikou team had actually made a sizeable loss: the demands of mobilization and the nationally important role that Li Shunda's model team was playing meant that this distortion and deception were covered up by officials.[20] The steady process of collectivization would also actually impoverish many rural communities, few of which lived from farming alone. 'Sideline' activities – handicrafts, or petty trading – were forbidden as unsocialist. Seasonal migration had been vital in many places, but this was also prevented. Little room was left for error or chance in the rural economy. This, and the gap between ideal and reality, would in time lead to an unimaginable cataclysm across the land.

At all times in this narrative it was the peasant – guided and enlightened by the party – who acted, who nurtured and grew the collective, set ambitious targets and exceeded them. The Wang Lung path – of settling comfortably and complacently into prosperity when it was achieved – was always presented and rejected. The farmer, once seen as little more than a beast at the mercy of his passions, moved steadily to the fore in the iconography of the new state. In 'Old China' peasants had gone overseas in their hundreds of thousands to labour like slaves or desperately grub around chimerical fields of gold in California or Australia, and face pogroms and discriminatory legislation around the Pacific. In 'New China' they were led by a government minister to view farms in the Ukraine in their newly cut suits.[21] Li Shunda was no ordinary peasant: he had joined the Communist Party in 1938, rose steadily through its ranks, and had been adopted as a focus for propaganda as early as 1945, when accounts of his activities had started to be published. He joined the National People's Congress in 1954 and would have a national political career until his death in 1983 that mirrored the vicissitudes of China's revolution. Li Shunda did well out of the revolution, as did countless numbers of others whose poverty and political luck certainly did not make them appear angelic.[22] Here was something truly new, nonetheless, a man once landless, from the rural underclass in a poor province, who had a name, and a place in the government of the Chinese state. This was truly revolutionary, for all the limitations of the man himself, and the murderous hypocrisies of the enterprise.

A figure often portrayed alongside Li Shunda and discussed in the story of Xikou's development was its female deputy chair, Shen Jilan. This too was new. If the peasant had not been seen or heard in Old China, neither had the country's women. Their position had been central to late Qing and early republican reformist thought: China could not become modern, it was asserted, unless its women were released from legal and cultural bondage. China's strength was sapped because half of its people were unable to contribute to its revival. The charge sheet was long: arranged marriage, foot binding, impaired access to education and employment, sequestration of women from public sight, and a patriarchal culture that degraded and enslaved them. This also degraded and enslaved China, it was argued. Foreign observers, blithely disregarding the gender inequalities of their own societies, also accorded the position of women a key role in their valuations of civilizational standing. China, in their view, fell comprehensively short. 'What happens after Nora leaves home?' asked Lu Xun in a famous 1923 talk to female students at Peking Normal University, discussing Henrik Ibsen's play A Doll's House, at the end of which the heroine walks out on her husband and her family to discover herself. The play had developed a life of its own in Chinese political and cultural debates, as Ibsen's implicitly caustic view of the family chimed with May Fourth Movement critiques.[23] Either Nora would return to her husband, or she would go 'to the bad', Lu said. This needed a political solution. Ibsen was interested in poetry, Lu declared, not the practical consequences that any woman in his society – or yours, he told his audience – had to face. In China, unless Nora had 'economic rights' she would be faced with the same choice. And securing those would be harder even than securing political rights.

Up to a point this picture of women's status was a caricature, although the fundamental outlines of gender inequality were certainly well mapped out. But while women's legal and political rights remained limited during the republic, more of them were being schooled, and for longer; more of them worked outside the home (where most had of course always worked), and across an increasing range of employment; and more of them were figures in the nation's public sphere. They taught in schools and universities, worked in social, cultural and political organizations. They were artists, writers and actors. A sustained campaign of suffragist activism after 1912 drove women's political rights into the mainstream as well as into provincial constitutions and, by the 1940s, the national constitution. Great numbers of women were involved in reform circles and revolutionary activity. Every aspiring saviour of her nation had heard of Qiu Jin, the anti-Qing revolutionary and head of a girl's school, who had been executed in 1907, and of Xie Bingying, who had fought in the Nationalist revolution and whose diary had been a best-seller. Xie's work was translated into English by Lin Yutang in 1934, and her memoir as *Girl Rebel* by Lin's daughters in 1940, feeding a growing English-language market for accounts of women's life in China. This had once largely been confined to accounts of the Empress Dowager Cixi, or missionary writings about Chinese Christians, but it now grew broader, and increasingly featured Chinese women who spoke or wrote for themselves.[24]

The greater part of women's political activism was more reformist. Scores of new women's groups and associations were formed in the first two decades of the republic after 1911. And nationalist activists looked to women consumers as the key link in the drive to fight imperialism through the consumption of 'national products': Chinese-made goods.[25] Women had power as consumers themselves, and as arbiters of family consumption, and through the education of children. The National Goods movement, it was asserted, could succeed or fail, on the basis of women's choices. The competing forces of cosmopolitan internationalism and patriotic consumption ultimately left women culturally and politically vulnerable. How could a woman be patriotically modern? And meanwhile, though there was a vibrant women's press, Shanghai's urban modernity was characterized by that sexualization of women's bodies. They had emerged out of cultural sequestration to be displayed as objects of male desire on the pages of the monthly Chinese magazine *Modern Sketch*.

New China was different, it was claimed. On 1 May 1950 the government issued its new Marriage Law, which was heralded as the revolutionary pick that smashed the feudal lock holding back women's progress. It enacted a right to divorce, abolished arranged marriage and marriage by purchase, asserted the equal status of men and women in marriage and their equal rights to property. The law established a new role for the state as registrar of marriages, but only of men and women who were of a new legal age, and with some consanguinity and other prohibitions. It also asserted its role in compulsory mediation proceedings that were built into the divorce process. Implementation of the act was accompanied by mass campaigns as well as violence. There were some spectacular rises in divorce rates. The law alone did not solve what Lu Xun outlined as Nora's underlying problem, but it had a revolutionary impact, particularly in rural China.[26] Its implementation in the countryside, however inconsistent and at times hesitant, was one key fact that distinguished the law from its predecessors; the other was its centrality to the myths of the new state. Women were seen to be moving into prominent positions: Xikou county's Shen Jilan would also become a National Deputy in 1954.[27]

Like the land-reform narrative, the story of the rapid liberation of China's women was much heralded. The new Marriage Law was published in English, and women's narratives of their new lives and ambitions were relayed in the English-language magazine *Women in China Today*. This was more than simple propaganda, but it played a central role within the story of New China sanctioned by the state. However, like the peasant story, the new history in Old China that was fashioned for women was relentlessly bleak. The Old Society was the site of feudal tyranny and patriarchal violence, in which women had no rights under the law, and in which infanticide and enforced prostitution were common. The tentative sexual liberation of the 1920s and the 1930s was recast as immoral and its cultural manifestations as simply pornographic. This story denied any agency to women when it had of course existed, unless it fitted the revolutionary myth – and this was, again, precisely the point.

The country's historians also had to reconsider their understanding of the course of modern Chinese history to accommodate these shifts in values. New China's model peasants, for example, needed to be kitted out with a new past in Old China.[28] Even the left had once routinely pilloried the rural upsurges of the nineteenth century, not least the Boxer uprising, as 'superstitious' and 'xenophobic'. The episode affronted their sense of how China could only be saved by being modern. Even when their hostility started to relent during the Nationalist revolution, when Boxer xenophobia began to be reinterpreted as prototype anti-imperialism, they remained profoundly ambivalent about the nature of Boxer beliefs, though impressed by their collective power.[29] But now the shape of modern history demanded a retelling that placed both proletarian and rural struggle at its heart. The Boxers were recast as anti-imperialist patriots who, although they lacked advanced political consciousness (as the language of the times had it), were engaged in a political struggle. Anti-missionary pogroms in 1900 found resonant echoes in the attack on Catholic and Protestant missionaries in 1950–51.

Mao Zedong had set out a template for understanding the role of the peasant in a key textbook for the party published in 1939. China had a uniquely rich history of large-scale peasant uprisings, he argued. These were 'the real motive forces of historical development in Chinese feudal society'. It required a little dexterity to fit these into Marxist orthodoxy, but each revolt destroyed the existing feudal regime and 'more or less furthered the growth of the social productive forces', even if each was itself defeated. Such historic peasant movements lacked the 'correct' proletarian leadership needed, however, and their transient successes merely ushered in a change in dynasty, but no revolution.[30] Guided by this, researchers set about reclaiming a lost history from the distortions and condescension of their predecessors. Projects were launched to recover what traces might be found of the Taiping rebels. Field trips sought out the sites of their origins in Guangxi province in 1954, hunted for objects and manuscripts, and secured testimonies and tales about them. In Tianjin, surviving Boxers were located and interviewed in 1958. Research teams went into the Shandong countryside conducting interviews, and looking for songs and other tangible and intangible relics of the great uprising.[31]

Few would now question the need to understand such episodes as the Taiping civil war or the Boxer uprising. The defining feature of post-war historical research internationally was the rise to pre-eminence of new forms of social and cultural history, and of 'history from below'. The focus almost exclusively on elites and rulers in China's established tradition of history writing was not unusual. The projects launched in the 1950s uncovered a tremendous and rich range of new materials that could reshape understandings of events previously known only from government records that were hostile or dismissive, and there was a systematic effort to popularize this new history through exhibitions, historical sites and museum displays. A Taiping Heavenly Kingdom Museum was opened in Nanjing in 1958. When the Museum of the History of the Chinese Revolution opened in 1961, both the Taiping civil war and the Boxer uprising were amongst the core elements in what was presented as the 'Old Democratic Revolution'.[32]

The difficulty for Chinese scholars was balancing praise for the peasant heroes of the past with the fact of their recurrent failure. Only the Chinese Communist Party helped break that cycle. Researchers also had to find ways to navigate the fact that Taiping beliefs were fundamentally based in an indigenized Protestant Christianity, and that the Boxer world view was shaped by a congeries of popular beliefs that, like Christianity, were under systematic attack by the new regime. It was safer by far to focus on Taiping land redistribution and gender politics (its legal code proscribed foot binding), and Boxer anti-imperialism (as its xenophobia was presented). The difficulty for scholarship more widely was a different one. China's past was made an instrument of China's present. What did not serve contemporary needs was largely irrelevant, and its study suspect. We now know a great deal more about the history of riot and rebellion in China, because this was seen as providing a pre-history for the revolution, but it has come at the cost of an understanding of great swathes of its past that served no useful political function in the modern world.

The recovery of a proud peasant history was one strand amongst other appropriations of once denigrated forms and experiences for New China's new national political culture. Others reshaped the arts and significantly expanded the range of what was considered to be 'culture'. The most immediate manifestation of this was a physical one: to celebrate the revolution urban China began to dance as its peasants danced. The eruption of the rural into the cities came initially in two forms. The most obvious was the soldiery itself, largely rural in origin. But the most ostentatious was the celebratory dance that was hastily learned by students and others in the newly liberated cities and performed – often with more exuberance than precision – in victory parades and on days of national celebration. This was the *yangge*, the 'rice-sprout song', based on a Shaanxi province dance form but modernized after 1943 in the Yan'an base area as part of a drive instigated by Mao Zedong's directives on art and literature, namely to create art forms deriving from and intended for the masses. Colourful costumes, spirited movements, drums, gongs and clashing cymbals made for a distinctive style. The *yangge* was relatively easy to learn, and it had the further nationalist virtue of being Chinese, but it would fall out of favour after the early 1950s, as it came to be seen as unsophisticated in comparison with the new forms and styles that were brought from the Soviet Union.[33] The foxtrot and other ballroom styles continued to hold the attention of dancegoers for a while yet.

The People's Republic of China also staked a claim to be preserving the cultural relics and treasures that had been central to new understandings of the country that flourished overseas in the 1930s – especially where there was a tale of foreign theft and Guomindang neglect to be highlighted, such as over the Dunhuang treasures, or of the remains of 'Peking Man' mistakenly believed to have been stolen by Americans.[34] As part of wider moves to protect China's cultural patrimony from the Japanese invasion, moves that included the shipping overseas of collections from libraries in Beijing and the peripatetic career of the Palace Museum collections, American diplomats had agreed to help ship the Peking Man fossils overseas in late 1941. But having reached US military custody by early December, the remains disappeared in the chaos after Pearl Harbor. Even though these particular finds were deemed to have provided scientific proof of Engels's theory that 'Labour Created Man' (for labour was concluded to be the decisive factor in evolution), China's new revolutionary culture was in fact its primary one.[35] The authorities had been swift to raise new monuments to mark the imperialist violence of the past, and to seek out revolutionary relics and display them. The gallows from which the early leader Li Dazhao was hanged, and the scythe used to execute a fourteen-year-old village girl who was assisting the Red Army, were amongst hundreds of items quickly located.[36] In Guangzhou a new and imposing memorial was unveiled in 1950 to commemorate those killed in the 1925 Shaji Massacre, replacing a much smaller one erected in 1926. The Museum of the History of the Chinese Revolution was one of 'Ten Great Buildings' constructed in Beijing, and was located in the spatial heart of the state, on the east side of a newly expanded Tiananmen Square. The very shape of the capital now showcased the narrative that was being established. Across China museums and memorial halls were constructed at sites of resistance, revolution, or oppression, or those with associations to revolutionary leaders or heroes. These often had to make do with artefacts that were, at best, tenuously linked to their subjects, or which, as with Shanghai's park sign, were faked but which gained a patina of authenticity through display and through description.

Telling stories was central to the business of the state. The new government had moved quickly to formalize and control its management of foreign affairs, which included the flow of information. New China's projection of itself was carefully controlled. Major tools in its portfolio of activity included its official news agency (*Xinhua*: New China News Agency), its foreign-language publication programme, and its management of foreign visits. Restrictions placed on the entrance of visitors and the tight management of their movement within China, and on the publication of data as well as the export of all forms of publication, made it difficult to secure information. As a result, Hong Kong became a major site of what was known as 'China watching', by which foreign diplomats, intelligence agencies, journalists and academics sifted what they could from the scraps of information that seeped out of the country across its only accessible land border with a non-communist administration. Chinese refugees were able to make their way across the border relatively easily until 1962. The China watchers interviewed them as well as the foreign nationals who continued to trickle out from Shanghai and other cities as their assets were finally surrendered against liabilities, or who were released from jail. Runes were read and statements and photographs parsed. But Cold War politics meant that much information casting a bad light on the new regime was simply distrusted or ignored by liberal or leftist opinion overseas or, equally, exaggerated by anti-communists. It was difficult to know what was actually going on.

This was partly the point. The new regime immediately began to publish accounts of its transformation of the country in foreign languages, including Esperanto; it also began radio broadcasts overseas, starting its first English operations in Morse code. Neither of these particular initiatives would have secured large audiences. However, the magazines *People's China* (from January 1950), *Chinese Literature* (1950), *China Pictorial* (from January 1951) and *China Reconstructs* (from January 1952) became widely circulated vehicles for this cultural and political campaign.[37] Soong Ching-ling, Sun Yat-sen's widow, was nominal editor of *China Reconstructs*, and other 'democratic personages' not affiliated to the Communist Party and regularly used in foreign-relations activity were listed as the writers of articles. A Foreign Languages Press was established in 1952 to 'use foreign languages to explain China, and books to communicate to the world'. Leadership texts, fiction and folk tales, biographies and reports delivered the Beijing line overseas in an increasing range of different tongues as its ambitions for influence and global political leadership grew. By 1959, Radio Peking was beaming out programmes in twenty-four different languages, and aiming English broadcasts to the United States, Australia and New Zealand, Southeast and South Asia, and Western Europe.[38] Another cultural journal, *Eastern Horizons*, was published in Hong Kong and was ostensibly independent, but was part of the same official stable. There was continuity here with the efforts of the Guomindang to communicate to foreign publics through the journals it subsidized, its cultural diplomacy, and through its pugnacious engagement with foreign film studios. The communist government's efforts were much more systematic and thorough despite continuing difficulties over securing and retaining linguistically able staff. Most Chinese who had fluency in foreign languages had problematic class backgrounds, or had lived overseas, and the commitment of some foreign nationals flagged as the regime mounted its attacks on the USSR. But the communist efforts were less influential than those of their predecessors, for the Nationalists had had so many more allies and able interlocutors overseas.

An eclectic cadre of foreign nationals had become vital to this work. They came from a wide range of backgrounds, reflecting, still, the internationalized history of pre-1949 China. The New Zealander Rewi Alley, a former Shanghai Municipal Council fireman and factory inspector, was one prolific propagandist. Europe's anti-Semitic regimes had pushed others to China: Israel Epstein and Sam Ginsbourg were from Russian Jewish families that had fled to Manchuria to escape Tsarist-era persecution. Epstein had worked for treaty-port newspapers in Tianjin, Shanghai and Hong Kong, and increasingly during the war worked with groups on the left.[39] Germanophone audiences were addressed by Ruth Weiss and Eva Siao (Sandberg), leftist Jews from Germany and Austria respectively. The Japanese economist Yokogawa Jirō's radical beliefs had seen him lose a government job in Japan, and then suffer arrest and imprisonment when he worked in the South Manchurian Railroad Research Department. Yokogawa remained in China after the war. The entanglement of love and politics conspired to bring Gladys Tayler, the daughter of a London Missionary Society educationalist, back to China. Born in Beijing, she became the first student of Chinese at the University of Oxford, married Yang Xianyi, a student of classics, and worked with him for decades at the Foreign Languages Press.[40] Denise LeBreton came out with her husband, Li Fengbai, whom she had met when he studied in France. Although born in Shanghai, Esther Cheo, who worked for Radio Peking for eleven years, was the child of another such student romance in London.

These foreign foot soldiers in China's war of words had also been drawn to the country by the China National Relief and Rehabilitation Administration, which brought New York dairy farmer William Hinton back to China as a tractor technician after he had worked there during the war for the US Office of Wartime Information. His sister Joan, a nuclear physicist who had worked on the Manhattan Project, was inspired to follow him in 1948 and worked on livestock initiatives, but the move meant that unsubstantiated allegations of treason and espionage were to dog her until her death in Beijing in 2010: instead of breeding sheep in China, she was charged with 'breeding atoms'. Others were despatched by fraternal communist parties: Alan Winnington and Michael Shapiro came to work for the New China News Agency at the command of the Communist Party of Great Britain (CPGB). Although born in Chengdu into a Canadian missionary family, the anthropologist Isabel Brown and her husband David Crook came to China in 1947 at the CPGB's request to research a book about land reform.[41] Crook was a British communist, who had fought in the Spanish Civil War and spied for the KGB on Trotskyists in Spain – most notoriously on George Orwell and his wife Eileen Blair – and in Shanghai. The veteran radical Anna Louise Strong – who had crossed Manchuria with Mikhail Borodin in 1927 – made Beijing her home from 1958 until her death in 1970, mailing out a regular 'Letter from China' that rehearsed whatever party line was then dominant. There were several score of others, including a Japanese aristocrat, twenty-two deserters from the United Nations forces in Korea (twenty-one Americans and one Briton), and two Marxist economists driven out of the United States after being fingered as Soviet espionage suspects in 1952.[42]

The foreign experts were relatively well paid, housed, fed and treated, and in the 1950s generally cossetted from the political storms that would consume China. This would not last, but in the meantime their memoirs often paint a picture of a world that Ann Bridge might recognize, and might have sketched in her novel *Peking Picnic* (1932), not least in its happy distance from the harsher realities of the revolution. In fact they had more in common with the Jesuit mathematicians and cartographers who had served the Ming and the Qing than with the thousands of foreign advisors who had worked in the republic. They were mostly technical experts, used to help the government pursue its propaganda and cultural diplomacy aims. The key difference was that, unlike the Jesuits, their chief loyalty was to the regime itself, and to China. In return the Chinese Communist Party did not always see them as anything more than useful hired hands. Even so, many were granted Chinese nationality, lived on in the country for decades and were highly honoured by the party.[43] These experts had a higher profile internationally than might normally be the case for literary translators, language teachers and propagandists, for they were often used to host or meet visiting delegations, or were sought out by visitors hoping to get some more information off the record. Some became well known within China itself, being assembled for parades and demonstrations, and speaking at rallies and other political events. The ranks of the 'true believers' and 'three hundred percenters' were augmented by supporters of the regime overseas, such as Edgar Snow, the Swedish radical Jan Myrdal or the Canadian former missionary James G. Endicott, all of whom also served, and uncritically and loudly proclaimed their support for the state, whichever way the Beijing wind happened to blow, although at a safe geographical distance from its icy chills.[44]

China's foreign servants were successful advocates for it. Few of the influential or widely read accounts published overseas of land reform, for example, were free of this tight management of information, or of the shaping of the narrative conveyed, or were unrelated to this group of foreign 'friends of China'. The narrative of that process began slowly to receive a wider and wider circulation overseas through reports based on participant observation during the land-reform process by the Crooks and William Hinton, or later interviews in villages by Michael Shapiro, Jack Chen or Jan Myrdal. David Crook later wrote that he 'hoped to learn' from the processes underway in the already 'Liberated Areas', and 'later to teach how twentieth-century Britain might be made a new utopia' from this example.[45] *Revolution in a Chinese Village* (1959), the Crooks' book – the first of three – was researched over eight months of residence in a Hebei village in 1948. At roughly the same time William Hinton also spent eight months in a village not far away across the border in Shanxi province, accompanying a party work team, and would later publish the result as *Fanshen* (1966). The book appeared much later than the

Crooks' volume because Hinton's notes were seized by the American authorities on his return to the United States in 1953, and not returned to him for five years. The policing of information was hardly the sole prerogative of the PRC.

All these writers were firmly of the communist left, and this shaped the tone of the body of material which ranged from the professional and impressively documented to the astoundingly superficial and naive, but cumulatively they outlined a story of how rural China had 'stood up', and achieved a 'fanshen' (literally 'turned the body') – a jargon term meaning that they had transformed themselves, their thinking and their villages. Violence was not glossed over (it was already a source of disquiet even in the most sympathetic political circles overseas), but nobody lingered on it. Michael Shapiro would have had his readers believe that 'Surprisingly few landlords were killed.'[46] In many cases those who died were presented as having been involved in wartime treason or other obvious crimes. Who, after all, could object to the execution of a traitor? But the traumas and extremes of wartime were often presented as the normal state of affairs. And some of the sketches of the evils of the past were simply risible. Jack Chen, for example, claimed that:

> The landlords forced tenants to pay from forty-five to over seventy per cent of the output of the land rented. They charged interest on loans of several hundred per cent a year. And to this was added the whole appalling burden of ruthless soldiery, police, secret agents, ignorance, superstition, corrupt courts, press gangs, forced labour, and acts of rape and murder.[47]

It is a wonder anybody was still alive in the countryside by 1949. However, such statements would find their way into school textbooks and popular histories overseas. An important shift had occurred in understandings of China overseas, but one caricature had largely been substituted for another. Land reform was analysed in what seemed to be academic monographs, published by academic presses, but these accounts were mostly in fact written by true believers. This work would also energize and inspire a new generation. Radicals across the world of 1968 were drawn to *Fanshen* in particular, and to Mao-ist political stances in general. Leftist scholarship and intellectual posturing found affirmation in the gospel of the Chinese revolution according to William Hinton.[48] Here was something novel, a lesson for the world from China, a glimpse of a possible 'new utopia'.

Although it presented itself to global publics through the tightly controlled propaganda machine in Beijing, China did not actually lack for visitors; there were roughly 8,000 to 10,000 a year in the 1950s.[49] They were queuing up to get in from the moment the new state was established, and it spent increasing amounts of money on easing their way. One of the first was a British communist and union official, Marian Ramelson, who arrived in December 1949 for an Asian Women's conference. 'China is free,' she reported on her return, 'the fact lights up the East as a blazing sun.'[50] In this way Ramelson was a pioneer pilgrim on what became a well-trodden path to revelation. There was light, laughter, order, unity and co-operation at the end of the Trans-Siberian Railway, or a flight to Beijing, or the border crossing at Hong Kong. There were no flies (a recurring theme); the trains ran on time; women and peasants stood proud; workers were well housed; all was right with the world of the East. Americans were technically barred by the United States government from visiting, but there were regular delegations from Britain starting in 1951. These were organized by the Britain–China Friendship Association, a communist front organization, and from 1955 onwards by a business group, the 'Icebreakers' (later known as the 48 Group) – to the fury of once-dominant companies like Jardine Matheson (who saw them as 'ridiculously uninformed businessmen').[51] The former British Prime Minister Clement Attlee led an official Labour Party visit in 1954; in 1955 Jean-Paul Sartre and Simone de Beauvoir came, saw and extolled at length the 'limitless' prospects, not only for China, but for all, as 'this new China embodies a particularly exciting moment in history: that in which man, so long reduced to dreaming of what humanity might be, is setting out to become it'. Pan-Africanist intellectuals W. E. B. Du Bois and Shirley Garner visited twice.[52] Some pilgrims were so impressed that they decided to return and work for the Foreign Languages Press. Returnees rushed to print and to give talks. There were exceptions – Clement Attlee for one – but like most travellers their responses to what they saw were fixed before they arrived. They had expected to find Jerusalem – and there it was.

By the end of the 1950s, as its dispute with the Soviet Union intensified, the PRC's foreign-policy concerns encouraged a big push to develop its profile in Africa, Asia and Latin America. Fifteen hundred Latin Americans visited in delegations between 1949 and 1960. Amongst them were former presidents, artists, the Chilean poet Pablo Neruda and the Brazilian novelist Jorge Amado, peace activists and scientists. Back home these visitors were prominent amongst those setting up 'friendship associations' and similar groups, and writing and talking positively about New China. African nationalists too started to find their way to China, finding a warm reception when they did so. In 1956 there were 435 delegations from non-communist countries. In the last three years of the decade there were eighty-four delegations just from the Belgian Congo: the communist and the non-aligned world beat a path to China's door.[53] For those who could not make the journey, Radio Peking's anti-colonial agenda provided either inspiration or an unsettling challenge to the information order internationally, and within many individual territories depending on the listener.

Nothing had been left to chance. These were minutely managed and choreographed visits, prepared with great attention to the detail of the political position, and potential, of the visitors.[54] The itineraries were limited, and the accounts of them become quite repetitive. Visitors had guides and translators, and these provided voluminous reports on their charges. The vanity of many a pilgrim was tickled by the cordiality of the receptions accorded, but the state also wheeled those potentially most useful into meetings with senior party leaders. Concern about managing visitors and visits had its obverse overseas. The British government did what it could, when it could, to discredit, discomfort and disable the more vociferous and prominent in the pro-PRC lobby, especially during the Korean War. The former diplomat Sir John Pratt, a long-time critic of the China coast British, was removed from the Foreign Office's seat on the Universities' China Committee. Monica Felton, a senior civil-service town planner, was sacked after she visited British prisoners of war in Korea. A Foreign Office China expert, Derek Bryan, who with Liao Hong Ying, his wife, was prominent in pro-PRC circles, found himself facing a posting to Peru, took the hint and resigned. The Foreign Office's Information

withdrawal of Soviet assistance; they had drawn on their training in Europe and America, gleaned what they could from scraps of information available to them, and improvised and designed their own path to 16 October's 'Great victory for the Chinese people', but Chinese scientists and technicians developed the weapon themselves in a staggering feat of defiant self-reliance. So this was a New China indeed, equipped with a strong state that could direct enormous resources and human ingenuity to focus single-mindedly on such a spectacular project. It was a militant state too, with global political ambitions to fight and defeat imperialism, into which category it increasingly came to include the USSR, and it was equipped now with nuclear weapons.

Moreover, it was not afraid of war. After all, said Mao, more than once, terrifying Nikita Khrushchev, amongst many others, if half of humanity perished in a nuclear war, half would survive; we would prevail, and 'get to work producing more babies than ever before', but 'imperialism would be razed to the ground'.[68]

10

Monsters and Demons

It was scissors that made young Jim Ballard shudder, metal blades wielded by ranks of Chinese women; that, and the spectacle of an irresistible force, advancing steadily in line, but wholly consumed in its own business, shouting slogans and performing an insular drama of revolution. The British writer J. G. Ballard was born in Shanghai's International Settlement in 1930, where his father managed a calico printing mill, and left after being released from a Japanese internment camp in 1945. He would echo twice in his writings a familiar childhood sight: the rows of Chinese 'weedy-women' employed to tend the lawns of Shanghai householders.[1] The first occasion was in his story 'A Place and a Time to Die', published in the autumn of 1969, which responded directly to what was formally called the Great Proletarian Cultural Revolution, then three years old.[2] This upheaval was the greatest of New China's mass movements, and it beguiled, inspired and shocked observers in equal measure. Old narratives and fears about China were given new life, and the 'Yellow Peril' was dressed anew as a 'Red' one. China was never weaker, but never seemed more dangerous, confident and unpredictable than at this moment.

Ballard imagined the advance of 'a vast throng' – a million-strong force – moving on an unnamed town in a half-conquered continent that might be North America. Two men prepare to make a suicidal last stand in the town's defence, but find themselves pushed aside and ignored by an onward rush of 'gong-beating and chanting soldiers' and:

> civilians, carrying no weapons or webbing, the women with small red booklets in their hands. On poles over their heads they held giant blown-up photographs of party leaders and generals.

'They're not interested in us! They're not interested at all!' one of the men realizes as they either brush past, or surround and harangue him, but without seeming to notice his actual presence. They are going through the agitprop motions of revolutionary indignation and enthusiasm in a spirit of solipsistic rage. Later Ballard drew more explicitly on the same well of memory in his autobiographical novel *Empire of the Sun*. There, eleven-year-old Jim watches the women work on a lawn in 1941 and 'always felt a faint shiver of horror when he strayed too close to them', for 'he could visualize what would happen if he fainted in their path'. His host offers an old thought, that there were so many Chinese they could stretch from pole to pole: 'They could weed the whole world?' the young boy asks. 'If you want to put it like that,' comes the reply.

Weeding the world: China certainly seemed to have declared war on it by the end of 1969, and on itself, and Shanghai headquartered this new struggle. Mao was based there or nearby for eight months after November 1965. It was the city in which a first salvo in the new struggle was fired through an article on a play, first published in the newspaper *Wenhui bao* on 10 November 1965; it was the city that was run by a revolutionary 'People's Commune', which overthrew the municipal administration in January 1967; and the city from which the group dominating the movement nationally emerged, not least the former Shanghai actress Lan Ping, now known as Jiang Qing, who was Mao's wife. With Mao, this cabal would play a leading role in retrieving control of the state from those they alleged were returning it to capitalism. But Shanghai was also still the capital city of Chinese cosmopolitanism, which had been given new life – with a distinctly more enhanced East European flavour – through the strong cultural interaction with the Communist bloc before the Sino-Soviet split. The city was battered and bruised, but its cosmopolitanism was still more pronounced there than anywhere else in China. It was an obvious target.

The country was never more militant than in 1966–9: it confronted the British and the Portuguese in Hong Kong and in Macao, it poured weapons into North Vietnam and sent army construction brigades and air-defence units as well; it fomented revolutionary movements in Burma and Cambodia; it fought a fitful border war with the USSR.

Its diplomats abroad handed out revolutionary propaganda and paraphernalia to anybody who came within range – deluging them with badges, books and pamphlets – as well as giving cash to militants. It trained guerrillas and revolutionary cadres in China, and dispatched advisors overseas. Its city squares and stadiums filled up with vast rallies denouncing imperialists and revisionists. At one point a million people – a vast throng – paraded past the British compound in Beijing, and 'Red Guards' – militant youth – later stormed and burned the mission, as well as part of the Soviet Embassy. Other embassy sieges took in the Indonesians, Mongolians and Indians, amongst others. Indian, French, British and Russian diplomats and their families were manhandled, and Chinese diplomats and students clashed with security forces in London, Rangoon, Paris, Moscow and Jakarta. Diplomatic relations with China were broken off by many states in response to these incidents. Effigies of foreign leaders were hanged and burned on Beijing streets in what became a predictable repertoire of scripted rage.[3]

But there was more rhetorical fury than policy in all of this; in truth there was almost no policy at all for the better part of a year, and it was replaced by a recurring and repetitive cycle of polemics against the enemies of China's revolution. The reason for this was a decisive turn to class struggle in politics and a deliberate scaling back of all foreign-relations activities; the Foreign Ministry itself imploded in January 1967 when it was seized by radical leftists. The Third World internationalism the government had avidly pursued after its Bandung triumph had peaked in 1964 and then fragmented. Many of its foreign friends had recoiled from an erstwhile partner that espoused solidarity with their regimes, but at the same time actively supported insurgent communist parties aiming to topple them. Fraternity with fellow parties and diplomacy did not easily mix. There had been a historic and warm set of meetings with Indian leaders, starting in 1954 when Nehru visited Beijing: 'In spite of differences in our ideologies and social systems,' Mao asserted in their first meeting, 'we have an overriding common point, that is, all of us have to cope with imperialism.' But what Nehru articulated as the 'common experience' of having 'suffered from foreign rule', and the shared challenges of development, did not prevent a turn to war in 1962 over unresolved border issues.[4] Liu Shaoqi, as Chinese head of state, had made a triumphant formal visit to Indonesia in April 1963, but the powerful Indonesia Communist Party (PKI) botched a coup in September 1965, and its suppression afterwards was accompanied by a genocidal pogrom that consumed half a million lives, most of them ethnically Chinese Indonesians. Zhou Enlai's tour of African capitals in 1964 had turned disastrous over suspicions of Chinese intentions. His assertion in Tanzania in 1965 that Africa was 'ripe for revolution' sounded the death knell for China's Third World diplomacy. A planned second Bandung conference was cancelled.[5] The Chinese still had their Albanian friends, but little else except their rhetoric.

Even so, there was a consistent recurring theme in China's fulminations against the world of its enemies: and that was anti-imperialism. And not just on its own domestic account: Chinese rhetoric consistently represented the country as the global centre and headquarters of world revolution, to which those struggling overseas looked for inspiration. But as well as opposition to the American intervention in Vietnam, or the Dominican Republic, for example, or the Arab-Israeli war, or whatever the battle that was currently being fought, there was the unfinished business of the past: the foreign-controlled colonies that still occupied two tiny footholds on China's southern coast; the contested borders with the USSR and India that were legacies of the 1860 treaty with Tsarist Russia, and the 1914 Simla Accord between the government of British India and Tibet; and the permeation of China itself even after seventeen years of the new regime with the culture, relics and evidence of its pre-revolutionary history. The Russian legacy was also wrapped up in the Sino-Soviet ideological dispute, and 'anti-revisionism', the second great theme in China's rhetoric.

If its actual foreign policy was a shambles, the country's militant Maoism was taken up globally. This became possibly the single most successful export beyond its immediate cultural realm of any of the philosophical or political ideas that had ever emerged within China in the modern era. The political fellow travellers of the 1950s were succeeded by far greater numbers of Maoist adepts, toting their copies of the iconic 'Little Red Book' (*Quotations from Chairman Mao Tse-tung*) in 'London, Paris, Rome, Berlin' – as the British leftist slogan of 1968 had it – in America, Japan and Australia; but also, and more devastatingly, in Arusha, Naxalbari, Ayacucho and Tirana, in the shape of Tanzanian President Julius Nyerere's *ujamaa* development programme, the West Bengal Naxalite insurgency, Peru's Sendero Luminoso (Shining Path) rebellion, and – of course – in Albania.[6] A Maoist chic would settle in amongst the fashionable left, or simply the fashionable, but deadly, real Maoist insurgencies still linger in 2017.

Never had a theatrical review had such a devastating impact. For the cue for this upheaval was just that: an attack on a play that damned it as a 'poisonous weed'. The play *Hai Rui Dismissed from Office* was hardly good theatre, but then it had been written for political purposes, not as drama. The author, Wu Han, was China's leading expert on Ming Dynasty history, and had been commissioned to write it in 1960 by a Beijing opera company to assist the drive to correct deliberate misreporting of results by cadres during the Great Leap Forward period. Hai Rui was an upright Ming official who had been punished for his honesty, and Mao had called on cadres to emulate him and report problems and data accurately and honestly, without fear of the consequences. However, by 1964, Mao and others had come to see Wu Han's play as a thinly veiled criticism. In this interpretation the figure of Hai Rui was assumed to stand in for Marshal Peng Dehuai, the Korean War hero and veteran party leader, who had been disgraced at Mao's behest in 1959 for his opposition to the Great Leap Forward. This didactic work of drama provided a pretext for a move by Mao to confront those he perceived as his opponents within the leadership. These were the men who had rolled back some of the ultra-socialist measures of the Great Leap Forward in order to revive the economy after the famine. Jiang Qing served as his emissary to Shanghai to get the article written, and Mao personally revised drafts of it.[7]

Wu Han was an incidental target. There was a policy difference within the leadership between those aiming for a more pragmatic, bureaucratic development model, and Mao, who saw that course as inexorably leading to corruption of the party, and the abandonment of class struggle. Mao was sensitive also to parallels in the ousting of Nikita Khrushchev by his Soviet Politburo colleagues in October 1964 for reasons that might also have been applied to himself: Khrushchev was deemed unpredictable, a source of 'hare-brained schemes', and someone who had overriden the practice of collective leadership (which Mao certainly had, by attacking Peng Dehuai). Wu Han was a professor at Tsinghua University, but he was also an official in the Beijing city government, and the campaign against him was implicitly an attack on Beijing's mayor, Peng Zhen, a senior and powerful figure within the party. This was to serve as the prompt for a wider shake-up of the nation, during which Mao aimed to outflank his opponents by calling on the powerless to criticize and overthrow the leadership elite, once revolutionary in ethos and character, but now getting too comfortable in its enjoyment of the fruits of victory and control. At least, this was Mao's formulation. As a result, too, a new generation that had not known the revolution would experience struggle, and new leaders would emerge from the masses across the nation. 'In history it is always the new arrivals who are more progressive,' Mao had told a visiting French politician in 1964, 'and that is why the younger generation will outstrip us.'[8] The criticism of Wu Han was taken up more widely. Peng Zhen was attacked for trying to protect his subordinate, and the party leadership started to fragment. The robustly organized state structure that the CCP had now established had delivered the atomic bomb; but, in Mao's analysis, the party's strengths were also profound revolutionary weaknesses, for it would foster complacency, and thereby a counter-revolution too.

What this meant in practice was that quite swiftly party leaders and administrators at all levels faced a mass insurgency from radical opponents, who fought the established elite, fought each other and fought the army. The first response of those attacked was to seize control of events themselves, sending in 'work teams' to investigate and criticize staff within their own departments, singling out easy targets from people with already-known politically difficult backgrounds, or those who had been labelled 'rightists' in 1957. But these tactical moves were outflanked by Mao's call on 5 August 1966 for a wider revolt and undermined by more radical factions who heeded that injunction to, as he put it, 'Bombard the Headquarters'. The work teams were attacked. Government buildings were taken over by new revolutionary groups, archives were seized, and at mass rallies the newly deposed leadership was paraded, ill-treated and denounced. Violence was sanctioned from the very top.

It became a revolt of the young. Schoolchildren formed themselves into 'Red Guard' units and struggled against and sometimes killed their teachers; gangs of them ransacked the homes of alleged class enemies; neighbour imprisoned neighbour; 'rich peasants', 'landlords' and all the other class enemies and counter-revolutionaries were dragged out again and beaten, jailed, or killed. Huge numbers of people committed suicide. There were mass killings in the country-side, and even well-attested incidents of cannibalism where the organs or the flesh of those murdered was eaten by their killers. Pitched battles were fought in several major cities between thousands of insurgents and soldiers, involving spears, clubs and rifles, as well as tanks, artillery and even warplanes. Liu Shaoqi, China's President, died of medical neglect in prison, as did Peng Dehuai. In a ferocious campaign of destruction targeting the 'four olds' – old thoughts, customs, culture and habits – China's cultural heritage was savaged. Temples and heritage sites, cultural artefacts, books and works of art were trashed, burned or broken.

Hundreds of thousands of homes were ransacked; people destroyed their own possessions or sold or disposed of them to try to obliterate evidence of their pasts. The paper-recycling industry was a standout economic success in this period as people queued up to dispose of books and private papers. Tens of thousands of people classified as 'landlords' or with other 'bad' labels were expelled from their homes in the cities and forced to move to their rural places of origin. At least one and a half million people were killed or committed suicide, mostly between 1967 and 1971; very large numbers were permanently maimed; tens of millions underwent the terror and torture of being oppressed in successive campaigns and waves of violence.[9]

It seemed to many observers and many caught within it to be a massive fit of collective madness, a delusional and inexplicable descent into chaos. How else could one describe a political campaign in which a state immolated itself; in which Buddhist statues were paraded in dunce hats, and then burned; and in which the domestic cats of Beijing were systematically slaughtered, and then laid out 'at the roadside with their front paws tied together'.[10] Yet once unleashed it was in many instances a revolt driven by the real grievances and fears of a shifting coalition of the disaffected, ambitious and afraid.

Included amongst these were the children of party officials and leaders – those who had done well out of the new dispensation – who went on the offensive to protect themselves, their perquisites and their future careers. In Shanghai, meanwhile, many younger workers found themselves facing declining workplace security and living standards in the post-Leap period of economic adjustment. They were excluded from the privileges of a better-paid older generation and these grievances fuelled a grassroots uprising against the status quo in the mills and factories of the city. It was virtually impossible not to be involved; and it was vitally important not be on the wrong side.

It was also carnivalesque. For many concerned it was liberating and invigorating. The normal tight restraints of age, position and gender were loosened dramatically and swiftly; young people travelled across China, riding for free on the massively expanded railway system to 'exchange experiences' of struggle. They poured into Beijing (11 million in four months after mid-August 1966, according to one report).[11] This was the lighter side of the release from discipline: seeing the country, excitement, sex, journeys of personal discovery, and the taste of power and of respect.[12] The darker side to carnival was inescapably intertwined with this: violence, cruelty and murder, paranoia, intolerance and a degradation of all social relations. There was much opportunity for crime and simple hooliganism. And Beijing stank as a result; its sanitation infrastructure was unable to cope with the sudden influx. One hundred and sixty thousand people died as a wave of cerebral-spinal meningitis was stoked and carried by the millions on the move.[13] Ultimately there was a shattering betrayal, when the revolutionary young, their purpose served, were suppressed from late 1968 onwards, and in many cases with great violence. The lives and careers of an entire 'lost' generation were distorted and degraded. But for many of those involved, especially the young, this was, while it lasted, a blissful dawn in which to be alive: China seemed theirs to remake.

But really, what was there left to do? What had New China not already gained? Visual surveys of Shanghai, for example, prepared for the tenth anniversary of the revolution, provide a triumphant view of the city's new dignity, and contrast the degraded past with the refreshed present.[14] Workers now enjoyed rowing in boats on a new lake in People's Park, the former site of the exclusive Shanghai Race Club. The Bund, 'springboard for economic imperialism', was now a 'majestic and beautiful' site of recreation for the people, and foreign soldiers and statues of imperialists like Sir Harry Parkes no longer guarded it. The riverside park, which once barred 'Dogs and Chinese', now accommodated retired workers who could sit there chatting with their grandchildren. The 'stood-up' people of Shanghai had also reclaimed Nanjing Road from the perpetrators of the 1925 May Thirtieth Massacre. There were estates of model houses for workers, instead of squatter shacks, and pestilential open sewers had been removed. The people of the city had washed 'clean the filth and stains inflicted by the colonialists'.

Shanghai was a chastened city. The 'Chinese people's blood and sweat sucking imperialist Canidrome' had been rebuilt as a Cultural Plaza with the capacity to hold 14,000 people. Dogs no longer chased the 'electric rabbit'; ballet dancers from Novosibirsk performed there instead. What were described as 'pornographic' films, like the Ronald Reagan vehicle *Stallion Road*, were no longer poisoning young people; 'obscene' and 'reactionary' magazines had been replaced with educational material. Foreign musicians no longer shrilled their 'lewd' music at Ciro's, which instead now reverberated to educational songs performed in a traditional voice and string genre by the Shanghai People's Pingtan troupe. It was all very worthy and creditable, and the old 'sink of iniquity', the 'city of sin', had certainly been cleaned up and transformed. A lively, non-official world persisted nonetheless, and Hong Kong-made films and fashions were quietly popular and influential, but it was hardly surprising that large numbers of people had volunteered to leave Shanghai altogether.

Tens of thousands took work assignments in the northwest or in Manchuria, as part of a massive drive to relocate industry and expertise in the cause of a more geographically balanced industrial development strategy.[15] They did not all go willingly, but they were not all conscripted. Shanghai had represented the biggest challenge for the CCP as it came to power. There had been discussion early on about relocating its industries, which would serve multiple purposes: helping development elsewhere in China; assuaging security concerns about over-concentration of strategic resources in one place (and that place coastal) and breaking the monopoly power of this dangerous, historically compromised city. Some industries were actually moved – 145 factories in their entirety between 1955 and 1960 – and the city was not a priority site for initiatives under the First Five Year Plan. It grew nonetheless, and some of Shanghai's people certainly were relocated. As early as July 1951 university graduates in Shanghai were being firmly directed to employment elsewhere in China. In September 1952, 1,200 left in one much-publicized troupe from Shanghai's station, heading to Manchuria to support the Korean War effort. In the 1950s tens of thousands were sent to Xinjiang and to other west China provinces. Between 1963 and 1966, 70,000 young people left for Xinjiang, and another 100,000 went to the countryside.[16] This was a national policy, but Shanghai was a particularly prominent target.

A very different destination for the Shanghai exodus had been Hong Kong. Between 1945 and 1951, when border controls went into operation, 1.4 million refugees settled in the colony, and at least another 420,000 came in the following ten years.[17] By 1961 it has been estimated that 100,000 of these refugees had come from Shanghai. A significant group of them brought capital, expertise and networks; some relocated their businesses, others transferred their shipping interests. Amongst them were some of the most prominent and experienced of Shanghai business families. Their role in Hong Kong's rapid post-war industrialization was crucial, most obviously in the cotton-spinning industry, which was 'virtually a Shanghai enclave'. They invested in new plant, ordering it from overseas, or making use of substantial amounts of equipment that was held up in Hong Kong warehouses as a result of political uncertainty and inflation in the late 1940s, and then the trade embargo with China. The peak of Shanghai's capital flight to Hong Kong was 1948–9, but it also continued, covertly, where it could, after the communist seizure of power. Most refugees, of course, had little to bring, but those new mills, and hundreds of other new factories that were established as Hong Kong's economy rapidly grew, needed labour. This rapid influx generated great stress on the colony's infrastructure, but it also fuelled its growth.

'To outward appearances little has changed,' remarked the outgoing Shanghai British consul in June 1966, 'the same imperialist buildings range imposingly along the bund'.[18] But these were now denuded of their former occupants. British China firms had steadily been relocating their company registration since the later 1930s in the face of Nationalist Government legislation, the expected demise of extraterritoriality and the Japanese invasion, but this accelerated after 1945. Although it had always had a distinctively different culture, partly derived from its place within the Chinese treaty ports, but partly also from its place within the circuit of British colonies, Hong Kong nonetheless provided a comfortably familiar home from home for some of the China British amongst the 23,000 Britons who lived there. The same bank dominated the waterfront (and the same bronze lions as well guarding its entrance); cricket was also played in the heart of the city centre, and the ponies raced at Happy Valley; and the Hong Kong Club was an agreeable respite for the displaced residents from the Shanghai Club. They had all the pomp of British official life that they had been used to in Shanghai, and then more, much more, as Hong Kong had its Governor and all the ceremonial that clustered around him. And from 1963 onwards there was also a Canidrome, albeit in Macao, but there were also casinos there, all to sweeten the taste of exile.

In China itself the rump foreign presence was tiny. In 1964 the total number of resident Russians, formerly the largest of the foreign communities, was down to 1,326, most of them living in Xinjiang. There were 2,730 foreign nationals in Shanghai at the start of 1965, but 2,092 of these were African, Asian or Latin American students. There were only sixty-five others resident in the city who were not diplomatic staff. There were forty-two Britons in 1962 (most of them the elderly ethnically Chinese widows of British men), and five French nationals. The number steadily declined even further: in his 1964–6 term of service, Consul David Brookfield recorded five deaths and one christening; others left the city as lingering foreign interests were wound up. Aside from a Polish shipping agency and a Pakistan International Airways office that opened in 1964, there were only three resident foreign firms by the end of 1965, all of them British. A fourth, the Banque Sino-Belge, was, with its manager and his family, a hostage rather than a going concern, and had been since he had arrived to wind up its business in 1952. There were twenty-seven Indians, mostly Sikhs running dairies, and only six Russians remained, who were outnumbered ten to one by Tibetans, of all the historically unlikeliest of Shanghai's residents.[19] Small pockets of foreign nationals lingered in Tianjin and Beijing itself. British diplomats retained a watching brief to look after their welfare when they were not, as one visitor, George Gale, reported with disbelief, organizing treasure hunts in the pleasant but underused grounds of the embassy. The British had finally to abandon the old legation in 1959. It was packed with history: archives (including Chinese ones captured in 1858 in Guangzhou), memorial plaques, monuments, ancient bronze cannon, and detritus left by passing residents, including the fantasist and fraud Sir Edmund Backhouse.[20] Some of this was shipped back to Britain, some given away and some sold for scrap, having long been surplus to any possible requirement other than pride, if not self-deception, for some decades past.

The number of Europeans in Shanghai actually increased in 1965, doubling in size overnight when thirty foreign experts arrived to teach at the Shanghai Foreign Language Institute. All the contradictory features that characterized such groups in China throughout the century were replicated even in this small, cosmopolitan crowd: ideological zeal and naivety, arrogant self-interest and even simple Sinophobia.[21] Most of this motley group had little to do with the foreign community that gathered en masse – fewer each year – for an annual Christmas service at the British Consulate. This was officially now the 'Office of the British Chargé d'Affaires taking care of British nationals' affairs in Shanghai', but visitors passed through its consulate gateposts on which were placed the royal coat of arms. Amongst those who came in 1965 were some whose families had a long history in the former treaty port: Constance Martin's grandfather had been the first chief of the settlement police, back in 1854, and there were men with historically resonant surnames: Robert Vyvyan Dent, whose father had been born in the old Dent & Co. *hong* on the Bund in 1862 when the family firm still rode high, wide and handsome amongst the British China companies, its only rival Jardine Matheson. Dent lived with his wife and son Louis in a large house on the former Avenue du Roi Albert. Husheng Pin Mesny's father arrived in Shanghai in 1860, and had carved out a career as a Taiping civil war gun-runner and post-war mercenary and military advisor. W. R.

McBain's family business had commenced in Shanghai in the 1870s, and he had himself served on the Shanghai Municipal Council in 1925–6 during the May Thirtieth Movement.[22] McBain too had once owned a building on the Bund, now let to Shell. Visiting foreign journalists in the 1950s like George Gale had nosed out surviving Russian tailors, or even bars and bar girls, but there were only now these relics of what seemed to be truly an Edwardian era. Brookfield and his successor still kept an old-fashioned establishment of servants that would have done the elder Dent or McBain proud back in Shanghailander days, listing, in 1967, 'No. 1 Boy, No. 2 Boy, House Coolie, Cook, Wash Amah, Baby Amah, Gardener', many of them having long served the consulate. The weedy-women still cut the British Consulate grass – 'the lawns were perfection', remembered a British diplomat – over which a 160-foot flagstaff still towered, and on which the Union Jack was raised, though only on fifteen occasions every year (so as not to provoke controversy).[23] So possibly the only man in China who was still called formally a 'coolie' worked at the British Consulate, on a site marked out in 1842 when Queen Victoria's troops occupied the city in the First Opium War.

If the formerly dominant British presence was but a slight whisper of its old self, how had the world changed for Liu Nianyi – the Cambridge-educated Shanghai businessman who with his father had enjoyed a mutually profitable collaboration with the CNRRA after the war? In 1965, like other 'national capitalists' who had stayed on or returned after 1949, Liu retained some of the fruits and status of his past: in his case a 5 per cent share of the earnings of the former family match factory, through which he could afford to support a car, a maid and a comfortable house. That year French photographer Marc Riboud secured a portrait of Liu and his wife, Xia Tianjin. A statuette of Mao Zedong graced a mantelpiece, but jade ornaments filled a display cabinet behind them. Liu stood, arms crossed and confident beside the elegantly presented Xia. Here was a 'happy capitalist', read the caption. His father had given him the English name Julius – in homage to Caesar; Liu still looked the part. The family were among the Shanghai capitalists that foreign reporters regularly got to interview. Visitors were amazed when they saw these men marching in National Day parades. 'Lunacy,' thought the journalist

James Cameron; that or hypocrisy. 'I can't complain,' Liu Nianyi's younger brother Liu Gongcheng (once Leonardo) had told Cameron a few years earlier: 'I expected to see the liberation chop my head off; instead it saved my life.' It will also have helped that he had been a member of the Communist Party since he had spent a year in Yan'an in 1938–9. When in due course the cement plant that Liu managed was transferred wholly to state ownership, he expected to be retained as manager. And, he said, 'I might add that there are nowadays no disputes with the workers': happy capitalism indeed.[24]

It could not last. On 23 August 1966 the young cultural revolutionaries got to work to overhaul Shanghai.[25] Against a backdrop of relentless noise from gongs, drums, chanting and blaring loudspeakers, they painted slogans, hung banners and pasted posters across the city. Streets and buildings were renamed: Nanjing Road should become 'Anti-Imperialism Road', decided the Red Guards; the Huangpu River should be 'Anti-Imperialism River'; the city should be renamed 'Anti-Imperialism City'. They competed with each other over the new names, but there was little scope for imagination. The Great World leisure centre became 'East is Red', and a massive statue of Mao would eventually grace its frontage. Surviving old inscriptions on foundation stones and on the fronts of formerly foreign-owned buildings were chiselled, drilled or burned off, plastered over with cement, or painted over. The British Consulate was told to remove the royal coat of arms, and did so to pre-empt their being ripped off (and consequent 'greater loss of face'). Foreign car marques were altered: Austin became Anti-Imperialism, Ford was Anti-Revisionism. The library in the old Race Club was trashed; the museum was invaded and wrecked.

The Shanghai skyline changed almost overnight. There was a systematic assault on religious buildings: mosques, temples and churches were ransacked and religious symbols and icons were destroyed. The City God, Jing'an and Longhua temples lost their relics and scriptures. Xujiahui and Holy Trinity cathedrals lost their landmark spires and towers; crosses were removed. The three Sikh Gurdwaras were taken over. A Parsi prayer room and cemetery on Fuzhou Road were broken into and seized. Monks and nuns were ill-treated; Shanghai's Imam was beaten (Beijing's was killed). Cemeteries were attacked and all but a handful of tombstones destroyed. Two posters on the front of the

Customs House declared that 'The chimes from the Customs building still ring with the ghostly sounds of imperialism', and that 'The East is Red' should be substituted instead. Within a week a new clock mechanism was installed and the song, a homage to Mao Zedong, was blasted out across the city through forty loudspeakers. Next door the bronze lions, still on guard outside the former Hongkong and Shanghai Bank, which had become the city government headquarters, were removed. Shanghai had Mao Zedong thought: what need had it of lions?

What need had Shanghai of Hong Kong-style fashions, or hairstyles? Squads of young revolutionaries confronted hairdressers' and coffee shops for encouraging 'teddy boys and flappers', and ordered them to close. People wearing fashionable clothes, shoes or hairstyles were accosted in the street: hair might be shorn on the spot, clothing ripped off. Young girls quickly cut off their own plaits. Shoe stores ran out of canvas shoes as leather was abandoned. The stylish young woman photographed by Marc Riboud a year earlier, with her smart trouser suit, white gloves, lipstick and chiffon scarf, would not have stood a chance. The visual propaganda of New Shanghai had once offered a bourgeois vision of the 'happy life' that 'Chairman Mao' had given the Shanghai proletariat, but now it was necessary to dress down, look like a worker and forget neatly ironed creases.[26] Confectioners abandoned selling foreign-style pastries; flower sellers shut up shop; goldfish were banned. One British diplomat reported seeing agitprop teams of twelve- to thirteen-year-old schoolgirls setting up on the streets, performing dances, chanting slogans and pledging loyalty to Mao, 'in the best evangelical-Salvation Army style'.[27] The sartorial 'sins' of the past were paid for by Wang Guangmei, wife of Liu Shaoqi, who was later paraded in front of hostile crowds at Tsinghua University in Beijing in high heels, a *qipao* that she had worn on the 1963 state visit to Indonesia, and with a chain of table-tennis balls hanging around her neck to represent the pearls that had completed the ensemble. Her accusers taunted her: you 'insulted us. By wearing this dress to flirt with Sukarno in Indonesia, you have put the Chinese people to shame and insulted the Chinese people as a whole.'[28] You were what you wore, and you might pay for it. It was hardly Wang's greatest transgression in radical eyes, but it provided one focus for her degradation and humiliation.

In Shanghai, away from the Bund and the Nanjing Road, violence was unleashed in every street and lane, and in home after home. The houses of alleged 'black' elements were invaded by Red Guards. They came for fifty-one-year-old Nien Cheng on the evening of 30 August 1966. She had been able to make some preparations after witnessing assaults on her neighbours, but nothing could prepare her for what happened. A gang of activists stormed into the house, locked her into one of the rooms, and then seized, destroyed, or despoiled the contents of the home she shared with her daughter. Cheng's clothes were cut to ribbons; her Ming Dynasty porcelain was stamped on; her books were thrown on a bonfire in her garden; furnishings were broken; her record collection was smashed up. 'Down with the running dog of imperialism' was written with her own lipstick on the wall above her bed. Mattresses and soft furniture were ripped open in a search for hidden gold and weapons. It was not the only visit she had. And it happened in 84,221 other homes in Shanghai alone in the two weeks after 23 August 1966. It will have happened to Liu Nianyi. Significant amounts of currency, bonds and precious metals were seized, and other valuables were removed from houses if they survived the despoliation – or theft – and were 'presented to the state' by Red Guards. Almost five and a half million books and 3,300,000 'cultural relics' were seized, and were later processed by the antiquities authorities in the city. The size of the seizures was evidence of the scale of the purge of private property. Between 1 and 25 September gangs of middle-school Red Guards beat more than 10,000 people, eleven of whom died. Another report counted 707 suicides and 354 deaths related to home invasions that month. The numbers can be calculated because the rampages of the young were closely followed and guided by officials, who provided information on those to be targeted. In Beijing, neighbourhood offices or police stations posted up lists of residents to be attacked, noting their names, ages, 'class origin' and 'crime': landlord, counter-revolutionary, bad element, 'dragging feet since revolution'.[29] This was a licensed campaign of violence.

Nien Cheng – Yao Nianyuan – was the daughter of a Beijing government official. She had studied at Yenching University and then at the London School of Economics, met her future husband there and followed him on his Guomindang Foreign Ministry postings. She had been a prominent speaker for China's cause during the war at rallies and meetings in Britain, the United States and also Australia, where they had lived when he was involved in setting up the first Chinese Embassy there. Her husband was running the foreign-affairs office in Shanghai when the city fell to the Communists in 1949, after which he had become General Manager of Shell in the city. After his death in 1957, Nien Cheng had taken over as advisor to the firm's British management until it was closed down in early 1966.[30] This was the generation that had consolidated China's standing in the international community, and that had itself fought to drive back imperialism. Cheng's lifestyle was unashamedly that of the cosmopolitan Shanghai bourgeois. She enjoyed European classical music, drank wine, ate buttered toast for breakfast and was fluent in English. Every two years she was able to make a trip to Hong Kong, where she stocked up on things that could no longer be found in Shanghai. The British diplomats knew her well. Her beautifully appointed house had nine bedrooms, four bathrooms, a piano and a fine collection of antiques and art; she was attended to by a cook, a maid and a gardener. Now she was accused of being a spy.

After a month of struggle sessions (forums of public humiliation and torture), Cheng was imprisoned, and would not be released for over six years. Her alleged crime was 'divulging information about the grain supply situation in Shanghai', by putting her name to a letter of advice to a British woman moving to the city in 1957. But she would only learn this in 1972. Cheng's Australia-born daughter, a young film actress, was abducted in June 1967, tortured in a political struggle session and killed. Both Liu brothers were attacked and denounced in a session broadcast on television.[31] Liu Nianyi fell to his death from the family's former headquarters building on 28 December 1967. This was an attack on the unfinished business of revolution, but it was also a merciless attack on China's cosmopolitans, its history, and the decades of the permeation of Chinese culture and society with global currents and influences.

The Cultural Revolution was riddled with this politically sanctioned xenophobia, a violent rejection of all manifestations of foreign culture, ideas and influences. Study in London, family overseas, a facility with foreign languages – Wang Guangmei spoke French, English and Russian – a taste for foreign products or style, these were all poisonous markers taken to denote a treason of the spirit, and of intent. Although this contrasted sharply with the internationalist solidarity so regularly espoused in political life, it was also quite clearly related to the nationalistic campaigns and thought that had shaped the Chinese revolution throughout the century. It had more in common with Chiang Kai-shek's denunciation of the poisonous influence of foreign power in Shanghai, and the waves of 'National Products' campaigns and movements to boycott foreign goods, than with the millenarianism of the Boxers. It seemed mad, but it was absolutely modern. Those rebels back in 1900 had believed that their world had gone awry because it had been polluted by foreign gods and their adherents. But Chiang and the boycott campaigners were involved in calculated political projects. So were the cultural revolutionaries.

Nothing was untouched, but the world of music was one of the most profoundly affected. One of the first individual targets of the upsurge in denunciations in Shanghai in June 1966 was the composer He Luding, Director of the Shanghai Conservatory of Music. The decade of eager Sino-Soviet friendship had brought about a rich programme of cultural exchanges and placements, for they had brought more than just tractor factories and fertilizer plants. There was the Novosibirsk ballet, but also many other musicians, singers and dancers.[32] The development of expertise in what was called 'New Music' – the composition and performance of Chinese work developed from the European classical tradition – had been as much a part of the nationalistic transformation of Chinese culture and society since 1919 as the adoption of the colloquial language in writing. A new music would help bring into existence a new China. The former Shanghai Municipal Council symphony orchestra – China's first, established in 1879 – provided the basis around which the Conservatory established in Shanghai in 1927 by Cai Yuanpei had built up a rich culture of musical training and expertise. Shanghai's European refugee communities had included many talented musicians, and the orchestra had attracted international stars to the city to perform.[33] In the 1950s this had been enhanced further by Russian and other socialist bloc interchanges. The piano in particular had been taken to heart in China, alongside some, but not all, of the Western canon: Mozart, Beethoven, Brahms and Schubert certainly struck a chord. There were tensions between the high cultural priorities of the Soviet bloc advisors, and the revolutionary ambitions of official Chinese cultural policies, but for urban cosmopolitans and musicians this was a rich and fertile period. And it was a matter of great national pride when twenty-one-year-old Shanghai-born Fou Ts'ong (Fu Cong) won third prize at the prestigious Chopin International Piano Competition in Warsaw in 1955, with a performance that received 'thunderous applause and cheers', as *Renmin ribao* (*People's Daily*, the official party newspaper) reported.[34] China applauded too. Fou was the first Asian, let alone the first Chinese, to win at such an event.

Fou had been talent-spotted by a Polish musician and studied in Poland for two years before his success, but his victory, stated his father, Fu Lei, a well-known Francophile translator, was due to the 'intensely Chinese education' he had given his son. And the Chinese, after all, Fu continued, had always 'assimilated the best of whatever foreign influences have touched their culture'. It was, therefore, a truly Chinese triumph, and the approving notice in *Renmin ribao* seemed to confirm this.[35] In 1956, Mao Zedong had delivered a talk to 'music workers' that was echoed in Fu's comments: 'we should learn from abroad and use what we learn to create things Chinese,' Mao argued. There should be no rejection, but also no unthinking mimicry of foreign things. So this was a careful argument for Fu Lei to use. It was not careful enough, however, and Fu's public trumpeting of his son and his own educational methods were sticks with which he was severely beaten in the 1957 anti-rightist campaign: he had not accorded proper respect to the party.

It was a greater shock two years later when Fou Ts'ong defected to Britain, but it would have been grist to the mill of those deeply suspicious of the inherent internationalism of the musical community in Shanghai, and whose view was the opposite of Fu Lei's. The Conservatory had bowed to pressure to incorporate the training of Chinese instruments in its activities – and minority musicians as well (including some of those Shanghai Tibetans), but with little real enthusiasm. Its composers tramped into the countryside and off to Yan'an, along the route of the Long March, and down into the Anyuan coal mines.

They interviewed old cadres, peasants and workers about their personal histories, and they fashioned the results into their revolutionary symphonies and cantatas. Its staff responded, as they had to, to the demands of the Great Leap Forward for demands for 'more' and 'better' (though perhaps not 'faster') compositions.[36] The Conservatory had launched an annual festival in 1960 – 'Shanghai Spring' – but in the wintry atmosphere that set in a few years later European classical music was suppressed by party fiat in favour of Chinese 'national music'. In 1966 performances in factories, barracks and villages were the centrepiece of the festival, and 'bourgeois "authorities" ' and their 'restrictions and conventions' were denounced.[37] Over 70 per cent of the performers, it was claimed, were 'amateur worker, peasant and soldier artists' who pledged to create 'more and better songs and dances worthy of our era' through holding 'to the party's Central Committee and to Chairman Mao'. So out went Bach, Beethoven and Strauss, and all ears were tuned instead to 'Forward, Glorious Workers of Shanghai!' and 'The Red Army Fears Not the Trials of the Long March'.

China applauded a different music now. And Fu Lei and Zhu Meifu, his wife, took their own lives on 2 September 1966, three days after Red Guards from the Conservatory of Music had occupied and laid waste to their home.[38] Other victims of the Cultural Revolution at the Conservatory included pianist Li Cuizhen, a friend of Nien Cheng's since student days in 1930s London, who had first studied at the Conservatory in 1929 and thereafter taught there. Her children lived in Australia; her husband had worked in Hong Kong, as she had for a while after his death in 1957. She stood little chance, but thought that having always steered clear of political engagement she would be left with her piano and her students. But on 9 September 1966, after a struggle session led by those same students during which she was forced – 'as a running dog of British imperialism' – to crawl on the ground under a barrier in front of the college gate, Li gassed herself. The Shanghai Symphony Orchestra conductor Lu Hongen was detained early in the campaign. By all accounts mentally ill, but denied treatment, he was brought back to the Conservatory for struggle sessions, during which he was deemed to have committed a counter-revolutionary offence by ill-treating a copy of the Little Red Book.

On 27 April 1968 he was put on trial before a large crowd at the former Canidrome – now renamed Cultural Revolution Square – in an event that was broadcast live on television to audiences assembled in workplaces across the city. Lu and seven others were given death sentences and immediately taken away and shot. The crowd cheered the verdict, clapped and shouted slogans, and then sang 'Sailing the Seas Depends on the Helmsman': 'Mao Zedong thought is a never setting sun' the song concludes.[39] At least seventeen Conservatory staff died in the heat of that sun. Others were maimed by beatings; fingers were broken. A large number of people were imprisoned, mostly on site. By 1970, a later report laconically notes, there were again 250 students, but there were also thirty improvised solitary confinement cells – and eighty of its staff served time in them.[40]

They sang in praise of Mao the Helmsman, the Risen Sun, the People's Saviour, in Hong Kong too. The British colony was on guard from 29 January 1967 because of the disorder over the border, but also specifically in response to a month-long assault on the Portuguese authorities in Macao. A planning dispute over a communist school had sparked riots and a left-wing uprising there that had finally been suppressed by the Portuguese. But in the aftermath the negotiated formal resolution of the episode, during which Portuguese minds had been focused by the arrival of Chinese naval vessels in Macao's harbour, had effectively been a surrender of de facto control. The colonial administration had to renounce the use of force, dismiss some senior officials and agree to pay compensation. Its authority remained in name, but was significantly compromised. It was not its own master in what was still its own house. Those Chinese ships, and the units of PLA soldiers that were deployed on Macao's borders, were also used to prevent militant Red Guards attacking the colony. The status quo best suited China, which benefited, not least economically, from this gateway on the world, as well as the much larger one at Hong Kong.

Even so, the British in Hong Kong had no intention of ever being 'Macaoed', as some put it. The strains and stresses of its rapid industrialization and the continuing absorption of refugees from China had provided sparks for labour protest before, notably in 1956 and 1966, but on 6 May 1967 a strike over pay and conditions at an

19. Waiting for a trick, and for the Communists: Diamond Bar, Shanghai, May 1949.

20. Macao's economy in action: casino, 1949.

21. Erasing the shame of the past: Shanghai Municipal Policeman's tombstone, 1954.

22. Soon to play a different tune: overseas Chinese from Vietnam in Xiamen, 1950.

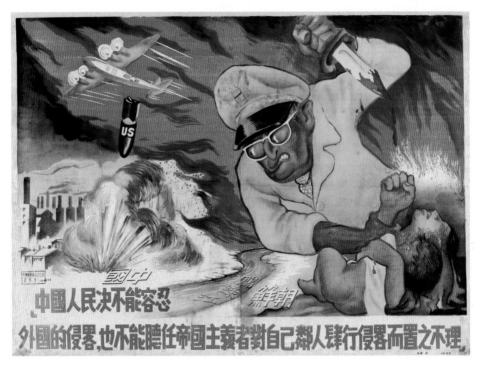

23. General Douglas MacArthur butchering civilians: Anti-American poster, Xu Ling, 1950. The text reads: 'The Chinese people absolutely cannot condone the encroachment of other countries, and cannot listen to whatever Imperialist who thinks that it can wantonly encroach its own neighbours without acting.'

24. Chinese cosmopolitan abroad: pianist Fou Ts'ong, 1960.

25. American Embassy, Taibei, under attack, May 1957.

26. Overtake Britain in Fifteen Years: Great Leap Forward poster, 1958.

27. Land reform and political terror as radical theatre, 1975.

28. Seduced by fantasy: Hong Kong on film, 1960.

29. Radical chic: Jean-Luc Godard's *La Chinoise* (1967).

30. The seductions of Maoism: *Lui* Magazine spread, 1967.

31. Fashioning socialism: womenswear feature from *China Reconstructs*, June 1956.

32. Modern China humiliated: Wang Guangmei and Tsinghua University Red Guards, 10 April 1967.

33. Decorating the British Mission, Beijing 1967: effigies of US President Lyndon Johnson, British Prime Minister Harold Wilson and Moshe Dayan.

34. Ping Pong diplomat: Glenn Cowan in China, 1971.

35. China opens up, to Wham!, 1985.

36. Down with Her Majesty as the handover nears, Hong Kong, 16 June 1997.

37. Never Forget National Humiliation, National Museum of China, 2011

artificial flower factory in Kowloon turned into a violent confrontation between the workers and the police.[41] Five days later the now radical-held Ministry of Foreign Affairs in Beijing issued a formal protest, and there were large-scale demonstrations in Beijing and in Guangzhou. Local Hong Kong communists took what they thought to be a strong hint. They were keen to improve their own revolutionary credentials, as these were compromised under the circumstances by their living in comfortable, capitalist Hong Kong. They formed an 'All Circles Anti-Persecution Struggle Committee', and instituted protests outside Government House and marches, supported by all the activist tools and theatre of the movement in China, and through the nine communist-aligned newspapers in the colony. Demonstrators surrounded the government administration building and recited lessons from the Little Red Book; and up went posters and banners. A general strike was launched in June. But demonstration turned to riot, and from rioting evolved a campaign of intimidation, and murder – and from July onwards, of bombing.

In total fifty-one people were killed. There were 250 bomb attacks, and another 1,500 devices were defused. A murderous assault on police from gunmen across the border in China on 8 July 1967 left five dead. Governor Sir David Trench gave up on his initial 'softly-softly' approach in the face of the violence, and when it became clear that the leftists had largely alienated the Hong Kong public. Reports of the disorder across the border, which directly affected the family and kin of many residents, will hardly have helped. All the well-oiled tools of the British counter-insurgency tool kit were deployed. This had been honed in Malaya, Kenya and Cyprus. A positive 'hearts and minds' propaganda campaign was backed up by steel: detention without trial; closure of the three most inflammatory newspapers and indictments against editors and publishers (three of whom were jailed); and dismissal of striking government workers. The army, with Royal Air Force helicopters, was brought in to back up a programme of police strikes at the bases of trade unions and the Struggle Committee. The British administration won. Few in Hong Kong mourned the defeat of the communists, but there had been rage in China as events escalated.

Shanghai felt it first. On 16 May 1967 the consulate was besieged by demonstrators, and a car ferrying the family of the consul, Peter Hewitt, was attacked. Then a crowd of Red Guards stormed into the compound, he reported, burned an effigy, painted 'anti-British and pro-Mao signs on all the walls and daubed the Queen's portrait, our coats of arms and the cinema screen':

> For the next 3½ hours I was jostled up and down between the gates and the house, which was being ransacked, from time to time being thumped and hit with the small beflagged sticks and having my neck nearly broken by furious efforts to force my head down in submission to Mao.

The British had their 'sentimental reasons' – as the head of mission put it in March 1966 – for wishing to retain the large complex on the Bund; but as a site it engendered that different sentiment in Chinese thinking, of an imperialist relic, a little bridgehead still squatting on the Huangpu waterfront.[42] Long have they 'yearned to gambol on our lawns', reflected Hewitt. Over the next five days he retrieved what had not been destroyed, burned all files, performed a regular ritual of receiving formal protests from Red Guards, and then withdrew by plane to Beijing, he and a colleague having had to run a gauntlet to the aircraft only to find themselves being harangued through loud-hailers by the plane's crew during the entire journey north. It had little to do with Hong Kong, he mused finally, and more to do with nationalism.

Six months later, to the tune of 'The East is Red', the flag of the People's Republic of China was raised over what was simply described as '33 Zhongshan Road' – to avoid giving any legitimacy to the British occupation of the site. It had been 'the headquarters for aggression against China', announced Shanghai radio as the site was confiscated by the city government.[43] This was a 'great victory in the fight against revisionism and imperialism', it was announced. 'It fully reflects the greatness and prestige of China.' After a little discussion the British decided to take no retaliatory action. After all, they could not win. And 'anyway', remarked one official in London, '122 years without rent isn't bad'.[44]

Beijing was next. A piano and a heavy brass lectern, a memorial of the 1900 siege of the legations by the Boxers, were used in a last-ditch defence of the mission – but to no avail. Culture and history failed: thrown against a door, even these heavy items could not hold back the crowd. On the hot evening of 22 August 1967, after some weeks of steadily rising tension, including earlier incursions involving the local foreign experts – including some of the Britons – a 10,000-strong crowd of Red Guards broke into the compound. Protests over David Trench's suppression of communist newspapers and the conviction and jailing of several journalists were the ostensible causes. The twenty-three British staff marooned inside the mission rapidly put an 'Armageddon' emergency plan into operation as the mob, shouting 'Sha! Sha!' – 'Kill! Kill!' – ran towards the building. But the staff were forced to evacuate their safe zone in the face of the assault and smoke from the fires that had been set. As they left they were seized, beaten and kicked. Many were forced to kneel and bow their heads for photographs, for their assailants had come equipped to record their humiliation. The Albanians in their embassy across the road came out in their night clothes to watch the fun, looking on, it was reported, 'with glee'. The Britons were eventually pulled out and brought away by PLA soldiers, and none were badly hurt, though parts of the mission were ruined and equipment was destroyed. Some consolation was taken by Donald Hopson, the head of mission, as he drew to a close his laconic report to London, from the fact that the signed photograph of the Queen that he had hurriedly placed securely in a safe was only slightly singed.[45]

The studied presentation of pluck and sangfroid in the despatches could not hide a very difficult position. After all, wrote the Far Eastern Department chief Arthur de la Mare, 'in any contest in bloody-mindedness the Chinese will always get the better of us'.[46] In many ways this was a perfect statement of the weakness of the British position, or of any other power, and not just at this point in the history of the People's Republic and its foreign relations. British diplomats would be denied exit visas for a year afterwards, but they were at least better off in their confinement than the dozens of British and other foreign nationals who now started to be swept into various types of formal and ad hoc detention.

The only British journalist in Beijing, Anthony Grey of Reuters, had been placed under 'house arrest' on 21 July 1967 in retaliation for the conviction in Hong Kong of a leftist journalist. On 18 August, Red Guards violently took over the house in which Grey was confined, beat and 'jet-planed him', stabbed and hanged his cat, and proceeded to keep him confined to one room in the building for the next two years. Every morning Grey was woken by his guards singing 'The East is Red'; their daily political study sessions concluded with 'Sailing the Seas Depends on the Helmsman'; and they sang the 'Internationale' as he ate dinner. A more solitary confinement would have been easier. The White Russian freelance journalist, Harbin-born Serge Kost, was in detention for eight years in Shanghai before he was even charged with any offence, and it was another seven before he was released.[47] Photography proved the undoing of several detainees. Engineer George Watt decided to confess to espionage in Lanzhou, where he was one of a group of foreign engineers overseeing construction of a polythene plant, and was jailed for three years. Watt reasoned it was the only way to secure any hope of release. Immediately after sentencing he was paraded in front of a mass rally and ritually humiliated. A German colleague was also jailed. Hong Kong-based journalist Norman Barrymaine was seized and imprisoned for nineteen months for taking photographs in the harbour at Shanghai. An Italian mariner arrested with him was not released for nearly three years. By this point there were at least twelve Britons in detention, a dozen Japanese, five West Germans and another twelve Americans. The last small group of foreign nuns in China had been beaten and humiliated in August 1966, and their convent in Beijing and its icons smashed up. They were then expelled from the country. Tourism to China from Western Europe and Asia, which had commenced in 1963, sputtered on into 1967 and then collapsed.[48] Few who were not ardent political pilgrims would risk visiting.

There were other arrests, detentions and what was in all but name hostage-taking. Most foreign students were ordered home in September 1966, and many foreign experts also departed: their numbers declined from 411 to 59. Some initially threw themselves into the cultural revolutionary fray, but their ideological enthusiasm would not protect them from eventual accusations of espionage.[49] David Crook, Michael Shapiro, Sidney Rittenberg, Gladys Yang, Israel Epstein and his British wife Elsie Fairfax-Cholmondley were amongst at least seventeen of the 'friends of China' who were detained for various lengths of time. British diplomats were bemused to be asked to exert themselves making representations on behalf of people like Fairfax-Cholmondley, who had been spotted in a crowd that invaded the mission in June, smashed up the Queen's portrait in the reception hall, pulled down the flag and burned it. But they did what they could. A few unfortunates amongst the tiny communities of ageing foreign nationals were scooped up. The elderly W. R. McBain and Constance Martin in Shanghai could only think in retrospect that the fact they had earlier been awarded official honours (an OBE and MBE respectively) had somehow raised suspicions. Louis Dent's home in Shanghai was invaded by Red Guards in September 1966, and many of his possessions were destroyed. His Chinese companion was beaten and taken away, and Dent's attackers spent two weeks camped out in his house. It was four years before he was permitted to leave China. At its lowest, the total number of foreign nationals resident in Shanghai dipped to seventy people. It is not clear whether this number includes or excludes those who were in jail.[50]

Sino-Soviet relations would take the darkest turn, however. The two-week siege of the Soviet Embassy in early 1967 had been the most spectacular, even if it lacked the pyrotechnic finale that was visited on the British. Hundreds of thousands of demonstrators surrounded the Soviet Embassy and detained the staff. When groups of diplomatic families were permitted to leave, they were manhandled and abused all the way to their aircraft. An elaborate working mannequin of Alexei Kosygin dangling from a gallows was deployed at Beijing's airport in their honour: the Russian Premier held a bloodstained dagger and a truncheon in his hands, and was made to jerk about in a *danse macabre*.[51] Nobody laughed. At the same time, however, the real Kosygin was being feted in London, to which he was making a state visit, and enjoying the first state banquet ever given a Soviet leader. This was grist to the mill of those charging the Russians with 'revisionism' and a drive to 'restore capitalism', and of colluding with the United States to partition China – a charge that was later laid before a startled Henry Kissinger by Zhou Enlai – but it exposed the fact that the international environment was now changing in ways that might leave the Chinese little room for manoeuvre.

Like the British, the Russians had other sites of potential conflict with China outside the embassy compound in Beijing: the two countries shared a 2,700-mile border. As the embassy siege was lifted in February 1967, news reports also noted that some 500 Chinese women and children had set up camp on an uninhabited island in the Amur River, whose control was one of 600 such that were subject to dispute.[52] On 2 March 1969, Soviet border guards based close to Damanskii Island (Zhenbao dao), which stood in the Ussuri River 150 miles from Khabarovsk, thought they were participating in what had become a wearyingly repetitive performance: Chinese men were deliberately intruding onto the mile-long, two-thirds of a mile wide, island. So the guards linked arms and walked in a line to push them back. Unexpectedly, the Chinese dispersed, a second line of men behind them began shooting, and 300 hidden PLA soldiers opened up a murderous crossfire from entrenched positions dug in on the island overnight. They killed thirty of the Russians, including wounded men who had initially been taken prisoner. Artillery also began to bombard the Soviet border guards. Two weeks later a much larger and bloodier engagement took place on the island, in which the Chinese suffered significant casualties.

For five days after this battle Soviet strategic rocket forces – equipped with nuclear weapons – were placed on alert. The first Damanskii Island encounter was – by Chinese reckoning – the 4,189th Soviet 'provocation' on the border since 15 October 1964. This was the day on which five years of negotiation aimed at settling disputes about the long common border had broken down. It was also the day before the first Chinese atomic bomb test, but even though China had exploded three bombs by March 1969, there was little they could still do at this stage in terms of using them. 'Explosion of our hydrogen bomb has given you British and American bastards the hump', was one piece of invective that Anthony Grey faced in 1967.[53] But this was, in the argot of the times, a paper tiger: an empty assertion. The Soviet arsenal was far more powerful than anything the Chinese could muster, and the Russians now repeatedly reminded the Chinese of this fact.

The borders that the People's Republic had inherited were brittle legacies of the Qing's degraded sovereignty.[54] Although it kept its concerns about them on its agenda, the Guomindang had never secured control of significant parts of China's heartland, let alone the border regions and frontiers that the old republic had nominally taken over in 1912. Mongolia had become independent; Xinjiang was never under its control; and Tibet had enjoyed de facto independence. A Soviet airlift of PLA troops had assisted the reconquest of Xinjiang in 1949, and in 1950 the army had invaded and suborned Tibet, enhancing Chinese control further and with great violence after crushing the rebellion of 1959. The PRC by the end of the 1950s now largely sat within most of the formally recognized borders of the Qing, but this also brought it into protracted dispute with its neighbours. The boundaries were often unclearly demarcated, and historic transfers of sovereignty remained controversial. There was the boundary with India, for example, marked in places with a 'line' named after Sir Henry McMahon, 'an English gentleman who one day drew a border', as Mao once described him. There was the Soviet Far East in its entirety, detached from the Qing in the 1860 Convention of Peking. And 'we have yet to settle that account', remarked Mao in 1964 to the consternation of the Russians. China was in fact in dispute with every single one of its neighbours by land, and at sea as well, in disputes over the ownership of various reefs, shoals and small islands. Most of these twenty-three separate disputes would be resolved peacefully, but in March 1969 realpolitik was subordinated to a callous and violent assertion of Chinese sovereignty on Damanskii Island.

It was a matter of islands, but also of the state itself. The Warsaw Pact invasion of Czechoslovakia in August 1968 had deeply troubled the Chinese leadership. The articulation of the 'Brezhnev Doctrine' in its aftermath, by which the USSR argued that the internal evolution of any single socialist state was a matter of concern for all, seemed to lay out a potential pretext for a similar intervention in China. And the issue of the border, which had been sketched out in 1860 across territories not charted in any great detail, was a further problem. The Damanskii Island incident seems to have been deliberately staged as a forceful demonstration of Chinese intent, and was instigated by Mao and the senior leadership. In their eyes it was a pre-emptive counter-attack; but it proved a dangerous misjudgement.

The Chinese were bewildered by the scale of Soviet anger; the Russians, in turn, were aghast at the Chinese adventure, and there was panic. 'A nightmare vision of invasion by millions of Chinese made the Soviet leaders almost frantic', a senior defector later stated.[55] When Premier Kosygin attempted to use the Moscow-Beijing telephone hotline in March 1969 to discuss a resolution, he was rebuffed by the operators in the Chinese capital, who were under orders not to connect him. A Soviet military build-up on the borders, underway since 1964, had already placed Soviet troops in Mongolia, only 300 miles from Beijing. Now more were deployed. The immediate crisis seemed to start to be de-escalated in September when Kosygin finally met senior Chinese leaders at Beijing's airport, although in the aftermath the Chinese began to feel that this had been a feint. The PLA was put on combat readiness on 1 October – China's National Day – and again on 20 October when a Soviet delegation flew in for a second meeting.

From the summer of 1969 onwards the Chinese state prepared for an expected onslaught, as it counted up hundreds more incidents, including a large-scale encounter on the USSR–Xinjiang border. The government ordered a crash programme of air-raid-shelter construction, including what became an extensive underground system in Beijing that could accommodate 100,000 people. Emergency food and other supplies were stockpiled, and urban evacuation and air-raid plans drawn up and tested. Government archives were evacuated from the capital, and shipped southwest. At short notice, ahead of that one key moment of fear on 20 October 1969, the entire senior leadership of the PRC was rapidly dispersed across the country for fear of a Soviet nuclear strike on Beijing that could otherwise decapitate the state at a single blow. The Chinese armed forces were placed on alert, and for the first time on an offensive nuclear attack footing. A decade earlier there had been steel furnaces in every backyard; now there were air-raid shelters.

The border conflict with the USSR went badly for China, and had hardly achieved Mao's aims. But it did, in time, generate a negotiated process that would start to resolve specific disputes. The need for mass mobilization to build up civil defence capacity and for militia training was also used by Mao to try to bring to an end what had effectively become a state of civil war in many of the provinces, and with some measure of success. The fallout from this violent adventure did involve the bringing to a close the most anarchic phase of the Cultural Revolution, although it hardly stopped the blood flowing. For its part, Soviet public opinion – dissidents no less than any other group – was as alarmed as the Kremlin. Yevgeny Yevtuschenko dashed off a poem about 'The new Batu Khans,/Bombs rattling in their quivers', joining a sanctioned and 'near hysterical' public discourse about a Mongol, 'Yellow Peril' threat from China. Jokes circulated fashioning grim – and often racist – humour out of fears of China's immense population and the danger it posed. There was sober analysis as well, such as that of the dissident Andrei Amalrik, written at the height of the crisis, which posed the 'China threat' as an existential one for the USSR.[56]

It was in this context that J. G. Ballard imagined his Red Guard army conquering North America. Satirist though he was, Ballard was not alone. In 1967 three-quarters of Americans polled by Gallup nominated China as a 'greater threat to world peace' than the USSR, a proportion that had been rising steadily throughout the 1960s but accelerated with China's A-bomb tests and the onset of the Cultural Revolution. Another Gallup survey in 1967 found 75 per cent of respondents held 'deeply negative' views of China. The polls were accompanied by a startling resurgence in 'Yellow Peril' fears and fantasies. These were voiced by American politicians – not least Secretary of State Dean Rusk, in October 1967, who expressed his concern about 'a billion Chinese on the mainland armed with nuclear weapons' – as well as in its popular culture. A 1966 poll of the American public's view of Chinese people found that a significant proportion chose the qualities 'sly', 'treacherous', 'warlike', 'cruel' and 'ignorant'. Given these concerns, the fact that 37 per cent found them 'hardworking' was hardly positive.[57] In Cold War culture, Chinese industriousness could fuel a plot to tunnel under the Pacific and explode nuclear weapons beneath Los Angeles – in the risible, but popular, MGM film *Battle beneath the Earth* (1967).[58] The novelist Sax Rohmer, who had created the character of Dr Fu Manchu, died in 1959. But this master criminal, played by Christopher Lee, still infected cinema screens with his world-conquering ambitions. The most popular China-set movies of the 1960s included *The Manchurian Candidate* (1962), which played on Korean War 'brainwashing' fears and communist plots to take over America; *55 Days at Peking* (1963), set during the siege of the legations in 1900; and *The Sand Pebbles* (1966), about a US Navy gunboat on the Yangzi in the 1920s. Each presented portrayals of beleaguered Westerners facing Chinese mobs. If the British diplomats assailed in Beijing in 1967 were mistaken when they reported that the crowds attacking them were shouting 'Kill!', as seems probable, it is certainly what they – or any consumer of popular culture – expected to hear.

But if the greater part of public and political opinion overseas was hostile to China, Maoism itself was embraced by a substantial and noisy minority in the radical political and cultural upsurge that came to be associated with the student protest movement, the May 1968 events in France, and the rise of the Western European, North American and Japanese New Left. The origins of this pre-dated the May 1968 events. For those who embraced Maoism and especially the Cultural Revolution, events in China offered the spectacle of a youth rebellion, an anti-authoritarian agenda, and – in Red Guard actions – a repertoire of tactics and approaches that resonated with the emerging political counterculture. Here too was a Third World power, led by a philosopher-poet, providing both inspiration and material support for revolution and for resistance in Vietnam. Radicals found there was immense shock value to be had from performing as Red Guards. This was a particular feature in West Germany, but Maoism stirred controversy wherever the dominant media discourse on China and the Cultural Revolution was hostile – which was nearly everywhere. The usual foreign fellow travellers rolled out their uncritical support. One British visitor in August 1966 reported seeing 'little visible roughness, and so much evident good humour' in Shanghai. The Red Guards were 'like school prefects or scout leaders'. And whichever way the East wind blew it blew sweetly for the Cambridge University lecturer Joan Robinson, for example, or the scientist Joseph Needham, but it was with the young new generation that the Cultural Revolution truly took hold.[59]

Aside from the *Peking Review* – launched in French, German, Spanish and Japanese editions in 1963–4 – there were two pivotal texts for this movement. The first of these was the Little Red Book itself, the selection of gobbets of Mao Zedong's writings that was prepared for PLA political training by the Chairman's ambitious acolyte Lin Biao, and published in 1964. The book enjoyed widespread circulation overseas, not just through the hundreds of thousands of copies shipped out by the Foreign Languages Press, but also through other translations that were published in German, French and Italian. It sold 100,000 copies in Germany alone in 1967; the Black Panthers studied it; radical film-makers in Germany and America made films using it; Edward Albee gutted it for a piece of theatre. Physically it was also an instantly recognizable item.[60] Its texts, wrenched out of any context, took on a life of their own: 'A revolution is not a dinner party' and 'Political power grows out of the barrel of a gun' were recognized and discussed (and satirized) far from Beijing. If the book found a ready political audience, it also had aesthetic power, as indeed did the entire visual culture of the Cultural Revolution. In Jean-Luc Godard's 1967 film *La Chinoise* the apartment shared by the radical Maoist faction at the centre of the story is awash with copies of the book, ranked on shelves by the score, piled up on the furniture, and used as symbolic weapons. The walls are decorated with Maoist slogans, Chinese propaganda posters and newspaper articles about Mao. 'It's the Little Red Book that makes it all move' went the chorus of an unlikely, and catchy, 1967 French pop song, 'Mao Mao', which was used in Godard's film.

A second key text that made it all move was William Hinton's *Fanshen*, which entered bookstores in the midst of the early phase of the Cultural Revolution in late 1966. It was the book's portrayal of the processes of group sessions, self-criticism and 'speaking bitterness' that found the readiest audience. This reading of Hinton's account proved important for Women's Liberation Movement activists – as 'consciousness raising' – and Weatherman Underground radicals, amongst others.[61] Elsewhere, within the broader and often narcissistic radical culture that emerged in the late 1960s, this could also be simply asinine: how might tensions inherent in communal living be resolved, asked a 1971 handbook? 'Maoism' was offered as one of the answers; but it was a nominal Maoism, appropriated and adapted for other purposes, and which took its place alongside encounter and sense-awareness groups in the communal pharmacopeia.[62] Playwright

David Hare and Joint Stock Theatre adapted *Fanshen* successfully for stage and BBC television in 1975. For Hare it was 'A play for Europe' and about revolution, and what that meant, but the play took the book seriously, and Hinton intervened to make sure that it did, while Hare instructed actors approaching the text to 'identify with the techniques of the fanshen and use them in the production – group discussion, self-criticism and so on'.[63]

And so on: in many ways this was simply a new phase in the long history of chinoiserie, and never since the 1935–6 Royal Academy Exhibition had China had such an impact. The Little Red Book offered more than its shiny plastic covers: it was in foreign minds a symbol, a gesture and a fad. Radical chic took the Little Red Book, the PLA cap with its red star, the Mao suit and the poster, blending them into the repertoire that embraced images of Che Guevara and Lenin, and all the fusion iconography of radical protest and dissent. At its most facile, Brigitte Bardot, Sammy Davis Jr, Alain Delon and the designer Valentino were photographed in variations of the Mao suit, alongside 'Le tout Paris', as *Vogue* announced in September 1967, for the city had gone 'mad for Mao'. So for a while the suit was a fashion feature, dressing the Western body, or in *Lui* – France's answer to *Playboy* – revealing it. What began as Parisian radical chic and haute couture made its way steadily into the mass market, where anybody could afford to 'look like a cool coolie'. 'I don't read much,' revealed the singer Marianne Faithfull in a 1967 interview, 'but I have read his Little Red Book of sayings and I know what he is about.'[64]

There was more to this than celebrity trouser suits. To differing extents across West European and North American society, Maoist groups, factions and parties played a distinctive and disruptive role in far-left politics. Generational and political disenchantment with established communist parties was heightened further by the invasion of Czechoslovakia in 1968. The Cultural Revolution offered a language of mass participatory politics and opposition to establishment power that found a ready audience amongst those who thought the parties of the West European left complicit in the established status quo, or unredeemable clients of the USSR. It was stoked too by a growing consciousness of 'Third World' national liberation movements, and opposition to American involvement in the Vietnam

War. African-American Black Power activists found inspiration and practical support in China's example. Politically engaged students from Asia, Africa and Latin America studying in Europe were important in shaping this movement. In West Germany, Maoism flourished within radical student politics, and as a form of theatrical direct action. In France, Maoism played a vibrant role, and would also have a far-reaching impact in the intellectual mainstream through the work of Jean-Paul Sartre, Simone de Beauvoir, Julia Kristeva, Michel Foucault and Louis Althusser. In 1970 the French government suppressed the Maoists' newspaper and organization, prompting an unlikely chorus of protest from, amongst others, the singer Mick Jagger, the socialist politician François Mitterrand and Sartre.[65]

In many cases this Maoism bore as much relation to Chinese reality as Alain Delon's trouser suit did to the clothes worn on the streets of Beijing. It was a form of political orientalism appropriating all the props and forms of the Cultural Revolution, but lacking any grounding in the objective reality of the Chinese experience. In fact, the less grounding there was, the more foreign Maoism flourished: too much reality proved unbearable, and increasing understandings of the course of events in the 1970s eroded most Maoist support.[66] But if there was Maoist chic, there was also Maoist terror. It was from these milieus that groups emerged which pursued armed struggle: the Red Army Faction in West Germany (the Baader-Meinhof Gang), and the Red Brigades and Prima Linea in Italy. An important scene in Godard's *La Chinoise* had mocked such terrorism as lacking any base in society, or, by implication, in reality: but these groups bombed and killed until eventually they were curtailed by police action, and they helped generate a sense of profound political crisis that was to have a chilling effect on civil liberties in West Germany and Italy. Worse havoc was unleashed in India, and especially in South America. Long before the Cultural Revolution, the Chinese had provided training for cadres from fraternal parties. Amongst those who visited China in 1965, and then again in 1967, was the Peruvian communist Abimael Guzmán, who in 1980 would launch the Shining Path (Sendero Luminoso) insurgency that would lead to some 60,000 deaths over the course of a twelve-year war.

To the extent that it was acknowledged by China, this new wave of support and emulation overseas was subsumed within a wider Cultural Revolution-era discourse on the inspirational impact of the PRC – and the Helmsman – on the global revolutionary movement. In this imagining, national liberation movements and communist revolutionaries internationally looked on China – and not the Soviet Union – as the headquarters of the struggle against imperialism.[67] Mao was the revolutionary world's 'saviour'; and the 'Red Sun in the Hearts of the People of the World'. From 'five continents' pilgrims made their way to Shaoshan, sleepless with excitement, and overjoyed – *Renmin ribao* assured its readers – with the prospect of tracing the Helmsman's route to his home. They dashed off bad verse about the 'Beacon for the people of the world', and studied his work, finding that only if they were equipped with Mao Zedong Thought could they hope to be victorious in their struggles, in Western Europe as much as anywhere else.[68] When twenty-five British Maoists paraded outside the Chinese Legation in London in the aftermath of the burning of the British Mission in Beijing, and chanted slogans from their Little Red Books, to the bemusement of curious onlookers, they were politely invited in by the diplomats inside, serenaded each other with Chinese and English renditions of 'The East is Red' and 'Sailing the Seas Depends on the Helmsman', and then departed, each with a colour photograph of Mao as a gift.[69]

Such surreal episodes highlight the existential confusion of China's international relationship with the rest of the world by the end of the 1960s. The PRC's relations with foreign states and cultures were key issues threading through much of the high political infighting of the Cultural Revolution era, as well as its everyday political action. Whether it was Wang Guangmei being assailed for humiliating the Chinese people on the diplomatic stage, or Nien Cheng's collection of Beethoven records, the Shanghai British Consulate's gateposts, or the bloody fight over uninhabited Damanskii Island, the politics of the foreign, saturated with issues of national dignity and humiliation, was central to the Cultural Revolution. It was far from being the only issue, but it was the only issue that came close to threatening international conflict, while developments in the arena of Sino-Soviet relations played a key part in both the onset of the campaign and the curtailment of its most violent phases in late 1969.

The problems of China's place in the world were hardly resolved by its purge of dead European composers, renaming of streets, jailing of geriatric foreign residents, or choir practice in China's London Legation. This cultural war on the West simply attracted derision overseas. And China was now ringed by enemies: Soviet tanks were on Beijing's doorstep; Taiwan, Japan, the Philippines and South Korea hosted American troops and facilities; China was as mired as the United States in the Vietnam stalemate. Little now existed by way of routine diplomatic intercourse with the world, let alone engagement in the symbolic gatherings of the international community in sport, cultural events or other spheres. To all intents and purposes China was a pariah state. The world's most populous nation was still excluded from the United Nations; and the President of the world's most powerful nation – the United States – did not even do the People's Republic of China the courtesy in public of using its official name: it was 'Red China', or 'Communist China'.

So when President Richard Nixon, a long-term Red-baiting Republican, deliberately used the title 'People's Republic of China' in 1970, it was a political gesture to be mulled over in Beijing. In response to this, and other discreet signals that the two leaderships had been exchanging, the Chinese turned to history, and in an extraordinary piece of symbolic choreography Edgar Snow was invited to Beijing. On 1 October 1970 he was pointedly placed alongside Mao Zedong on the Tiananmen viewing platform during the National Day parade. A photograph of this American, the man who had first been used to help communicate the Chinese revolution to the world thirty-four years earlier, was published on the cover of *Renmin ribao*, together with Mao's statement that 'The peoples of the world, including the American people, are our friends.'[70] The Chinese also turned to the unlikeliest of all historical diplomatic vehicles, and to something that Snow himself had noted a 'bizarre' passion for amongst the Red Army in Yan'an in 1936: they turned to ping-pong.

11

Unfinished Business

Zhou Enlai would say that they had set a small ball flying to move a big one, and that they played ping-pong for the world. In April 1971 in a surprise move that grabbed global attention, not least in the White House, the United States table-tennis team received a hastily dispatched, last-minute invitation to join a friendly tournament in Beijing. This was scheduled to take place immediately after the World Championships in Nagoya that involved both the Chinese and Americans. The newly emphasized line that 'The peoples of the world, including the American people, are our friends' shaped the behaviour of the Chinese team in Japan as they interacted, stiffly and awkwardly at first, with these new friends. Both sets of players and officials circled each other during the tournament looking for an opening, as rapprochement was the mood of the moment across the Pacific as well: at the same time as anxieties about the threat the country posed had peaked, opinion polling in the United States also showed a steadily growing percentage of Americans in favour of resuming formal contact with China.

The most dramatic incident in Nagoya proved to be what has become a much-mythologized accidental encounter on the Chinese team's bus, when the young American player Glenn Cowan, whose hair, clothes and outlook could not have been further removed from the Chinese, climbed on to it and shared some inchoate radical-chic thoughts about oppression with them. Gifts and platitudes were then exchanged. Behind this chance encounter lay a great deal of planning in China and a readiness to seize the moment and act, for events in Nagoya were being monitored very closely from Beijing. Zhou Enlai personally called the Chinese team with instructions; and Mao

Zedong, drifting off to sleep on the night of 6 April, gave instructions that an invitation to visit China be issued.

So, three days later, at Chinese expense, the fifteen Americans flew to Hong Kong and then crossed into China.[1] This was the largest group of American citizens to enter the country since fifteen leftists had attended the 1952 Peace Conference. 'It boggles the mind', one US State Department official admitted, and well it might. Here were Glenn Cowan, eighteen-year-old John Tannehill (who declared Mao 'the greatest moral and intellectual leader in the world today'), Guyana-born United Nations clerk George Brathwaite and fifteen-year-old Judy Bochenski being hosted with the rest of the team at a formal meeting with Zhou Enlai. It was seventeen years since American officials had come close to Zhou, at the Geneva talks, and then Secretary of State John Foster Dulles had deliberately and sullenly evaded being introduced to him. The lead US negotiator, former CIA chief Walter Bedell Smith, had been careful to keep a coffee cup in his right hand, to avoid shaking Zhou's. 'He used his left hand to shake my arm,' recalled Zhou in 1972. 'You do not take a drink ... with the criminal at the bar,' declared the US Assistant Secretary for Far Eastern Affairs, the pathologically anti-communist Walter S. Robertson. At Geneva they were 'bringing them before the bar of world opinion', he declared.[2]

Still, Chinese and American diplomats had met and talked 136 times between 1955 and 1970, first in Geneva and then in Warsaw. There were just over one hundred meetings between their respective ambassadors up to 1960, and then fewer in the 1960s, not least as US involvement in Vietnam intensified after 1964.[3] However, for all this State Department talking, the breakthrough was not led by the China experts, but through an intensely political process driven by Richard Nixon, and shaped by his National Security Advisor, Henry Kissinger. The 1972 presidential elections were firmly in their minds.

Rapprochement was certainly not helped by Edgar Snow, because, for all that he was prominent in Chinese eyes, he was largely *persona non grata* to American officials. The depths of Chinese insularity by 1970 were demonstrated by this assumption that Washington would understand Beijing's own pointed gesture involving Snow, their

American 'Friend'. But Snow was history, and part of that discredited history of fellow travellers and alleged communists. McCarthyite mud still stuck. For related reasons, Canadians were bewildered to discover, after normalization of relations in 1971, that the most famous foreigner in the People's Republic of China was a long-dead Canadian doctor, Norman Bethune. Mao had written a eulogy about him that would be widely and repeatedly circulated, but Bethune's life, work and death in China in 1939 were unknown beyond leftist circles back home. 'I like rightists,' Mao told Nixon at their first meeting in Beijing in February 1972. And only a rightist, Kissinger had told Zhou the previous year on his secret visit to China, could effect any rapprochement, because of the entrenched power of the pro-Chiang Kai-shek and anti-communist lobby in the United States.

The Chinese also issued visas for seven journalists working for American news organizations – another first – while every member of the US table-tennis team seemed to be doubling as a freelance for other agencies and papers. George Brathwaite filed reports for *Ebony*. The maximum coverage possible was squeezed out of the opportunity, including an extended prime-time television news report about this 'love feast' on NBC, a *Time* cover story ('China: A Whole New Game') and twenty-one pages from 'Inside China Today' in *Life*.[4] It was hardly all positive: images of Mao were omnipresent, everyone was dressed alike, and drably, children and adults marched along in a 'modified goose step'. John Tannehill was pilloried for his comments in the conservative press, however mainstream these were within youth culture. Opposition to rapprochement remained vocal and unforgiving. Moreover – setting aside jailed foreign experts – five Americans were held in detention in China: two CIA agents captured in 1952 (a third, held since 1951, had died in prison in 1970); two pilots shot down after flying into Chinese airspace by accident; and a woman who had been seized from a yacht that had strayed into Chinese territorial waters in 1968, and was being held secretly.[5] As the table-tennis team left China, the May issue of *China Reconstructs* was heading to the printers, devoted in large part to invectives against American aggression, and outlining how 'The world's people fight US imperialism' and, of course, its 'running dogs'.[6]

But, once the ball had been sent spinning, events moved quickly.

The stridency of the Chinese attacks was indicative both of its assessment of the 'extreme isolation' of the Nixon administration (as Chinese polemics put it) and America's resulting strategic need to engage with China, and of residual concern within the Chinese leadership about the propriety of talking with the enemy. Nixon, for one, had been making his position clear on the need to reintegrate China into the international community for some years in articles and speeches, including his 1969 inaugural address. Some trade and travel restrictions were being lifted just as the table-tennis episode unfolded. Kissinger had paved the way for the 1972 presidential visit in three days of talks in July 1971, during which he offered a commitment to a set of fundamental changes in US policy, affirming its support for a 'One China' policy and committing itself to withdrawing troops from Taiwan and to the normalization of relations with Beijing.[7] He was taken by surprise at the importance of the emphasis placed by the Chinese on the issue of Taiwan, when his own focus was on the great game: outflanking the USSR. Kissinger highlighted the readiness of the United States to co-operate in responding to what he presented as the common threat to China's north, and in 1972 he plied the Chinese with detailed intelligence reports on the Soviet military position along China's borders.[8]

Throughout the discussions in 1971 and 1972 the words 'dignity' and 'honour' were used again and again by both the American visitors and their Chinese hosts. Nixon wanted peace with honour, or at least an honourable withdrawal, for US troops from Vietnam. The Chinese reiterated the simple fact that, as they saw it, the Americans had never accorded them the dignity of recognition of any sort. The 1954 Geneva talks set the standard against which the Americans wished themselves to be judged. The symbolism of Dulles's failure then even to shake Zhou's hand – literally or metaphorically – when Anthony Eden for the British, for example, had secured an immediate introduction, followed by 'a deal of handshakes', and three dinners, hung in the air.[9] Nixon made explicit amends, and shook Zhou's hand, once, twice, again and again, in public and in private. The issue of Taiwan, however, which had been made into such a stubborn stain on China's dignity through two decades of invective and propaganda, could not be resolved by pumping hands.

The greatest problem for the Americans was their continuing commitment to Chiang Kai-shek: for all that they were driven by global realpolitik, they were still tangled up in the past. They also worried about the effect of any 'betrayal' of one ally on the confidence of their other partners. Nixon himself, now aiming at re-election partly on a peace-with-China ticket, had first run for office in autumn 1950 on a China-containment platform. He had claimed then that the refugee government and its Taiwan bastion were all that stood between Communist China and 'the coast of California'.[10] Nixon twice visited the embattled island as Eisenhower's Vice President. In 1971–2 the Republic of China's publicity machine was happy to remind Nixon of these visits and of his long history of vocal support. By 1971, Chiang Kai-shek had devolved effective power to his son, Chiang Ching-kuo, but he remained President and party chairman. He also remained largely loathed by foreign officials who actually had to deal with him, and he, for his part, continued routinely to blame the British when things did not go his way, their aim being, as ever (as he put it in 1950), 'to choke to death the soul and spirit of the Asian people'.[11]

Bonds of sympathy with the Americans aside, the Republic of China maintained an extensive and effective lobbying network in the United States. This has been anathematized as a sinister, shadowy organization, hands deep in Taiwan's pocket. But it was much more amorphous, for the ROC's supporters had many motives and they were mainly strongly rooted historically in the tight interaction between China and foreign interests across the decades since 1917. There were ideological anti-communists, exiles from the former treaty ports whose interests were financial or sentimental, Christian groups and Churches aghast at religious repression, Chinese-Americans and others. There were political activists, businessmen, former missionaries and Nationalist Government advisors. There were certainly organized lobbying groups, such as the 'Committee of One Million', led by a tireless former missionary, now congressman, Walter H. Judd. But the cultural diplomacy of the 1930s, the work of Pearl Buck and Lin Yutang, and the wartime United China Relief publicity campaigns continued to bear fruit in the indivisible identification of the Nationalists, indeed of Chiang Kai-shek, with China and the Chinese – even in wretched defeat.[12] And how could the real-life equivalents of Pearl Buck's character Wang Lung and his family be left to Joseph Stalin's tender mercies? These ties and sympathies evolved and strengthened after 1950, helped not least by the tens of thousands of students from Taiwan who had pursued graduate research in America – and by the dark twists and turns in 'Red' China's own sanguine politics.

In October 1971 the annual United Nations ritual vote on the admittance of the PRC to membership in place of the ROC finally produced the long-awaited upset. In fact it quite 'astonished' the Chinese – as Zhou Enlai put it later to British Prime Minister Edward Heath – for they thought it would take another year and were unprepared.[13] In 1970 they had diplomatic relations with forty-five states; by October 1972 with seventy-six. Foreign ministers from France, Canada, Japan, West Germany and Britain made visits to China after Nixon. On Taiwan there was shock and dismay at what became a rapid degradation of the international status of the ROC. But Nationalist diplomats packed up their offices at the UN in New York with quiet dignity, and the state set out to explore other ways of maintaining its profile. Some of its allies hoped for a de facto 'Two Chinas' policy – or more accurately 'One China, but not now' – that would enable them to maintain support for the Chiang government, but pressure from Beijing would force most of them to switch to formal recognition.

Diplomatic recognition had meant acceptance, however belated, of political reality. But it certainly did not resolve all existing issues, and in particular three spectres now haunted the new landscape: those of territorial degradation, of colonialism and of the war, that is, of Taiwan, of Hong Kong and Macao, and of the Japanese invasion – of the past still present in any and every encounter. Journalists on the table-tennis visit found this out at the Summer Palace in 1971, when they were accosted by a seventy-eight-year-old whose story in outline was very much that of China's formerly cosmopolitan past. Named as T. S. Tsai, he spoke fluent English, which had been used and refined in Europe during the First World War, presumably in relation to work with the Chinese Labour Corps; and he had then worked in China for an American company until 1948, he said. 'Chairman Mao has given us back our pride,' Tsai said, a phrase that was highlighted in

Life. 'There are no beggars here now.'[14] We can sketch out his probable travails after 1949: as a capitalist with experience of study and work abroad, Tsai would have been on the sharp end of various campaigns in the 1950s and 1960s. In the xenophobic summer of 1966 he would have been attacked and humiliated. He was still there, however, wearing a Mao badge, and quick to say the right thing, but adorned too with all that he represented of the once cosmopolitan and open China of the past.

Spectres of yesterday visited too. On 25 September 1972 a former payroll clerk in the Kwantung Army, now Prime Minister of Japan, Tanaka Kakuei, alighted at Beijing's airport from a Japan Air Lines plane that had flown directly from Tokyo – the first such flight for over two decades. Live television relayed Tanaka's reception by Zhou Enlai, the Japanese flag fluttering over the terminal building, and 360 PLA troops formed an honour guard with a band that played the Japanese national anthem.[15] The last time Tanaka Kakuei had heard that anthem in China was in Manchuria, in 1940, before he was invalided out of the army. He had then embarked on an increasingly intertwined business and political career that had seen him become Prime Minister just two months before he flew to China in the aftermath of the 'Nixon shock' – the rapprochement with Beijing – to start a process of normalization of Sino-Japanese relations.

The war met Tanaka at the airport. The honour guard at Beijing also played the Chinese national anthem, the 'March of the Volunteers', a stirring call to arms against the Japanese that dated from 1935. In fact the two states were technically still at war, for Beijing did not recognize the 1952 peace treaty that Japan had signed with the Republic of China. But a rapid process of change followed in the wake of the Tanaka visit in which the Japanese withdrew diplomatic recognition from the Republic in Taiwan; the Chinese renounced any claim for war reparations, and all pledged for peace. But the war persisted nonetheless, represented in Beijing also by Tanaka's inescapable companion, his own record as a minor functionary in the army of occupation. Ōhira Masayoshi, his Foreign Minister (and successor as Prime Minister), came with a shadow too, a year's service on secondment from the Finance Ministry in 1939–40 to an office of the Kōain, the Asia Development Board, in Zhangjiakou in Inner Mongolia.

In the talks in 1972 the Chinese did not push for war reparations in economic terms, for they knew the 'bitterness' of such impositions, Zhou had told Tanaka. But moral reparation was to become the touchstone of Sino-Japanese relations, and on this point successive Japanese governments would in future – in Chinese eyes – fail to deliver adequate or sincere restitution. This developing 'history problem' was foreshadowed right at the beginning, in the Great Hall of the People on the first day of the 1972 visit during the welcoming banquet for the Japanese, when Tanaka apologized for the 'unhappy path' that Sino-Japanese relations had taken in the recent past, and for the 'great trouble' (*meiwaku*) that had been caused to the Chinese people. Translated directly into Chinese as *mafan* ('bother') this last phrase was a wholly inappropriate description of the scale of the impact of the invasion. Zhou, in private the following day, told Prime Minister Tanaka that he accepted the 'sincerity' of the apology, but rejected the language. 'In China,' he said, 'this expression is only used for very small things.'[16] Thereafter, a conflict over words would start to grow, and from 1982 onwards the war was fought all over again on the question of the language used in the history textbooks that were approved for use in schools by Japan's Ministry of Education, and whether that language deliberately made very small things from very big ones – where it mentioned them at all.

The British rapprochement developed with less fanfare, although a table-tennis team had also been invited to China in April 1971.[17] The response to the crisis of 1967, and to the detention of British subjects, was in general persistent and constructive, and a slow re-engagement produced no major shocks along the way. On 13 March 1972 representation was finally raised to ambassadorial level, and the British closed their remaining consulate in Taiwan. The Foreign Secretary, and former Prime Minister, Sir Alec Douglas-Home, visited Beijing in October that year, and Edward Heath (then Leader of the Opposition) went in May 1974. Douglas-Home's flight included a large cohort of journalists, as well as an emergency delivery to the embassy of instant coffee, fruit juice, cornflakes and baked beans: British embassies to China were now rather less grandiose than they had been in the gilded past.[18] British diplomats managed to steer the Ministry of Foreign Affairs protocol officers away from their suggestion that the PLA band in attendance serenade the formal banquet for Douglas-Home with 'representative and suitable English folk music', which turned out to be a 1930s drinking song 'Here we are again, happy as can be/All good pals and jolly good company'.[19] But, keeping secret the fact that they had sourced it from the band of the Royal Hong Kong Police, the British did provide music for the 'Eton Boating Song' – another first for the Great Hall of the People (and 'too good' a prospect to miss, so they thought).

The key strategic interest of the Chinese lay in encouraging a strong Western European bloc to counter the USSR, against which they expressed what Douglas-Home thought 'virulent hatred' – Tanaka received a seventy-five-minute lecture from Zhou Enlai on the Russians.[20] What to say about history, however, was a pressing concern for the British ahead of their talks. 'Relations between China and Britain', went the approved final text of Douglas-Home's speech at the formal welcoming banquet, 'have been uneven.' But it was the first Western country to recognize the new state in 1950, he reminded his listeners. Finding the right words was always a challenge, as the tortuously edited drafts of this speech make clear:

> It is a matter of history that relations between China and Britain have ~~at times~~ been ~~chequered~~ uneven. ~~I do not want to~~ I will not examine the reasons for this now. [~~I think it enough to say that the nineteenth century was a period in our history when attitudes in my country towards the rest of the world were very remote indeed different from the attitudes which prevail today.~~] ~~I want~~ Rather I wish to speak of the present and the future~~, rather than of the past~~.[21]

Fine wishes, but it was in fact difficult to keep Chinese leaders off the topic of the 'uneven' past, as Zhou Enlai would 'revert' to it again and again in discussion (about Geneva in particular). It was hardly 'very remote'. Well, 'leaving aside questions of history', Douglas-Home asked in exasperation at one point in their talks, 'what should we do about the current situation?'[22]

In the British discussions in 1972 and 1974 there had been no sustained focus on Hong Kong. It was a 'matter that had been left over by history', said Zhou. But the Chinese would 'take no "surprise action"', he assured Douglas-Home. They would not 'take over the colony by force'. This was just as well: in 1967, in the wake of the confrontation, the British had explored all possible scenarios for the defence of the colony and concluded that, as in 1941, this would be impossible.[23] There would be negotiation when the ninety-nine-year lease on the New Territories, secured by treaty in 1898, came closer – but not in the foreseeable future. 'It was a question for the younger generation,' Mao Zedong told Edward Heath in 1974, and pointed to the other senior leaders in his study with them, although only one of those, the tough, wiry Deng Xiaoping, would survive the political twists and turns of the following two years. 'I always remember the date of the treaty,' said Zhou at the same meeting, 'because it was the year in which I was born.'[24] The personal and the political were consciously intertwined.

Instead of such thorny issues, the new relationships were tested first in softer areas that promised early wins for 'friendship', and for re-establishing China's image overseas. The hunger for news from China was intense. The table-tennis team had been accompanied by journalists; the diplomats and politicians travelling to China were always greatly outnumbered by them. The country's propaganda and news machine still poured out magazines and books that delivered its own breathlessly positive vision of its achievements; Radio Peking still fought its corner of the international airwaves. The Nixon delegation flew with over one hundred journalists and broadcast technicians in a second jet, who then used a specially imported satellite relay station that was set up at Beijing's airport to report on the visit. On this occasion Nixon travelled light: 450 had accompanied him to Romania in 1969.[25] Douglas-Home flew with a VC-10 full of reporters; Tanaka's trip was extensively covered. But this was only the start.

Visas for journalists, exhibitions and animal exchanges, language teaching and film-making, music, drama and art, all formed the subjects of a new phase of cultural diplomacy. And everybody wanted pandas. In return Nixon gave musk ox; Douglas-Home offered Père David's deer (native to China, but by 1972 only surviving in captivity in Britain); Tanaka offered red-crowned cranes. Animal diplomacy had a rich history in the People's Republic, even if a British diplomat cynically jested in 1959 that the Chinese would in fact be 'really happy' to have some caged imperialists, capitalists and foreign missionaries in Beijing's zoo. Now Britain's Royal Shakespeare Company hoped to despatch Peter Brook's production of *The Tempest* to China, and hoped to host a 'Peking Opera' company in return (but the embassy in London ignored letter after letter). Perhaps the London Philharmonic Orchestra might visit? After all there was more to British musical life than 'The Eton Boating Song'. They did, and so did the Philadelphia Orchestra, but they were rarely heard by any but a chosen few. And the hopes of China's musicians that this heralded a relaxation in cultural policy were quashed by a new campaign in 1974 against European music.[26]

The most significant initiative was the one that seemed least connected to the communist era: a globe-circling exhibition of breathtaking new archaeological discoveries. After his appointment as British ambassador to China in 1972, Sir John Addis – himself a collector and connoisseur – pursued the Palace Museum for an exhibition, highlighting the 'great effect' of the 1935–6 Burlington House show.[27] Addis had his eye on the collection of post-1949 archaeological finds on show in Beijing in May 1972. This exhibition would eventually spend two years circumnavigating the globe, appearing in Paris in the summer of 1973, then moving via the Royal Academy in London to Vienna and Stockholm, and on to Toronto, Washington, DC, Kansas City and San Francisco. Elements of it then went on to Australia, the Philippines and Hong Kong, where examples of 'Terracotta Army' figures from the 1974 uncovering of the tomb of the first Emperor, Qin Shi Huangdi, gained their first unveiling. In London the show's attendance outstripped its famous predecessor: over 770,000 people visited the Royal Academy, which had been hired for the show, and where China's national flag and the Union Jack flew together. Books and television documentaries fed another China boom. The Han Dynasty bronze flying horse and jade funeral suit of Lady Dou Wan instantly became iconic, standing out even within an exhibition that offered a revelatory view of China's deep past. This show matched the aspirations of each side: for the British it gave substance to the new relationship; and for the Chinese it showed that Beijing was in fact an attentive guardian of China's heritage.

This was an intensely political initiative. The Chinese and British signed a bilateral treaty to underpin the exhibition. The show had its debut in Paris to mark the fact that the French, not the British, had established full diplomatic relations first. There it was named 'Trésors d'art chinois'; in London it was to be 'The Genius of China'. Here was the initial problem: neither of the adjectives linked to China in these titles had any connection to class politics. Although it was formally organized by a 'Chinese Exhibition Council', the Royal Academy show was shaped by Times Newspapers, which sponsored it. The devil was partly in the treaty detail, where the exhibits were itemized and ordered in a Marxist chronological schema that the Chinese subsequently demanded be used in the display and catalogue. They wanted primitive society, slave society and feudal society. They were instead presented with a simple chronological narrative, uninflected by Marx, and with texts smoothed by the *Times* journalists. 'You are not people from whom I take orders,' declared the newspaper's chairman when the Chinese Embassy threatened to abandon the exhibition at the last moment unless the apolitical title was dropped.[28] The politics of the title, commentary and periodization, as well as the exhibition's relations with other Chinese materials on display in museums such as Kansas City's Nelson-Atkins – which had a fine Tang Dynasty Buddhist relief, hacked from its site in Henan's Longmen Caves in the 1930s – and the guest list at the press reception, would dog the show. By the time it reached Washington, DC, the Chinese had produced their own catalogue, and secured a veto even over other materials that might be sold in the museum gift store. There was to be no 'treasure' and no 'genius' on show. Memories of Burlington House worked both ways: Xia Nai, the leading archaeologist on the Chinese side, had visited the 1935–6 show when studying for his doctorate in London, and still had his ticket. He also still had memories of the controversy over presentation and interpretation. This was not simply the politics of the Cultural Revolution, but came from the longer history of conflict over who spoke for China.[29]

The cultural politics of modern drama and art also remained unforgiving. Even seemingly minor details such as the specific Beethoven symphony that China's Central Philharmonic Orchestra should play on Kissinger's second visit in 1971 was discussed by Mao's wife Jiang Qing and Zhou Enlai. So was the question of how this concession to styles that were politically condemned would be balanced by the staging for Kissinger of a revolutionary opera, and which one. The Central Philharmonic Orchestra had not played Beethoven for over five years; Kissinger found the opera a work of 'truly stupefying boredom'.[30] Nonetheless, this was revolutionary China's culture. Britain's pro-PRC Society for Anglo-Chinese Understanding organized a festival of contemporary films from China in the autumn of 1971 in London, providing the first British outings of filmed stagings of *Taking Tiger Mountain by Strategy*, and *Red Detachment of Women* (to which Nixon was treated in Beijing the following March), as well as documentaries. The politically committed may have appreciated them, but they were 'exotic rather than aesthetically compelling', thought one reviewer, and 'a little goes a very long way'.[31] They were very poorly attended. A later touring exhibition of peasant paintings from Huxian was more successful, for this was a less overtly didactic genre, but it was still based on an iconography limited to tractors, pigs and mounds of cabbages.

No single cultural project evoked as much controversy as Michelangelo Antonioni's television film *Chung Kuo, Cina*, which was subjected from 30 January 1974 onwards to a full-scale campaign of virulent political criticism. As a well-known anti-fascist, Antonioni might have seemed a safe bet for the Italian state broadcaster, RAI, when it proposed a documentary after the two countries had established diplomatic relations in November 1970. Filmed in China in the spring of 1972, a version was shown in the United States in December that year, and the final three-hour version was unveiled in February 1973. Through a series of staged and impromptu episodes – Antonioni had no choice over the itinerary – and with an occasional and laconic commentary, the film provided an atmospheric series of visual impressions of the country and its people. Antonioni did not fulfil his brief in Chinese eyes: his colour palette was too muted – there were no strident revolutionary reds; the film's gaze was too obtrusive; its commentary was seemingly too offhand and negative; its camera angles belittled great revolutionary construction achievements; and the team had snatched several scenes without permission, while others were filmed with hidden cameras. The judgement was comprehensive. The film was deemed a 'serious Anti-China provocation'. Instead of a heroic, sharply coloured portrait of a peasant achievement,

Antonioni showed a pig urinating in a scruffy village street, a woman with bound feet, people drying clothes, girls queuing to have their photographs taken. A puppet-show sequence seemed to comment purposefully on staged scenes of schoolchildren performing revolutionary skits. This was 'grave contempt', and showed 'disrespect'. 'Any Chinese with any national pride cannot but be greatly angered on seeing this film,' announced the *People's Daily*.[32] Chinese diplomats launched a concerted effort to have the film suppressed in countries across Western Europe, threatening to break off cultural relations if it was broadcast. As Antonioni wryly noted, the only government to conform to the demand was the military junta in Greece – strange bedfellows for Maoist China.

The bewildered Italian was partly the pawn in the late moves of Jiang Qing and the Cultural Revolution leftists to attack Zhou Enlai and secure the succession of power after the ailing Mao's death. Foreign students who began to arrive in China in the early 1970s were confronted when they took photographs of scenes that might reflect negatively on the country, and forced to destroy their films.[33] But the politics of representation and the determination to shape or control it had that much longer history stretching back to Theodore Tu's sojourn in Hollywood on the set of *The Good Earth*, and Chinese student protests in Europe and America over films and plays. And Pearl Buck herself, whose career had revolved around trying to bring America to a more real understanding of China and its people, was sharply rebuffed, at Zhou's direction, when, buoyed up by the US–China rapprochement, she asked in 1972 for permission to revisit the country of her birth. This was refused because of her 'attitude of distortion, smear and vilification towards the people of New China and its leaders'.[34]

Zhou did, however, authorize an old friend, the Dutch film-maker Joris Ivens, who had first worked with the Chinese Communists in 1936, to film what would become a twelve-hour documentary, *How Yukong Moved the Mountains* (1976). In this instance the Chinese got what they wanted, an unmediated and uncritical – but no less remarkable – presentation of Cultural Revolution China and its people. Even though 130,000 patiently sat through it in Paris after its release in March 1976, the film had a short political life. With Mao's death in September that year, and the arrest of Jiang Qing and those soon to be labelled the 'Gang of Four', the culture that Ivens portrayed would start to be broken up.

So the sense of history pervaded the new relations being established in the early 1970s. But it lingered elsewhere too, it seemed. One issue that pervaded all these meetings was that of the Nationalist Government on Taiwan, where the entire state structure that had been supplanted on 1 October 1949 still existed. Half of the legislators elected in 1948 to the Legislative Yuan moved with it to the island redoubt, and most of the 750 members of the National Assembly, and there they formally represented constituencies across China until 1991, unless death, senility or boredom had taken them earlier. This was surreal, but logical. The constitution was still in effect; even the calendar used was that initiated in 1912, dating the years since the establishment of the Republic of China.[35] The only prominent element of its former network of power that it left behind were the gangster auxiliaries of Du Yuesheng, who himself died in Hong Kong in 1951. (The Green Gang leader Huang Jinrong was last spotted in a deliberately humiliating photograph from 1951, published in the Shanghai press, sweeping the streets outside the Great World, the entertainment complex he had formerly owned.)[36] The refugee state of Taiwan was at the same time the PRC's competitor for international recognition, a military threat dominating its southeast (with 100,000 troops on the offshore islands), and a sharp rebuke to its poverty and underdevelopment. Taiwan came to offer an alternative Chinese modernity, and a safe haven for China's culture and traditions, its literature, arts and language. Its own substantial propaganda efforts made sure that this was known to the world. So the Republic of China posed an existential threat; and it also represented the past, alive and kicking, and for much of its early history it hungered for a crisis in China that it could exploit to re-establish itself.

In the 1950s, Taiwan, the Penghu island group and the other twenty-five small islands the Guomindang controlled, some within artillery range of the mainland, had been a temporary fix. The Republic of China reorganized its military forces, conducted a bloody purge of communist and other suspects, and prepared itself to defend the province from attack and to reoccupy the mainland. The Guomindang was thoroughly reformed and remodelled as an effective, disciplined Leninist party organization. New bodies for social mobilization were created, and political commissars were placed in the reformed army. In fact, the Guomindang consciously remodelled itself closely on its triumphant opponent and, ironies aside, this was a reminder of the common historical ancestry of the two parties, and their shared nationalist agenda. But in January 1950, in the midst of this reform and revitalization of the demoralized party, President Truman stated clearly that the United States would not defend the island against invasion – and his analysts had concluded that the Nationalist forces could at that stage not defend it themselves. The Communists prepared their forces for an assault, rapidly developing an air force with Soviet aid and assistance. In April 1950 they captured Hainan Island from Nationalist forces with relative ease.

The onset of the Korean War altered this strategy completely: it was probably the single biggest piece of luck that Chiang Kai-shek ever had, and certainly did him far more good than any amount of lobbying. Chiang's offers to send troops were declined, despite General Douglas MacArthur's attempts to bounce Truman into authorizing acceptance. But there was substantial involvement of Nationalist personnel in the Korea conflict after the intervention of the PLA nonetheless, in psychological warfare operations and in dealing with PLA prisoners of war. And the American right was able to emphasize, as Nixon had, the ROC's role in what US defence planners came to see as a defence chain stretching south from Japan (and protecting the 'coast of California'). The United States signed a Mutual Defence Treaty with the ROC in 1954, and despatched what would become one of its largest overseas Military Assistance Advisory Groups, along with a package of military aid that provided aircraft, weapons and training, and that would help the island develop its own defence industries. For thirty years the US Navy patrolled the turbulent waters of the Straits.[37] The Nationalists were able to complete the overhaul of their military forces, drawing increasingly on the conscripted manpower of the people of Taiwan. On two occasions by 1958 the United States considered using nuclear weapons against China in defence of the island. Meanwhile, it served as a base for U2 aircraft espionage operations in East Asia and covert operations across the region including into Tibet.

Guerrillas from ROC-held islands harried the Chinese coast, conducting assaults into the mid-1960s. The CIA and other US organs supported these and other Nationalist military operations on the mainland, and launched attacks from northern Burma until the heroin trade that Nationalist forces controlled there became too grave an international scandal and they were evacuated to Taiwan. ROC agencies also worked out of Macao and Hong Kong, nearly claiming Zhou Enlai's life in 1955, at the height of his 'peace offensive' when it seemed possible that the plausible face of Chinese diplomacy might be nudging America towards considering recognition of the People's Republic.[38]

Although the institutions of the Republic of China were relocated to Taiwan, they were kept in suspended animation, for it was placed under a martial-law regime that lasted thirty-eight years until it was lifted in 1987. As well as facing an active threat from PRC infiltration and espionage – an estimated 1,500 agents were sent into the island, 1,100 of whom were captured and executed – the Taiwan Garrison Command implemented martial law enforcing a zealous censorship policy, suppressing political activity, and in particular stifling indigenous Taiwanese opinion.[39] The island felt like an armed camp: it was meant to. The party launched a 'total mobilization' programme to prepare for war.[40] Military police guarded highways and city streets and buildings. Into the mid-1980s Taiwan's built environment – its schools, barracks, government offices – was plastered with slogans promoting its revanchist principles: the province was the 'island bastion of the Republic of China', and the springboard for recovery of the mainland from the 'Communist bandits'. The militarization of society was comprehensive: school and university students underwent compulsory military training, and the armed forces developed an extensive network of media organizations. Stories from China's deep past of national salvation after bitter defeat were drawn on and widely disseminated in army ideological training and in the highly politicized education system. One popular figure was Koxinga (Zheng Chenggong), the Ming loyalist general who had resisted the Manchu invaders from Taiwan, having seized it from the Dutch in 1661, and who was, as the story told it, aiming to restore Ming rule on the mainland.[41] The mainland was a 'place of no sun', the state-approved primary-school textbooks told pupils into the early 1980s, and its students' nine million compatriots lacked freedom, food and shelter. Relieving their suffering was 'everybody's duty'.[42] Chiang Kai-shek regularly bombarded his unreceptive and at times disbelieving American allies with new plans for invasion that were nonetheless puffed up in more sympathetic newspapers.[43]

Under Japanese colonial rule, Taiwan had undergone an economic transformation that left it with an infrastructure for development – including a highly literate and well-educated population – that weathered great destruction from American bombing during the war, and the depredations of the Guomindang takeover of the island after 1945.[44] A successful programme of agrarian reform (aided by the confiscation of vast landholdings from Japanese official and private interests), investment in education, and a fifteen-year programme of economic aid from the United States built on this success, and assisted the construction of a successful and from the late 1950s onwards an export-led economy that brought growth and prosperity to the island. What the Guomindang had preached on the mainland, its American-trained technocrats finally had the opportunity to deliver in Taiwan: radical land reform, stability and economic development. But it was also a state born in terror: an estimated 10,000 Taiwanese were killed during and after the February 1947 uprising, and another 1,000 in 1949. Officially there were almost 30,000 arrests for political offences during the decades of martial law, and an estimated 1,500 to 5,000 executions. It was a police state. Even the provincial governor, the Princeton graduate and former Shanghai mayor K. C. Wu, fled in fear in 1953.[45] Although it retained its weapons of force and terror, after the crisis of the early 1950s its deployment of them proved an exception rather than a rule. Despite maintaining martial law and a ban on the formation of political parties, the Guomindang allowed forms of local elections from early on that helped it slowly start to co-opt into its island state the Taiwanese who had been bruised, battered and terrorized by the transition to Chinese rule.

The Republic of China on Taiwan increasingly exemplified a powerful model of a successful authoritarian development state, whose success it broadcast through an extensive programme of overseas technical assistance and aid that it used to compete for influence in

Africa and the Americas. It also invested heavily in projects to show-case itself as a bastion providing a respite for China's cultural heritage. The fleets that shipped 800,000 demoralized soldiers and the bullion reserves of the Bank of China to Taiwan in 1949 also brought intel-lectuals, artists and scholars, 3,000 crates containing the finest items of the already much-travelled National Palace Museum collection, Ming and Qing state archives, a great cache of rare books and manu-scripts from the National Central Library and other treasures. The National Palace collections were displayed in a new National Palace Museum built north of Taibei; the research institutes of Academia Sinica were re-established east of the city. In 'Free China', despite a heavy-handed political censorship, Chinese were able to pursue cul-tural and religious practices and traditions and engage in scholarship. The history of peasant revolution did not disturb research agendas. Cultural diplomacy programmes brought language students and overseas Chinese to the island. The Chinese written script survived there unreformed – on the mainland it was officially simplified in the 1950s and 1960s as part of a literacy drive. The rhetoric of this delib-erate political project was made manifestly more and more real as the Communists reformed, revised and ravaged Chinese society and cul-ture in the 1950s and 1960s. But these initiatives also came at the cost of the systematic suppression of research from a Taiwanese, rather than a Chinese, perspective, namely research into the island's lan-guage, history and cultures.

The ROC was no less attentive to its perceived duty of protecting China's territorial sovereignty. It was not afraid to test the patience of even its anti-communist ally South Korea, in outlining its claims on territories now within the borders of North Korea. It laid claim to the Senkaku/Diaoyutai islands and vigorously protested when the United States passed these to Japan in 1972 when it ended the occupation of Okinawa, and to reefs and islands in the South China Sea. Closer to home, the Guomindang vigorously suppressed the Taiwan Independ-ence Movement until the mid-1980s and was still using sedition laws against independence activists until 1992. In its language policies it even discriminated against Minnanhua (Hokkien), the majority lan-guage on the island, and yet more stringently against the Japanese that most islanders spoke who had grown up under colonial rule. The

Nationalists never pursued anything but a One China policy, basing their hopes for a triumphant return on a collapse of the mainland regime, a strategy that seemed to be given new life by the cataclysm of the Great Leap famine, which prompted an upsurge in coastal operations by ROC forces. It seems clear that continuing contacts between Chiang and Zhou Enlai, passed through an intermediary in Hong Kong, focused in the main on co-ordination of a strategy to prevent any 'One China, One Taiwan' option being engineered by the Americans.[46]

At the same time, the assertion of sovereignty and dignity characterized the often-tense relationship with the United States. The 1949 'China White Paper' and related American statements blaming Chiang's leadership for the Nationalist collapse long rankled. That Truman had 'ignored our sovereignty' and treated the republic 'worse than a colonial nation' were characteristic entries in the Generalissimo's diaries. But Chiang would console himself with the belief that British influence generally lay behind his American disappointments.[47] However, like the Soviet advisors in the PRC, American personnel in Taiwan – whose numbers peaked at close to 10,000 in the late 1960s – enjoyed full diplomatic immunity: in effect they had extraterritorial rights that reminded many observers of older times and struggles. The pay and accommodation of the Americans were vastly superior to those of their ROC peers: they lived in foreign-style housing compounds, accessed their own stores, drove imported cars and generally led segregated lives. Sex was often a flashpoint. Single men had resources that allowed them to outcompete their Chinese colleagues, and created a service industry of bars and sex workers. 'Let me check your wallet', runs one pointed phrase in a Chinese handbook of helpfully transliterated 'American': 'We cohabit', 'How much you pay me?', 'Don't break my heart'.[48] This was entirely of the pattern of the impact across the globe of the half a million American personnel and their dependants stationed overseas, but its salience in Taiwan was heightened by its pre-history as extraterritoriality, and the Nationalist project to eradicate colonialism. The acquittal by a court martial of an American advisor charged with manslaughter in a shooting incident provoked a riot on 24 May 1957 in Taibei, and the ransacking of the American Embassy and the headquarters of other agencies.

Huang Zhenwu, the city's garrison commander, was not swift to act that day: and he was the man who had killed John Thorburn back in 1931. 'Kick out the American devils', read one slogan painted on the embassy wall. 'When anybody kills Chinese he's not guilty', complained another, and 'Don't act like Russians', stated a third.[49]

What was in practice a 'Two China' policy came under greater and greater strains from the People's Republic as the 1970s progressed, and on 15 December 1978, over three years after the death of Chiang Kai-shek, and two years after that of Mao, President Jimmy Carter gave the ROC two weeks' notice of a final switch to recognition of the PRC.[50] Shortly afterwards, Deng Xiaoping made a strikingly successful visit to the United States that prompted a love feast far greater than any witnessed in the days of ping-pong and the Nixon visit. The sight of diminutive Deng in a ten-gallon Stetson at a rodeo in Simonton, Texas, seemed to offer a whole new politics, if not a new way of conceiving the world. Gone, it seemed for good, were the 'ChiComs' and 'Reds' of US establishment speech. But the United States Congress had reacted by enacting a Taiwan Relations Act that substantially ameliorated the practical consequences of what many saw as a betrayal, including Ronald Reagan, Carter's successor.

Old politics stayed put. The United States continued to supply weapons and technology to its ally, although the remaining American official presence was withdrawn. Reagan only abandoned his attempt to reinstate relations with the Nationalists in 1984. Despite the shock, the Republic of China's economy continued to grow, and under the pragmatic presidency of Chiang Ching-kuo the ROC would move to end martial law and legalize the creation of new parties; his successor as Guomindang leader and President, the Taiwanese Lee Teng-hui, would oversee what became a highly successful transition to democracy. Having lost the presidency in 2000, the Guomindang would even be voted back into power in 2008. Given its track record of repression and violence, this was a significant moment. The continuing challenge presented by Taiwan to the PRC lay not only in the persistence of partition, but in this transition into a genuinely Chinese model democracy, and a plural society that developed on China's border. This hardly pleased everybody in the Nationalist camp. It was mob rule, announced Chiang Kai-shek's adopted son, Chiang

Wei-kuo; Madame Chiang moved permanently to Long Island in disgust. She was not much missed.

Chiang Kai-shek's body would lie mouldering in exile far from the family's preferred burial place in his hometown of Xikou, in Zhejiang. Interment there would have been a fine symbol of China's indivisibility, but there was solace to be had from the fact that the Generalissimo's ultimate strategic objective remained visible. Having been regained from the Japanese, Taiwan was not again formally detached, neither as a result of American policy nor by the independence movement, despite the strategic or nationalistic imperative behind arguments that it should be. True, it was not formally joined either, but in practical terms its status remained in abeyance. The long, long project of holding together China's territorial integrity – and of perpetuating the borders of the Qing Empire – was maintained. In 1981 the People's Republic definitively shifted its policy and announced the first version of what became its 'Nine point proposal' for reunification, articulating what would become its 'one country, two systems' policy. Under this, Taiwan could keep its political and economic system, even its armed forces, but it needed to acknowledge the necessity and inevitability of reunification and recognize the PRC as the central government of China: the flag of the People's Republic would fly in Taibei. These were substantial concessions made by the communist leaders to their old friends and former classmates who led the Guomindang: even Deng Xiaoping and Chiang Ching-kuo had studied together back in Moscow in 1926. Nonetheless, Beijing reserved the right to use force, clarifying later that it would only consider doing so if there was a declaration of independence or foreign intervention. But Taiwan did not bite.

By 1949, of the territories lost as colonies only two remained: Macao and Hong Kong.[51] Nobody liked the word 'colony', however, not even the British, and by 1984 it had virtually disappeared from official use there, but Hong Kong was still a British colony nonetheless. This was a technical description of its formal legal status in British and in international law, although this was not recognized by the Chinese, who saw it simply as illegally occupied territory. Beijing had swiftly used its new UN membership to demand the removal of Macao and Hong Kong from the organization's list of 'colonial territories'. The British evaded a confrontation about this, reserving all rights, by simply ceasing to send annual reports on the colony to the UN – as it was obliged to do. There was, thereafter, no cause for discussion of the colony's status.[52] Hong Kong had been administered through the Colonial Office, and then the Foreign & Colonial Office, later the Foreign & Commonwealth Office, as British government departments were reorganized to make sense of a dwindling colonial empire. Its administrators and officials were Britons, who often circulated through the wider network of British colonies as they secured promotion in the colonial services (until, that is, there was little for them to relocate within). Sir David Trench, Governor of Hong Kong between 1964 and 1971, had come from the Solomon Islands, which provided in every respect a surreal experience to qualify a man to govern Hong Kong; but it was a perfectly valid one, for one colony was much like any other. Governors were primarily responsible to their territories, and had considerable autonomy. They were not puppets of the London government. They were not beholden to it for funds (although the British Treasury ultimately underwrote the administration's funding), nor did they contribute any, and they were increasingly attuned to local public opinion.

What could be more colonial in style and ethos than the great pantomime of the arrival of a Governor in the territory: Sir David Wilson was the last career civil servant to govern Hong Kong (although unlike most of his predecessors he had never had any ties to the old colonial services). His arrival on 9 April 1987 by plane was one of the few concessions to modernity of the ceremonial that marked his installation. But then it was back in time to the high noon of empire: kitted out in his official uniform, sword at his side, Wilson boarded the gubernatorial launch and crossed the traffic-stilled harbour, accompanied by Royal Navy and police vessels, cocked hat on his head, its ostrich feathers in place, to follow most of his twenty-six predecessors in formally landing at Queen's Pier on Hong Kong Island. Nepali soldiers of the Gurkha Regiment provided a guard of honour for their new commander in chief – the British had been stationing South Asian troops in the colony since 1841 – aircraft flew past in formation and a seventeen-gun salute was fired. At the ceremonial swearing-in Wilson undertook:

to well and truly serve Our Sovereign Lady Queen Elizabeth in the office of Governor, and I will do right to all manner of people after the laws and usages of this Colony, without fear or favour, affection or ill will. So help me God.

This text dated back to 1869, and was delivered, as was the entire ceremony, in English. The commitment to the responsibility apart, this was a performance of a type that few Britons ever actually took entirely seriously, but equally few actually ever seriously questioned. It took place in Hong Kong, on a Chinese stage, and it was anchored in the 1842 Treaty of Nanjing.[53]

The Governor had an authority that was constitutionally tempered by advisory Executive and Legislative councils that included officials and appointees from outside the administration. He could be as sensitive to their advice as he chose, but on the whole by the 1980s was far more receptive to the opinion of the business and other interests represented there. Like other colonies Hong Kong had its own specialist cadre of officials, the Hong Kong Cadets, from which Chinese were barred until 1946, and its distinctive legal tradition.[54] But like all colonies the greater part of its staff was indigenous. They had had to show that they knew English, which they used at work, and through which they communicated officially with their fellow Cantonese speakers. At school they learned any history but Hong Kong's, and they learned very little of modern China's. The British official establishment had actually grown after the riots in 1967 – when there were an estimated 61,000 British officials and their dependants – as the military presence was increased to provide a better internal security capacity.[55] In 1950 'local' – Chinese – staff were a minority, often a tiny one, in most parts of the civil service. By 1977 this had substantially been reversed, but still only 32 per cent of 'Directorate' (senior) appointments were held by local men and women, and less than half of senior police positions. Expatriate Britons held the rest, and 550 new recruits came from Britain that same year.[56] There were still 3,200 British civil servants (and 1,600 military personnel) in 1982. Despite a 'localization' policy in staff recruitment and progression, men and women continued to be recruited from London until 1994 when the last five British recruits flew out to join the Royal Hong Kong Police.[57]

Lesser functionaries arrived with far less fanfare than the Governor, but were inducted rapidly into the certainties and psychological and other trappings of British colonial life, not least the functional, if not explicit, racism that shaped its social and cultural interactions – or more accurately in most cases, its lack of them.[58] A non-commissioned officer in the armed forces, for example, was generally provided with subsidized accommodation, could afford a live-in servant, and a lifestyle and status generally more comfortable than those which could be secured in Britain, let alone by most of Hong Kong's residents. And this was without the expatriate allowances enjoyed by civil servants. This was not enough for some, however: until the late 1970s, Hong Kong was also permeated by systemic corruption at all levels throughout the administration, a factor that provided the single biggest threat to the legitimacy of British control. After the high-profile case of the British police officer Peter Godber, a new Independent Commission Against Corruption went to war with such singular success that the force mutinied, and an amnesty for historical crimes was agreed.[59]

There were high-profile cases of corruption even in the colony's earliest days, but it was exacerbated after the Second World War by Hong Kong's demographic history, its population exploding as refugees poured across the border in the late 1940s, and then steadily through the 1950s and 1960s. It was also aided by language. English was the sole official language of government until 1974 when barely a quarter of the population spoke or read it. But even when the administration had committed itself to bilingualism, utility companies routinely billed customers in English. Until the end of British rule jurors were required to know English.[60] Racist zoning laws restricting residence on the Peak and parts of Cheung Chau Island to 'non-Chinese' were repealed in 1946. Yet in the 1960s the cricket club ground in the heart of the city centre served as a continuing proxy for a history of racist exclusion of the majority of the population that had existed in one form or another from the earliest days of the colony. For how many Chinese played cricket? And the ground was not otherwise open to the public, even though it was held on a government lease. This 'revived unpleasant memories', one local paper commented, 'of a notice prohibiting "Chinese and dogs" from entering a park in Shanghai'.[61] In 1978 the cricket ground became a public park.

From the 1960s onwards a quite unique local identity began to coalesce in Hong Kong. It was outward-looking, urban and Cantonese. Although the colony's borders remained porous, and many of its people retained ties to their places of origin, rising levels of education and relative prosperity, a successful local film industry and later Cantonese pop music drove the process. A baby boom in the late 1950s and early 1960s meant that half of the population was less than twenty years old in the 1961 and 1971 census.[62] Hong Kong was young, and it spoke Cantonese. Television, radio and a large and vibrant press nurtured a confident new popular culture and its local icons, and assimilated elements from the diverse worlds of its multinational resident foreign communities, the fast-developing tourist industry, and the territory's openness to global fashions and cultural currents. The colonial government worked to foster this (it was vital to its economy, and its political stability), but it had its own dynamic. Hong Kong fashion, film and music had a long reach and influenced diaspora Chinese communities across the globe, and in China itself. This quite distinct identity increasingly set Hong Kong residents further and further apart from their mainland roots. 'Would you like to go to China?' Paul McCartney was asked when the Beatles visited Hong Kong in June 1964. 'I thought this was China,' he replied. But increasingly it wasn't. The 1967 riots demonstrated quite dramatically that the great majority of Hong Kong people identified with a set of values that distinguished them from those of their roots – the greater part of the colony's population by far was formed of immigrants and their locally born children.

Unlike most colonies Hong Kong was a runaway economic success. Its outward-looking character was vital to its export-led economy. By 1967 it had the fifth-busiest port in the world, and if it had been a country it would have ranked twenty-fifth globally amongst trading economies. Britain benefited substantially from this: orders were placed by the Hong Kong government or local companies with British suppliers, for example, but there was no revenue transfer to London (a fact that Chinese negotiators would fail to understand, for it did not fit their political models of imperialism, nor their suspicions of the British). On balance, the British themselves concluded that the overall economic effect in 1982 was 'about even' for the United

Kingdom. Hong Kong increasingly attracted a non-British foreign presence from the 1960s onwards, and in the 1980s this grew as its role as an international instead of a mostly regional financial hub rapidly developed. But it remained in form and legal fact a colonial society.[63] The colony had gained in value too, as a springboard from which the British might 'get in on the ground floor of modernization' in China itself, as the then ambassador Percy Cradock put it in 1979, with the reform policy of the Deng Xiaoping leadership beginning to be developed after 1978.[64]

Margaret Thatcher, who became British Prime Minister in 1979, was smitten with Hong Kong. She had first visited it two years earlier and it was obviously all she ever wanted Britain to be. Thatcher saw it as a model low-regulation, low-tax economic success, secured by the rule of law and – belatedly – honest and efficient British administration.[65] Hong Kong's oligarchs beat a path to the welcoming door of 10 Downing Street: Lord Kadoorie, Sir Y. K. Pao, Eric Hotung and Henry Keswick (Jardines) all proffered schemes, advice and offers of assistance in discussions with China. She could not always quite grasp what 'Y. K.' was actually proposing, Thatcher would say, but she helped launch his ships and her files are full of his letters. Hong Kong's reality was much more complex and qualified than the picture that so appealed to the Prime Minister: but the vision mattered more. The social consequences of this form of governance were largely discounted in this understanding of its strengths and successes. Income inequality was the highest in Asia, and high by general global standards.[66] Buoyed up by British victory in June 1982 in the conflict with Argentina over the Falkland Islands, Thatcher was in no mood to accept any surrender of the colony and its people to a Marxist regime when she visited Beijing in September of that year.

But the Iron Lady failed. The 'younger generation' of Chinese leaders whose historic role, Mao had said, would be to deal with this problem that was left over from history was led by Deng Xiaoping, the great survivor. Deng was a pragmatist, but over Hong Kong he was first and foremost an anti-imperialist nationalist for whom the historic task of the civil war was yet unfinished. The British had been warned: in 1979 they had attempted to propose a technical legal fix to the looming problem of the impact on property leases of the termination date on the ninety-nine-year 1898 lease on the New Territories. These could only run until 1997 unless measures of some sort were taken. The Hong Kong government was concerned about what would become with each passing year an increasingly difficult problem that, it was believed, would steadily undermine business confidence and drive investors to Singapore or Japan. In a landmark visit to Beijing in March 1979, the then governor Sir Murray MacLehose was given a curt 'rebuff' – his term – when he raised the issue and sprang a potential solution on Deng Xiaoping. In the aftermath various attempts to clarify the situation were parried as 'unnecessary and inappropriate'. It was barely discussed during the then premier Hua Guofeng's visit to Britain in November 1979, with Hua simply stating that Hong Kong was 'Chinese territory'. However, both the British and the Chinese began planning for the future.[67]

So Margaret Thatcher set out in September 1982 to enlighten the Chinese leadership on just what it was that made Hong Kong so prosperous, and the key to that – in her eyes – was British administration. In the interim the Chinese had developed the 'one country, two systems' principle, which, while aimed at the greater prize of Taiwan, they applied equally to Hong Kong, which would become a 'special administrative zone' and so a pilot for the grander scheme of reunification. But at the Great Hall of the People on the morning of 23 September the Prime Minister told Premier Zhao Ziyang that this proposal would be 'disastrous': the economy would 'collapse', and that would bring 'discredit' to both Britain and China. Moreover, the British had a 'moral obligation to the people of Hong Kong, which we must honour'. She 'felt deeply' about this, underscoring her words firmly in her own copy of the minutes.[68] For her listeners it was an abrasive and insulting message: here was the ghost of Victorian gunboat warmonger Sir Harry Parkes, or the muscular proconsul Sir Miles Lampson reading the riot act, lecturing the Qing and the warlords.

So Zhao made himself equally clear: 'China would not maintain the prosperity of Hong Kong and develop it at the expense of recovering sovereignty', a principle it would place above 'prosperity and stability'.[69] Deng Xiaoping, the following day, was no less firm. The British appeared to be proposing an extension to their control of

Hong Kong – which they were, in the form of what they called a 'management contract' to secure administrative control.[70] But 'If sovereignty were not recovered,' Deng replied, 'it would mean that the new China was like the China of the Qing Dynasty and the present leaders were like Li Hongzhang' – the senior Qing official, reviled by nationalists for allegedly selling out China to a foreign power in the 1895 Treaty of Shimonoseki with Japan, and the 1898 treaty with the British. Deng, like Zhao, stated that the government's credibility was at stake, and that they were beholden to a popular nationalism that expected retrocession. And it will do you good, too, he said, in a remark that needled the British Prime Minister, 'it would mean that Britain's colonial era had been brought to an end. This would rebound to British credit.'

Deng spoke for the imperatives of history. Thatcher barely understood them, and she was hardly well briefed. The Prime Minister had to hand in her FCO briefing papers, 'A Hasty Guide to the History of China', which passed over in silence the British role in the assault on China: here there was no Opium or Arrow War, no Boxer uprising, no May Thirtieth, no Shakee Massacre; Sir Francis Aglen did not control the republic's finances; the great sway that Britain held in China until the 1930s was ignored; there were no gunboats at Wanxian; HMS *Amethyst* had never fired on the PLA. The history of Sino-British relations had been described by Douglas-Home as 'uneven' in 1972; in her brief historical survey of relations at the welcoming banquet in the Great Hall of the People, Thatcher commented euphemistically that the record of political relations between Britain and China was 'more varied' than the rich history of cultural interaction she also laid claim to and placed greatest emphasis on. But had not the British helped Sun Yat-sen escape from his Qing captors at the Legation in London in 1896, and had not the two countries stood side by side and alone against fascism for twelve months in 1940–41? How swiftly the British forgot their history in China. That same dark period was made acutely worse for Chongqing when Churchill's government shut the Burma Road, the only supply route to Chiang's regime, and then when its imperial forces collapsed in the face of the Japanese assault.[71] For many this was the moment of Britain's greatest betrayal of China, not its finest hour of embattled solidarity. And Thatcher's request to Zhao for the return of the old Shanghai consulate building on the Bund hardly demonstrated a sensitive understanding of the power and meaning of the past.

Deeply suspicious about British intentions, the Chinese promptly refused to open negotiations unless the British first conceded that they did not have sovereignty over any part of Hong Kong. And you do not speak for Hong Kong's people, the Chinese said, we do. They are Chinese people; they know their history. Margaret Thatcher lambasted the initial solutions to the impasse proposed by the FCO as 'pathetic' on the grounds that 'WE HAVE . . . THE TREATIES.' The Chinese launched a barrage of strident propaganda highlighting not least of all the historical inequities in Britain's acquisition of Hong Kong; the colony's stock market and currency tumbled, supermarkets were cleared out by panicked residents.[72] At the same time Hong Kong audiences were treated to local film director Li Han-hsiang's sumptuously styled epic *The Burning of the Summer Palace* (*Huoshao Yuanming yuan*). This was a pungently nationalistic account of the 1860 north China campaign and the single act that was becoming talismanic of Anglo-French vandalism – just in case not all Hong Kong people quite 'knew their history'.

Still the British clung on, hoping to find a way to give 'them the outer form of what they wanted but to fill that form with the substance of our requirements' – that old song again, *you ming wu shi*.[73] From July 1983, having all but conceded the point, as the Chinese saw it, formal negotiations began that led to the abandonment of the attempt to secure any sort of formal British administrative link, in the Sino-British Joint Declaration of 26 September 1984. This was explicitly not a 'treaty': 'A rose by any other name,' noted one leading Chinese negotiator, well primed with Shakespeare, 'would smell as sweet.' He 'loathed the word and assumed he did not need to explain why'.[74] But he did, because the British and Chinese still spoke different political languages, and worked with different understandings of the potency of the past, or even of its facts. But the British hardly listened to the 'ponderous repetitions', 'usual tedious repetitions' and 'monologues' to which they were treated on the subject. The Chinese, complained Ambassador Percy Cradock, used 'emotive language', like 'imperialism', but it was a meaningful and technical description and in Beijing's eyes a source of 'historical trauma', and a living threat.[75] We are not 'playing cards', Cradock would say at one point, nor do we think you are playing 'cards or ping pong'. Well, Chinese officials answered, you are 'day dreaming', 'trying to replace the old unequal treaties with a new one'.[76]

The Joint Declaration proved to be the start, not the end, of controversy, and in Chinese eyes it marked the immediate end of any British free hand in the colony. This took the British by surprise. But the Chinese worked with such a rigid caricature of British 'colonialism' that it had already proved a substantial obstacle and would continue to do so during the negotiations that also followed. These lurched from crisis to crisis, over infrastructure projects; the alleged favouring of British companies in tender decisions (Jardine Matheson was singled out for particular invective, salted with the history of the opium trade); Hong Kong government finance policies; and, under the last Governor, the Conservative Party politician Chris Patten, over democratic reform.[77] While part of Hong Kong's purported value lay in the fact that it was deemed to be a 'free world enclave on the Chinese mainland', its people were colonial subjects who may have had economic freedom, and were subject to a stable and fair legal system, but had no political rights. The plans for genuine constitutional development in Hong Kong – developed by colonial administrators back in London and in captivity in the colony during the dark months following its catastrophic defeat by Japanese forces in December 1941 – had by 1952 been abandoned.[78] The administration had evolved by the 1980s an effective ability to respond to public opinion without conceding anything by way of formal democratic representation. Governors had largely consulted the oligarchs, although they had become increasingly sensitive to the press. But a new generation of Hong Kong residents pushed instead for the dignity of a democracy that would complement Hong Kong's free press and society. This would not be achieved.

Governor Patten and Jardine Matheson grew resigned to serving as punchbags for Chinese anger over Hong Kong. Macao had an easier time of it. As news arrived of Portugal's Carnation Revolution in April 1974, the territory seemed 'as sleepy as ever'. The dogs ran that night at the colony's Canidrome, and the casinos remained open around the clock.[79] The new government in Portugal was committed to divesting itself of the country's colonial empire – or, technically, of its overseas provinces, for Portugal, unlike the United Kingdom, formally denied that it held colonies (through a constitutional amendment in 1951). It was also intent on formally recognizing the government in Beijing, for, despite its long-standing modus vivendi with the People's Republic over the governance of Macao, Portugal still held to its recognition of the Republic of China in Taiwan. Whilst the territory itself prepared to commemorate the bicentenary of the birth of the great China coast artist George Chinnery in May 1974 – by renaming a street, issuing stamps, holding a church service and placing a memorial plaque on his tomb – the Portuguese authorities now looked forward, and looked to secure a resolution to the Macao anomaly. A secret clause in the 1975 recognition agreement surrendered any claim to sovereignty and pledged Portugal to retrocession, but this would take longer to negotiate, and there was no terminal date to concentrate minds (though perhaps, they later thought, the 450th anniversary of its establishment). The return of the colony that was not in fact a colony, according to its Governor in a statement in 1981, but Chinese territory under Portuguese administration, became subordinate to the bigger prize at Hong Kong. Formal talks opened in 1986 and the Chinese began negotiations by simply presenting the British Hong Kong Joint Declaration text.[80] The Macao government slept on after an agreement on Hong Kong was reached in 1987. Macao failed to localize its civil service or deal effectively with a wave of gangster violence – or to generally subordinate its powers, despite constitutional developments, to pro-Beijing groups, and the interests running the casinos that largely drove its tourism-reliant economy.

Dealing with the past legacies of Portugal's four centuries in China, and Britain's two centuries, caused occasional shrill outbursts from Beijing, but the level of disquiet and invective over the PRC's newly established relationship with Japan was of a different order. In 1971 and 1972, Kissinger and Nixon had encountered a strong vein of suspicion about Japanese ambitions. Not only did Zhou Enlai articulate a fear of Japan moving to turn Taiwan into a client state of some sort, but he also argued that the Japanese aimed to reassert themselves more widely back in China. The Chinese would not let go of the war; and as they found themselves in 1972 dealing with Japanese leaders who had served that wartime state, and served it in China, there were some grounds for hesitancy, even if, initially, only emotional ones.

In the chaotic aftermath of surrender and during the American-led occupation, more than five million soldiers and settlers had returned to Japan bringing home stories of atrocity, cruelty and corruption. The Tokyo war crimes tribunal reinforced these, providing ample documentary evidence of military violence and barbarity that was officially sanctioned by commanders at all levels, or casually inflicted by soldiers operating within a colonialist war machine. Historians and activists, including Okinawans murdered by the Japanese military, had been engaged ever since in making sure that this was recorded appropriately in the country's Education Ministry-approved school textbooks. From 1953 onwards the Japanese historian Ienaga Saburō had battled through the Japanese legal system to force the ministry to acknowledge the country's wartime record.[81] But as Japan grew in economic strength, so memories faded, and older justifications for the war began to re-emerge in conservative circles. Neo-nationalists claimed again that the Japanese had been fighting a war to liberate Asia from European colonialism and American hegemony, and to protect it from communism. The Japanese were victims too, others argued, in Hiroshima and Nagasaki, and in all the cities firebombed by the United States Air Force, and they did not look far beyond these catastrophes to the wider war.

It was a public sensation, then, when a prominent crusading journalist, Honda Katsuichi, started filing a series of reports from China in 1971 in the mass circulation *Asahi Shimbun* newspaper, which recorded in detail his interviews with survivors of Japanese atrocities. Honda's approach and style highlighted and humanized the personal stories of the experiences of Chinese men and women at the hands of individual Japanese. It rescued atrocity from anonymity, formed a devastating indictment of the Imperial Army's war crimes, and was published in book form in the months before Prime Minister Tanaka's journey to China. Other journalists accompanying the visit reported back from symbolic sites of the conflict, such as the Marco Polo Bridge just outside Beijing, confronting the past as Tanaka himself clumsily attempted to, in his remarks at the state banquet. The final joint statement in 1972 acknowledged that Japan was 'keenly conscious of the responsibility for the serious damage that Japan caused in the past to the Chinese people through war, and deeply reproaches itself'.[82] But this was only the start of exchanges between the two governments on the issue of their recent history.

In its sanctioning of areas and themes for historical research after 1949, the Chinese state had not generally emphasized the Japanese invasion of China after 1931. Mao Zedong often teased visitors by expressing his gratitude to the Japanese for invading China, saving his party from almost certain destruction at the hands of Chiang Kai-shek, and galvanizing the nation to fight. China had been defiant, had been roused and had emerged victorious. The war was certainly taught and discussed, and remembered and commemorated, by the state at all levels, and by veterans, victims and their families.[83] Wartime experience provided the matter, too, of films, novels and memoirs. 'People's diplomacy' initiatives involving visits by Japanese delegations had time and again to plan and manage popular responses to the reappearance of the former invader and potential protest (and the Japanese had always been the largest cohort amongst pre-Cultural Revolution visitors). Anger persisted. But the broadsides fired at the Japanese government in the summer of 1982 over its handling of a controversy over school textbook descriptions of the invasion were startling.[84] An ongoing domestic political campaign led by Japanese conservatives critical of what they saw as entrenched leftist bias in state-approved textbooks became a full-scale diplomatic incident that affected Japan's relations with a host of nations. This only subsided when the Japanese provided sufficient commitments to revise problematic terms whereby the 'Japanese invasion' of China, had become, for example, 'the Japanese advance'. These revisions long pre-dated 1982 and the revisionist textbooks were used in a small minority of schools, but concerns at home, and elsewhere in Asia, about Japan's more assertive international profile fuelled the crisis.

So the war was far from over. It was fought and refought. There were more battles over the textbooks, over the form of official Japanese government statements, and over official and private remembrance of Japan's war dead by ministers and leading politicians at the

Yasukuni Shrine in Tokyo. There was controversy over the extent or even historical veracity of accounts of specific episodes, such as the extensive massacres in the winter of 1937–8 that had quickly become known as the 'Rape of Nanjing'. There were disputes over the record of Japanese biological and chemical warfare in China, over medical atrocities committed against Chinese, and over the forced conscription into sex-slavery of Asian 'comfort women' by the Imperial Army. Nanjing massacre 'denialists' 'proved' that 'only' 6,000 or perhaps 40,000 soldiers had been killed at Nanjing. (The Tokyo tribunal concluded that 260,000 men and women, civilians and soldiers, were killed.) Honda Katsuichi provided additional telling testimony from interviews with survivors from the city and its vicinity; in a best-selling polemic a Chinese-American writer, Iris Chang, 'proved' that a 'holocaust' had taken place. Academics, veterans, journalists and politicians joined the fray. The popular nationalism to which Deng Xiaoping had held himself to account in 1982 was inflamed by these controversies.[85] There has never been any reasonable doubt that the soldiers of the armies of Japan perpetrated a war of bestial violence in China, as they did elsewhere in the many theatres of the conflict, and that its wider occupation establishment was responsible for further war crimes. The documentary evidence is incontrovertible. But finding a common language to describe what happened, why and when, over the decades of Sino-Japanese conflict, proved an intractable problem: even when the Chinese and Japanese governments established an official 'Joint History Research Committee' to try to compose a shared narrative, it failed to bridge the gap.

Dismay at Japanese neo-nationalist rewriting of the history of the war was not confined to China, nor was denial of the complexity of the horrors of the war a uniquely Japanese phenomenon.[86] But in the aftermath of the 1982 textbook incident the Chinese government encouraged a systematic programme to upgrade history museums and sites of remembrance, or construct new ones. A Nanjing Massacre Memorial Hall was opened in 1985 on the site of a mass grave that had recently been uncovered. Museums to showcase the medical atrocities perpetrated by the Japanese Army's Unit 731, and to mark the outbreak of war in 1931, were opened in 1985 and 1991. A War of Resistance Museum was established in 1987.[87] Chinese scholars combed archives around the world searching for overlooked documentary evidence, publishing the results in a voluminous compendium. A feature of this drive was the incorporation of the wartime role of the National Government into the narrative presented, and a re-evaluation of the role of the Nationalists and of Chiang Kai-shek. The prime focus in communist narratives, and in analysis amongst scholars overseas, had always been on the wartime resistance of the Red Army. The Guomindang barely featured, or they did so as traitors and cowards, still damned by Theodore White and their other wartime critics. Now, as part of the process of opening the door to Taiwan, they were placed back in the story of China's struggle.

As China continued to become more accessible to foreign visitors, the novelty started to wear off, but a deeper engagement could also start to be explored. There were more and more exchanges of language and other students, and some bizarre initiatives: the American comedian Bob Hope visited and filmed a television special in 1979; the French electronic musician Jean-Michel Jarre performed in China in 1981 (the laser show at least went down well); *Sesame Street*'s 'Big Bird' came in 1983; and the British pop group Wham! played two concerts in 1985. This last visit was an expensive publicity stunt that achieved its aim of securing extensive publicity for the group in the United States. By this point the strictures on what music was permissible were unravelling, and senior leaders no longer vetted programmes piece by piece, although Foreign Minister Zhou Nan, once heard quoting Shakespeare, hosted a banquet and attended the Wham! concert. Vice Minister of Culture Zhou Weizhi, known for his Korean War-era patriotic anthems, hosted a visit of the duo to the ministry, and reminisced about hearing Paul Robeson sing in Prague. Robeson was well known in China for his version – in Chinese – of what became the national anthem, 'March of the Volunteers'. 'I'm afraid we're ... out of touch with that,' replied the musicians. 'We don't actually know who Robeson is.' Wham! began their concert in Guangzhou with 'Love Machine'. Their manager, who had dreamed up the venture had, like many Britons, a link to the old world of the treaty ports: as a salesman for Asiatic Petroleum, his father had lived in Guangzhou and Hong Kong for two years after 1929. 'Overall,' remarked one British diplomat in the aftermath of the concerts, there was 'a certain lack of mutual understanding'. More in the tradition of exchanges from the era of Sino-Soviet interaction was the arrival in 1983 of American playwright Arthur Miller to direct *Death of a Salesman* with a Chinese cast at the Beijing People's Art Theatre. Its star, and Miller's collaborator on the project, was Ying Ruocheng, another Vice Minister for Culture, and formerly, amongst other roles, a spy engaged in 'battle' with British diplomats.[88] This was clearly a different phase in the normalization of relations.

By the time the British-produced television documentary *Heart of the Dragon* came to air internationally in twelve one-hour parts in 1984 – for Chinese critics could never complain that the country was not given enough screen time – explicit reference to politics was largely absent. The programme's object was to portray 'some of the *truth* about Chinese culture', and the essential 'timelessness' of its cultural core, not 'Revolutionary' or 'New' China, but the culture that had weathered the storm.[89] Politics was never absent, of course. During the filming of one scene amongst patients in a Harbin asylum, an inmate who might or might not have had good reason to be there was caught pronouncing on the changes starting to develop in reform-era China. Playing with words and with current slogans, he shouted out his own 'four modernizations': meals would be 'state-banquetized; clothes Westernized; the whole country mansionized; transport limousinized'. He would not prove to be far wrong.

If the right understanding of the past needed to be established over the Nanjing Massacre, or Unit 731, and if the historic task of closing the open wounds of history – such as Hong Kong and Macao – needed to be achieved, China's 'reform and opening up' (*gaige kaifang*) was fraught with this deeper peril. The political reverse course might unlock confusion and corruption; capitalist and colonialist demons and monsters from the black history of national humiliation might move straight back in. As China embarked on its reform policies after 1978, every development was attended by this danger. One key vehicle was its establishment of 'Special Economic Zones' (SEZs), starting with four in Guangdong province in 1979.[90] These were export-oriented manufacturing zones that were designed to draw in foreign currency and capital, expertise and technology, to assist in China's post-Mao economic modernization and development. They would also provide employment, training in foreign practices and exposure to foreign ideas. The first such enterprise, a Hong Kong-registered ship-breaking facility, was authorized in January 1979. Its raw material was China's antiquated shipping stock, and the market for the scrap metal was Hong Kong. So products of China's socialist state enterprise were quite literally to be torn apart in the new era. Eight months later the four zones were established just north of Hong Kong at Shenzhen, at Zhuhai, just north of Macao, at Shantou and in Fujian. These were all areas formerly deemed strategically too insecure to warrant state investment. Shanghai, historically the obvious choice for such a venture, was still deemed too untrustworthy, for its comprador past was too strong.

Critics of the SEZs believed that they heralded the reintroduction of capitalism, and that money incentives, let alone the corruption and crime which inevitably followed, threatened to demoralize if not destroy the Communist Party in Guangdong province. Their supporters saw a profound transformation take place. The small town of Shenzhen swiftly became a city of high-rise blocks; new factories were built at a breakneck pace and, despite setbacks and difficulties, Hong Kong and overseas investors came calling. Another fourteen SEZs were announced in 1984, and all of them were former treaty ports. Shanghai was among these but would not be let off its leash until 1992. The impact of the reforms on China's economy and society was spectacular, but suspicion of the consequences was also profound. Crackdowns on crime and corruption, and on 'spiritual pollution' (pornography – very broadly defined – and 'bourgeois liberalism'), were launched to keep a balance between ideological orthodoxy and reform. The routine theatre of public show trials, the parading of groups of those condemned through city streets, and then their immediate execution, accounted for over 5,000 lives in 1983. But after a relatively short period, the campaign lapsed. After all, 'Time is money', as one contemporary slogan decorating the Sichuan countryside had it.

History became a rallying point and a tool of reform. As their contribution to the country's Seventh Five Year Plan of 1986–90, researchers undertook systematic studies of the history of China's treaty ports. Urban historians found themselves suddenly in demand.

Officials wanted to know how these prototype special economic zones had developed? What had gone right, what had gone wrong? How might an understanding of the achievements of the past serve economic development in the present? What did planners and administrators need to watch out for? The Shanghai capitalists were let back out of their cage. But part of the answer was carefully complemented by a new rash of books published at the same time narrating and cataloguing China's national humiliation. These research projects were not designed to rehash the critiques of the past, but to support what Deng Xiaoping called China's 'second revolution'.[91] History mattered still, but the history that now mattered more was that of the once vilified, free-wheeling open culture of the treaty ports.

This about-turn was strongly checked in 1989. Over two months from 15 April of that year, Tiananmen Square in Beijing became the symbolic centre of a nationwide upsurge of protest that found support from those angry at corruption, at the effects of the steep inflation that followed the abolition of price controls, and of continuing rigid restraints on freedom of expression and choice. Students at Beijing's universities led the way, acutely conscious of their historic role in political protest movements. They were joined by people from all walks of life and from across China in a challenge to the status quo that prompted the violent crackdown of 4 June and after on what was officially labelled a 'counter-revolutionary rebellion'. Unprecedentedly, events unfolded in real time across foreign television and radio networks. China had never before secured such exposure to foreign audiences, and it could not have looked worse. This time the state simply did not care. Anyway, 'Westerners will forget,' said Deng Xiaoping in advance of the violence.[92] The country's historic rapprochement with the Soviet Union in May, heralded by Mikhail Gorbachev's visit to Beijing, was overshadowed by the protests, angering and humiliating senior leaders.

In the aftermath of the crackdown, the state punished those it claimed had directed events. But it also formally embarked in 1991 on a new programme of 'patriotic education'.[93] The Tiananmen postmortem concluded that the bigger problem actually lay in the fact that in the rush towards reform the horrors of the past had been obscured. The achievements of the Communist Party in rescuing China from its dismembered, emasculated and degraded state had been forgotten. So all China was to receive this history lesson, at school, at work and at leisure. Television channels poured out historical dramas and documentaries. New books rolled off the presses. Up sprouted new museums and official sites of memory through which these lessons were to be taught.[94]

History had always been central in the creation of 'New China', as we have seen, but the generations coming of age after 1980 had no direct experience from which to draw the essential comparisons with the 'old society', and with what a weak China had suffered at the hands of its stronger enemies. They needed instruction. The state now invested heavily in sites of party congresses, treaty signings and massacres. It built new memorials recording landmark strikes, and at prisons and Red Army headquarters, and to commemorate resistance fighting. Memorials at cemeteries, the old communist 'base areas' and hilltop Soviets, homes of former leaders, sites of enemy surrender, and of atrocity, were established, upgraded or refreshed. Guomindang leaders and stories of anti-Japanese resistance were not forgotten – and there was even a Lin Yutang Memorial Hall – but they were placed in the ideological context of the 'United Front' with the Communists, and they were also balanced with monuments at former National Government prison camps. These were places for pilgrimage and for commemoration – by school groups, teams from party and state organizations, and a rapidly growing constituency of Chinese tourists. Prices were kept low. New roads and hotels were built, and guidebooks prepared. Promotion was undertaken on television, and through trade fairs, expositions and Red Tourism festivals. Tourist receipts helped offset the costs.

It helped that pieces of the true cross had seemed to multiply in great number when needed. Mao's birthplace, Shaoshan, employed 110 people by 2010, guarding 40,000 cultural relics, including 6,000 'personal items' from the Chairman's later years. Mao was now remembered through at least fourteen memorial sites across the nation, including at least three former homes, and the Chairman himself still lay in state, embalmed, in a Memorial Hall in the middle of Tiananmen Square. A bed he once slept in is displayed in the former official residence of the German Governor of Qingdao. One hundred of these places were designated 'National Bases for Patriotic Education' in 1996; and these would later overlap with another 100 officially designated 'Classic Red Tourism Sites'. Textbooks and teaching were reinvigorated with an avowedly nationalist agenda in which China as victim was given as much emphasis as China the eventual victor. The prime Maoist injunction had been 'Never Forget Class Struggle'; in reform China it was 'Never Forget National Humiliation', and never forget the leading role of the Chinese Communist Party in righting the wrongs of history. Through normalization in the 1970s, and reform in the 1980s, it had seemed that the wounds of the past might start to be healed. But by the 1990s it was apparent that they were to be kept open and raw, carefully tended by the extensive machinery of a modern propaganda state.

12

Haunted by History

What did 1997 mean? On 1 July that year the People's Republic of China resumed the exercise of sovereignty over Hong Kong. China's senior leadership and British government ministers and officials took part in a punctiliously choreographed midnight handover ceremony. Rain poured down, and tears were shed for all the reasons that tears might be shed: sadness, joy, fear, confusion, or relief. The departing Governor stepped aboard the British royal yacht *Britannia* just after midnight and sailed away. The Union Jack had been pulled down at midnight, the five stars of China's flag raised in its stead, and the colony's own standard was at the same time surmounted by that of the new Special Administrative Region. Other symbols of colonial rule were being removed as midnight passed, and many had already been superseded by 1997. In Beijing there were fireworks in Tiananmen Square. A digital clock that had been placed in front of the Museum of Revolutionary History, and which had been counting down the days and seconds since 1994, reached zero. Crowds chanted as the seconds ticked down. A century of humiliation had been 'washed away' as the rain fell in Hong Kong.

There had been other ways of looking forward to this moment than the clock. (This was one of several; there was one at the Hong Kong–Shenzhen border, and another in Beijing at the ruins of the Yuanming Yuan, the old Summer Palace looted and burned down by French and British troops in 1860.) One that had stuck with me was a music video that seemed to be endlessly repeated in 1994 on a satellite music channel – itself a phenomenon that was bewildering for a visitor to China – and that I had watched in a Shanghai hotel room. A young woman faced the camera, strumming a guitar. Her name was Ai Jing, and at the age of twenty-four she had a hit across and beyond the Chinese-speaking world with a catchy song, 'My 1997'. It takes the form of a jaunty folk riff periodically interrupted by passages in a Chinese opera style, in which she narrates her journey from Shenyang in the far northeast, through Beijing, to Shanghai's Bund and down south to the border with Hong Kong. Visually the film makes the same shifts from past to present. But the song is about the future: 'when will I be able to visit Hong Kong?' she asks from Guangzhou. It is a cheeky song, lamenting at once a Hong Kong lover, but Hong Kong itself as a lover, perhaps, certainly as a future for the Chinese. The song and video's celebratory climax presents a sensual longing for urban freedom and modernity. On the cover of the CD itself Ai Jing was photographed in Hong Kong's Lan Kwai Fong bar district. 'What is it like? What are Hong Kong people like?' Ai asks. In the years before the handover of the last significantly sized British colony, the Chinese government was sponsoring academic research and film-makers. In these endeavours it was making Hong Kong the focus for a celebration of China's new strength, and a reminder of past weakness and humiliation. Culture still mattered; it was no less a political sphere than it had been in the most hectic days of the Maoist era, or even during the more cosmopolitan republic.[1] So Ai Jing's song deftly struck the right political notes, and subverted them. Her 1997 was not about national humiliation, but about personal liberation.

Late colonial Hong Kong had boomed as a British imperial city was transformed into a global capitalist hub. The disputes between the British and the Chinese diplomats continued almost up to the last moment. Signs of that old treaty-port world remained in abundance after the formal symbols of British power were removed, but many of the new expatriates of the 1990s and after were looking north, waiting for China, diving in whenever opportunity was opened up, finding partners, and chasing ancient fantasies of unlimited China markets.[2] For the Chinese government the question was how to manage it all, and how to bring the foreign back in without re-creating the past, and without surrendering sovereignty and dignity. Reclaiming Hong Kong was a grand affirmation of its triumph over history. The handover was a substantial exercise in political theatre, but it was also a landmark in the growing economic freedoms enjoyed by Chinese. After 1949 the city had inherited Shanghai's modernity. High-rise Hong Kong provided an alternative vision of China's present, and its soon-to-be-realized future. The return of Macao in 1999 was also accompanied by much fanfare, but the earlier return in 1997 was made significantly more important as a symbol, as its roots lay not in the Ming Dynasty but in the nineteenth-century British assault on China's sovereignty.

Ai Jing's video lingers in the mind, but there were orthodox cultural projects launched before 1997 that were intended to resonate widely as well. In one way the most mainstream of these was a big-budget film, *The Opium War*, which premiered with a showing for senior government leaders in the Great Hall of the People in Beijing on 9 June 1997, and which was described by its director, the veteran Chinese film-maker Xie Jin, as a 'special gift for the motherland and the people . . . to ensure we and our descendants forever remember the humiliation the nation once suffered'. Hong Kong's Shanghai-born incoming senior leaders – Chief Executive Tung Chee-hwa and Legislative Council President Rita Fan – attended the Hong Kong premiere three days later. The film had already been endorsed by no less a figure than Deng Xiaoping's successor, the Communist Party leader Jiang Zemin, and patriotically minded backers had put up the funds. Group bookings by government and other official and party units produced a good deal of the receipts. Hong Kong's origins in the conflict over the opium trade and in the British bid to seize 'the entire East . . . the Nineteenth century' mattered most in this retelling (and the ambition was put into the mouth of Queen Victoria). The film was by some measure the most expensive then yet made in China. Its script delivered a more nuanced understanding of the British position than might have been expected; however, the significant point is that ultimately the project was not rooted in Hong Kong's present but in China's past. Hong Kong was not what its people had made it by 1997, and what they might make it afterwards, but was to be remembered as an historical act of theft, with its origins in a squalid criminal enterprise and the weakness and chauvinism of the Qing.[3]

It was not in fact the first time in modern Chinese history that a retrocession had been commemorated with a film about the Opium

War. The earlier occasion had been the premiere of the 1943 Japanese-sponsored Chinese movie *Wanshou liufang* (*Eternity*), screened in Nanjing for the benefit of collaborationist president Wang Jingwei. That, too, had been an officially directed project, and it was released to mark the handover of the International Settlement to the quisling Shanghai Special Municipality on 1 August 1943. At the very least this coincidence of rituals demonstrates the centrality of nationalism and anti-imperialism to all twentieth-century political projects in China. The Chinese Communist Party and Wang Jingwei, once allies, later the bitterest of opponents, played tunes from the same narrow repertoire.[4] This is not to suggest any equation between the CCP and Wang Jingwei's regime, but to highlight the centrality of these issues of humiliation in understanding the competing forms of nationalism that have emerged in modern China.

Over the next thirty years the world that Ai Jing's song laid claim to was brought to China. The state enterprises that her lyrics mention her father working in have folded, and have been broken up for scrap like those ships that were the fuel for the first foreign business established in China. These enterprises were swept aside by the massive programme of renewal and economic development that began with those contentious reforms in Guangdong province in 1979. Economic growth brought profound social and cultural transformation that is still unfolding, and there are now bar districts like Lan Kwai Fong all over China.[5] Hong Kong is still very different, providing a distinctive modern Chinese culture with different values; but like Macao it is also partly irrelevant to the story of change in China itself. A quarter of a million foreign nationals live in Shanghai, for example, which has hungrily embraced all the trappings of its ambitions to be a world-class city, and all the greyer and darker ones too.[6] Only the rickshaws are missing from the streets.

There are plenty of those in the museums, however, for the past is bigger business than ever in China. An estimated 10,000 'Red Tourism' sites and half a billion visits to them in 2011 accounted for one-fifth of all Chinese domestic tourism.[7] Heritage initiatives with little political flavouring have also made progress in the generally unequal battle with the bulldozer and property speculation. Some of this apparent political elision is striking: Tianjin's former Italian concession was revamped as the 'Italian-style scenic district' after 2004. In this case an Italian colonial enterprise now serves as an example of cosmopolitan heritage style.[8] The repackaging of the colonial as the cosmopolitan is now quite common. It serves the purpose too of stressing continuities over time despite China's shutdown during the Maoist era. The iconic modern skyline in China is still Shanghai's. Its high-rises were the stuff of the movies viewed across the nation in the 1930s and 1940s, and this persisted. But now the vista representing Shanghai in its room at the Great Hall of the People in Beijing is of the Pudong skyline, across the river from the Bund. To appreciate this, which thousands of tourists from all over China do every day, one needs to turn one's back on the old Bund and its buildings, on the British Consulate, the headquarters of Jardine Matheson and Co., the Hongkong and Shanghai Bank, Sir Victor Sassoon's Cathay Hotel, the North China Daily News Building, Yokohama Specie Bank and the Shanghai Club.

But even when backs are turned the memory is kept alive. On 1 October every year, China's national day, city officials in Shanghai gather on the north end of the Bund at what is still called a park, although little trace of anything much like one remains. What dominates the site now is a 'Monument to the People's Heroes' that was unveiled in 1993.[9] Three granite pillars lean together at the top to form a three-sided obelisk reaching 60 metres into the air. They represent the 'eternal glory' of the 'people's heroes' who died in the liberation war, in revolutionary movements more widely since the 1919 May Fourth Movement and since the Opium War. In a sunken area around its base are seven bas-relief friezes depicting key incidents in the revolutionary history of the city down to 1949, culminating with students dancing the *yangge* in Shanghai's streets in May 1949. For some decades prior to 1943 another much less imposing obelisk stood close to this very same spot, a memorial erected in 1866 to the foreign officers of the Ever Victorious Army, the unit led by General Gordon that supported Qing forces in the battles around Shanghai against the Taiping. The city's histories, like all of China's, overlay and echo one another. And not far away you can read the twentieth century's changes on what was formerly the China headquarters of the British company Imperial Chemical Industries. Shorn now of the allegorical reliefs with which it was adorned on its unveiling in 1923, its own name is just still visible, and so are huge sets of Cultural Revolution slogans running down the building, wishing long life to the Great Helmsman Chairman Mao. It now houses a securities firm.

The annual ceremony at the memorial on the Bund is of fresh vintage. Recently the event commenced early in the morning with the playing of the national anthem by a military band, while the participants stood in contemplative silence. Then, without a word, the Shanghai Party Secretary, the Mayor and representatives from other official organizations stepped forward to lay wreaths in front of the obelisk. So the ceremony itself echoes another, the one that took place annually from 1924 to 1941, and then again from 1945 to 1948, on 11 November, Remembrance Day for the Allied dead of the world wars. That took place at the other end of the former International Settlement Bund, in front of Shanghai's tall war memorial. This is a powerful testament to the reach of imported practices and forms, and their acculturation – including the ceremonial silence, and the playing by a military band using European instruments, of a national anthem indebted to Western musical forms, and indeed to the very idea of a 'national anthem'. The concrete forms of memorialization – those obelisks – are linked in a similar way. But none of these are any less authentic facets of modern China and modern Chinese culture. Most of Shanghai's tourists do not pay any homage at the memorial, despite the fact that it is a 'patriotic education base'. Most do not even really visit that end of the promenade: the blindingly neon-lit Pudong skyline at night is the draw instead. Such is the pervasiveness still of the humiliation narrative that they hardly need to, for the stories it tells remain at the heart of the nationwide system of patriotic education.

Reactions to bilateral and other disputes that unfold or erupt today are still nearly always addressed through the prism of the past, or they are about that past. There were violent street and online protests during the Chinese-Japanese dispute over the Senkaku/Diaoyutai islands in 2012, which were inflamed by its coincidental timing with the anniversary of the Japanese Kwantung Army's attack on Manchuria on 18 September (usually simply '918' in Chinese). The islands themselves are another legacy issue from the longer history of territorial disintegration in the nineteenth century: 'No longer learn from Li Hongzhang,' shouted demonstrators in Nanchang, echoing Deng Xiaoping's curt rejoinder to Margaret Thatcher over Hong Kong.[10] 'Never forget National Humiliation; Remember 9.18; Recover the Diaoyu islands', ran another slogan. Since 2000 controversy over demands for the repatriation of artefacts looted from the Yuanming Yuan in 1860 has also gathered tremendous momentum. And over forty years after Prime Minister Tanaka's incompetent first apology, and the 1972 Sino-Japanese joint declaration, Japanese Prime Minister Abe's official statement in 2015 to mark the seventieth anniversary of the end of the Sino-Japanese War was closely read, and sharply criticized for its perceived inadequacies in Chinese and others' eyes. The sullen and resentful language of the text was a mark not only of Abe's own conservative politics and revisionist leanings, but also of a wider exasperation in Japan with the never-ending war. For China the past is becoming more important. And what's clear in all of this is that the Chinese state is now often playing catch-up, struggling to keep abreast of the popular nationalism that it has nurtured and encouraged, and which runs riot in social media, on foreign university campuses and sometimes in Chinese streets. The state needs to be agile, for its perceived inadequacies in defending China's honour have frequently diverted popular hostility towards it and away from Japan.

The story of the world outlined in this book is on the whole not well enough known. It certainly lives on in saga, romance or thriller, or through cinema – J. G. Ballard's autobiographical *Empire of the Sun*, mediated through Hollywood, for example. As we have seen, it was portrayed as romance back in the 1920s and especially in the 1930s, and this persists. But it is still too easily thought of as a sideshow, far away and involving people with whom there is little connection. In most cases there was always a profound asymmetry in relations: the West was always far more important in China than China seemed to be at home. As we have seen, this was not always in fact actually true, although it generally holds good. What it does mean is that a significant imbalance in knowledge and understanding persists. In 2011 I was invited to give a talk about *The Scramble for China* at the Foreign and Commonwealth Office in London. It seemed wise to signal in advance that I could not provide much by way of enlightenment on contemporary policy. I did not know what the then CCP leader Hu Jintao thought, or much about climate change or healthcare initiatives. I was not to worry, was the response, leave policy to us, but we really need to know more about the history. Our recruits have learned little of it before they join us, yet the Chinese still talk about it all the time. Given how profoundly modern China has been shaped by its relationship with the United Kingdom, this was a telling admission.

They know this well in China, of course. And in which other state does a new leadership team, on the day that it is unveiled, change into more sombre clothing, and make a pilgrimage to a history museum?[11] (What other state has so many history museums?) This is what Xi Jinping and the members of the Standing Committee of the Politburo did on 29 November 2012. The most powerful leaders in the land paid homage to the past through this visit to the National Museum of China, and its permanent display 'The Road to Rejuvenation' (the official translation of the Chinese *Fuxing zhi lu*). The design aesthetic in the first galleries is darkness. Art works and artefacts illustrate a stridently captioned narrative of China's story of humiliation and weakness from 1840 onwards. But then comes the light, and in the second set of galleries a different aesthetic decorates a record of events and triumphs since 1949 (and in a discreet and selective way some disasters). The exhibition concludes, or at least did on my own last visit – when it was thronged with school groups assiduously taking notes – by paying homage to China's space programme, and then with a display of mobile phones. The promise of a project that generates intense national pride, and the history of China's economic growth and individual prosperity, are both framed in a story of release from the shame of the past. The promise at the end of the black tunnel of history is a smartphone.

The story of the foreign presence in China in the twentieth century, as much as in the nineteenth century or in any part of China's modern history, is too important today to be left in the hands of the Chinese party-state and this approved script. Its sanctioned narrative is partial, self-serving and ultimately incendiary. A new nationalism in which angry demonstrators have been heard many times clamouring for war and for killing Japanese is pregnant with the potential for calamity. But this is not a Japanese problem alone. No nation complicit in the degradation of China after the 1830s – which includes most European states as well as the United States – is ultimately secure. Being effectively equipped with the facts might help us understand the roots of that rage. In this book I have aimed to show that world in all its complexity and all its contexts – and that word 'complexity' is no coy cover for nostalgia or an apologetics. The foreign presence in China in the twentieth century had more than its fair share of bigotry, racism, violence, greed, or simple callous indifference. This is on display in profusion in the National Museum of China. In that world, too, you can find collaboration, cohabitation, alliance and coalition. Many other voices also spoke for China and stood up for it against its enemies and against ignorance and prejudice overseas, and on China's streets. This is all but absent in the displays in Beijing. There was also self-delusion and self-conceit, as well as genuine humanitarian concern and disinterested technical interest. This was a world in which the imperatives or norms of a world in which colonial power was exercised overlapped with (and helped shape) new forms of globalization and the movement of people, goods and ideas. It was a world in which people in China incorporated into their lives all sorts of innovations that came from overseas, and equally made their own new culture, promiscuously mixing all sorts of foreign ingredients and indigenous ones too. Chinese of all political hues and none worked with and against the unequal and unjust exercise of foreign political power in China and the treatment of China in international forums and organizations. The Chinese Communist Party holds no monopoly of nationalistic virtue, and it was itself complicit in the continued degradation of Chinese sovereignty in the 1950s.

'The Chinese nation has suffered unusual hardship and sacrifice in the world's modern history,' said Xi Jinping in November 2012 at the end of his museum visit. Its people 'have never given in, have struggled ceaselessly, and have finally taken hold of their own destiny'. Xi's rhetoric then and since has promised a 'China dream', the 'great renewal of the Chinese nation' and individual aspiration, subsuming along the way the hopes of Ai Jing's song 'My 1997'. The China dream is grounded in this story of an unrelenting Chinese nightmare. We need to acknowledge that, and understand it, but we do not need to believe it.

Further Reading, Watching and Listening

One of the questions I was asked when I interviewed for my job at the University of Bristol in 1997 was about how I could teach the history of China to students who had no Chinese. What could they read? I was momentarily speechless, for in fact the volume of accessible English-language material on modern China was even then almost unmanageably large. Look for it, and you will find a surfeit of collections of primary documents, books, memoirs, travel writing and reportage, fiction, film, comics and magazines, and yet more. To be fair, my interlocutor's area of specialization was such that he had never felt the need to look. But this book argues that we all need to. And since then vast amounts of additional material have been made available for easy public access, and of course more advanced scholarly tools have yielded significant new collections of material. Since 1997 also, there has been a great growth in the number of scholars working on China in universities overseas, and in particular historians specializing in the modern era. I have learned much from their work.

Amongst the books I found particularly stimulating and accessible were (chronologically with my chapters, where you will find fuller references): Erez Manela, *The Wilsonian Moment* (2007); Frederick Wakeman Jr, *Policing Shanghai* (1995) and *The Shanghai Badlands* (1996); James Farrer and Andrew David Field, *Shanghai Nightscapes* (2015); Rana Mitter, *China's War with Japan, 1937–1945* (2013); Philip Snow, *The Fall of Hong Kong* (2003); Sergey Radchenko, *Two Suns in the Heavens* (2009); Austin Jersild, *The Sino-Soviet Alliance* (2014); Nancy Bernkopf Tucker, *The China Threat* (2012); Roderick MacFarquhar and Michael Schoenhals, *Mao's Last Revolution* (2006);

and William A. Callahan, *China: The Pessoptimist Nation* (2010) and *China Dreams* (2013). Frank Dikötter's readable and provocative 'People's Trilogy' (*Mao's Great Famine*, 2010, *The Tragedy of Liberation*, 2013, and *The Cultural Revolution*, 2016) has prompted intense and stimulating debate. China's recent decades have been wonderfully reported on by Peter Hessler in *River Town* (2001), *Oracle Bones* (2006) and *Country Driving* (2010). A fine and accessible background introduction drawing on recent scholarship can be found in *The Oxford Illustrated History of Modern China* (2016), edited by Jeffrey N. Wasserstrom.

Amongst the profusion of memoirs I found great delight in revisiting the books of Graham Peck (particularly *Two Kinds of Time*, 1950), Robert Payne's *Chungking Diary* (1945) and *China Awake* (1947), Esther Cheo Ying's *Black Country Girl in Red China* (1980) and Ying Ruocheng and Claire Conceison's *Voices Carry* (2009). I can also highly recommend the vastly different perspectives to be found in J. G. Ballard's *Miracles of Life* (2008), Joshua A. Fogel's translation of *Life Along the South Manchurian Railway: The Memoirs of Itō Takeo* (1988), the memoir of Macao's wartime British consul, John Reeves, *The Lone Flag* (2014), edited by Colin Day and Richard Garrett, and Arthur Miller's *Salesman in Beijing* (1984). Jean-Luc Godard's film *La Chinoise* (1967) remains mesmerizing, and Michelangelo Antonioni's *Chung Kuo, Cina* (1972), Joris Ivens's epic documentary *How Yukong Moved the Mountains* (1976) and the equally lengthy twelve-part 1984 television series *Heart of the Dragon* are all worth seeking out. The film of the 1985 China tour by Wham! (*Foreign Skies*, 1986) provides a surreal twist to reports from China's Reform Era; William A. Callahan's ethnographic shorts, including *Toilet Adventures* (2015), are well worth watching. The photographs taken in China by Cecil Beaton, Henri Cartier-Bresson, Jack Birns and Marc Riboud are often quite astonishing, and can be found in various collections of their work. Birns's photographs of Shanghai, Macao and Hong Kong can be viewed online through the LIFE Photo Archive.

My references will also guide you to openly accessible online sets of 1930s Chinese illustrated magazines (at the MIT Visualizing Cultures platform), US State Department, Presidential and Central

Intelligence Agency documents (through https://history.state.gov/, the CIA's Electronic Reading Room and the FDR Presidential Library's digital collections). The Wilson Center's Cold War International History Project has published online (with translations) a great volume of material secured from former Soviet bloc archives. You can easily find trenchant first-hand reports from the 1940s (through the Internet Archive, or CADAL Digital Library); Cultural Revolution posters (at chineseposters.net); Hong Kong government reports (through Hong Kong University Library's Digital Initiatives) or newspapers (through the Hong Kong Public Libraries MMIS system); Shanghai's premier French-language newspaper (*Le Journal de Shanghai*, on Gallica.fr); or the music of Hattori Ryoichi and the songs and films of Yoshiko Yamaguchi (Li Xianglan) on YouTube. It will then be even clearer why Yamaguchi's 'Candy-Selling Song' was such a cross-frontline hit in 1943. At Marxists.org or Bannedthought. net you can browse to your heart's delight through long runs of digitized copies of *People's China*, *China Reconstructs*, and much, much more. Christian Henriot's 'Virtual Cities Project' bursts at the seams with films, photographs, books and documents from China; and my own project, 'Historical Photographs of China', presents over 10,000 digitized historical photographs, including several used in this book.

So there is indeed, as I said even in 1997, plenty to read, watch and listen to.

Notes

INTRODUCTION

1 Excellent surveys include Peter Hays Gries, *China's New Nationalism: Pride, Politics, and Diplomacy* (Berkeley, CA: University of California Press, 2004); William A. Callahan, *China: The Pessoptimist Nation* (Oxford: Oxford University Press, 2010).

2 In this section I draw on Robert Bickers and Jeffrey N. Wasserstrom, 'Shanghai's "Chinese and Dogs Not Admitted" Sign: History, Legend and Contemporary Symbol', *China Quarterly* 142 (1995), pp. 444–66. While there has been a substantial literature on the topic since 1994, and further sightings of references to the signboard, the argument has not been proven wrong.

3 *Guangming ribao*, 13 June 1994, p. 3. The newspapers were: *Qingnian bao* (*Youth Post*), the mass circulation *Xinmin wanbao* (*Xinmin Evening News*), *Wenhui bao* (*Wenhui Daily*) and the party newspaper *Jiefang ribao* (*Liberation Daily*). *Shiji* published it in August 1994, and it was reproduced elsewhere. The rebuttal first appeared in *Dangshi xinxi bao* (*Party History Information News*) on 1 June 1994, and there were many other contributions to the controversy. It is worth noting that the editing of Xue Liyong's originally much longer article had excised a fuller account of the history of racist exclusion from the parks, and accentuated the story of the fake sign: it made for better copy in a popular magazine.

4 *The Times*, 4 January 1907, p. 3.

5 *North China Herald*, 15 November 1907, p. 428; the press pack can be found in a Shanghai Municipal Council Secretariat file in the Shanghai Municipal Archives: U1-3-1908, 'Notice Board of Municipal Parks: "No Dogs or Chinese Admitted" (1925–1931)'. Hong Kong: I have spotted disputes over the issue in the *South China Morning Post* in 1959, 1967, 1978, 1986, and in 1987.

6 At the park itself, in the texts on display that I saw in 2010 in the Bund History Memorial Hall, and in its 1999 semi-official guide, the story was presented as originating in a popular simplification and conflation of different items in the regulations. However, the display also includes a cartoon of recent vintage in which the offensive legend is clearly in place: personal observation, 8 October 2010; Gao Da, *Huangpu gongyuan jinxi* (*Huangpu Park Then and Now*) (Shanghai: Shanghai renmin meishu chubanshe, 1999), pp. 8–11, back cover.

I. ARMISTICE

1 *North China Herald* (hereafter *NCH*), 30 November 1918, pp. 532–9; *Shenbao*, 24 November 1918.

2 *NCH*, 7 December 1918, pp. 588–9; *Peking and Tientsin Times*, 29 November 1918, pp. 6–7; missionary Sidney Gamble's shots of the celebrations in the capital: rolls 212, 213, 217–19, in Sidney D. Gamble Photographs, David M. Rubenstein Rare Book & Manuscript Library, Duke University, Durham, North Carolina.

3 *Peking and Tientsin Times*, 22 November 1918, p. 7. On China and the conflict see Xu Guoqi, *China and the Great War* (Cambridge: Cambridge University Press, 2005).

4 Wilson to Xu, 10 October 1918, in *Papers Relating to the Foreign Relations of the United States, 1918* (U.S. Government Printing Office, 1918) (hereafter *FRUS*), p. 118.

5 *NCH*, 30 November 1918, pp. 542–3; Norman E. Saul, *The Life and Times of Charles R. Crane, 1858–1939: American Businessman, Philanthropist, and a Founder of Russian Studies in America* (Lanham, MD: Lexington Books, 2012).

6 Recent histories include: John Fitzgerald, *Big White Lie: Chinese Australians in White Australia* (Sydney: University of New South Wales Press, 2007); Erika Lee, *At America's Gates: Chinese Immigration during the Exclusion Era, 1882–1943* (Chapel Hill, NC: University of North Carolina Press, 2003); Lisa Rose Mar, *Brokering Belonging: Chinese in Canada's Exclusion Era, 1885–1945* (Oxford: Oxford University Press, 2010); see also James Belich, *Replenishing the Earth: The Settler Revolution and the Rise of the Anglo-World, 1783–1939* (Oxford: Oxford University Press, 2009); Elizabeth Sinn, *Pacific Crossing: California Gold, Chinese Migration, and the Making of Hong Kong* (Hong Kong: Hong Kong University Press, 2013); Stacey Bieler, *'Patriots' or 'Traitors'? A History of American-Educated Chinese Students* (London:

Routledge, 2009). On the Chinese Labour Corps see Xu Guoqi, *Strangers on the Western Front: Chinese Workers in the Great War* (Cambridge, MA: Harvard University Press, 2011).

7 Robert René Le Fernbach, *A Child's Primer of Things Chinese* (Tianjin: Tientsin Press Ltd, 1923), pp. 2–3.

8 Hans van de Ven, *From Friend to Comrade: The Founding of the Chinese Communist Party, 1920–1927* (Berkeley, CA: University of California Press, 1991); Li Dazhao, 'Bolshevism de Shengli' ('The Victory of Bolshevism'), *Xin Qingnian* 5:5 (15 October 1918), 442–8.

9 Translated by Yang Xianyi and Gladys Yang in Lu Xun, *Selected Works*, vol. 2 (Beijing: Foreign Languages Press, 1980), pp. 29–30.

10 *NCH*, 20 October 1917, p. 163; 7 September 1918, p. 586.

11 Henrietta Harrison, *The Making of the Republican Citizen: Political Ceremonies and Symbols in China 1911–1929* (Oxford: Oxford University Press, 2000); Antonia Finnane, *Changing Clothes in China: Fashion, History, Nation* (London: Hurst and Co., 2007); Frank Dikötter, *Things Modern: Material Culture and Everyday Life in China* (London: Hurst and Co., 2007).

12 This section draws on Wellington K. K. Chan, 'Selling Goods and Promoting a New Commercial Culture: The Four Premier Department Stores on Nanjing Road, 1917–1937', and Sherman Cochran, 'Transnational Origins of Advertising in Early Twentieth-Century China', both in Sherman Cochran (ed.), *Inventing Nanjing Road: Commercial Culture in Shanghai, 1900–1949* (Ithaca, NY: Cornell East Asia Series, 1999), pp. 19–36, 37–58; Karl Gerth, *China Made: Consumer Culture and the Creation of the Nation* (Cambridge, MA: Harvard University Asia Center, 2003), chapter 1.

13 Dikötter, *Things Modern*, pp. 177–81.

14 Arthur H. Smith, *Village Life in China: A Study in Sociology* (New York: Fleming H. Revell, 1899), p. 310.

15 For its development see Robert Bickers, *The Scramble for China: Foreign Devils in the Qing Empire, 1832–1914* (London: Allen Lane, 2011).

16 In the second of Sun Yat-sen's 1923 lectures collected as *San Min Chu I: The Three Principles of the People*, trans. Frank W. Price (Taipei: China Publishing Co., undated), pp. 13–14. For analysis see Marie-Claire Bergère, *Sun Yat-sen* (Stanford, CA: Stanford University Press, 1998), pp. 352–94.

17 Robert Bickers, 'British Concessions and Chinese Cities, 1910s–1930s', in Billy K. L. So and Madeleine Zelin (eds), *New Narratives of Urban*

Space in Republican Chinese Cities: Emerging Social, Legal and Governance Orders (Leiden: Brill, 2013), pp. 183–4.

18 *The China Year Book, 1919–20* (London: George Routledge and Sons, 1919), p. 624; Shanghai Municipal Council, *Annual Report 1920*, pp. 271a–75a; *North China Daily News* (hereafter *NCDN*), 21 November 1918. For a contemporary survey of this world see Arnold Wright and H. A. Cartwright (eds), *Twentieth-Century Impressions of Hongkong, Shanghai and Other Treaty Ports of China* (London: Lloyd's Greater Britain Publishing Company, 1908).

19 Carl Crow, *The Travelers' Handbook for China* (Shanghai: Carl Crow, 1920), pp. 297–9. On Macao see Jonathan Porter, *Macau: The Imaginary City* (Boulder, CO: Westview, 2000); on Macanese identity see João De Pina-Cabral, *Between Europe and China: Person, Culture and Emotion in Macao* (London: Bloomsbury Continuum, 2002).

20 *South China Morning Post* (hereafter *SCMP*), 31 January 1921, p. 3; *Hong Kong Hansard*, 3 October 1918, p. 73.

21 Statistics from 'Report on the Census of the Colony for 1921', passim, quotation from p. 159, *Sessional Papers 1921, Papers Laid before the Legislative Council of Hongkong 1921*, 15/1921. On the colony's history see John M. Carroll, *A Concise History of Hong Kong* (Lanham, MD: Rowman and Littlefield, 2007).

22 *SCMP*, 14 November 1918, p. 1.

23 The estimate is by Albert Feuerwerker, *The Foreign Establishment in China in the Early Twentieth Century* (Ann Arbor, MI: University of Michigan Center for Chinese Studies, 1976), p. 39.

24 Jane Hunter, *The Gospel of Gentility: American Women Missionaries in Turn-of-the-Century China* (New Haven, CT: Yale University Press, 1984).

25 Henrietta Harrison, ' "A Penny for the Little Chinese": The French Holy Childhood Association in China, 1843–1951', *American Historical Review* 113:1 (2008), pp. 72–92; see also Henrietta Harrison, *The Missionary's Curse and Other Tales from a Chinese Catholic Village* (Berkeley, CA: University of California Press, 2013).

26 'The Diocese of Anking' by the Right Reverend Daniel Trumbull Huntington, DD, Bishop of Anking (Hartford, CT: Church Missions Publishing, 1943).

27 All figures from *China Mission Year Book 1917* (Shanghai: Christian Literature Society for China, 1917), pp. 73–84.

28 Ryan Dunch, *Fuzhou Protestants and the Making of a Modern China, 1857–1927* (New Haven, CT: Yale University Press, 2001).

29 See Robert Bickers, *Empire Made Me: An Englishman Adrift in Shanghai* (London: Allen Lane, 2003); Eileen P. Scully, *Bargaining with the State from Afar: American Citizenship in Treaty Port China, 1844–1942* (New York: Columbia University Press, 2001).

30 See Stephen Platt, *Autumn in the Heavenly Kingdom: China, the West, and the Epic Story of the Taiping Civil War* (London: Atlantic Books, 2012); Jonathan D. Spence, *God's Chinese Son: The Taiping Heavenly Kingdom of Hong Xiuquan* (London: Harper Collins, 1996).

31 Shanghai Municipal Council (hereafter SMC), *Annual Report 1918*, pp. 58a–88a; SMC, *Annual Report 1919*, pp. 93a–95a.

32 Maritime Customs, *Decennial Reports on the Trade, Industries etc. of the Ports Open to Foreign Commerce . . . 1912–21, Volume 2: Southern and Frontier Ports* (Shanghai: Statistical Department of the Inspectorate General of Customs, 1924), pp. 2, 450–51; Feuerwerker, *Foreign Establishment in China*, p. 17. On the growth of the Japanese community in Shanghai see Joshua A. Fogel, *Maiden Voyage: The Senzaimaru and the Creation of Modern Sino-Japanese Relations* (Berkeley, CA: University of California Press, 2014).

33 'Hongkew Disturbances', report, SMC, *The Municipal Gazette*, 28 October 1918, pp. 330–44, quotation at p. 331.

34 This section draws on: Erez Manela, *The Wilsonian Moment: Self-Determination and the International Origins of Anticolonial Nationalism* (New York: Oxford University Press, 2007); Bruce A. Elleman, *Wilson and China: A Revised History of the Shandong Question* (Armonk, NY: M. E. Sharpe, 2002); Naoko Shimazu, *Japan, Race and Equality: The Racial Equality Proposal of 1919* (London: Routledge, 1998).

35 Baker diary, 30 April 1919; House to Wilson, 29 April 1919, Grayson diary, 30 April 1919, in Arthur S. Link (ed.), *The Papers of Woodrow Wilson*, vol. 58 (Princeton, NJ: Princeton University Press, 1988), pp. 270, 228–9, 244.

36 *The Deliberations of the Council of Four (March 24–June 28, 1919): Notes of the Official Interpreter Paul Mantoux*, trans. and ed. Arthur S. Link, vol. 1 (Princeton, NJ: Princeton University Press, 1992), pp. 336, 404–5; Baker diary, 30 April 1919, in *The Papers of Woodrow Wilson*, vol. 58, p. 271.

37 First made public in *The Times*, 6 May 1919, p. 13.

38 Elleman, *Wilson and China*, pp. 160–62.

39 Enclosure in Chengting T. Wang to Morrison, 4 March 1919, in Lo Hui-min (ed.), *The Correspondence of G. E. Morrison*, vol. 2 (Cambridge: Cambridge University Press, 1978), p. 728.

40 Chow Tse-Tsung, *The May Fourth Movement: Intellectual Revolution in Modern China* (Cambridge, MA: Harvard University Press, 1960), p. 166.

41 Pingyuan Chen, *Touches of History: An Entry into 'May Fourth' China*, trans. Michel Hockx (Leiden: Brill, 2011), p. 24.

42 Chow, *May Fourth Movement*, pp. 99–116; Chen, *Touches of History*, pp. 11–66.

43 SMC, *Annual Report 1915*, p. 51a; Gerth, *China Made*, pp. 133–46.

44 Joseph T. Chen, *The May Fourth Movement in Shanghai: The Making of a Social Movement in Modern China* (Leiden: Brill, 1971); Tiina Helena Airaksinen, *Love Your Country on Nanjing Road: The British and the May Fourth Movement in Shanghai* (Helsinki: Renvall Institute for Area and Cultural Studies, 2005).

45 Chow, *May Fourth Movement*, pp. 178–82.

46 Li Chien-nung, *The Political History of China, 1840–1928*, trans. Ssu-yu Teng and Jeremy Ingalls (Princeton, NJ: Van Nostrand, 1956), pp. 390–93.

47 SMC, *Annual Report 1919*, pp. 61a–63a. Some seven hundred remained under temporary or permanent exemptions, such as age or health.

2. MAKING REVOLUTION

1 Marie-Claire Bergère, *Sun Yat-sen* (Stanford, CA: Stanford University Press, 1998), pp. 299–301.

2 Jack J. Gerson, *Horatio Nelson Lay and Sino-British Relations 1854–1864* (Cambridge, MA: Harvard East Asia Monographs, 1972).

3 Shubing Jia, 'The Dissemination of Western Music through Catholic Missions in High Qing China (1662–1795)', unpublished thesis, University of Bristol, 2012.

4 Jonathan D. Spence, *To Change China: Western Advisers in China, 1620–1960* (Boston, MA: Little, Brown, 1969).

5 See, for example, John King Fairbank, *Trade and Diplomacy on the China Coast: The Opening of the Treaty Ports, 1842–1854* (1953) (Stanford, CA: Stanford University Press, 1969), pp. 341–6.

6 On Cohen see Daniel S. Levy, *Two-Gun Cohen: A Biography* (New York: St Martin's Press, 1997); on Borodin see Dan N. Jacobs, *Borodin: Stalin's Man in China* (Cambridge, MA: Harvard University Press, 1981).

7 Levy, *Two-Gun Cohen*, pp. 116–24; on Ch'en see Howard L. Boorman (ed.), *Biographical Dictionary of Republican China, Volume 1* (New York: Columbia University Press, 1967), pp. 180–83.

8   Stanley F. Wright, *China's Customs Revenue since the Revolution of 1911*, 3rd edition (Shanghai: Statistical Department of the Inspectorate General of Customs, 1935), pp. 295–9.

9   Leslie H. Dingyan Chen, *Chen Jiongming and the Federalist Movement* (Ann Arbor, MI: Center for Chinese Studies, University of Michigan, 1999).

10 *Hong Kong Telegraph*, 6 May 1921; Virgil K. Y. Ho, *Understanding Canton: Rethinking Popular Culture in the Republican Period* (Oxford: Oxford University Press, 2005), p. 345.

11 Bergère, *Sun Yat-sen*, pp. 304–14.

12 Sun Yat-sen, *The International Development of China* (New York: G. P. Putnam's Sons, 1922); Bergère, *Sun Yat-sen*, pp. 281–3.

13 C. Martin Wilbur, *Sun Yat-sen: Frustrated Patriot* (New York: Columbia University Press, 1976), pp. 105–8; J. Scott Matthews, 'Nippon Ford', in John C. Wood and Michael C. Wood (eds), *Henry Ford: Critical Evaluations in Business and Management* (Routledge: London, 2003), vol. 2, p. 83: for the letter see https://archive.org/details/808353-letter-from-dr-sun-yat-sen-to-henry-ford-and, accessed 4 July 2014.

14 *NCH*, 27 January 1923, p. 243; 3 February 1923, pp. 310, 289.

15 S. A. Smith, *A Road is Made: Communism in Shanghai 1920–1927* (Richmond, Surrey: Curzon Press, 2000); Hans van de Ven, *From Friend to Comrade: The Founding of the Chinese Communist Party, 1920–1927* (Berkeley, CA: University of California Press, 1992); on Comintern strategy see Alexander Vatlin and Stephen A. Smith, 'The Comintern', in Stephen A. Smith (ed.), *The Oxford Handbook of the History of Communism* (Oxford: Oxford University Press, 2014), pp. 187–202.

16 *Hongkong Daily Press*, 31 February 1923; Bergère, *Sun Yat-sen*, pp. 299–300; F. Gilbert Chan, 'An Alternative to Kuomintang-Communist Collaboration: Sun Yat-sen and Hong Kong, January–June 1923', *Modern Asian Studies* 13:1 (1979), pp. 127–39; Ming K. Chan (ed.), *Precarious Balance: Hong Kong Between China and Britain, 1842–1992* (Armonk, NY: M. E. Sharpe, 1994); Jung-fang Tsai, *Hong Kong in Chinese History: Community and Social Unrest in the British Colony, 1842–1913* (New York: Columbia University Press, 1993).

17 Jacobs, *Borodin*, p. 116.

18 Bruce A. Elleman, *Diplomacy and Deception: The Secret History of Sino-Soviet Diplomatic Relations, 1917–1927* (Armonk, NY: M. E. Sharpe, 1997); Akira Iriye, *After Imperialism: The Search for a New Order in the Far East, 1921–1931* (Cambridge, MA: Harvard University Press, 1965).

19 Stephen G. Craft, *V. K. Wellington Koo and the Emergence of Modern China* (Lexington, KY: University Press of Kentucky, 2004), pp. 66–71.

20 T. G. Otte, ' "Wee-ah-wee"? Britain at Weihaiwei, 1898–1930', in Greg Kennedy (ed.), *British Naval Strategy East of Suez 1900–2000: Influences and Actions* (London: Routledge, 2004), pp. 4–34; Pamela Atwell, *British Mandarins and Chinese Reformers: The British Administration of Weihaiwei (1898–1930) and the Territory's Return to Chinese Rule* (Hong Kong: Oxford University Press, 1985), pp. 128–9.

21 Wesley R. Fishel, *The End of Extraterritoriality in China* (Berkeley, CA: University of California Press, 1952), pp. 109–26.

22 On Guangzhou see Michael Tsin, *Nation, Governance, and Modernity in China: Canton, 1900–1927* (Stanford, CA: Stanford University Press, 1999); Ho, *Understanding Canton.*

23 See, for example, John Fitzgerald, *Awakening China: Politics, Culture, and Class in the Nationalist Revolution* (Stanford, CA: Stanford University Press, 1996).

24 *The China Year Book 1921–1922* (London: George Routledge and Sons, 1922), p. 24 (based on Post Office statistics).

25 Kwok Mon Fong, *Modern Canton Illustrated* (Guangzhou: China Photo-Engraving, 1924).

26 H. Staples-Smith, *Diary of Events and the Progress on Shameen, 1859–1938* (Hong Kong: Ye Olde Printerie, 1938); Robert Bickers, 'British Concessions and Chinese Cities, 1910s–1930s', in Billy K. L. So and Madeleine Zelin (eds), *New Narratives of Urban Space in Republican Chinese Cities: Emerging Social, Legal and Governance Orders* (Leiden: Brill, 2013), pp. 157–96.

27 Nora Waln, *The House of Exile* (1933) (Harmondsworth: Penguin, 1938), pp. 120–23; 'Shameen Traffic Regulations', 21 August 1924, in Canton No. 203, 13 November 1924: TNA, FO 228/3193; Staples-Smith, *Diary of Events and the Progress on Shameen*, p. 26.

28 Hallett Abend, *My Years in China, 1926–1941* (London: John Lane, The Bodley Head, 1944), p. 14; Victor Purcell, *Memoirs of a Malayan Official* (London: Cassel and Co., 1965), pp. 108–38; Staples-Smith, *Diary of Events and the Progress on Shameen*, p. 36; Carl Crow, *The Travellers Handbook for China* (Shanghai: Carl Crow, 1920), p. 294.

29 Liao Chengzhi, in 1938, quoted in Nym Wales, *Red Dust: Autobiographies of Chinese Communists* (Stanford, CA: Stanford University Press, 1952), p. 28.

30 Edward J. M. Rhoads, 'Lingnan's Response to Chinese Nationalism: The Shakee Incident (1925)', in Kwang-Ching Liu (ed.), *American*

Missionaries in China: Papers from Harvard Seminars (Cambridge, MA: East Asian Research Center, Harvard University, 1966), pp. 183–214; Dong Wang, *Managing God's Higher Learning: U.S.–China Cultural Encounter and Canton Christian College (Lingnan University), 1888–1952* (Lanham, MD: Lexington Books, 2007); Kenneth W. Rhea (ed.), *Canton in Revolution: The Collected Papers of Earl Swisher, 1925–1928* (Boulder, CO: Westview Press, 1977), p. 42; *NCH*, 24 June 1922, p. 869.

31 A. I. Cherepanov, *As Military Adviser in China*, trans. Sergei Sosinsky (Moscow: Progress Publishers, 1982).

32 Sergei Dalin, cited in Smith, *A Road is Made*, pp. 59–60.

33 'Memorandum of Interview Dr James M. Henry, President, Canton Christian College, had with M. M. Borodin, Advisor to Nationalist Government in Canton, December 31, 1925', *British Documents on Foreign Affairs* (hereafter *BDFA*), vol. 30 (Frederick, CO: University Publications of America, 1992), pp. 201–3.

34 C. Martin Wilbur and Julie Lien-ying How, *Missionaries of Revolution: Soviet Advisers and Nationalist China 1920–1927* (Cambridge, MA: Harvard University Press, 1989), pp. 8–13, 425; Jacobs, *Borodin*, pp. 155–6. This section more widely draws on these books and the memoirs cited here, notably Cherepanov, *As Military Adviser in China*, and Vera Vladimirovna Vishnyakova-Akimova, *Two Years in Revolutionary China 1925–1927* (Cambridge, MA: Harvard University Press, 1971).

35 'Minutes of a Special Meeting of Ratepayers', 3 November 1924, in Canton No. 203, 13 November 1924: TNA, FO 228/3193.

36 Tsin, *Nation, Governance, and Modernity in China*, pp. 78–82; John M. Carroll, *A Concise History of Hong Kong* (Lanham, MD: Rowman and Littlefield, 2007), pp. 97–9. On forms of protest see Jeffrey Wasserstrom, *Student Protests in Twentieth-Century China: The View from Shanghai* (Stanford, CA: Stanford University Press, 1991).

37 'A. Hilton-Johnson to Secretary and Commissioner General', 26 March 1922, in Shanghai Municipal Archives (hereafter SMA), U1-3-1718, 'Strikes in Settlement'.

38 Robert Bickers, *Empire Made Me: An Englishman Adrift in Shanghai* (London: Allen Lane, 2003), pp. 163–74; Richard W. Rigby, *The May 30 Movement: Events and Themes* (London: Wm Dawson and Sons, 1980); Nicholas Clifford, *Spoilt Children of Empire: Westerners in Shanghai and the Chinese Revolution of the 1920s* (Hanover, NH: Middlebury College Press, 1991).

39 Cherepanov, *As Military Adviser in China*, p. 178.

40 Wilbur and How, *Missionaries of Revolution*, p. 348, n. 18.

41 Nathaniel Peffer, *China: The Collapse of a Civilization* (London: George Routledge, 1931), p. 159.

42 This enigmatic trip to the north is discussed in Bergère, *Sun Yat-sen*, pp. 397–404.

43 David Strand, *An Unfinished Republic: Leading by Word and Deed in Modern China* (Berkeley, CA: University of California Press, 2011), pp. 236–82.

44 Wang Fan-hsi, *Chinese Revolutionary: Memoirs, 1919–49* (Oxford: Oxford University Press, 1980), pp. 22–7; Gregor Benton (ed. and trans.), *An Oppositionist for Life: Memoirs of the Chinese Revolutionary Zheng Chaolin* (Atlantic Highlands, NJ: Humanities Press, 1997), pp. 91, 137–56; Smith, *A Road is Made*, pp. 122–6; Vishnyakova-Akimova, *Two Years in Revolutionary China*, p. 208.

45 J. W. Jamieson to C. C. Wu, 22 June 1926, in 1926 (Cmd. 2636) China No. 1 (1926), *Papers Respecting the First Firing in the Shameen Affair of June 23, 1925*; P. D. Coates, *The China Consuls: British Consular Officers, 1843–1943* (Hong Kong: Oxford University Press, 1988), pp. 461–2; Putnam Weale, *The Port of Fragrance* (London: Noel Douglas, 1930), p. 253.

46 E. T. Schjöth, 'An account of what happened and my experiences during the first week of the Shameen struggle . . .', 27 March 1929, in SOAS, Papers of Sir Frederick Maze, PPMS2, 'Confidential Letters and Reports', vol. 18; *Guangzhou Shaji canan diaocha weiyuanhui baogaoshu* (Shaji Incident Investigation Committee Report) (Guangzhou, 1925); Wilbur and How, *Missionaries of Revolution*, pp. 155–9.

47 See, for example, André Malraux, *The Conquerors* (London: Jonathan Cape, 1929), and the original French edition *Les Conquérants* (Paris: Grasset, 1928); James W. Bennett, *The Yellow Corsair* (London: John Hamilton, 1928).

48 Quoted in Yang Tianshi, 'Perspectives on Chiang Kaishek's Early Thought from His Unpublished Diary', in Roland Felber et al. (eds), *The Chinese Revolution in the 1920s: Between Triumph and Disaster* (London: RoutledgeCurzon, 2002).

49 In a speech in Shantou on 12 November 1925; text in *BDFA*, vol. 30, p. 96. F110/1/10, 'Communicated by Mr Leefe', P&O, China Association.

50 Smith, *A Road is Made*, pp. 51–8.

51 The British colonial government in Hong Kong was apt at times to pursue an independent-minded policy of its own in south China, but an attempt at this time to seek London's support for an initiative to

fund anti-communist elements in Guangzhou was firmly rejected: Wilbur and How, *Missionaries of Revolution*, pp. 167–71.

52 'Characteristics of Prominent Men of the Kuomintang', May 1926, document no. 49, and 'Stepanov's Report on the March Twentieth Incident', document no. 50, in Wilbur and How, *Missionaries of Revolution*, pp. 697–707.

53 Rhoads, 'Lingnan's Response to Chinese Nationalism'.

54 This section draws on C. Martin Wilbur, *The Nationalist Revolution in China, 1923–1928* (Cambridge: Cambridge University Press, 1983).

55 This is the essential argument of Arthur Waldron, *From War to Nationalism: China's Turning Point, 1924–1925* (Cambridge: Cambridge University Press, 1995).

56 Edmund S. K. Fung, *The Diplomacy of Imperial Retreat: Britain's South China Policy, 1924–1931* (Hong Kong: Oxford University Press, 1991), pp. 101–13.

57 H. Owen Chapman, *The Chinese Revolution, 1926–27: A Record of the Period under Communist Control* (London: Constable, 1928), pp. 35–6, 158–62.

58 Churchill to Baldwin, 22 January 1927, Baldwin Papers, Cambridge University Library, vol. 115, ff. 205–8, quoted in Peter G. Clark, 'Britain and the Chinese Revolution, 1925–1927', unpublished thesis, University of London, 1973, p. 492; *Shanghai Defence Forces Souvenir*, vol. 1 (Shanghai: North-China Daily News and Herald, 1927).

59 United States National Archives and Records Administration (hereafter NARA), RG263, Shanghai Municipal Police Special Branch Files, IO 7563, T. P. Givens, 'Report on Anti-Southern Propaganda', 27 January 1927. The following section draws on Smith, *A Road is Made*, pp. 168–208, and Harold R. Isaacs, *The Tragedy of the Chinese Revolution* (1938) (New York: Atheneum, 1966), pp. 175–85. On Du see Brian G. Martin, *The Shanghai Green Gang: Politics and Organized Crime, 1919–1937* (Berkeley, CA: University of California Press, 1996).

60 Zhang Guotao, *The Rise of the Chinese Communist Party*, vol. 1 (Lawrence, KS: University Press of Kansas, 1971), pp. 617–18, 622–4, 639.

61 Robert C. North and Xenia J. Eudin, *M. N. Roy's Mission to China: The Communist-Kuomintang Split of 1927* (Berkeley, CA: University of California Press, 1963).

62 Percy Chen narrates the journey in his memoir, *China Called Me: My Life inside the Chinese Revolution* (Boston, MA: Little, Brown, 1979), pp. 125–77.

63 The melancholy afterlife of the advisors is detailed in Wilbur, *Missionaries of Revolution*, pp. 425–32.

64 Rhea (ed.), *Canton in Revolution*, p. 97.

3. GOOD EARTH

1 Leslie H. Dingyan Chen, *Chen Jiongming and the Federalist Movement* (Ann Arbor, MI: Center for Chinese Studies, University of Michigan, 1999); *NCH*, 24 June 1922, p. 387.

2 All quotations from the report in this chapter come from: P'eng P'ai, *Seeds of Peasant Revolution: Report on the Haifeng Peasant Movement*, trans. David Holoch (Ithaca, NY: Cornell East Asia Papers, 1973). I also draw on Fernando Galbiati, *P'eng P'ai and the Hai-Lu-Feng Soviet* (Stanford, CA: Stanford University Press, 1985). The movement in Haifeng and more widely forms the subject of Robert Marks, *Rural Revolution in South China: Peasants and the Making of History in Haifeng County, 1570–1930* (Madison, WI: University of Wisconsin Press, 1984); see also Roy Hofheinz Jr., *The Broken Wave: The Chinese Communist Peasant Movement, 1922–1928* (Cambridge, MA: Harvard University Press, 1977).

3 There was no effective or unproblematic census undertaken in China until 1953, and even that had its problems. Figures given in the 1920s range from 425 million to 475 million. The higher total may be more accurate: Ping-ti Ho, *Studies on the Population of China, 1368–1953* (Cambridge, MA: Harvard University Press, 1959); Lloyd Eastman, *Family, Fields, and Ancestors: Constancy and Change in China's Social and Economic History, 1550–1949* (New York: Oxford University Press, 1988).

4 Maurice Meisner, *Li Ta-chao and the Origins of Chinese Marxism* (Cambridge, MA: Harvard University Press, 1967), p. 56; Christopher T. Keaveney, *Beyond Brushtalk: Sino-Japanese Literary Exchange in the Interwar Period* (Hong Kong: Hong Kong University Press, 2008), pp. 85–96.

5 Galbiati, *P'eng P'ai and the Hai-Lu-Feng Soviet*; Marks, *Rural Revolution in South China*; Rolf G. Tiedemann, 'Rural Unrest in North China, 1868–1900: With Particular Reference to South Shandong', unpublished PhD thesis, University of London, 1992.

6 R. H. Tawney, *Land and Labour in China* (London: George Allen and Unwin, 1932), p. 77. On the famine trope see Walter H. Mallory, *China: Land of Famine* (New York: American Geographical Society, 1926).

7 On the modern history of ideas of the Chinese 'peasant' see Charles W. Hayford, 'The Storm over the Peasant: Orientalism and Rhetoric in Construing China', in Jeffrey Cox and Shelton Stromquist (eds), *Contesting the Master Narrative: Essays in Social History* (Iowa City, IA: University of Iowa Press, 1998), pp. 150–72; Myron L. Cohen, 'Cultural and Political Inventions in Modern China: The Case of the Chinese "Peasant"', *Daedalus* 122:2 (1993), pp. 151–70.

8 Tawney, *Land and Labour in China*, p. 25; Maxine Berg, *A Woman in History: Eileen Power, 1889* (Cambridge: Cambridge University Press, 1996), pp. 86–7, 105.

9 On the debate about the state of the rural economy in modern history see the discussions in: R. Bin Wong, 'Chinese Economic History and Development: A Note on the Myers-Huang Exchange', *Journal of Asian Studies* 51:3 (1992), pp. 600–611; Thomas G. Rawski and Lillian M. Li (eds), *Chinese History in Economic Perspective* (Berkeley, CA: University of California Press, 1992).

10 C. Martin Wilbur, *The Nationalist Revolution in China, 1923–1928* (Cambridge: Cambridge University Press, 1983), pp. 117–24; Robert C. North and Xenia J. Eudin, *M. N. Roy's Mission to China: The Communist-Kuomintang Split of 1927* (Berkeley, CA: University of California Press, 1963).

11 Joseph W. Esherick, *The Origins of the Boxer Uprising* (Berkeley, CA: University of California Press, 1987); Robert Hart, *These from the Land of Sinim: Essays on the Chinese Question* (London: Chapman and Hall, 1901), pp. 54–5.

12 Galbiati, *P'eng P'ai and the Hai-Lu-Feng Soviet*, p. 129.

13 Charles W. Hayford, *To the People: James Yen and Village China* (New York: Columbia University Press, 1990), pp. 53–9.

14 Gerald W. Berkley, 'The Canton Peasant Movement Training Institute', *Modern China* 1:2 (1975), pp. 161–79.

15 C. Martin Wilbur and Julie Lien-ying How, *Missionaries of Revolution: Soviet Advisers and Nationalist China 1920–1927* (Cambridge, MA: Harvard University Press, 1989).

16 Galbiati, *P'eng P'ai and the Hai-Lu-Feng Soviet*, pp. 278–83. See also Hofheinz, *Broken Wave*, pp. 234–62.

17 Galbiati, *P'eng P'ai and the Hai-Lu-Feng Soviet*, p. 294.

18 See, for example, James Ryan, *Lenin's Terror: The Ideological Origins of Early Soviet State Violence* (London: Routledge, 2012); Arno Mayer, *The Furies: Violence and Terror in the French and Russian Revolutions* (Princeton, NJ: Princeton University Press, 2000).

19 See, for example, Wang Qisheng, 'Dangyuan, dang zuzhi yu xiangcun shehui: Guangdong de Zhonggong dixia dang (1927–1932 nian)' ('The Membership and Organization of the Party and Rural Society: The CCP's Underground Party in Guangdong Province, 1927–1932'), *Jindai shi yanjiu* 5 (2002), pp. 1–44; Gordon Y. M. Chan, 'The Communists in Rural Guangdong, 1928–1936', *Journal of the Royal Asiatic Society* 13:1 (2003), pp. 77–97.

20 Gregor Benton, *Mountain Fires: The Red Army's Three-Year War in South China, 1934–1938* (Berkeley, CA: University of California Press, 1992).

21 Wilbur, *Nationalist Revolution in China*, pp. 65–8; Wilbur and How, *Missionaries of Revolution*, pp. 263–6.

22 All quotations here come from the text of 'Report on the Peasant Movement in Hunan', in Stuart R. Schram (ed.), *Mao's Road to Power: Revolutionary Writings, 1912–1949, Volume 2: National Revolution to Social Revolution, December 1920–June 1927* (Armonk, NY: M. E. Sharpe, 1997), pp. 429–64.

23 Stuart Schram, *The Thought of Mao Tse-tung* (Cambridge: Cambridge University Press, 1989), pp. 35–6; Dan N. Jacobs, *Borodin: Stalin's Man in China* (Cambridge, MA: Harvard University Press, 1981), pp. 253–4.

24 Randall E. Stross, *The Stubborn Earth: American Agriculturalists on Chinese Soil, 1898–1937* (Berkeley, CA: University of California Press, 1988), p. 171; Hilary Spurling, *Pearl Buck in China: Journey to the Good Earth* (New York: Simon and Schuster, 2010), pp. 157–61.

25 Henrietta Harrison, *The Making of the Republican Citizen: Political Ceremonies and Symbols in China, 1911–1929* (Oxford: Oxford University Press, 2000).

26 Tong Lam, *A Passion for Facts: Social Surveys and the Construction of the Chinese Nation-State, 1900–1949* (Berkeley, CA: University of California Press, 2011). The quotation is from Arthur H. Smith, *Village Life in China: A Study in Sociology* (New York: Fleming H. Revell Co., 1899), p. 17.

27 Stross, *Stubborn Earth*, pp. 110–15, 161–88; Spurling, *Pearl Buck in China*.

28 John Lossing Buck, *Chinese Farm Economy* (Chicago, IL: University of Chicago Press, 1930), pp. 426–7; Stross, *Stubborn Earth*, p. 166.

29 Peter Conn, *Pearl S. Buck: A Cultural Biography* (Cambridge: Cambridge University Press, 1996), pp. 64–6.

30 SOAS Library, Council for World Mission, London Missionary Society Archives, China personal, Box 13, Marjorie Clements letters, passim; quotation from letter to Mrs May, 15 December 1932.

and Republican China', *Comparative Studies in Society and History* 49:1 (2007), pp. 143–69.

36 Circular no. 4304, 9 September 1931, *Documents Illustrative of the Origin, Development, and Activities of the Chinese Customs Service*, vol. 4 (Shanghai: Statistical Department of the Inspectorate General of Customs, 1939), pp. 52–97.

37 Bridie Andrews, *The Making of Modern Chinese Medicine, 1850–1960* (Vancouver: University of British Columbia Press, 2014); *NCH*, 16 December 1930, p. 375.

38 Fung, *Diplomacy of Imperial Retreat*, pp. 201–14.

39 Killearn Diary, 1 October 1930; Pamela Atwell, *British Mandarins and Chinese Reformers: The British Administration of Weihaiwei (1898–1930) and the Territory's Return to Chinese Rule* (Hong Kong: Oxford University Press, 1985).

40 *NCH*, 11 November 1930, p. 188.

41 Robert Bickers, 'British Concessions and Chinese Cities, 1910s–1930s', in Billy K. L. So and Madeleine Zelin (eds), *New Narratives of Urban Space in Republican Chinese Cities: Emerging Social, Legal and Governance Orders* (Leiden: Brill, 2013), pp. 157–95.

42 See T. R. Jernigan, *Shooting in China* (Shanghai: Methodist Publishing House, 1908), and Henling Thomas Wade, *With Boat and Gun in the Yangtze Valley*, 2nd edition (Shanghai: Shanghai Mercury, 1910), and the pages of *The China Journal of Science and Arts*, published in Shanghai from 1923 to 1941. There were 150 houseboats registered at Shanghai in 1910: Wade, *With Boat and Gun*, pp. 100–101, on the idylls of which see J. O. P. Bland, *Houseboat Days in China* (London: Edward Arnold, 1909).

43 Wade, *With Boat and Gun*, p. 116.

44 SOAS, MS 186361, Royal Institute of International Affairs archives, Far East Department, China: Political, Box 9, Minutes of a Meeting held at Chatham House, 12 July 1929.

45 Memorandum of 27 May 1931: TNA, FO 371/15460, F2899; Akira Iriye, *After Imperialism: The Search for a New Order in the Far East, 1921–1931* (Cambridge, MA: Harvard University Press, 1965), pp. 286–9.

46 Robert Bickers, 'Death of a Young Shanghailander: The Thorburn Case and the Defence of the British Treaty Ports in China in 1931', *Modern Asian Studies* 30:2 (1996), pp. 271–300.

47 Patricia Allan, *Shanghai Picture-Verse*, with illustrations by Sapajou (Shanghai: Kelly and Walsh, 1939); Sir Frederick Bourne, *Gardening in*

Shanghai for Amateurs (Shanghai: Kelly and Walsh, 1915); Arthur de Carle Sowerby, *A Guide to the Fauna and Flora of a Shanghai Garden* (Shanghai: The China Journal Publishing Co., 1939).

48 *NCH*, 2 June 1931, pp. 298, 305. By May 1932, having gone north as far as Shenyang, they had headed south to Guangzhou, after which reports cease: *NCH*, 3 May 1932, p. 338. One of the pair may have been running a bar in Kunming during the war.

49 'Probe Reveals Britisher Took to Opium Pipe', *The China Press*, 20 March 1936, p. 1.

50 Taylor, *Generalissimo*, pp. 78-83; C. Martin Wilbur, *The Nationalist Revolution in China, 1923-1928* (Cambridge: Cambridge University Press, 1983), pp. 78-80; Shuge Wei, 'Beyond the Front Line: China's Rivalry with Japan in the English-Language Press over the Ji'nan Incident, 1928', *Modern Asian Studies* 48:1 (2014), pp. 188-224.

51 Report by Flt. Lt. O'Gowan, 7 May 1928: TNA, FO 228/3807.

52 Taylor, *Generalissimo*, pp. 79-82.

53 On the Japanese communities see: Peter Duus, Ramon H. Myers and Mark R. Peattie (eds), *The Japanese Informal Empire in China, 1895-1937* (Princeton, NJ: Princeton University Press, 2014); Christian Henriot, ' "Little Japan" in Shanghai: An Insulated Community, 1875-1945', in Robert Bickers and Christian Henriot (eds), *New Frontiers: Imperialism's New Communities in East Asia, 1842-1953* (Manchester: Manchester University Press, 2000), 146-69; Joshua A. Fogel, ' "Shanghai-Japan": The Japanese Residents' Association of Shanghai', *Journal of Asian Studies* 59:4 (2000), pp. 927-50. The occupation breakdown comes from internal data derived from the 1935 SMC census: SMA, U1-4-1227.

54 Peter Fleming, *One's Company* (London: Jonathan Cape, 1934), p. 175; Arnold J. Toynbee, *A Journey to China, or Things which are Seen* (London: Constable & Co., 1931), p. 202. On the development of Dalian see Robert John Perrins, ' "Great Connections": The Creation of a City, Dalian, 1905-1931: China and Japan on the Liaodong Peninsula', unpublished PhD thesis, University of York, 1997; and Christian A. Hess, 'From Colonial Jewel to Socialist Metropolis: Dalian, 1895-1955', unpublished PhD thesis, University of California San Diego, 2006.

55 Fogel, ' "Shanghai-Japan" ', pp. 930-31.

56 Toynbee, *Journey to China*, pp. 204-6; see also Louise Young, *Japan's Total Empire: Manchuria and the Culture of Wartime Imperialism* (Berkeley, CA: University of California Press, 1998), pp. 89-93.

57 To be fair, there were also foreign volunteer militias in several cities,

most notably in Shanghai, and there too the Municipal Council oversaw the operation from January 1927 onwards of a Russian Regiment, a paid company of Russian nationals with strong links to former Tsarist army formations: I. I. Kounin, *Eighty-Five Years of the SVC* (Shanghai: Cosmopolitan Press, 1938). None of these units bore any resemblance to the 10,000-strong Kwantung Army. This was its effective strength in 1931, and it was dramatically increased in size thereafter: Alvin D. Coox, 'The Kwantung Army Dimension', in Duus, Myers and Peattie (eds), *Japanese Informal Empire in China*, pp. 395–428.

58 On railway controversies in the 1929 conflict see the essays in Bruce A. Elleman and Stephen Kotkin (eds), *Manchurian Railways and the Opening of China: An International History* (Armonk, NY: M. E. Sharpe, 2010). A contemporary survey of the CER is provided by *North Manchuria and the Chinese Eastern Railway* (Harbin: C. E. R. Printing Office, 1924).

59 Karl Gerth, *China Made: Consumer Culture and the Creation of the Nation* (Cambridge, MA: Harvard University Asia Center, 2003).

60 Donald A. Jordan, *Chinese Boycotts versus Japanese Bombs: The Failure of China's 'Revolutionary Diplomacy', 1931–32* (Ann Arbor, MI: University of Michigan Press, 1991).

61 This section draws on Mark R. Peattie, *Ishiwara Kanji and Japan's Confrontation with the West* (Princeton, NJ: Princeton University Press, 1975); Rana Mitter, *The Manchurian Myth: Nationalism, Resistance, and Collaboration in Modern China* (Berkeley, CA: University of California Press, 2000); Yoshihisa Tak Matsusaka, *The Making of Japanese Manchuria, 1904–1932* (Cambridge, MA: Harvard University Asia Center, 2001).

62 Mitter, *Manchurian Myth*, pp. 20–71.

63 Mitter, *Manchurian Myth*, p. 75. See also Brooks, *Japan's Imperial Diplomacy*, pp. 140–42, on violent Japanese military threats against their own consuls.

64 It has, however, finally secured the disinterested analysis that it deserved in Prasenjit Duara, *Sovereignty and Authenticity: Manchukuo and the East Asian Modern* (Lanham, MD: Rowman and Littlefield, 2003).

65 Donald A. Jordan, *China's Trial by Fire: The Shanghai War of 1932* (Ann Arbor, MI: University of Michigan Press, 2001).

66 Thorne, *Limits of Foreign Policy*, pp. 276–83.

67 Duara, *Sovereignty and Authenticity*; Young, *Japan's Total Empire*.

68 *From Emperor to Citizen: The Autobiography of Aisin-Gioro Pu Yi*, trans. W. J. F. Jenner (Oxford: Oxford University Press, 1987), pp. 275–9; *NCH*, 7 March 1932, p. 362.

69 Albert Feuerwerker, *The Foreign Establishment in China in the Early Twentieth Century* (Ann Arbor, MI: Center for Chinese Studies, University of Michigan, 1976), p. 101.

5. CHINA IN THE MIND

1 Dowdy: *Manchester Guardian*, 28 November 1935, p. 9; Bell: *New Statesman*, 11 January 1936, p. 49; Watson: *New Statesman*, 25 April 1936, p. 630.

2 F. T. Cheng, *East and West: Episodes in a Sixty Years' Journey* (London: Hutchinson, 1951), p. 161; Jason Steuber, 'The Exhibition of Chinese Art at Burlington House, London, 1935–36', *The Burlington Magazine* 148 (August 2006), pp. 528–36.

3 On 'national extinction' see Rebecca E. Karl, *Staging the World: Chinese Nationalism at the Turn of the Twentieth Century* (Durham, NC: Duke University Press, 2002); on strategic logic see T. G. Otte, *The China Question: Great Power Rivalry and British Isolation, 1894–1905* (Oxford: Oxford University Press, 2007); more widely, Robert Bickers, *The Scramble for China: Foreign Devils in the Qing Empire, 1832–1914* (London: Allen Lane, 2011), pp. 344–5.

4 Gray Tuttle, *Tibetan Buddhists in the Making of Modern China* (New York: Columbia University Press, 2005); and Andrew D. W. Forbes, *Warlords and Muslims in Chinese Central Asia: A Political History of Republican Sinkiang, 1911–1949* (Cambridge: Cambridge University Press, 1986).

5 James Reardon-Anderson, *Reluctant Pioneers: China's Expansion Northward, 1644–1937* (Stanford, CA: Stanford University Press, 2005), pp. 255–61; Prasenjit Duara, *Sovereignty and Authenticity: Manchukuo and the East Asian Modern* (Lanham, MD: Rowman and Littlefield, 2003), pp. 56–8; *Report of the Commission of Enquiry* (Geneva: League of Nations, 1932), pp. 29, 38, 127.

6 J. L. Cranmer-Byng (ed.), *An Embassy to China: Being the Journal Kept by Lord Macartney during his Embassy to the Emperor Ch'ienlung, 1793–1794* (London: Longmans, 1961), p. 212.

7 Some of the extensive and still-growing literature on this includes: A. W. Appleton, *A Cycle of Cathay: The Chinese Vogue in England during*

the 17th and 18th Centuries (New York: Columbia University Press, 1951); David Beevers (ed.), *Chinese Whispers: Chinoiserie in Britain, 1650–1930* (Brighton: Royal Pavilion and Museums, Brighton and Hove, 2008); David Porter, *The Chinese Taste in Eighteenth-Century England* (Cambridge: Cambridge University Press, 2010).

8 Edward A. Ross, 'Sociological Observations in Inner China', *The American Journal of Sociology*, 16:6 (1911), p. 721, quoted in Charles W. Hayford, '*The Good Earth*, Revolution and the American Raj in China', in Elizabeth J. Lipscomb et al. (eds), *The Several Worlds of Pearl S. Buck: Essays Presented at a Centennial Symposium, Randolph-Macon Woman's College, March 26–28, 1992* (Westport, CT: Greenwood Press, 1994), p. 22.

9 T. H. Barrett, *Singular Listlessness: A Short History of Chinese Books and British Scholars* (London: Wellsweep, 1989).

10 J. O. P. Bland, *China: The Pity of It* (London: William Heinemann, 1932), p. 2.

11 Rodney Gilbert, *What's Wrong with China* (London: John Murray, 1926), pp. 41, 86.

12 Stimulating surveys include Nicholas Clifford, '*A Truthful Impression of the Country*': *British and American Travel Writing in China, 1880–1949* (Ann Arbor, MI: University of Michigan Press, 2001); Douglas Kerr and Julia Kuehn (eds), *A Century of Travels in China: Critical Essays on Travel Writing from the 1840s to the 1940s* (Hong Kong: Hong Kong University Press, 2007).

13 The exception was George Morrison, *The Times* correspondent from 1897 to 1912.

14 This paragraph draws on Emmanuel Cooper, *Bernard Leach: Life and Work* (New Haven, CT: Yale University Press, 2003), pp. 87–113, quotations from pp. 90, 93.

15 For a survey of the evolution of attitudes in China towards the Dunhuang expeditions see Justin M. Jacobs, 'Confronting Indiana Jones: Chinese Nationalism, Historical Imperialism, and the Criminalization of Aurel Stein and the Raiders of Dunhuang, 1899–1944', in Sherman Cochran and Paul G. Pickowicz (eds), *China on the Margins* (Ithaca, NY: Cornell University Press, 2010), pp. 65–90. For an overview of Stein's career see Susan Whitfield, *Aurel Stein on the Silk Road* (London: British Museum Press, 2004).

16 Quote in Minna Törmä, *Enchanted by Lohans: Osvald Sirén's Journey into Chinese Art* (Hong Kong: Hong Kong University Press, 2013), p. 58.

17   Charles W. Hayford, 'Chinese and American Characteristics: Arthur H. Smith and His China Book', in Suzanne Wilson Barnett and John King Fairbank (eds), *Christianity in China: Early Protestant Missionary Writings* (Cambridge, MA: Harvard University Press, 1985), pp. 155–74.

18   Krystyn R. Moon, *Yellowface: Creating the Chinese in American Popular Music and Performance, 1850s–1920s* (New Brunswick, NJ: Rutgers University Press, 2005); Anne Veronica Witchard, *Thomas Burke's Dark Chinoiserie: Limehouse Nights and the Queer Spell of Chinatown* (Farnham: Ashgate, 2009).

19   On Burke's Limehouse see Witchard, *Thomas Burke's Dark Chinoiserie.*

20   See Marek Kohn, *Dope Girls: The Birth of the British Drug Underground* (London: Lawrence and Wishart, 1992).

21   *The Play Pictorial* 248 (November 1922), p. 93.

22   J. Dyer Ball, *Things Chinese: or, Notes Connected with China* (1892) (Shanghai: Kelly and Walsh, 1925), 5th edition, revised by E. T. C. Werner. This section draws on Robert Bickers, *Britain in China: Community, Culture, and Colonialism* (Manchester: Manchester University Press, 1999), chapter 2, pp. 22–66.

23   See Moon, *Yellowface.*

24   On this topic see Akira Iriye, *Cultural Internationalism and World Order* (Baltimore, MD: Johns Hopkins University Press, 1997), and his *Global Community: The Role of International Organizations in the Making of the Contemporary World* (Berkeley, CA: University of California Press, 2002).

25   C. C. Wang (Wang Jiazhen), quoted in Alison Adcock Kaufman, 'In Pursuit of Equality and Respect: China's Diplomacy and the League of Nations', *Modern China* 40:4 (2014), p. 22.

26   L. T. Chen (Chen Liting), 'Preface', in *Symposium on Chinese Culture: Prepared for the Fourth Biennial Conference of the Institute of Pacific Relations* (Shanghai: China Institute of Pacific Relations, 1931).

27   *NCH*, 27 October 1931, pp. 125–6.

28   Cai Yuanpei quoted in Danian Hu, *China and Albert Einstein: The Reception of the Physicist and His Theory in China, 1917–1979* (Cambridge, MA: Harvard University Press, 2005), pp. 138–9.

29   *Report of the Commission of Enquiry*, p. 138.

30   Steuber, 'The Exhibition of Chinese Art at Burlington House, London, 1935–36', pp. 528–36.

31   Yiyou Wang, 'The Louvre from China: A Critical Study of C. T. Loo and the Framing of Chinese Art in the United States, 1915–1950',

unpublished PhD thesis, Ohio University, 2007, pp. 46–9; Di Yin Lu, 'Collecting China: Buying a Civilization in the Chinese Art Market, 1911–1945', unpublished paper, 2008. On the wider history of collecting at this time see, in addition to other work cited in this chapter, Warren I. Cohen, *East Asian Art and American Culture: A Study in International Relations* (New York: Columbia University Press, 1992); Judith Tybil Green, 'Britain's Chinese Collections: Private Collecting and the Invention of Chinese Art', unpublished DPhil thesis, University of Sussex, 2002; Valérie A. M. Jurgens, 'The Karlbeck Syndicate 1930–1934: Collecting and Scholarship on Chinese Art in Sweden and Britain', unpublished PhD thesis, School of Oriental and African Studies, 2010; Lara Jaishree Netting, *A Perpetual Fire: John C. Ferguson and His Quest for Chinese Art and Culture* (Hong Kong: Hong Kong University Press, 2013).

32 Memorandum dated 3 February 1934, quoted in Stacey Pierson, *Collectors, Collections and Museums: The Field of Chinese Ceramics in Britain, 1560–1960* (Bern: Peter Lang, 2007), p. 156. The exhibition is discussed in Pierson's chapter 3, pp. 154–66, and in Ellen Huang, 'China's China: Jingdezhen Porcelain and the Production of Art in the Nineteenth Century', unpublished PhD thesis, University of California San Diego, 2008, pp. 14–79.

33 *The New Yorker*, 28 December 1935, p. 53.

34 Jeannette Shambaugh Elliott, with David Shambaugh, *The Odyssey of China's Imperial Art Treasures* (Seattle, WA: University of Washington Press, 2005), pp. 73–81.

35 *NCH*, 10 April 1935, p. 57. The Shanghai exhibition has attracted recent critical analysis in its own right; see Guo Hui, 'Writing Chinese Art History in Early Twentieth-Century China', unpublished PhD thesis, Leiden University, 2010, pp. 138–69. On Guomindang relations with Du Yuesheng see Brian G. Martin, *The Shanghai Green Gang: Politics and Organized Crime* (Berkeley, CA: University of California Press, 1996).

36 *NCH*, 30 January 1935, p. 172; Frances Wood, 'Paul Pelliot, Aurel Stein and Chinese Opposition to the Royal Academy's International Exhibition of Chinese Art 1935–36', in Helen Wang (ed.), *Sir Aurel Stein: Colleagues and Collections* (London: British Museum Press, 2012); translations of the response to Beijing's protest, and of the sale rumours, are in TNA, FO 370/477, file 198.

37 R. C. Clive to S. Gaselee, 8 April 1935, and file: TNA, FO 370/477.

38 Cohen, *East Asian Art and American Culture*, p. 122.

39 Letter dated 3 December 1935, in Catherine Speck (ed.), *Heysen to Heysen: Selected Letters of Hans Heysen and Nora Heysen* (Canberra: National Library of Australia, 2011), pp. 49–50.

40 *Vogue*, 1 December 1935, p. 73.

41 Summaries in *NCH*, 28 December 1935, p. 537, and 4 December 1935, p. 414; *Manchester Guardian*, 16 October 1935, p. 10, and 31 January 1936, p. 8; *Daily Mail*, 18 May 1936, p. 25, and 23 July 1936, p. 9; *Times of India*, 11 August 1936, p. 12; *Western Daily News*, 8 April 1936, p. 13. For a study of the place of Chinese goods in British stores see Sarah Cheang, 'Selling China: Class, Gender and Orientalism at the Department Store', *Journal of Design History* 20:1 (2007), pp. 1–16.

42 *NCH*, 17 April 1935, p. 100, and 4 December 1935, p. 414.

43 Osbert Sitwell, *Escape with Me! An Oriental Sketchbook* (London: Macmillan, 1940), p. vii; George Kates, *The Years that were Fat: Peking, 1933–1940* (New York: Harper and Brothers, 1952), p. 8; John Blofeld, *City of Lingering Splendour: A Frank Account of Old Peking's Exotic Pleasures* (London: Hutchinson, 1961); Harold Acton, *Memoirs of an Aesthete* (London: Methuen, 1948); D. E. Mungello, *Western Queers in China: Flight to the Land of Oz* (Lanham, MD: Rowman and Littlefield, 2012); John King Fairbank, *Chinabound: A Fifty-Year Memoir* (New York: Harper and Row, 1982). See also here Patricia Laurence, *Lily Briscoe's Chinese Eyes: Bloomsbury, Modernism, and China* (Columbia, SC: University of South Carolina Press, 2003).

44 Cheng, *East and West*, p. 157.

45 The journey made some queasy, for the liner carrying the collection briefly ran aground at Gibraltar, vindicating for many in China their opposition on safety grounds to despatching the collections overseas. Escorted by a Royal Navy cruiser, the vessel carrying the cargo finally reached Shanghai safely in May 1936: *NCH*, 20 May 1936, p. 332.

46 *Manchester Guardian*, 4 April 1936, p. 15; *The Observer*, 5 April 1936, p. 10.

47 *The China Critic* 1:1, 31 May 1928, p. 1. For studies of the journal see Shuang Shen, *Cosmopolitan Publics: Anglophone Print Culture in Semi-Colonial Shanghai* (New Brunswick, NJ: Rutgers University Press, 2009), and the special issue of *China Heritage Quarterly* 30/31 (2012), http://www.chinaheritagequarterly.org/ (accessed September 2015).

48 On *T'ien Hsia* see Shen, *Cosmopolitan Publics*, and *China Heritage Quarterly* 19 (2009), http://www.chinaheritagequarterly.org/editorial.php?issue=019 (accessed September 2015).

49 'Lin Yu-t'ang', in Howard L. Boorman, *Biographical Dictionary of Republican China*, vol. 2 (New York: Columbia University Press, 1968), pp. 387–9; *NCH*, 26 July 1919, p. 230, 23 August 1919, p. 494; the description of the treatment of the students comes from fellow passenger Chih Meng (Meng Zhi), quoted in Madeline Y. Hsu, *The Good Immigrants: How the Yellow Peril Became the Model Minority* (Princeton, NJ: Princeton University Press, 2015), p. 72; more widely on this see Stacey Bieler, *'Patriots' or 'Traitors'? A History of American-Educated Chinese Students* (2004) (Abingdon: Routledge, 2015).

50 Harold R. Isaacs, *Scratches on Our Minds: American Images of China and India* (New York: John Day, 1958), p. 156.

51 Diran John Sohigian, 'Contagion of Laughter: The Rise of the Humor Phenomenon in Shanghai in the 1930s', *positions* 15:1 (2007), pp. 137–63.

52 Lin Yutang, *My Country and My People* (New York: John Day, 1935), pp. 5–15.

53 *NCH*, 26 December 1934, p. 513; Diana Yeh, *The Happy Hsiungs: Performing China and the Struggle for Modernity* (Hong Kong: Hong Kong University Press, 2014).

54 Chiang Yee, *The Chinese Eye: An Interpretation of Chinese Painting* (London: Methuen, 1935), p. 4; on Chiang see Da Zheng, *Chiang Yee, the Silent Traveller from the East: A Cultural Biography* (New Brunswick, NJ: Rutgers University Press, 2010), pp. 44–82.

55 Chiang Yee, *The Story of Ming* (London: Puffin, 1945); Chiang Yee, *Lo Cheng: The Boy who Wouldn't Keep Still* (London: Puffin, 1945).

56 It was helped in this case by Communist Party infighting, which led to betrayal of the group arrested: Frederic Wakeman Jr, *Policing Shanghai, 1927–1937* (Berkeley, CA: University of California Press, 1995), p. 174; Wang-chi Wong, *Politics and Literature in Shanghai: The Chinese League of Left-Wing Writers, 1930–1936* (Manchester: Manchester University Press, 1991), pp. 100–106; *Living China: Modern Chinese Short Stories*, compiled and edited by Edgar Snow (London: George G. Harrap, 1936).

57 John Sedgwick and Michael Pokorny, 'The Film Business in the United States and Britain during the 1930s', *Economic History Review* 58:1 (2005), p. 82.

58 Data from R. C. North, 'The Chinese Motion Picture Market', in US Department of Commerce (ed.), *Trade Information Bulletin* 467 (1927). For a survey see Zhiwei Xiao, 'Hollywood in China, 1897–1950: A Preliminary Survey', *The Chinese Historical Review* 12:1 (2005), pp. 71–95.

59 Zhiwei Xiao, 'Anti-Imperialism and Film Censorship during the Nanjing Decade, 1927–1937', in Sheldon Hsiao-peng Lu (ed.), *Transnational Chinese Cinemas: Identity, Nationhood, Gender* (Honolulu: University of Hawai'i Press, 1997), pp. 35–57, quotation on p. 41.

60 See correspondence in TNA: FO 228/3801, Dossier 23J 1928; on Shu see Robert A. Bickers, 'New Light on Lao She, London, and the London Missionary Society, 1921–1929', *Modern Chinese Literature* 8:1/2 (1994), pp. 21–39.

61 Marie Cambon, 'The Dream Palaces of Shanghai: American Films in China's Largest Metropolis', unpublished MA thesis, Simon Fraser University, 1986, pp. 88–9; Xiao, 'Anti-Imperialism and Film Censorship during the Nanjing Decade, 1927–1937', pp. 41–2; for a survey of the developing censorship infrastructure see Zhiwei Xiao, 'Prohibition, Politics and Nation-Building: A History of Film Censorship in China', in Daniel Biltereyst and Roel Vande Winkel (eds), *Silencing Cinema: Film Censorship around the World* (New York: Palgrave Macmillan, 2013), pp. 109–30.

62 Eric Smoodin, *Regarding Frank Capra: Audience, Celebrity, and American Film Studies, 1930–1960* (Durham, NC: Duke University Press, 2004), pp. 51–75, quotations from p. 72.

63 Quoted in Hye Seung Chung, *Hollywood Asian: Philip Ahn and the Politics of Cross-Ethnic Performance* (Philadelphia, PA: Temple University Press, 2006), pp. 100–101; on Paramount's business in China see Xiao, 'Hollywood in China', p. 81.

64 *Film Daily*, 9 November 1932, p. 8, and 2 December 1932, p. 10. Syndicated articles about his activities can be found in the *Bradford Era*, 22 January 1934; *San Antonio Light*, 12 November 1933; *Variety*, 6 January 1934, 9 January 1934, 29 August 1934, 14 September 1934. 'China Roars' was to have been filmed on location, but was never made.

65 Dorothy Jones, *The Portrayal of China and India on the American Screen, 1896–1955: The Evolution of Chinese and Indian Themes, Locales, and Characters as Portrayed on the American Screen* (Cambridge, MA: Center for International Studies, MIT, 1955), pp. 43–7; Zhiwei Xiao, 'Nationalism, Orientalism, and an Unequal Treatise of Ethnography: The Making of *The Good Earth*', in Susie Lan Cassel (ed.), *The Chinese in America: A History from Gold Mountain to the New Millennium* (Walnut Creek, CA: AltaMira Press, 2002), pp. 274–90; *FRUS*, 1929, vol. 2, pp. 620–22.

66 On Tu see *NCH*, 10 November 1928, p. 245; and a biographical sketch in the (San Bernadino) *Sun*, 15 December 1935.

67 Mark A. Vieira, *Irving Thalberg: Boy Wonder to Producer Prince* (Berkeley, CA: University of California Press, 2010), p. 326. Both men were in California in the late summer of 1936.

68 *Chinese Digest*, 30 October 1936, p. 9.

69 Xiao, 'Nationalism, Orientalism and an Unequal Treatise of Ethnography', pp. 282–4; the Wodehouse review was widely syndicated, see *Salt Lake Tribune*, 7 February 1937.

70 Jones, *Portrayal of China and India*, p. 47; Isaacs, *Scratches on Our Minds*, pp. 155–8.

71 For discussions of this see in particular Joshua A. Fogel, *The Literature of Travel in the Japanese Rediscovery of China, 1862–1945* (Stanford, CA: Stanford University Press, 1996), and Joshua A. Fogel, *Articulating the Sinosphere: Sino-Japanese Relations in Space and Time* (Cambridge, MA: Harvard University Press, 2009).

72 Lin, *My Country and My People*, p. 11.

73 Stephen R. MacKinnon and Oris Friesen, *China Reporting: An Oral History of American Journalism in the 1930s and 1940s* (Berkeley, CA: University of California Press, 1990), is a good survey. See also Paul French, *Through the Looking Glass: China's Foreign Journalists from Opium Wars to Mao* (Hong Kong: Hong Kong University Press, 2009); Clifford, 'A Truthful Impression of the Country', pp. 143–80.

74 Rana Mitter, *China's War with Japan, 1937–1945: The Struggle for Survival* (London: Allen Lane, 2013), pp. 73–91.

6. MONKEYS RIDING GREYHOUNDS

1 For the fullest accounts see NARA, RG 263, D8298/45, and *Shenbao*, 2 March 1939, p. 9; translated leaflet text as printed in *China Weekly Review*, 4 March 1939, p. 12; *Le Journal de Shanghai*, 2 March 1939, pp. 1 and 6.

2 'Translation of a handbill, copies of which were distributed in the Louza district in the evening of March 1, 1939, when bombs were thrown': NARA, RG 263, D8298/45. For more on this world of 'special' work see Frederic Wakeman Jr., *Spymaster: Dai Li and the Chinese Secret Service* (Berkeley, CA: University of California Press, 2003).

3 In discussing the conflict this chapter draws on Rana Mitter, *China's War with Japan, 1937–1945: The Struggle for Survival* (London: Allen Lane, 2013).

4 Mitter, *China's War with Japan*, pp. 119-40, 157-63. Eyewitness accounts of the events at Nanjing include Erwin Wickert (ed.), *The Good German of Nanking: The Diaries of John Rabe* (New York: Knopf, 1998), and Timothy Brook (ed.), *Documents on the Rape of Nanking* (Ann Arbor, MI: University of Michigan Press, 1999). Accounts of the continuing controversies about Nanjing can be found in Joshua A. Fogel (ed.), *The Nanjing Massacre in History and Historiography* (Berkeley, CA: University of California Press, 2000).

5 Shuge Wei, 'News as a Weapon: Hollington Tong and the Formation of the Guomindang Centralized Foreign Propaganda System, 1937-1938', *Twentieth-Century China* 39:2 (2014), pp. 118-43; Stephen R. MacKinnon, *Wuhan, 1938: War, Refugees, and the Making of Modern China* (Berkeley, CA: University of California Press, 2008), p. 105; 'Here War is Simple', in W. H. Auden and Christopher Isherwood, *Journey to a War* (London: Faber and Faber, 1939), p. 274.

6 Patricia Stranahan, *Underground: The Shanghai Communist Party and the Politics of Survival, 1927-1937* (Lanham, MD: Rowman and Littlefield, 1998), and Frederic Wakeman Jr, *Policing Shanghai, 1927-1937* (Berkeley, CA: University of California Press, 1995), pp. 132-61.

7 Key work on Shanghai during the war includes: Christian Henriot and Wen-hsin Yeh (eds), *In the Shadow of the Rising Sun: Shanghai under Japanese Occupation* (Cambridge: Cambridge University Press, 2004); Frederic Wakeman Jr., *The Shanghai Badlands: Wartime Terrorism and Urban Crime, 1937-1941* (Cambridge: Cambridge University Press, 1996); Wen-hsin Yeh (ed.), *Wartime Shanghai* (London: Routledge, 1998).

8 F. C. Jones, *Shanghai and Tientsin* (London: Royal Institute of International Affairs, 1940); Robert W. Barnett, *Economic Shanghai: Hostage to Politics, 1937-1941* (New York: Institute of Pacific Relations, 1941).

9 Christian Henriot, *Shanghai, 1927-1937: Municipal Power, Locality and Modernization*, trans. Noël Castelino (Berkeley, CA: University of California Press, 1993); Wakeman, *Policing Shanghai*; see also Mark Elvin, 'The Administration of Shanghai, 1905-1914', in Mark Elvin and G. William Skinner (eds), *The Chinese City between Two Worlds* (Stanford, CA: Stanford University Press, 1974), pp. 239-62.

10 Kerrie MacPherson, 'Designing China's Urban Future: The Greater Shanghai Plan, 1927-1937', *Planning Perspectives* 5 (1990), pp. 39-62.

11 On the European refugee experience see, amongst others: Gao Bei, *Shanghai Sanctuary: Chinese and Japanese Policy toward European Jewish Refugees during World War II* (New York: Oxford University Press, 2013); Antonia Finnane, *Far from Where? Jewish Journeys from Shanghai to Australia* (Carlton South: University of Melbourne Press, 1999); Marcia Reynders Ristaino, *Port of Last Resort: The Diaspora Communities of Shanghai* (Stanford, CA: Stanford University Press, 2001); James R. Ross, *Escape to Shanghai: A Jewish Community in China* (New York: Free Press, 1994).

12 Maurine Karns and Pat Patterson, *Shanghai: High Lights, Low Lights, Tael Lights* (Shanghai: Tridon Press, 1936), p. 40.

13 Edgar Snow, 'Americans in Shanghai', *The American Mercury* 20 (1930), p. 438.

14 Robert Bickers, *The Scramble for China: Foreign Devils in the Qing Empire, 1832–1914* (London: Allen Lane, 2011), p. 367.

15 Kathryn Meyer and Terry Parssinen, *Webs of Smoke: Smugglers, Warlords, Spies, and the History of the International Drug Trade* (Lanham, MD: Rowman and Littlefield, 1998), p. 164; *NCH*, 17 December 1921, p. 767.

16 *The Times*, 17 March 1928, p. 7.

17 Stirling Fessenden, 'Circular for Foreign Members: Hai Alai', 1 October 1930, enclosure in Shanghai no. 299, 5 November 1930, TNA: FO 371/15485. The controversy is explored in detail in Ning Jennifer Chang, 'Pure Sport or a Gambling Disgrace? Greyhound Racing and the Formation of Modern Shanghai', in Peter Zarrow (ed.), *Creating Chinese Modernity: Knowledge and Everyday Life, 1900–1940* (New York: Peter Lang, 2006), pp. 147–81; see also Frederic Wakeman Jr., 'Licensing Leisure: The Chinese Nationalists' Attempt to Regulate Shanghai, 1927–49', *Journal of Asian Studies* 54:1 (1995), pp. 19–42. Finances: T. P. Yang, 'Three Nights at the Dog-Race Course', *China Weekly Review*, 18 October 1930, pp. 245–6.

18 Interview with Frederick West, former station chief, Bubbling Well Station, 13 September 1996; Commissioner of Police to Secretary, SMC, 8 April 1929, U1-3-2660, SMA.

19 This paragraph draws on Brian G. Martin, *The Shanghai Green Gang: Politics and Organized Crime, 1919–1937* (Berkeley, CA: University of California Press, 1996), pp. 64–9, 73–4, 115–21; Fiori is quoted in Consul General J. F. Brenan to Sir Miles Lampson, 21 February 1931: TNA, FO 371/15485.

20 Calculated from Norman Miners, *Hong Kong under Imperial Rule, 1912–1941* (Hong Kong: Oxford University Press, 1987), p. 212.

21 Martin, *Shanghai Green Gang*, p. 115.

22 Council minutes, 21 May 1929, in SMA, U1-3-2660. Allman's wartime memoir tells the story of his Mexican responsibilities differently, as well it might: Norwood F. Allman, *Shanghai Lawyer* (New York: Whittlesey House, 1943).

23 Eileen P. Scully, *Bargaining with the State from Afar: American Citizenship in Treaty Port China, 1844–1942* (New York: Columbia University Press, 2001), pp. 187–92; *NCH*, 5 February 1936, p. 209; *NCH*, 24 July 1935, p. 139.

24 *Shanghai Evening Post and Mercury*, 9 September 1941; *NCDN*, 11 and 13 September 1941.

25 Barnett, *Economic Shanghai*; Lloyd E. Eastman, 'Facets of an Ambivalent Relationship: Smuggling, Puppets and Atrocities during the War, 1937–45', in Akira Iriye (ed.), *The Chinese and the Japanese: Essays in Political and Cultural Interactions* (Princeton, NJ: Princeton University Press, 1980), pp. 275–303; on Wang: Gerald E. Bunker, *The Peace Conspiracy: Wang Ching-wei and the China War, 1937–1941* (Cambridge, MA: Harvard University Press, 1972), and John Hunter Boyle, *China and Japan at War, 1937–1945: The Politics of Collaboration* (Stanford, CA: Stanford University Press, 1972).

26 Carroll Alcott, *My War with Japan* (New York: Henry Holt, 1943).

27 Shanghai Municipal Council, *Report for the Year 1938 and Budget for the Year 1939* (Shanghai: North-China Daily News and Herald, 1939).

28 In this section and throughout this chapter I draw on Andrew David Field, *Shanghai's Dancing World: Cabaret Culture and Urban Politics, 1919–1954* (Hong Kong: Chinese University Press, 2010), and James Farrer and Andrew David Field, *Shanghai Nightscapes: A Nocturnal Biography of a Global City* (Chicago, IL: University of Chicago Press, 2015).

29 Whitey Smith, with C. L. McDermott, *I Didn't Make a Million* (Manila: Philippine Education Co., 1956), p. 21.

30 Burnett Hershey, 'Jazz Latitude', *The New York Times Book Review and Magazine*, 25 June 1922, reprinted in Karl Koenig (ed.), *Jazz in Print, 1859–1929* (Hillsdale, New York: Pendragon Press, 2002), pp. 191–2.

31 Andrew F. Jones, 'Black Internationale: Notes on the Chinese Jazz Age', in E. Taylor Atkins (ed.), *Jazz Planet* (Jackson, MI: University Press

of Mississippi, 2003), pp. 225–43; E. Taylor Atkins, 'Jammin' on the Jazz Frontier: The Japanese Jazz Community in Interwar Shanghai', *Japanese Studies* 19:1 (1999), pp. 5–16; Szu-wei Chen, 'The Music Industry and Popular Song in 1930s and 1940s Shanghai: A Historical and Stylistic Analysis', unpublished PhD thesis, University of Stirling, 2007, pp. 153–4.

32 Henry Champly, *The Road to Shanghai: White Slave Traffic in Asia* (London: John Long, 1934), pp. 209 and 210. This was first published in 1933 in Paris, and went through at least thirty-eight editions and sales of 100,000 copies: Michael B. Miller, *Shanghai on the Métro: Spies, Intrigue, and the French between the Wars* (Berkeley, CA: University of California Press, 1994), pp. 181 and 246.

33 See Anne Frédérique Glaise, 'L'Évolution sanitaire et médicale de la Concession française de Shanghai entre 1850 et 1950', unpublished PhD thesis, Université Lumière Lyon 2, 2005, pp. 224–30; the extent of official involvement can be gauged from: Conseil d'administration municipale de la Concession française, *Compte rendu de la gestion pour l'exercice 1929–Budget 1930* (Shanghai: Imprimerie municipal, 1929), p. 16. On the Canidrome see also Buck Clayton, assisted by Nancy Miller Elliott, *Buck Clayton's Jazz World* (Basingstoke: Macmillan, 1986), pp. 69–76.

34 *China Press*, 15 April 1934, p. 5, and 22 May 1938, p. 32.

35 John Pal, *Shanghai Saga* (London: Jarrolds, 1963), pp. 159–60.

36 'Yellow' because deemed by its opponents as 'pornographic', which is the connotation delivered in Chinese: see Andrew F. Jones, *Yellow Music: Media Culture and Colonial Modernity in the Chinese Jazz Age* (Durham, NC: Duke University Press, 2001), p. 6; Szu-wei Chen, 'The Rise and Generic Features of Shanghai Popular Songs in the 1930s and 1940s', *Popular Music* 24:1 (2005), pp. 107–25; Carlton Benson, 'Back to Business as Usual: The Resurgence of Commercial Radio Broadcasting in *Gudao* Shanghai', in Henriot and Yeh (eds), *In the Shadow of the Rising Sun*, pp. 279–301.

37 Christian Henriot, *Prostitution and Sexuality in Shanghai: A Social History, 1849–1949* (Stanford, CA: Stanford University Press, 2001), p. 105.

38 Xiao Jianqing, *Manhua Shanghai* (*Shanghai in Cartoons*) (Shanghai: Shanghai jingwei shuju, 1936).

39 John A. Crespi (ed.), 'China's *Modern Sketch*: The Golden Era of Cartoon Art, 1934–1937', presents every page of most of the journal's issues, and three stimulating essays, on the MIT Visualizing Cultures platform, at http://ocw.mit.edu/ans7870/21f/21f.027/modern_sketch, accessed

September 2015. On Shanghai's cartooning world more widely see Paul Bevan, *A Modern Miscellany: Shanghai Cartoon Artists, Shao Xunmei's Circle and the Travels of Jack Chen, 1926–1938* (Leiden: Brill, 2016).

40 *Shidai manhua* 2 (February 1934), p. 28.

41 See the essays collected in Jason C. Kuo (ed.), *Visual Culture in Shanghai, 1850s–1930s* (Washington, DC: New Academia Publishing, 2007).

42 Quoted in R. Keith Schoppa, *Twentieth-Century China: A History in Documents* (New York: Oxford University Press, 2011), p. 80.

43 Hanchao Lu, *Beyond the Neon Lights: Everyday Shanghai in the Early Twentieth Century* (Berkeley, CA: University of California Press, 1999); Marcia R. Ristaino, *The Jacquinot Safe Zone: Wartime Refugees in Shanghai* (Stanford, CA: Stanford University Press, 2008); Christian Henriot, ' "Invisible Deaths, Silent Deaths": "Bodies Without Masters" in Republican Shanghai', *Journal of Social History* 43:2 (2009), pp. 407–37.

44 *NCH*, 8 December 1937, pp. 368–71; the best account of this period is Wakeman, *Shanghai Badlands*.

45 G. G. Philips to Sir Archibald Clark-Kerr, 29 June 1940: TNA, FO 676/435.

46 See TNA, FO 371/23454-5, FO 371/24684, FO 371/27631. On the political trajectory of the SMC and the Shanghai British see Robert Bickers, 'Settlers and Diplomats: The End of British Hegemony in the International Settlement, 1937–1945', in Henriot and Yeh (eds), *In the Shadow of the Rising Sun*, pp. 229–56.

47 Christian Henriot, 'Shanghai and the Experience of War', *European Journal of East Asian Studies* 5:2 (2006), pp. 215–45; Ristaino, *Jacquinot Safe Zone*.

48 Barnett, *Economic Shanghai*, pp. 131–9.

49 *Shenbao*, 16 March 1941, p. 7; *NCDN*, 19 March 1941, p. 445.

50 NARA, SMP D9454; this section draws on Kenneth Bonner Papers, private collection.

51 This section draws on Bickers, 'Settlers and Diplomats', in Henriot and Yeh (eds), *In the Shadow of the Rising Sun*, pp. 229–56.

52 SMC, *Municipal Gazette*, 1942, passim.

53 *SCMP*, 21 August 1937, p. 9.

54 *Administrative Reports for the Year 1936* (Hong Kong: Government Printer, 1936), p. 4; variants of Grayburn's comment are in John Haffenden, *William Empson: Among the Mandarins* (Oxford: Oxford University Press, 2005), p. 483; Christopher Isherwood, *Christopher*

and His Kind (1977) (London: Village Books, 2012), p. 310; Frank H. H. King, *The Hongkong Bank between the Wars and the Bank Interned, 1919–1945* (Cambridge: Cambridge University Press, 1988), p. 567.

55 Philip Snow, *The Fall of Hong Kong: Britain, China and the Japanese Occupation* (New Haven, CT: Yale University Press, 2004), pp. 27–36.

56 Vivian Wai Yan Kong, ' "Clearing the Decks": The Evacuation of British Women and Children from Hong Kong to Australia in 1940', unpublished MPhil dissertation, University of Hong Kong, 2015.

57 Tim Luard, *Escape from Hong Kong: Admiral Chan Chak's Christmas Day Dash, 1941* (Hong Kong: Hong Kong University Press, 2012).

58 L. T. Ride, 'A Report on Conditions in Hong Kong Subsequent to the Surrender, and on the Events which Led up to my Escape from the Prisoner-of-War Camp in Sham-shui-po', February 1942, in War Office to A. L. Scott, Foreign Office, 25 May 1942, F4000/1193/10: TNA, FO 371/31679. For accounts of the battle see Snow, *The Fall of Hong Kong*, and Kwong Chi Man and Tsoi Yiu Lun, *Eastern Fortress: A Military History of Hong Kong, 1840–1970* (Hong Kong: Hong Kong University Press, 2014), pp. 161–224.

59 *SCMP*, 15 December 1941, p. 3. See also Gwen Dew, *Prisoner of the Japs* (New York: Alfred A. Knopf, 1943), pp. 51–5.

60 The charge was led by US journalist Cecil Brown: 'Malay Jungle War', *Life*, 12 January 1942, pp. 32–8; *Daily Express*, 14 January 1942, pp. 1 and 4; *Daily Mirror*, 15 January 1942, p. 3; David Low cartoon, *Evening Standard*, 22 January 1942.

61 Emily Hahn, *China to Me* (1944) (London: Virago Press, 1986), pp. 300–305; 'The Hong-Kong Incident: Court-Martial Story of Film', *The Times*, 3 September 1946, p. 2.

62 Little Diaries, December 1941.

63 Howard Payne Diary, April 1942: Bristol Record Office, 2002/027, Payne Papers, 1939–45.

64 Hope Danby, *My Boy Chang* (London: Victor Gollancz, 1955), pp. 187–93; J. E. Hoare, *Embassies in the East: The Story of the British Embassies in Japan, China and Korea from 1859 to the Present* (Richmond, Surrey: Curzon Press, 1999), pp. 60–63; Hugh Trevor-Roper, *Hermit of Peking: The Hidden Life of Sir Edmund Backhouse* (Penguin: Harmondsworth, 1978); Derek Sandhaus (ed.), *Décadence Mandchoue: The China Memoirs of Sir Edmund Trelawny Backhouse* (Hong Kong: Earnshaw Books, 2011).

65 Judith and Arthur Hart Burling, 'Collecting in Wartime Shanghai', *Apollo* 40:1 (July 1944), pp. 49–50, iii; Di Yin Lu, 'On a Shoestring:

Small-Time Entrepreneurs and the International Market for Chinese Curios, 1921–1949', *Archives of Asian Art* 63:1 (2013), pp. 87–102.

66 NARA, SMP N615; H. G. W. Woodhead, 'The Japanese Occupation of Shanghai: Some Personal Experiences', Chatham House lecture, 12 November 1942: TNA RIIA/8/875; 'Conditions in Shanghai', 5 May 1942: TNA, WO 208/378a; Intercept, 'Sandy' to Sir Victor Sassoon, 23 July 1942: TNA, WO 387b; *The Spectator*, 22 May 1942, p. 480.

67 Quotations from Imperial War Museum (hereafter IWM), Documents 2155, 'Private Papers of Miss J. Main'. On internment and repatriation see Greg Leck's encyclopedic *Captives of Empire: The Japanese Internment of Allied Civilians in China, 1941–1945* (Bangor, PA: Shandy Press, 2006). See also Hugh Collar, *Captive in Shanghai: A Story of Internment in World War II* (Hong Kong: Oxford University Press, 1980).

68 Major General E. C. Hayes, Commanding British Troops in China, report to H. M. Ambassador and Lt. Gen. Carton de Wiart, 13 September 1945: private collection. The impact of two years of enforced teetotalism on a hard-drinking society also needs factoring in; see J. G. Ballard, *Miracles of Life: Shanghai to Shepperton. An Autobiography* (London: Fourth Estate, 2008), p. 74.

69 IWM, Documents 3454, 'Private Papers of W. C. Henry'. This was Karoly M. Pate, the Japanese-born son of a British merchant.

70 This paragraph draws on: NARA, RG266, OSS files, E182, Box 141, folder 86, 'Summary Report on Indian Political Activities in Japanese-Occupied China', 1 March 1946; and Ristaino, *Port of Last Resort*, pp. 190–213.

71 K. C. Chan, 'The Abrogation of British Extraterritoriality in China 1942–43: A Study of Anglo-American-Chinese Relations', *Modern Asian Studies* 11:2 (1977), pp. 257–91.

72 SMA, U1-4-1828.

73 SMA, U1-4-966, 'Rendition of Settlement'. Okazaki would later take part in a very different surrender ceremony, of the Japanese Empire to the Allies on the USS *Missouri* on 2 September 1945 in Tokyo Bay.

74 'Greater Shanghai March Song': SMA, R22-2-723; *Shanghai Times*, 2 May 1943, 1 and 4 August 1943; on Li Xianglan: Norman Smith, *Intoxicating Manchuria: Alcohol, Opium and Culture in China's Northeast* (Vancouver: University of British Columbia Press, 2012), pp. 1–3; Shelley Stephenson, 'A Star by Any Other Name: The (After) Lives of Li Xianglan', *Quarterly Review of Film and Video* 19:1 (2002), pp. 1–13; Poshek Fu, *Between Shanghai and Hong Kong: The Politics of Chinese Cinemas* (Stanford, CA: Stanford University Press, 2003), pp. 108–18.

7. ALLIES OF A KIND

1 Arthur N. Young, *China's Nation-Building Effort, 1927–1937* (Stanford, CA: Hoover Institution Press, 1971), p. 73; Arthur N. Young, *China's Wartime Finance and Inflation, 1937–1945* (Cambridge, MA: Harvard University Press, 1965), table 40, p. 332.

2 P. D. Coates, *The China Consuls: British Consular Officers, 1843–1943* (Hong Kong: Oxford University Press, 1988), p. 300.

3 Based on statistics in Maritime Customs, *Service List, Sixty-Seventh Issue (corrected to 1st June 1941)* (Shanghai: Statistical Department of the Inspectorate General of Customs, 1941).

4 Stanley Wright to Basil (Dick) Foster Hall, 23 January 1944, S. F. Wright Papers, Special Collections, Library, Queen's University Belfast; Circulars nos 5769, 5771, in 679 (1) 26920, *Inspector General's Circulars*, vol. 28, Second Series, nos 5701–5868, 1938–42. This section draws on Robert Bickers, 'Purloined Letters: History and the Chinese Maritime Customs Service', *Modern Asian Studies* 40:3 (2006), pp. 691–723, and 'The Chinese Maritime Customs at War, 1941–45', *Journal of Imperial and Commonwealth History* 36:2 (2008), pp. 295–311.

5 Owen Gander Diary, p. 16, O. D. Gander Papers, 86/44/1, IWM.

6 Maze to A. Feragen, 13 December 1941, copy attached to Mrs E. Krogseth to Tso Chang-chin, 3 December 1945, in Second Historical Archives of China, Chinese Customs Archive (hereafter SHAC) 679(9), 2152. There was controversy later about what precisely Maze had said, or even what he had intended it to mean. See Benjamin Geoffrey White, ' "A Question of Principle with Political Implications": Investigating Collaboration in the Chinese Maritime Customs Service, 1945–1946', *Modern Asian Studies* 44:3 (2010), pp. 517–46.

7 Chungking no. 260, 27 August 1942, F6301/1689/10, TNA: FO 371/31679.

8 Chungking no. 202, 7 July 1942, F5218/1689/10, TNA: FO 371/31679.

9 B. E. F. Gage, 'Report on a Visit to Lanchow September 8 to October 1, 1942', in Chungking no. 416, 14 October 1942, F7657/1689/10, TNA: FO 371/31679.

10 Little Diary, 10 August 1943.

11 Rolla Rouse to L. K. Little, 6 May 1943, LKL Correspondence, 1941–4.

12 Little Diary, 7–9 and 27 August 1943.

13 Little Diary, 10 August 1943.

14 This section draws on James J. Matthews, 'The Union Jack on the Upper Yangzi: The Treaty Port of Chongqing, 1891–1943', unpublished PhD thesis, York University, Toronto, Ontario, 1999, and Lee McIsaac, 'The City as Nation: Creating a Wartime Capital in Chongqing', in Joseph W. Esherick (ed.), *Remaking the Chinese City: Modernity and National Identity, 1900–1950* (Honolulu: University of Hawai'i Press, 2001), pp. 174–81; 'Special Chungking Number', *West China Missionary News* 40:5 (May 1939).

15 W. Somerset Maugham, *On a Chinese Screen* (London: William Heinemann, 1922), pp. 231–5.

16 *China Press*, 20 January 1936, p. 12; 10 November 1931, p. 11; H. G. W. Woodhead, *The Yangtze and its Problems* (Shanghai: Mercury Press, 1931), pp. 53–4; *NCH*, 23 December 1936, p. 490.

17 *NCH*, 16 January 1935, p. 91; 21 April 1937, p. 100.

18 Robert A. Kapp, *Szechwan and the Chinese Republic: Provincial Militarism and Central Power, 1911–1938* (New Haven, CT: Yale University Press, 1973); Anne Reinhardt, ' "Decolonisation" on the Periphery: Liu Xiang and Shipping Rights Recovery at Chongqing, 1926–38', *Journal of Imperial and Commonwealth History* 36:2 (2008), pp. 259–74; 'Confidential Memorandum for Inspector General', 10 February 1944, in Harvard University, Houghton Library, Lester Knox Little Papers, Ms Am 1999.1, 'Letters, Memoranda etc Relating to Customs Affairs 1941 to 1944'.

19 Joshua H. Howard, *Workers at War: Labor in China's Arsenals, 1937–1953* (Stanford, CA: Stanford University Press, 2004), pp. 52–63; Randall Gould, 'My Impression of Chungking', *China Critic*, 18 May 1939, pp. 102–6; buses: Gerald Samson, *The Far East Ablaze* (London: Herbert Joseph, 1945), p. 160; Jeanette Shambaugh, with David Shambaugh, *The Odyssey of China's Imperial Art Treasures* (Seattle, WA: University of Washington Press, 2005), pp. 86–7.

20 *Life*, 12 June 1939, pp. 30 and 33.

21 Joy Homer, *Dawn Watch in China* (Boston, MA: Houghton Mifflin, 1941), p. 255.

22 Graham Peck, *Two Kinds of Time* (Boston, MA: Houghton Mifflin, 1950), pp. 385–8, 425; Homer, *Dawn Watch in China*, p. 71, and *China after Four Years of War* (Chungking: China Publishing Company, 1941), pp. 173–8.

23 Lin Yutang, *The Vigil of a Nation* (London: William Heinemann, 1946), p. 37.

24 Lin, *Vigil of a Nation*, pp. 50–51.

25 John D. Plating, *The Hump: America's Strategy for Keeping China in World War II* (College Station, TX: Texas A&M University Press, 2011).

26 Wilma Fairbank, *America's Cultural Experiment in China, 1942–1949* (Washington, DC: Bureau of Educational and Cultural Affairs, 1976), pp. 43–56.

27 Stephen R. MacKinnon and Oris Friesen, *China Reporting: An Oral History of American Journalism in the 1930s and 1940s* (Berkeley, CA: University of California Press, 1990), pp. 48–78; Peck, *Two Kinds of Time*, p. 428.

28 Emily Hahn, *China to Me* (1944) (London: Virago Press, 1986), pp. 113, 199–200; Robert Payne, *Chungking Diary* (London: William Heinemann, 1945), p. 86; D. F. Karaka, *Chungking Diary* (Bombay: Thacker and Co., 1942), p. 12.

29 Matthew D. Johnson, 'Propaganda and Sovereignty in Wartime China: Morale Operations and Psychological Warfare under the Office of War Information', *Modern Asian Studies* 45:2 (2011), pp. 303–44; Harrison Forman, 'The Voice of China', *Collier's*, 17 June 1944, p. 85; *SCMP*, 13 March 1940, p. 13; *China Weekly Review*, 6 May 1939, p. 292; Bill Lascher, 'Radio Free China', *Boom* 4:1 (2014), pp. 11–17.

30 Harold R. Rattenbury, *Face to Face with China* (London: George G. Harrap and Co., 1945), p. 5; Cecil Beaton, *Far East* (London: B. T. Batsford, 1945), *Chinese Album* (London: B. T. Batsford, 1945), and *The Years Between: Diary 1939–44* (London: Weidenfeld and Nicolson, 1965), p. 332; 'Prevailing China', *Vogue*, 15 November 1944, p. 104.

31 *FRUS*, 1943, *China*, p. 483; Saul Steinberg, 'Fourteenth Air Force: China Theater', *New Yorker*, 15 January 1944, pp. 18–19, and 5 February 1944, pp. 20–21; *China Theater: An Informal Notebook of Useful Information for Military Men in China* (Washington, DC: US Government Printing Office, 1943); Jane Kramer, 'Mission to China', *New Yorker*, 15 July 2000, pp. 58–65. On tensions see Wesley M. Bagby, *The Eagle-Dragon Alliance: America's Relations with China in World War II* (Newark, NJ: University of Delaware Press, 1992), pp. 101–3.

32 *Why We Fight: The Battle for China* (Dir. Frank Capra, 1944); Elizabeth Rawitsch, *Frank Capra's Eastern Horizons: American Identity and the Cinema of International Relations* (London: I. B. Tauris, 2014), pp. 115–34.

33 Hemingway: quoted in Joyce Hoffmann, *Theodore H. White and Journalism as Illusion* (Columbia, MI: University of Missouri Press, 1995), p. 54; Martha Gellhorn, *Travels with Myself and Another: Five Journeys from Hell* (1978) (London: Eland, 2002), p. 53.

34 *The New York Times*, 27 December 1941, p. 21; *Life*, 12 January 1941, pp. 26–7; Chiang Yee, *Chin-Pao and the Giant Pandas* (London: Country Life, 1942); Chiang Yee, *The Story of Ming* (Harmondsworth: Puffin, 1945). Ming garnered an editorial in *The Times* after her death: 30 December 1944, p. 5.

35 T. Christopher Jespersen, *American Images of China, 1931–1949* (Stanford, CA: Stanford University Press, 1996), pp. 82–107.

36 *Hastings and St Leonards Observer*, 17 September 1938, p. 2; *The Canberra Times*, 16 December 1941, p. 2. On campaigns to support China see Arthur Clegg, *Aid China: Memoir of a Forgotten Campaign* (Beijing: New World Press, 1989), and Tom Buchanan, *East Wind: China and the British Left, 1925–1976* (Oxford: Oxford University Press, 2012).

37 Theodore H. White and Annalee Jacoby, *Thunder out of China* (New York: William Sloane Associates, 1946), p. 3.

38 Hsiao Ch'ien (Xiao Qian), *China but not Cathay* (London: Pilot Press, 1942), pp. 1 and 130; Hsiao Ch'ien, *Traveller without a Map* (Stanford, CA: Stanford University Press, 1990), pp. 84–8.

39 Little Diary, 9 October 1943.

40 'Visit to China', in *Selected Works of Jawaharlal Nehru, Volume 10* (New Delhi: Orient Longman, 1977), pp. 73–114; 'Detestable Policy', *SCMP*, 3 September 1939, p. 4; Chiang Kai-shek telegram to T. V. Soong, 24 February 1942, in Franklin D. Roosevelt Presidential Library and Museum, President's Secretary's File (PSF), Box 2; Guido Samarani, 'Shaping the Future of Asia: Chiang Kai-shek, Nehru and China–India Relations during the Second World War Period', *Working Papers in Contemporary Asian Studies* 11 (Centre for East and South-East Asian Studies, Lund University, 2005). Intelligence: Richard J. Aldrich, *Intelligence and the War against Japan: Britain, America and the Politics of Secret Service* (Cambridge: Cambridge University Press, 2000), pp. 150–55; 'The Memoirs of Kenneth Morison Bourne', unpublished manuscript, 1971, private collection, pp. 96–7.

41 On discussions about handling reports of atrocities see file 'Situation in Hong Kong', TNA: FO 371/31671; on Harrop, 'No Woman was Safe in the Streets', *Daily Mail*, 13 March 1942; Phyllis Harrop, *Hong Kong Incident* (London: Eyre and Spottiswode, 1943), and private information.

42 *Daily Express*, 12 March 1942, p. 1; *Punch*, 18 March 1942, p. 221.

43 John Pownall Reeves, *The Lone Flag: Memoir of the British Consul in Macao during World War II*, ed. Colin Day and Richard Garrett (Hong Kong: Hong Kong University Press, 2014), passim, quotation from p. 107, statistic from p. 14.

44 This section draws on Edwin Ride, *BAAG: Hong Kong Resistance, 1942–1945* (Hong Kong: Oxford University Press, 1981); and Chan Sui-jeung, *East River Column: Hong Kong Guerrillas in the Second World War and After* (Hong Kong: Hong Kong University Press, 2009).

45 Philip Snow, *The Fall of Hong Kong: Britain, China and the Japanese Occupation* (New Haven, CT: Yale University Press, 2003), p. 155. This section draws further on this account.

46 The statue survived the war, and was discovered with other monuments in 1946 and returned: *China Mail*, 17 September 1946, p. 1, and 18 October 1946, p. 1.

47 On internment see: Geoffrey Charles Emerson, *Hong Kong Internment, 1942–1945: Life in the Japanese Civilian Camp at Stanley* (Hong Kong: Hong Kong University Press, 2008); Bernice Archer, *The Internment of Western Civilians under the Japanese, 1941–1945: A Patchwork of Internment* (London: RoutledgeCurzon, 2004); on Franklin and camp politics see Alan Birch, 'Confinement and Constitutional Conflict in Occupied Hong Kong 1941–45', *Hong Kong Law Journal* 3:3 (1973), pp. 293–318.

48 Kent Fedorowich, 'Decolonization Deferred? The Re-establishment of Colonial Rule in Hong Kong, 1942–45', *Journal of Imperial and Commonwealth History* 28:3 (2000), pp. 25–50; Felicia Yap, 'A "New Angle of Vision": British Imperial Reappraisal of Hong Kong during the Second World War', *Journal of Imperial and Commonwealth History* 42:1 (2014), pp. 86–113.

49 Steve Tsang, *Hong Kong: An Appointment with China* (London: I. B. Tauris, 1997), pp. 34–9.

50 *The Times*, 11 November 1942, p. 4.

51 Jay Taylor, *The Generalissimo: Chiang Kai-shek and the Struggle for Modern China* (Cambridge, MA: Belknap Press, 2011), pp. 245–52; Field Marshal Lord Alanbrooke, *War Diaries, 1939–1945*, ed. Alex Danchev and Daniel Todman (London: Weidenfeld and Nicolson, 2001), p. 480. On Cairo see Keith Sainsbury, *The Turning Point: Roosevelt, Stalin, Churchill, and Chiang Kai-shek, 1943. The Moscow, Cairo, and Tehran Conferences* (Oxford: Oxford University Press, 1986).

52 *FRUS, 1943, China*, pp. 476–9.

53 Little Diary, 3 August 1944, 6 November 1944 and 23 June 1944.

54 Rana Mitter, *China's War with Japan, 1937–1945: The Struggle for Survival* (London: Allen Lane, 2013), pp. 323–6.

55 Luoyang, Semi-Official no. 134, 20 June 1944: Harvard University, Houghton Library, Lester Knox Little Papers, Ms Am 1999.1, 'Letters, Memoranda etc Relating to Customs Affairs 1941 to 1944'.

56 'First Informal Impressions of the North Shensi Communist Base', 28 July 1944, in Joseph W. Esherick (ed.), *Lost Chance in China: The World War II Dispatches of John S. Service* (New York: Random House, 1974), pp. 178–81. Dancing: Peter Vladimirov, *The Vladimirov Diaries: Yenan, China, 1942–1945* (New York: Doubleday, 1975), p. 296, 19 November 1944.

57 Quoted in Stuart Gelder, *The Chinese Communists* (London: Victor Gollancz, 1946), p. xxxviii.

58 *The New York Times*, 20 August 1944, p. 23.

59 Harrison Forman, *Report from Red China* (New York: Henry Holt, 1945), p. 177. See also 'Interview with Mao Tze-Tung – August 10, 1944', Harrison Forman Diary, China, June–August 1944, Harrison Forman Papers, Special Collections and University Archives, University of Oregon Libraries.

60 *The New York Times*, 6 October 1944, p. 12; Vladimirov, *Vladimirov Diaries*, pp. 214–15, 3 April 1944. Michael Lindsay, *The Unknown War: North China 1937–1945* (London: Bergstrom and Boyle Books, 1975); Hsiao Li Lindsay, *Bold Plum: With the Guerrillas in China's War against Japan* (Morrisville, NC: Lulu Press, 2007).

61 Vladimirov, *Vladimirov Diaries*, pp. 297–8, 23 November 1944.

62 Robert Bickers, 'The Business of a Secret War: Operation "Remorse" and SOE Salesmanship in Wartime China', *Intelligence and National Security* 16:4 (2001), pp. 11–37.

63 White and Jacoby, *Thunder out of China*, p. 114. Exchange-rate issues were a continuing American concern; see, for example, Franklin D. Roosevelt Presidential Library and Museum, PSF, Series 3, Box 27, 'China, January–June 1944', passim.

64 Lin Yutang, *Between Tears and Laughter* (New York: John Day, 1943), quotations from pp. 117, 2–4.

65 Lin, *Between Tears and Laughter*, pp. 89 and 5; Qian Suoqiao, *Liberal Cosmopolitan: Lin Yutang and Middling Chinese Modernity* (Leiden: Brill, 2011), p. 183; *The New York Times*, 1 August 1943, p. BR3, and 4 August 1943, p. 13.

66 Minute, 31 May 1943, on Chungking no. 886, 21 April 1943, F2351/632/10, TNA: FO 371/35813. This section draws on correspondence in this file about Chiang's book, its continuation in TNA: FO 371/35813 (which also contains a widely circulated unofficial summary translation,

highlighting key points that worried foreign commentators), and FO 371/53722, and *FRUS*, 1943, *China*, pp. 244–7, 252, 310–12, 347–8, and *FRUS*, 1944, *China*, pp. 472–4, 708–11. An unauthorized translation of the book, highlighting differences between its two Chinese editions and with highly critical commentary by the editor, Philip Jaffe, appeared as *China's Destiny and Chinese Economic Theory* (New York: Roy Publishers, 1947); an authorized translation by Wang Zhonghui, with an introduction by Lin Yutang, was published the same year.

67 John King Fairbank, *Chinabound: A Fifty-Year Memoir* (New York: Harper and Row, 1982), p. 452; Robert Payne, *China Awake* (New York: William Heinemann, 1947), pp. 244–5.

68 Pearl S. Buck, 'A Warning about China', *Life*, 10 May 1943, pp. 53–4. On Luce's support see Jespersen, *American Images of China*.

69 James Farrer and Andrew David Field, *Shanghai Nightscapes: A Nocturnal Biography of a Global City* (Chicago, IL: University of Chicago Press, 2015), pp. 131–2.

8. FOREIGN EXPERTS

1 Shamian: *SCMP*, 3 May 1946, p. 12, 18 August 1946, p. 4, and 16 March 1947, p. 6; 10 December 1947, p. 16; *The Observer*, 27 February 1949, p. 6; riot: *SCMP*, 17–19 January 1948, passim; *Shenbao*, 17 January 1948, p. 1. For a full account see Zhang Junyi, '1948 nian Guangzhou Shamian shijian zhi shimo: yi Song Ziwen dang'an wei zhongxin' ('The History of the 1948 Shamian Incident in Guangzhou: A Study based on the T. V. Soong Papers'), *Zhongguo shehui kexue* 6 (2008), pp. 185–200.

2 This paragraph draws on Peter Wesley-Smith, *Unequal Treaty, 1898–1997: China, Great Britain, and Hong Kong's New Territories* (Hong Kong: Oxford University Press, 1998), pp. 177–88; *SCMP*, 6 January 1948, pp. 1 and 11; *China Mail*, 6 January 1948, p. 1; *Wah Kiu Yat Po*, 6 January 1948, p. 4. See also the Foreign Office minute of 4 February 1948, in S. R. Ashton, G. Bennett and K. A. Hamilton (eds), *Documents on British Policy Overseas, Series 1, Volume 8: Britain and China, 1945–1950* (London: Routledge, 2013), pp. 126–31.

3 Alexander Grantham, *Via Ports: From Hong Kong to Hong Kong* (Hong Kong: Hong Kong University Press, 1965), pp. 130–33; *Shenbao*, 18 January 1948, p. 4; *SCMP*, 18–19 January 1948, passim.

4 *SCMP*, 30 January 1948, p. 1; *Shenbao*, 17 January 1948, p. 1.

5 See *FRUS*, 1948, vol. 8, *The Far East: China*, pp. 46–55, for US reports and analysis of events; quotation from p. 50.

6 Shun-hsin Chou, *The Chinese Inflation, 1937–1949* (New York: Columbia University Press, 1963), p. 34.

7 *Shenbao*, 1 February 1948, p. 4; Andrew David Field, *Shanghai's Dancing World: Cabaret Culture and Urban Politics, 1919–1954* (Hong Kong: Chinese University Press, 2010), pp. 232–61; Ma Jun, *1948 nian: Shanghai wuchao an. Dui yiqi Minguo nüxing jiti baoli kangyi shijian de yanjiu* (*1948: Shanghai Dance Unrest. Towards the Study of Republican Women's Collective Protest*) (Shanghai: Shang- hai guji chubanshe, 2005).

8 A good taste of this can be found in Joseph W. Esherick (ed.), *Lost Chance in China: The World War II Despatches of John S. Service* (New York: Random House, 1974).

9 Lloyd E. Eastman, 'Who Lost China? Chiang Kai-shek Testifies', *China Quarterly* 88 (1981), pp. 658–68.

10 A good entry into this topic is Robert P. Newman's *Owen Lattimore and the 'Loss' of China* (Berkeley, CA: University of California Press, 1992).

11 Frederic Wakeman Jr, *Spymaster: Dai Li and the Chinese Secret Service* (Berkeley, CA: University of California Press, 2003), pp. 344–6; Robert Payne, *China Awake* (London: William Heinemann, 1947), p. 419; Wen Yidou quoted in Pei-kai Cheng and Michael Lestz, with Jonathan D. Spence, *The Search for Modern China: A Documentary Collection* (New York: W. W. Norton, 1999), pp. 337–8.

12 Suzanne Pepper, *Civil War in China: The Political Struggle, 1945– 1949*, 2nd edition (Lanham, MD: Rowman and Littlefield, 1999); Odd Arne Westad, *Decisive Encounters: The Chinese Civil War, 1946– 1950* (Stanford, CA: Stanford University Press, 2003); Diana Lary, *China's Civil War: A Social History, 1945–1949* (Cambridge: Cam- bridge University Press, 2015), quotation from p. 126.

13 Two good general surveys of the wider history of foreign involvement in the advising of China are Jonathan D. Spence, *To Change China: Western Advisers in China, 1620–1960* (Boston, MA: Little, Brown, 1969), and James C. Thomson Jr., *While China Faced West: American Reformers in Nationalist China, 1928–1937* (Cambridge, MA: Harvard University Press, 1969).

14 Robert Bickers, ' "Good Work for China in Every Possible Direction": The Foreign Inspectorate of the Chinese Maritime Customs, 1854–1950', in Bryna Goodman and David S. G. Goodman (eds), *Twentieth-Century Colonialism and China: Localities, the Everyday and the World*

(London: Routledge, 2012), pp. 25–36; Hans van de Ven, *Breaking with the Past: The Maritime Customs Service and the Global Origins of Modernity in China* (New York: Columbia University Press, 2014).

15 See, amongst other work, Ryan Dunch, *Fuzhou Protestants and the Making of a Modern China, 1857–1927* (New Haven, CT: Yale University Press, 2001); Jun Xing, *Baptized in the Fire of Revolution: The American Social Gospel and the YMCA in China, 1919–1937* (Bethlehem, PA: Lehigh University Press, 1996).

16 Albert Feuerwerker, *The Foreign Establishment in China in the Early Twentieth Century* (Ann Arbor, MI: Center for Chinese Studies, University of Michigan, 1976), p. 39.

17 Andrew J. Nathan, *A History of the China International Famine Relief Commission* (Cambridge, MA: East Asian Research Center, Harvard University, 1965). A good survey is Andrea Janku, 'The Internationalization of Disaster Relief in Early Twentieth-Century China', *Berliner China-Hefte/Chinese History and Society* 43 (2013), pp. 6–28.

18 In the late Ming and into the eighteenth century during the Qing, extensive use was made at court of foreign architects, mathematicians, musicians and cartographers: Liam Matthew Brockey, *Journey to the East: The Jesuit Mission to China, 1579–1724* (Cambridge, MA: Harvard University Press, 2007).

19 H. G. W. Woodhead and H. T. Montague Bell, *China Year Book, 1914* (London: George Routledge and Sons, 1914), p. 312; Lo Hui-min (ed.), *The Correspondence of G. E. Morrison*, 2 vols (Cambridge: Cambridge University Press, 1976, 1978).

20 F. A. Sutton, *One Arm Sutton* (London: Macmillan, 1933).

21 See Arthur N. Young, *China and the Helping Hand, 1937–1945* (Cambridge, MA: Harvard University Press, 1962) and *China's Wartime Finance and Inflation, 1937–1945* (Cambridge, MA: Harvard University Press, 1965); Antony Best, 'The Leith-Ross Mission and British Policy towards East Asia, 1934–7', *The International History Review* 35:4 (2013), pp. 681–701.

22 *The China Year Book 1936* (Shanghai: North-China Daily News and Herald, 1936), p. 158.

23 William C. Kirby, *Germany and Republican China* (Stanford, CA: Stanford University Press, 1984), passim.

24 Hans van de Ven, *War and Nationalism in China, 1925–1945* (London: RoutledgeCurzon, 2003), pp. 19–63; Jay Taylor, *The Generalissimo: Chiang Kai-shek and the Struggle for Modern China* (Cambridge, MA: Belknap Press, 2011), pp. 286–95.

25 Stillwell: most recently Taylor, *The Generalissimo*; and van de Ven, *War and Nationalism in China*, pp. 19–63; Germans: Kirby, *Germany and Republican China*; Japanese: Donald G. Gillin and Charles Etter, 'Staying On: Japanese Soldiers and Civilians in China, 1945–1949', *Journal of Asian Studies* 42:3 (1983), pp. 497–518; Okamura: Barak Kushner, 'Ghosts of the Japanese Imperial Army: The "White Group" (*Baituan*) and Early Post-War Sino-Japanese Relations', *Past and Present* 218, Supplement 8 (2013), pp. 117–50; see also 'Political Information: Japanese Activities in Shanghai, Nanking and North China', 6 November 1947, Central Intelligence Group intelligence report SO 10724, CIA Freedom of Information Act Electronic Reading Room (hereafter CIAFOI), at http://www.foia.cia.gov/document/519697ee993294098d50d1dc, accessed 10 October 2015.

26 Aglaia De Angeli, 'Early 1930s China: State, Fascism and Law', unpublished paper presented at the Seventeenth Biennial Conference of the European Association for Chinese Studies, Lund, 2008; but see the case studies in Jedidiah J. Kroncke, *The Futility of Law and Development: China and the Dangers of Exporting American Law* (New York: Oxford University Press, 2016).

27 Michael H. Hunt, 'The American Remission of the Boxer Indemnity: A Reappraisal', *Journal of Asian Studies* 31:3 (1972), pp. 539–59.

28 This estimate comes from a 1954 survey cited in Stacey Bieler, '*Patriots*' or '*Traitors*'? A History of American-Educated Chinese Students (Armonk, NY: M. E. Sharpe, 2004), p. 381.

29 Laurence D. Schneider, 'The Rockefeller Foundation, the China Foundation, and the Development of Modern Science in China', *Social Science and Medicine* 16:12 (1982), pp. 1217–21; Charlotte Furth, *Ting Wenchiang: Science and China's New Culture* (Cambridge, MA: Harvard University Press, 1970), pp. 34–58.

30 Chan Lau Kit-ching and Peter Cunich (eds), *An Impossible Dream: Hong Kong University from Foundation to Re-establishment, 1910–1950* (Oxford: Oxford University Press, 2002), pp. 201–3.

31 The history of the Boxer Indemnity is covered in Stanley F. Wright, *China's Customs Revenue since the Revolution of 1911*, 3rd edition, revised and enlarged with the assistance of John H. Cubbon (Shanghai: Statistical Department of the Inspectorate General of Customs, 1935), pp. 169–230, and appendix 3, pp. 442–591; see also Frank H. H. King, 'The Boxer Indemnity: "Nothing but Bad"', *Modern Asian Studies* 40:3 (2006), pp. 663–89.

32 The first person to benefit from this was John Lossing Buck's second wife, Lomay Chang: *The New York Times*, 4 June 1944, p. 40, and 14 August 1944, p. 8.

33 Milton T. Stauffer (ed.), *The Christian Occupation of China: A General Survey of the Numerical Strength and Geographical Distributon [sic] of the Christian Forces in China ... 1918–1921* (Shanghai: China Continuation Committee, 1922), pp. 419, 425, 429.

34 This section draws principally on Mary Brown Bullock, *An American Transplant: The Rockefeller Foundation and Peking Union Medical College* (Berkeley, CA: University of California Press, 1980); Mary Brown Bullock, *The Oil Prince's Legacy: Rockefeller Philanthropy in China* (Washington, DC: Woodrow Wilson Center Press, 2011); John Z. Bowers, *Western Medicine in a Chinese Palace: Peking Union Medical College, 1917–1951* (Philadelphia, PA: The Josiah Macy Jr. Foundation, 1972). See also Warren I. Cohen, *The Chinese Connection: Roger S. Greene, Thomas W. Lamont, George E. Sokolsky and American-East Asian Relations* (New York: Columbia University Press, 1978), pp. 7–40.

35 See 'Activities of the China Medical Board', in *Addresses and Papers: Dedication Ceremonies and Medical Conference, Peking Union Medical College, September 15–22, 1921* (Peking: Peking Union Medical College, 1922), p. 4. On SOCONY see Sherman Cochran, *Encountering Chinese Networks: Western, Japanese, and Chinese Corporations in China, 1880–1937* (Berkeley, CA: University of California Press, 2000), pp. 12–43.

36 Jeffrey W. Cody, *Building in China: Henry K. Murphy's 'Adaptive Architecture', 1914–1935* (Hong Kong: Chinese University Press, 2001), p. 76. On the legation see J. E. Hoare, *Embassies in the East: The Story of the British Embassies in Japan, China and Korea from 1859 to the Present* (Richmond, Surrey: Curzon Press, 1999), pp. 17–92.

37 *NCH*, 3 September 1921, p. 698; Bullock, *An American Transplant*, p. 113.

38 This was Chen Sibang, a British-trained, Singapore-born medical advisor to the Interior Ministry: *Addresses and Papers: Dedication Ceremonies and Medical Conference*, p. 49.

39 The phrase is from Bowers, *Western Medicine in a Chinese Palace*, p. 77.

40 Although see Bullock, *An American Transplant*, pp. 1–23, especially pp. 18–20.

41 Zuoyue Wang, 'Saving China through Science: The Science Society of China, Scientific Nationalism, and Civil Society in Republican China', *Osiris* 17 (2002), pp. 291–322.

42 SHAC 679(1), 3611, 'Dossier: Meteorology, 1923–1934', Acting Coast Inspector Terry to I. G. Maze, 10 March 1934; *The Academia Sinica*

and Its National Research Institutes (Nanking: Academia Sinica, 1931), pp. 79–80.

43 Robert Bickers, ' "Throwing Light on Natural Laws": Meteorology on the China Coast, 1869–1912', in Robert Bickers and Isabella Jackson (eds), *Treaty Ports in Modern China: Law, Land and Power* (London: Routledge, 2016), pp. 179–200.

44 Lewis Pyenson, *Civilizing Mission: Exact Sciences and French Overseas Expansion, 1830–1940* (Baltimore, MD: Johns Hopkins University Press, 1993); Augustín Udías, *Searching the Heavens and the Earth: The History of Jesuit Observatories* (Dordrecht: Kluwer Academic Publishers, 2003).

45 Pyenson, *Civilizing Mission*, p. 180; SHAC 679(1), 3853, 'History of the Customs Meteorological Service'.

46 Kirby, *Germany and Republican China*, chapter 4; William C. Kirby, 'The Chinese War Economy', in James C. Hsiung and Steven I. Levine (eds), *China's Bitter Victory: The War with Japan, 1937–1945* (Armonk, NY: M. E. Sharpe, 1992), pp. 185–212.

47 SHAC 679(1), 3852, 'Meteorology, 1937–1945', appendix X of letter from Coast Inspector Carrel to I. G. Maze, 16 November 1937.

48 Pyenson, *Civilizing Mission*, p. 176; P. H. B. Kent to Sir Archibald Clark-Kerr, 27 June 1942, TNA: FO 371/31668.

49 This paragraph draws on Bullock, *An American Transplant*, pp. 100–116, 126–7, quotation from p. 196.

50 Robert Bickers, 'The Chinese Maritime Customs at War, 1941–45', *Journal of Imperial and Commonwealth History* 36:2 (2008), pp. 305–7. Soong's comment comes in an interview with IG L. K. Little: Little Diaries, 8 November 1946. Nonetheless, when Pritchard died from TB shortly after his appointment, his successor was Chinese.

51 As *The Times* put it, 20 February 1947, p. 6. See Wen Kegang, *Zhongguo qixiang shi* (*History of Meteorology in China*) (Beijing: Qixiang chubanshe, 2004), p. 338.

52 *Shanghai Evening Post and Mercury* (New York), 11 September 1945, p. 1. See also John Dower, *Embracing Defeat: Japan in the Wake of World War II* (London: Allen Lane, 1999), pp. 59, 112–19.

53 Frederic Wakeman Jr, ' "Liberation": The Shanghai Police, 1942–1952', in Yves Chevrier, Alain Roux and Xiaohong Xiao-Planes (eds), *Citadins et citoyens dans la Chine du XXe siècle: Essais d'histoire sociale. En hommage à Marie-Claire Bergère* (Paris: Éditions de la Maison des sciences de l'homme, 2010), p. 506.

54 *Shanghai Evening Post and Mercury* (New York), 13 September 1946, pp. 1, 8; 18 October 1946, p. 4, Chang Ning, 'Cong Paoma ting dao

Renmin guangchang: Shanghai Paomating shouhui yundong, 1946–1951' ('From Racecourse to People's Square: The Campaign for the Retrocession of the Shanghai Racecourse, 1946–1951'), *Zhongyang yanjiu yuan Jindai lishi yanjiu suo jikan* 48 (2005), pp. 97–136.

55 *UNRRA in China, 1945–1947* (Washington, DC: United Nations Relief and Rehabilitation Administration, 1948), pp. 190–281.

56 *Life*, 13 May 1946, pp. 29–35; Pepper, *Civil War in China*, pp. 152–3; Lloyd E. Eastman, *Seeds of Destruction: Nationalist China in War and Revolution, 1937–1949* (Stanford, CA: Stanford University Press, 1984), pp. 71–3.

57 Payne, *China Awake*, p. 421.

58 Recorded in William G. Sewell, *I Stayed in China* (London: George Allen and Unwin, 1966), p. 169.

59 Micah S. Muscolino, *The Ecology of War in China* (Cambridge: Cambridge University Press, 2015), pp. 172–235; Rana Mitter, *China's War with Japan, 1937–1945: The Struggle for Survival* (London: Allen Lane, 2013), p. 57.

60 Sherman Cochran and Andrew Hsieh, *The Lius of Shanghai* (Cambridge, MA: Harvard University Press, 2013), pp. 263–7.

61 For example, 'CNRRA Charges', *China Mail*, 30 September 1947; 'CNRRA Men Jailed for Corruption', *NCDN*, 2 April 1948, p. 3.

62 *UNRRA in China*, pp. 69–72.

63 T. Y. Lin (Lin Daoyang), Guangdong regional director 1945–6, quoted in Lester K. Little diary, 26 September 1946.

64 Rana Mitter, 'Imperialism, Transnationalism, and the Reconstruction of Post-War China: UNRRA in China, 1944–7', *Past and Present* 218, Supplement 8 (2013), pp. 51–69; *UNRRA in China*, p. 210.

65 George H. Kerr, *Formosa Betrayed* (Boston, MA: Houghton Mifflin, 1965), p. 158.

66 Dower, *Embracing Defeat*, pp. 48–53. Different but still significant figures can be found in Louise Young, *Japan's Total Empire: Manchuria and the Culture of Wartime Imperialism* (Berkeley, CA: University of California Press, 1998), pp. 408–11.

67 Indians: *NCDN*, 30 November 1945, 2 December 1945; Marcia Reynders Ristaino, *Port of Last Resort: The Diaspora Communities of Shanghai* (Stanford, CA: Stanford University Press, 2001), pp. 242–72.

68 *Shenbao*, 21 November 1947, p. 4; *NCDN*, 21 November 1921, p. 3; Archer had also tasted jail life in Hong Kong: *SCMP*, 24 May 1940, p. 8; *SCMP*, 20 September 1947, p. 12; *NCDN*, 18 February 1949, p. 5; *SCMP*, 27 July 1956, p. 8. Archer was eventually released and deported to Hong Kong in 1956.

69 On this case see Robert Shaffer, 'A Rape in Beijing, December 1946: GIs, Nationalist Protests, and U.S. Foreign Policy', *Pacific Historical Review* 69:1 (2000), pp. 31–64; Yanqiu Zheng, 'A Specter of Extraterritoriality: The Legal Status of U.S. Troops in China, 1943–1947', *Journal of American-East Asian Relations* 22:1 (2015), pp. 17–44. Images: Adam Cathcart, 'Atrocities, Insults, and "Jeep Girls": Depictions of the U.S. Military in China, 1945–1949', *International Journal of Comic Art* 10:1 (2008), pp. 140–54. See also Mark F. Wilkinson, 'American Military Misconduct in Shanghai and the Chinese Civil War: The Case of Zang Dayaozi', *Journal of American-East Asian Relations* 17:2 (2010), pp. 146–73. On wartime agitation against women consorting with American soldiers see Graham Peck, *Two Kinds of Time* (Boston, MA: Houghton Mifflin, 1950), p. 636, and *Shanghai Evening Post and Mercury* (hereafter *SEPM*) (New York), 15 June 1945, pp. 1–2.

70 First published in *Life Magazine*, 17 October 1949, pp. 129–38, 141–2, these were later reprinted in Henri Cartier-Bresson, *China in Transition: A Moment in History* (London: Thames and Hudson, 1956).

71 Jürgen Osterhammel, 'Imperialism in Transition: British Business and the Chinese Authorities, 1931–37', *China Quarterly* 98 (1984), pp. 282–3.

72 *FRUS*, 1949, vol. 8, *The Far East: China*, pp. 1303–27, quotation from Clark, Canton, to Secretary of State, 5 August 1949, p. 1308. See this volume more widely for American officials' experience at the hands of the Communists.

73 The key documents are in S. R. Ashton, G. Bennett and K. A. Hamilton (eds), *Documents on British Policy Overseas, Series 1, Volume 8: Britain and China, 1945–1950* (London: Frank Cass, 2002), pp. 397–402, 417–26. The course of events is discussed in David Clayton, *Imperialism Revisited: Political and Economic Relations between Britain and China, 1950–54* (Basingstoke: Macmillan, 1997).

74 'Cable, Mao Zedong [via Kovalev] to Stalin', 14 June 1949, Archive of the President of the Russian Federation (hereafter APRF), f. 45, op. 1, d. 331, ll. 101–11. Reprinted in Andrei Ledovskii, Raisa Mirovitskaia and Vladimir Miasnikov, *Sovetsko-Kitaiskie Otnosheniia*, vol. 5, book 2, 1946–February 1950 (Moscow: Pamiatniki Istoricheskoi Mysli, 2005), pp. 141–6. Translated for the Cold War International History Project, History and Public Policy Program, Wilson Center (hereafter CWIHP), by Sergey Radchenko at http://digitalarchive.wilsoncenter.org/document/113377.

75 *United States Relations with China, with Special Reference to the Period 1944-49* (Washington, DC: Department of State, 1949); Nancy Bernkopf Tucker (ed.), *China Confidential: American Diplomats and Sino-American Relations, 1945-1996* (New York: Columbia University Press, 2001), pp. 24 and 62.

76 'Cable, Kovalev to Stalin, Report on the 22 May 1949 CCP CC Politburo Discussion', 23 May 1949, APRF, f. 45, op. 1, d. 331, ll. 66-9. Reprinted in Ledovskii, Mirovitskaia and Miasnikov, *Sovetsko-Kitaiskie Otnosheniia*, vol. 5, book 2, pp. 132-4. Translated for CWIHP by Sergey Radchenko at http://digitalarchive.wilsoncenter.org/document/113365.

77 *NCDN*, 24 April 1949, pp. 1-2; A. C. S. Trivett, ' "Topside Jossman" or "The Indiscretions of a Dean" ', unpublished memoir, *c.* 1966, p. 103. The Canadian Alexander C. S. Trivett (1890-1981) was Dean of Holy Trinity from 1928 to 1951; Malcolm H. Murfett, *Hostage on the Yangtze: Britain, China and the Amethyst Crisis of 1949* (Annapolis, MD: Naval Institute Press, 1991).

78 *Chicago Tribune*, 23 April 1949, p. 5; John Leighton Stuart, *Fifty Years in China: The Memoirs of John Leighton Stuart, Missionary and Ambassador* (New York: Random House, 1954), p. 234.

79 On this process see Thomas N. Thompson, *China's Nationalization of Foreign Firms: The Politics of Hostage Capitalism, 1949-57* (Baltimore, MD: School of Law, University of Maryland Occasional Papers, no. 6, 1979). Fresh analysis of the course of this process can now be found in Jonathan J. Howlett, 'Accelerated Transition: British Enterprises in Shanghai and the Transition to Socialism', *European Journal of East Asian Studies* 13:2 (2014), pp. 163-87, and ' "The British Boss is Gone and Will Never Return": Communist Takeovers of British Companies in Shanghai (1949-1954)', *Modern Asian Studies* 47:6 (2013), pp. 1941-76.

80 'Record of Conversation between I. V. Stalin and . . . Mao Zedong [in Moscow] on 16 December 1949', APRF, f. 45, op. 1, d. 329, ll. 9-17. Translated by Danny Rozas, at http://digitalarchive.wilsoncenter.org/document/111240; Zhu Kezhen, 'Zhongguo qixiang xuehui diyijie daibiao dahui kaimu ci' ('Opening Statement, First Session of the General Assembly of the Chinese Meteorological Society', 15 April 1951), and Zhu Kezhen, 'Zhongguo guoqu zai qixiang xue shang de chengjiu' ('China's Past Achievements in Meteorology', 1951), in *Zhu Kezhen quanji* (*Complete Works of Coching Chu*), vol. 3 (Shanghai: Shanghai keji jiaoyu chubanshe, 2004), pp. 56, 59-60.

81 Bullock, *An American Transplant*, pp. 206-8; Report from *Daily*

News Release (Beijing), 22 June 1952, reproduced in Peter Lum, *Peking 1950–1953* (London: Robert Hale, 1958), p. 181; *Renmin ribao*, 10 June 1952, p. 3. Over twenty-five years later this charge was still being made in history classes at Peking University (Frances Wood, personal communication).

82 *SCMP*, 25 March 1951, p. 12; 5 February 1952, p. 1; 16 December 1952, p. 1; 31 July 1953, p. 4.

83 Steve Tsang, *Hong Kong: An Appointment with China* (London: I. B. Tauris, 1997), p. 69; Chi-kwan Mark, *Hong Kong and the Cold War: Anglo-American Relations 1949–1957* (Oxford: Oxford University Press, 2004), pp. 26–30; Moisés Silva Fernandes, 'Macao in Sino-Portuguese Relations, 1949–1955', *Portuguese Studies Review* 16:1 (2008), pp. 153–70; Grantham, *Via Ports*, pp. 185–8; *SCMP*, 18 October 1949, pp. 1 and 9; 21 October 1949, p. 8.

84 Robert Bickers, *Britain in China: Community, Culture, and Colonialism* (Manchester: Manchester University Press, 1999), pp. 92–5; Jane Hunter, *The Gospel of Gentility: American Women Missionaries in Turn-of-the-Century China* (New Haven, CT: Yale University Press, 1984). A good survey of the wider debate about the relationship between missions and colonialism is Dana L. Robert, 'Introduction', in Dana L. Robert (ed.), *Converting Colonialism: Visions and Realities in Mission History, 1706–1914* (Grand Rapids, MI: William B. Eerdmans, 2008), pp. 1–20.

85 Sewell, *I Stayed in China*, p. 160.

86 *Nanfang ribao*, 15 and 16 December 1950, translated in Canton no. 44, 18 December 1950, TNA: FO 371/92330.

87 George Hood, *Neither Bang nor Whimper: The End of a Missionary Era in China* (Singapore: Presbyterian Church in Singapore, 1991), pp. 102–12; Gao Wangzhi, 'Y. T. Wu: A Christian Leader under Communism', in Daniel H. Bays (ed.), *Christianity in China: From the Eighteenth Century to the Present* (Stanford, CA: Stanford University Press, 1996), pp. 338–52; manifesto text: Francis Price Jones (ed.), *Documents of the Three-Self Movement: Source Materials for the Study of the Protestant Church in Communist China* (New York: National Council of the Churches of Christ in the United States of American, 1963), pp. 19–20.

88 Paul P. Mariani, *Church Militant: Bishop Kung and Catholic Resistance in Communist Shanghai* (Cambridge, MA: Harvard University Press, 2011); on orphanage trials see extensive correspondence in TNA: FO 371/92230, 92331; on Tianjin see Robert Bickers, *The*

Scramble for China: Foreign Devils in the Qing Empire, 1832–1914 (London: Allen Lane, 2011), pp. 231–6.

89 Yang Kuisong, 'Reconsidering the Campaign to Suppress Counter-Revolutionaries', *China Quarterly* 193 (2008), pp. 102–21; Julia C. Strauss, 'Paternalist Terror: The Campaign to Suppress Counter-Revolutionaries and Regime Consolidation in the People's Republic of China, 1950–1953', *Comparative Studies in Society and History* 44:1 (2002), pp. 80–105; Frank Dikötter, *The Tragedy of Liberation: A History of the Chinese Revolution, 1945–57* (London: Bloomsbury, 2013); on covert action see Frank Holober, *Raiders of the China Coast: CIA Covert Operations during the Korean War* (Annapolis, MD: Naval Institute Press, 1999); James Lilley, with Jeffrey Lilley, *China Hands: Nine Decades of Adventure, Espionage, and Diplomacy in Asia* (New York: PublicAffairs, 2004).

90 For documentation on the Beijing case see TNA: FO 371/92332. The men were most likely part of an American intelligence network of some description, but the elaborate assassination plot was a Chinese fabrication: CIAFOI: Director's Log, 11 September 1951, at http://www.foia.cia.gov/sites/default/files/document_conversions/1700319/1951-09-01.pdf.

91 *NCDN*, 21 October 1950, p. 2.

92 *Jiefang ribao* 693 (29 April 1951) and 754 (1 July 1951); *New China News Agency*, 4 June 1951; *Manchester Guardian*, 14 November 1951, p. 6; John Craig William Keating, *A Protestant Church in Communist China: Moore Memorial Church Shanghai, 1949–1989* (Bethlehem, PA: Lehigh University Church, 2012), p. 99; *Jiefang ribao* 754 (1 July 1951).

93 Frederick C. Teiwes, 'Establishment and Consolidation of the New Regime', in Roderick MacFarquhar and John K. Fairbank (eds), *The Cambridge History of China, Volume 14: The People's Republic, Part 1: The Emergence of Revolutionary China, 1949–1965* (Cambridge: Cambridge University Press, 1987), pp. 88–92.

94 Strauss, 'Paternalist Terror', p. 87; 'On the correct handling of contradictions among the people' (speaking notes), in Roderick MacFarquhar, Timothy Cheek and Eugene Wu (eds), *The Secret Speeches of Chairman Mao: From the Hundred Flowers to the Great Leap Forward* (Cambridge, MA: Council on East Asian Studies, Harvard University, 1989), p. 142.

95 Shanghai no. 266, 5 June 1951, in TNA: FO 371/92332.

96 *NCDN*, 3 August and 17 December 1950, 25 February 1951; Ewo Brewery: Shanghai nos 76, 79, 82, in TNA: FO 371/99283, file FC1105/43.

97 Details from a CIA survey, 'Soviet Economic Installations and Personnel in Communist China', 6 October 1954, pp. 11–15: CIAFOI, at http://www.foia.cia.gov/sites/default/files/document_conversions/89801/DOC_0000474341.pdf, accessed 21 October 2015. This section is indebted to: Deborah A. Kaple, 'Soviet Advisors in China in the 1950s', in Odd Arne Westad (ed.), *Brothers in Arms: The Rise and Fall of the Sino-Soviet Alliance, 1945–1963* (Washington, DC: Woodrow Wilson Center Press, 1998), pp. 117–40; Austin Jersild, *The Sino-Soviet Alliance: An International History* (Chapel Hill, NC: University of North Carolina Press, 2014).

98 Suzanne Pepper, 'Education for the New Order', in MacFarquhar and Fairbank (eds), *The Cambridge History of China, Volume 14*, pp. 201–2.

99 The most comprehensive surveys are Thomas P. Bernstein and Hua-Yu Li (eds), *China Learns from the Soviet Union, 1949–Present* (Plymouth: Lexington Books, 2010), and Yan Li, 'In Search of a Socialist Modernity: The Chinese Introduction of Soviet Culture', unpublished PhD thesis, Northeastern University, 2012.

100 Odd Arne Westad, *Restless Empire: China and the World since 1750* (London: The Bodley Head, 2012), p. 305.

101 Shu Guang Zhang, *Economic Cold War: America's Embargo against China and the Sino-Soviet Alliance, 1949–1963* (Washington, DC: Woodrow Wilson Center Press, 2001), p. 163; see also Lorenz M. Lüthi, *The Sino-Soviet Split: Cold War in the Communist World* (Princeton, NJ: Princeton University Press, 2008), pp. 39–41. The figures vary across different accounts, and were the subject of charge and counter-charge as the alliance fell apart.

102 'Letter . . . [from] Aleksei Vasil'evich Stozhenko', 1956, Russian State Archive of Contemporary History, f. 5, op. 28, r. 5200, d. 506, ll. 94–7. Obtained and translated for CWIHP by Austin Jersild, at http://digitalarchive.wilsoncenter.org/document/116815.

103 Guangzhou: *SCMP*, 7 April 1951, p. 12; 7 September 1951, p. 12; Bin Zhongjun, *Shamian* (Guangzhou: Guangdong renmin chubanshe), pp. 133–9. This paragraph draws on: Mikhail A. Klochko, *Soviet Scientist in China*, trans. Andrew MacAndrew (London: Hollis and Carter, 1963), pp. 56–69; Anne-Marie Brady, *Making the Foreign Serve China: Managing Foreigners in the People's Republic* (Lanham, MD: Rowman and Littlefield, 2003), pp. 86–8; Michael Schoenhals, *Spying for the People: Mao's Secret Agents, 1949–1967* (New York: Cambridge University Press, 2013), pp. 102–9.

104 Sergei N. Goncharov, John W. Lewis and Xue Litai, *Uncertain Partners: Stalin, Mao, and the Korean War* (Stanford, CA: Stanford University Press, 1993), pp. 125–6; Shu Guang Zhang, 'Sino-Soviet Economic Cooperation', in Westad (ed.), *Brothers in Arms*, p. 199. Text and analysis in 'Relations between the Chinese Communist Regime and the USSR: Their Present Character and Probable Future Courses', National Intelligence Estimate 58, 10 September 1952: CIA FOI, at http://www.cia.gov/library/readingroom/docs/DOC_0001086032.pdf.

105 Pepper, 'Education for the New Order', p. 202.

106 Christian A. Hess, 'Big Brother is Watching: Local Sino-Soviet Relations and the Building of New Dalian, 1945–55', in Jeremy Brown and Paul G. Pickowicz (eds), *Dilemmas of Victory: The Early Years of the People's Republic of China* (Cambridge, MA: Harvard University Press, 2007), pp. 160–83.

107 Charles Kraus, 'Creating a Soviet "Semi-Colony"? Sino-Soviet Cooperation and Its Demise in Xinjiang, 1949–1955', *Chinese Historical Review* 17:2 (2010), pp. 129–65.

108 Nicholas R. Lardy, 'Economic Recovery and the 1st Five-Year Plan', in MacFarquhar and Fairbank (eds), *The Cambridge History of China, Volume 14*, p. 149.

109 *Peking Review*, 6 June 1966, pp. 6–7. The history of this alliance is explored in Elez Biberaj, *Albania and China: A Study of an Unequal Alliance* (Boulder, CO, and London: Westview Press, 1986). See also Harry Hamm, *Albania: China's Beachhead in Europe*, trans. Victor Andersen (London: Weidenfeld and Nicolson, 1963).

9. LIGHT OF ASIA

1 Him Mark Lai, *Chinese American Transnational Politics* (Chicago, IL: University of Illinois Press, 2010), p. 95; *China Weekly Review*, 14 November 1936, pp. 377–9, and 21 November 1936, pp. 420–29; *Life*, 25 January 1937, pp. 9–14; and 1 February 1937, pp. 42–5.

2 Anne-Marie Brady, *Making the Foreign Serve China: Managing Foreigners in the People's Republic* (Lanham, MD: Rowman and Littlefield, 2003), pp. 46–7; A. T. Steele, *The American People and China* (New York: McGraw-Hill, 1966), p. 171.

3 Edgar Snow, *Red Star over China* (1937) (Harmondsworth: Penguin Books, 1972, revised and enlarged edition), p. 157. On Snow's venture see Robert M. Farnsworth, *From Vagabond to Journalist: Edgar Snow in Asia, 1928–1941* (Columbia, MI: University of Missouri

Press, 1996), pp. 213–52; S. Bernard Thomas, *Season of High Adventure: Edgar Snow in China* (Berkeley, CA: University of California Press, 1996), pp. 126–89.

4 T. Christopher Jespersen, *American Images of China, 1931–1949* (Stanford, CA: Stanford University Press, 1996), pp. 130–31.

5 Kathryn Weathersby, 'Deceiving the Deceivers: Moscow, Beijing, Pyongyang, and the Allegations of Bacteriological Weapons Use in Korea', Cold War International History Project *Bulletin* 11 (1998), pp. 176–85; Milton Leitenberg, 'New Russian Evidence on the Korean War Biological Warfare Allegations: Background and Analysis', Cold War International History Project *Bulletin* 11 (1998), pp. 185–99.

6 Lucien Bianco, *Peasants without the Party: Grass-Roots Movements in Twentieth-Century China* (Armonk, NY: M. E. Sharpe, 2001); Stephen R. Platt, *Autumn in the Heavenly Kingdom: China, the West, and the Epic Story of the Taiping Civil War* (New York: Knopf, 2012); Paul A. Cohen, *History in Three Keys: The Boxers as Event, Experience and Myth* (New York: Columbia University Press, 1997).

7 Chang-tai Hung, *Going to the People: Chinese Intellectuals and Folk Literature, 1918–1937* (Cambridge, MA: Council on East Asian Studies, Harvard University, 1985); James A. Flath, *The Cult of Happiness: Nianhua, Art and History in Rural North China* (Vancouver: University of British Columbia Press, 2004); David Holm, *Art and Ideology in Revolutionary China* (Oxford: Clarendon Press, 1991).

8 William C. Kirby, *Germany and Republican China* (Stanford, CA: Stanford University Press, 1984), pp. 76–101.

9 Pearl Buck, 'Introduction' (1949), *The Good Earth* (London: Methuen and Co., 1953).

10 Theodore H. White and Annalee Jacoby, *Thunder out of China* (New York: William Sloane Associates, 1946), pp. 20–32, 201–5.

11 James Bertram, *Unconquered: Journal of a Year's Adventures among the Fighting Peasants of North China* (New York: John Day Press, 1939); George Hogg, *I See a New China* (London: Victor Gollancz, 1945).

12 Editorial on 'Chinese "Communism" in Action', *The Times*, 25 January 1945, p. 5; on British views more widely see Brian Porter, *Britain and the Rise of Communist China: A Study of British Attitudes, 1945–1954* (London: Oxford University Press, 1967), pp. 1–24.

13 'Record of Conversation between I. V. Stalin and . . . Mao Zedong [in Moscow] on 16 December 1949', APRF, f. 45, op. 1, d. 329, ll. 9–17. Translated by Danny Rozas, at http://digitalarchive.wilsoncenter.org/document/111240.

14 Nicholas R. Lardy, 'Economic Recovery and the 1st Five-Year Plan', in Roderick MacFarquhar and John K. Fairbank (eds), *The Cambridge History of China, Volume 14: The People's Republic, Part 1: The Emergence of Revolutionary China, 1949–1965* (Cambridge: Cambridge University Press, 1987), pp. 144–84.

15 Peter J. Seybolt, *Throwing the Emperor from his Horse: Portrait of a Village Leader in China, 1923–1995* (Boulder, CO: Westview Press, 1996), pp. 35–6; Huang Shu-min, *The Spiral Road: Change in a Chinese Village through the Eyes of a Communist Party Leader*, 2nd edition (Boulder, CO: Westview Press, 1998), pp. 46–7; Edward Friedman, Paul G. Pickowicz and Mark Selden, with Kay Ann Johnson, *Chinese Village, Socialist State* (New Haven, CT: Yale University Press, 1991), pp. 104–7.

16 William Hinton, *Fanshen: A Documentary of Revolution in a Chinese Village* (New York: Monthly Review Press, 1966), p. 141; Isabel and David Crook, *Revolution in a Chinese Village: Ten Mile Inn* (London: Routledge and Kegan Paul, 1959), p. 151.

17 For a succinct survey see Frederick C. Teiwes, 'Establishment and Consolidation of the New Regime', in MacFarquhar and Fairbank (eds), *The Cambridge History of China, Volume 14*, pp. 83–8. See also Frank Dikötter, *The Tragedy of Liberation: A History of the Chinese Revolution, 1945–57* (London: Bloomsbury, 2013).

18 This section draws on Sun Tan-wei, 'A Village Moves to Socialism', supplement to *China Reconstructs*, October 1956; 'A Peasants' Letter to Chairman Mao', *People's China*, 1 July 1950, p. 14; on 'Li Shunda' see Wolfgang Bartke, *Who Was Who in the People's Republic of China* (Munich: K. G. Saur, 1997), p. 239; Xing Long, 'Zai cunzhuang yu guojia zhi jian: Laodong mofan Li Shunda de geren shenguo shi' ('Between Village and Nation: The Personal Life of Model Worker Li Shunda'), *Shanxi daxue xuebao (Zhexue yu shehui kexue ban)* 30:3 (2007), pp. 143–53.

19 *Shanxi ribao (Shanxi Daily)*, 27 September 1952. On the delegation see Friedman, Pickowicz and Selden, with Johnson, *Chinese Village, Socialist State*, pp. 130–32.

20 Xing Long, 'Zai cunzhuang yu guojia zhi jian', p. 148.

21 William C. Kirby, 'China's Internationalization in the Early People's Republic: Dreams of a Socialist World Economy', *China Quarterly* 188 (2006), pp. 878–9.

22 Huang, *Spiral Road*, pp. 47–8, and passim.

23 Lu Xun, 'What Happens after Nora Leaves Home?', in Hua R. Lan and Vanessa L. Fong (eds), *Women in Republican China: A Source-*

book (Armonk, NY: M. E. Sharpe, 1999), pp. 176–81; Elisabeth Eide, *China's Ibsen: From Ibsen to Ibsenism* (London: Curzon Press, 1987).

24 Louise Edwards, *Gender, Politics, and Democracy: Women's Suffrage in China* (Stanford, CA: Stanford University Press, 2008); on Qiu Jin: Joan Judge, *The Precious Raft of History: The Past, the West and the Woman Question in China* (Stanford, CA: Stanford University Press, 2008); Xie Bingying: Lin Yutang, *Letters of a Chinese Amazon and War-Time Essays* (Shanghai: Commercial Press, 1934); Hsieh Ping-ying, *Girl Rebel: The Autobiography of Hsieh Ping-ying* (New York: John Day Company, 1940), and also *Autobiography of a Chinese Girl: A Genuine Autobiography*, trans. Tsui Chi (London: George Allen and Unwin, 1943).

25 The best survey is Karl Gerth, *China Made: Consumer Culture and the Creation of the Nation* (Cambridge, MA: Harvard University Asia Center, 2003), pp. 285–332, from which this section draws.

26 Neil J. Diamant, *Revolutionizing the Family: Politics, Love and Divorce in Urban and Rural China, 1949–1968* (Berkeley, CA: University of California Press, 2000); for an example of the accompanying propaganda see Li Fengjin, *How the New Marriage Law Helped Chinese Women Stand Up*, ed. and trans. Susan Glosser (Portland, OR: Opal Mogus Books, 2005).

27 For some years up to the time of writing, she has been notorious for her record over six decades at the National People's Congresses of voting in favour of every resolution proposed.

28 A good early discussion is James P. Harrison, 'Chinese Communist Interpretations of the Chinese Peasant Wars', in Albert Feuerwerker (ed.), *History in Communist China* (Cambridge, MA: The MIT Press, 1968), pp. 189–215.

29 Cohen, *History in Three Keys*, pp. 227–34, 241–51.

30 Mao Zedong, 'The Chinese Revolution and the Chinese Communist Party', December 1939, in *Selected Works of Mao Tse-tung, Volume 2* (Beijing: Foreign Languages Press, 1975), pp. 305–34.

31 Luke S. K. Kwong, 'Oral History in China: A Preliminary Review', *Oral History Review* 20:1–2 (1992), pp. 23–50; see also Cohen, *History in Three Keys*, pp. 321–2, n. 97.

32 Chang-tai Hung, *Mao's New World: Political Culture in the Early People's Republic* (Ithaca, NY: Cornell University Press, 2011), pp. 111–26.

33 This paragraph draws on Chang-tai Hung, 'The Dance of Revolution: *Yangge* in Beijing in the Early 1950s', *China Quarterly* 181 (2005), pp.

82–99; see also David Holm, 'Folk Art as Propaganda: The *Yangge* Movement in Yan'an', in Bonnie S. McDougall (ed.), *Popular Chinese Literature and Performing Arts in the People's Republic of China, 1949–1979* (Berkeley, CA: University of California Press, 1984), pp. 3–35.

34 James A. Flath, 'Managing Historical Capital in Shandong: Museum, Monument, and Memory in Provincial China', *The Public Historian* 24:2 (2002), pp. 41–59; Sigrid Schmalzer, *The People's Peking Man: Popular Science and Human Identity in Twentieth-Century China* (Chicago, IL: University of Chicago Press, 2008), pp. 102–3.

35 Pei Wen-chung, 'New Light on Peking Man', *China Reconstructs* 3:4 (1954), pp. 33–5. For a survey of the affair see Jia Lanpo and Huang Weiwen, *The Story of Peking Man: From Archaeology to Mystery* (Beijing: Foreign Languages Press; Hong Kong: Oxford University Press, 1990).

36 Hung, *Mao's New World*, pp. 111–26.

37 Brady, *Making the Foreign Serve China*, pp. 90–91; Cagdas Ungor, 'Reaching the Distant Comrade: Chinese Communist Propaganda Abroad 1949–1976', unpublished PhD thesis, State University of New York at Binghamton, 2009; Lanjun Xu, 'Translation and Internationalism', in Alexander C. Cook (ed.), *Mao's Little Red Book: A Global History* (New York: Cambridge University Press, 2014), pp. 76–95.

38 'The Voice of Peace, Construction and Friendship', *China Pictorial*, 5 April 1959. Esther Cheo Ying, *Black Country Girl in Red China* (London: Hutchinson, 1980); Sidney Rittenberg and Amanda Bennett, *The Man Who Stayed Behind* (Durham, NC: Duke University Press, 2001).

39 Anne-Marie Brady, *Friend of China: The Myth of Rewi Alley* (London: Taylor and Francis, 2004); Israel Epstein, *My China Eye: Memoirs of a Jew and a Journalist* (San Francisco, CA: Long River Press, 2005); Sam Ginsbourg, *My First Sixty Years in China* (Beijing: New World Press, 1982). For surveys see Margaret Stanley, *Foreigners in Areas of China under Communist Jurisdiction before 1949: Biographical Notes and a Comprehensive Bibliography of the Yenan Hui* (Lawrence, KS: University of Kansas, 1987).

40 Takeo Itō, *Life along the South Manchurian Railway*, trans. Joshua A. Fogel (Armonk, NY: M. E. Sharpe, 1988), p. 190; 'Obituary' (Yokogawa Jiro), *Sino-Japanese Studies* 2:2 (1990), p. 2; Yang Xianyi, *White Tiger: An Autobiography of Yang Xianyi* (Hong Kong: Chinese University Press, 2002).

41 William Hinton, *Iron Oxen: A Documentary of Revolution in Chinese Farming* (New York: Monthly Review Press, 1970); Joan Hinton: *Southeast Weekly Bulletin*, 6 January 1966; Isabel Crook, 'Preface', in Isabel Brown Crook and Christina Kelley Gilmartin, with Yu Xiji, *Prosperity's Predicament: Identity, Reform, and Resistance in Rural Wartime China* (Lanham, MD: Rowman and Littlefield, 2013), p. xvii. See also Communist Party of Australia exchanges: Lachlan Strahan, *Australia's China: Changing Perceptions from the 1930s to the 1990s* (Cambridge: Cambridge University Press, 1996), pp. 181–208.

42 Alan Winnington, *Breakfast with Mao: Memoirs of a Foreign Correspondent* (London: Lawrence and Wishart, 1986); *Hampstead Heath to Tian An Men: The Autobiography of David Crook*, at http://www.davidcrook.net (1990); James M. Broughton, 'The Case against Harry Dexter White: Still Not Proven', IMF Working Paper WP/00/149 (August 2000).

43 Brady, *Making the Foreign Serve China*, p. 132; Cheo Ying, *Black Country Girl in Red China*, pp. 156–7.

44 On Myrdal: Perry Johansson, 'Mao and the Swedish United Front against the USA', in Zheng Yangwen, Hong Liu and Michael Szonyi (eds), *The Cold War in Asia: The Battle for Hearts and Minds* (Leiden: Brill, 2010), pp. 223–5; Stephen Endicott, *James G. Endicott: Rebel Out of China* (Toronto: University of Toronto Press, 1980).

45 Crook, *Hampstead Heath to Tian An Men*, chapter 8, p. 8, at http://www.davidcrook.net/pdf/DC11_Chapter8.pdf, accessed 1 October 2015; William H. Hinton, 'Background Notes to *Fanshen*', *Monthly Review* 55:5 (2003); Daniel Raymond Husman, 'Long Bow: Memory and Politics in a Chinese Village', unpublished PhD thesis, University of California, Berkeley, 2011, pp. 13–15.

46 Tom Buchanan, *East Wind: China and the British Left, 1925–1976* (Oxford: Oxford University Press, 2012), pp. 136–41; Michael Shapiro, *Changing China* (London: Lawrence and Wishart, 1958), p. 46. The belief that there was, for example, a 'relatively rare resort to coercion in China to bring peasants to socialism', had a long life: Vivenne Shue, *Peasant China in Transition: The Dynamics of Development toward Socialism, 1949–1956* (Berkeley, CA: University of California Press, 1980), p. 7.

47 Jack Chen, *New Earth: How the Peasants in One Chinese County Solved the Problems of Poverty* (Peking: New World Press, 1957), p. 23.

48 David Hare, 'Author's Preface', *Fanshen* (London: Faber and Faber, 1976).

49 Herbert Passin, *China's Cultural Diplomacy* (New York: Praeger, 1963), p. 1.

50 Buchanan, *East Wind*, pp. 115 and 117.

51 Percy Timberlake, *The 48 Group: The Story of the Icebreakers in China* (London: The 48 Group Club, 1994); Buchanan, *East Wind*, pp. 156–9; John Keswick, quoted in James Tuck-Hong Tang, *Britain's Encounter with Revolutionary China, 1949–54* (Basingstoke: Macmillan, 1992), p. 160.

52 Yunxiang Gao, 'W. E. B. and Shirley Graham Du Bois in Maoist China', *Du Bois Review* 10:1 (2013), pp. 59–85; Matthew D. Johnson, 'From Peace to the Panthers: PRC Engagement with African-American Transnational Networks, 1949–1979', *Past and Present* 218, Supplement 8 (2013), pp. 233–57; Simone de Beauvoir, *The Long March: An Account of Modern China* (*La Longue marche*, 1957), paperback edition (London: Phoenix Press, 2001), p. 501.

53 Matthew D. Rothwell, *Transpacific Revolutionaries: The Chinese Revolution in Latin America* (London: Routledge, 2013), pp. 20–21; Passin, *China's Cultural Diplomacy*, pp. 1–12; Philip Snow, *The Star Raft: China's Encounter with Africa* (London: Weidenfeld and Nicolson, 1988), pp. 72–4.

54 Gordon Barrett, 'Foreign Policy, Propaganda, and Scientific Exchange: Scientists in China's Cold War Foreign Relations', unpublished PhD thesis, University of Bristol, 2015.

55 Mark Clapson, 'The Rise and Fall of Monica Felton, British Town Planner and Peace Activist, 1930s to 1950s', *Planning Perspectives* 30:2 (2015), pp. 211–29; Buchanan, *East Wind*, pp. 130–35.

56 Tom Buchanan, 'The Courage of Galileo: Joseph Needham and the "Germ Warfare" Allegations in the Korean War', *History* 86:284 (2001), pp. 503–22; Ruth Rogaski, 'Nature, Annihilation, and Modernity: China's Korean War Germ-Warfare Experience Reconsidered', *Journal of Asian Studies* 61:2 (2002), pp. 381–415.

57 Hung, *Mao's New World*, pp. 25–72.

58 *China Reconstructs* 6 (November/December 1952), pp. 1–5, 28–32; Brady, *Friend of China*, pp. 68–73; Crook, *Hampstead Heath to Tian An Men*, chapter 10, p. 21.

59 Preface, *What We Saw in China, by 15 Americans* (New York: Weekly Guardian Associates, 1952); Joan Hinton, 'A Statement to the Japanese Delegation', in *Important Documents of the Peace Conference of*

the Asian and Pacific Regions, October 2–12, 1952, Peking (Beijing: Secretariat of the Peace Conference of the Asian and Pacific Regions, 1952).

60 George McTurnan Kahin, *The Asian-African Conference, Bandung, Indonesia, April 1955* (Port Washington, NY: Kennikar Press, 1972).

61 James Cameron, *Mandarin Red: A Journey behind the 'Bamboo Curtain'* (London: Michael Joseph, 1955), pp. 250–51.

62 Zhou Xun, *The Great Famine in China, 1958–1962: A Documentary History,* (New Haven, CT: Yale University Press, 2012), p. 80.

63 Nicholas R. Lardy, 'The Chinese Economy under Stress, 1958–1965', in MacFarquhar and Fairbank (eds), *The Cambridge History of China, Volume 14,* pp. 363–78; Frank Dikötter, *Mao's Great Famine: The History of China's Most Devastating Catastrophe, 1958–62* (London: Bloomsbury, 2010); Felix Wemheuer, 'Dealing with Responsibility for the Great Leap Famine in the People's Republic of China', *China Quarterly* 201 (2010), pp. 176–94.

64 Joan Robinson, *Reports from China: 1953–1976* (London: Anglo-Chinese Educational Institute, 1977), p. 45.

65 Guo Wu, 'Recalling Bitterness: Historiography, Memory, and Myth in Maoist China', *Twentieth-Century China* 39:3 (2014), pp. 245–68.

66 Xiaobing Li, *China's Battle for Korea: The 1951 Spring Offensive* (Bloomington, IN: Indiana University Press, 2014), pp. 239–41.

67 John Wilson Lewis and Xue Litai, *China Builds the Bomb* (Stanford, CA: Stanford University Press, 1988).

68 Lewis and Xue, *China Builds the Bomb,* p. 66.

10. MONSTERS AND DEMONS

1 J. G. Ballard, *Miracles of Life: Shanghai to Shepperton. An Autobiography* (London: Fourth Estate, 2008).

2 J. G. Ballard, 'A Place and a Time to Die', *New Worlds* (September/ October 1969), pp. 4–5; J. G. Ballard, *Empire of the Sun* (1984) (London: Fourth Estate, 2012), pp. 26 and 29.

3 Roderick MacFarquhar and Michael Schoenhals, *Mao's Last Revolution* (Cambridge, MA: The Belknap Press of Harvard University Press, 2006), pp. 222–7. The 'British Masses' – to use the head of mission's phrase – relieved the tedium and retaliated in early August with 'operation effigy', dashing out at night to cut down effigies of Prime Minister Harold Wilson that were hanging outside: Peking Despatch no. 23, 8 August 1967, TNA: FCO 21/33.

4   'Minutes of Chairman Mao Zedong's First Meeting with Nehru', 19 October 1954, PRC Ministry of Foreign Affairs 204-00007-01, 1–10, at http://digitalarchive.wilsoncenter.org/document/117825, accessed 1 November 2015.

5   Thomas Robinson, 'China Confronts the Soviet Union: Warfare and Diplomacy on China's Inner Asian Frontiers', in Roderick MacFarquhar and John K. Fairbank (eds), *The Cambridge History of China, Volume 15: The People's Republic, Part 2: Revolutions within the Chinese Revolution, 1966–1982* (Cambridge: Cambridge University Press, 1991), pp. 227–31; Peter Van Ness, *Revolution and Chinese Foreign Policy: Peking's Support for Wars of National Liberation* (Berkeley, CA: University of California Press, 1970).

6   Alexander C. Cook (ed.), *Mao's Little Red Book: A Global History* (New York: Cambridge University Press, 2014).

7   This section draws on MacFarquhar and Schoenhals, *Mao's Last Revolution*, and Michael Schoenhals (ed.), *China's Cultural Revolution, 1966–1969: Not a Dinner Party* (Armonk, NY: M. E. Sharpe, 1996). Li Zhensheng, *Red-Color News Soldier* (London: Phaidon, 2003), provides an extraordinary visual record of events through the lens of a single photojournalist. See also Frank Dikötter, *The Cultural Revolution: A People's History, 1962–1976* (London: Bloomsbury, 2016).

8   'Verbatim of talk between French delegation and Mao Tse-tung at Hangchow, September 11, 1964', in Peking to FO, CS1015/272, 29 July 1967, TNA: FO 371/186984.

9   Yang Su, *Collective Killings in Rural China during the Cultural Revolution* (New York: Cambridge University Press, 2011), pp. 37–8. The vast majority of deaths were rural.

10 Boyd to Wilson, 31 August 1966, FC1015/141, TNA: FO 371/186982.

11 Peking to FO, 19 December 1966, 1018/66, FC1018/262, TNA: FO 371/186984.

12 Emily Honig, 'Socialist Sex: The Cultural Revolution Revisited', *Modern China* 29:2 (2003), pp. 143–75.

13 MacFarquhar and Schoenhals, *Mao's Last Revolution*, p. 113.

14 Dong Weikun (ed.), *Shanghai jinxi* (*Shanghai Yesterday and Today*) (Shanghai: Shanghai renmin meishu chubanshe, 1958); *Shanghai* (Shanghai: Shanghai renmin duiwai wenhua xiehui Shanghai shi fenhui bian, 1958). The broader history of this genre is surveyed in Martin Parr and WassinkLundgren (comps), *The Chinese Photobook: From the 1900s to the Present* (New York: Aperture, 2015).

15 Lynn T. White III, *Careers in Shanghai: The Social Guidance of Personal Energies in a Developing Chinese City, 1949–1966* (Berkeley, CA: University of California Press, 1978), pp. 56–61; Richard Gaulton, 'Political Mobilization in Shanghai, 1949–1951', in Christopher Howe (ed.), *Shanghai: Revolution and Development in an Asian Metropolis* (Cambridge: Cambridge University Press, 1981), pp. 45–7. The wider programme, which included millions, nationally, is assessed in Thomas P. Bernstein, *Up to the Mountains and Down to the Villages: The Transfer of Youth from Urban to Rural China* (New Haven, CT: Yale University Press, 1977).

16 D. S. Brookfield to Peking, 3 July 1966, FC1015/91, TNA: FO 371/186980.

17 The key source is Wong Siu-lun, *Emigrant Entrepreneurs: Shanghai Industrialists in Hong Kong* (Hong Kong: Oxford University Press, 1988), from which the data are drawn, quotation from p. 13. Capital was also relocated from Southeast Asia as Chinese entrepreneurs found themselves increasingly uncomfortable in several newly independent states. See also David R. Meyer, *Hong Kong as a Global Metropolis* (Cambridge: Cambridge University Press, 2000).

18 D. S. Brookfield to Peking, 3 July 1966, FC1015/91, TNA: FO 371/186980.

19 He Yaping, 'Jianguo yilai Shanghai waiguo renkou bianqian yu renkou guojihua yanjiu' ('Population Change and Internationalization in Shanghai since 1949'), *Shehui kexue* 9 (2009), p. 67; *SCMP*, 6 October 1962, p. 18; 4 February 1964, p. 26; 26 April 1966, p. 18; *The Times of India*, 20 September 1963, p. 3; Linda Benson and Ingvar Svanberg, 'The Russians in Xinjiang: From Immigrants to National Minority', *Central Asian Survey* 8:2 (1989), p. 120.

20 George Stafford Gale, *No Flies in China* (New York: George Morrow and Co., 1955), pp. 77–81; J. E. Hoare, *Embassies in the East: The Story of the British Embassies in Japan, China and Korea from 1859 to the Present* (Richmond, Surrey: Curzon Press, 1999), pp. 74–7.

21 For accounts, Colin Mackerras and Neale Hunter, *China Observed* (Melbourne: Nelson, 1967), pp. 170–73; Sophia Knight, *Window on Shanghai: Letters from China, 1965–67* (London: André Deutsch, 1967), passim.

22 Martin: *NCH*, 23 November 1938, p. 347; Dent: *SCMP*, 19 December 1970, p. 9, and 3 July 1982, p. 8; Mesny: *NCH*, 20 December 1919, pp. 769 and 795; McBain: *NCH*, 18 February 1904, pp. 338–9, and 25 February 1904, p. 363; *SCMP*, 23 April 1971, p. 1; 'Domestic

Servants in Shanghai', 9 June 1967; TNA: FCO 21/33. Journalists: Gale, *No Flies in China*, pp. 153–6.

23 Douglas Hurd, in M. D. Kandiah (ed.), *Witness Seminar: The Role and Functions of the British Embassy in Beijing, 7 June 2012* (London: Foreign and Commonwealth Office, 2013), p. 19; *SCMP*, 21 January 1963, p. 8.

24 *The Sunday Times Magazine*, 10 October 1965, pp. 18–19; see also K. S. Karol, *China: The Other Communism* (London: Heinemann, 1967), p. 233 and photograph after p. 314; James Cameron, *Mandarin Red: A Journey behind the 'Bamboo Curtain'* (London: Michael Joseph, 1955), pp. 224 and 194–8; Sherman Cochran and Andrew Hsieh, *The Lius of Shanghai* (Cambridge, MA: Harvard University Press, 2013), pp. 206–15. See also Christopher Russell Leighton, 'Capitalists, Cadres and Culture in 1950s China', unpublished PhD thesis, Harvard University, 2010.

25 This and the following paragraph draw on: *South China Morning Post*, 8 September 1966, p. 16; TNA: FO 371/186982, Shanghai no. 510/14/66, 29 August 1966; Andrew G. Walder, *Chang Ch'un-ch'iao and Shanghai's January Revolution* (Ann Arbor, MI: University of Michigan Center for Chinese Studies, 1978), pp. 18–19; Denise Y. Ho, 'Revolutionizing Antiquity: The Shanghai Cultural Bureaucracy in the Cultural Revolution, 1966–1968', *China Quarterly* 207 (2011), pp. 692–3; Chi Ti, ' "The East is Red" Rings out over Shanghai', *China Reconstructs* (February 1967), p. 10; Colin Mackerras and Neale Hunter, *China Observed* (London: Sphere Books, 1968), p. 140; face: TNA: FO 371/187045, FO telegram to Peking, 25 August 1966.

26 Honig, 'Socialist Sex', p. 148; Nien Cheng, *Life and Death in Shanghai* (London: Grafton, 1986), pp. 58–9; Riboud: *The Sunday Times*, 10 October 1965, p. 26; Xin Liliang, 'Chairman Mao Gives us a Happy Life' ('Mao zhuxi gei women de xingfu shenghuo') (1954); Chinese posters at http://chineseposters.net/gallery/e16-269.php.

27 Percy Cradock to J. B. Denson, 27 September 1966: TNA, FO 371/186983.

28 Schoenhals (ed.), *China's Cultural Revolution, 1966–1969*, p. 106; Antonia Finnane, *Changing Clothes in China: Fashion, History, Nation* (London: Hurst and Co., 2007), pp. 227–40.

29 Boyd to Wilson, 31 August 1966, FC1015/141: TNA, FO 371/186982; MacFarquhar and Schoenhals, *Mao's Last Revolution*, pp. 117–18; Elizabeth J. Perry and Li Xun, *Proletarian Power: Shanghai in the Cultural*

Revolution (Boulder, CO: Westview, 1997), pp. 11–12, 201, n. 20; Ho, 'Revolutionizing Antiquity', p. 701.

30 See TNA: FO 371/181020.

31 Cheng, *Life and Death in Shanghai*, pp. 63–84, 317–19; Cochran and Hsieh, *The Lius of Shanghai*, pp. 351–2.

32 Austin Jersild, *The Sino-Soviet Alliance: An International History* (Chapel Hill, NC: University of North Carolina Press, 2014), pp. 93–7, 149–55.

33 Robert Bickers, ' "The Greatest Cultural Asset East of Suez": The History and Politics of the Shanghai Municipal Orchestra and Public Band, 1881–1946', in Chi-hsiun Chang (ed.), *China and the World in the Twentieth Century: Selected Essays, Volume 2* (Nankang: Institute of Modern History, Academia Sinica, 2001), pp. 835–75; Chen Xieyang (chief ed.), *The 120th Anniversary Album of the Shanghai Symphony Orchestra (1879–1999)* (Shanghai: Shanghai Symphony Orchestra, 1999).

34 *Renmin ribao*, 24 March 1955.

35 Fu Lei, 'My Son Fu Tsung', *China Reconstructs* (April 1957), pp. 9–11; Richard Curt Kraus, *Pianos and Politics in China: Middle-Class Ambitions and the Struggle over Western Music* (New York: Oxford University Press, 1989), pp. 70–99.

36 Kraus, *Pianos and Politics*, pp. 106–7.

37 *Peking Review*, 8 June 1962; *Chinese Literature*, September 1963, p. 115, and August 1966, pp. 141–2; *Peking Review*, 10 June 1966, pp. 6–8.

38 Kraus, *Pianos and Politics*, p. 93.

39 Cheng, *Life and Death in Shanghai*, pp. 44–54; *Jiefang ribao*, 28 April 1968; Sheila Melvin and Jindong Cai, *Rhapsody in Red: How Western Classical Music Became Chinese* (New York: Algora Publishing, 2007), pp. 233–4, 240.

40 Liao Fangzhou, 'Downbeats and Upbeats', *Global Times*, 2 December 2013; Xu Yanqin, 'Wenge shiqi Zhongguo tanqin gaibian qu de yishu tezheng' ('Artistic Characteristics of Chinese Piano Transcriptions of the Cultural Revolution'), *Wenxue jiaoyu* (March, 2007), p. 134.

41 This section draws on the essays in Robert Bickers and Ray Yep (eds), *May Days in Hong Kong: Riot and Emergency in 1967* (Hong Kong: Hong Kong University Press, 2009).

42 D. C. Hopson to E. Bollard, 15 March 1966, FC 1891/3 TNA, FO 371/187045. This paragraph draws on reports in TNA: FCO 21/33, particularly P. M. Hewitt to D. C. Hopson, 29 June 1967.

43 *The Times*, 14 September 1967, p. 5.

44 'British Premises in Shanghai', 15 September 1967, Rodgers minute, 16 September 1967, in TNA, FO 371/187045. The diplomats could

find no record of the consulate ever paying a peppercorn ground rent on the site, as required by the original lease.

45 D. C. Hopson to George Brown, 31 August 1967, 'The Burning of the British Office in Peking'; and D. C. Hopson to J. B. Denson, 14 September, enclosing personal statements by the British staff, in TNA, FC 21/34. Accounts of events are given in Hoare, *Embassies in the East*, pp. 82–6; Anthony Grey, *Hostage in Peking* (London: Michael Joseph, 1970), pp. 120–32.

46 A. J. de la Mare minute, 15 September 1967, on TNA: FCO 21/34, 'British Premises in Shanghai'; Chi-kwan Mark, 'Hostage Diplomacy: Britain, China, and the Politics of Negotiation, 1967–1969', *Diplomacy & Statecraft* 20:3 (2009), pp. 473–93.

47 Grey, *Hostage in Peking*; George Watt, *China 'Spy'* (London: Johnson, 1972). Watt's guilt is still taken as a fact in China; Kost: 'A Tolerant Man Savours Freedom', *SCMP*, 19 February 1986, p. 31. It was another four years before Kost managed to leave the country.

48 M. Uysal, Lu Wei and L. M. Reid, 'Development of International Tourism in PR China', *Tourism Management* 7:2 (1986), pp. 113–19; 'British Agents Plan More Routes to China', *The Times*, 16 July 1965, p. 18.

49 Anne-Marie Brady, *Making the Foreign Serve China: Managing Foreigners in the People's Republic* (Lanham, MD: Rowman and Littlefield, 2003), pp. 146–69.

50 Honours: *SCMP*, 3 April 1970, p. 1; *SCMP*, 12 October 1969, p. 1; He, 'Jianguo yilai Shanghai waiguo renkou bianqian yu renkou guojihua yanjiu', p. 67.

51 *SCMP*, 5 February 1967, p. 1.

52 This section draws on: *SCMP*, 13 February 1967, p. 18; Thomas W. Robinson, 'The Sino-Soviet Border Dispute: Background, Development and the March 1969 Clashes', *American Political Science Review* 66:4 (1972), pp. 1175–202; Yang Kuisong, 'The Sino-Soviet Border Clash of 1969: From Zhenbao Island to Sino-American *Rapprochement*', *Cold War History* 1:1 (2000), pp. 21–52; Christian F. Ostermann, 'East German Documents on the Border Conflict, 1969', Cold War International History Project *Bulletin* 6/7 (1995–6), pp. 186–93.

53 Grey, *Hostage in Peking*, p. 72

54 A comprehensive survey is provided by M. Taylor Fravel, *Strong Borders, Secure Nation: Cooperation and Conflict in China's Territorial Disputes* (Princeton, NJ: Princeton University Press, 2008).

55 Arkady N. Shevchenko, *Breaking with Moscow* (London: Jonathan Cape, 1985), p. 164.

56 Elizabeth McGuire, 'The Book that Bombed: Mao's Little Red Thing in the Soviet Union', in Cook (ed.), *Mao's Little Red Book*, pp. 149–50; Elizabeth McGuire, 'China, the Fun House Mirror: Soviet Reactions to the Chinese Cultural Revolution, 1966–1969', Berkeley Program in Soviet and Post-Soviet Studies Working Paper (spring 2001), pp. 25–34; Yevtuschenko's 'On the Red Ussuri Snow', published in *Literaturnaya Gazeta*, no. 12, 19 March 1969: translation from *Studies in Comparative Communism* 2:3/4 (1969), pp. 211–13; Andrei Amalrik, *Will the Soviet Union Survive until 1984?* (London: Allen Lane, 1970).

57 Harold R. Isaacs, *Scratches on Our Minds: American Images of China and India* (New York: John Day, 1958); William G. Mayer, *The Changing American Mind: How and Why American Public Opinion Changed between 1960 and 1988* (Ann Arbor, MI: University of Michigan Press, 1993), pp. 58–9, 420. Rusk denied the charge, but the trope was ever close to the surface: *Chicago Defender*, 15 March 1967, p. 13; *The New York Times*, 15 October 1967, p. 204; *The Washington Post*, 17 October 1967, p. A1.

58 On film see Naomi Greene, *From Fu Manchu to Kung Fu Panda: Images of China in American Film* (Hong Kong: Hong Kong University Press, 2014), pp. 95–150.

59 See Tom Buchanan, *East Wind: China and the British Left, 1925–1976* (Oxford: Oxford University Press, 2012), pp. 199–204; Richard Wolin, *The Wind from the East: French Intellectuals, the Cultural Revolution, and the Legacy of the 1960s* (Princeton, NJ: Princeton University Press, 2010); Edward P. Morgan, *The 60s Experience: Hard Lessons about Modern America* (Philadelphia, PA: Temple University Press, 1991); Quinn Slobodian, *Foreign Front: Third World Politics in Sixties West Germany* (Durham, NC: Duke University Press, 2012). The quotation is from Frida Knight, 'Another View of the Red Guards', *Society for Anglo-Chinese Understanding News*, 1:12 (October 1966), pp. 1–2.

60 Lanjun Xu, 'Translation and Internationalism', in Cook (ed.), *Mao's Little Red Book*, pp. 85–6; Slobodian, *Foreign Front*, p. 286.

61 Carol Hanisch, 'Impact of the Chinese Cultural Revolution on the Women's Liberation Movement', in *Women of the World, Unite: Writings by Carol Hanisch* (1996), at http://www.carolhanisch.org/Speeches/ChinaWLMSpeech/ChinaWLspeech.html.

62 Clem Gorman, *Making Communes* (Bottisham: Whole Earth Tools, 1971), p. 96. It should be noted that 'Maoism' does not exist as a Chi-

nese term. Instead, the formation used is 'Mao Zedong Thought' (*Mao Zedong sixiang*).

63 Hare has since disowned the comment: David Hare, *Fanshen* (London: Faber and Faber, 1976), pp. 7–10; David Hare, *Writing Left-Handed* (London: Faber and Faber, 1991), pp. 64–72; 'After *Fanshen*: A Discussion . . .', in David Bradby, Louis James and Bernard Sharratt (eds), *Performance and Politics in Popular Drama: Aspects of Popular Entertainment in Theatre, Film and Television, 1800–1976* (Cambridge: Cambridge University Press, 1980), pp. 297–314.

64 *Vogue*, September 1967, p. 231; 'Le Petite Livre *Rose* de Mao', *Lui*, June 1967, pp. 46–53; *Life*, 10 December 1971, pp. 59–65; *Daily Mail*, 10 October 1967, p. 6.

65 Wolin, *The Wind from the East*, pp. 197–203.

66 Robeson Taj Frazier, *The East is Black: Cold War China in the Black Radical Imagination* (Durham, NC: Duke University Press, 2014).

67 See Zachary A. Scarlett, 'China after the Sino-Soviet Split: Maoist Politics, Global Narratives, and the Imagination of the World', unpublished PhD thesis, Northeastern University, 2013, pp. 169–238.

68 *Peking Review*, 22 July 1966, pp. 6–11.

69 *Daily Mail*, 28 August 1967, p. 2; *Peking Review*, 8 September 1967, pp. 28–9.

70 *Renmin ribao*, 25 December 1970, p. 1; Edgar Snow, *Red Star over China* (1937) (Harmondsworth: Penguin Books, 1972, revised and enlarged edition), p. 324.

11. UNFINISHED BUSINESS

1 Xu Guoqi, *Olympic Dreams: China and Sports, 1895–2008* (Cambridge, MA: Harvard University Press, 2008), pp. 117–48; Tim Broggan, *Ping-Pong Oddity* (1999), chapter 5, online at http://www.usatt.net/articles/ppoddity05.shtml.

2 Boggled: Marshall Green, Assistant Secretary for Far Eastern Affairs, quoted in *The New York Times*, 18 April 1971, p. E1; Tannehill: *The New York Times*, 13 April 1971, p. 14; Dulles: *The New York Times*, 23 May 1954, p. SM10; Evelyn Shuckburgh, *Descent to Suez: Diaries 1951–56* (London: Weidenfeld and Nicolson, 1986), pp. 163–4, 185–6; Zhou, in 'Memorandum of Conversation . . . Monday, February 21, 1972, 5:58 p.m.–6:55 p.m.', at http://nsarchive.gwu.edu/nsa/publications/DOC_readers/kissinger/nixzhou/11-01.htm.

3 Yafeng Xia, *Negotiating with the Enemy: U.S.–China Talks during the Cold War, 1949–1972* (Bloomington, IN: Indiana University Press, 2006).

4 George Brathwaite, 'My China Visit as a Ping Pong Diplomat', *Ebony*, November 1971, pp. 84–92; 'NBC News Special Report: American Ping Pong Team Visits China', 20 April 1971; *Time*, 26 April 1971; *Life*, 30 April 1971.

5 The yacht's owner had allegedly killed himself while in Chinese hands: Mary Ann Harbert, *Captivity: 44 Months in Red China* (New York: Delacourt Press, 1973).

6 Shih Ta-peng, 'US Imperialism Means War and Aggression', *China Reconstructs* (May 1971), p. 12.

7 Robert Accinelli, 'In Pursuit of a Modus Vivendi: The Taiwan Issue and Sino-American Rapprochement, 1969–1972', in William C. Kirby, Robert S. Ross and Gong Li (eds), *Normalization of U.S.–China Relations: An International History* (Cambridge, MA: Harvard University Asia Center, 2005), pp. 9–55.

8 There is a substantial literature on the 1971–2 visits. As well as the self-serving accounts of Kissinger and Nixon, which newer documents show to be quite incomplete, more material has now emerged from Chinese sources. I have used: Evelyn Goh, *Constructing the U.S. Rapprochement with China, 1961–1974* (Cambridge: Cambridge University Press, 2004); Henry Kissinger, *White House Years* (London: Phoenix Press, 2000); and the National Security Archive Electronic Briefing Books.

9 Shuckburgh, *Descent to Suez*, p. 178; how literal the refusal to shake hands actually was remains a subject of disagreement, but see Nancy Bernkopf Tucker, *The China Threat: Memories, Myths, and Realities in the 1950s* (New York: Columbia University Press, 2012), pp. 28 and 64–5.

10 *Oakland Tribune*, 28 September 1950, p. 6.

11 Jay Taylor, *The Generalissimo: Chiang Kai-shek and the Struggle for Modern China* (Cambridge, MA: Harvard University Press, 2009), p. 426.

12 See especially Joyce Mao, *Asia First: China and the Making of Modern American Conservatism* (Chicago, IL: University of Chicago Press, 2015), and Stanley D. Bachrack, *The Committee of One Million: 'China Lobby' Politics, 1953–1971* (New York: Columbia University Press, 1976).

13 'Record of conversation between . . . Edward Heath . . . and Premier Chou En-lai . . . 27 May 1974', TNA: FCO 21/1240.

14 *Life*, 30 April 1971, pp. 25 and 34; *SCMP*, 22 April 1971, p. 18.

15 Robert Hoppens, *The China Problem in Postwar Japan: Japanese National Identity and Sino-Japanese Relations* (London: Bloomsbury Academic, 2015), pp. 80–98; *The New York Times*, 25 September 1972, pp. 1–2.

16 Hoppens, *The China Problem*, pp. 86–91.

17 A good survey is Robert Boardman, *Britain and the People's Republic of China 1949–74* (Basingstoke: Macmillan, 1976).

18 A. V. Waters to H. Llewellyn Davies, 19 September 1972, TNA: FCO 21/993.

19 E. J. Richardson to H. Llewellyn Davies, 8 November 1972, TNA: FCO 21/995.

20 A. Douglas-Home, 'A Fleeting Visit to Peking', 6 November 1972, FCO, 21/995; Tanaka: United States Embassy (Japan), Confidential, Cable, 16 October 1972: Digital National Security Archive collection, Japan and the US, 1960–76.

21 'Secretary of State's Visit to China', K. M. Wilford drafting edits, 19 October 1972, TNA: FCO 21/994.

22 'Record of conversation between the Prime Minister of China and the Foreign & Commonwealth Secretary ... 1 November 1972', TNA: FCO 21/995.

23 Sir Anthony Galsworthy, 'The Possibility of a British Withdrawal from Hong Kong', 31 May 1967, TNA: DEFE 13/857; and 'Cabinet Ministerial Committee on Hong Kong', Minutes, 22 September 1967; and 'Feasibility Study on Evacuation of Hong Kong', 20 September 1967, TNA: CAB 134/2945.

24 'Meeting between Chair Mao Tse-tung and Mr. Heath, 25 May 1974', TNA: FCO 21/1240.

25 'Memorandum of Conversation', Kissinger and Zhou, 20 October 1971, National Security Archive Electronic Briefing Book No. 70, at nsarchive.gwu.edu/NSAEBB/NSAEBB70/doc10.pdf, accessed 16 December 2015.

26 This section draws on: file on 'Cultural Relations between China and UK', TNA: FCO 21/1007; file on 'Exchange of Wild Animals by China as Tokens of Friendship', 1959, TNA: FO 371/141348; Boardman, *Britain and the People's Republic of China*; and Amy Jane Barnes, *Museum Representations of Maoist China: From Cultural Revolution to Commie Kitsch* (Farnham: Ashgate, 2014); Richard Curt Kraus, *Pianos and Politics in China: Middle-Class Ambitions and the Struggle over Western Music* (New York: Oxford University Press, 1989), pp. 169–73.

27 My sources here are: 'Cultural Relations between China and UK', TNA: FCO 21/1007; Royal Academy Archives, 'Genius of China Files', RAA/EXH/1/16/1–2; Royal Society Archives, NCUACS/2/1/88, Great Britain China Centre records in papers of Sir Harold Thompson.

28 *Editor-in-Chief: The Fleet Street Memoirs of Sir Denis Hamilton* (London: Hamish Hamilton, 1989), pp. 154–6. The exhibition is generally known as 'The Genius of China', but in fact *The Times* was more diplomatic in its advertising, for all of Hamilton's bluster, and simply referred to it as 'The Chinese Exhibition'. Toronto's Royal Ontario Museum used the British catalogue, written by the art historian William Watson, head of London University's Percival David Foundation, but dropped the title.

29 *The Genius of China: An Exhibition of Archaeological Finds of the People's Republic of China Held at the Royal Academy, London . . .* (London: Times Newspapers, 1973); Tracey L-D Lu, *Museums in China: Power, Politics and Identities* (London: Routledge, 2014), pp. 132–3; 'Chinese Change Catalogue in US Exhibition', *The Times*, 31 December 1974, p. 9. Longmen Caves: Karl E. Meyer and Shareen Blair Brysac, *The China Collectors: America's Century-Long Hunt for Asian Art Treasures* (New York: Palgrave Macmillan, 2015), pp. 90–101; Xia Nai's attitude in general to foreign scholars of Chinese archaeology, and the wider political context, are discussed in Enzheng Tong, 'Thirty Years of Chinese Archaeology (1949–1979)', in Philip L. Kohl and Clare Fawcett (eds), *Nationalism, Politics and the Practice of Archaeology* (Cambridge: Cambridge University Press, 1995), pp. 177–97; ticket: *The Times*, 29 September 1973, p. 1.

30 Adam Cathcart, 'Nixon, Kissinger and Musical Diplomacy in the Opening of China, 1971–1973', *Yonsei Journal of International Studies* 4:1 (2012), pp. 131–9.

31 *The Times*, 24 September 1971, p. 9, and 5 October 1971, p. 14.

32 *A Vicious Motive, Despicable Tricks – A Criticism of M. Antonioni's Anti-China Film China* (Beijing: Foreign Languages Press, 1974). On this affair see Jiwei Xiao, 'A Traveller's Glance: Antonioni in China', *New Left Review* 79 (2013), pp. 103–20; Xin Liu, 'China's Reception of Michelangelo Antonioni's *Chung Kuo*', *Journal of Italian Cinema & Media Studies* 2:1 (2014), pp. 23–40; Sun Hongyun, 'Two Chinas? Joris Ivens' *Yukong* and Antonioni's *China*', *Studies in Documentary Film* 3:1 (2009), pp. 45–59.

33 Beverley Hooper, *Inside Peking: A Personal Report* (London: Macdonald and Jane's, 1979), pp. 75–7; Isabel Hilton, 'Struggling with

Antonioni', 24 October 2012, *ChinaFile*, at https://www.chinafile.com/struggling-antonioni, accessed 1 December 2015.

34 Hilary Spurling, *Pearl Buck in China: Journey to the Good Earth* (New York: Simon and Schuster, 2010), p. 251.

35 Except where specified, this section draws on Ralph Clough, 'Taiwan under Nationalist Rule, 1949–1982', in Roderick MacFarquhar and John K. Fairbank (eds), *The Cambridge History of China, Volume 15: The People's Republic, Part 2: Revolutions within the Chinese Revolution, 1966–1982* (Cambridge: Cambridge University Press, 1991), pp. 815–74; Taylor, *Generalissimo*; and Tucker, *The China Threat*.

36 *Xinwenbao*, 20 May 1951, and *Dagongbao*, 20 May 1951.

37 Bruce A. Elleman, *High Seas Buffer: The Taiwan Patrol Force, 1950–1979* (Newport, RI: Naval War College Press, 2012).

38 Steve Tsang, 'Target Zhou Enlai: The "Kashmir Princess" Incident of 1955', *China Quarterly* 139 (1994), pp. 766–82.

39 'Memorial in Beijing Sheds Light on Communist Spies', *SCMP*, 16 February 2014.

40 Tehyun Ma, 'Mobilizing Taiwan: The Building of the Chinese Nationalist State on Taiwan, 1945–1955', unpublished PhD, University of Bristol, 2010.

41 Paul A. Cohen, *History and Popular Memory: The Power of Story in Moments of Crisis* (New York: Columbia University Press, 2014), pp. 94–104; Ralph C. Croizier, *Koxinga and Chinese Nationalism: History, Myth, and the Hero* (Cambridge, MA: East Asian Research Center, Harvard University, 1977). The claims for Koxinga's intention to restore Ming rule after 1681 are disputed.

42 *Guomin xiaoxue Guoyu keben* (*Elementary School Mandarin Textbook*), Book 6 (Taibei: Taiwan shudian, 1981), pp. 75–6.

43 Duncan Norton-Taylor, 'The Sword Aimed at Red China', *Life International*, 27 January 1967, pp. 80–85. This originally appeared in *Fortune*.

44 Sources for this section include John W. Garver, *The Sino-American Alliance: Nationalist China and American Cold War Strategy in Asia* (London: Routledge, 2015). Taylor's biographies of Chiang Kai-shek and his son, and Murray A. Rubinstein (ed.), *Taiwan: A New History* (Armonk, NY: M. E. Sharpe, 1999).

45 Political executions largely ceased after 1954: Jay Taylor, *The Generalissimo's Son: Chiang Ching-kuo and the Revolutions in China and Taiwan* (Cambridge, MA: Harvard University Press, 2000), pp. 211–12, 221; Taylor, *Generalissimo*, pp. 464–5; M. Taylor Fravel, 'Towards

Civilian Supremacy: Civil-Military Relations in Taiwan's Democratization', *Armed Forces & Society* 29:1 (2002), pp. 57–84.

46 Taylor, *Generalissimo*, pp. 501 and 549.

47 Taylor, *Generalissimo*, pp. 426 and 437.

48 Wu Ming (ed.), *Meiguo hua (American)* (Taibei: Zhongtai shudian, 1983), pp. 59 and 63.

49 *The New York Times*, 26 May 1957, pp. 1 and 37. The incident, and the wider history of US military assistance, is explored in Stephen G. Craft, *American Justice in Taiwan: The 1957 Riots and Cold War Foreign Policy* (Lexington, KY: University Press of Kentucky, 2016).

50 On this see the papers in Kirby, Ross and Li (eds), *Normalization of U.S.–China Relations*.

51 The date from which Portuguese Macao took its formal establishment was 1557. For Sino-Portuguese relations and Macao after 1949 see Moisés Silva Fernandes, *Confluência de Interesses: Macau nas Relações Luso-Chinesas Contemporâneas, 1945–2005* (Lisbon: Ministério dos Negocios Estrangeiros, 2008).

52 See J. E. Holmes to John Coles, 6 December 1982, TNA: PREM 19/1053.

53 *SCMP*, 10 April 1987, pp. 1–3.

54 Steve Tsang, *Governing Hong Kong: Administrative Officers from the Nineteenth Century to the Handover to China, 1862–1997* (London: I. B. Tauris, 2007).

55 This number includes Gurkha soldiers, and is more accurately, but coyly, 'British Commonwealth' inhabitants: details here and below from Defence Review Working Party, 'Hong Kong', January 1968, TNA: T317/902.

56 *SCMP*, 21 May 1971, p. 10, and 31 March 1978, p. 8.

57 *SCMP*, 10 December 1994, p. 6, and 19 August 1995, p. 5.

58 This section draws on Mark Hampton, *Hong Kong and British Culture, 1945–97* (Manchester: Manchester University Press, 2016), and personal information.

59 Henry Lethbridge, *Hard Graft in Hong Kong: Scandal, Corruption, the ICAC* (Hong Kong: Oxford University Press, 1985); Ray Yep, 'The Crusade against Corruption in Hong Kong in the 1970s: Governor MacLehose as a Zealous Reformer or Reluctant Hero?', *China Information* 27:2 (2013), pp. 197–221.

60 *SCMP*, 26 March 1966, p. 6; 14 March 1975, p. 7; 9 March 1973, p. 8; 28 October 1996, p. 6.

61 A *Tin Tin Yat Po* editorial quoted in *SCMP*, 14 August 1968, p. 11; 9 March 1969, p. 1.

62 Fan Shuh Ching, *The Population of Hong Kong* (Hong Kong: Committee for International Coordination of National Research in Demography, 1974). More widely this section draws on David Faure, 'Reflections on being Chinese in Hong Kong', in Judith M. Brown and Rosemary Foot (eds), *Hong Kong's Transitions, 1842–1997* (Basingstoke: Macmillan Press, 1997), pp. 103–20; Helen F. Siu, 'Remade in Hong Kong: Weaving into the Chinese Cultural Tapestry', in Tao Tao Liu and David Faure (eds), *Unity and Diversity: Local Cultures and Identities in China* (Hong Kong: Hong Kong University Press, 1996), pp. 177–96; on the colonial administration's work see, for example, TNA: FCO 40/105–6, 'Disturbances in Hong Kong: Propaganda'.

63 These developments are the subject of Catherine R. Schenk, *Hong Kong as an International Financial Centre: Emergence and Development 1945–65* (London: Routledge, 2001), and David R. Meyer, *Hong Kong as a Global Metropolis* (Cambridge: Cambridge University Press, 2000).

64 Beijing no. 432, 11 May 1979, TNA: PREM 19/963.

65 In this she was not alone: Hampton, *Hong Kong and British Culture*, pp. 42–71.

66 Leo F. Goodstadt, *Poverty in the Midst of Affluence: How Hong Kong Mismanaged Its Prosperity* (Hong Kong: Hong Kong University Press, 2014), p. 73.

67 Lord Carrington minute, 9 October 1979, TNA: PREM 19/789; 'Record of a discussion between the Prime Minister and Premier Hua Guofeng', 1 November 1979, TNA: PREM 19/3.

68 Thatcher Mss, Churchhill Archive Centre, THRC 1/10/39-2 f52.

69 The records of the meetings with the Chinese leadership are in TNA: PREM 19/962. For a recent analysis see Chi-kwan Mark, 'To "Educate" Deng Xiaoping in Capitalism: Thatcher's Visit to China and the Future of Hong Kong in 1982', *Cold War History*, forthcoming 2017. For a wider survey of the Hong Kong negotiations from which this section draws see Steve Tsang, *Hong Kong: An Appointment with China* (London: I. B. Tauris, 1997).

70 FCO, 'The Future of Hong Kong: A Special Study', August 1982, TNA: PREM 19/792.

71 'A Hasty Guide to the History of China', September 1982, TNA: PREM 19/962; 'Speech at Chinese Welcoming Banquet, 22 September 1982', Margaret Thatcher Foundation, archives, www.margaretthatcher.org/document/105022.

72 Examples and discussion in TNA: PREM 19/1053. Thatcher's comments can be found scribbled on PM/83/17, 'Future of Hong Kong'.

73 The comment was Percy Cradock's, 'Note of a Meeting, 5 September 1983 at 10 Downing Street', TNA: PREM 19/1057.

74 Zhou Nan, quoted in Beijing no. 571, Cradock, 21 June 1983, TNA: PREM 19/1055.

75 Zhao Ziyang to Margaret Thatcher, 28 April 1983, text in Beijing no. 439, 12 May 1983, TNA: PREM 19/1055.

76 Cradock discussions with Yao Kang, in Beijing no. 932, 23 September 1983, and Beijing no. 927, 22 September 1983, TNA: PREM 19/1057.

77 Patten's roller-coaster ride is chronicled in his own book *East and West* (London: Macmillan, 1998), and Jonathan Dimbleby, *The Last Governor: Chris Patten and the Handover of Hong Kong* (London: Little, Brown and Company, 1997).

78 Wm. Roger Louis, 'Hong Kong: The Critical Phase, 1945–1949', *American Historical Review* 102:4 (1997), pp. 1052–84.

79 *SCMP*, 27 April 1974, p. 1.

80 *SCMP*, 31 May 1974, p. 5. This section draws on Cathryn H. Clayton, *Sovereignty at the Edge: Macau and the Question of Chineseness* (Cambridge, MA: Harvard University Asia Center, 2009); Moisés Silva Fernandes, 'The Normalization of Portuguese-Chinese Relations and Macao's Handover to Mainland China, 1974–1979', *China: An International Journal* 13:1 (2015), pp. 3–21; and Lo Shiu-hing, 'Aspects of Political Development in Macao', *China Quarterly* 120 (1989), pp. 837–51.

81 Yoshiko Nozaki, *War Memory, Nationalism and Education in Postwar Japan, 1945–2007: The Japanese History Textbook Controversy and Ienega Saburo's Court Challenges* (London: Routledge, 2008); Ienaga Saburo, *The Pacific War: 1931–1945* (New York: Pantheon Books, 1978). On the post-war period see John Dower, *Embracing Defeat: Japan in the Wake of World War II* (London: Allen Lane, 1999).

82 Hoppens, *The China Problem*, pp. 62–3, 95–6.

83 Yang Chan, 'Reconsidering the Sino-Japanese history problem: remembrance of the Fifteen-year War in mainland China prior to the 1982 textbook incident', unpublished PhD thesis, University of Bristol, 2014.

84 Caroline Rose, *Interpreting History in Sino-Japanese Relations: A Case Study in Political Decision-Making* (London: Routledge, 1998).

85 Iris Chang, *The Rape of Nanking: The Forgotten Holocaust of World War II* (New York: Basic Books, 1997); Honda Katsuichi, *The Nanjing Massacre: A Japanese Journalist Confronts Japan's National Shame* (Armonk, NY: M. E. Sharpe, 1999); Jing-Bao Nie, Nanyan Guo, Mark Selden and Arthur Kleinman, *Japan's Wartime Medical Atrocities:*

Comparative Inquiries in Science, History, and Ethics (Abingdon: Routledge, 2010); Joshua A. Fogel (ed.), *The Nanjing Massacre in History and Historiography* (Berkeley, CA: University of California Press, 2000); Bob Tadashi Wakabayashi (ed.), *The Nanking Atrocity 1937–38: Complicating the Picture* (New York: Berghahn Books, 2007).

86 The viciousness of the Pacific War, on both sides, is discussed in John W. Dower, *War without Mercy: Race and Power in the Pacific War* (New York: Pantheon Books, 1986). See also Kai Bird and Lawrence Lifschultz (eds), *Hiroshima's Shadow: Writings on the Denial of History and the Smithsonian Controversy* (Stony Creek, NY: Pamphleteer's Press, 1998).

87 On these museums see: Kirk A. Denton, 'Heroic Resistance and Victims of Atrocity: Negotiating the Memory of Japanese Imperialism in Chinese Museums', *Asia-Pacific Journal* 5:10 (2007), at http://japanfocus. net/-Kirk_A_-Denton/2547/article.html, accessed 15 January 2016; Rana Mitter, 'Educating Citizens through War Museums in Modern China', in Véronique Bénéï (ed.), *Manufacturing Citizenship: Education and Nationalism in Europe, South Asia and China* (London: Routledge, 2005), pp. 129–42.

88 *SCMP*, 26 October 1981, p. 10, 'How Wham! Baffled Chinese Youth in First Pop Concert', *Guardian*, 9 May 2005; the exchange at the ministry is in the film *Foreign Skies* (1986, dir. Lindsay Anderson); Simon Napier-Bell, *I'm Coming to Take You to Lunch* (New York: Wenner Books, 2009), p. 47; Rod Wye, Beijing, to John Boyd, FCO, 18 April 1985, PC293/301/2, at http://www.theguardian.com/politics/foi/images/0,9069,1480049,00.html; Ying Ruocheng and Claire Conceison, *Voices Carry: Behind Bars and Backstage during China's Revolution and Reform* (Lanham, MD: Rowman and Littlefield, 2009), p. xxiii; Arthur Miller, *Salesman in Beijing* (London: Methuen, 1984).

89 Hugh Baker, series Chief Editorial Consultant, quoted in Cao Qing, *China under Western Gaze: Representing China in British Television Documentaries, 1980–2000* (Singapore: World Scientific Publishing, 2014), p. 221; Alasdair Clayre, *Heart of the Dragon* (London: Harvill Press, 1984), p. 103.

90 This section draws on Ezra F. Vogel, *Deng Xiaoping and the Transformation of China* (Cambridge, MA: Belknap Press of Harvard University Press, 2011), pp. 394–422.

91 Liu Haiyan and Kristin Stapleton, 'Chinese Urban History: State of the Field', *China Information* 20:3 (2006), pp. 391–427.

92 Vogel, *Deng Xiaoping*, pp. 595–639, quotation from p. 617.

93 William A. Callahan, *China: The Pessoptimist Nation* (Oxford: Oxford University Press, 2010).

94 See the several hundred entries in *Zhongguo jinianguan* (English title given as *Chinese Museum Guide*) (Shanghai: Zhongguo bowuguan xie-hui jinianguan zhuanye weiyuanhui, 2010), Shaoshan at pp. 579–80.

12. HAUNTED BY HISTORY

1 Geremie R. Barmé, *In the Red: On Contemporary Chinese Culture* (New York: Columbia University Press, 1999). For an additional reading of Ai Jing's song see Nimrod Baranovitch, *China's New Voices: Popular Music, Ethnicity, Gender, and Politics, 1978–1997* (Berkeley, CA: University of California Press, 2003), pp. 162–72.

2 For a good account of this see Joe Studwell, *The China Dream: The Elusive Quest for the Greatest Untapped Market on Earth* (London: Profile Books, 2002).

3 Xie Jin is quoted in a Reuters report on 9 June 1997, 'Britain and China Refight Opium War on Film'; 'China's Epic Exorcism', *The Guardian*, 12 June 1997, p. 17. This discussion draws on two essays by Zhiwei Xiao: 'The Opium War: History, Politics and Propaganda', *Asian Cinema* 11:1 (2000), pp. 68–83, and 'Nationalism in Chinese Popular Culture: A Case Study of *The Opium War*', in C. X. George Wei and Xiaoyuan Liu (eds), *Exploring Nationalisms of China: Themes and Conflicts* (Westport, CT: Greenwood Press, 2002), pp. 41–54.

4 There is continuity too in the use of the Shanghai park sign: *Shanghai zujie de heimu* (*The Dark Side of the Shanghai Concessions*) (Shanghai: Shanghai tebie shi, Xuanchuan bu, 1943).

5 Excellent guides to these changes are provided in Peter Hessler's books *River Town: Two Years on the Yangtze* (New York: HarperCollins, 2001), *Oracle Bones: A Journey through Time in China* (New York: HarperCollins, 2006), and *Country Driving: A Chinese Road Trip* (New York: HarperCollins, 2010), and Duncan Hewitt, *Getting Rich First: Life in a Changing China* (London: Chatto and Windus, 2007).

6 See James Farrer and Andrew David Field, *Shanghai Nightscapes: A Nocturnal Biography of a Global City* (Chicago, IL: University of Chicago Press, 2015). A good discussion about the impact of new overseas residence in the city is James Farrer, 'Foreigner Street: Urban Citizenship in Multicultural Shanghai', in Nam-Kook Kim (ed.), *Multicultural Challenges and Redefining Identity in East Asia* (Farnham: Ashgate, 2013), pp. 17–43.

7 Louisa Lim, *The People's Republic of Amnesia: Tiananmen Revisited* (New York: Oxford University Press, 2014), pp. 148–50.

8 Maurizio Marinelli, 'The "New I-Style Town": From Italian Concession to Commercial Attraction', *China Heritage Quarterly* 21 (2010), at http://www.chinaheritagequarterly.org.

9 Details here from personal visits and Gao Da, *Huangpu gongyuan jinxi* (*Huangpu Park Today and Yesterday*) (Shanghai: Shanghai renmin meishu chubanshe, 1999).

10 This section draws on: Annetta Fotopoulos, 'Understanding the Zodiac Saga in China: World Cultural Heritage, National Humiliation, and Evolving Narratives', *Modern China* 41:6 (2015), pp. 603–30; Peter Hays Gries, Derek Steiger and Tao Wang, 'Popular Nationalism and China's Japan Policy: The Diaoyu Islands Protests, 2012–2013', *Journal of Contemporary China* (early online, 26 November 2015). See also the papers in Jing Wang and Winnie Won Yin Wong (eds), 'Reconsidering the 2006 MIT Visualizing Cultures Controversy', special issue of *positions: east asia critique* 23:1 (2015). See also William A. Callahan, *China Dreams: 20 Visions of the Future* (New York: Oxford University Press, 2013), and his *China: The Pessoptimist Nation* (Oxford: Oxford University Press, 2010).

11 For a comprehensive study of this museum and a note on its tortuous record of openings and closings, and rearrangement of displays and historical judgements, see Anne Hennings, 'The National Museum of China: Building Memory, Shaping History, Presenting Identity', unpublished PhD thesis, Ruperto Carola University of Heidelberg, 2012; see pp. 152–70 on the 'Road to Rejuvenation'. On Xi's visit see *Renmin ribao*, 30 November 2012, p. 1, and 'Xi Pledges "Great renewal of Chinese nation"', at http://news.xinhuanet.com/english/china/2012-11-29/c_132008231.htm.

Index